Shojo Beat

VAMPIRE KNIGHT

Story & Art by
Matsuri Hino

Vol. 19

VAMPIRE KNIGHT

Contents

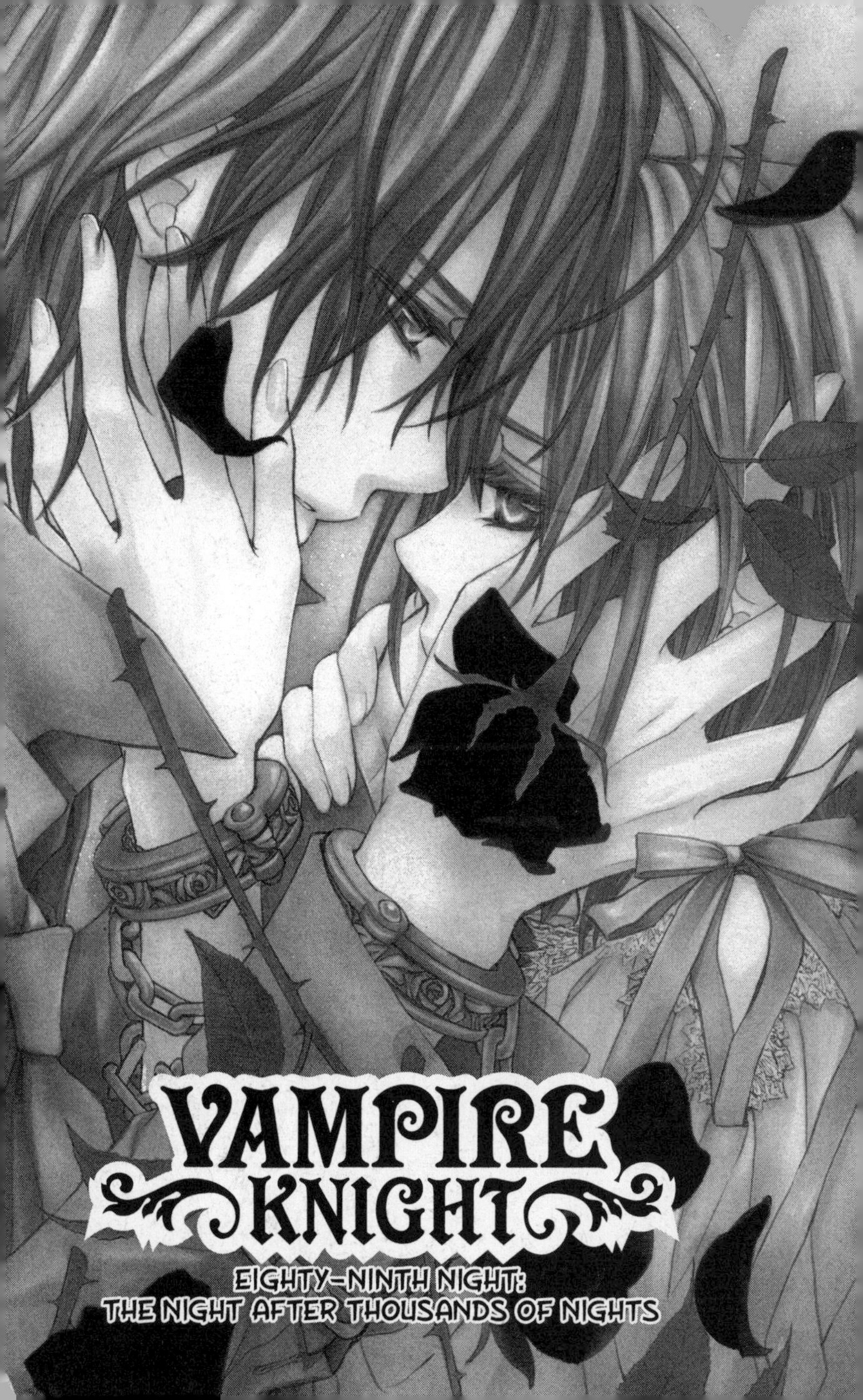
VAMPIRE
KNIGHT
EIGHTY-NINTH NIGHT:
THE NIGHT AFTER THOUSANDS OF NIGHTS

In the previous volume...

After the death of Sara Shirabuki, Yuki and Zero go in pursuit of Kaname and find the pureblood Isaya at the masquerade. Kaname appears before Isaya and tells him he plans to sacrifice himself to take the place of the origin metal to create vampire hunter weapons.

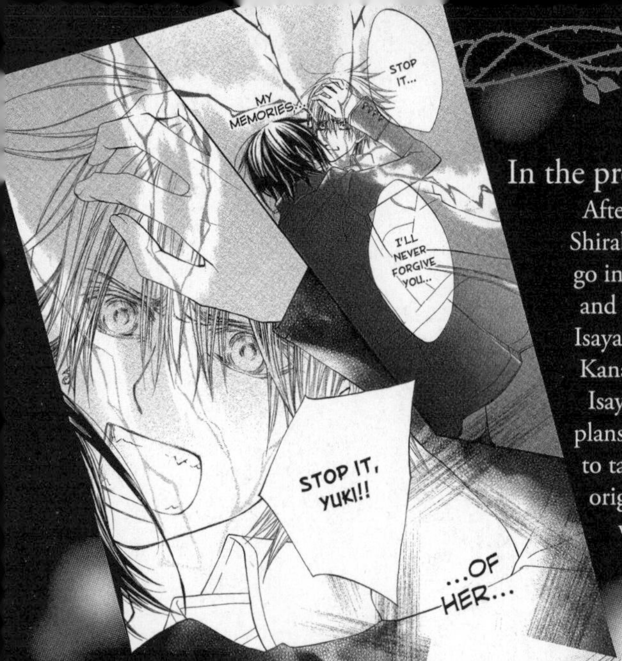
STOP IT...
MY MEMORIES...
I'LL NEVER FORGIVE YOU...
STOP IT, YUKI!!
...OF HER...

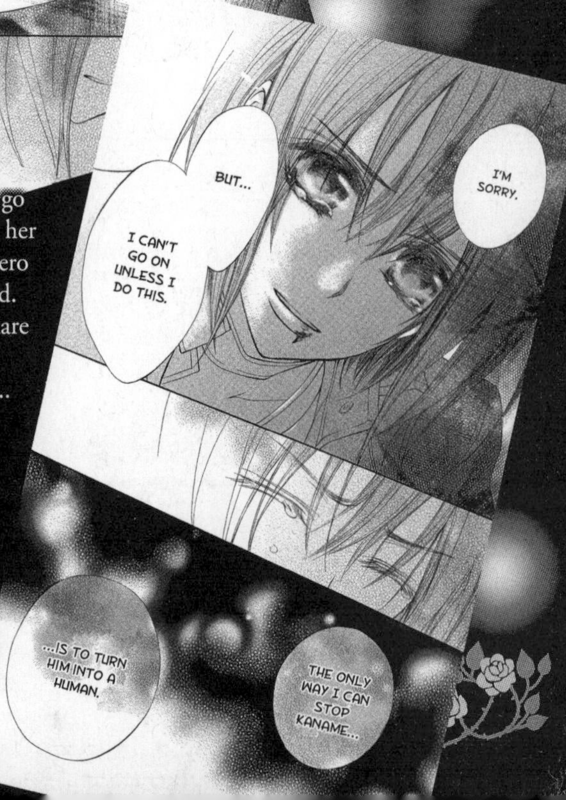
I'M SORRY.
BUT...
I CAN'T GO ON UNLESS I DO THIS.
THE ONLY WAY I CAN STOP KANAME...
...IS TO TURN HIM INTO A HUMAN.

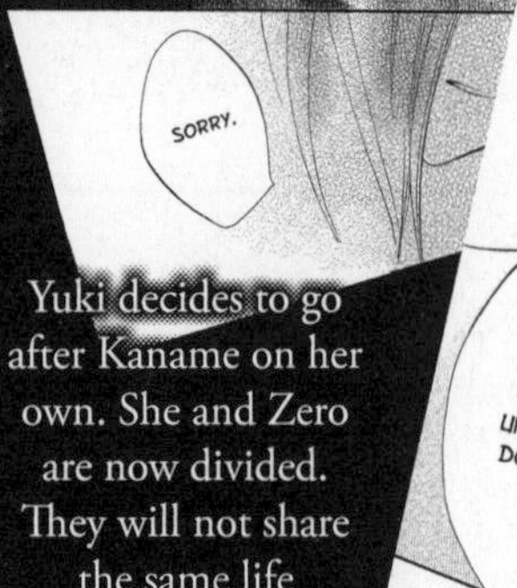
SORRY.

Yuki decides to go after Kaname on her own. She and Zero are now divided. They will not share the same life span together...

Yuki sinks her teeth into Zero's neck to erase his memories of her...!

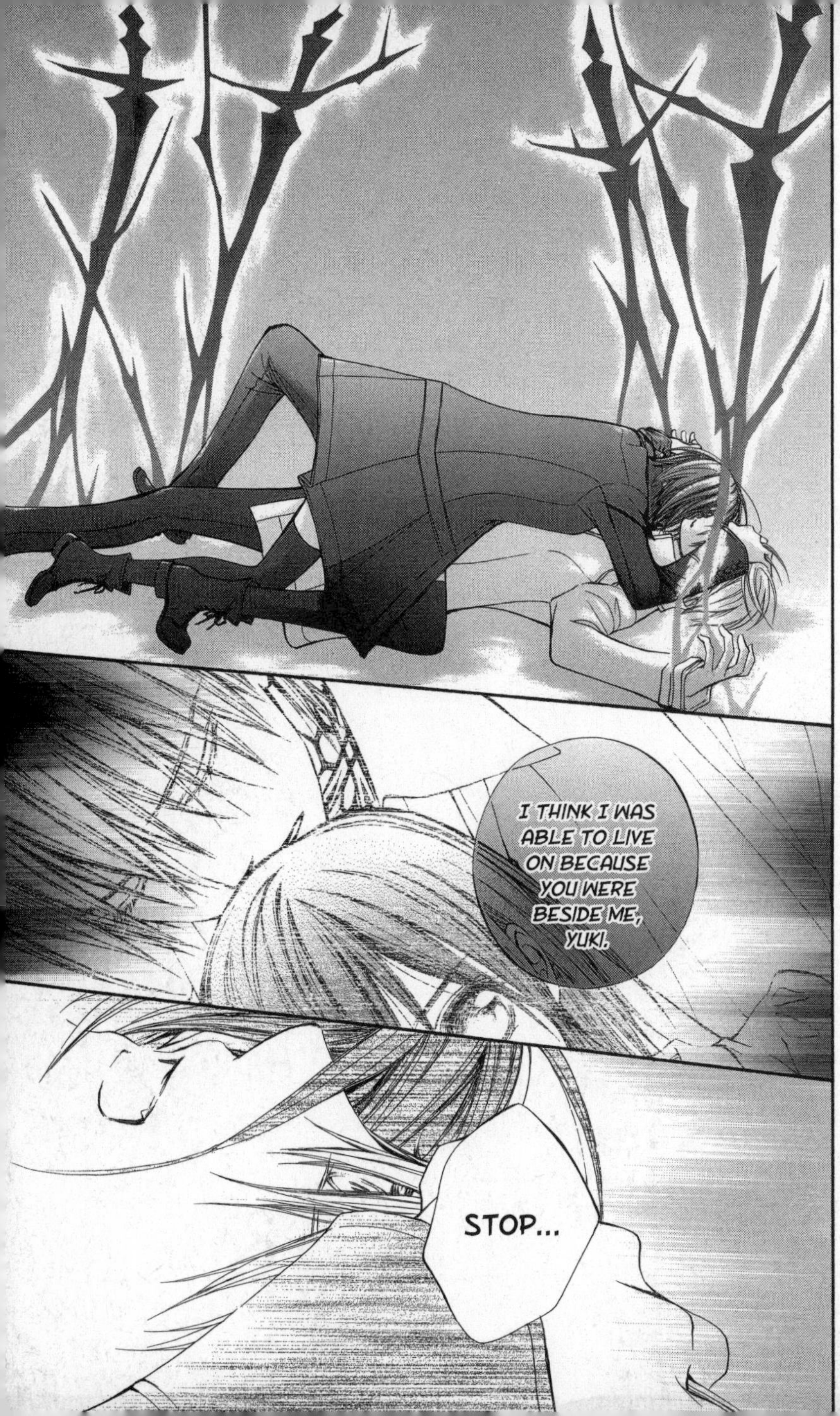
I THINK I WAS ABLE TO LIVE ON BECAUSE YOU WERE BESIDE ME, YUKI.
STOP...

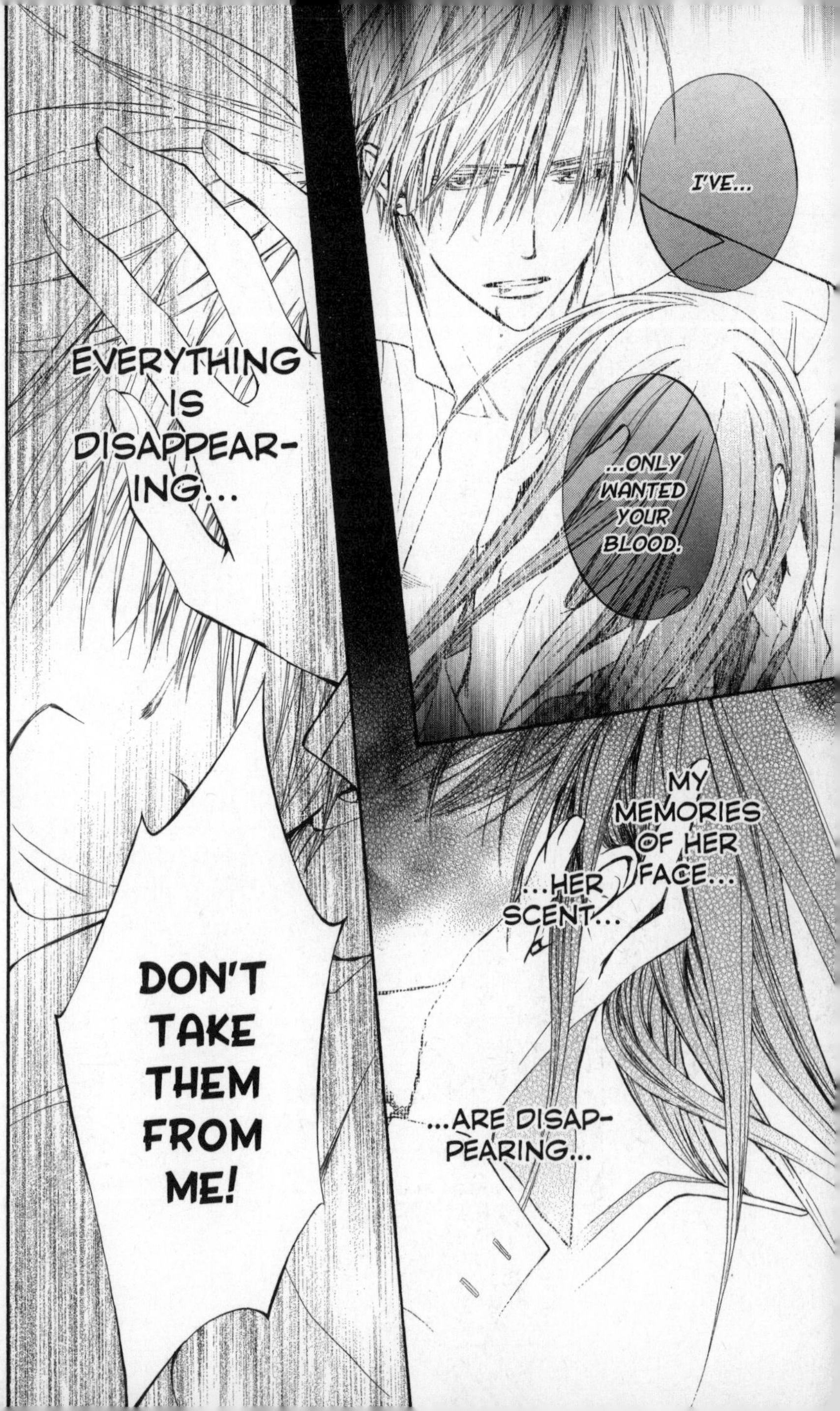
I'VE...
...ONLY WANTED YOUR BLOOD.
MY MEMORIES OF HER FACE...
...HER SCENT...
...ARE DISAPPEARING...
EVERYTHING IS DISAPPEARING...
DON'T TAKE THEM FROM ME!

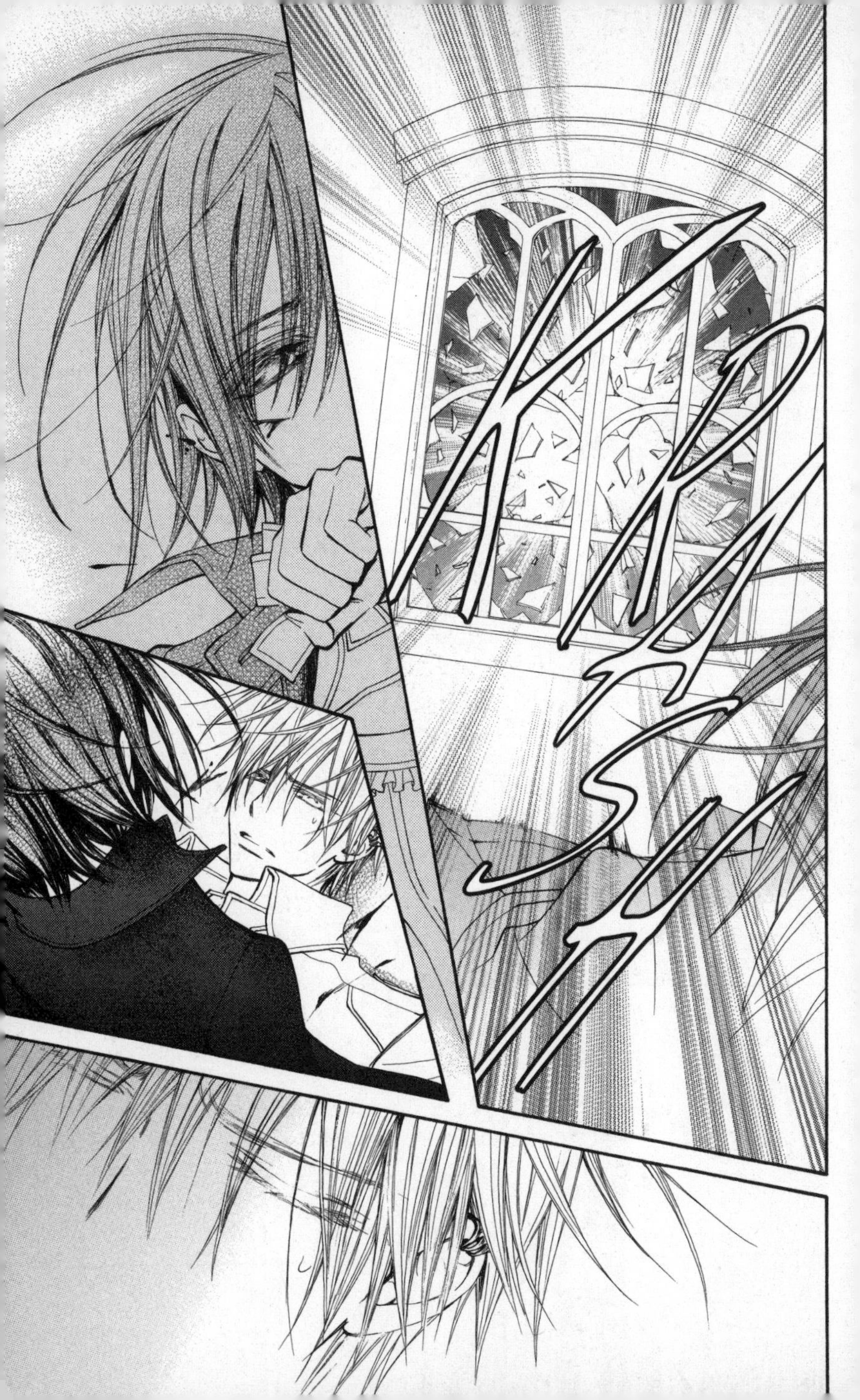
KRASH

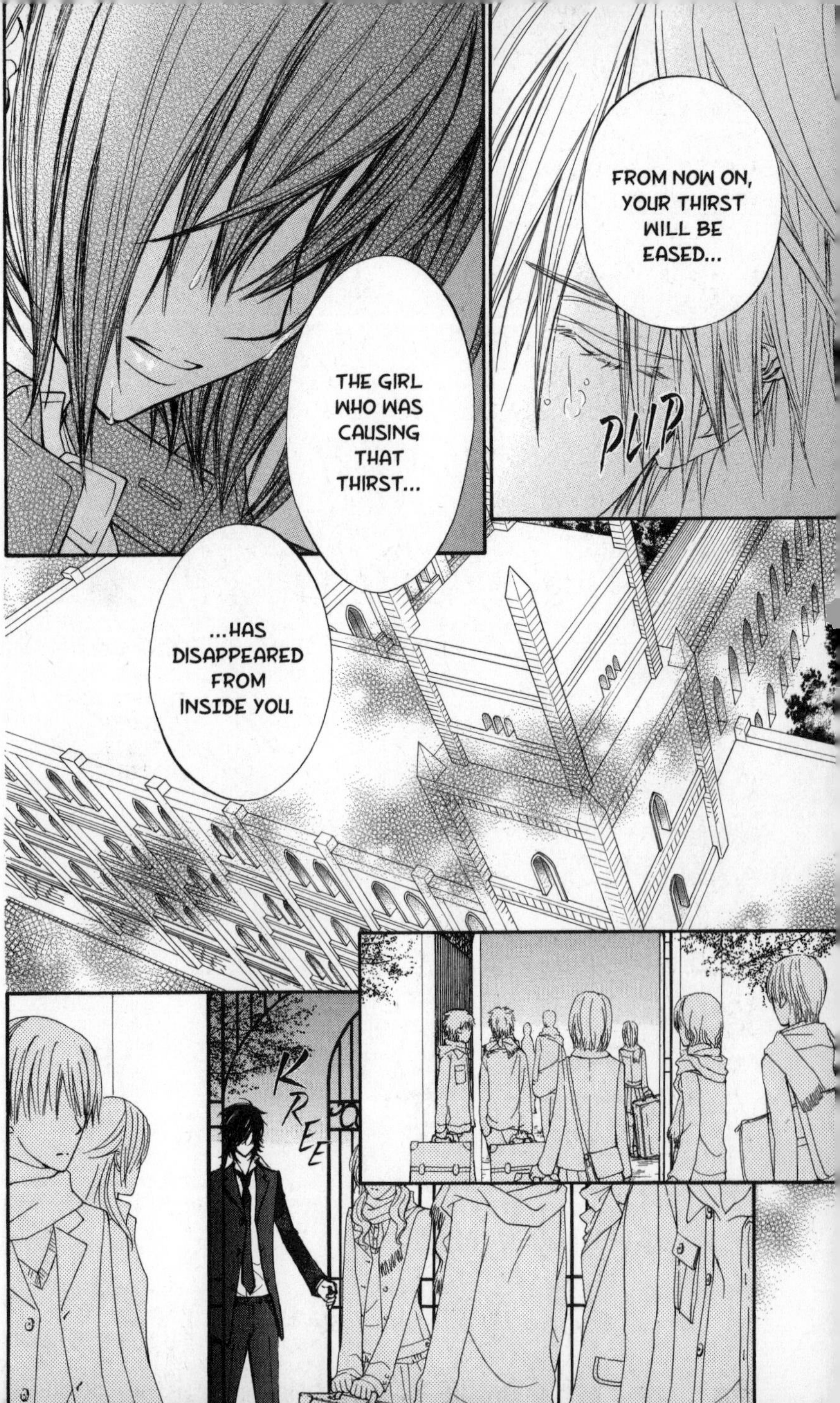
FROM NOW ON, YOUR THIRST WILL BE EASED...
PLIP
THE GIRL WHO WAS CAUSING THAT THIRST...
...HAS DISAPPEARED FROM INSIDE YOU.
KREE

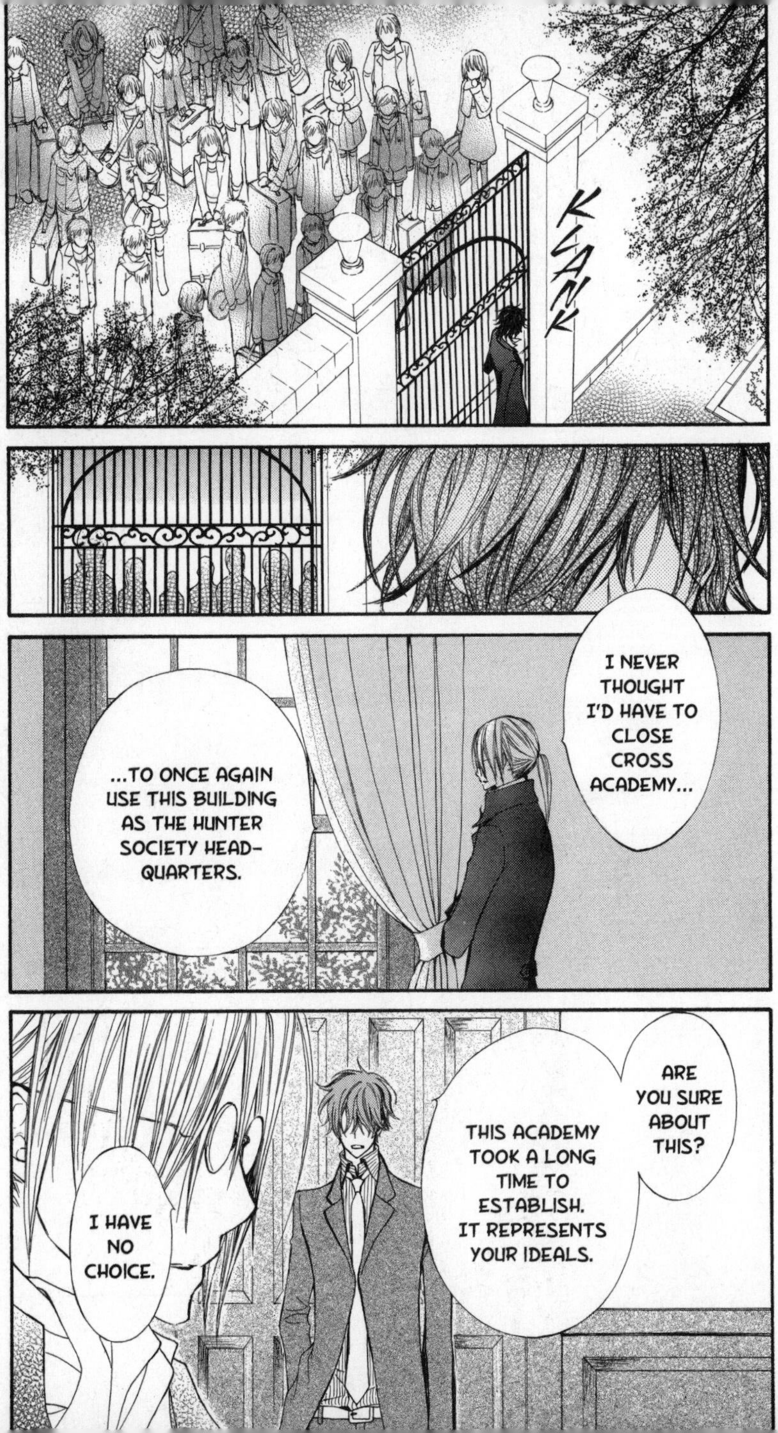
KLANK
I NEVER THOUGHT I'D HAVE TO CLOSE CROSS ACADEMY...
...TO ONCE AGAIN USE THIS BUILDING AS THE HUNTER SOCIETY HEAD-QUARTERS.
ARE YOU SURE ABOUT THIS?
THIS ACADEMY TOOK A LONG TIME TO ESTABLISH. IT REPRESENTS YOUR IDEALS.
I HAVE NO CHOICE.

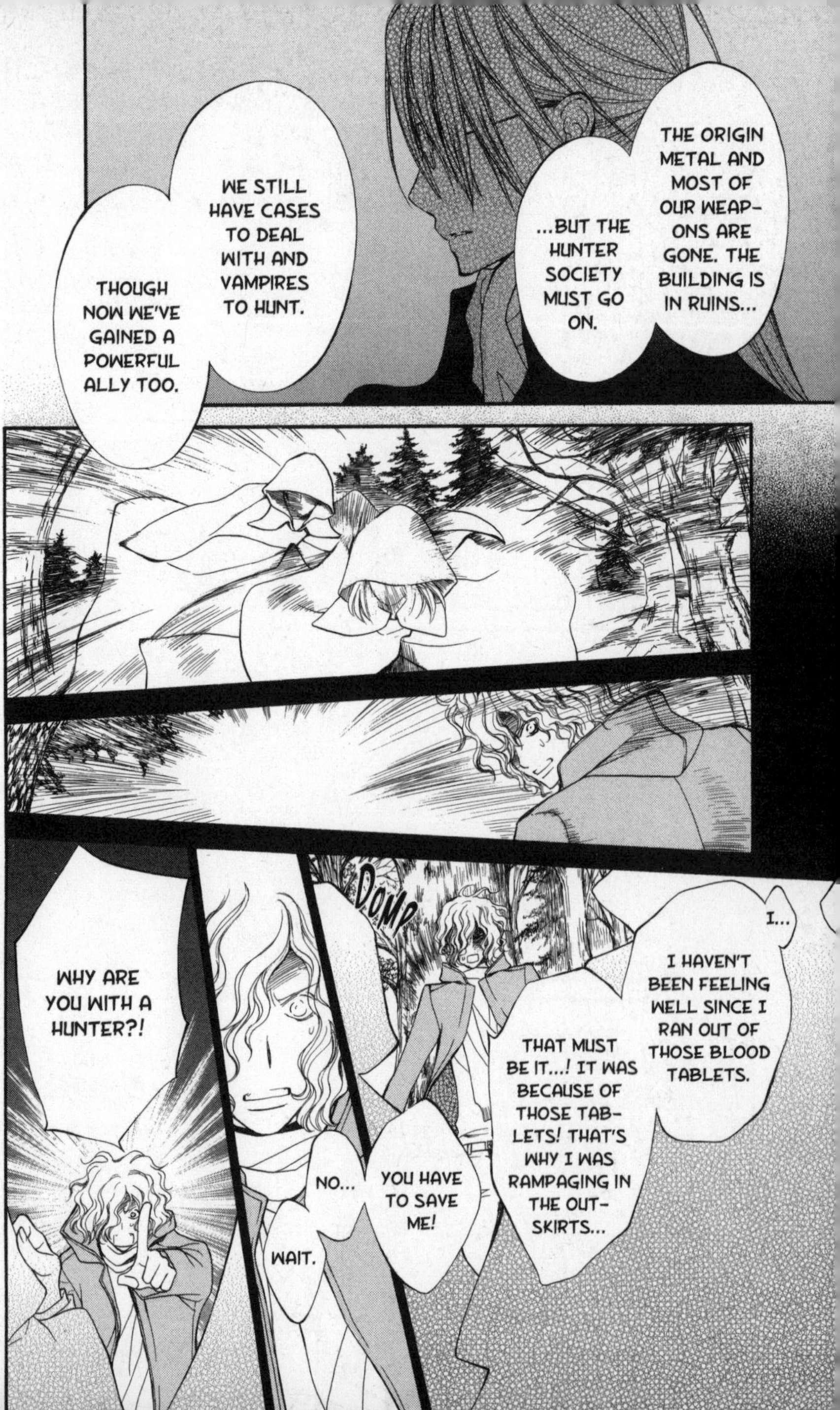
THE ORIGIN METAL AND MOST OF OUR WEAPONS ARE GONE. THE BUILDING IS IN RUINS...
...BUT THE HUNTER SOCIETY MUST GO ON.
WE STILL HAVE CASES TO DEAL WITH AND VAMPIRES TO HUNT.
THOUGH NOW WE'VE GAINED A POWERFUL ALLY TOO.
DOMP
I...
I HAVEN'T BEEN FEELING WELL SINCE I RAN OUT OF THOSE BLOOD TABLETS.
THAT MUST BE IT...! IT WAS BECAUSE OF THOSE TABLETS! THAT'S WHY I WAS RAMPAGING IN THE OUTSKIRTS...
YOU HAVE TO SAVE ME!
NO...
WAIT.
WHY ARE YOU WITH A HUNTER?!

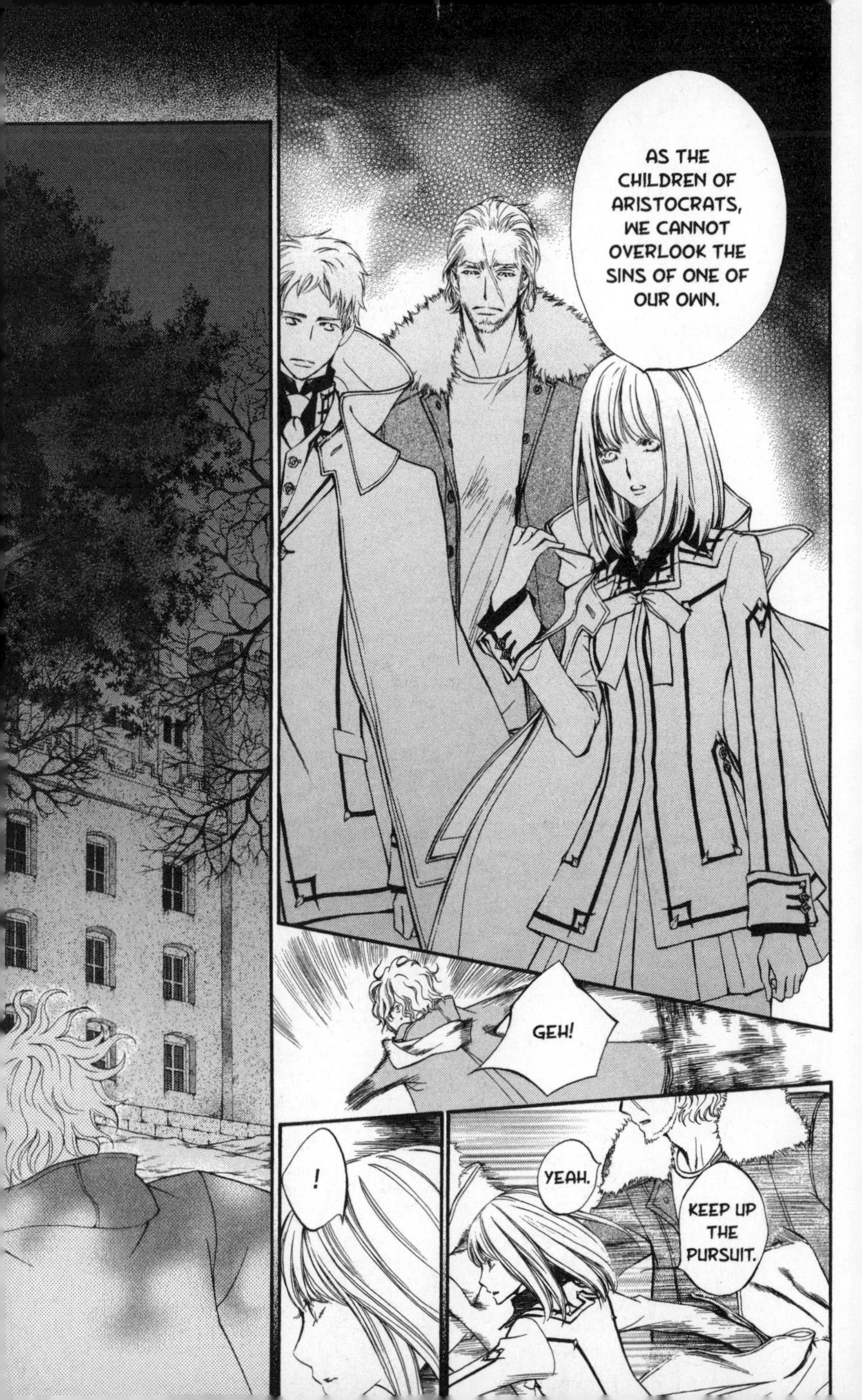
AS THE CHILDREN OF ARISTOCRATS, WE CANNOT OVERLOOK THE SINS OF ONE OF OUR OWN.
GEH!
YEAH.
KEEP UP THE PURSUIT.
!

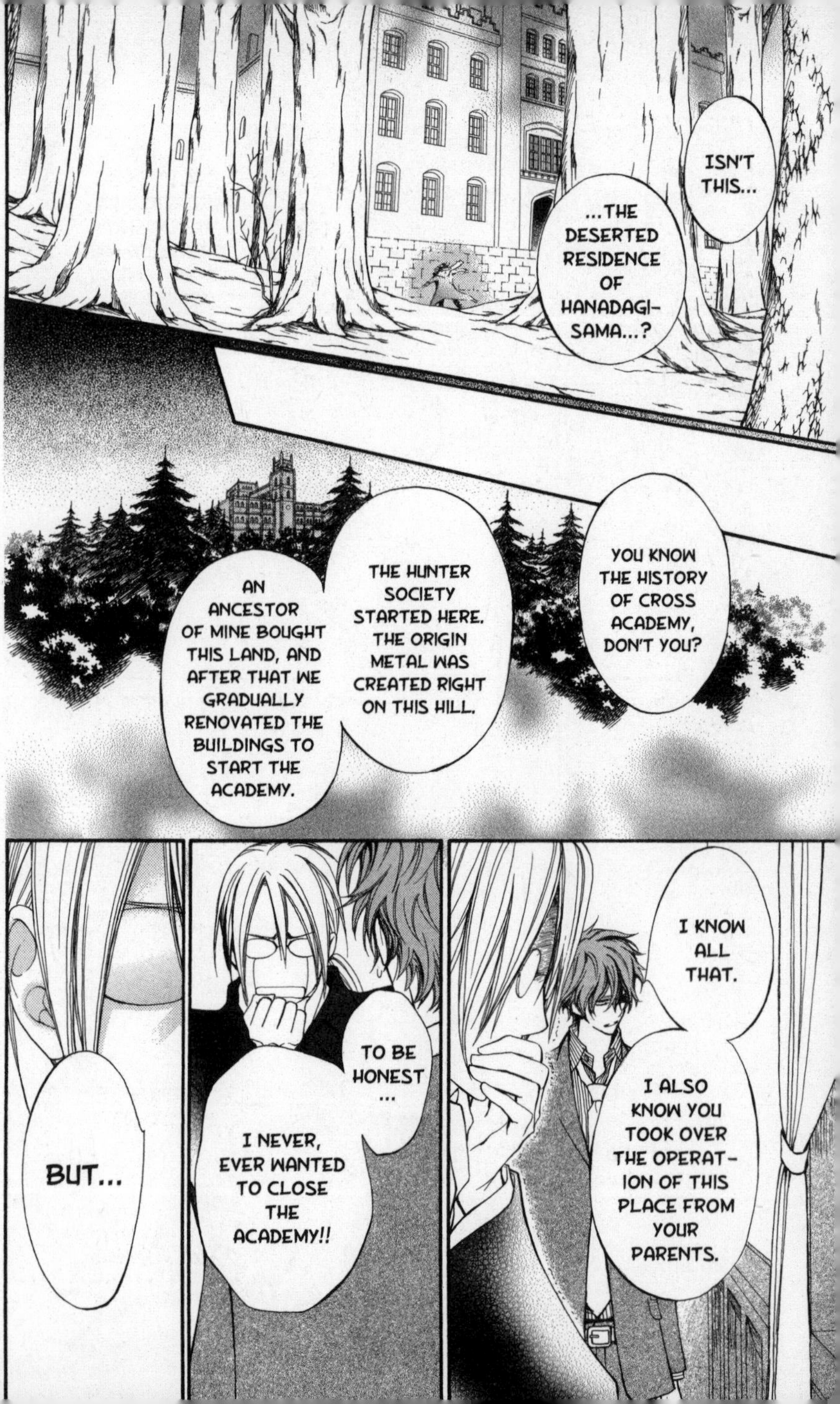
ISN'T THIS...
...THE DESERTED RESIDENCE OF HANADAGI-SAMA...?
YOU KNOW THE HISTORY OF CROSS ACADEMY, DON'T YOU?
THE HUNTER SOCIETY STARTED HERE. THE ORIGIN METAL WAS CREATED RIGHT ON THIS HILL.
AN ANCESTOR OF MINE BOUGHT THIS LAND, AND AFTER THAT WE GRADUALLY RENOVATED THE BUILDINGS TO START THE ACADEMY.
I KNOW ALL THAT.
I ALSO KNOW YOU TOOK OVER THE OPERAT-ION OF THIS PLACE FROM YOUR PARENTS.
TO BE HONEST...
I NEVER, EVER WANTED TO CLOSE THE ACADEMY!!
BUT...

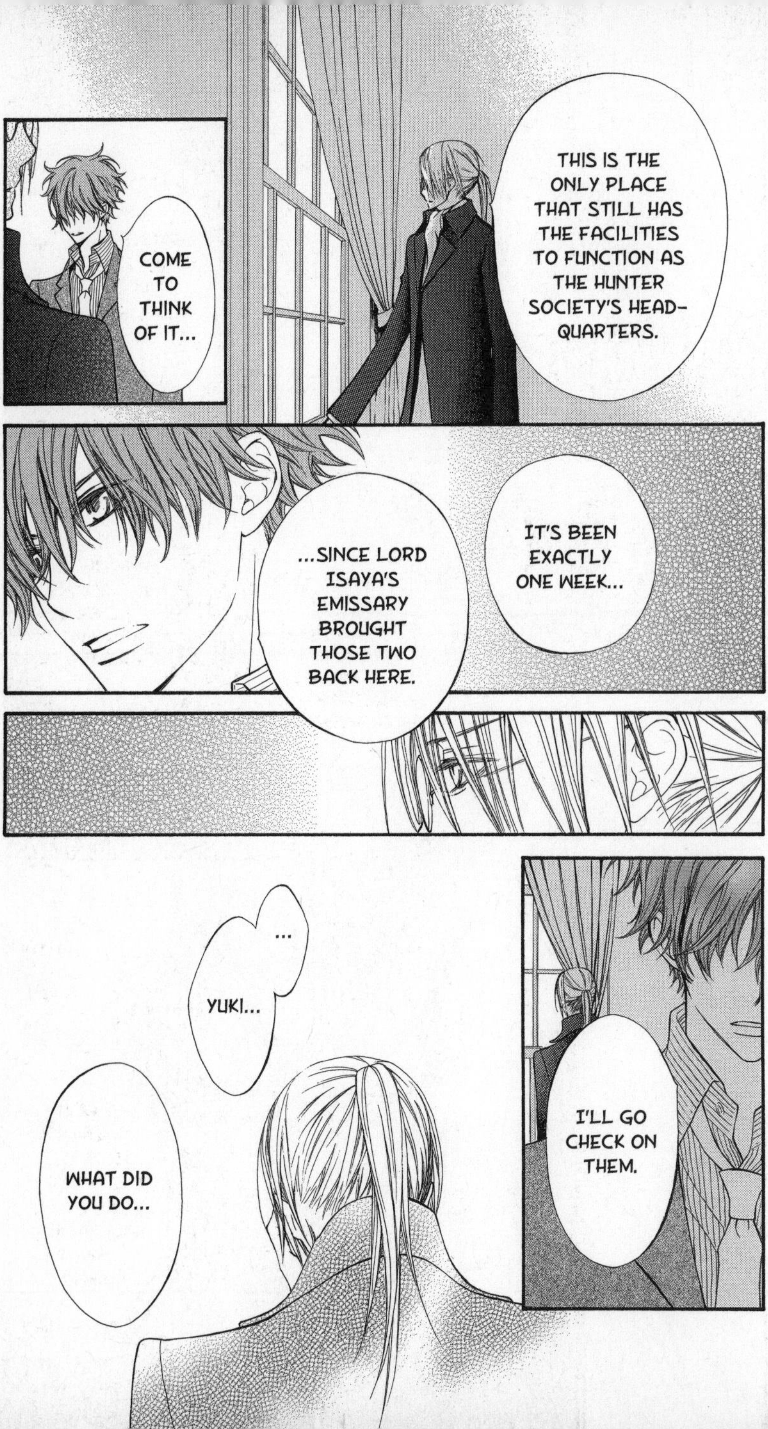
THIS IS THE ONLY PLACE THAT STILL HAS THE FACILITIES TO FUNCTION AS THE HUNTER SOCIETY'S HEAD-QUARTERS.
COME TO THINK OF IT...
IT'S BEEN EXACTLY ONE WEEK...
...SINCE LORD ISAYA'S EMISSARY BROUGHT THOSE TWO BACK HERE.
I'LL GO CHECK ON THEM.
...
YUKI...
WHAT DID YOU DO...

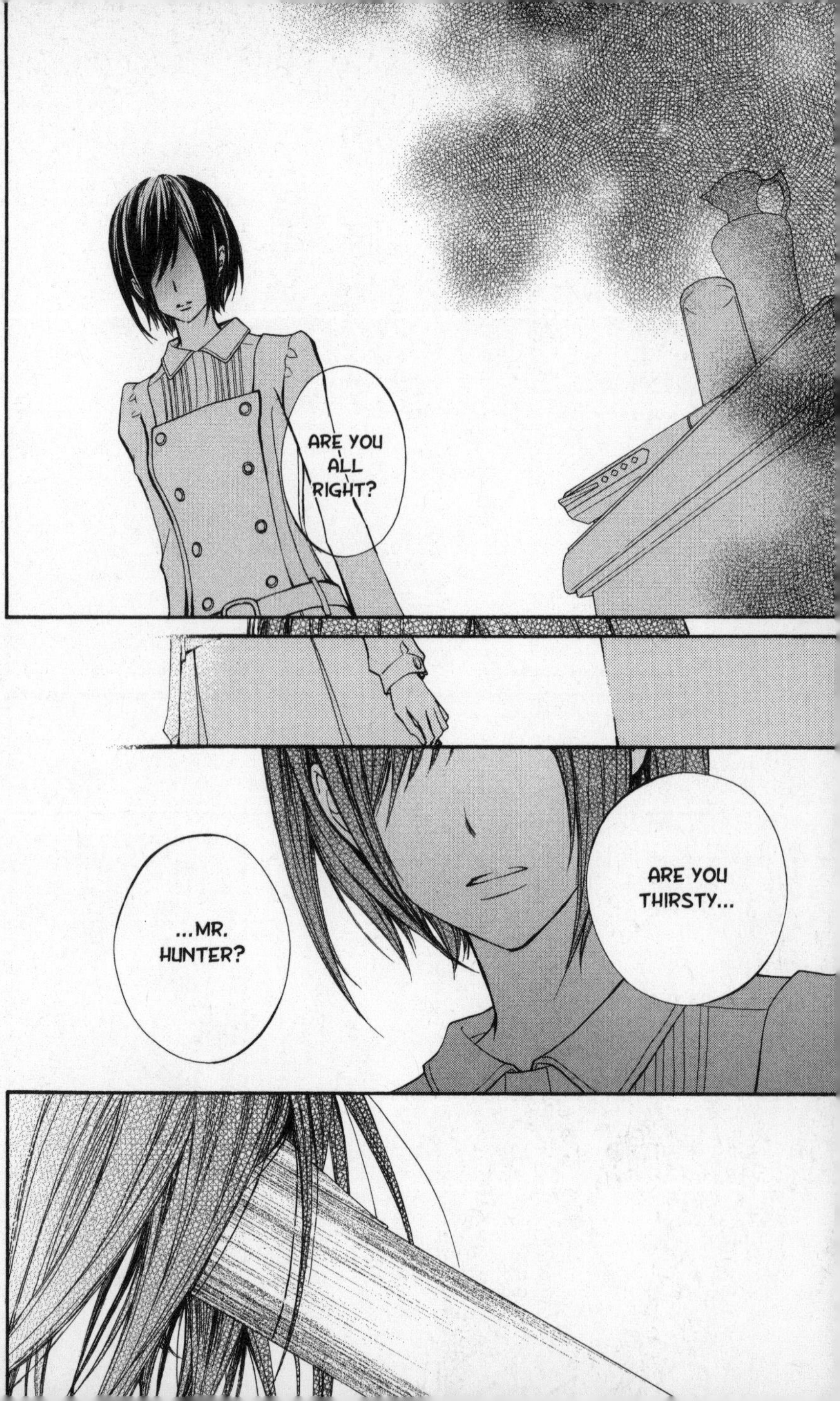
ARE YOU ALL RIGHT?
ARE YOU THIRSTY...
...MR. HUNTER?

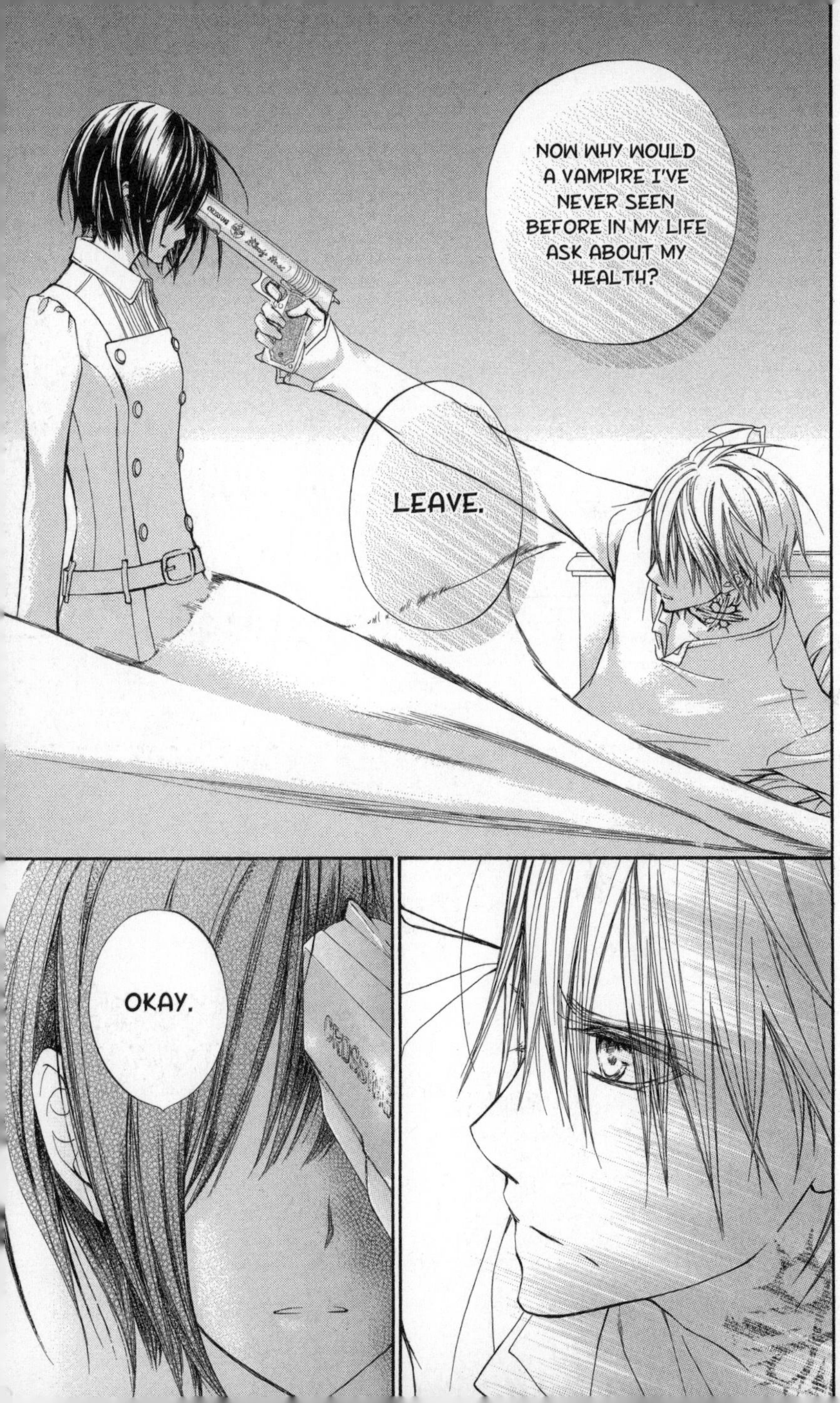
NOW WHY WOULD A VAMPIRE I'VE NEVER SEEN BEFORE IN MY LIFE ASK ABOUT MY HEALTH?
LEAVE.
OKAY.

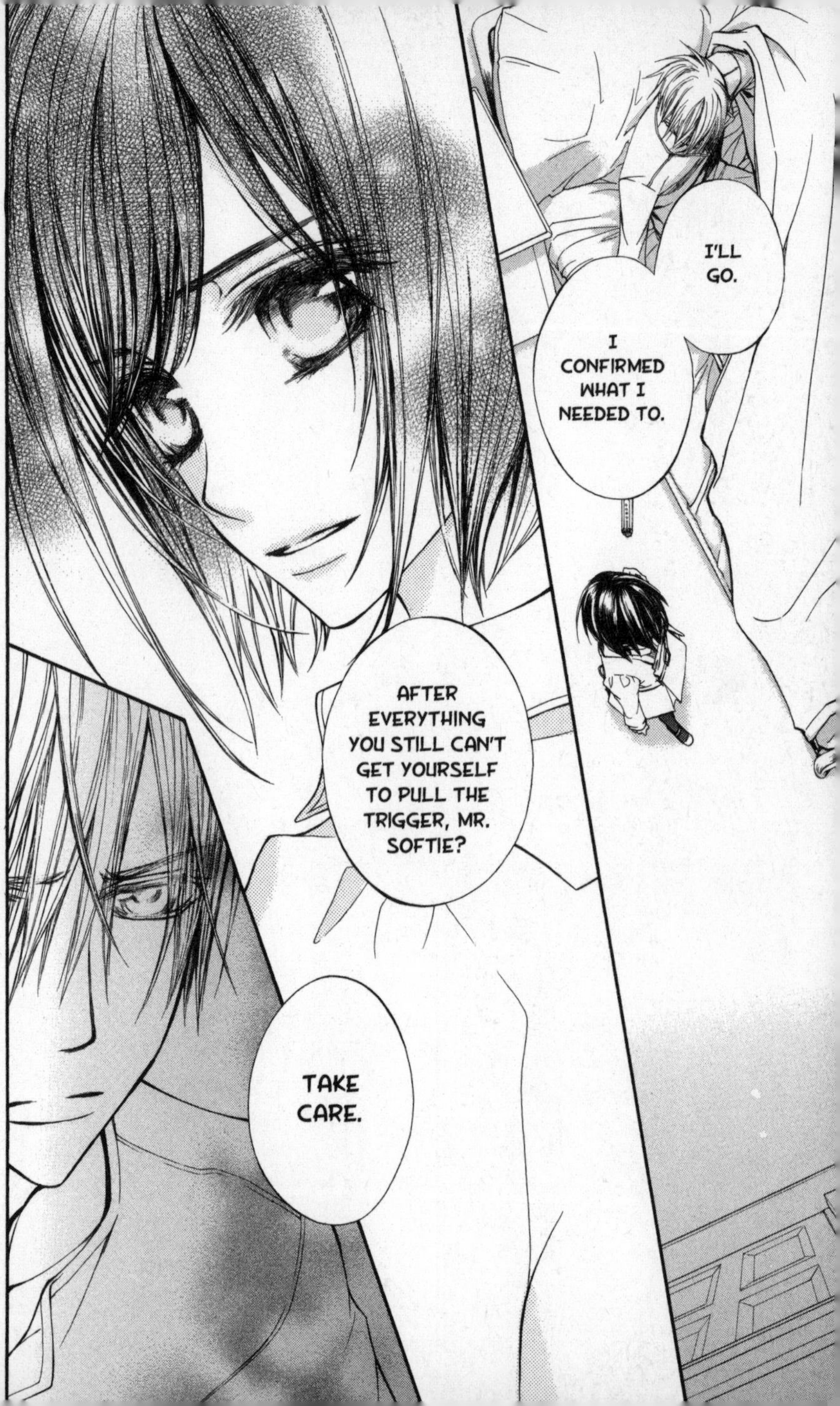
I'LL GO.
I CONFIRMED WHAT I NEEDED TO.
AFTER EVERYTHING YOU STILL CAN'T GET YOURSELF TO PULL THE TRIGGER, MR. SOFTIE?
TAKE CARE.

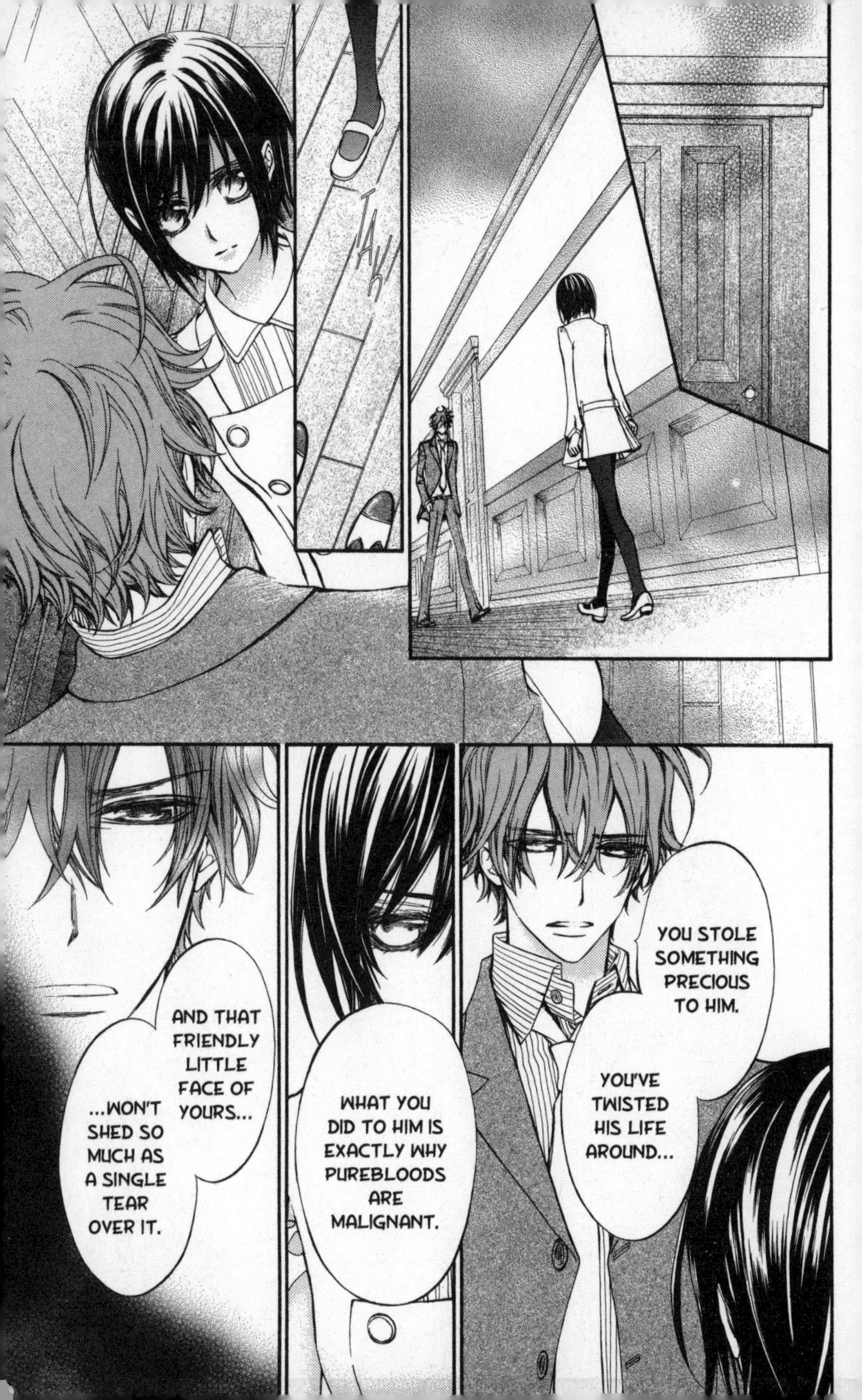
TAK!
YOU STOLE SOMETHING PRECIOUS TO HIM.
YOU'VE TWISTED HIS LIFE AROUND...
WHAT YOU DID TO HIM IS EXACTLY WHY PUREBLOODS ARE MALIGNANT.
AND THAT FRIENDLY LITTLE FACE OF YOURS...
...WON'T SHED SO MUCH AS A SINGLE TEAR OVER IT.

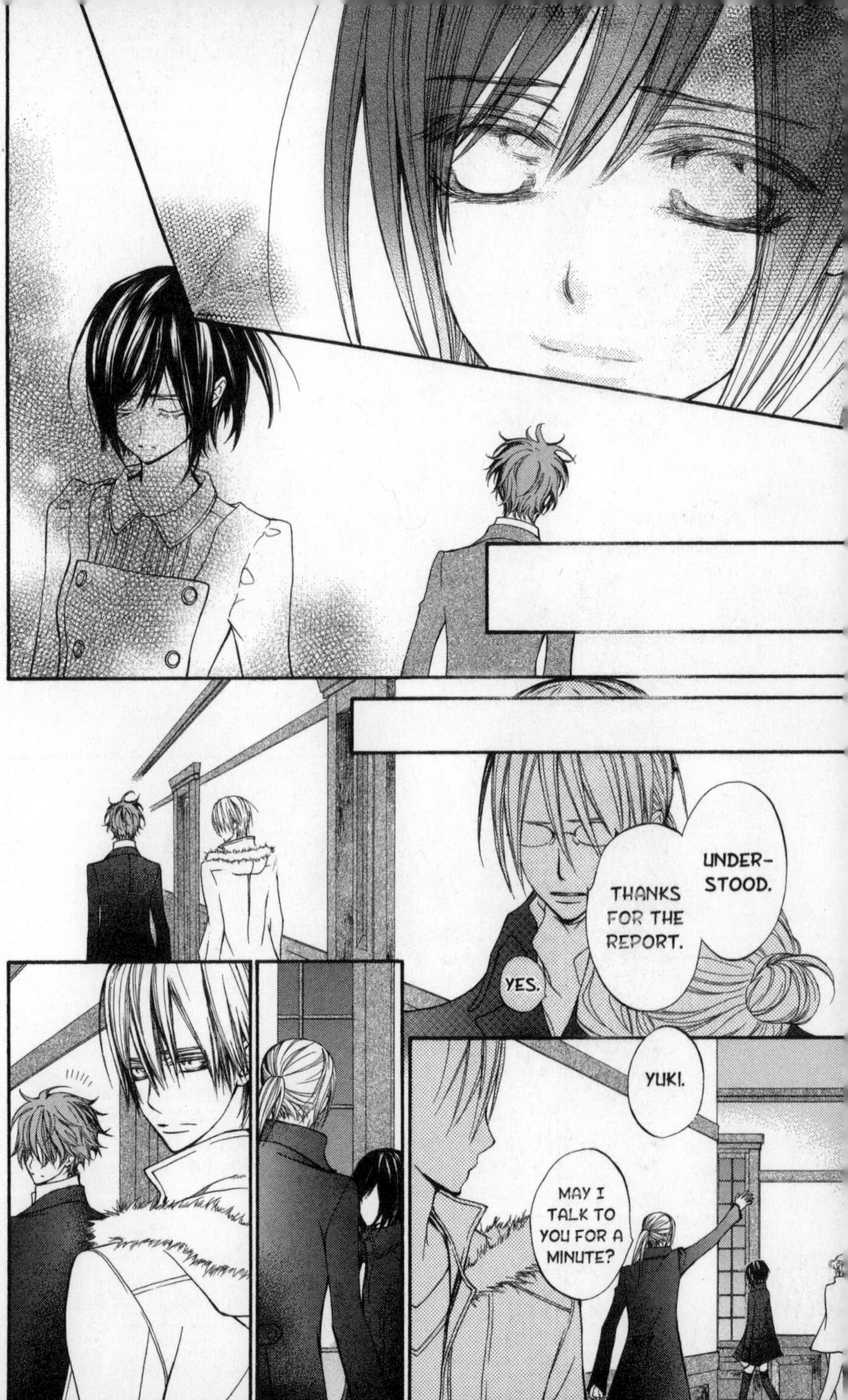
UNDER-STOOD.
THANKS FOR THE REPORT.
YES.
YUKI.
MAY I TALK TO YOU FOR A MINUTE?

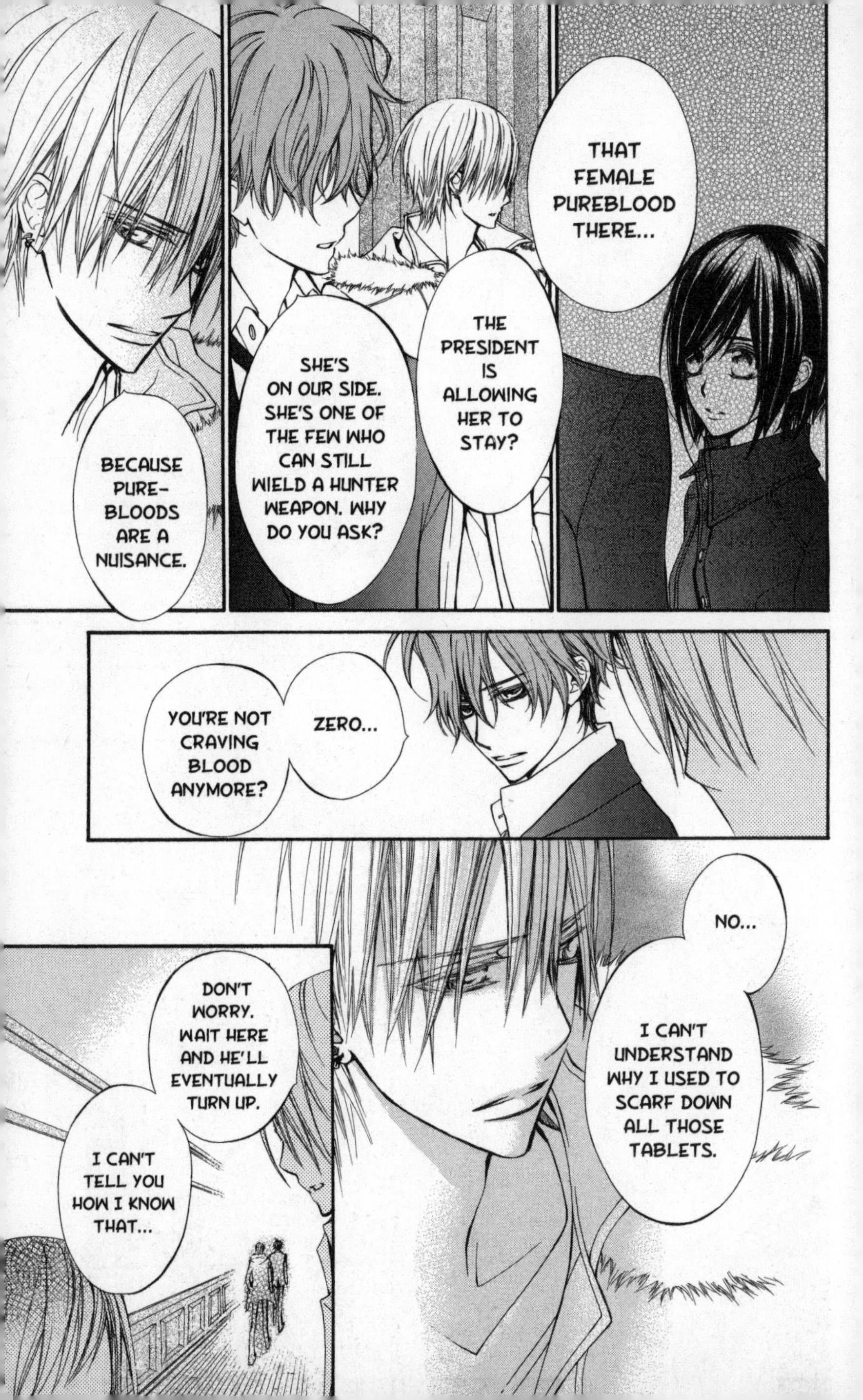
THAT FEMALE PUREBLOOD THERE...
THE PRESIDENT IS ALLOWING HER TO STAY?
SHE'S ON OUR SIDE. SHE'S ONE OF THE FEW WHO CAN STILL WIELD A HUNTER WEAPON. WHY DO YOU ASK?
BECAUSE PURE-BLOODS ARE A NUISANCE.
ZERO...
YOU'RE NOT CRAVING BLOOD ANYMORE?
NO...
I CAN'T UNDERSTAND WHY I USED TO SCARF DOWN ALL THOSE TABLETS.
DON'T WORRY. WAIT HERE AND HE'LL EVENTUALLY TURN UP.
I CAN'T TELL YOU HOW I KNOW THAT...

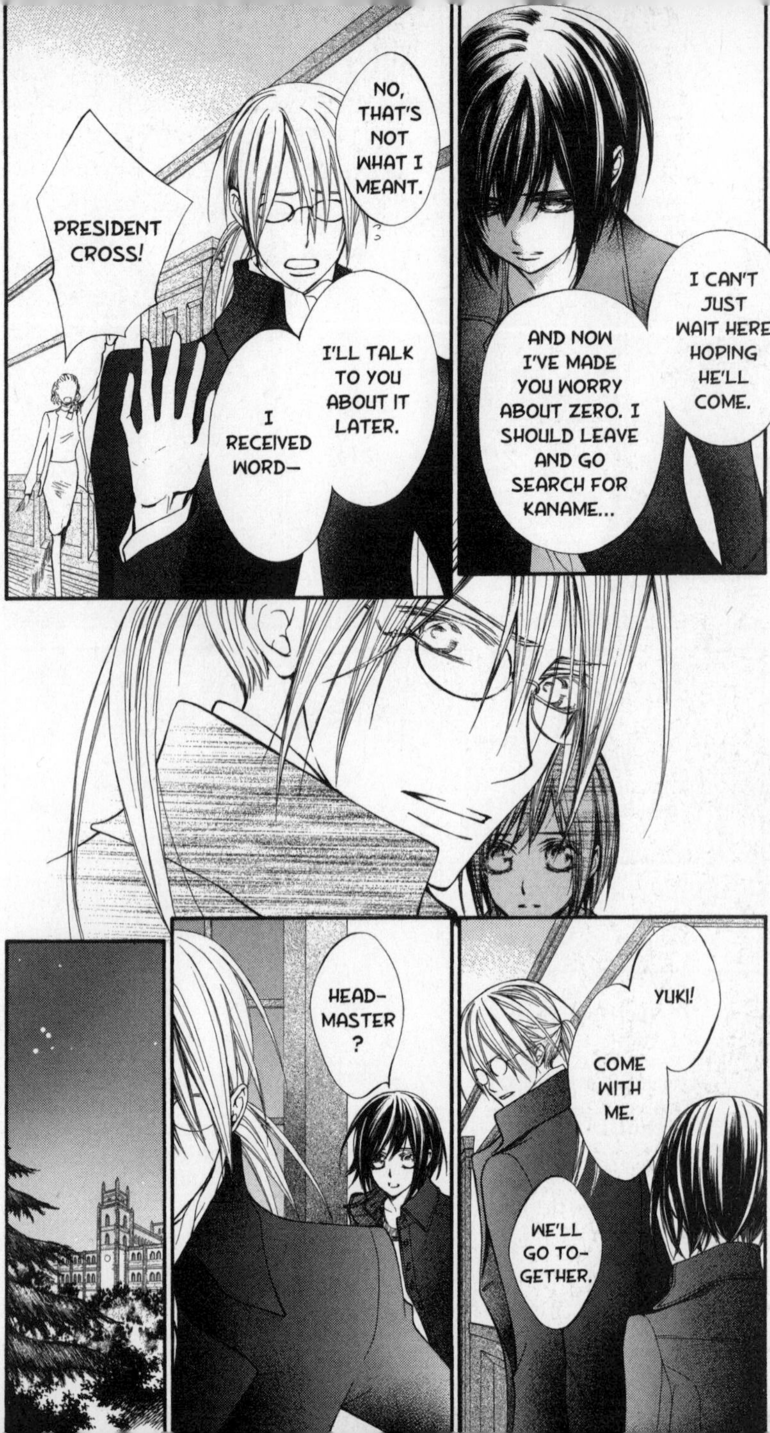
I CAN'T JUST WAIT HERE HOPING HE'LL COME.
AND NOW I'VE MADE YOU WORRY ABOUT ZERO. I SHOULD LEAVE AND GO SEARCH FOR KANAME...
NO, THAT'S NOT WHAT I MEANT.
PRESIDENT CROSS!
I'LL TALK TO YOU ABOUT IT LATER.
I RECEIVED WORD—
YUKI!
COME WITH ME.
WE'LL GO TO-GETHER.
HEAD-MASTER?

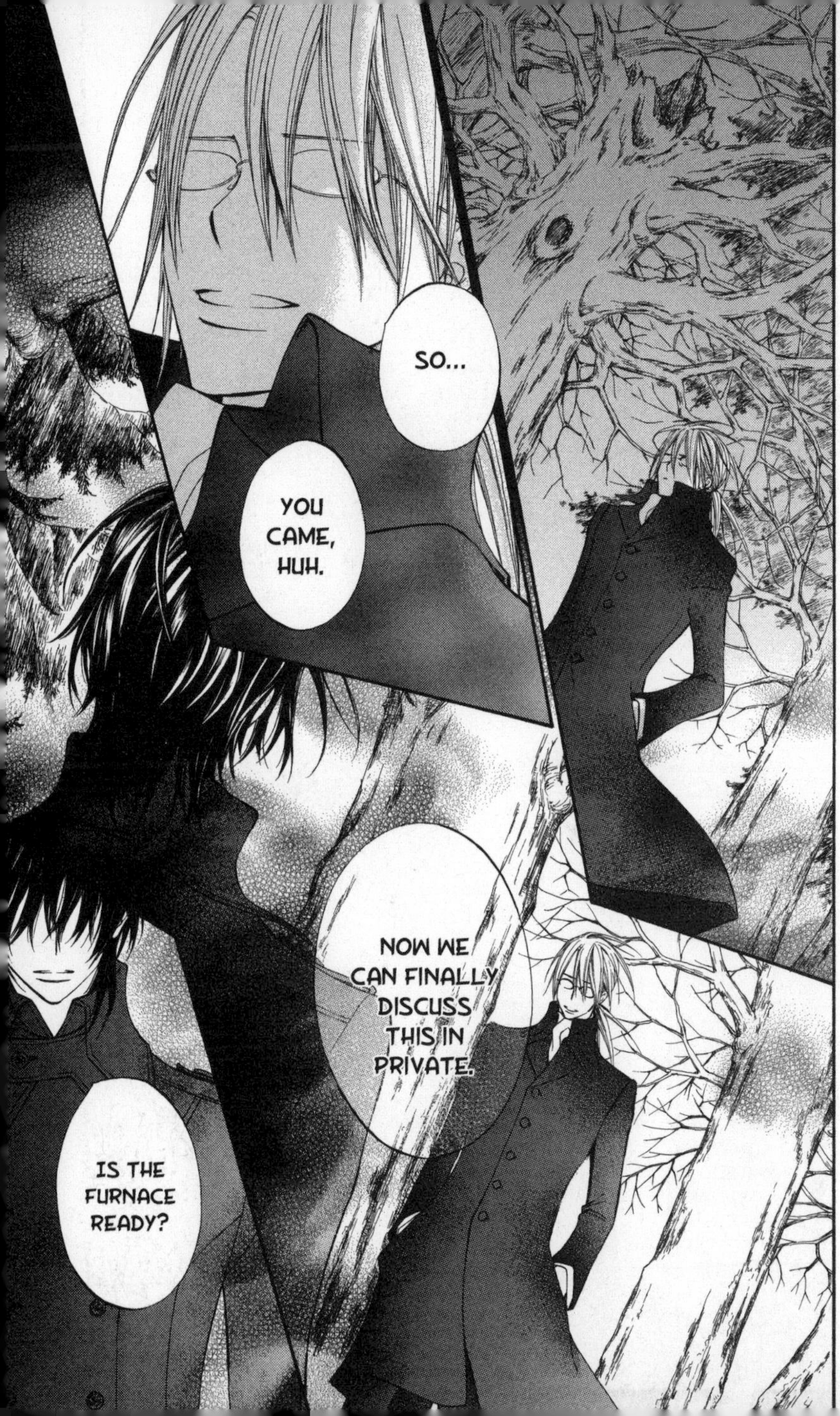
SO...
YOU CAME, HUH.
NOW WE CAN FINALLY DISCUSS THIS IN PRIVATE.
IS THE FURNACE READY?

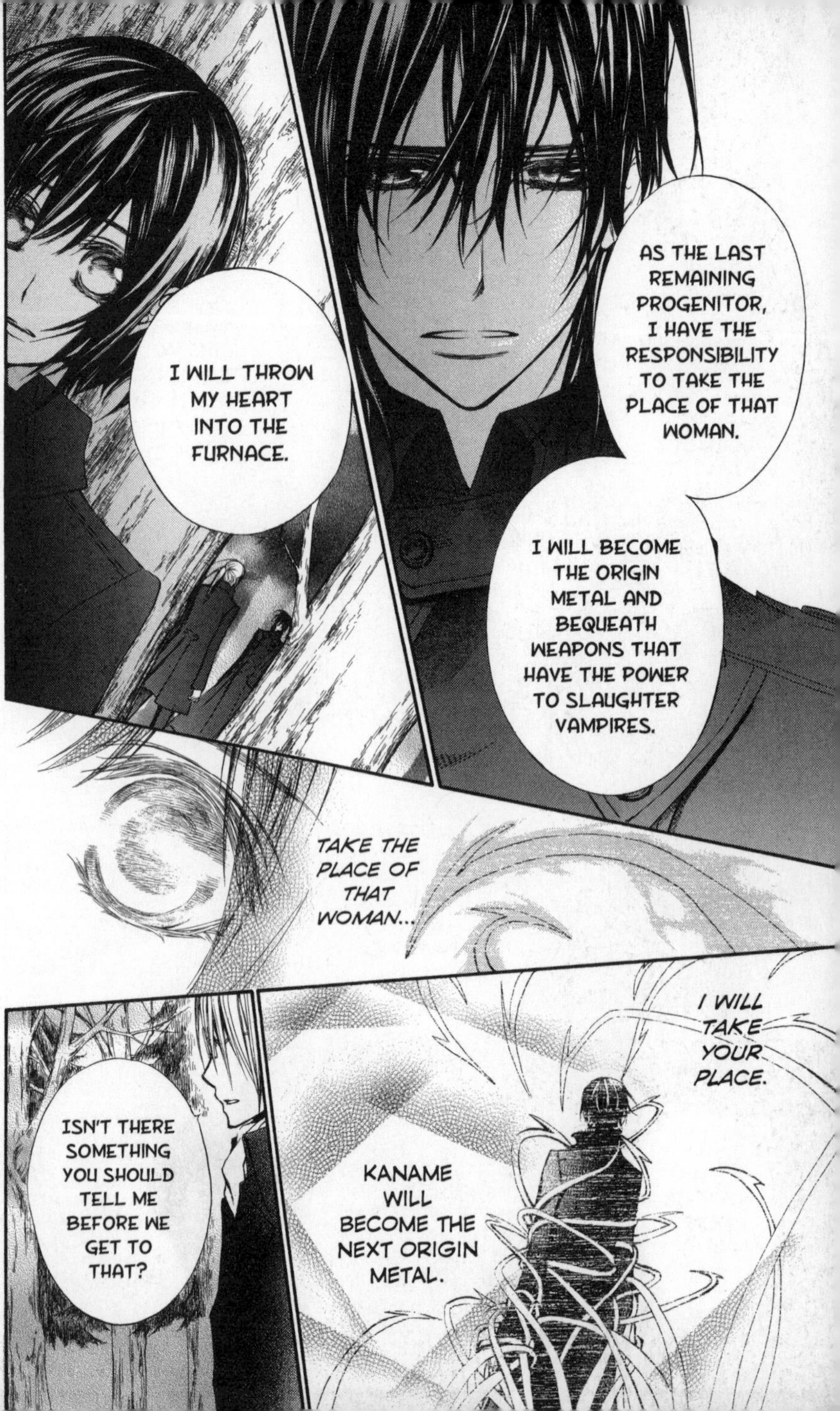
AS THE LAST REMAINING PROGENITOR, I HAVE THE RESPONSIBILITY TO TAKE THE PLACE OF THAT WOMAN.
I WILL BECOME THE ORIGIN METAL AND BEQUEATH WEAPONS THAT HAVE THE POWER TO SLAUGHTER VAMPIRES.
I WILL THROW MY HEART INTO THE FURNACE.
TAKE THE PLACE OF THAT WOMAN...
I WILL TAKE YOUR PLACE.
KANAME WILL BECOME THE NEXT ORIGIN METAL.
ISN'T THERE SOMETHING YOU SHOULD TELL ME BEFORE WE GET TO THAT?

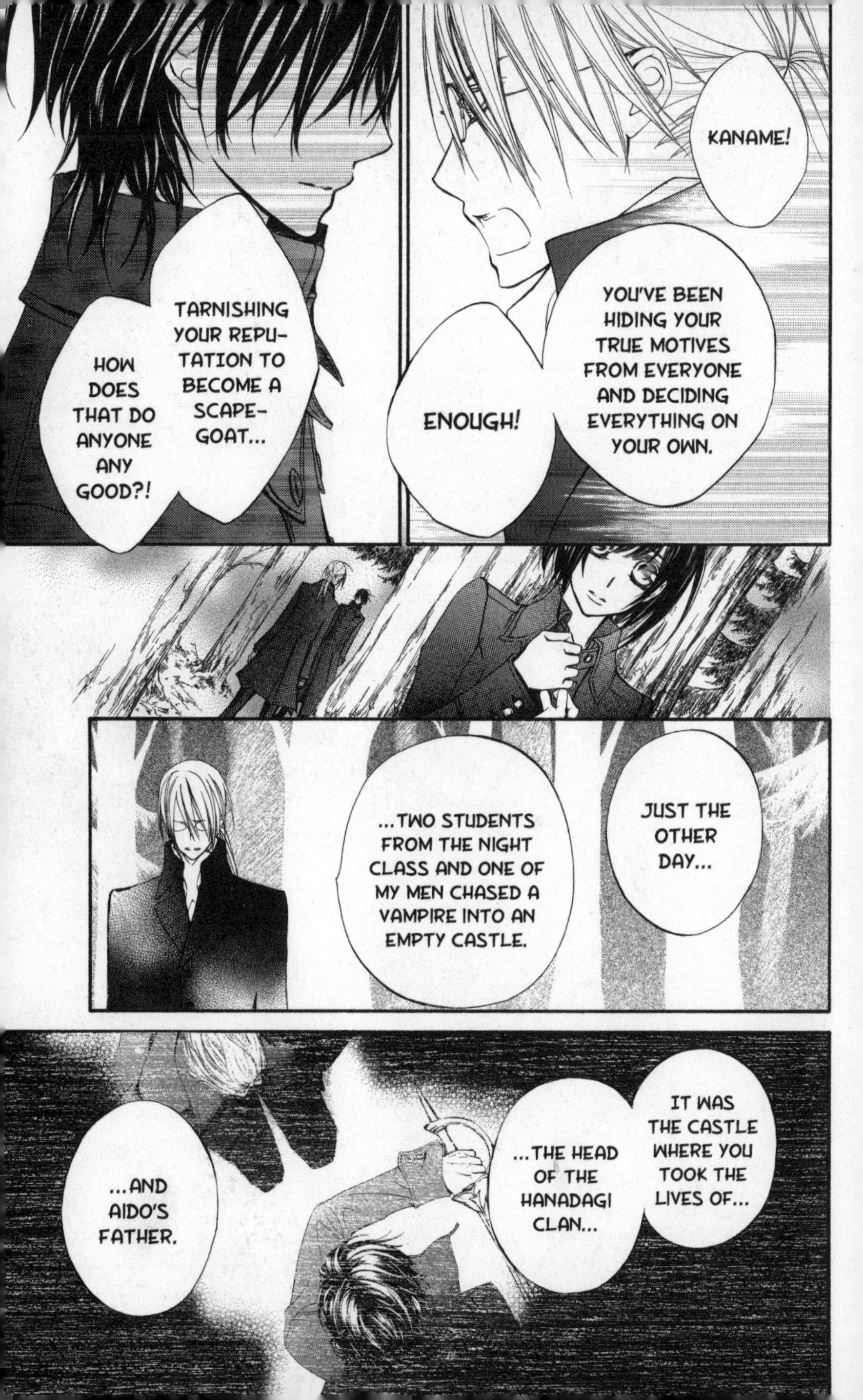
KANAME!
YOU'VE BEEN HIDING YOUR TRUE MOTIVES FROM EVERYONE AND DECIDING EVERYTHING ON YOUR OWN.
ENOUGH!
TARNISHING YOUR REPU-TATION TO BECOME A SCAPE-GOAT...
HOW DOES THAT DO ANYONE ANY GOOD?!
JUST THE OTHER DAY...
...TWO STUDENTS FROM THE NIGHT CLASS AND ONE OF MY MEN CHASED A VAMPIRE INTO AN EMPTY CASTLE.
IT WAS THE CASTLE WHERE YOU TOOK THE LIVES OF...
...THE HEAD OF THE HANADAGI CLAN...
...AND AIDO'S FATHER.

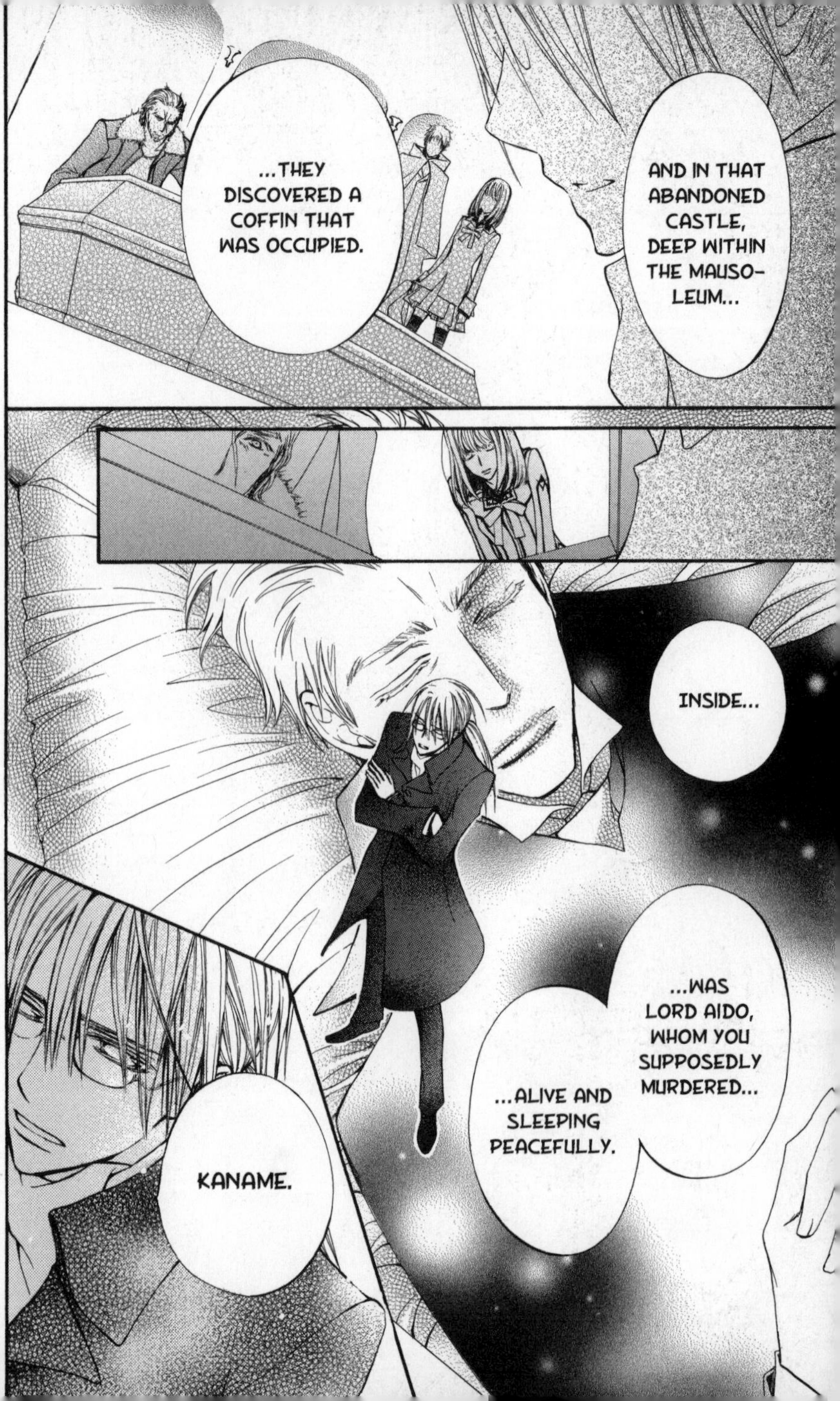
AND IN THAT ABANDONED CASTLE, DEEP WITHIN THE MAUSO-LEUM...
...THEY DISCOVERED A COFFIN THAT WAS OCCUPIED.
INSIDE...
...WAS LORD AIDO, WHOM YOU SUPPOSEDLY MURDERED...
...ALIVE AND SLEEPING PEACEFULLY.
KANAME.

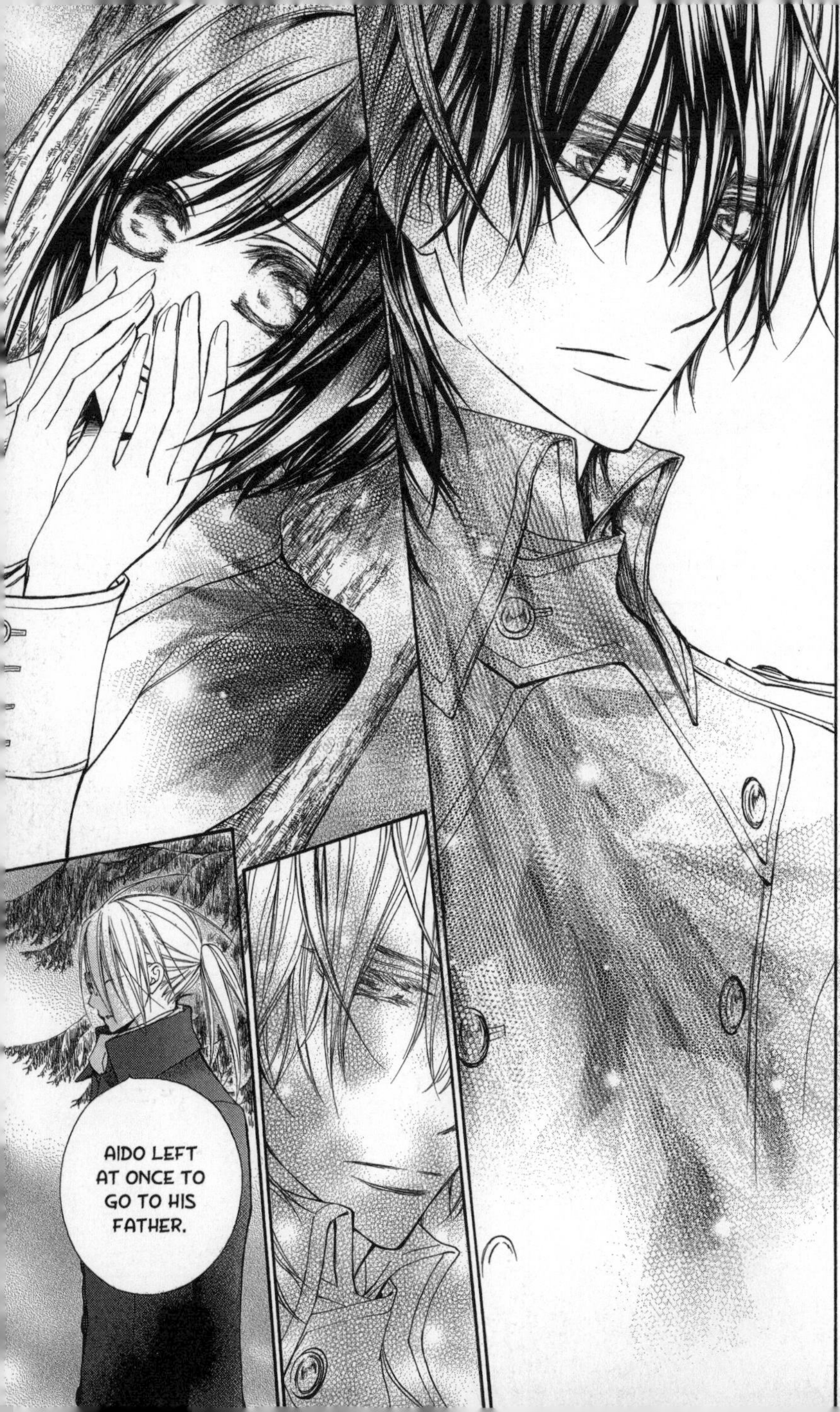
AIDO LEFT AT ONCE TO GO TO HIS FATHER.

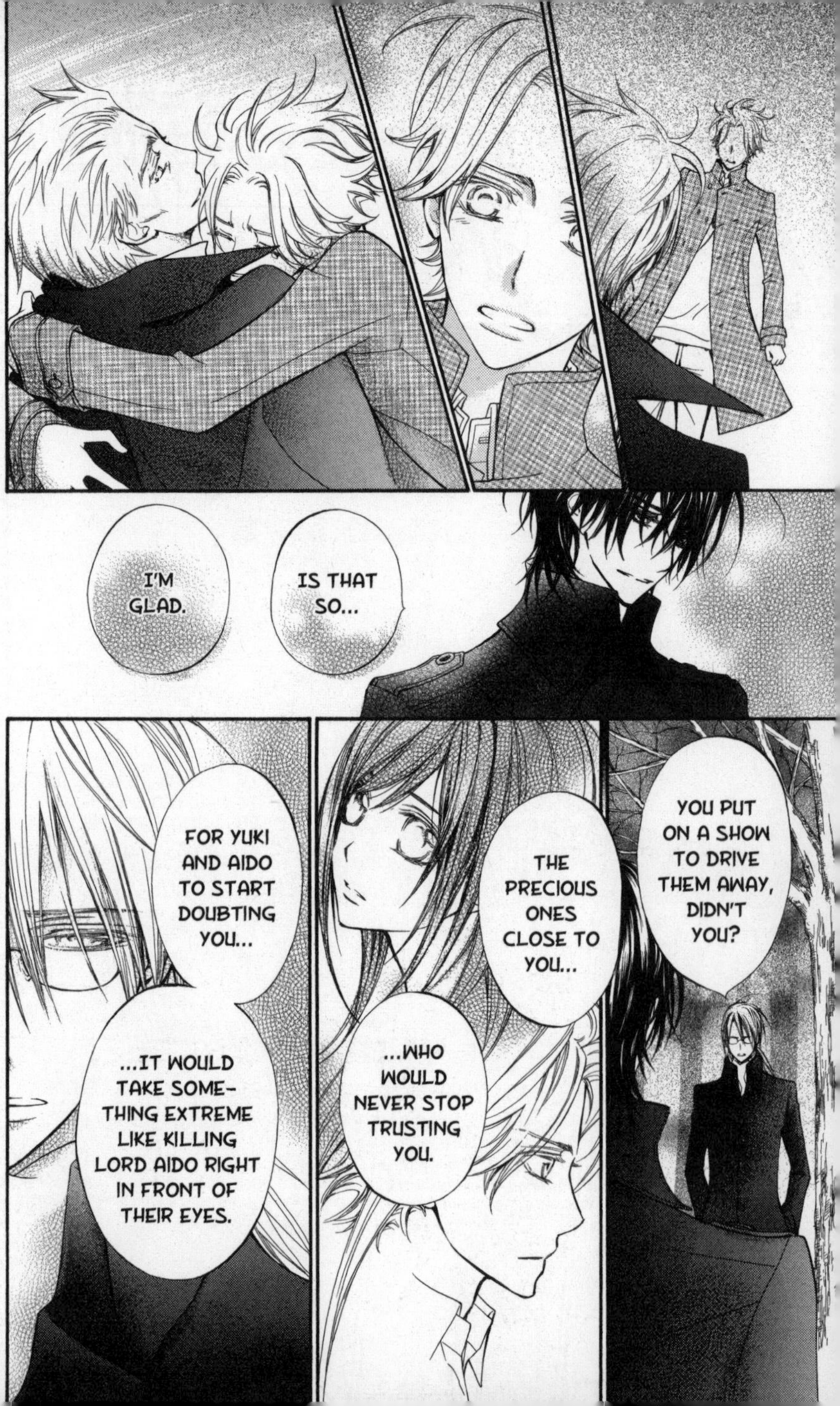
IS THAT SO...
I'M GLAD.
YOU PUT ON A SHOW TO DRIVE THEM AWAY, DIDN'T YOU?
THE PRECIOUS ONES CLOSE TO YOU...
...WHO WOULD NEVER STOP TRUSTING YOU.
FOR YUKI AND AIDO TO START DOUBTING YOU...
...IT WOULD TAKE SOME-THING EXTREME LIKE KILLING LORD AIDO RIGHT IN FRONT OF THEIR EYES.

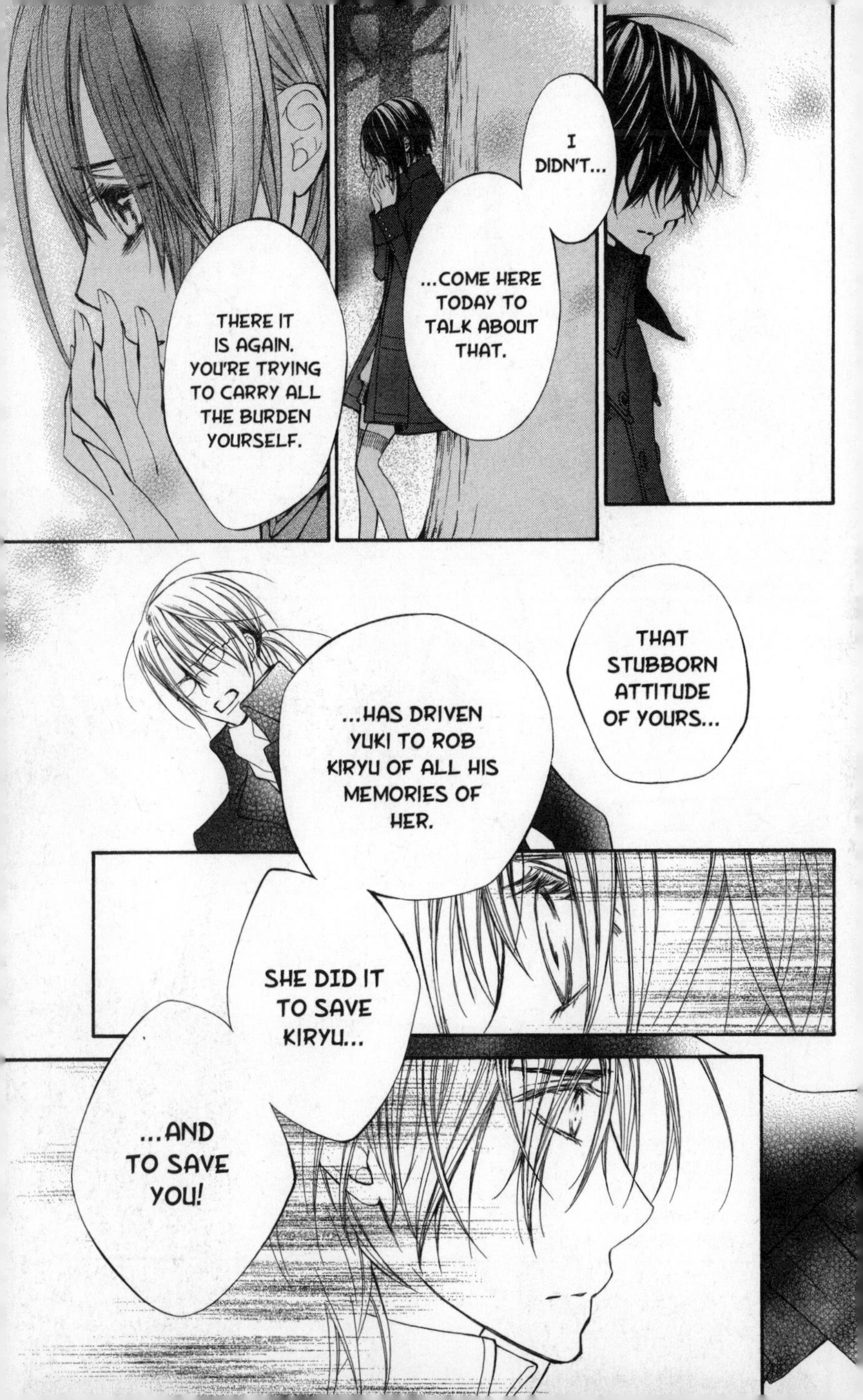
I DIDN'T...
...COME HERE TODAY TO TALK ABOUT THAT.
THERE IT IS AGAIN. YOU'RE TRYING TO CARRY ALL THE BURDEN YOURSELF.
THAT STUBBORN ATTITUDE OF YOURS...
...HAS DRIVEN YUKI TO ROB KIRYU OF ALL HIS MEMORIES OF HER.
SHE DID IT TO SAVE KIRYU...
...AND TO SAVE YOU!

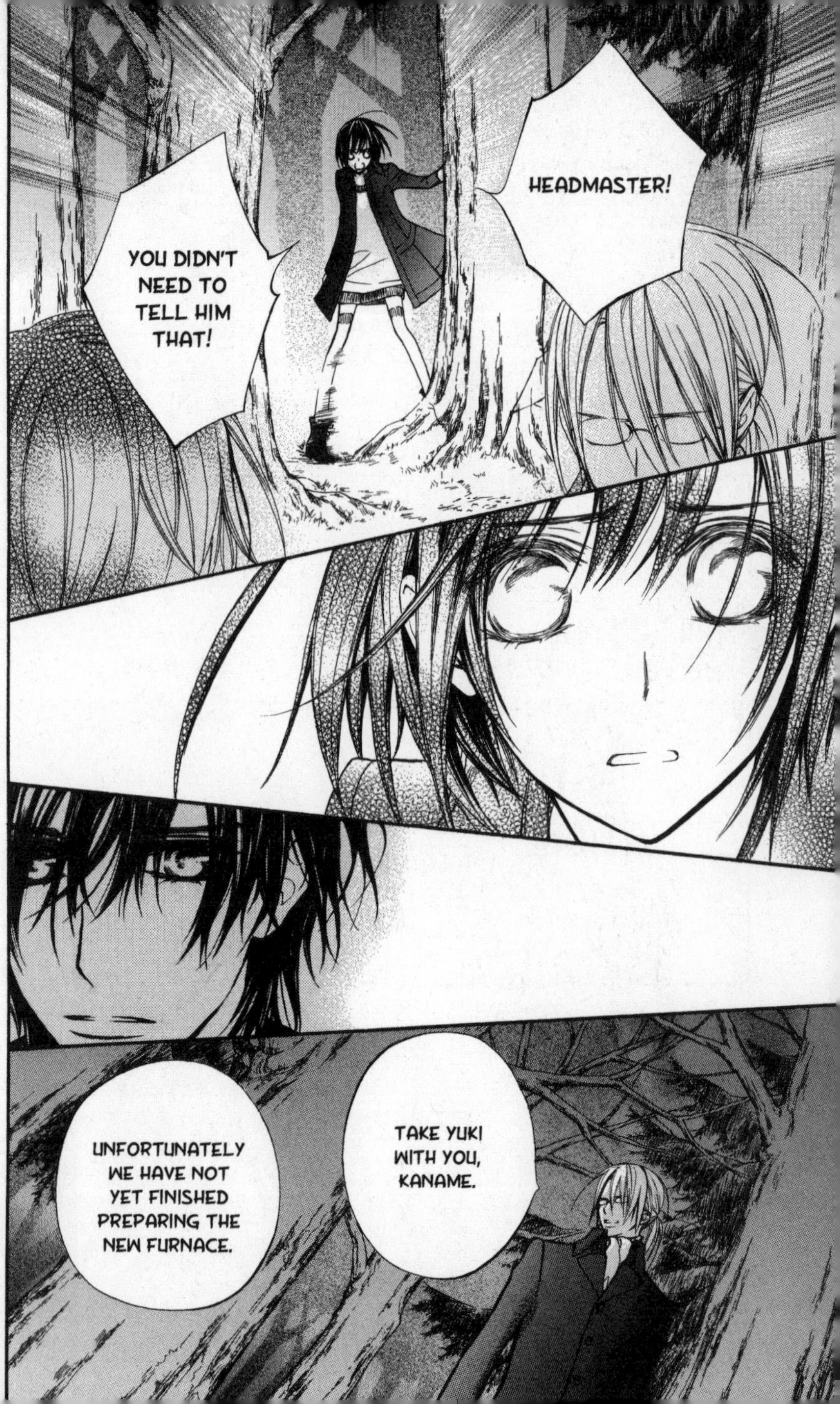
HEADMASTER!
YOU DIDN'T NEED TO TELL HIM THAT!
TAKE YUKI WITH YOU, KANAME.
UNFORTUNATELY WE HAVE NOT YET FINISHED PREPARING THE NEW FURNACE.

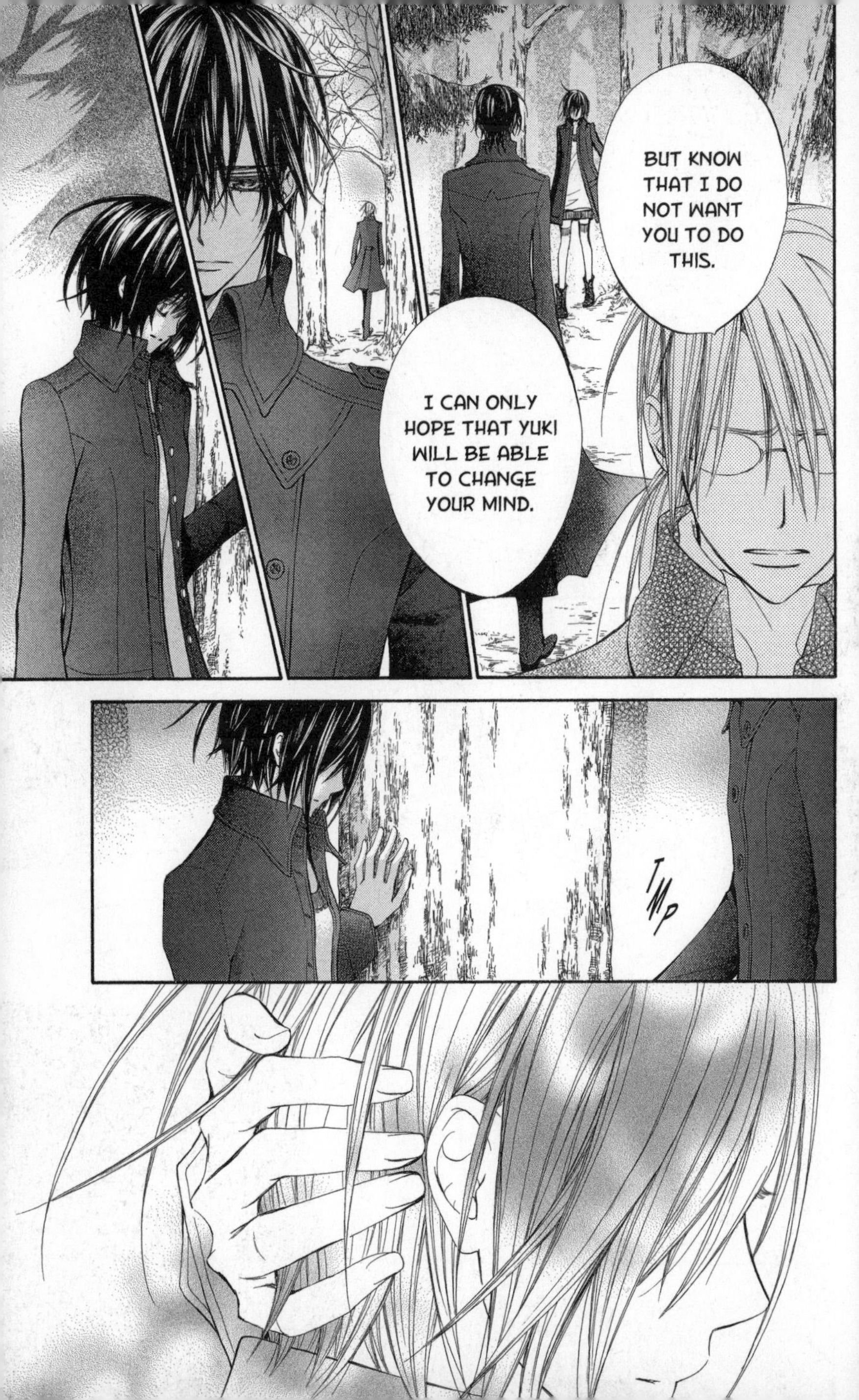
BUT KNOW THAT I DO NOT WANT YOU TO DO THIS.
I CAN ONLY HOPE THAT YUKI WILL BE ABLE TO CHANGE YOUR MIND.
TMP

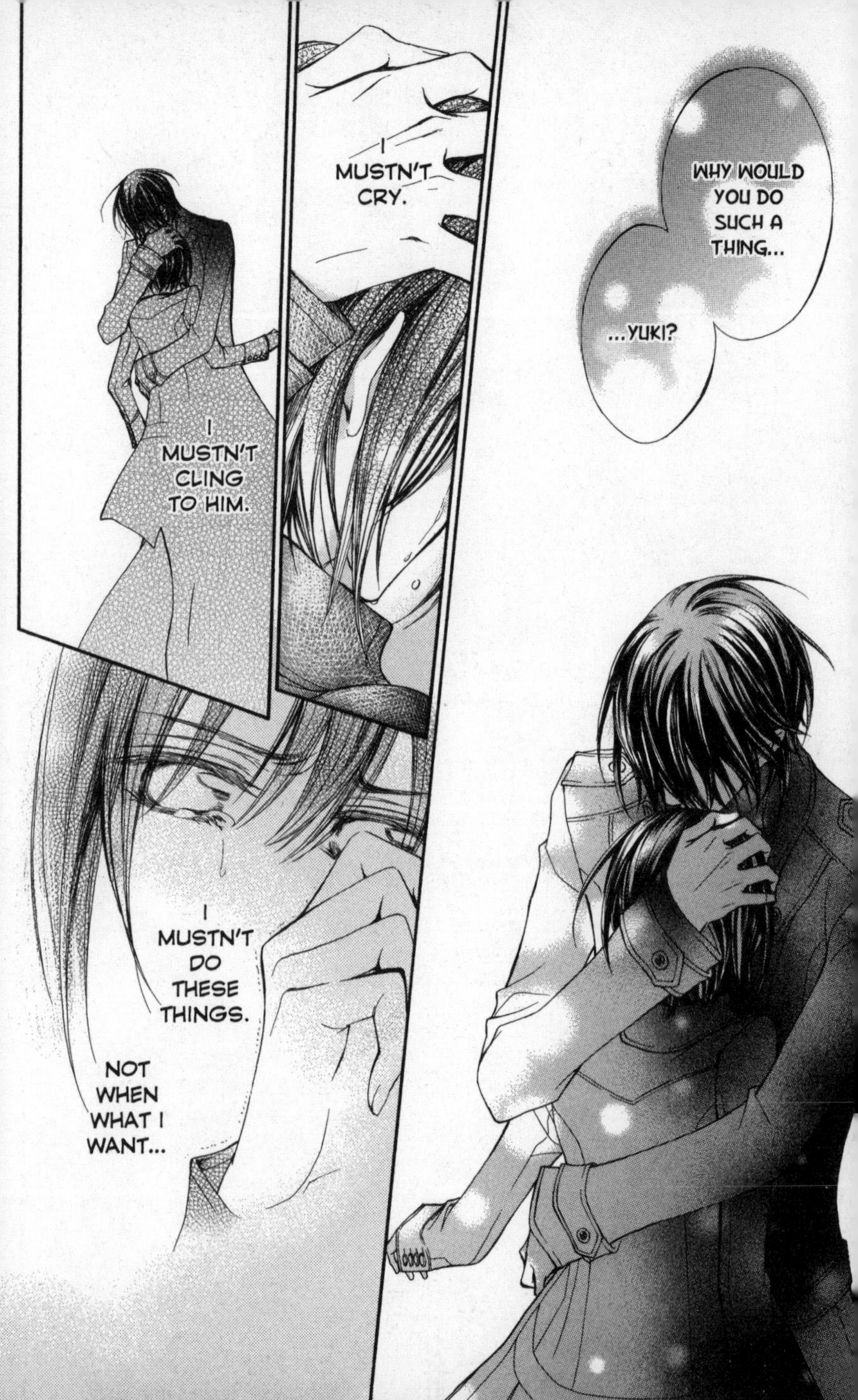
WHY WOULD YOU DO SUCH A THING...
...YUKI?
I MUSTN'T CRY.
I MUSTN'T CLING TO HIM.
I MUSTN'T DO THESE THINGS.
NOT WHEN WHAT I WANT...

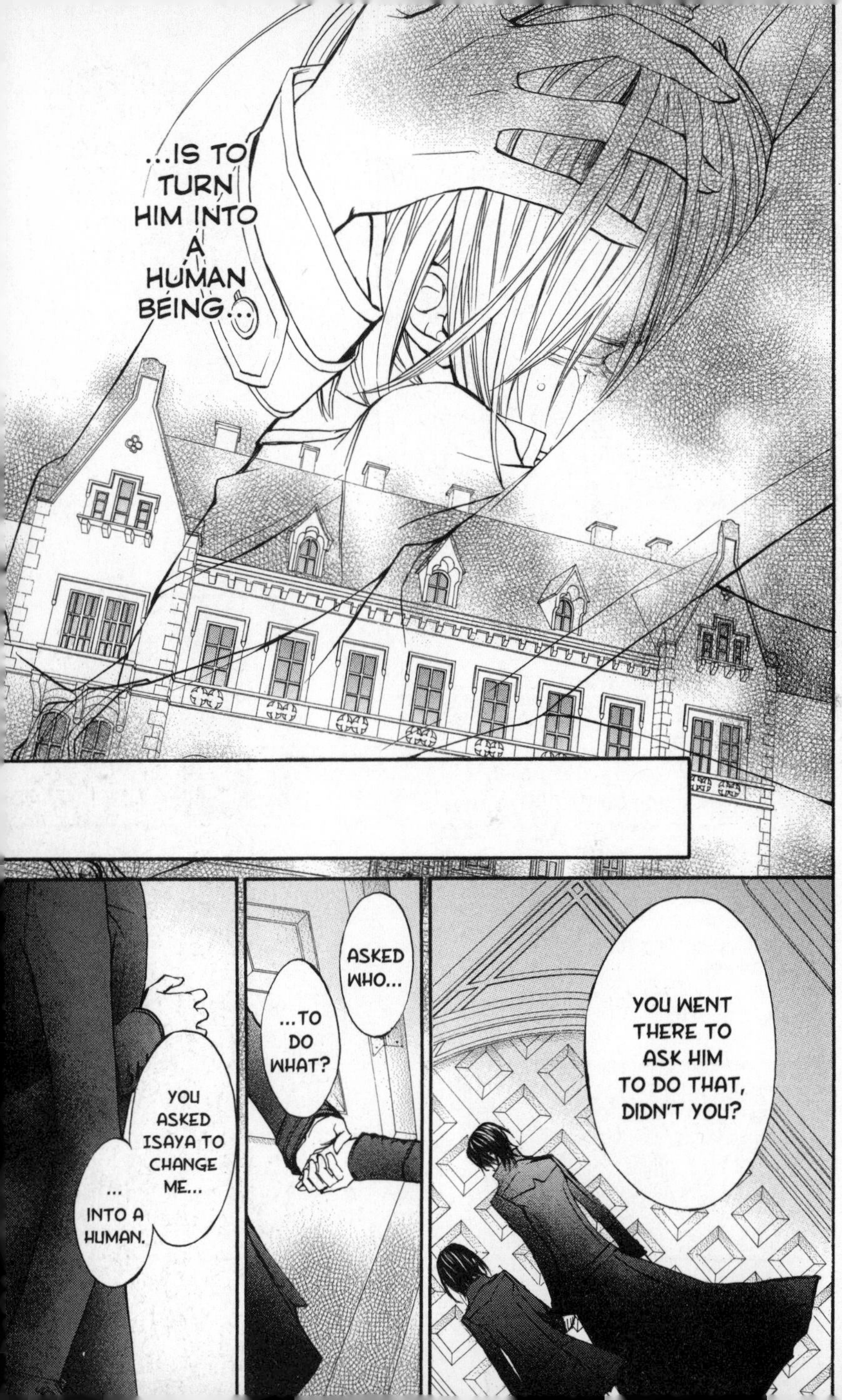
...IS TO TURN HIM INTO A HUMAN BEING...
YOU WENT THERE TO ASK HIM TO DO THAT, DIDN'T YOU?
ASKED WHO...
...TO DO WHAT?
YOU ASKED ISAYA TO CHANGE ME...
... INTO A HUMAN.

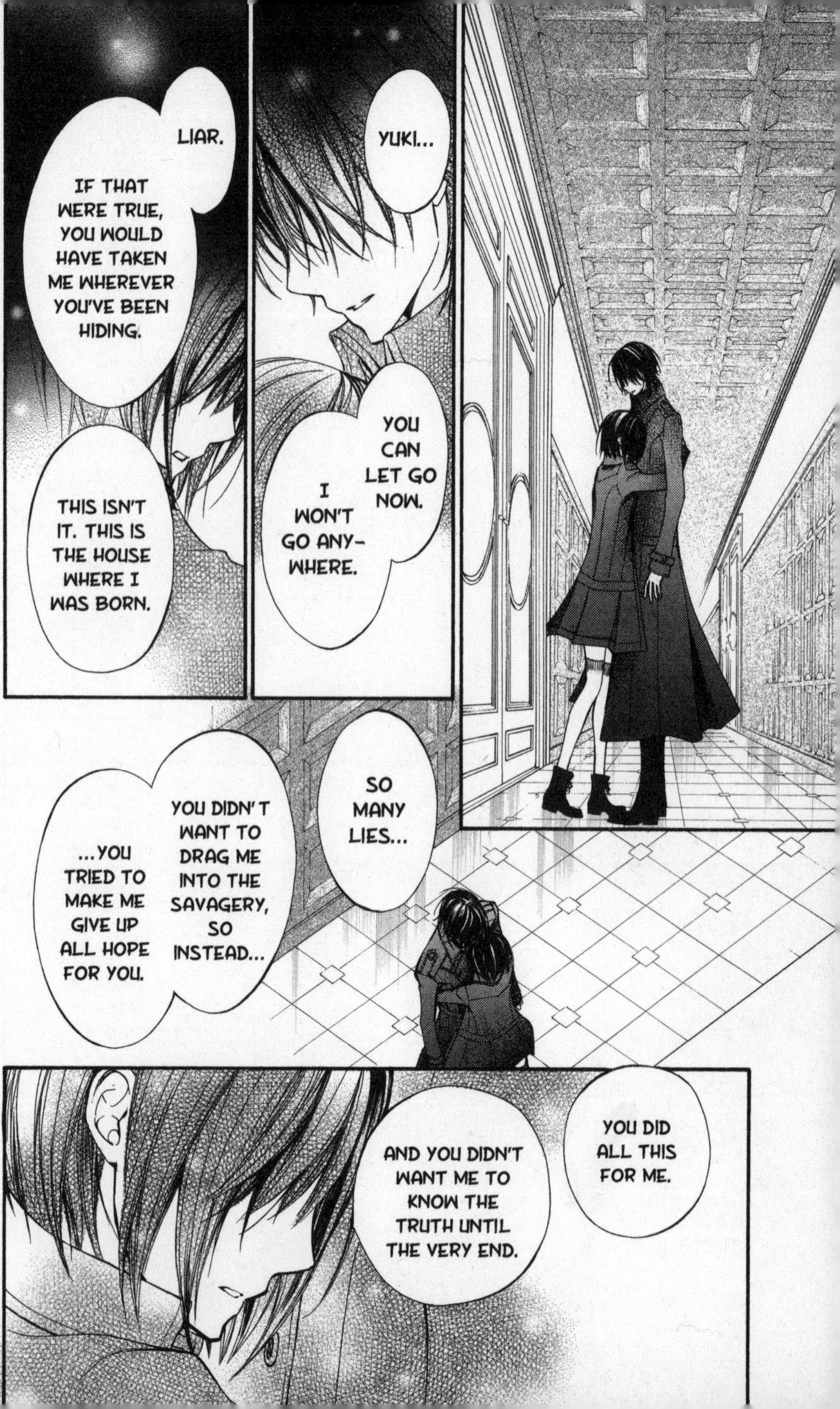
YUKI...
YOU CAN LET GO NOW.
I WON'T GO ANYWHERE.
LIAR.
IF THAT WERE TRUE, YOU WOULD HAVE TAKEN ME WHEREVER YOU'VE BEEN HIDING.
THIS ISN'T IT. THIS IS THE HOUSE WHERE I WAS BORN.
SO MANY LIES...
YOU DIDN'T WANT TO DRAG ME INTO THE SAVAGERY, SO INSTEAD...
...YOU TRIED TO MAKE ME GIVE UP ALL HOPE FOR YOU.
YOU DID ALL THIS FOR ME.
AND YOU DIDN'T WANT ME TO KNOW THE TRUTH UNTIL THE VERY END.

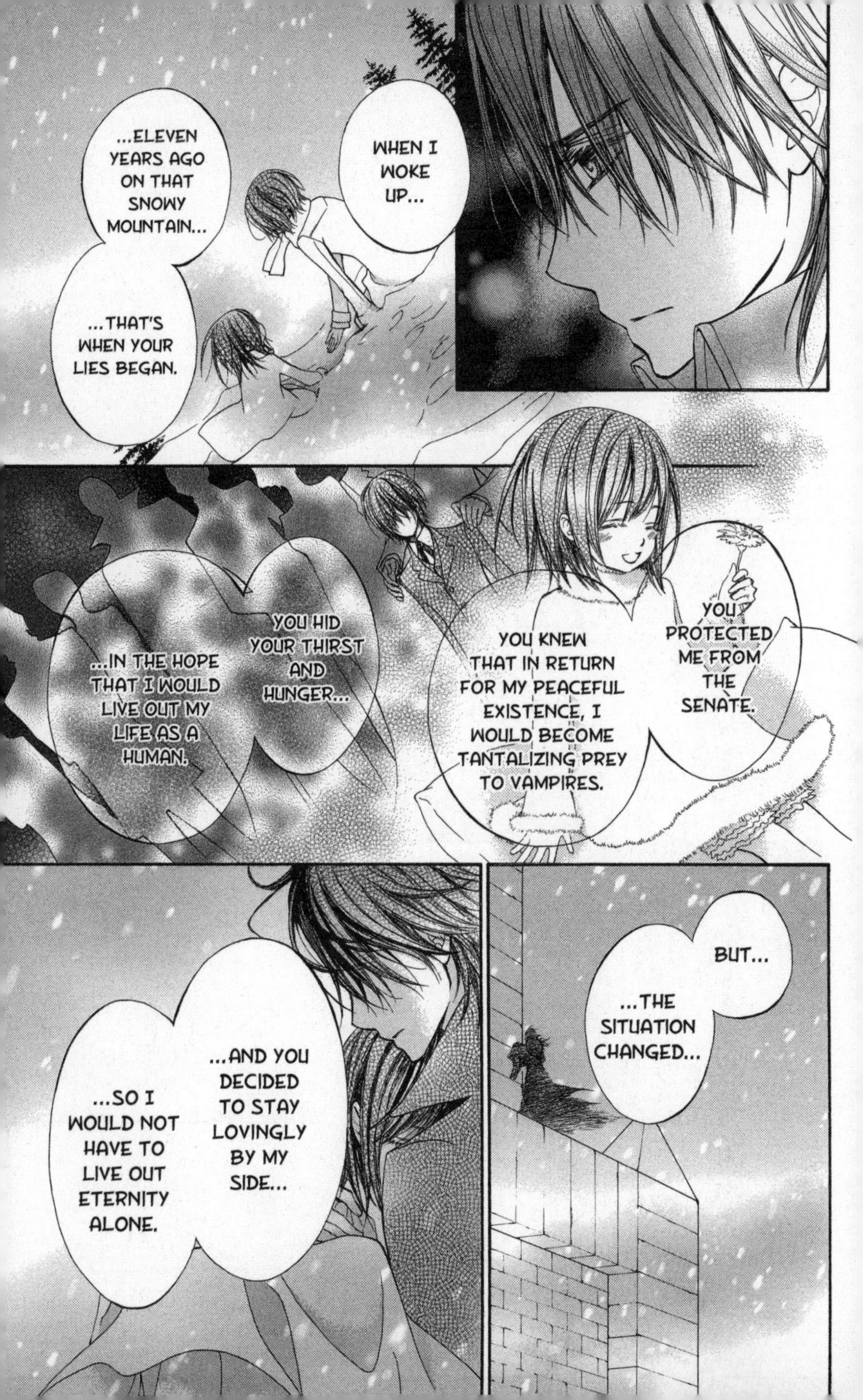
WHEN I WOKE UP...
...ELEVEN YEARS AGO ON THAT SNOWY MOUNTAIN...
...THAT'S WHEN YOUR LIES BEGAN.
YOU PROTECTED ME FROM THE SENATE.
YOU KNEW THAT IN RETURN FOR MY PEACEFUL EXISTENCE, I WOULD BECOME TANTALIZING PREY TO VAMPIRES.
YOU HID YOUR THIRST AND HUNGER...
...IN THE HOPE THAT I WOULD LIVE OUT MY LIFE AS A HUMAN.
BUT...
...THE SITUATION CHANGED...
...AND YOU DECIDED TO STAY LOVINGLY BY MY SIDE...
...SO I WOULD NOT HAVE TO LIVE OUT ETERNITY ALONE.

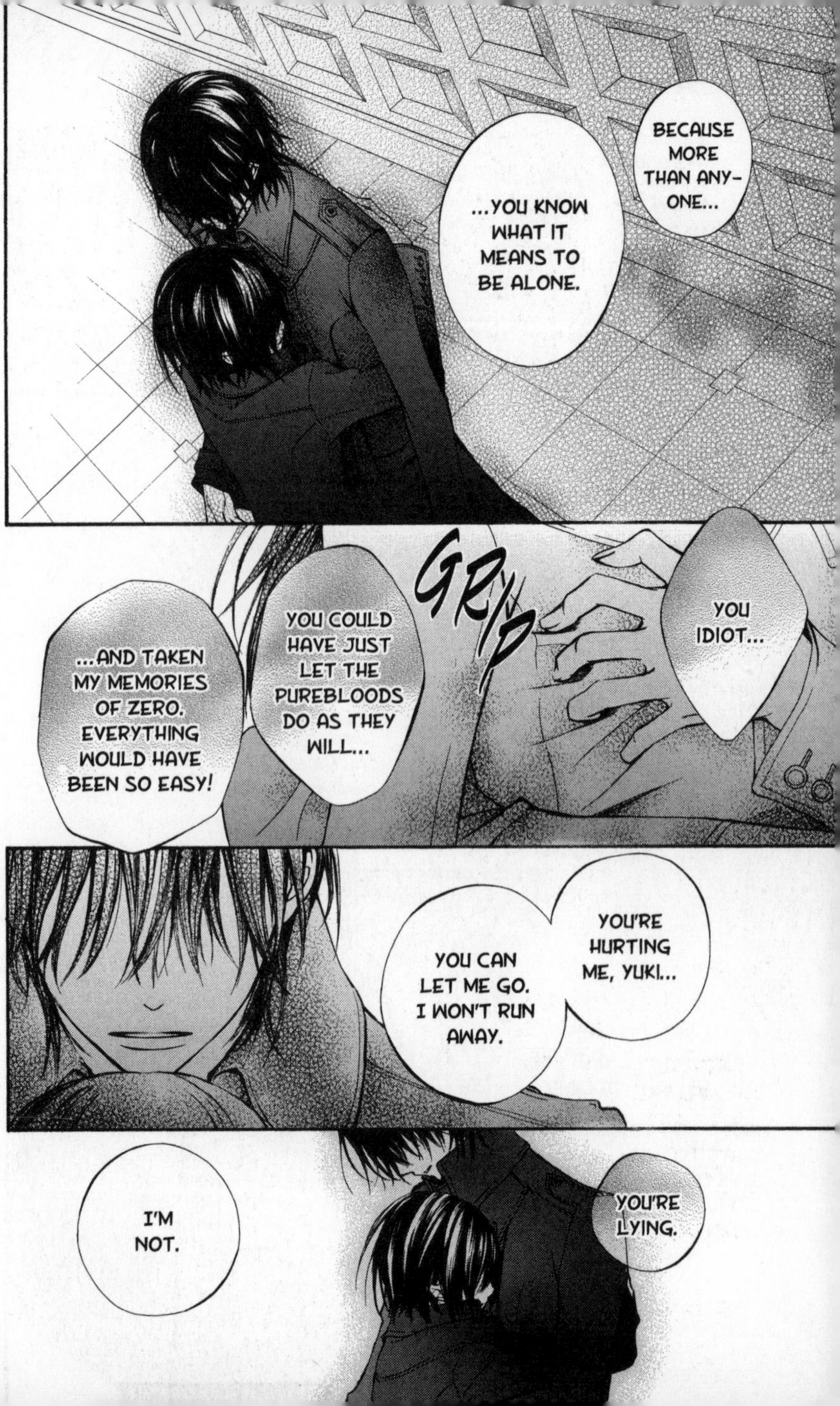
BECAUSE MORE THAN ANY-ONE...
...YOU KNOW WHAT IT MEANS TO BE ALONE.
YOU IDIOT...
GRIP
YOU COULD HAVE JUST LET THE PUREBLOODS DO AS THEY WILL...
...AND TAKEN MY MEMORIES OF ZERO. EVERYTHING WOULD HAVE BEEN SO EASY!
YOU'RE HURTING ME, YUKI...
YOU CAN LET ME GO. I WON'T RUN AWAY.
YOU'RE LYING.
I'M NOT.

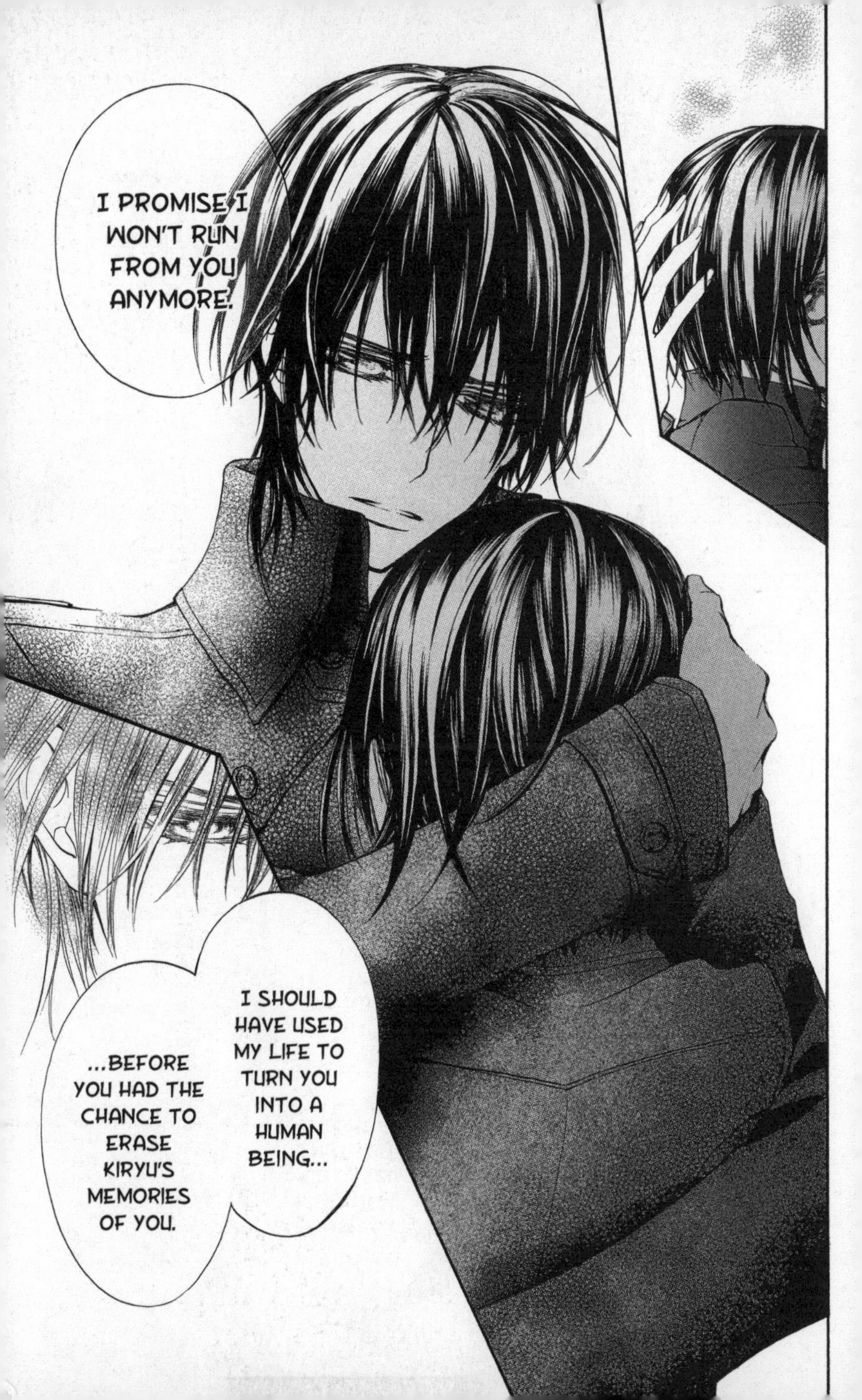
I PROMISE I WON'T RUN FROM YOU ANYMORE.
I SHOULD HAVE USED MY LIFE TO TURN YOU INTO A HUMAN BEING...
...BEFORE YOU HAD THE CHANCE TO ERASE KIRYU'S MEMORIES OF YOU.

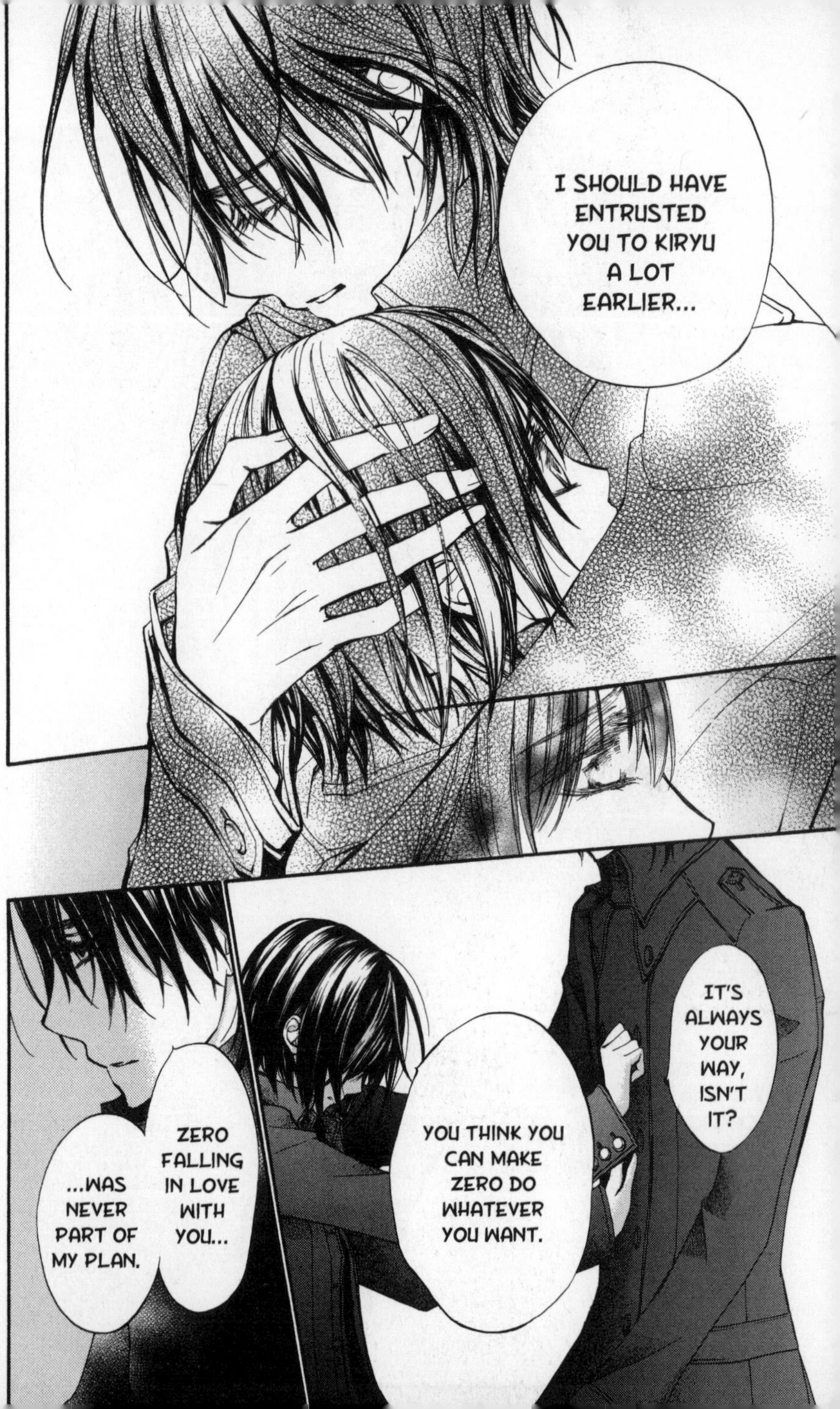
I SHOULD HAVE ENTRUSTED YOU TO KIRYU A LOT EARLIER...
IT'S ALWAYS YOUR WAY, ISN'T IT?
YOU THINK YOU CAN MAKE ZERO DO WHATEVER YOU WANT.
ZERO FALLING IN LOVE WITH YOU...
...WAS NEVER PART OF MY PLAN.

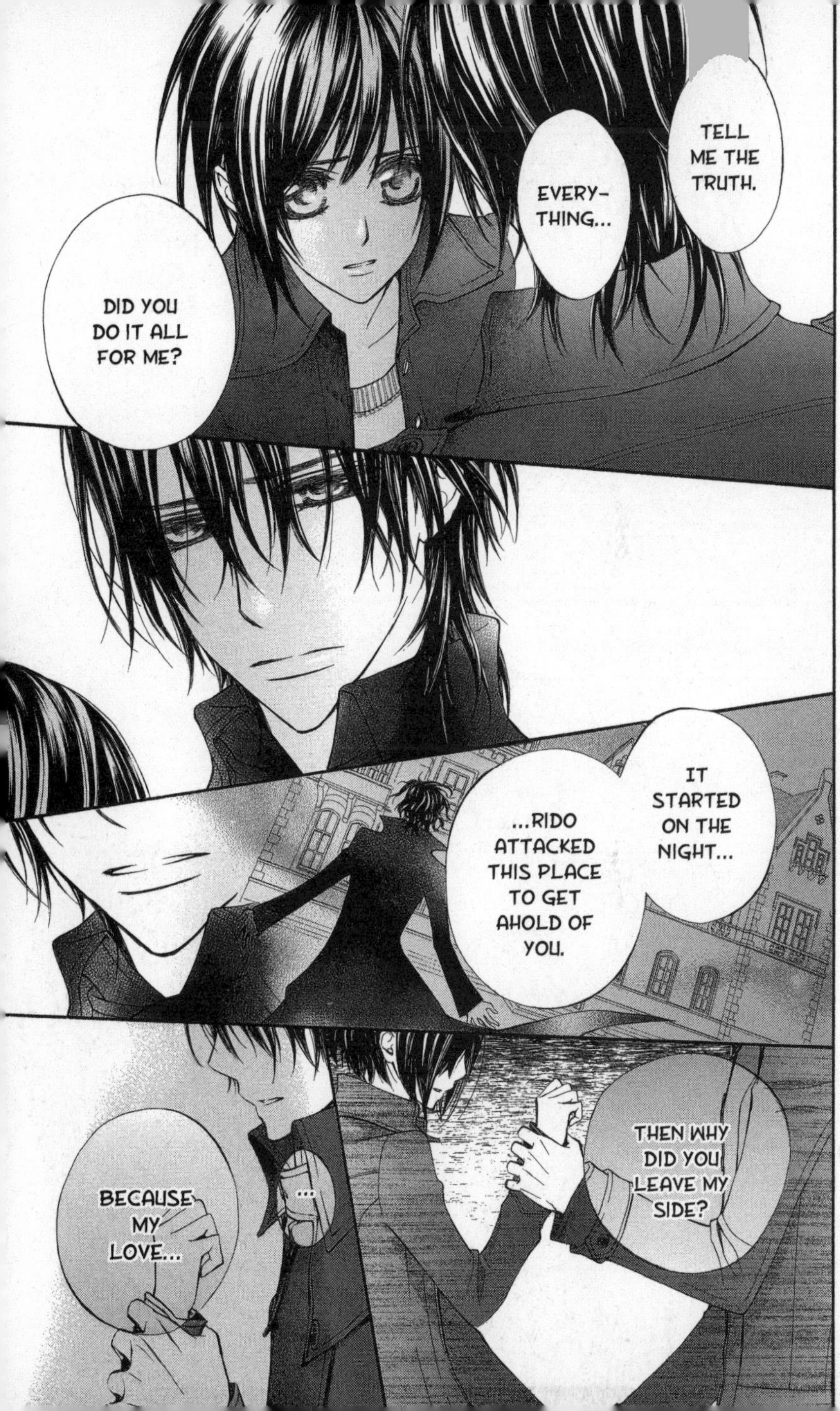
TELL ME THE TRUTH.
EVERY-THING...
DID YOU DO IT ALL FOR ME?
IT STARTED ON THE NIGHT...
...RIDO ATTACKED THIS PLACE TO GET AHOLD OF YOU.
THEN WHY DID YOU LEAVE MY SIDE?
...
BECAUSE MY LOVE...

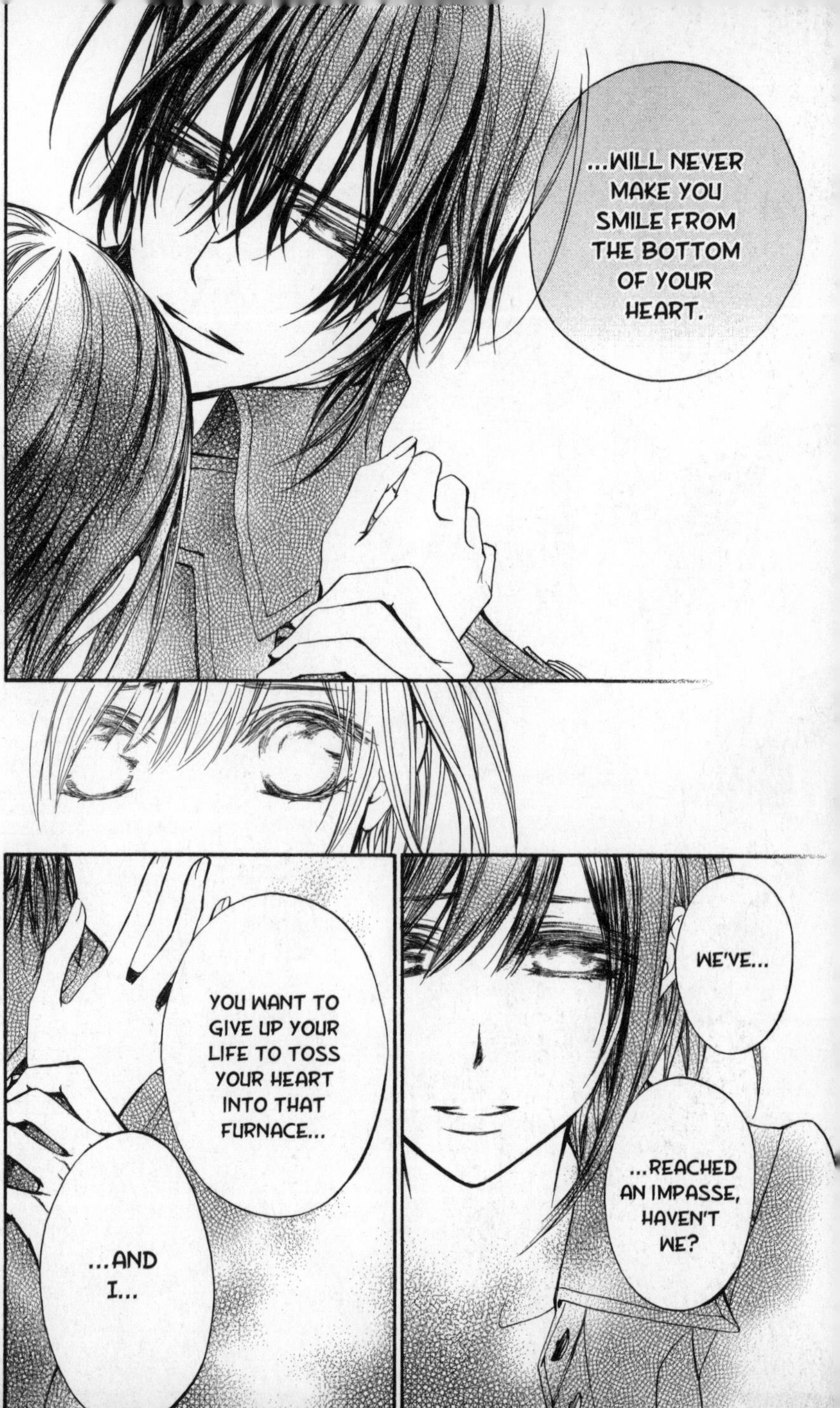
...WILL NEVER MAKE YOU SMILE FROM THE BOTTOM OF YOUR HEART.
WE'VE...
...REACHED AN IMPASSE, HAVEN'T WE?
YOU WANT TO GIVE UP YOUR LIFE TO TOSS YOUR HEART INTO THAT FURNACE...
...AND I...

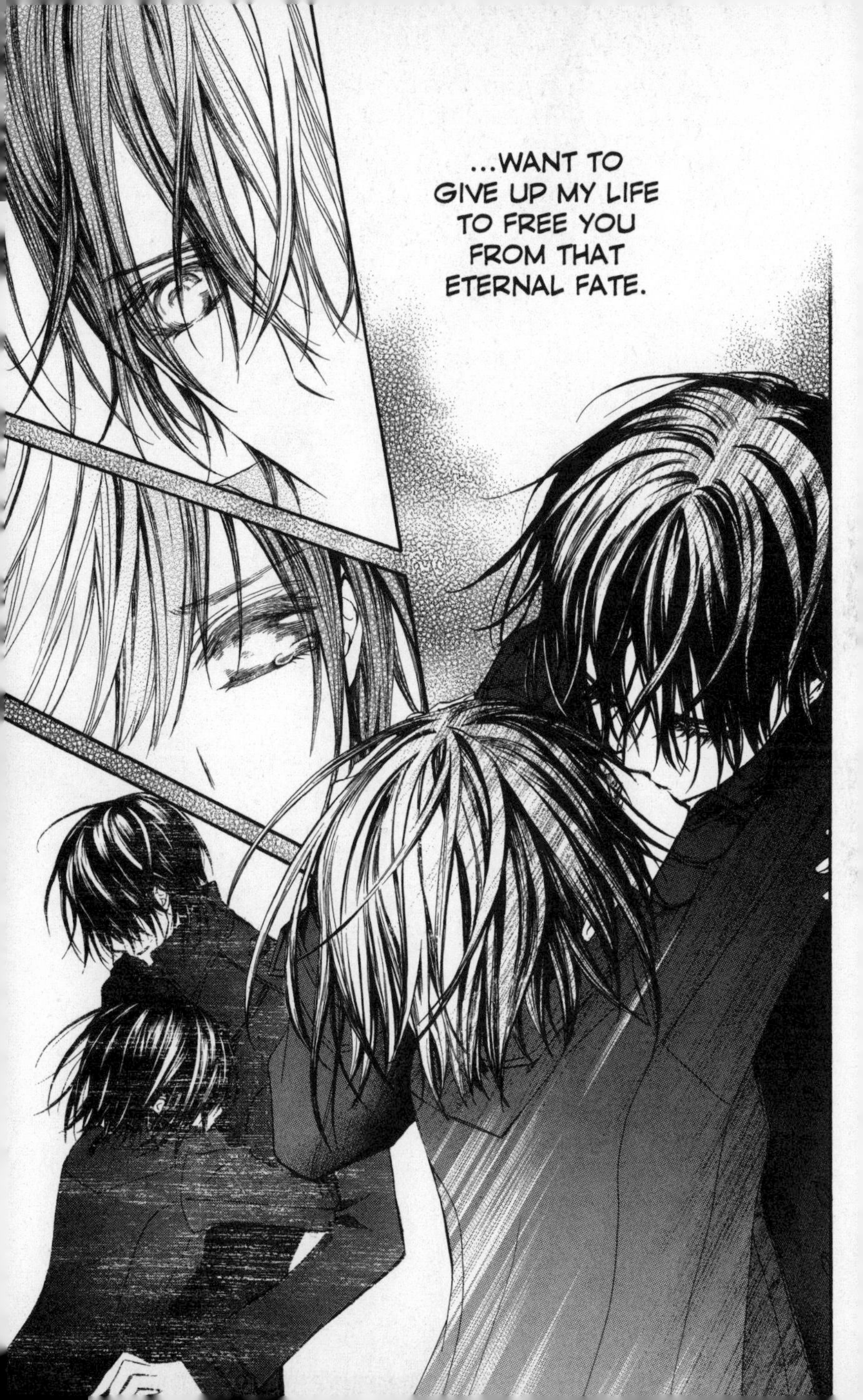
...WANT TO GIVE UP MY LIFE TO FREE YOU FROM THAT ETERNAL FATE.

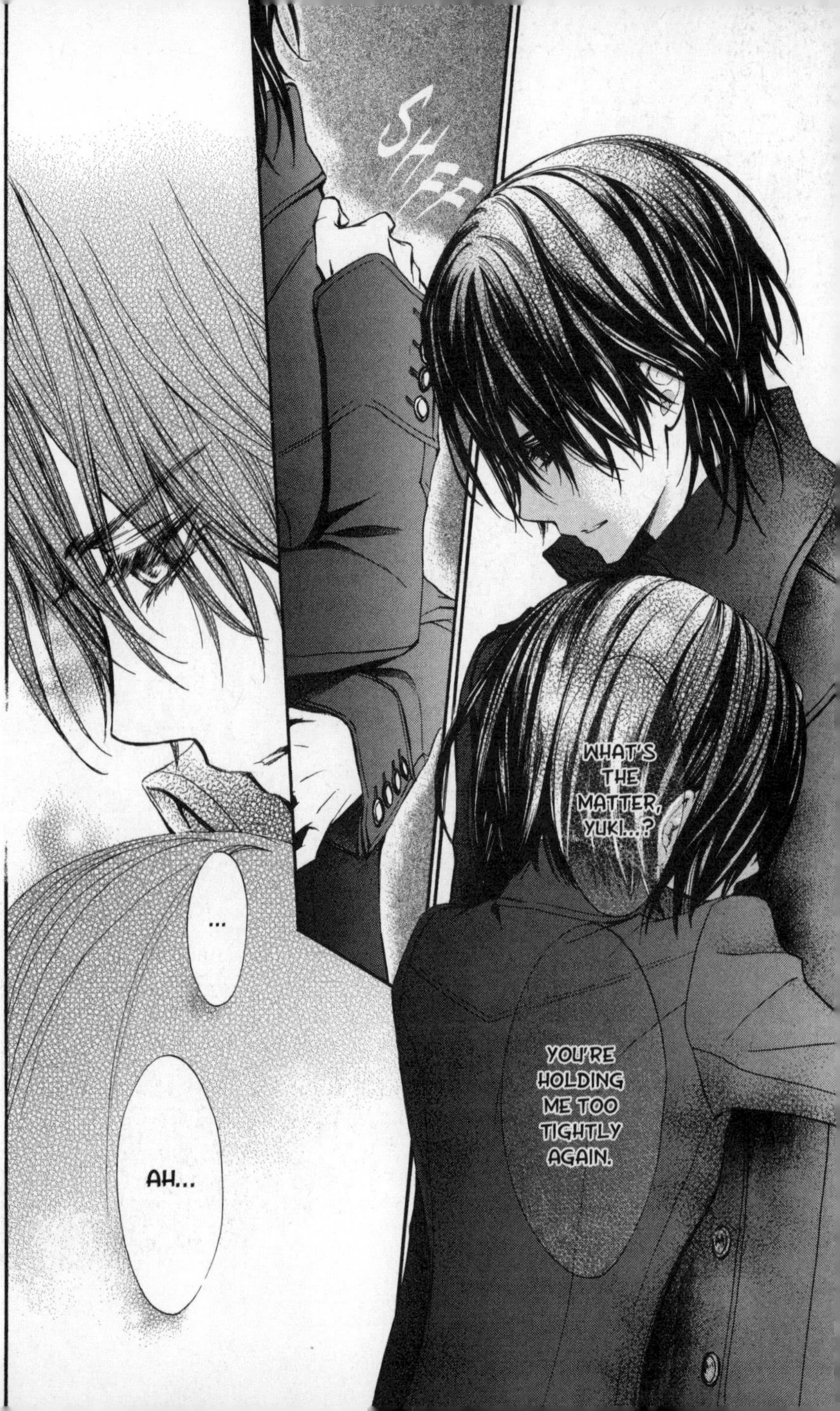
SHFF
WHAT'S THE MATTER, YUKI...?
YOU'RE HOLDING ME TOO TIGHTLY AGAIN.
...
AH...

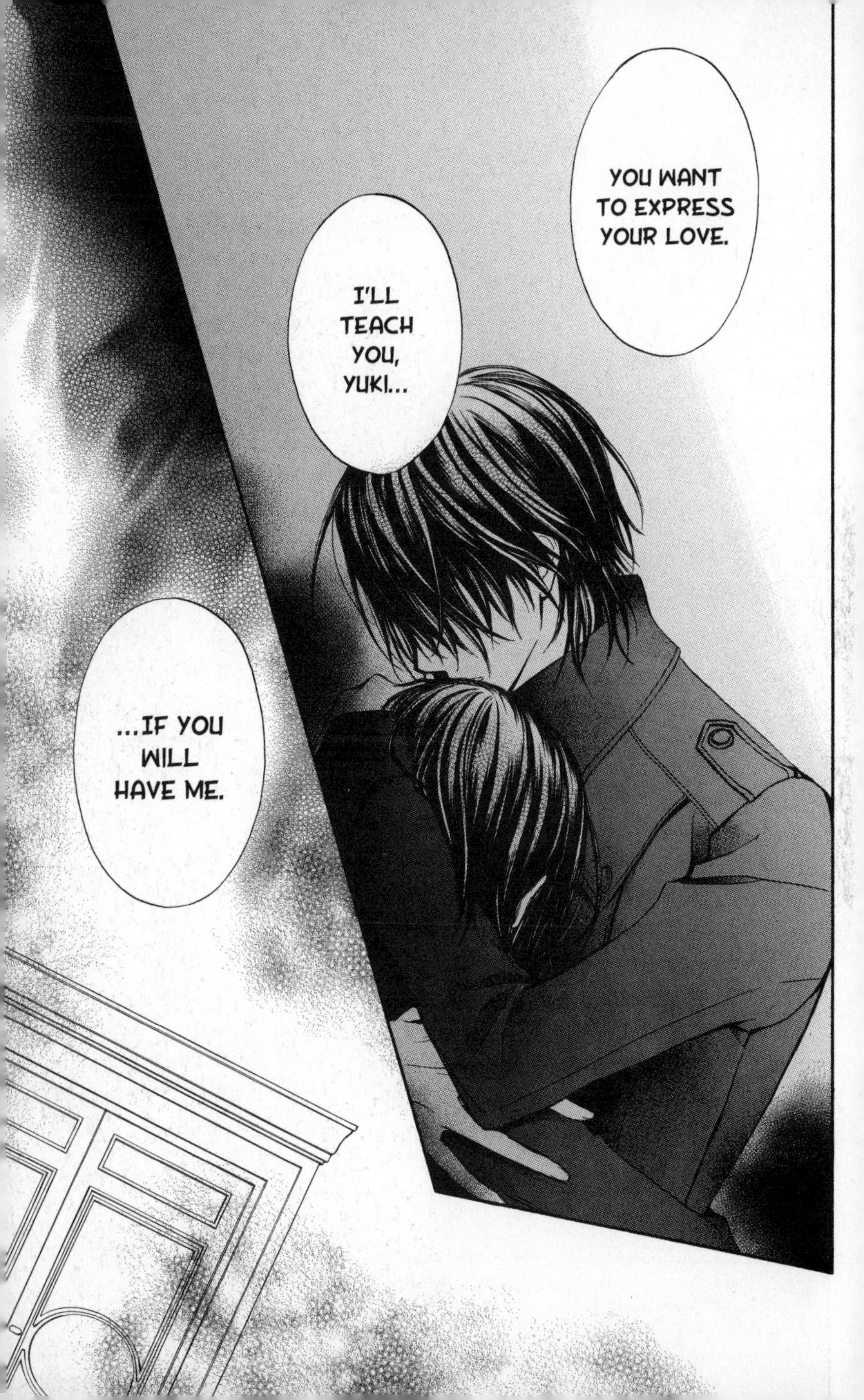
YOU WANT TO EXPRESS YOUR LOVE.
I'LL TEACH YOU, YUKI...
...IF YOU WILL HAVE ME.

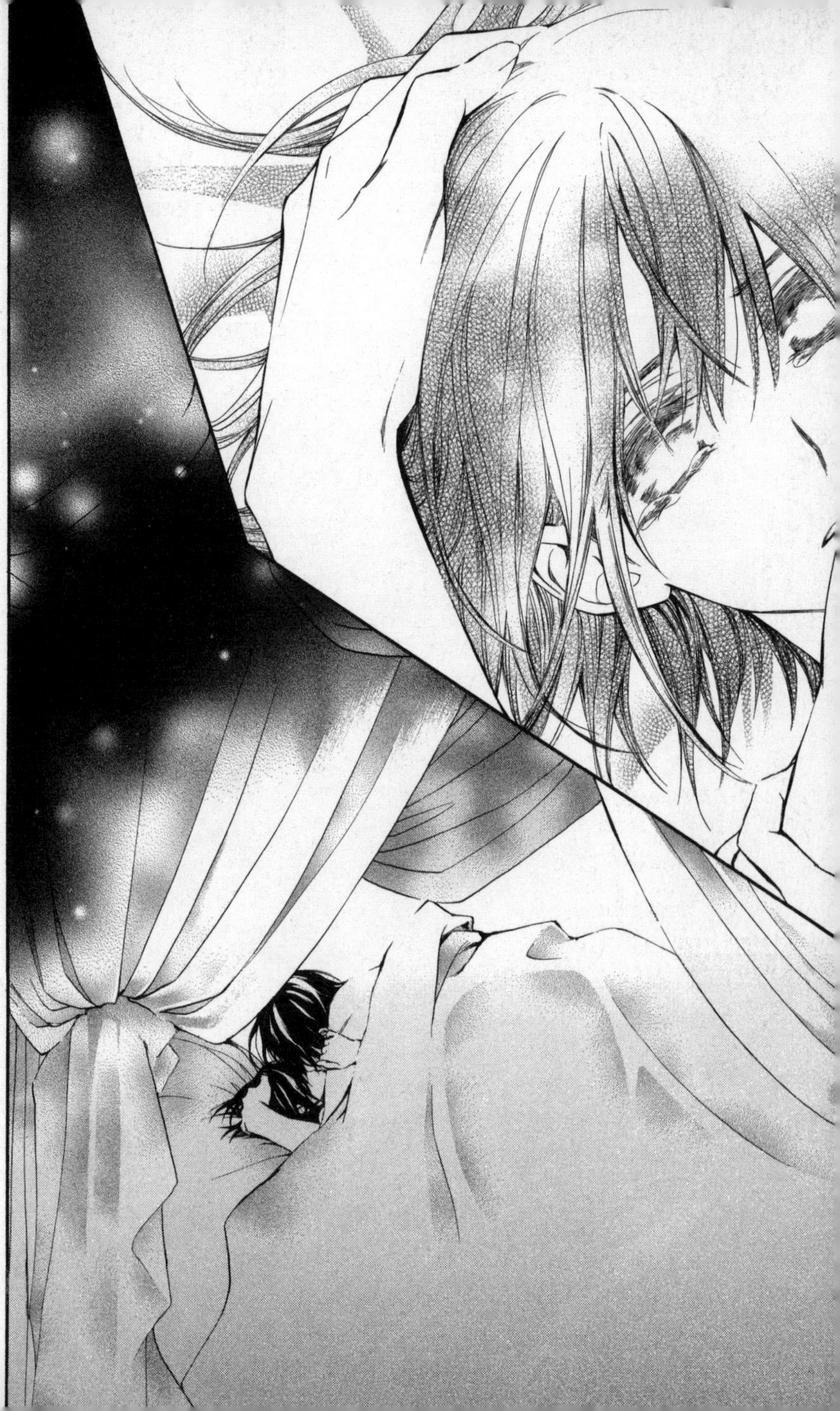

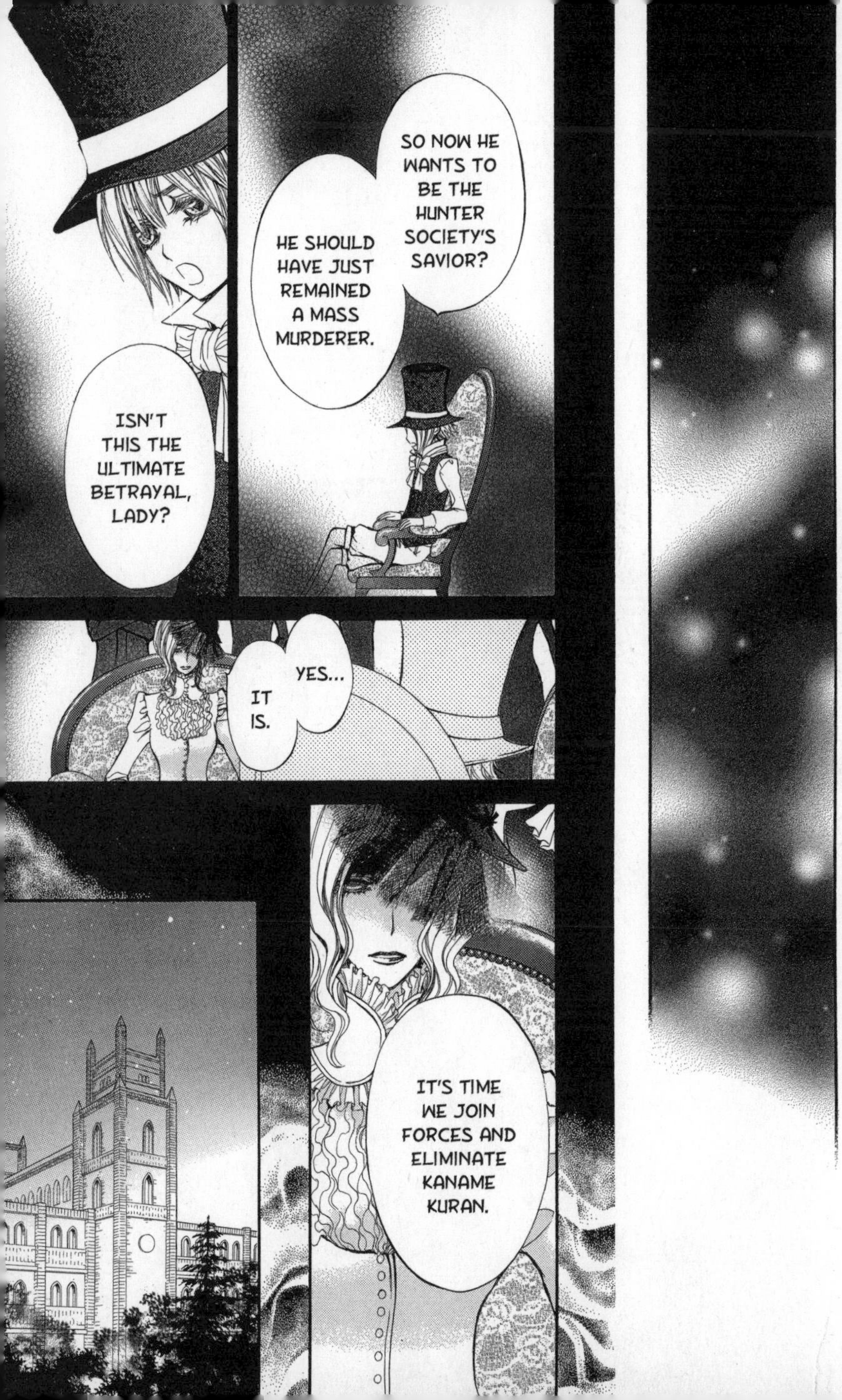
SO NOW HE WANTS TO BE THE HUNTER SOCIETY'S SAVIOR?
HE SHOULD HAVE JUST REMAINED A MASS MURDERER.
ISN'T THIS THE ULTIMATE BETRAYAL, LADY?
YES... IT IS.
IT'S TIME WE JOIN FORCES AND ELIMINATE KANAME KURAN.

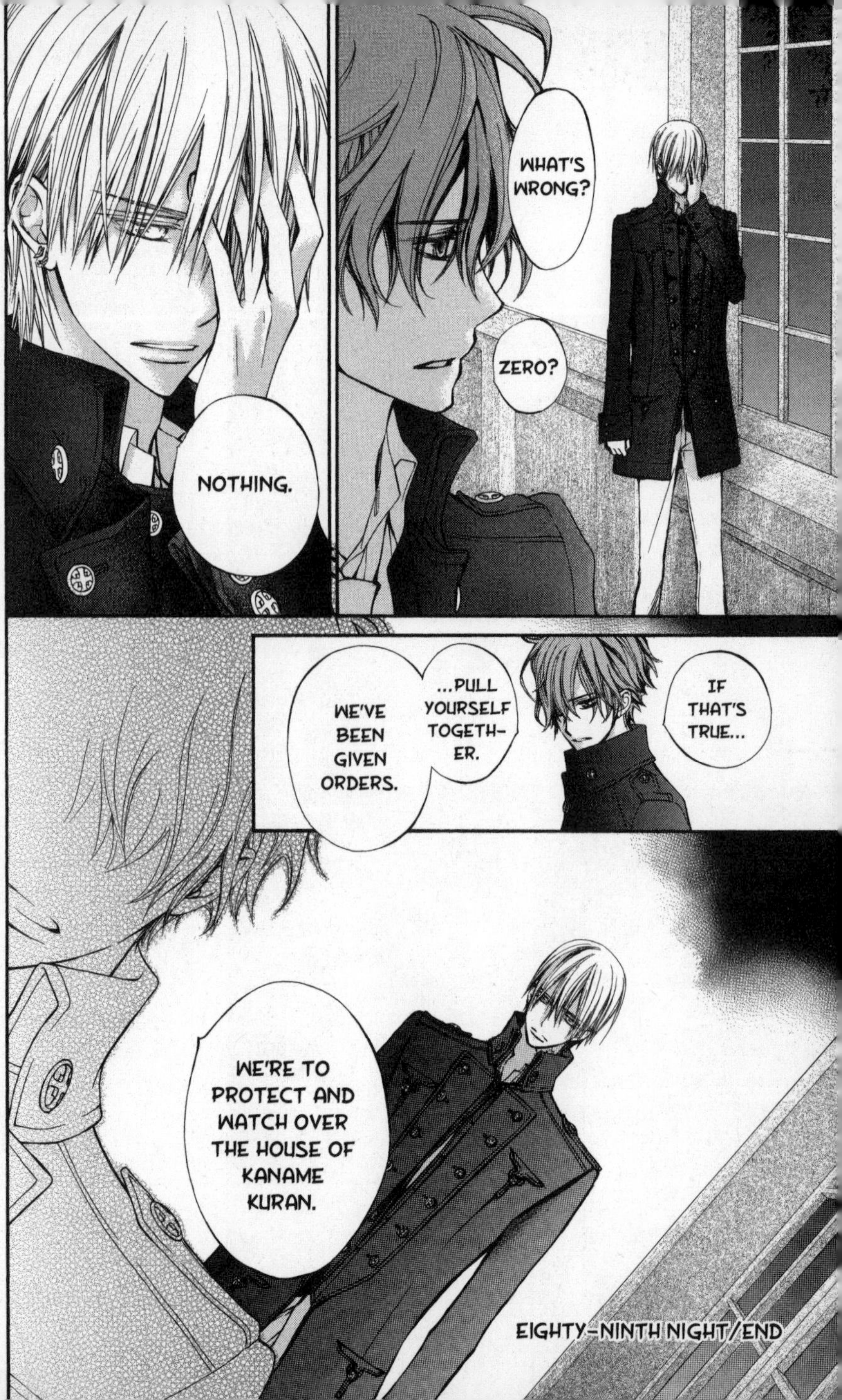
WHAT'S WRONG?
ZERO?
NOTHING.
IF THAT'S TRUE...
...PULL YOURSELF TOGETH-ER.
WE'VE BEEN GIVEN ORDERS.
WE'RE TO PROTECT AND WATCH OVER THE HOUSE OF KANAME KURAN.
EIGHTY-NINTH NIGHT/END

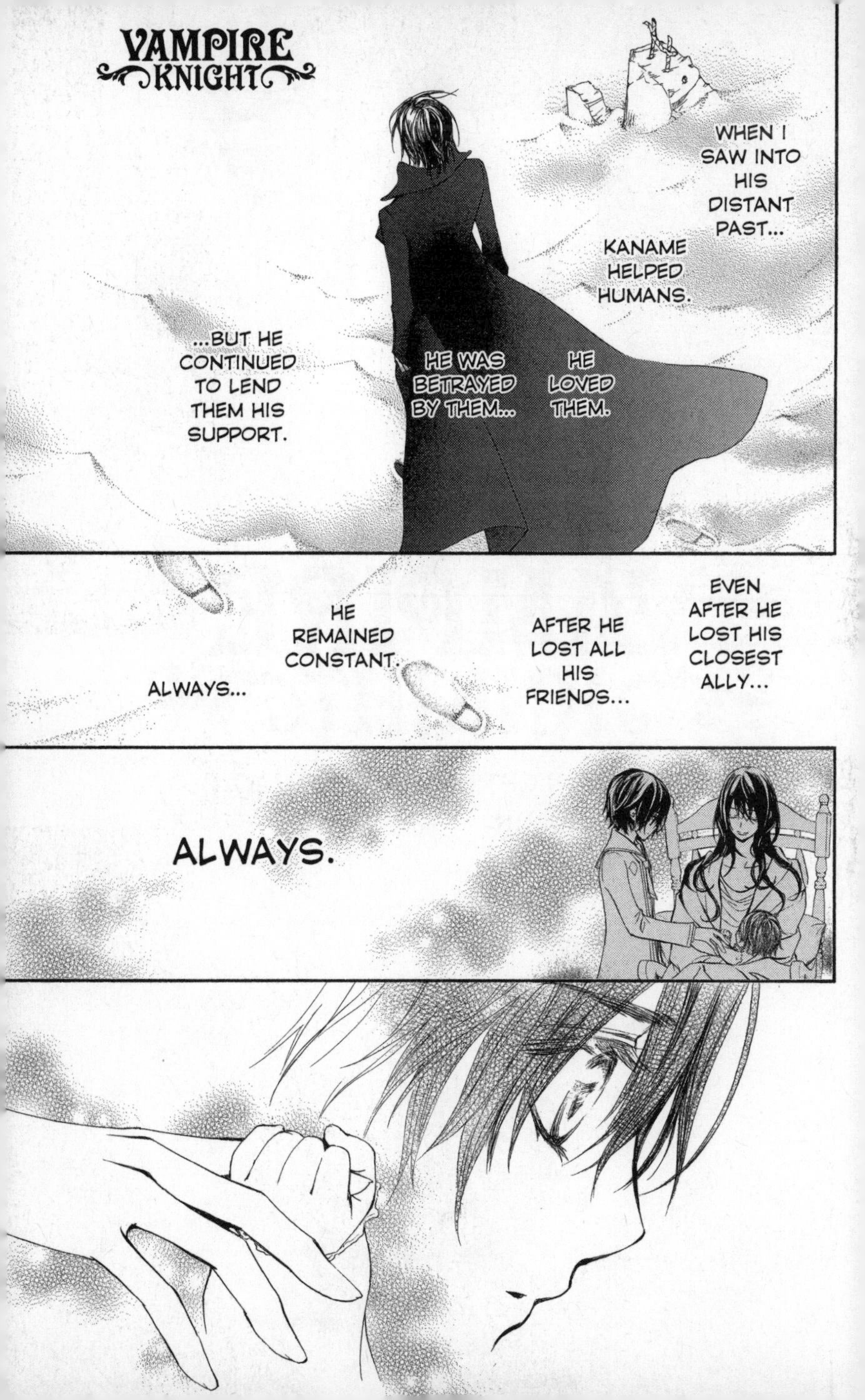
VAMPIRE KNIGHT
WHEN I SAW INTO HIS DISTANT PAST...
KANAME HELPED HUMANS.
HE LOVED THEM.
HE WAS BETRAYED BY THEM...
...BUT HE CONTINUED TO LEND THEM HIS SUPPORT.
EVEN AFTER HE LOST HIS CLOSEST ALLY...
AFTER HE LOST ALL HIS FRIENDS...
HE REMAINED CONSTANT.
ALWAYS...
ALWAYS.

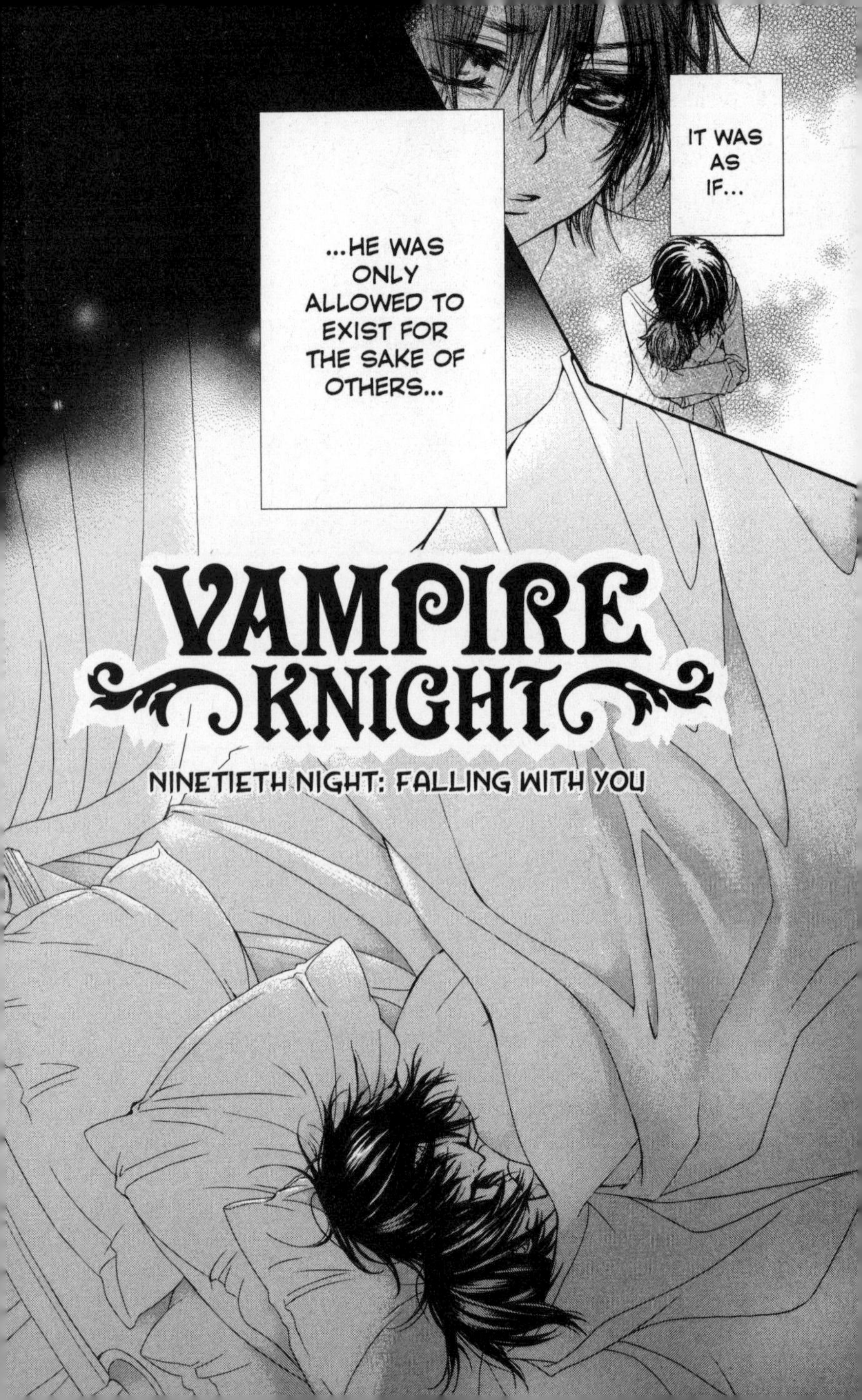
IT WAS AS IF...
...HE WAS ONLY ALLOWED TO EXIST FOR THE SAKE OF OTHERS...
VAMPIRE KNIGHT
NINETIETH NIGHT: FALLING WITH YOU

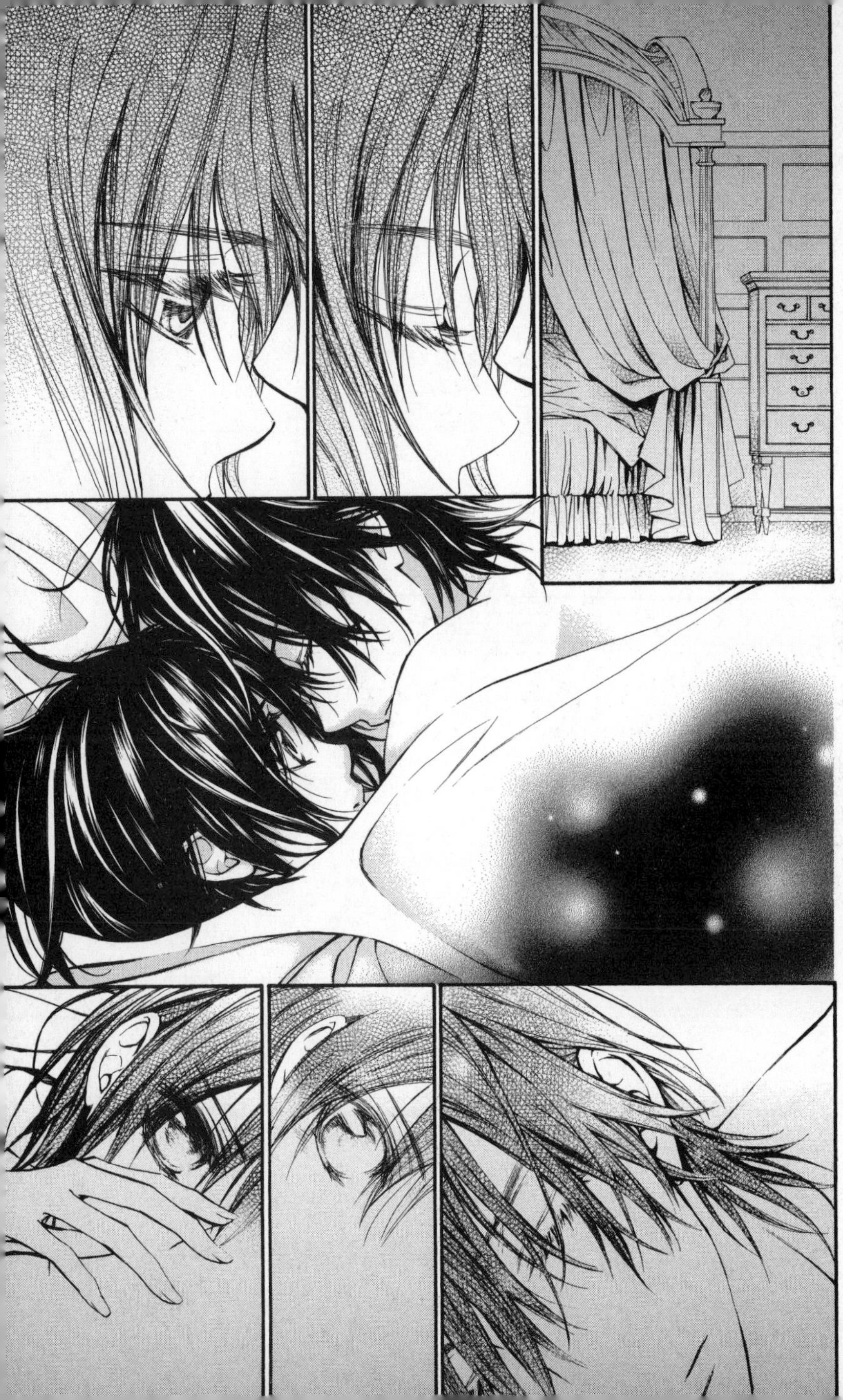

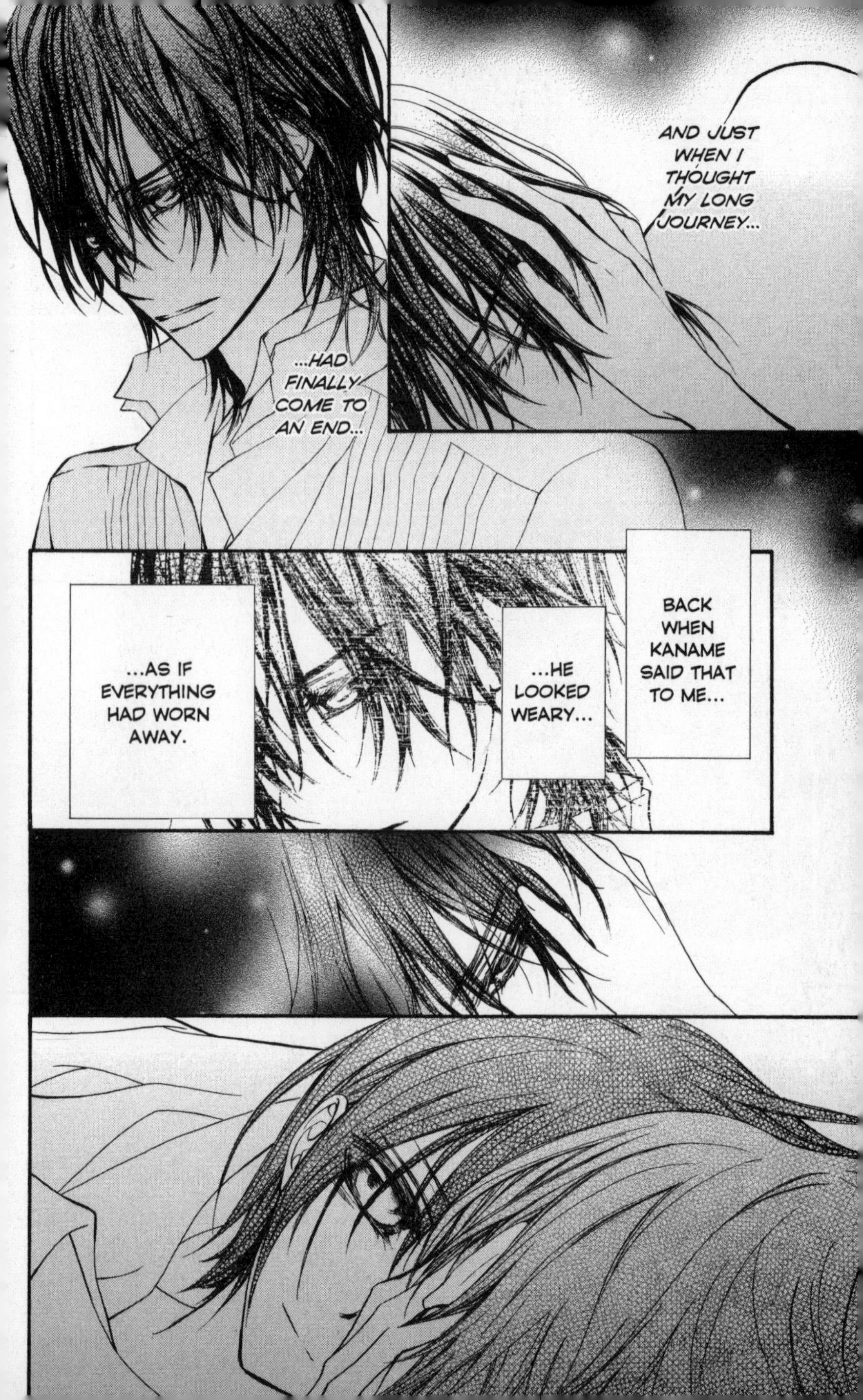
AND JUST WHEN I THOUGHT MY LONG JOURNEY...
...HAD FINALLY COME TO AN END...
BACK WHEN KANAME SAID THAT TO ME...
...HE LOOKED WEARY...
...AS IF EVERYTHING HAD WORN AWAY.

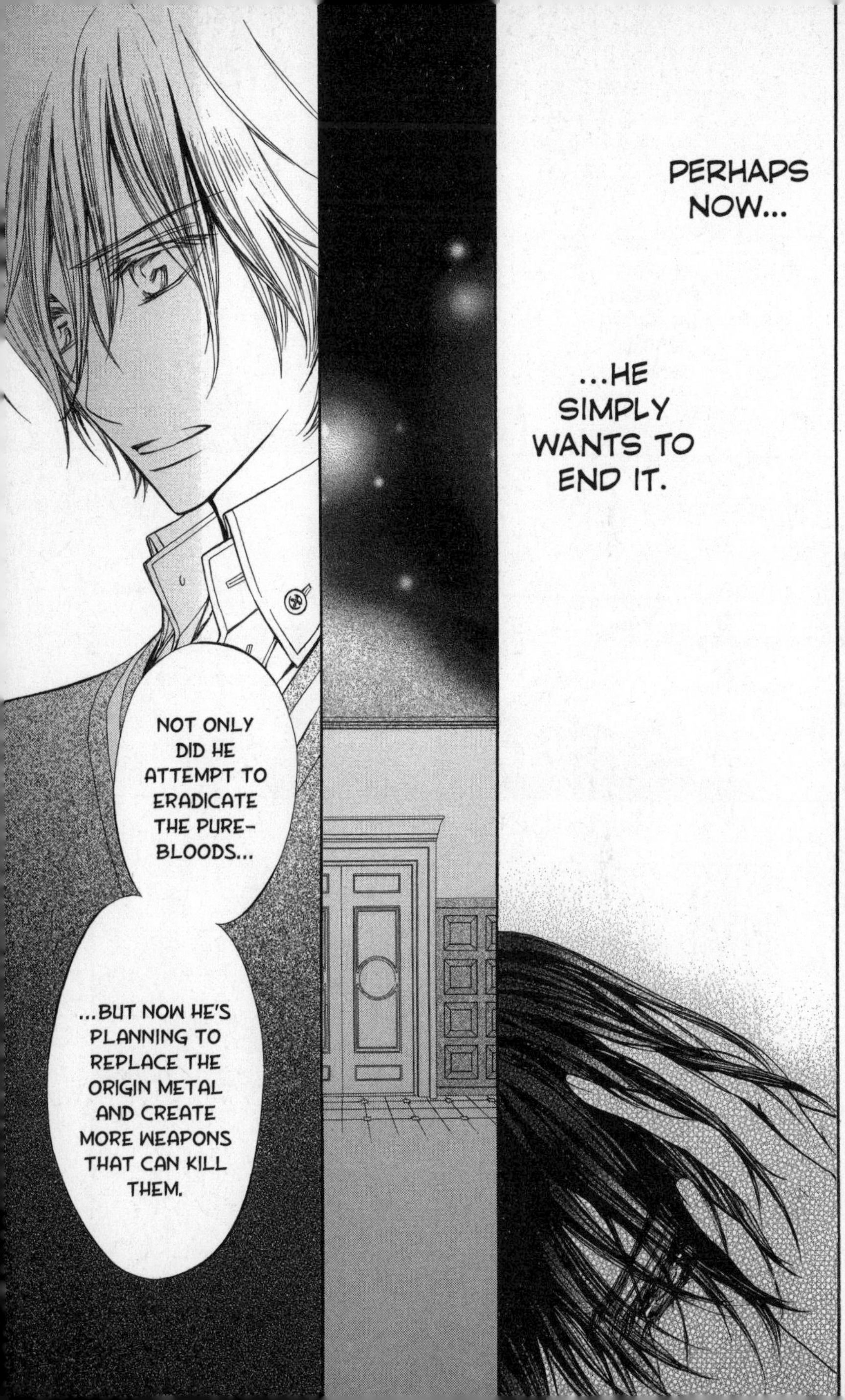
PERHAPS NOW...
...HE SIMPLY WANTS TO END IT.
NOT ONLY DID HE ATTEMPT TO ERADICATE THE PURE-BLOODS...
...BUT NOW HE'S PLANNING TO REPLACE THE ORIGIN METAL AND CREATE MORE WEAPONS THAT CAN KILL THEM.

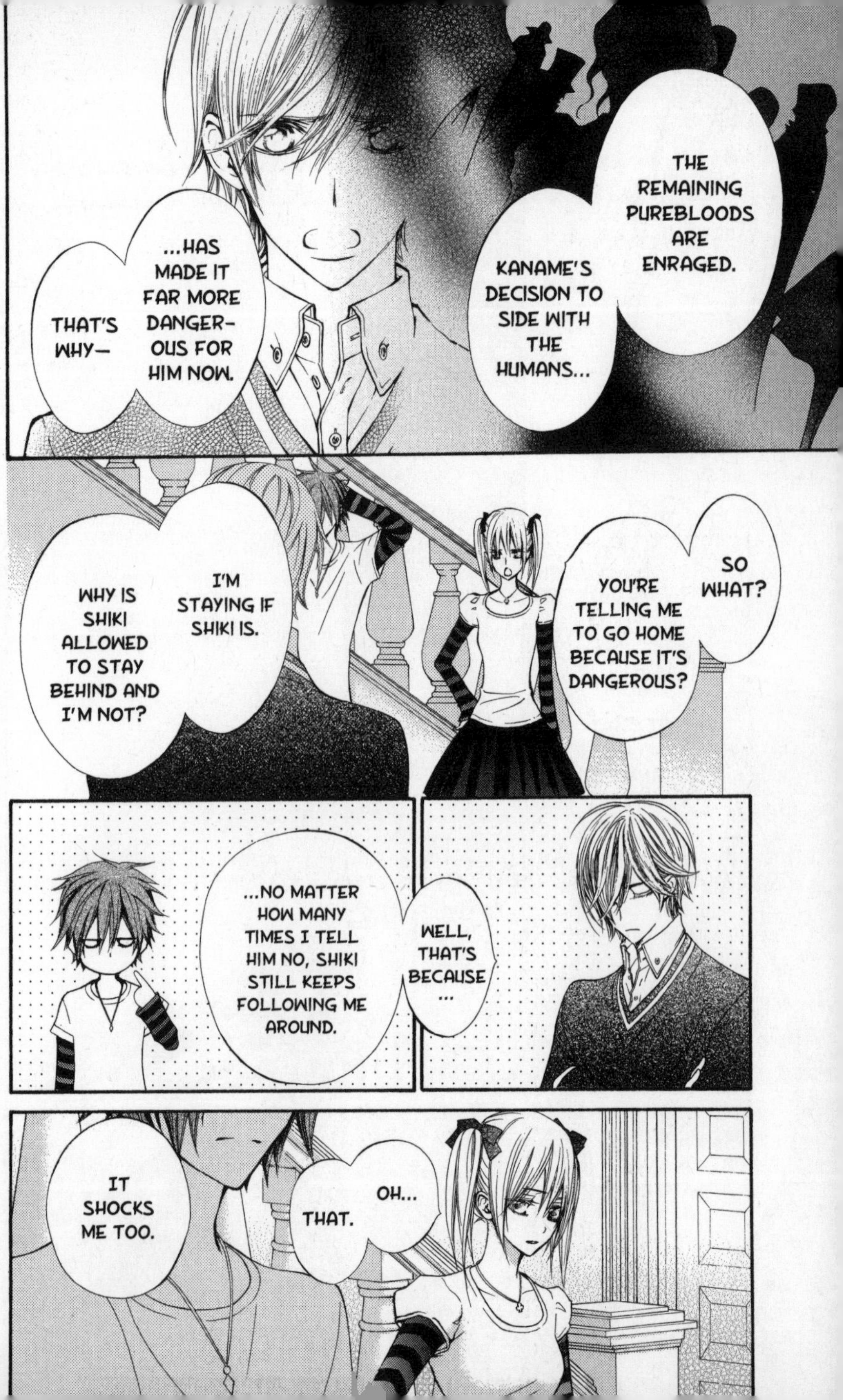
THE REMAINING PUREBLOODS ARE ENRAGED.
KANAME'S DECISION TO SIDE WITH THE HUMANS...
...HAS MADE IT FAR MORE DANGER-OUS FOR HIM NOW.
THAT'S WHY—
SO WHAT?
YOU'RE TELLING ME TO GO HOME BECAUSE IT'S DANGEROUS?
I'M STAYING IF SHIKI IS.
WHY IS SHIKI ALLOWED TO STAY BEHIND AND I'M NOT?
WELL, THAT'S BECAUSE ...
...NO MATTER HOW MANY TIMES I TELL HIM NO, SHIKI STILL KEEPS FOLLOWING ME AROUND.
OH...
THAT.
IT SHOCKS ME TOO.

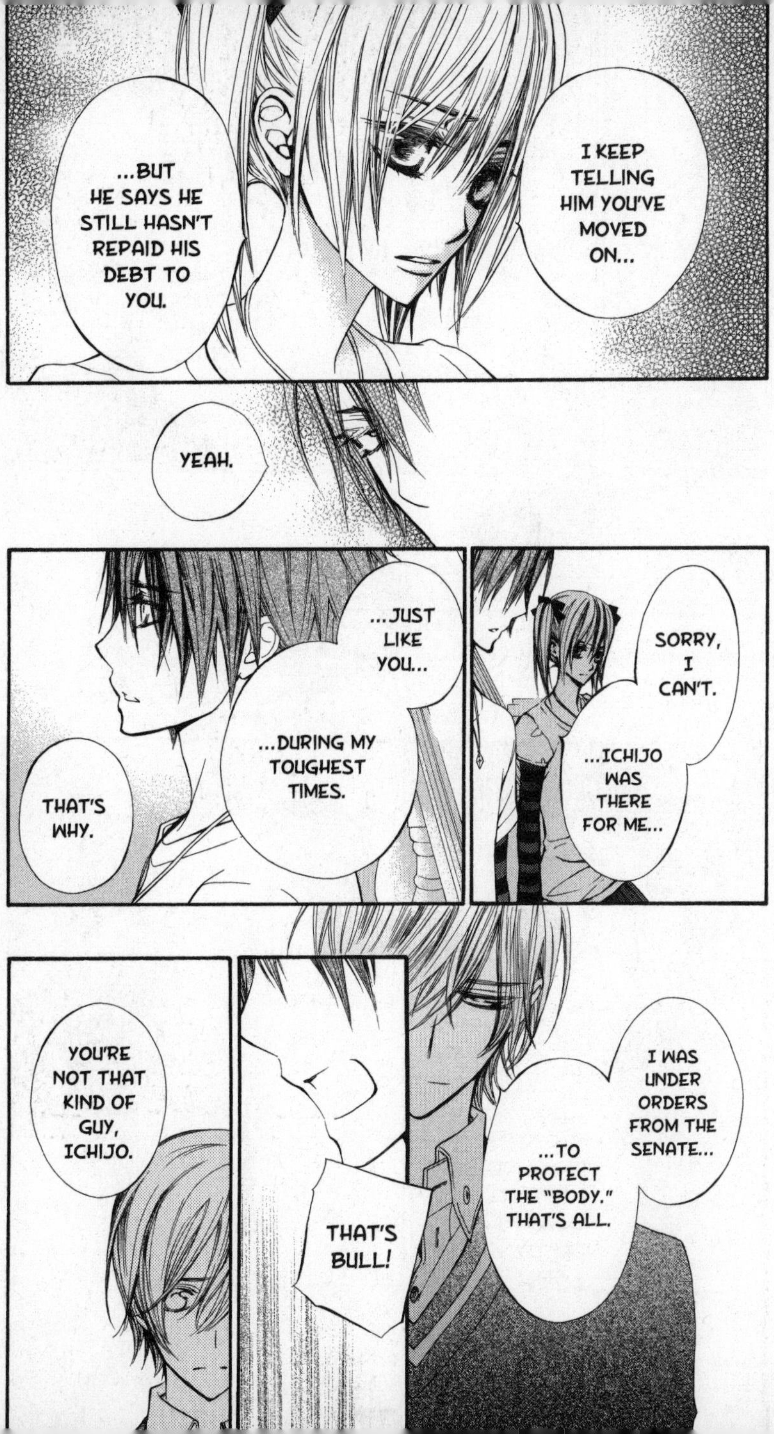
I KEEP TELLING HIM YOU'VE MOVED ON...
...BUT HE SAYS HE STILL HASN'T REPAID HIS DEBT TO YOU.
YEAH.
SORRY, I CAN'T.
...ICHIJO WAS THERE FOR ME...
...JUST LIKE YOU...
...DURING MY TOUGHEST TIMES.
THAT'S WHY.
I WAS UNDER ORDERS FROM THE SENATE...
...TO PROTECT THE "BODY." THAT'S ALL.
THAT'S BULL!
YOU'RE NOT THAT KIND OF GUY, ICHIJO.

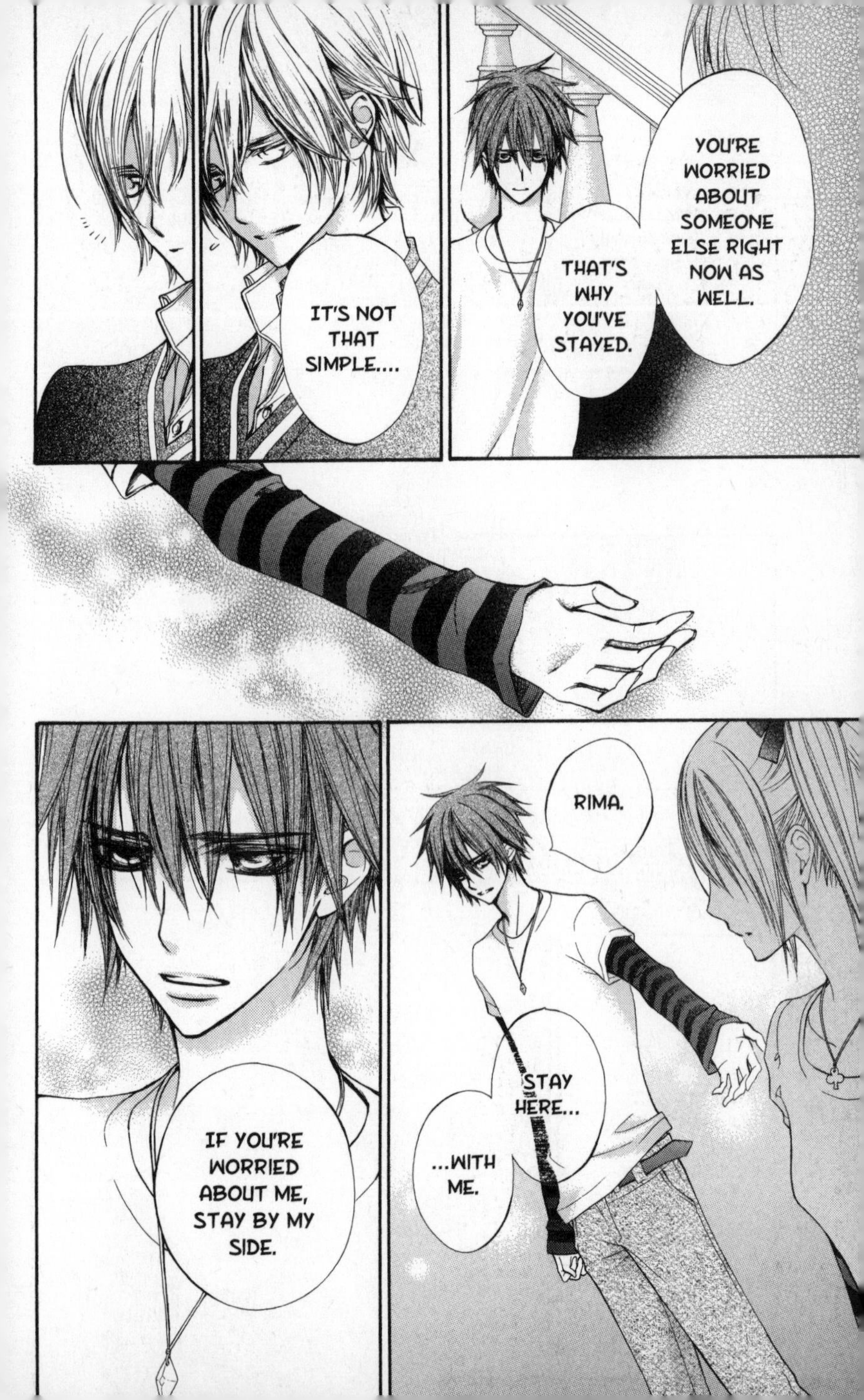
YOU'RE WORRIED ABOUT SOMEONE ELSE RIGHT NOW AS WELL.
THAT'S WHY YOU'VE STAYED.
IT'S NOT THAT SIMPLE....
RIMA.
STAY HERE...
...WITH ME.
IF YOU'RE WORRIED ABOUT ME, STAY BY MY SIDE.

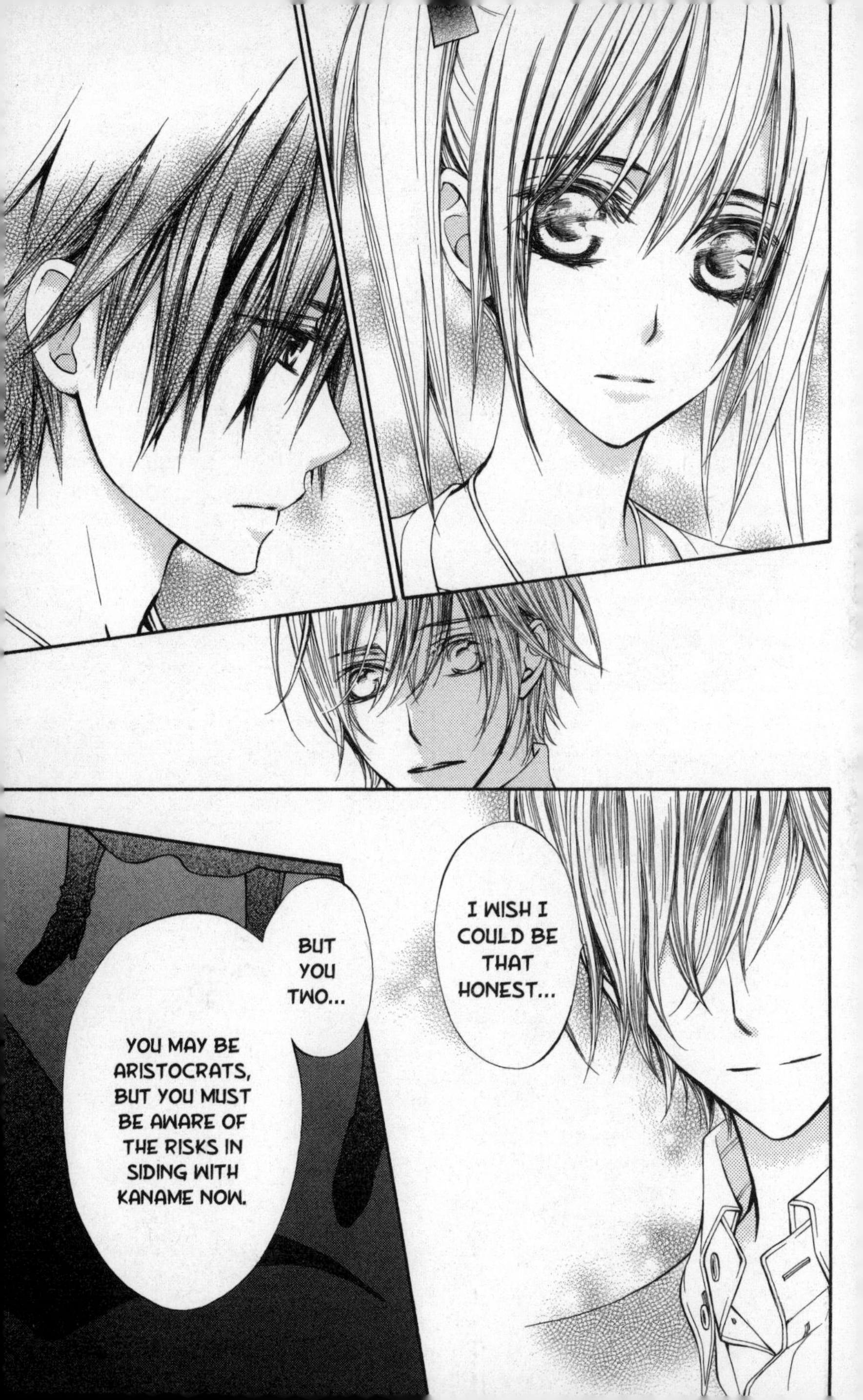
I WISH I COULD BE THAT HONEST...
BUT YOU TWO...
YOU MAY BE ARISTOCRATS, BUT YOU MUST BE AWARE OF THE RISKS IN SIDING WITH KANAME NOW.

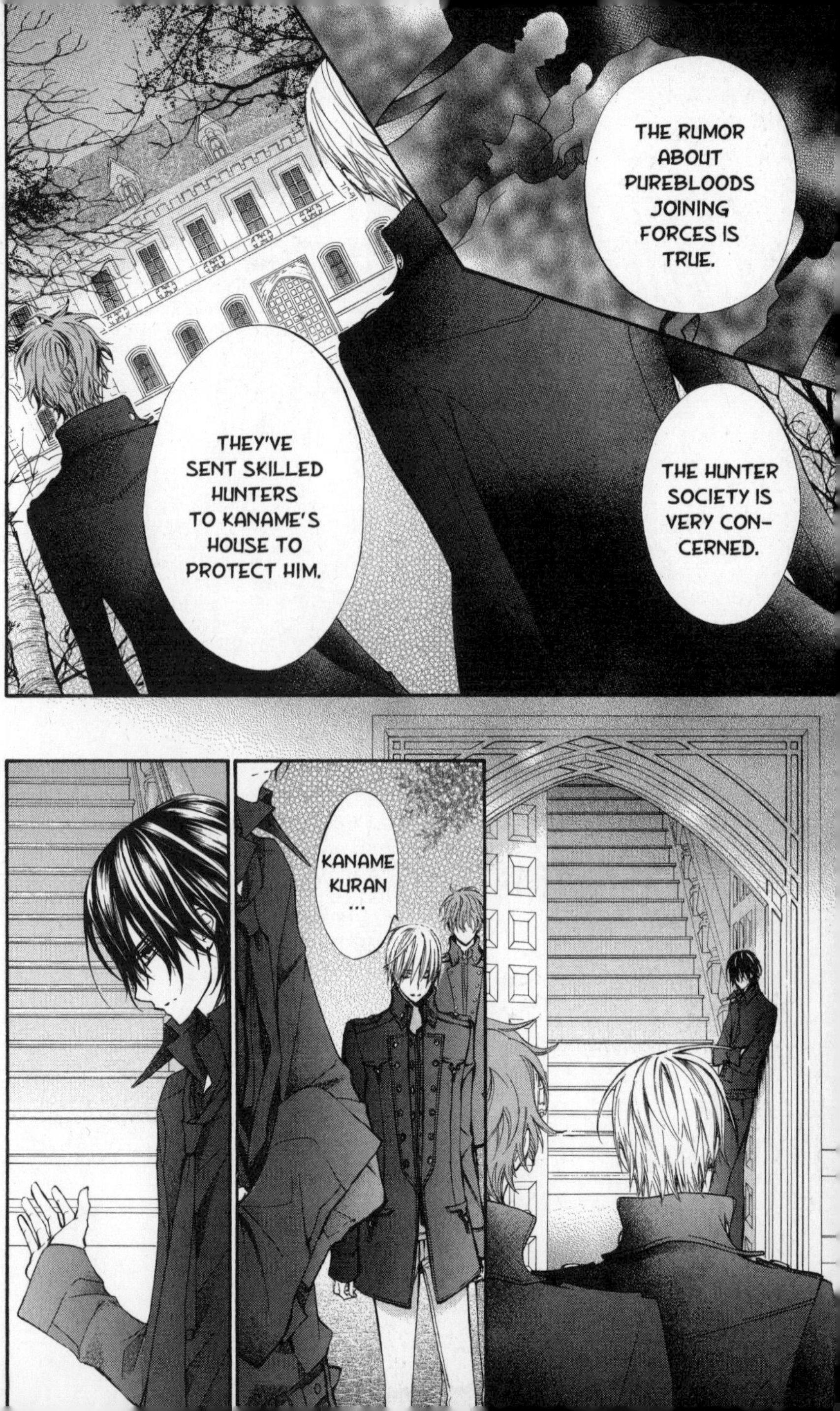
THE RUMOR ABOUT PUREBLOODS JOINING FORCES IS TRUE.
THE HUNTER SOCIETY IS VERY CON-CERNED.
THEY'VE SENT SKILLED HUNTERS TO KANAME'S HOUSE TO PROTECT HIM.
KANAME KURAN ...

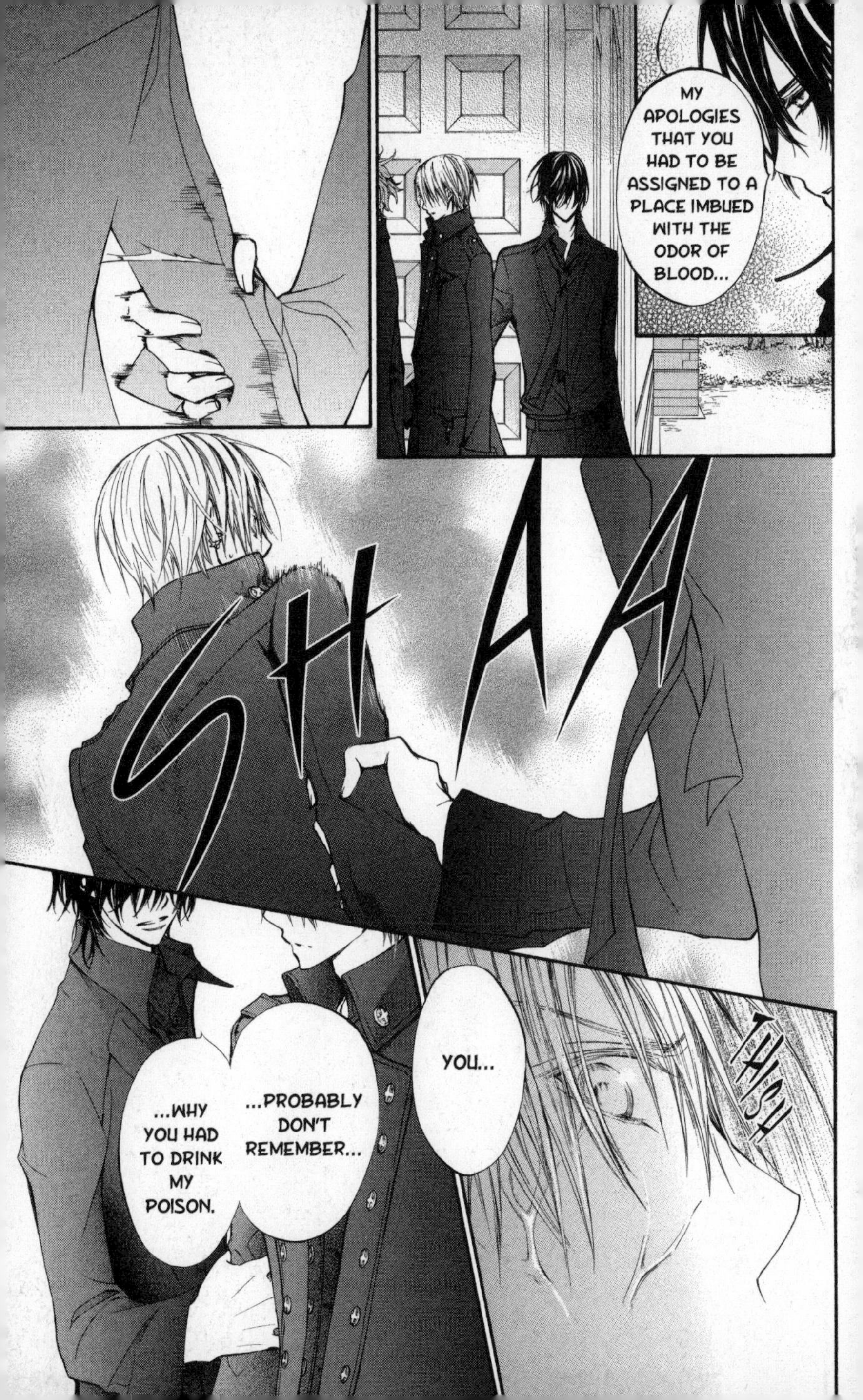
MY APOLOGIES THAT YOU HAD TO BE ASSIGNED TO A PLACE IMBUED WITH THE ODOR OF BLOOD...
SHAA
THSH
YOU...
...PROBABLY DON'T REMEMBER...
...WHY YOU HAD TO DRINK MY POISON.

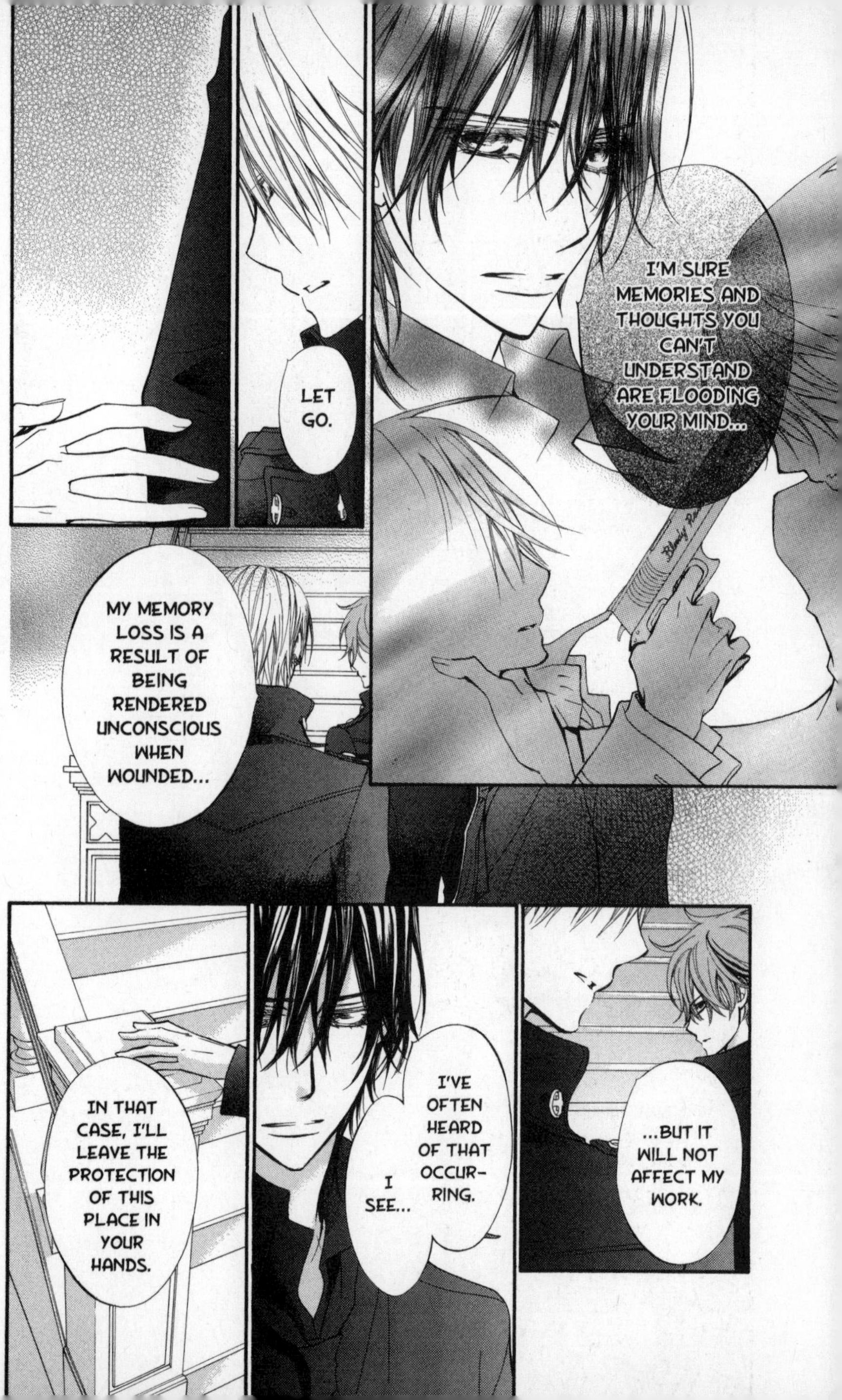
I'M SURE MEMORIES AND THOUGHTS YOU CAN'T UNDERSTAND ARE FLOODING YOUR MIND...
LET GO.
MY MEMORY LOSS IS A RESULT OF BEING RENDERED UNCONSCIOUS WHEN WOUNDED...
...BUT IT WILL NOT AFFECT MY WORK.
I'VE OFTEN HEARD OF THAT OCCUR-RING.
I SEE...
IN THAT CASE, I'LL LEAVE THE PROTECTION OF THIS PLACE IN YOUR HANDS.

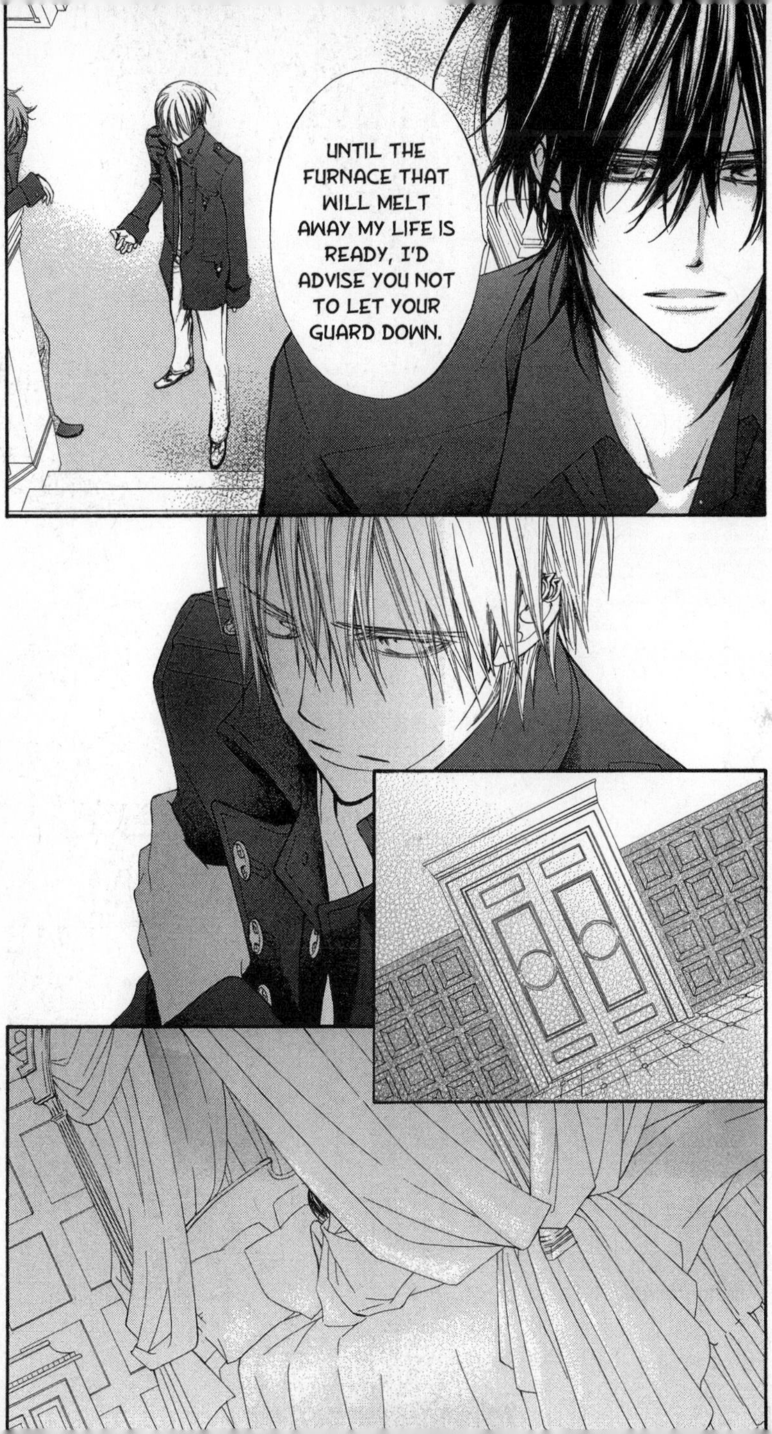
UNTIL THE FURNACE THAT WILL MELT AWAY MY LIFE IS READY, I'D ADVISE YOU NOT TO LET YOUR GUARD DOWN.

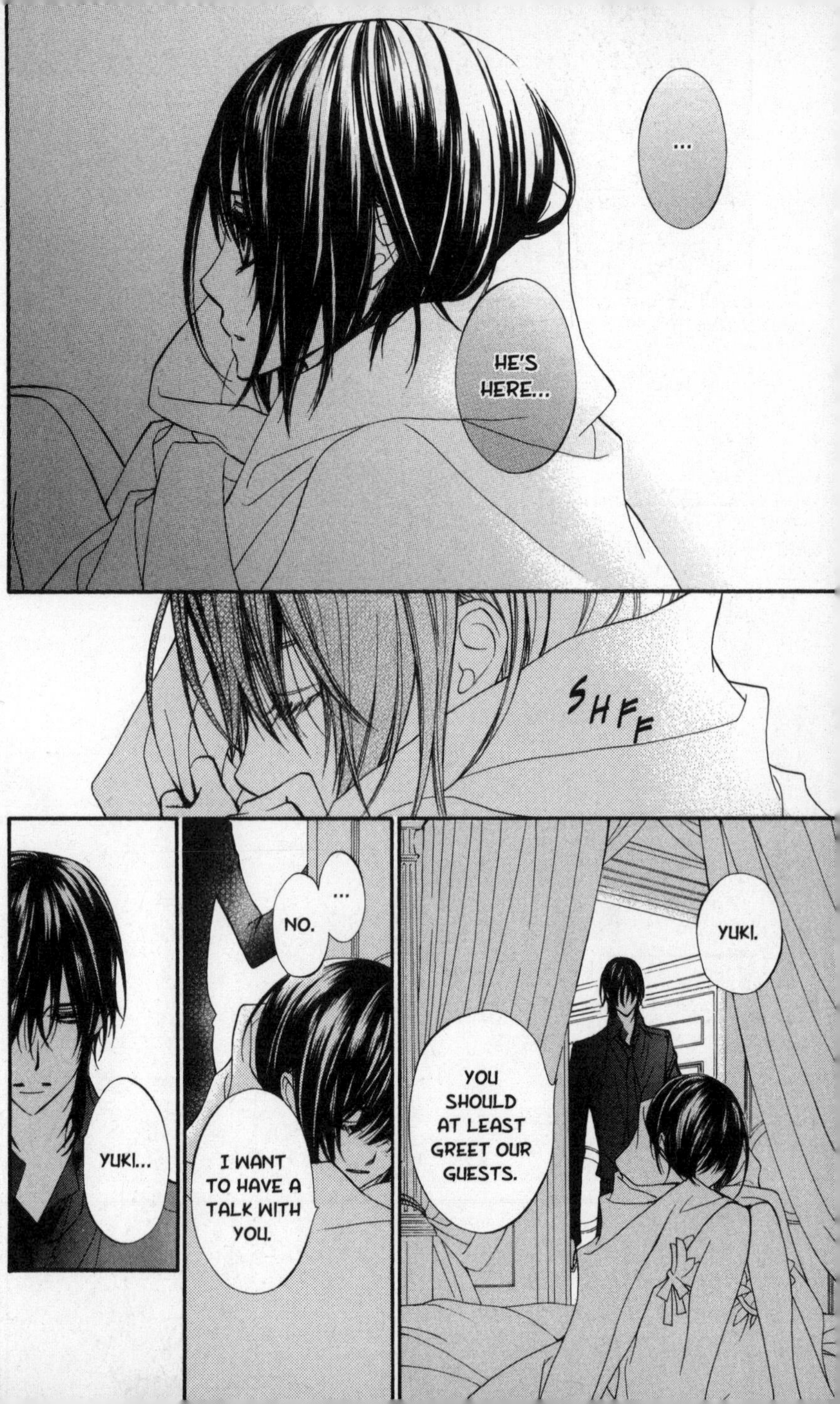
...
HE'S HERE...
SHFF
YUKI.
YOU SHOULD AT LEAST GREET OUR GUESTS.
...
NO.
I WANT TO HAVE A TALK WITH YOU.
YUKI...

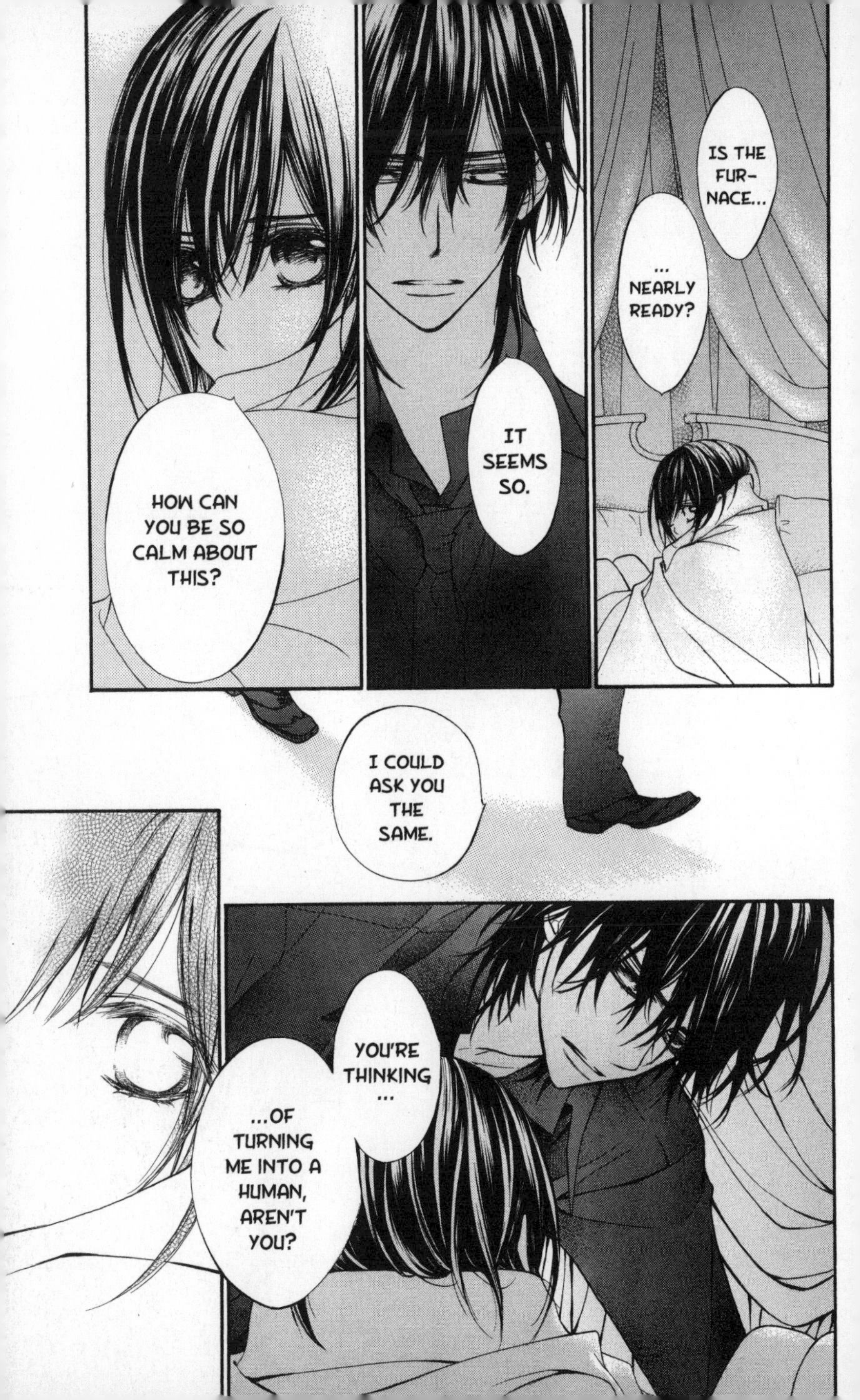
IS THE FUR-NACE...
...NEARLY READY?
IT SEEMS SO.
HOW CAN YOU BE SO CALM ABOUT THIS?
I COULD ASK YOU THE SAME.
YOU'RE THINKING...
...OF TURNING ME INTO A HUMAN, AREN'T YOU?

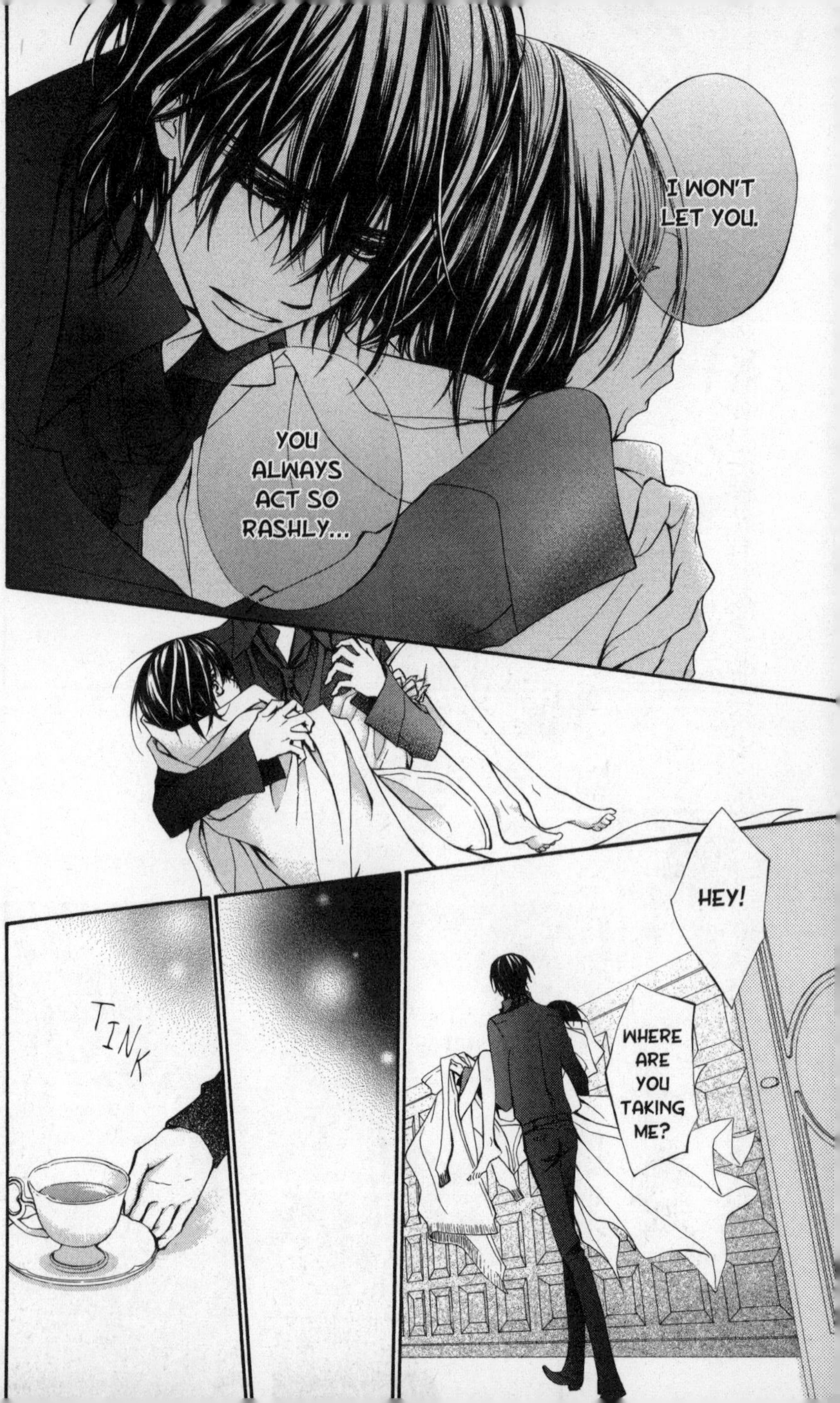
I WON'T LET YOU.
YOU ALWAYS ACT SO RASHLY...
HEY!
WHERE ARE YOU TAKING ME?
TINK

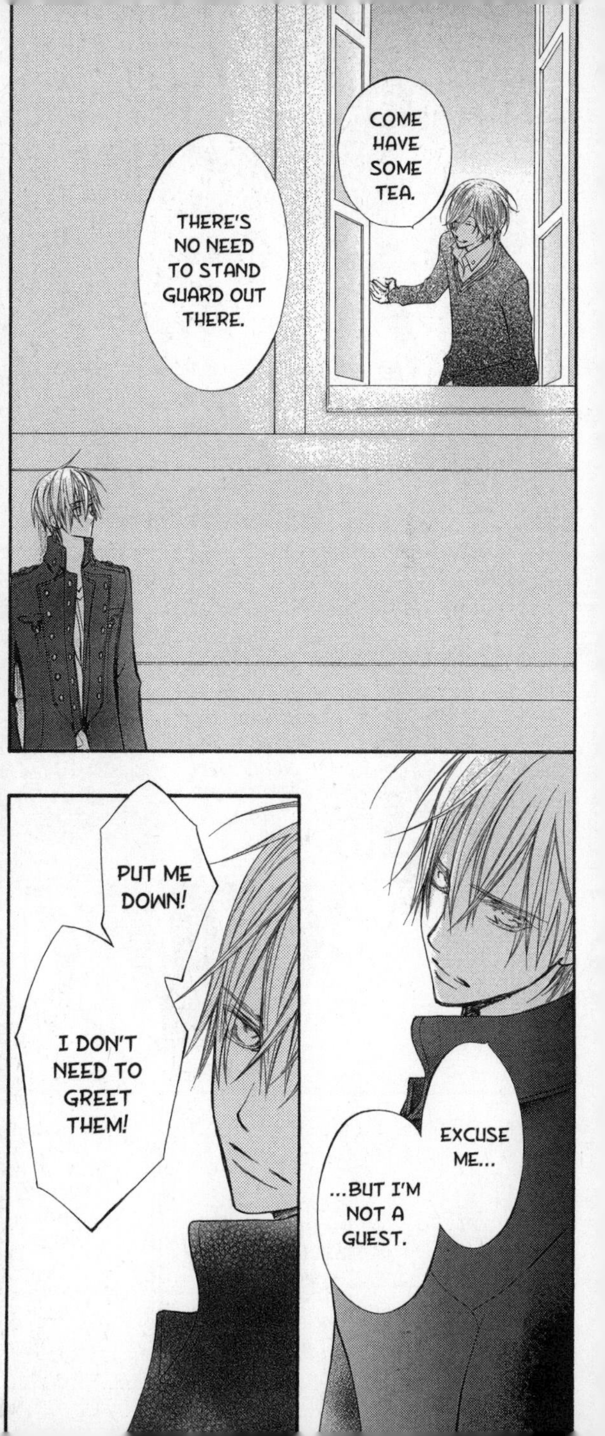
COME HAVE SOME TEA.
THERE'S NO NEED TO STAND GUARD OUT THERE.
EXCUSE ME...
...BUT I'M NOT A GUEST.
PUT ME DOWN!
I DON'T NEED TO GREET THEM!

I

Here is Volume 19. I would like to thank you all from the bottom of my heart for supporting this series to the very end. This series would not have continued without the support of the readers. And if there is even one person out there who thought it was great or enjoyed a part of the story, I'm sure the characters created by this imperfect mangaka will feel honored. I too will feel honored for spending the past eight and a half years on this work. And of course so will my editor who spent just as much effort on it, and my assistants... And... And...

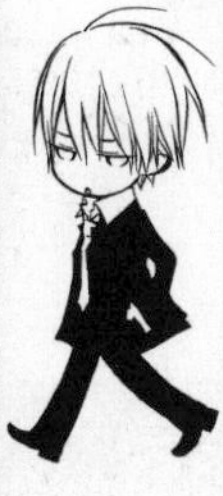

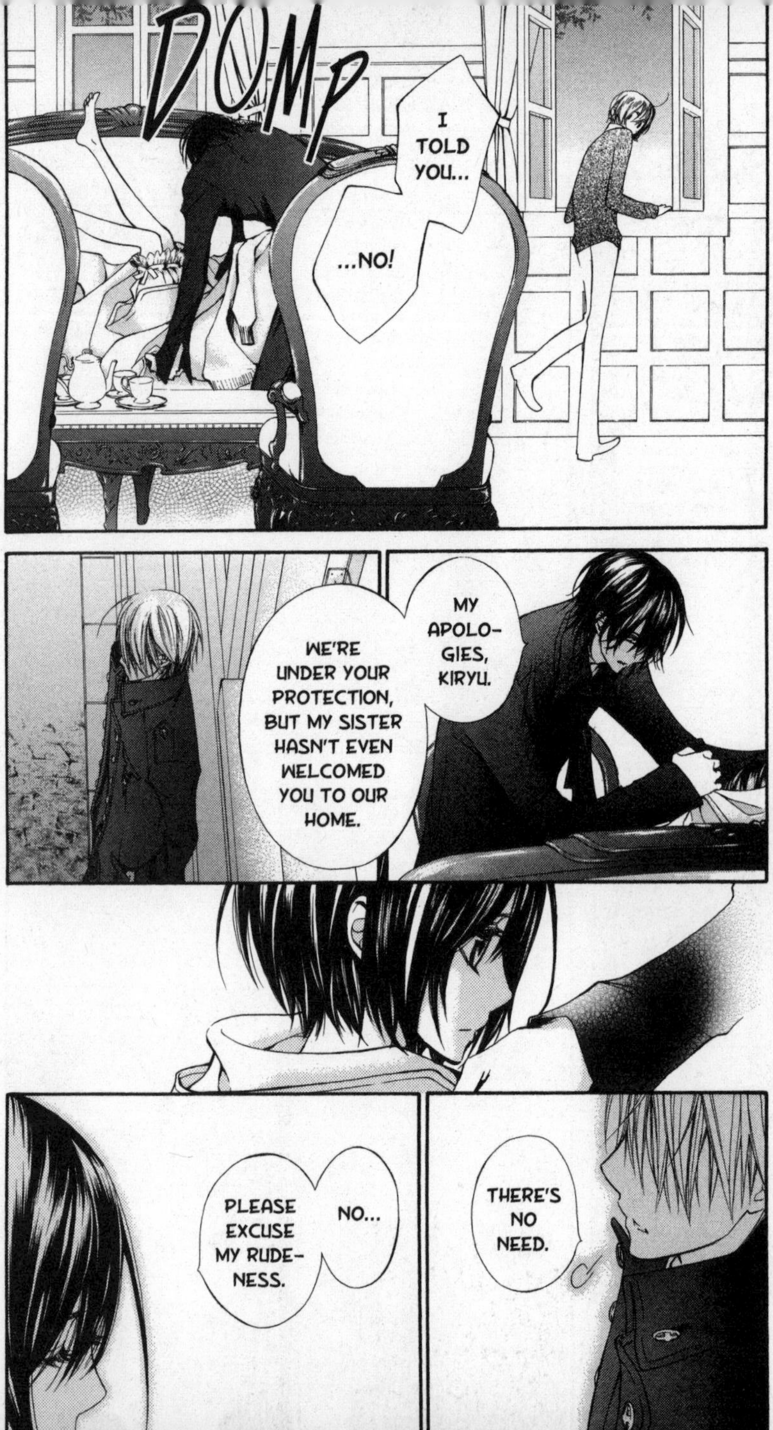
DOMP
I TOLD YOU...
...NO!
MY APOLO-GIES, KIRYU.
WE'RE UNDER YOUR PROTECTION, BUT MY SISTER HASN'T EVEN WELCOMED YOU TO OUR HOME.
THERE'S NO NEED.
NO...
PLEASE EXCUSE MY RUDE-NESS.

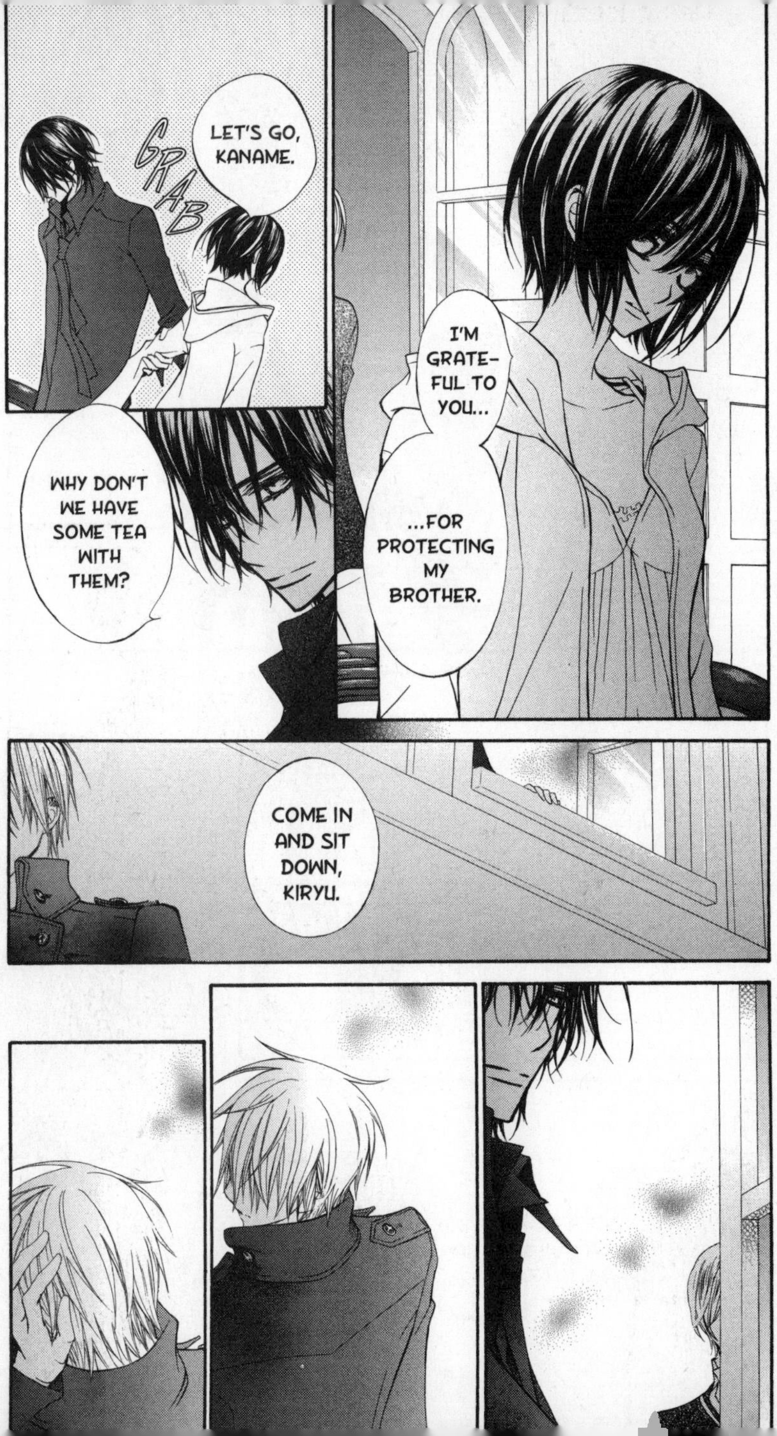
I'M GRATEFUL TO YOU...
...FOR PROTECTING MY BROTHER.
LET'S GO, KANAME.
GRAB
WHY DON'T WE HAVE SOME TEA WITH THEM?
COME IN AND SIT DOWN, KIRYU.

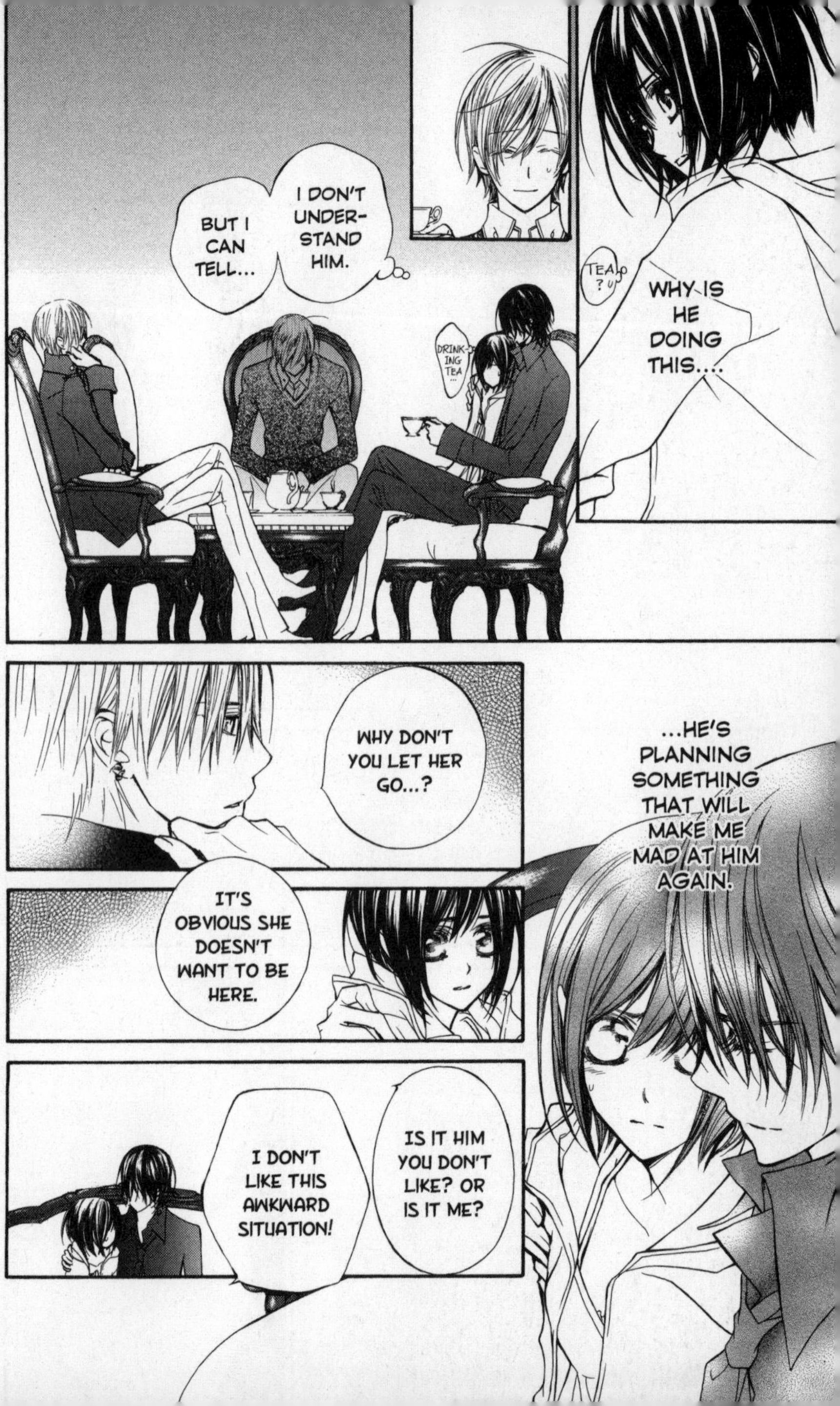
TEA?
WHY IS HE DOING THIS....
DRINKING TEA...
I DON'T UNDERSTAND HIM.
BUT I CAN TELL...
...HE'S PLANNING SOMETHING THAT WILL MAKE ME MAD AT HIM AGAIN.
WHY DON'T YOU LET HER GO...?
IT'S OBVIOUS SHE DOESN'T WANT TO BE HERE.
IS IT HIM YOU DON'T LIKE? OR IS IT ME?
I DON'T LIKE THIS AWKWARD SITUATION!

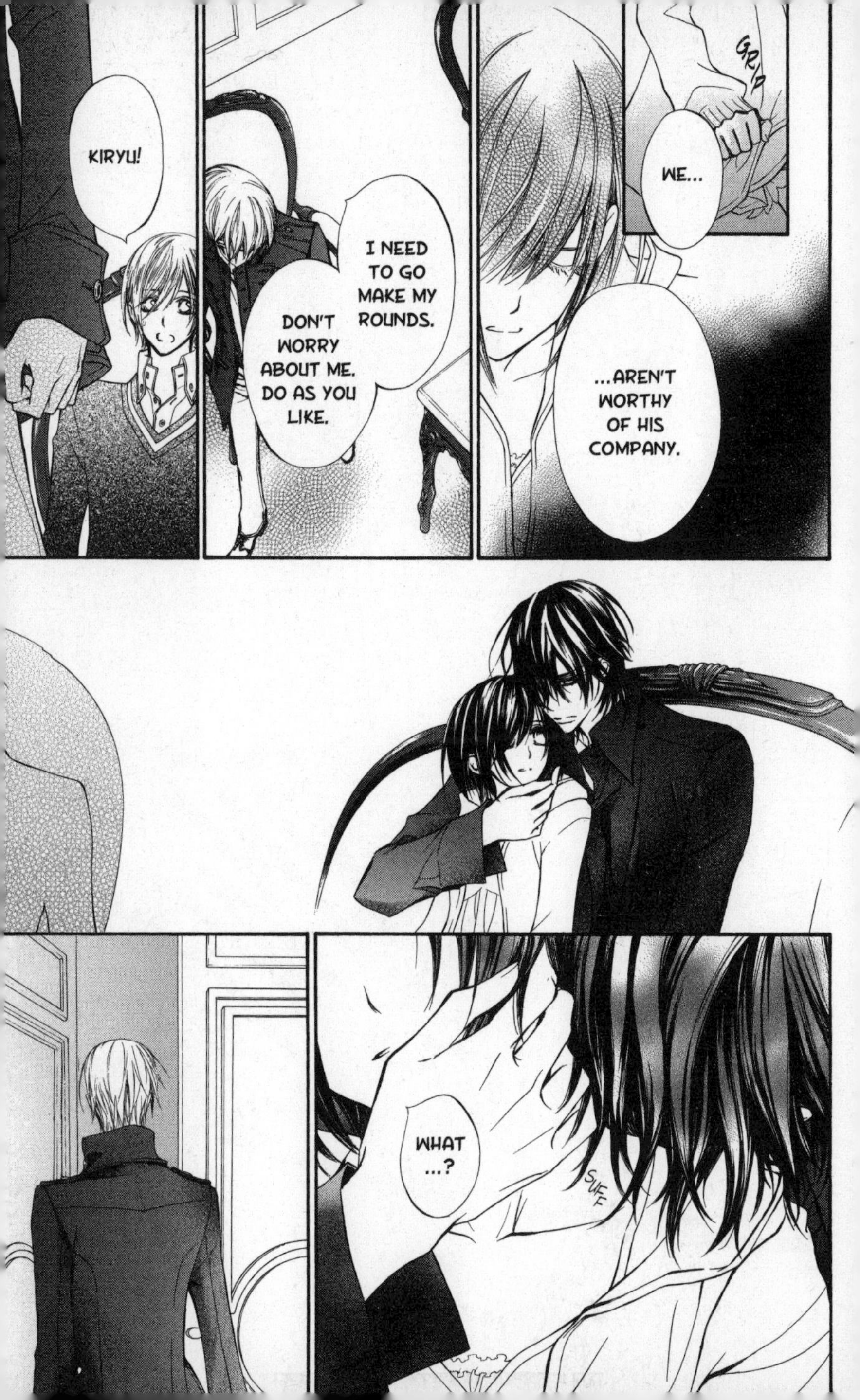
GRIP
WE...
...AREN'T WORTHY OF HIS COMPANY.
I NEED TO GO MAKE MY ROUNDS.
DON'T WORRY ABOUT ME. DO AS YOU LIKE.
KIRYU!
WHAT ...?
SUFF

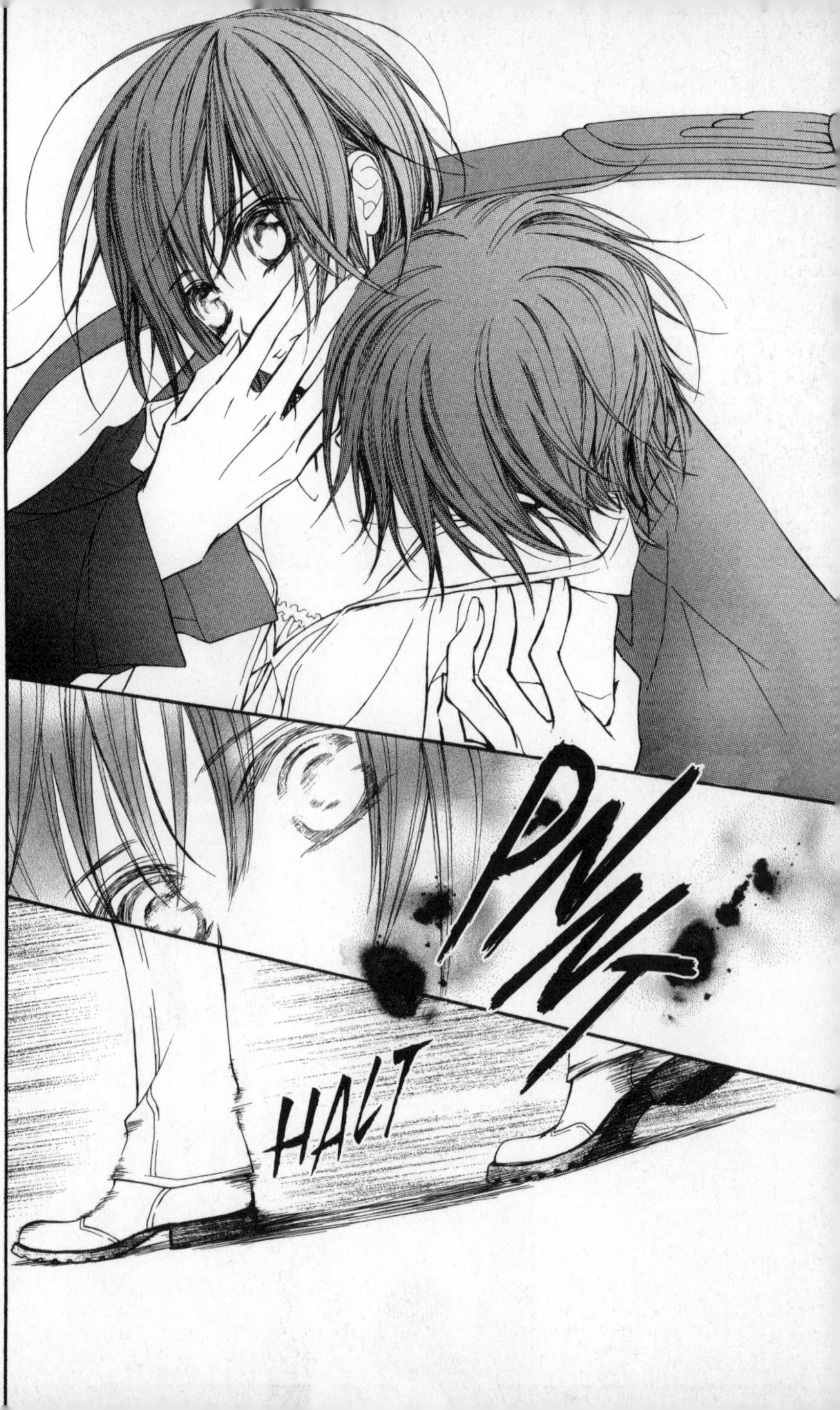
PWNT
HALT

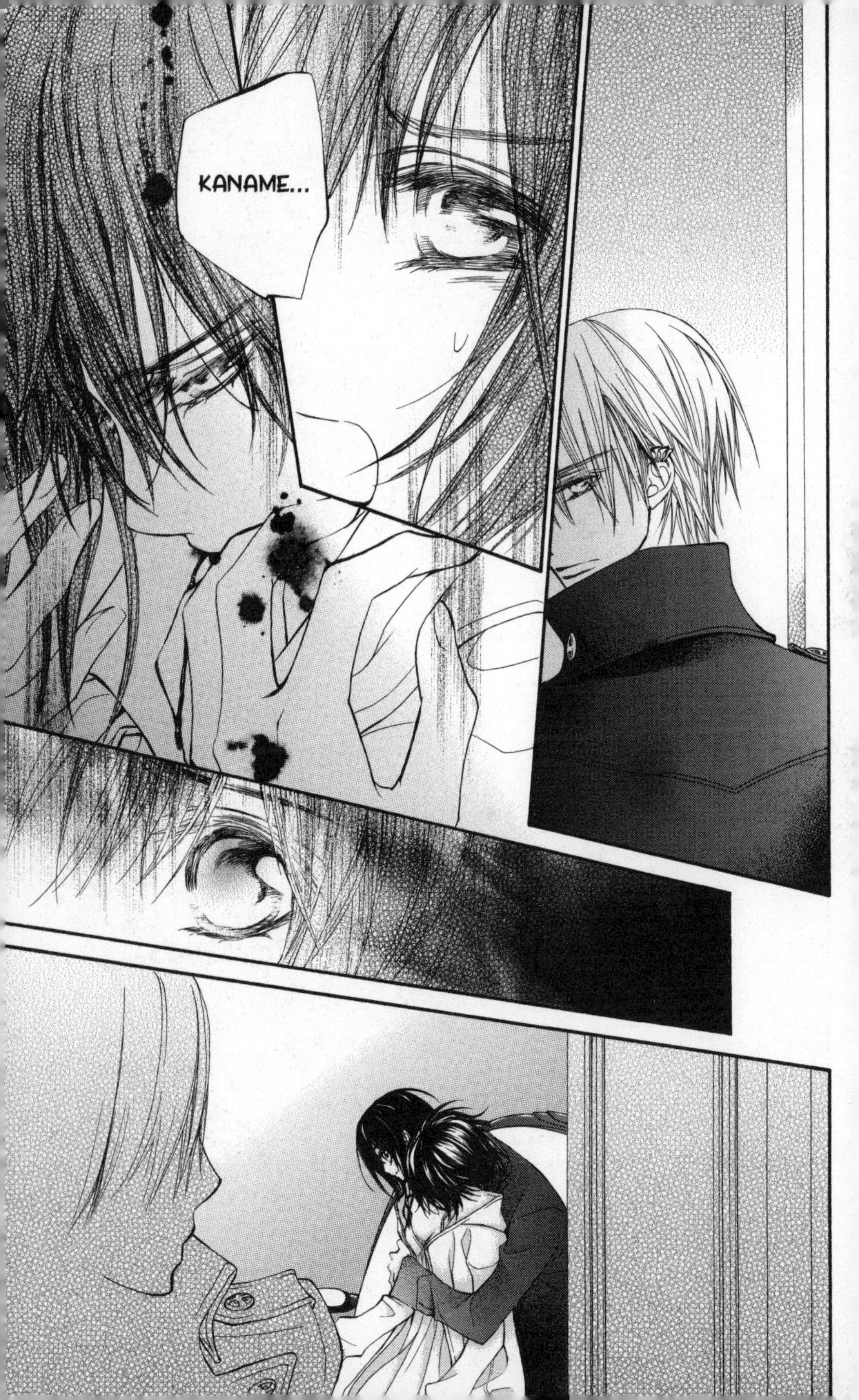
KANAME...

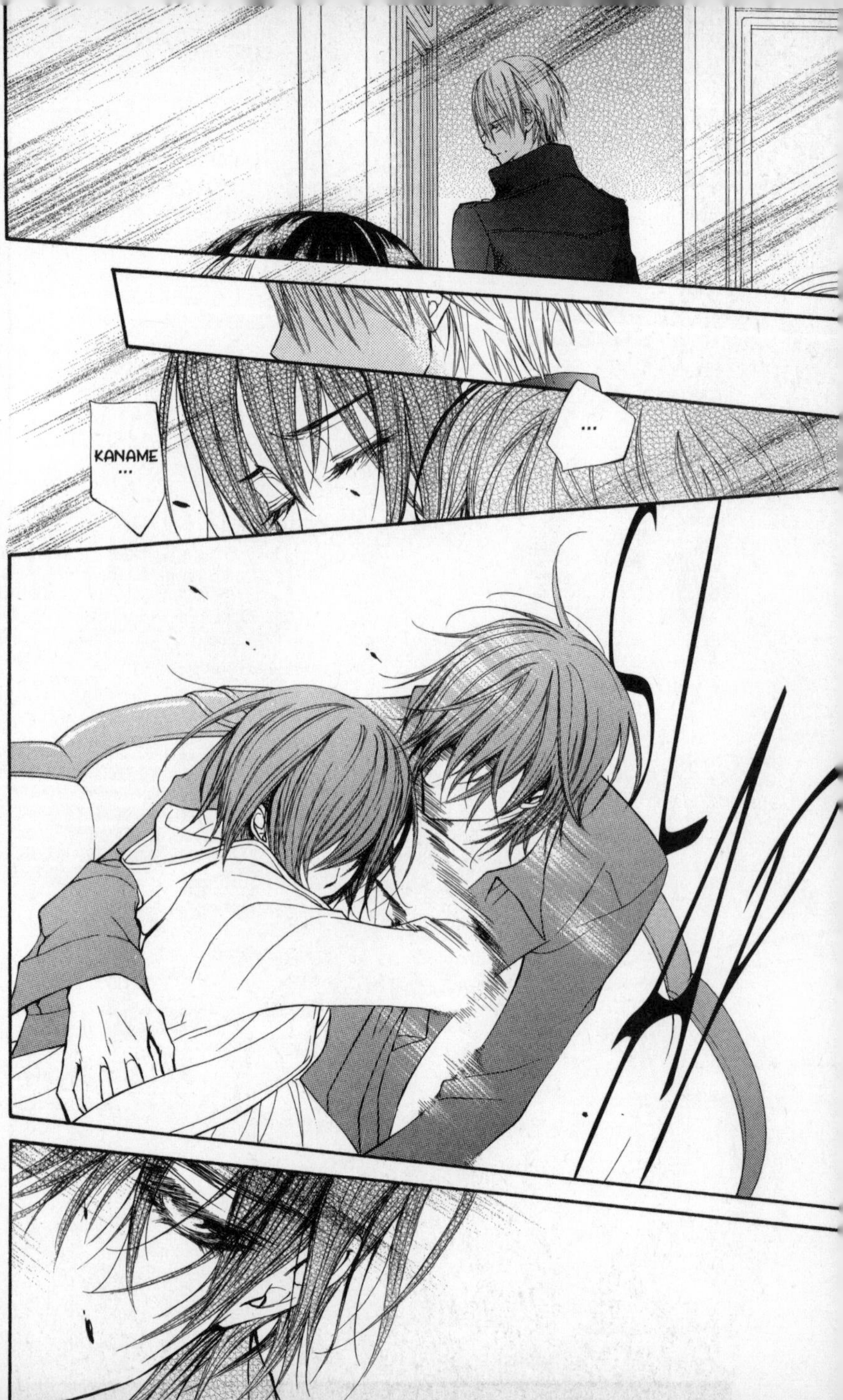
...
KANAME ...

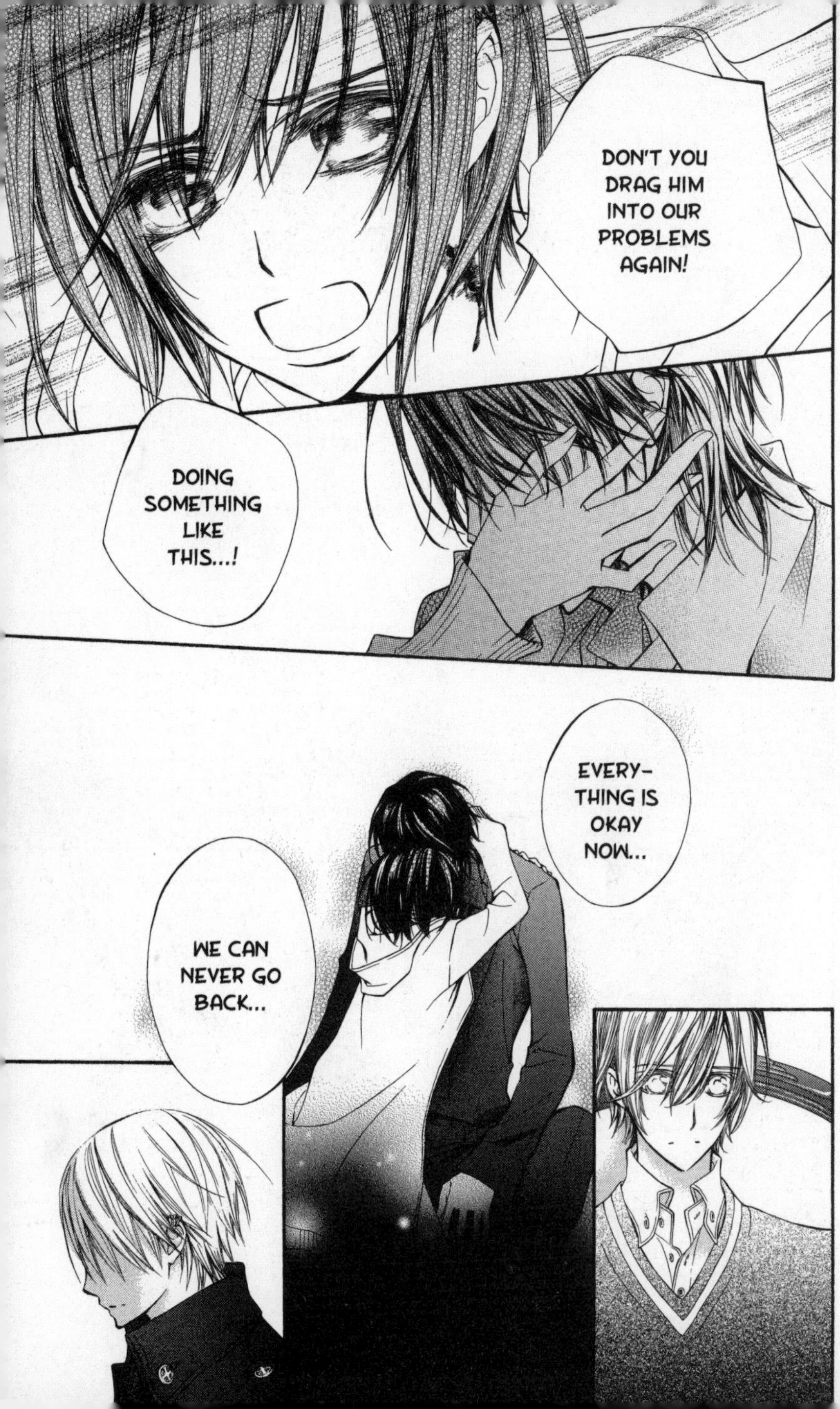
DON'T YOU DRAG HIM INTO OUR PROBLEMS AGAIN!
DOING SOMETHING LIKE THIS...!
EVERY-THING IS OKAY NOW...
WE CAN NEVER GO BACK...

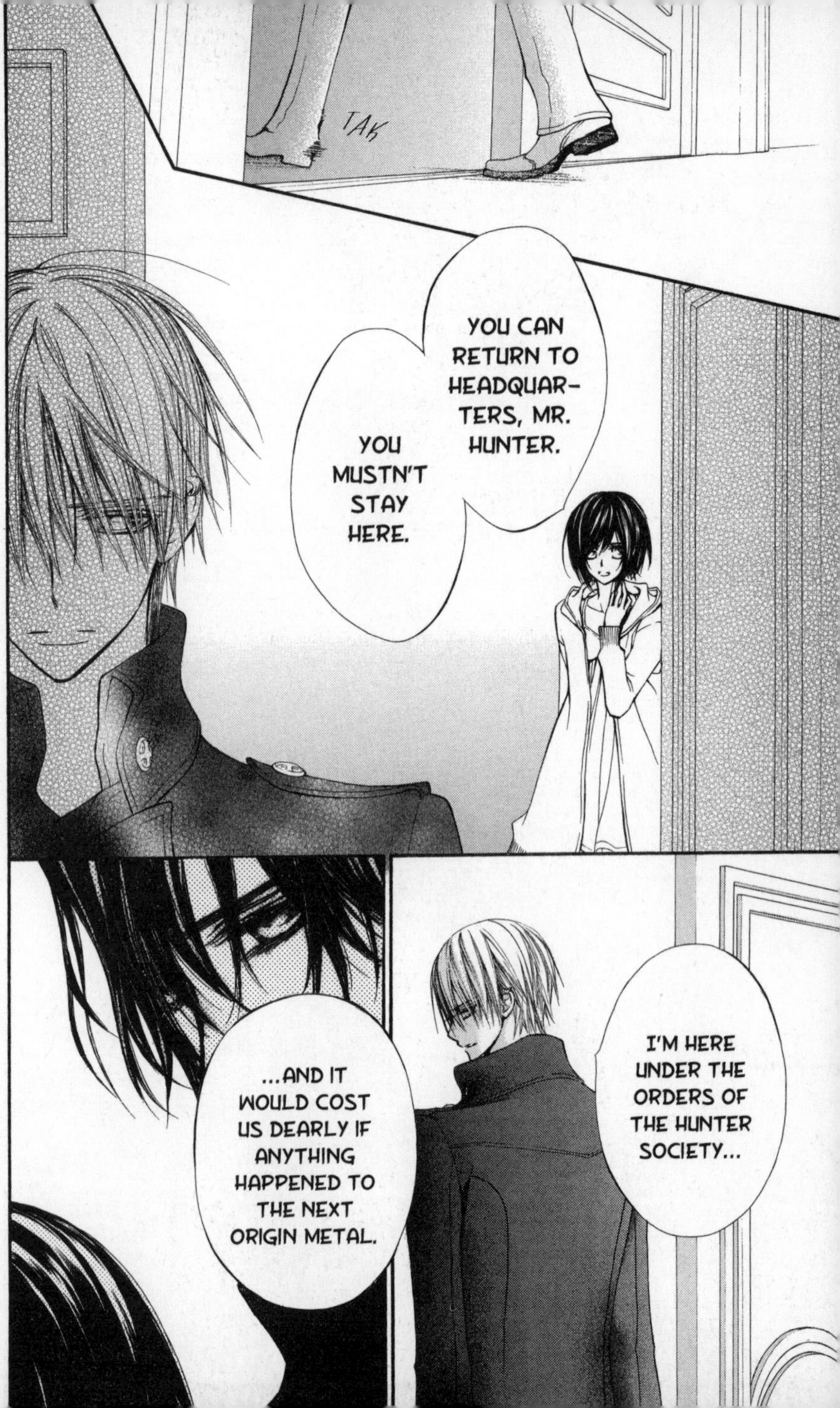
TAK
YOU CAN RETURN TO HEADQUARTERS, MR. HUNTER.
YOU MUSTN'T STAY HERE.
I'M HERE UNDER THE ORDERS OF THE HUNTER SOCIETY...
...AND IT WOULD COST US DEARLY IF ANYTHING HAPPENED TO THE NEXT ORIGIN METAL.

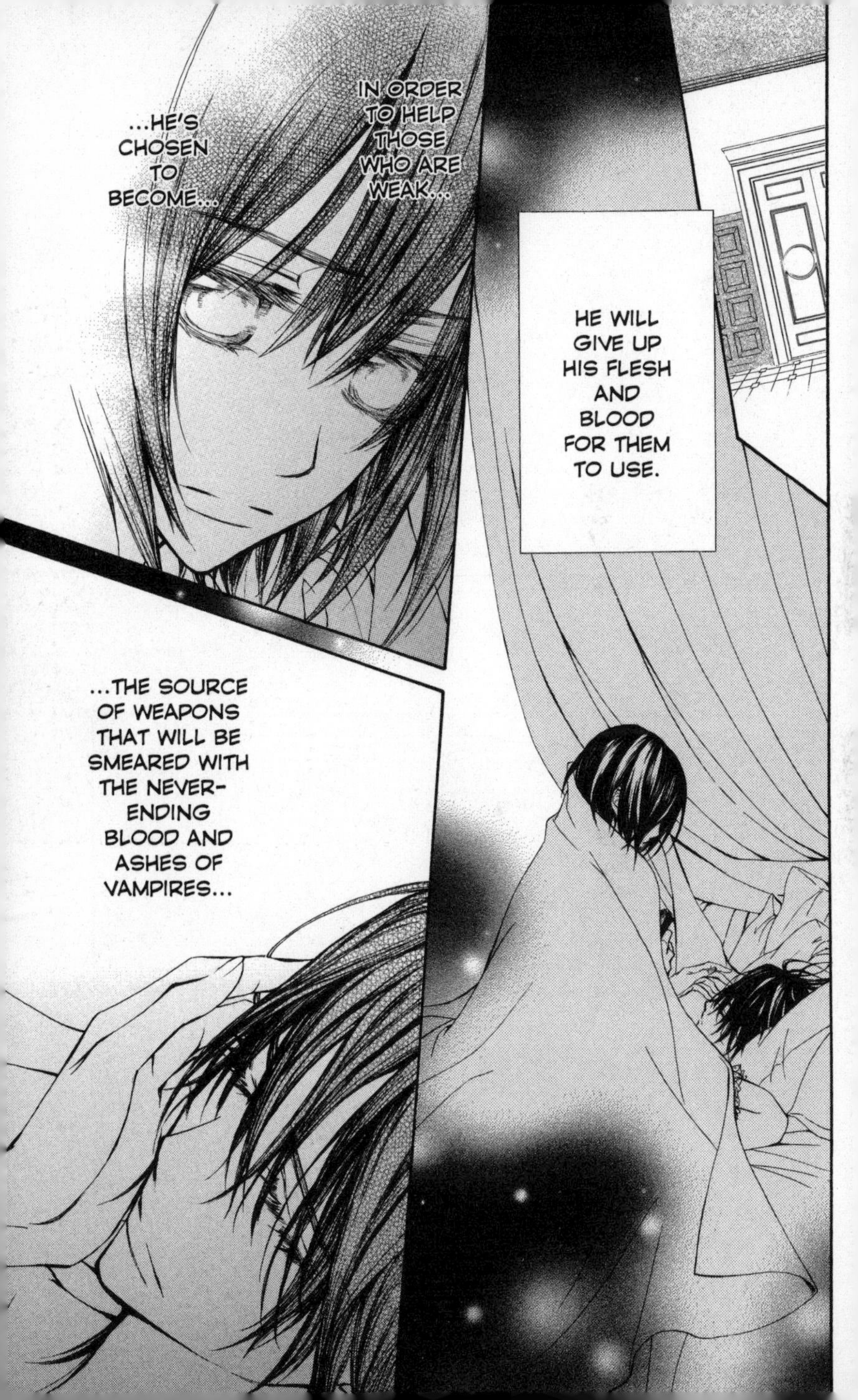
HE WILL GIVE UP HIS FLESH AND BLOOD FOR THEM TO USE.
IN ORDER TO HELP THOSE WHO ARE WEAK...
...HE'S CHOSEN TO BECOME...
...THE SOURCE OF WEAPONS THAT WILL BE SMEARED WITH THE NEVER-ENDING BLOOD AND ASHES OF VAMPIRES...

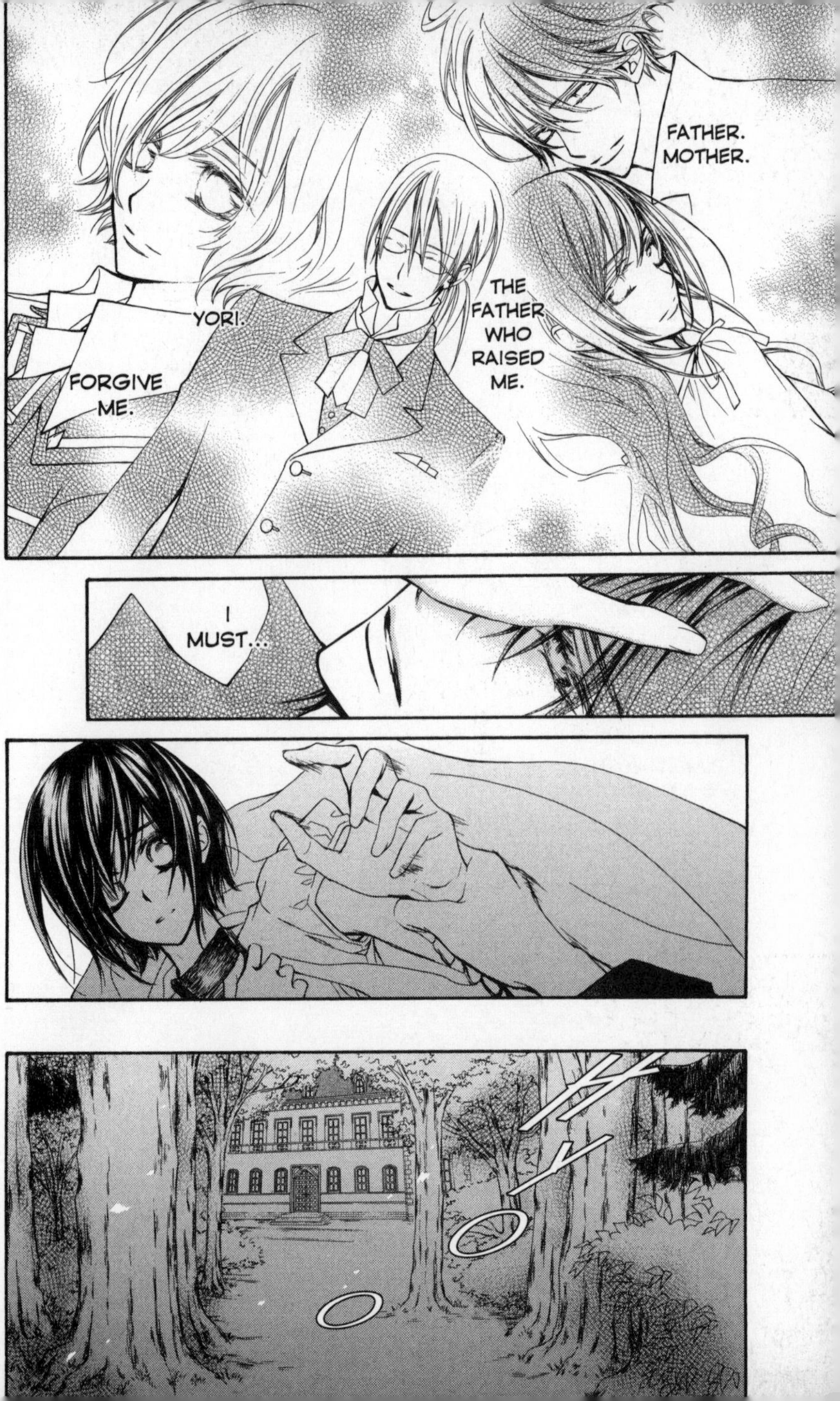
FATHER. MOTHER.
THE FATHER WHO RAISED ME.
YORI.
FORGIVE ME.
I MUST...

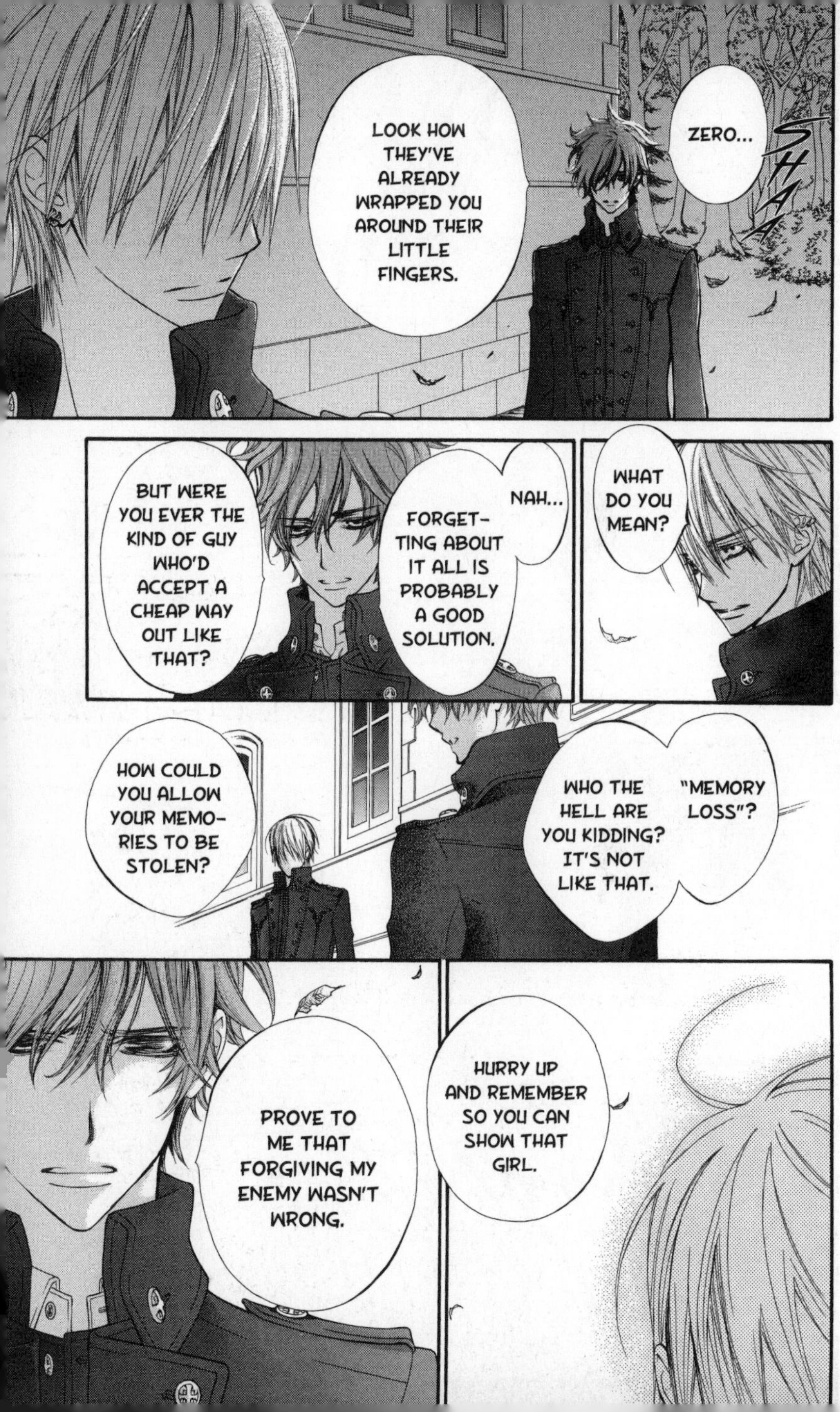
ZERO...
SHAA
LOOK HOW THEY'VE ALREADY WRAPPED YOU AROUND THEIR LITTLE FINGERS.
WHAT DO YOU MEAN?
NAH... FORGET-TING ABOUT IT ALL IS PROBABLY A GOOD SOLUTION.
BUT WERE YOU EVER THE KIND OF GUY WHO'D ACCEPT A CHEAP WAY OUT LIKE THAT?
"MEMORY LOSS"?
WHO THE HELL ARE YOU KIDDING? IT'S NOT LIKE THAT.
HOW COULD YOU ALLOW YOUR MEMO-RIES TO BE STOLEN?
HURRY UP AND REMEMBER SO YOU CAN SHOW THAT GIRL.
PROVE TO ME THAT FORGIVING MY ENEMY WASN'T WRONG.

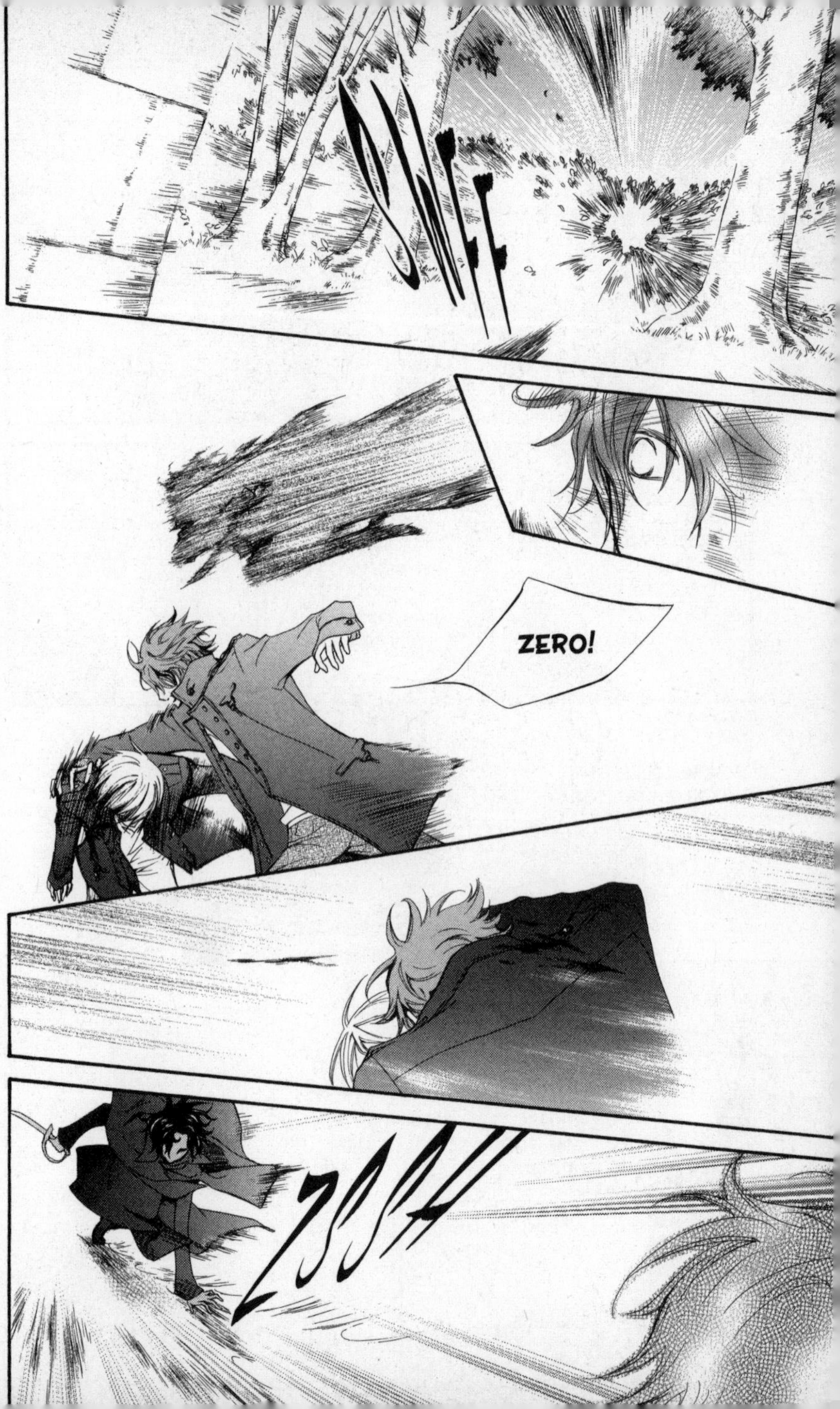
SHFF
ZERO!

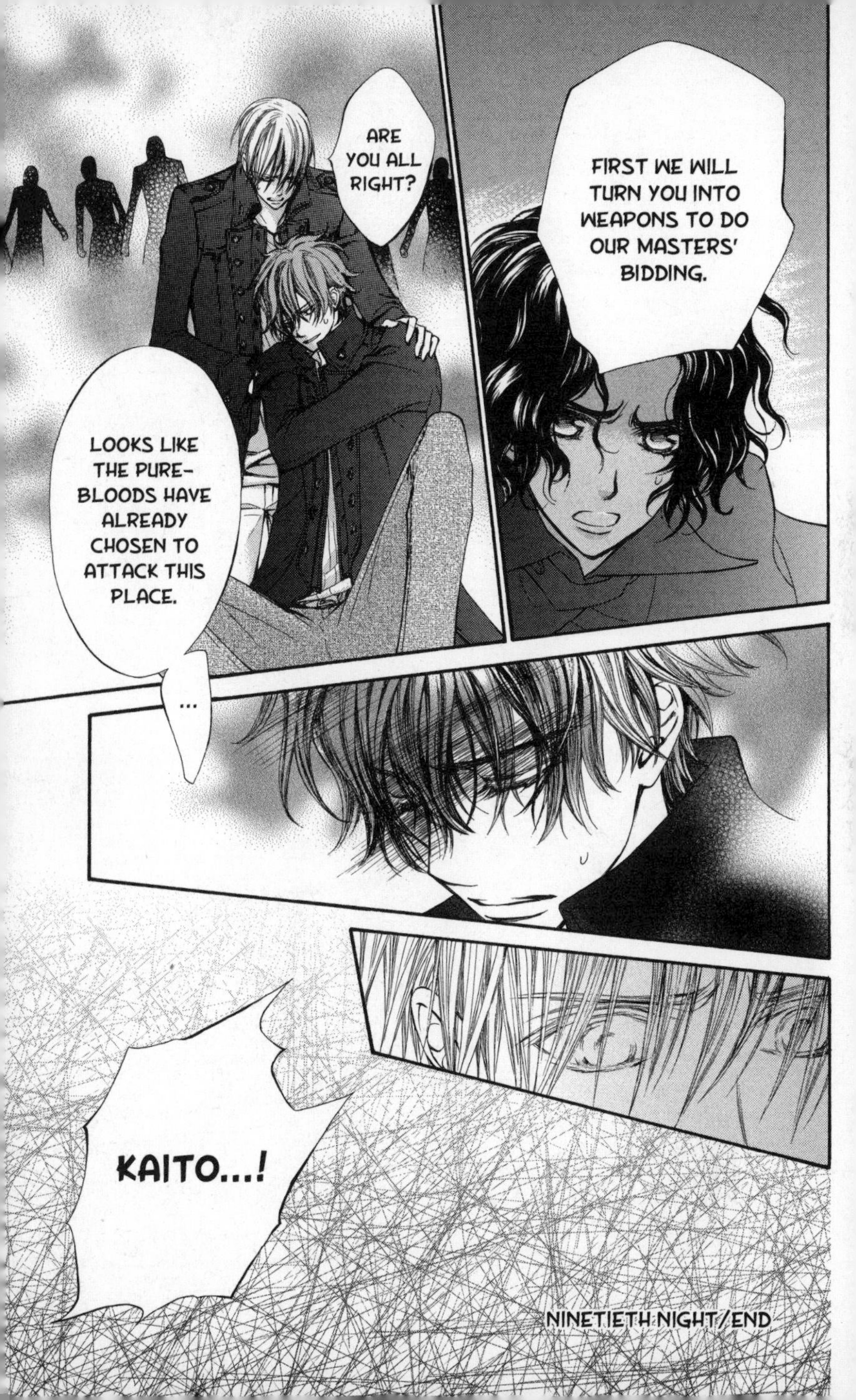
FIRST WE WILL TURN YOU INTO WEAPONS TO DO OUR MASTERS' BIDDING.
ARE YOU ALL RIGHT?
LOOKS LIKE THE PURE-BLOODS HAVE ALREADY CHOSEN TO ATTACK THIS PLACE.
...
KAITO...!
NINETIETH NIGHT/END

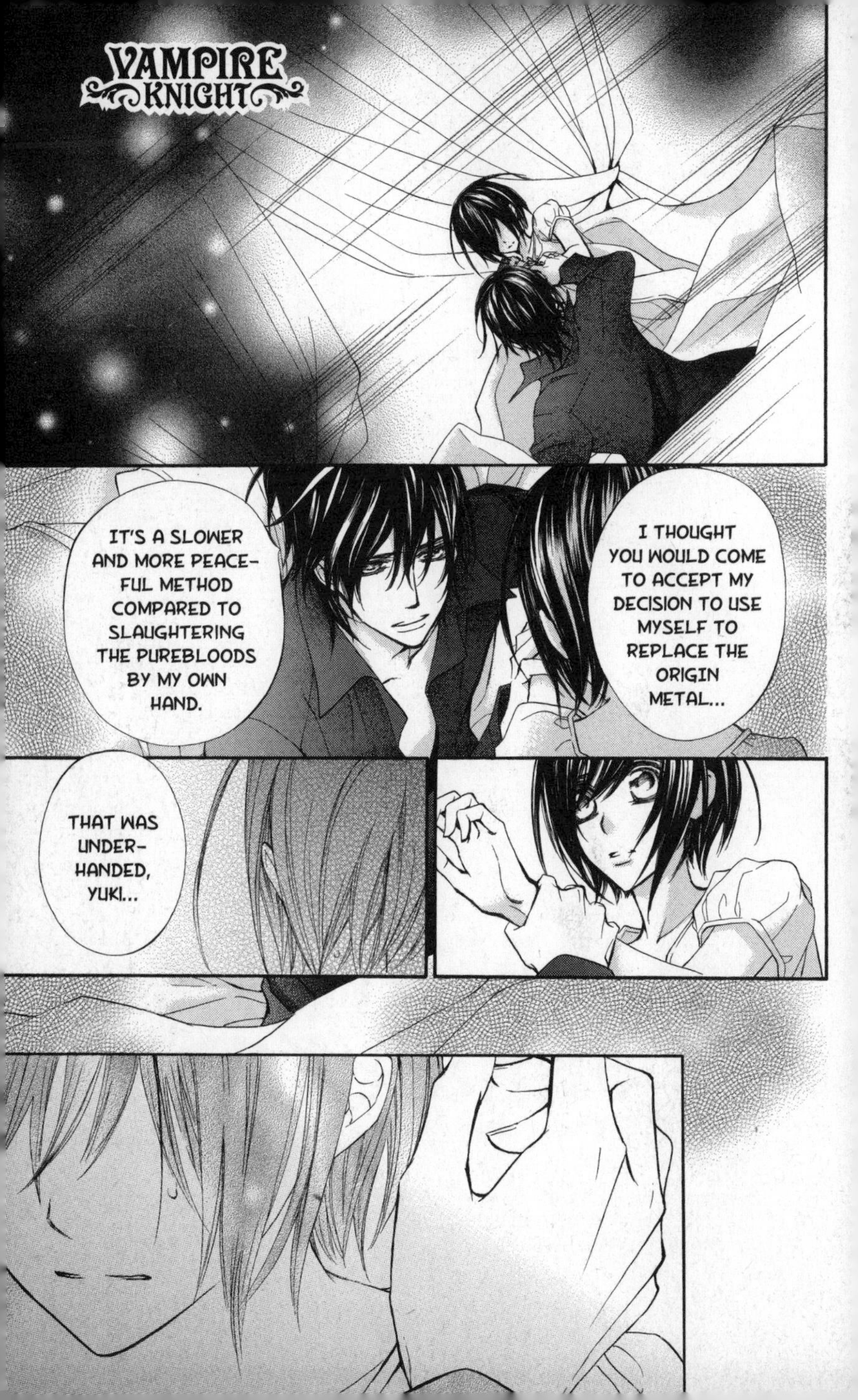
VAMPIRE KNIGHT
I THOUGHT YOU WOULD COME TO ACCEPT MY DECISION TO USE MYSELF TO REPLACE THE ORIGIN METAL...
IT'S A SLOWER AND MORE PEACE-FUL METHOD COMPARED TO SLAUGHTERING THE PUREBLOODS BY MY OWN HAND.
THAT WAS UNDER-HANDED, YUKI...

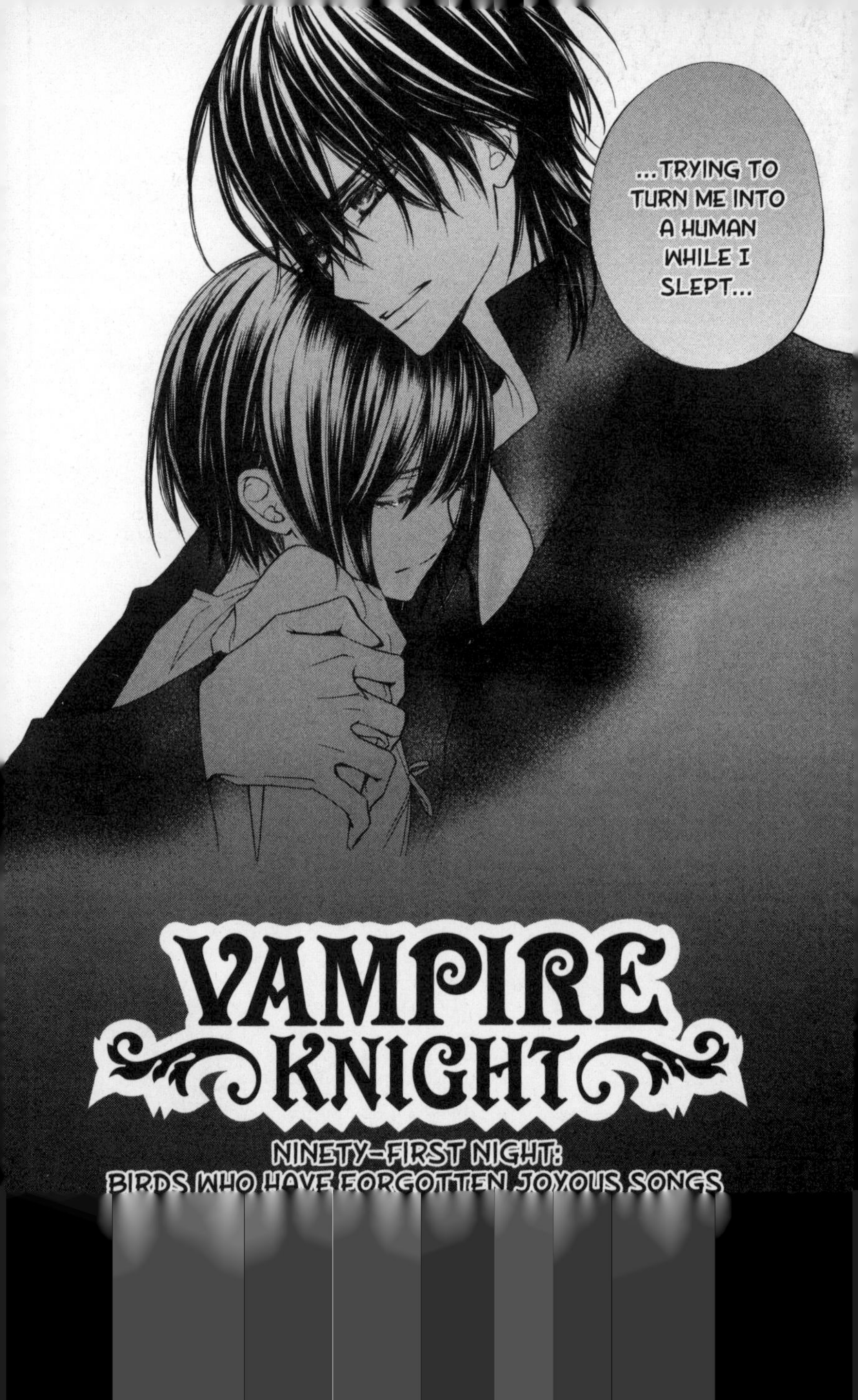
...TRYING TO TURN ME INTO A HUMAN WHILE I SLEPT...
VAMPIRE KNIGHT
NINETY-FIRST NIGHT:
BIRDS WHO HAVE FORGOTTEN JOYOUS SONGS

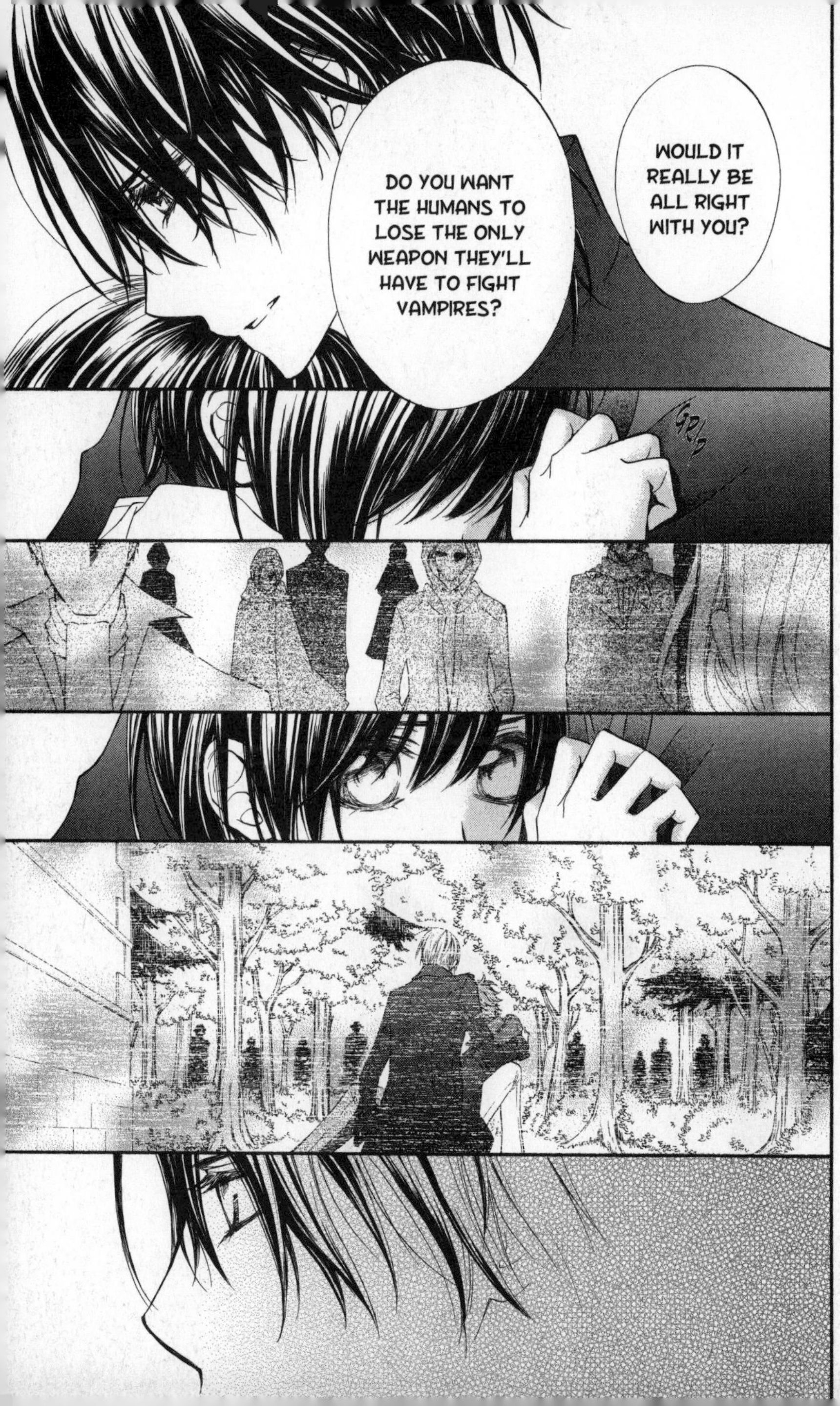
WOULD IT REALLY BE ALL RIGHT WITH YOU?
DO YOU WANT THE HUMANS TO LOSE THE ONLY WEAPON THEY'LL HAVE TO FIGHT VAMPIRES?
GRIP

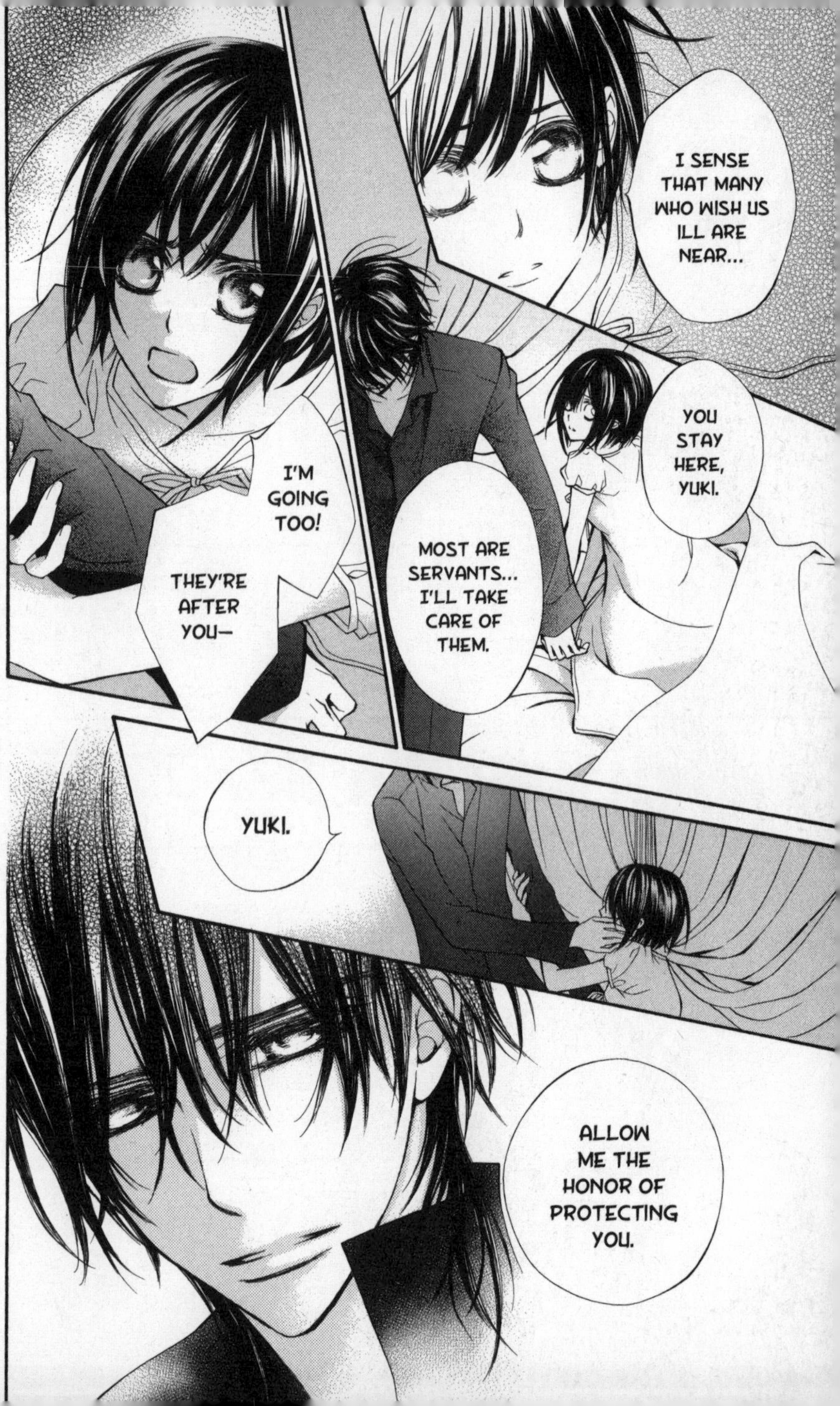
I SENSE THAT MANY WHO WISH US ILL ARE NEAR...
YOU STAY HERE, YUKI.
MOST ARE SERVANTS... I'LL TAKE CARE OF THEM.
I'M GOING TOO!
THEY'RE AFTER YOU—
YUKI.
ALLOW ME THE HONOR OF PROTECTING YOU.

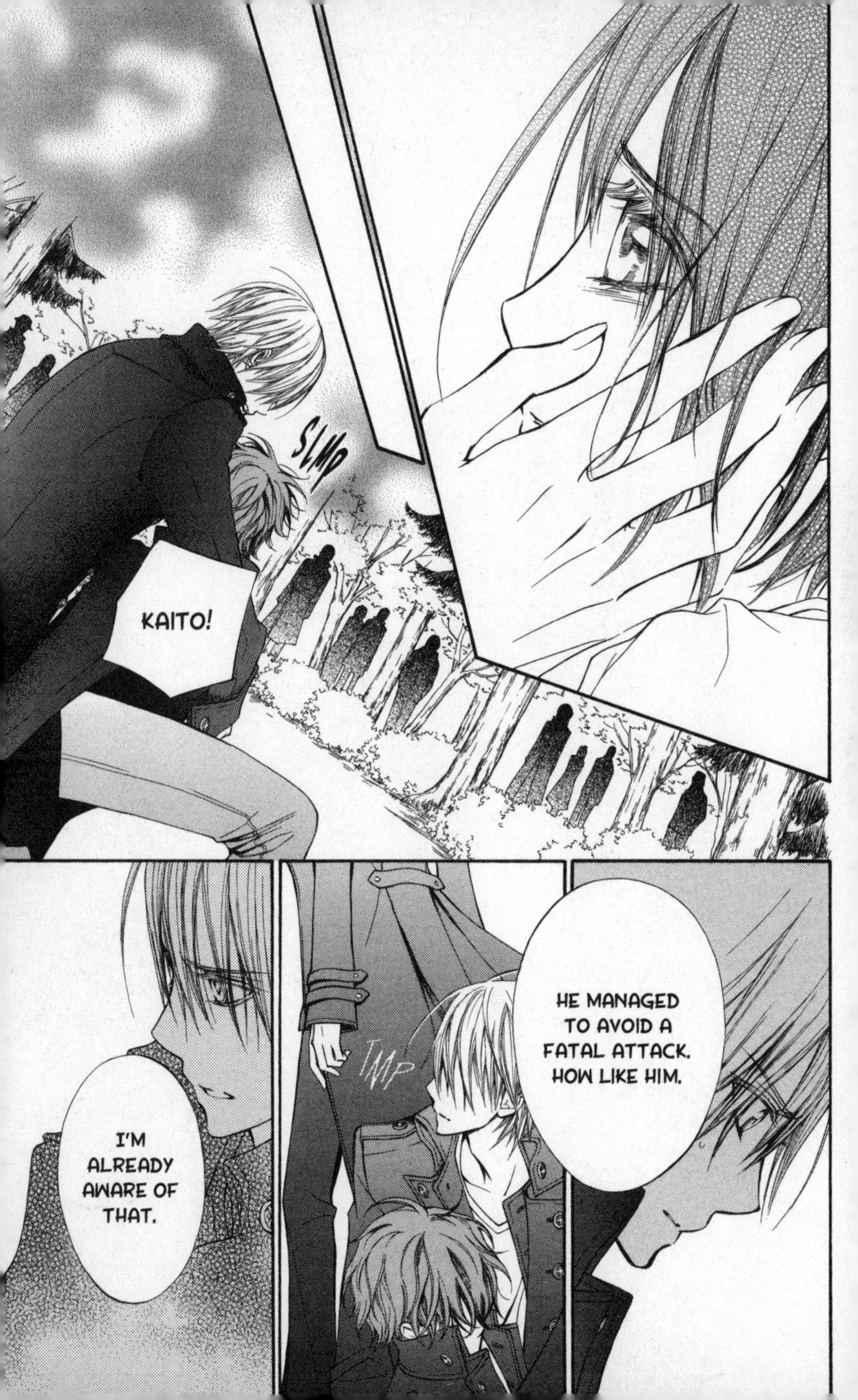
KAITO!
HE MANAGED TO AVOID A FATAL ATTACK. HOW LIKE HIM.
TMP
I'M ALREADY AWARE OF THAT.

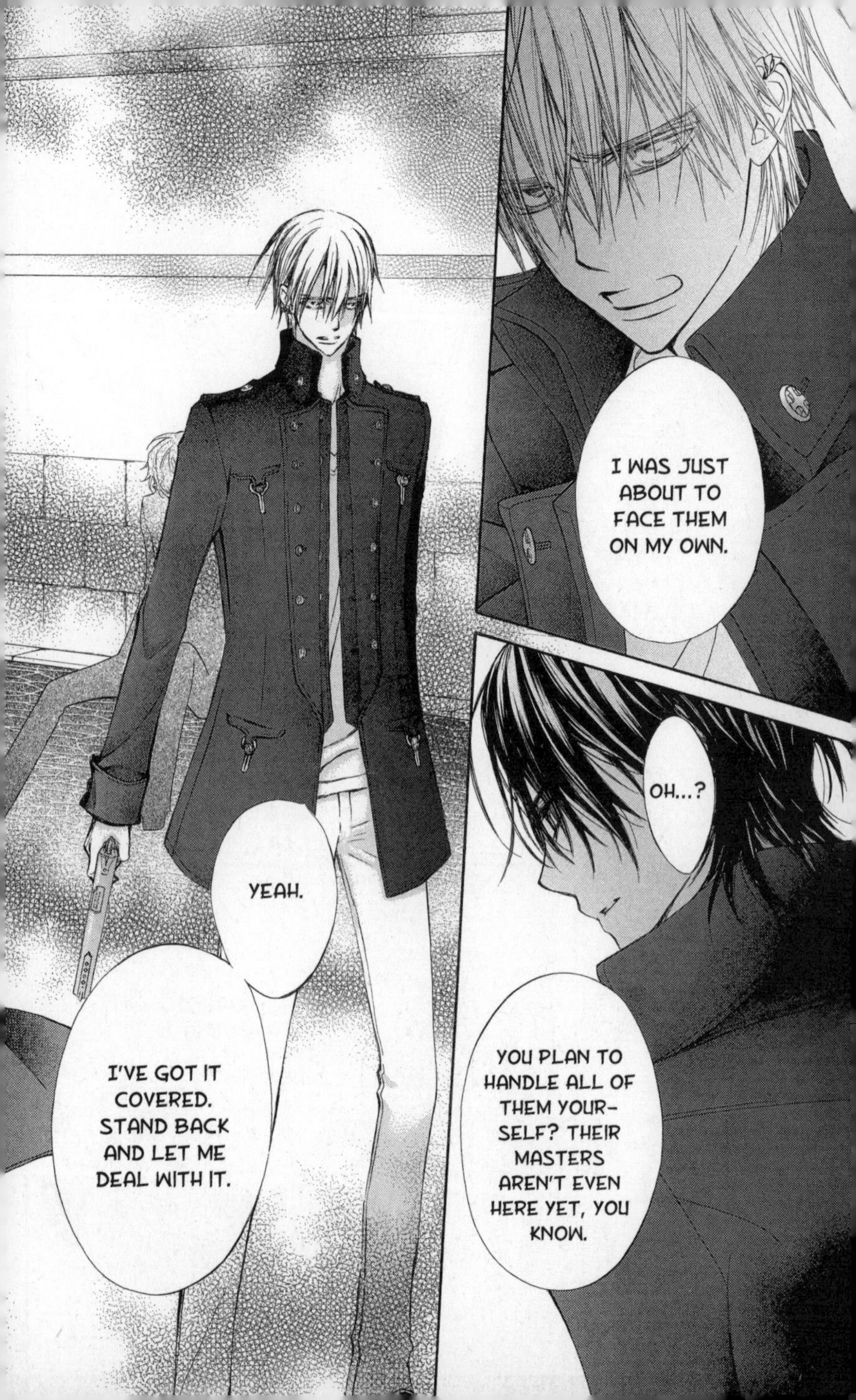
I WAS JUST ABOUT TO FACE THEM ON MY OWN.
OH...?
YOU PLAN TO HANDLE ALL OF THEM YOUR-SELF? THEIR MASTERS AREN'T EVEN HERE YET, YOU KNOW.
YEAH.
I'VE GOT IT COVERED. STAND BACK AND LET ME DEAL WITH IT.

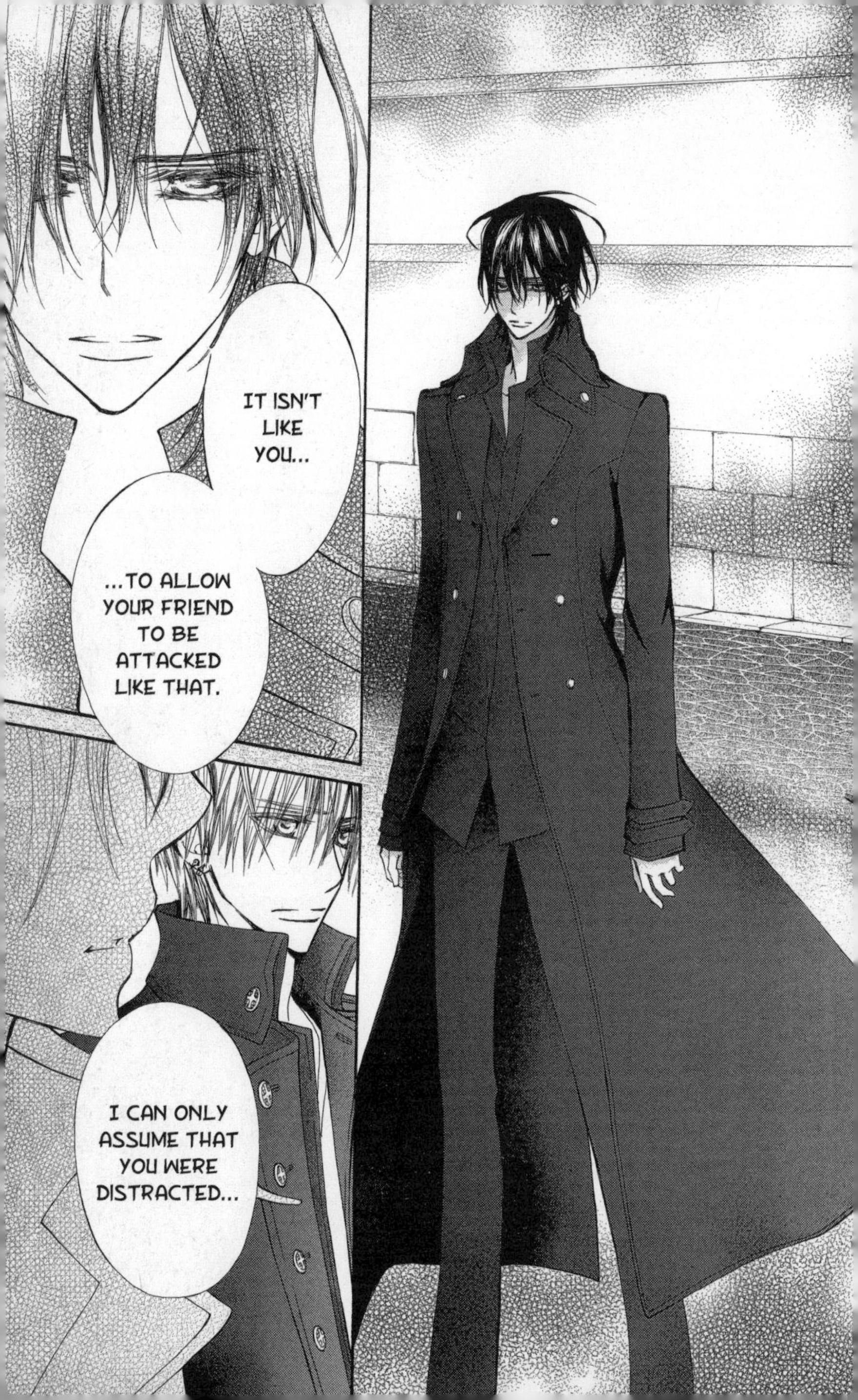
IT ISN'T LIKE YOU...
...TO ALLOW YOUR FRIEND TO BE ATTACKED LIKE THAT.
I CAN ONLY ASSUME THAT YOU WERE DISTRACTED...

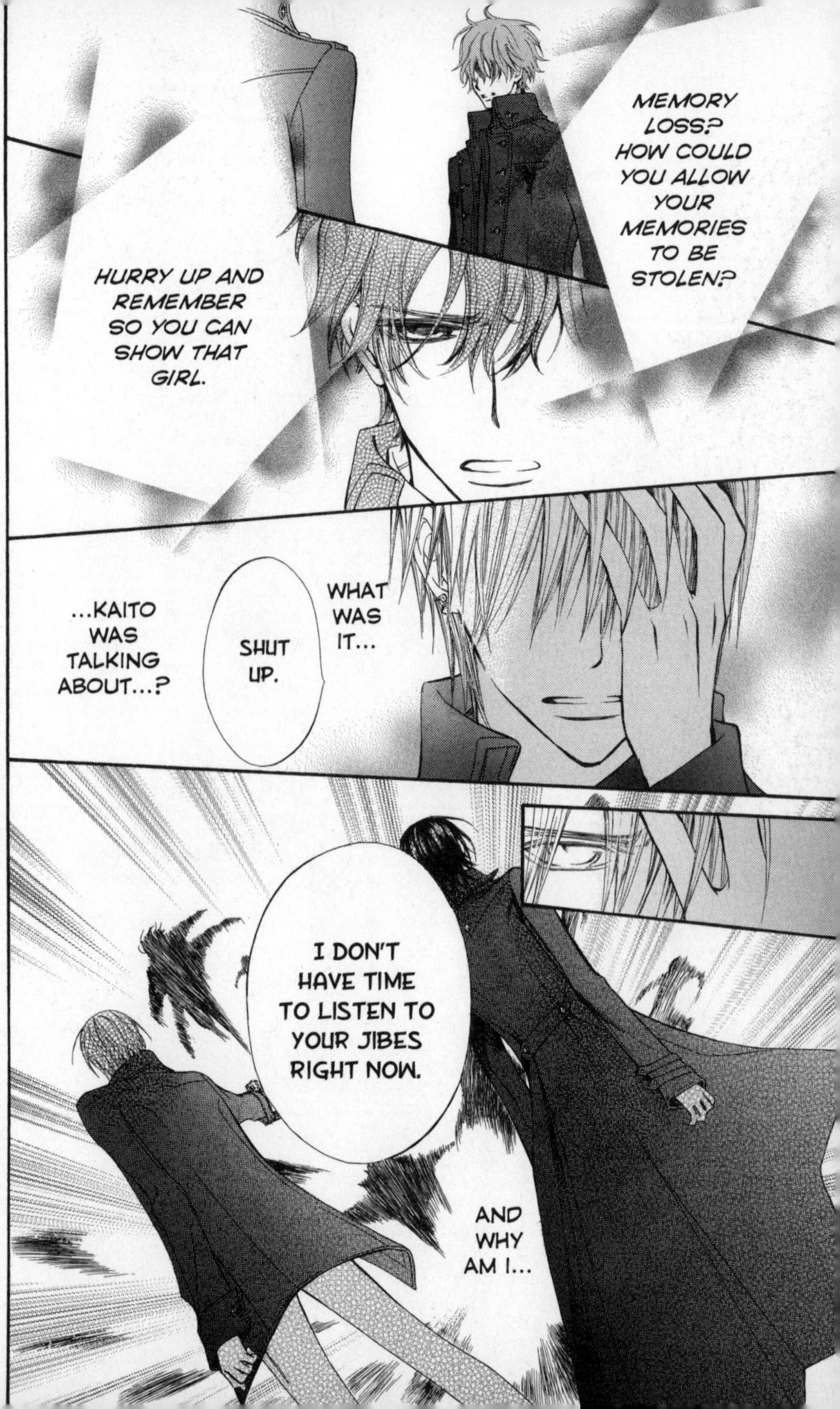
MEMORY LOSS? HOW COULD YOU ALLOW YOUR MEMORIES TO BE STOLEN?
HURRY UP AND REMEMBER SO YOU CAN SHOW THAT GIRL.
WHAT WAS IT...
SHUT UP.
...KAITO WAS TALKING ABOUT...?
I DON'T HAVE TIME TO LISTEN TO YOUR JIBES RIGHT NOW.
AND WHY AM I...

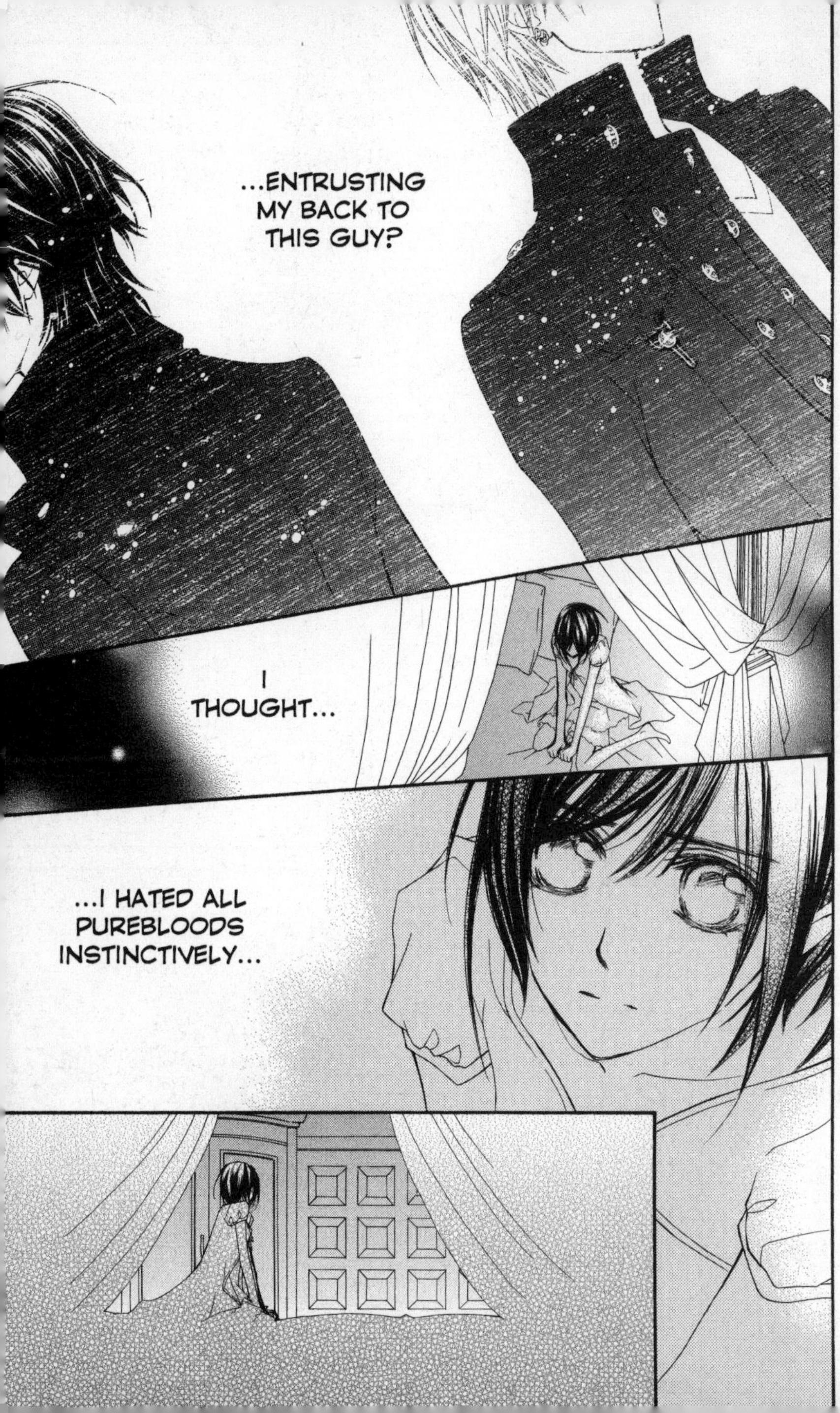
...ENTRUSTING MY BACK TO THIS GUY?
I THOUGHT...
...I HATED ALL PUREBLOODS INSTINCTIVELY...

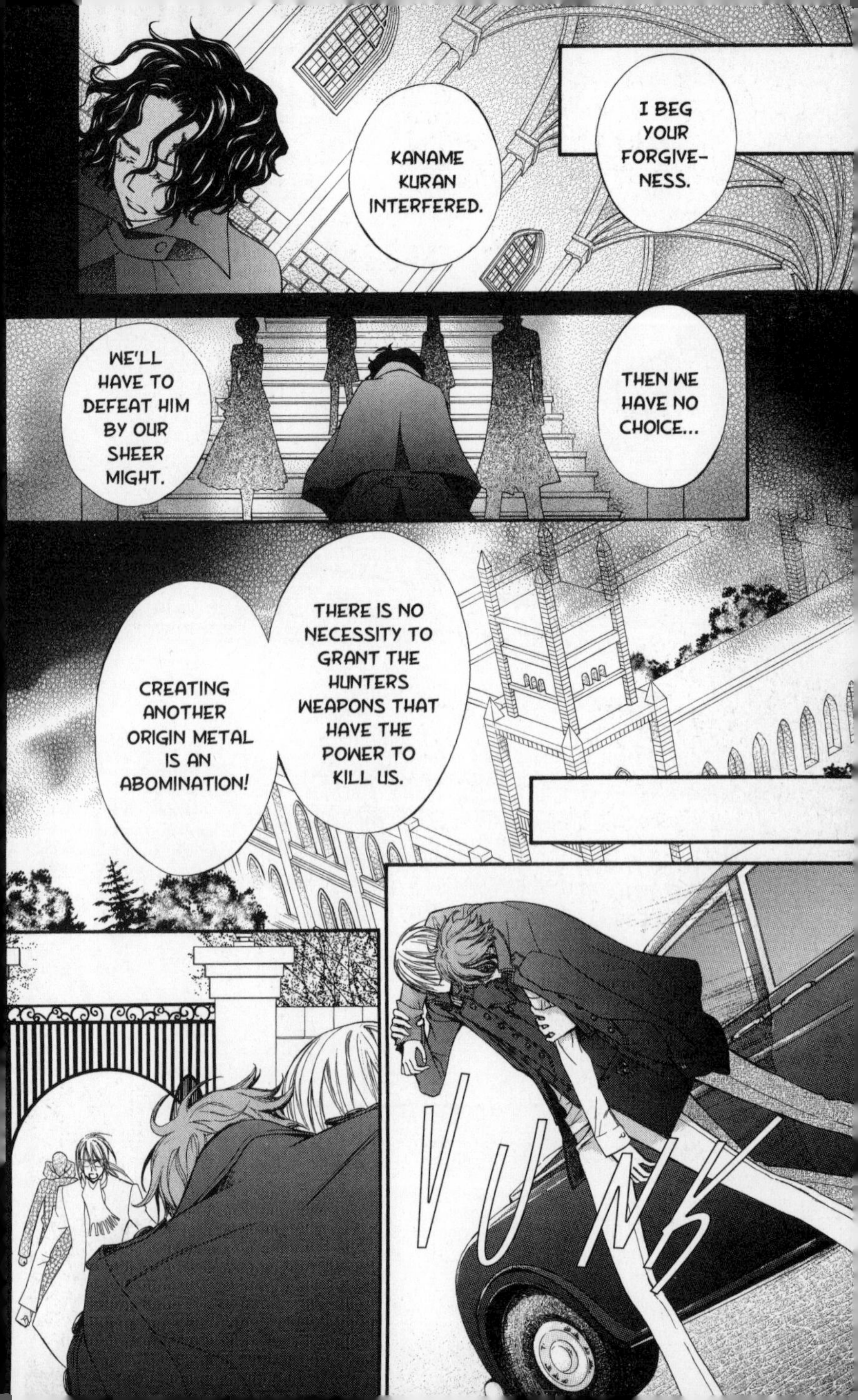
I BEG YOUR FORGIVE-NESS.
KANAME KURAN INTERFERED.
THEN WE HAVE NO CHOICE...
WE'LL HAVE TO DEFEAT HIM BY OUR SHEER MIGHT.
THERE IS NO NECESSITY TO GRANT THE HUNTERS WEAPONS THAT HAVE THE POWER TO KILL US.
CREATING ANOTHER ORIGIN METAL IS AN ABOMINATION!
VUNK

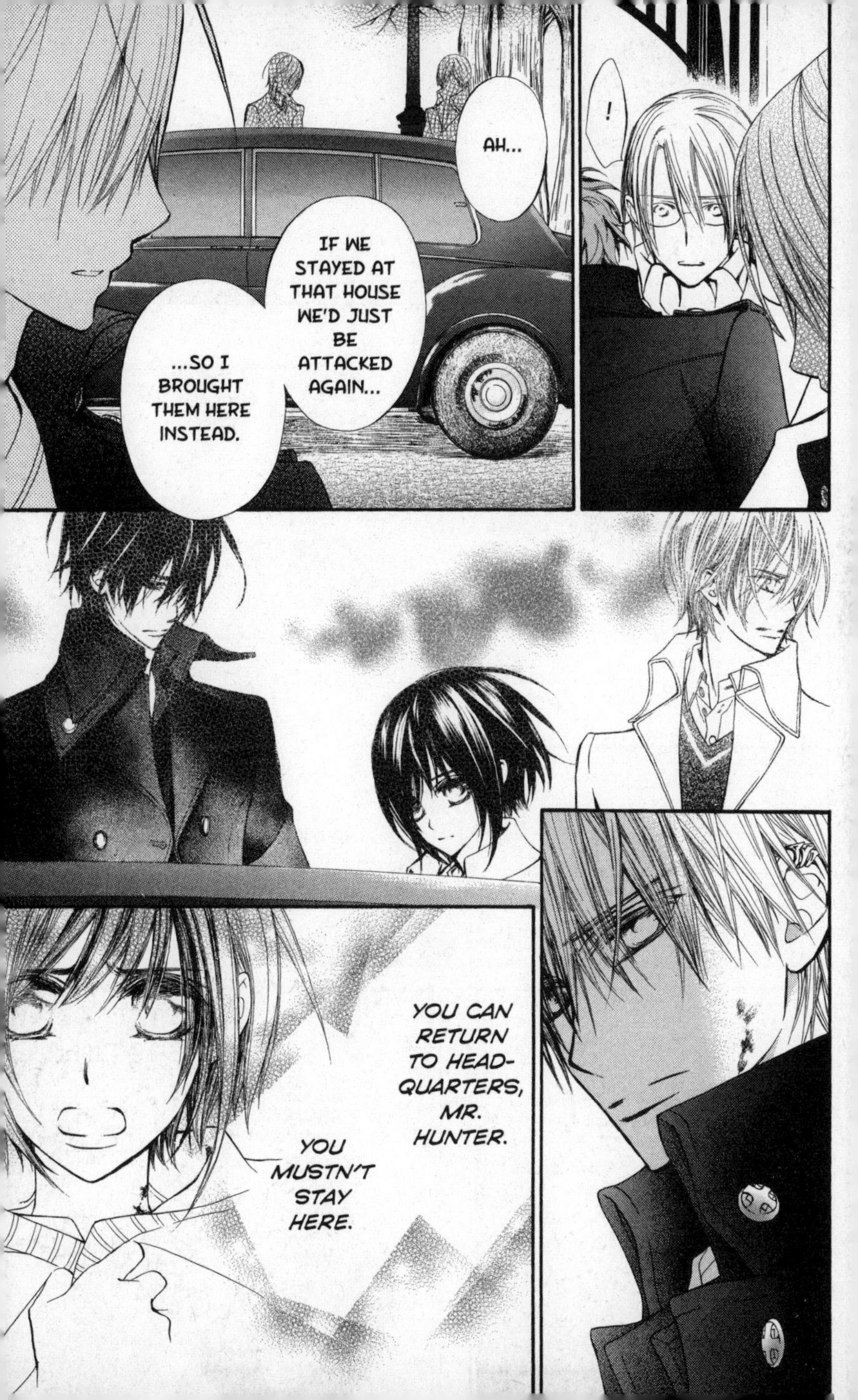
!
AH...
IF WE STAYED AT THAT HOUSE WE'D JUST BE ATTACKED AGAIN...
...SO I BROUGHT THEM HERE INSTEAD.
YOU CAN RETURN TO HEAD-QUARTERS, MR. HUNTER.
YOU MUSTN'T STAY HERE.

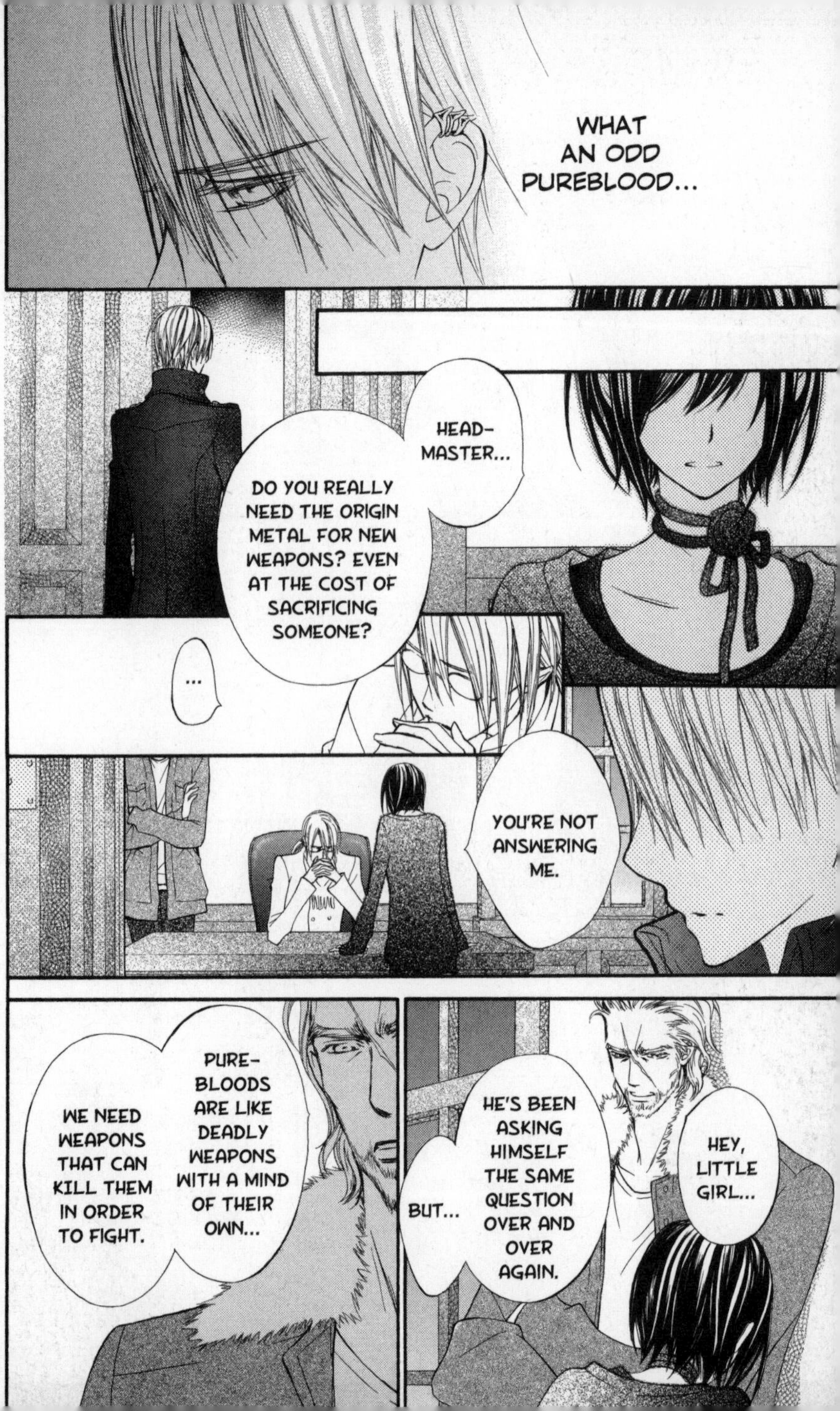
WHAT AN ODD PUREBLOOD...
HEAD-MASTER...
DO YOU REALLY NEED THE ORIGIN METAL FOR NEW WEAPONS? EVEN AT THE COST OF SACRIFICING SOMEONE?
...
YOU'RE NOT ANSWERING ME.
HEY, LITTLE GIRL...
HE'S BEEN ASKING HIMSELF THE SAME QUESTION OVER AND OVER AGAIN.
BUT...
PURE-BLOODS ARE LIKE DEADLY WEAPONS WITH A MIND OF THEIR OWN...
WE NEED WEAPONS THAT CAN KILL THEM IN ORDER TO FIGHT.

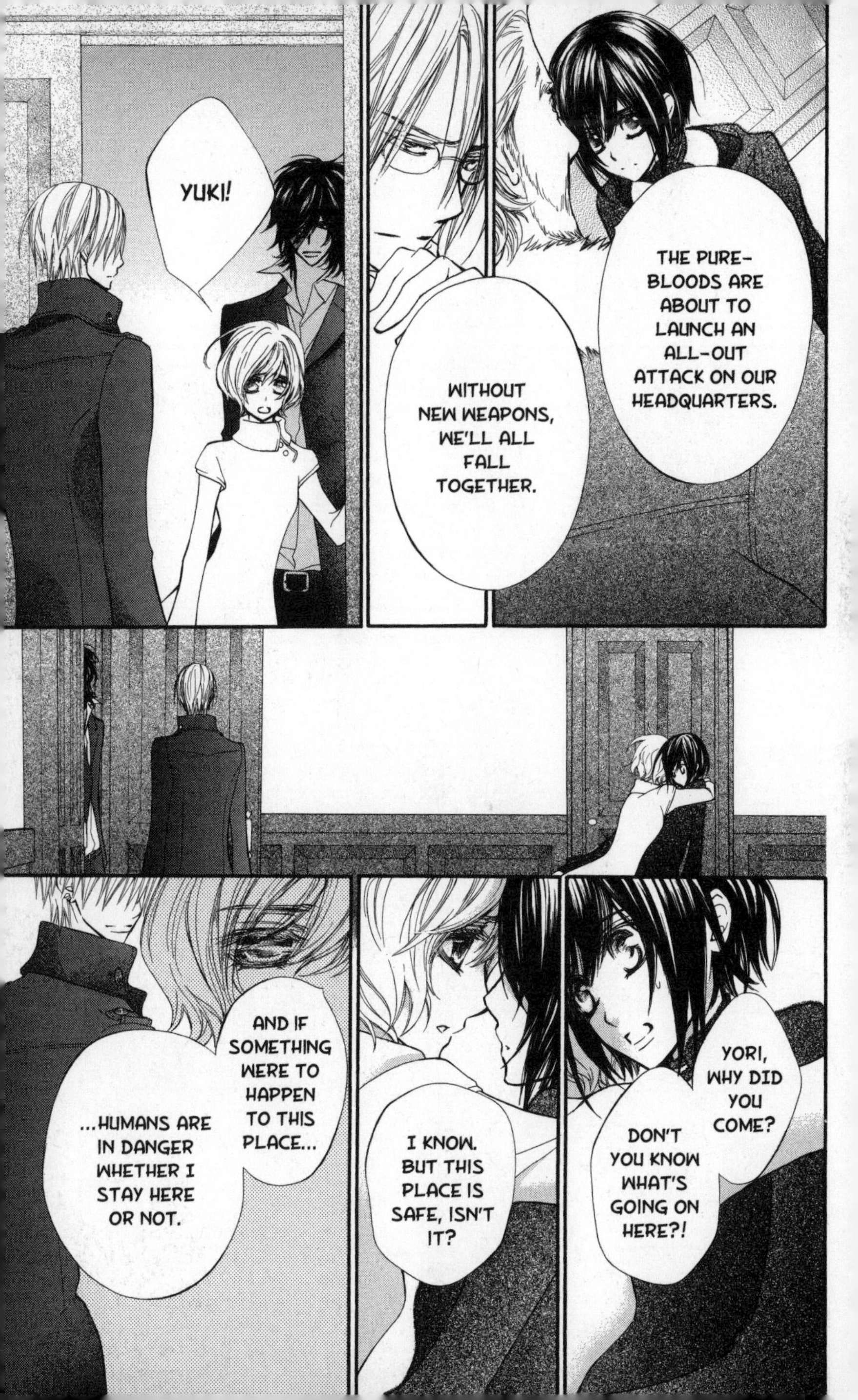
THE PURE-BLOODS ARE ABOUT TO LAUNCH AN ALL-OUT ATTACK ON OUR HEADQUARTERS.
WITHOUT NEW WEAPONS, WE'LL ALL FALL TOGETHER.
YUKI!
YORI, WHY DID YOU COME?
DON'T YOU KNOW WHAT'S GOING ON HERE?!
I KNOW. BUT THIS PLACE IS SAFE, ISN'T IT?
AND IF SOMETHING WERE TO HAPPEN TO THIS PLACE...
...HUMANS ARE IN DANGER WHETHER I STAY HERE OR NOT.

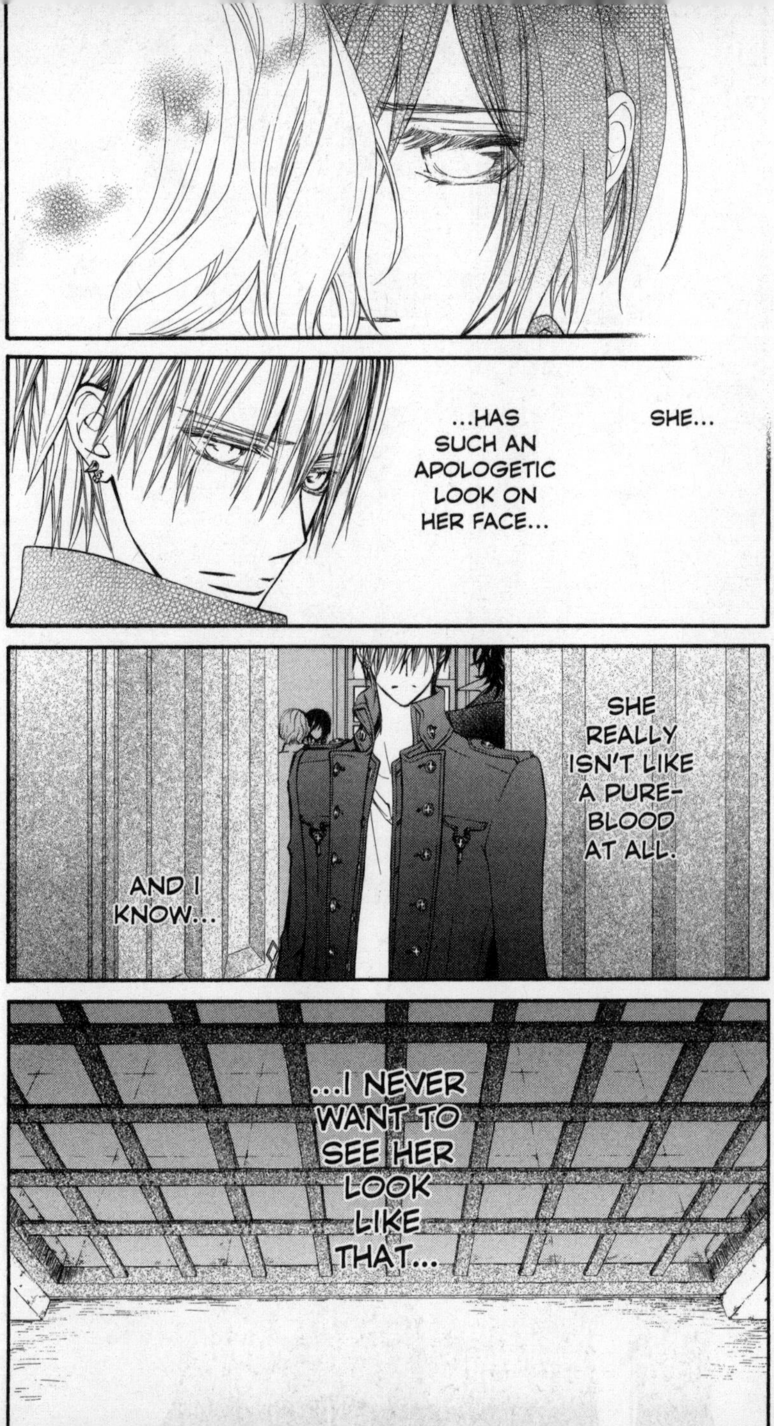
SHE...
...HAS SUCH AN APOLOGETIC LOOK ON HER FACE...
SHE REALLY ISN'T LIKE A PURE-BLOOD AT ALL.
AND I KNOW...
...I NEVER WANT TO SEE HER LOOK LIKE THAT...

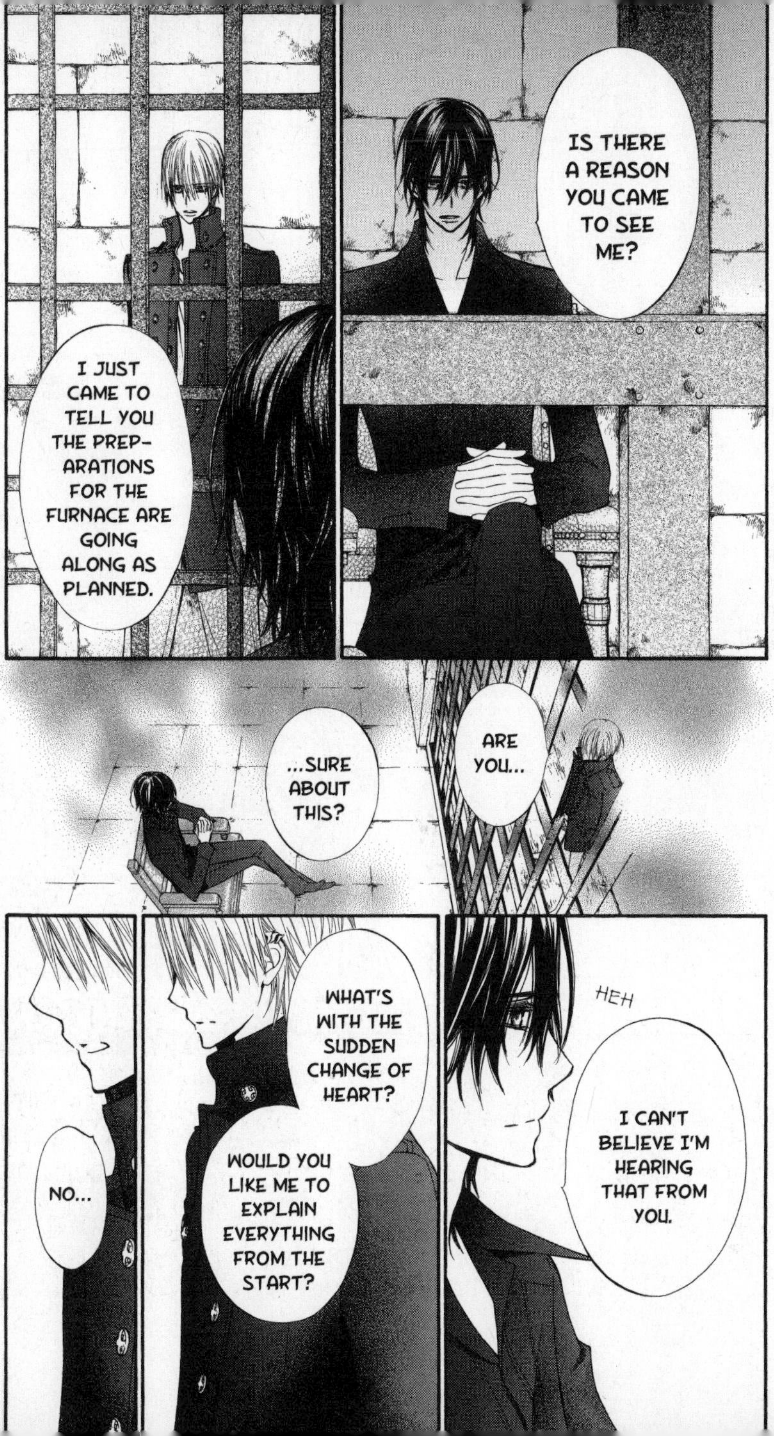
IS THERE A REASON YOU CAME TO SEE ME?
I JUST CAME TO TELL YOU THE PREP-ARATIONS FOR THE FURNACE ARE GOING ALONG AS PLANNED.
ARE YOU...
...SURE ABOUT THIS?
HEH
I CAN'T BELIEVE I'M HEARING THAT FROM YOU.
WHAT'S WITH THE SUDDEN CHANGE OF HEART?
WOULD YOU LIKE ME TO EXPLAIN EVERYTHING FROM THE START?
NO...

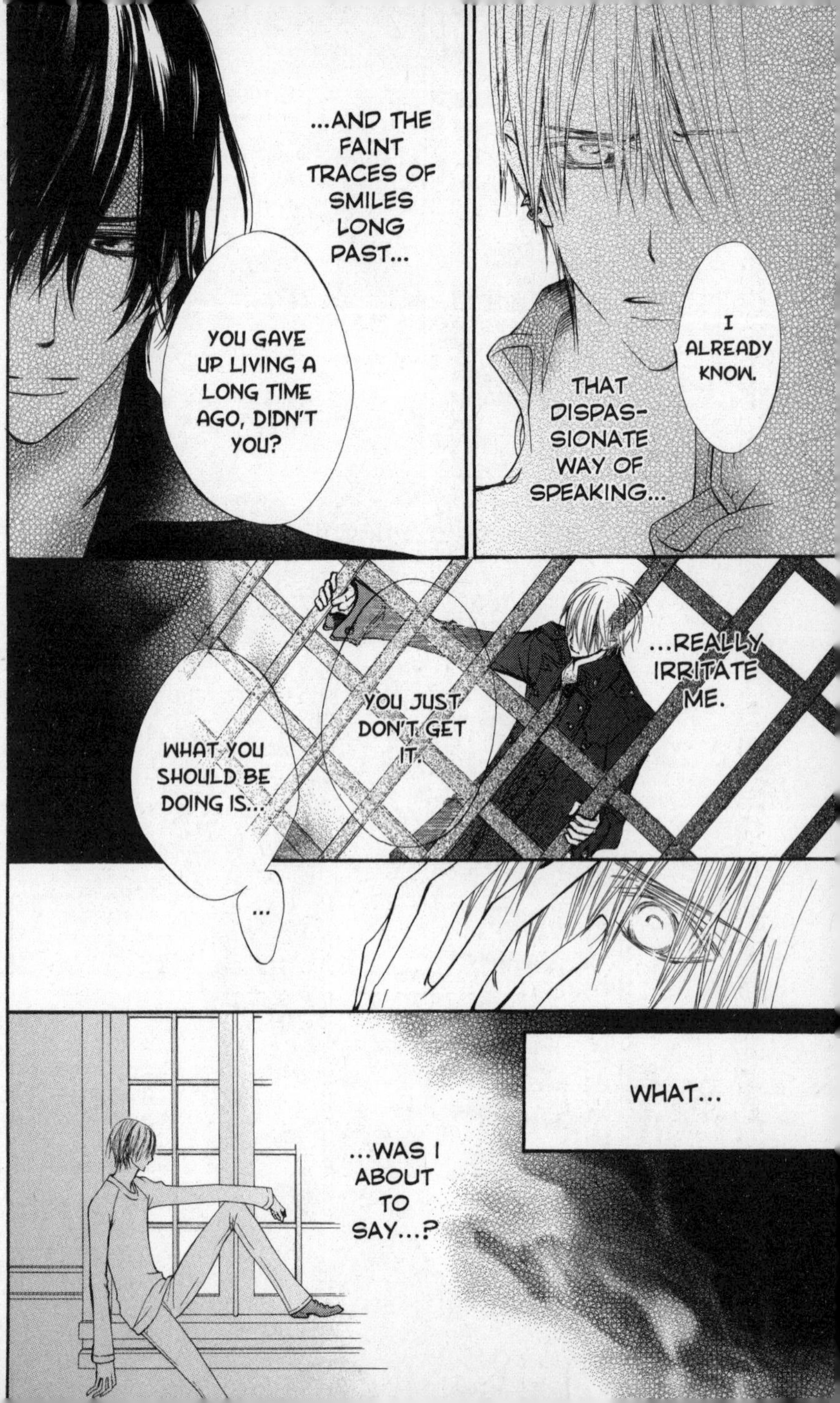
I ALREADY KNOW.
THAT DISPAS-SIONATE WAY OF SPEAKING...
...AND THE FAINT TRACES OF SMILES LONG PAST...
YOU GAVE UP LIVING A LONG TIME AGO, DIDN'T YOU?
...REALLY IRRITATE ME.
YOU JUST DON'T GET IT.
WHAT YOU SHOULD BE DOING IS...
...
WHAT...
...WAS I ABOUT TO SAY...?

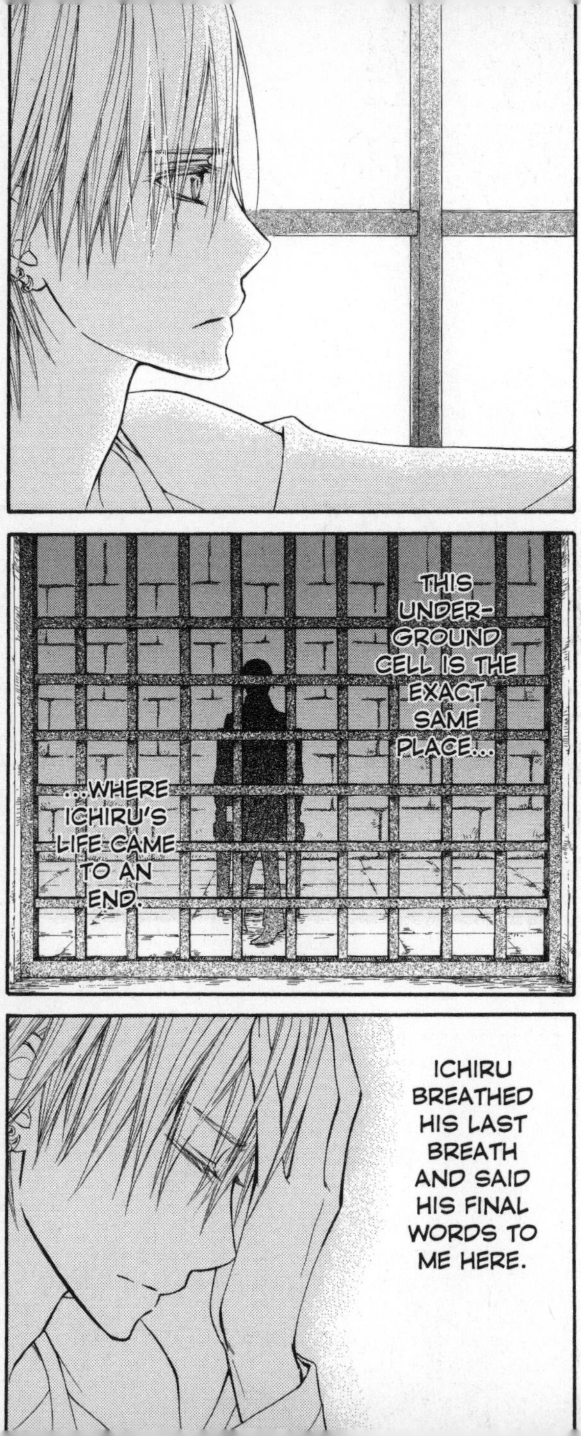
THIS UNDER-GROUND CELL IS THE EXACT SAME PLACE...
...WHERE ICHIRU'S LIFE CAME TO AN END.
ICHIRU BREATHED HIS LAST BREATH AND SAID HIS FINAL WORDS TO ME HERE.

II

Ending the series before volume 20 was something I had planned on from the start. It is up to the readers to decide whether they enjoyed the story or not, but I for one am glad... I have been able to complete the story within the original schedule. I put everything I had into creating this series, so that is all the more reason for me to have various thoughts about this series. And I feel it is also time for me to think about what I want to do for the latter half of my life. The best thing would be for me to sort out my thoughts, rejuvenate my spirit, energy, and mind so I can work on another series again.

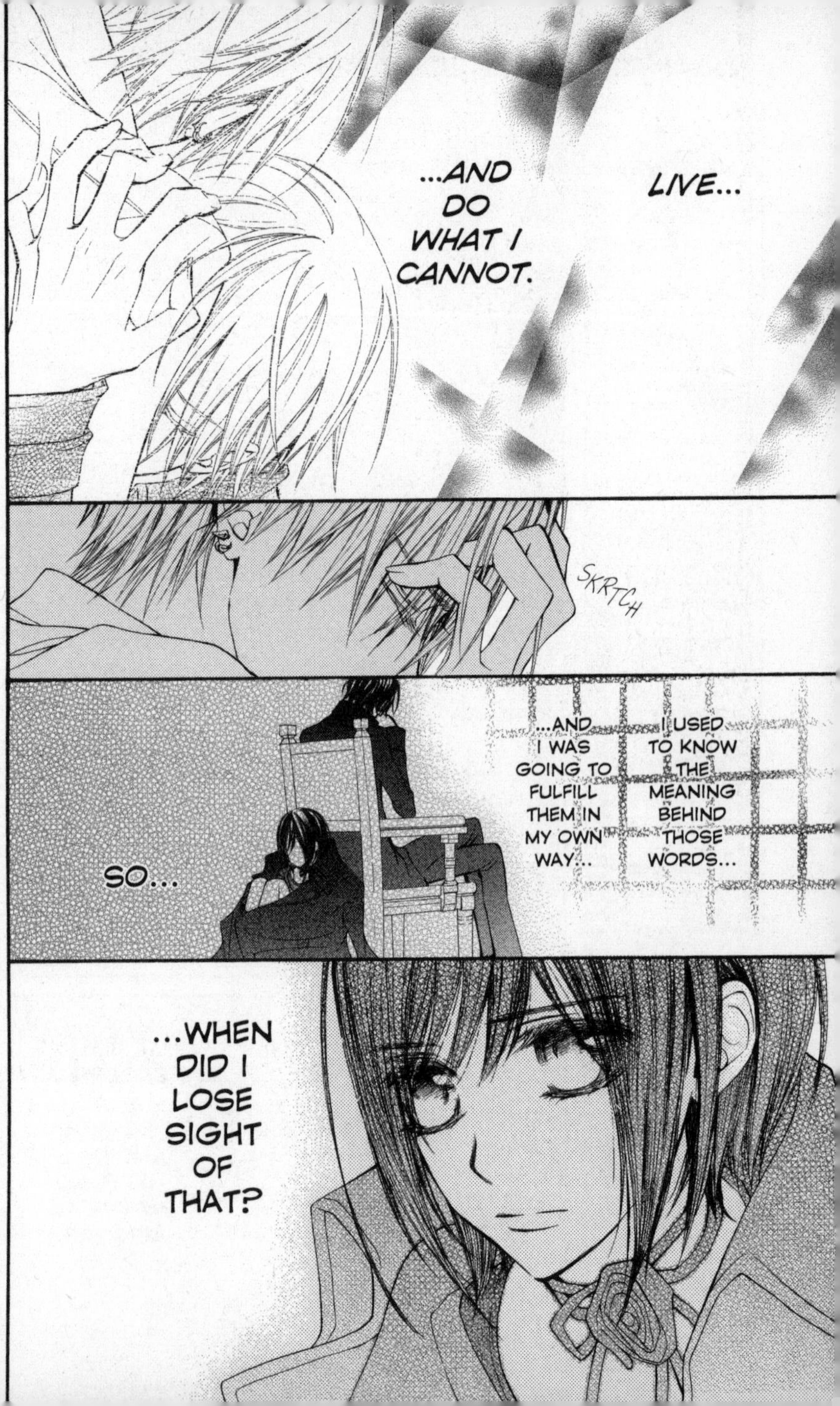
LIVE...
...AND DO WHAT I CANNOT.
SKRTCH
I USED TO KNOW THE MEANING BEHIND THOSE WORDS...
...AND I WAS GOING TO FULFILL THEM IN MY OWN WAY...
SO...
...WHEN DID I LOSE SIGHT OF THAT?

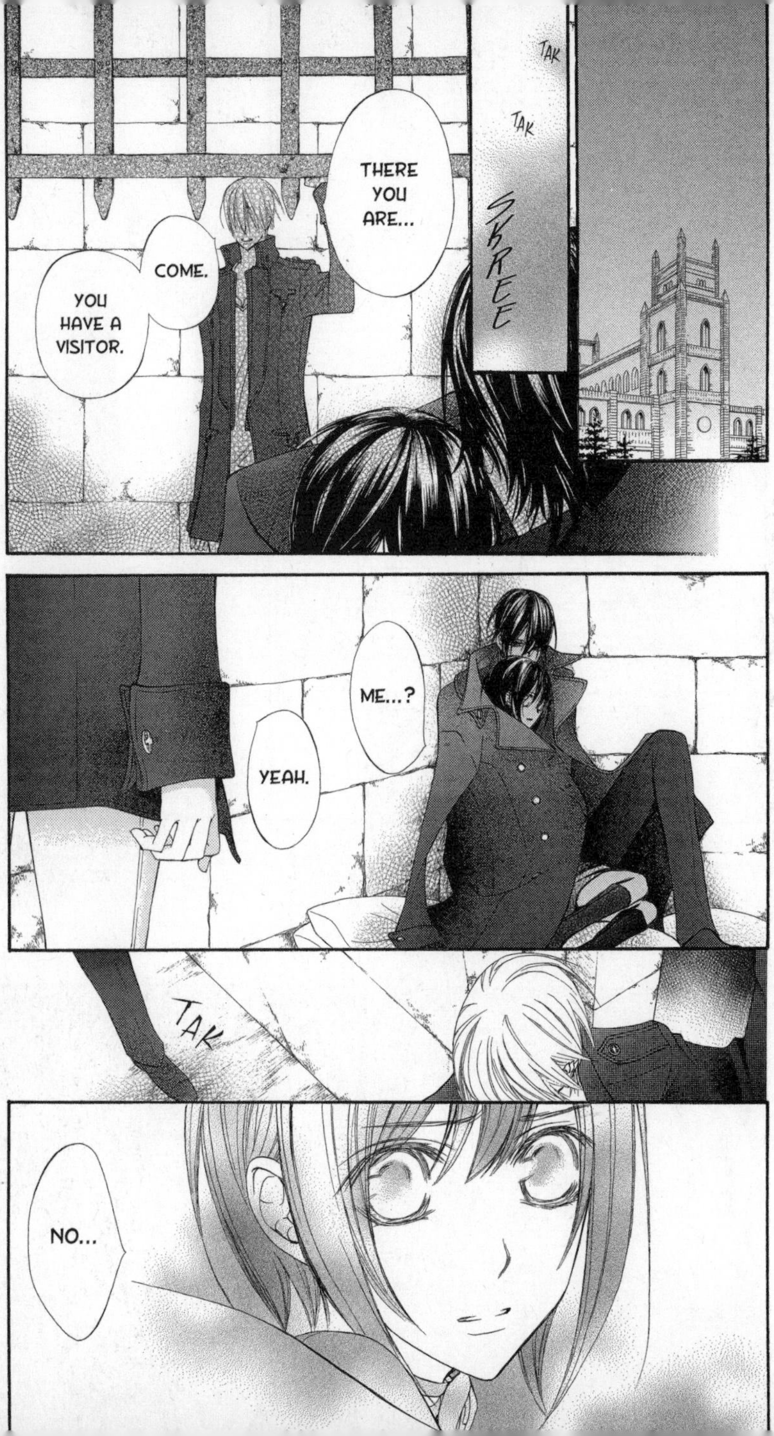
TAK
TAK
SKREE
THERE YOU ARE...
COME.
YOU HAVE A VISITOR.
ME...?
YEAH.
TAK
NO...

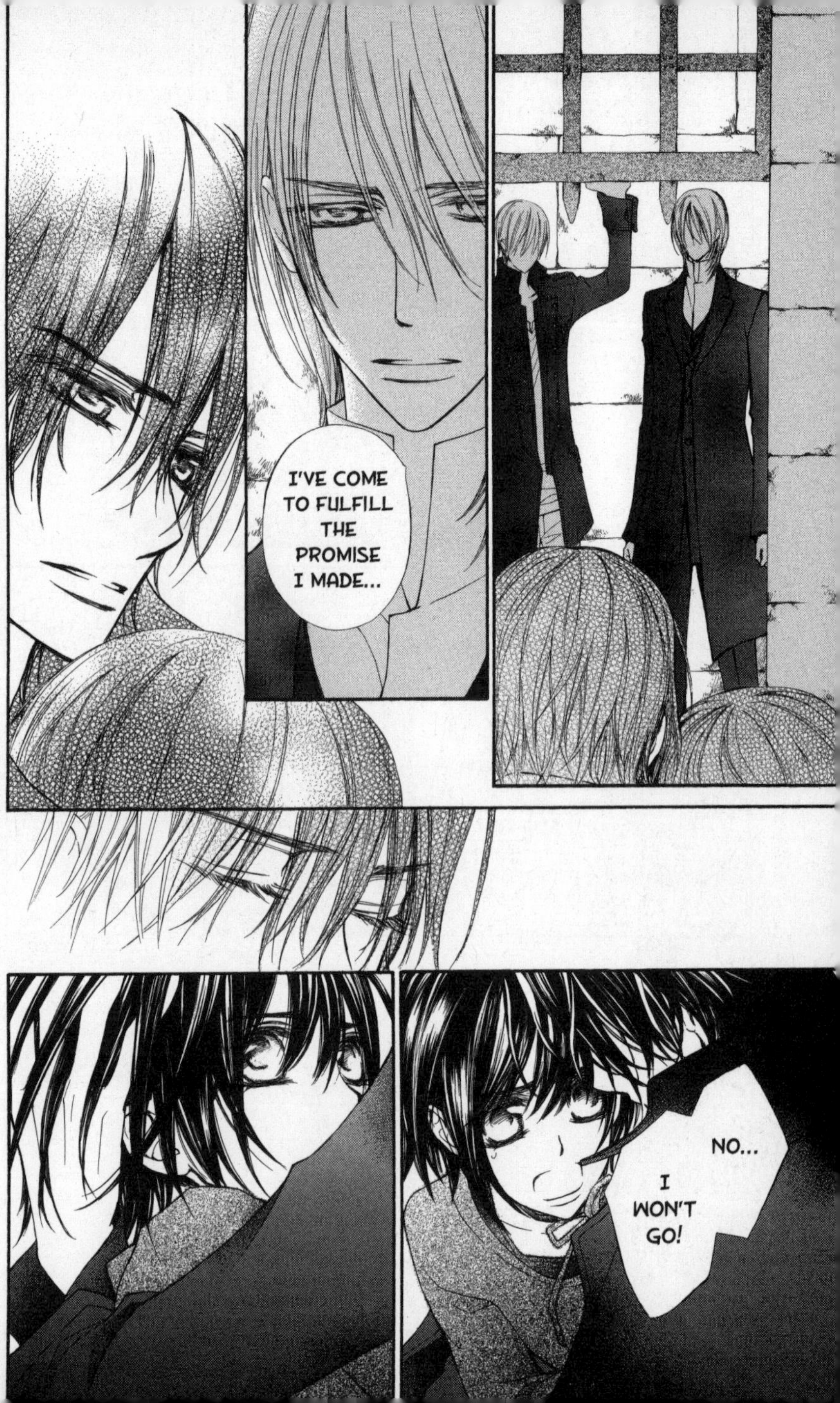
I'VE COME TO FULFILL THE PROMISE I MADE...
NO...
I WON'T GO!

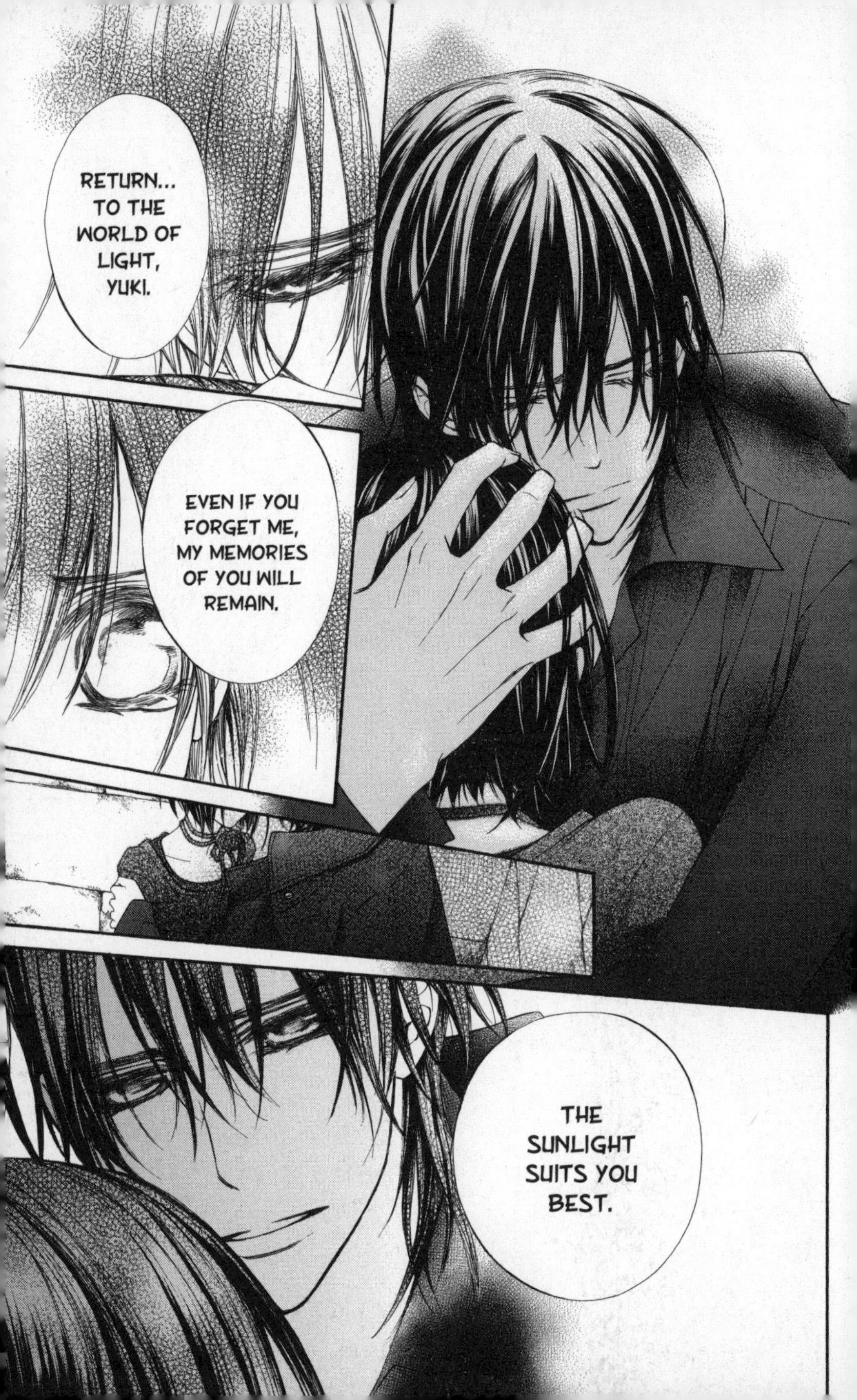
RETURN... TO THE WORLD OF LIGHT, YUKI.
EVEN IF YOU FORGET ME, MY MEMORIES OF YOU WILL REMAIN.
THE SUNLIGHT SUITS YOU BEST.

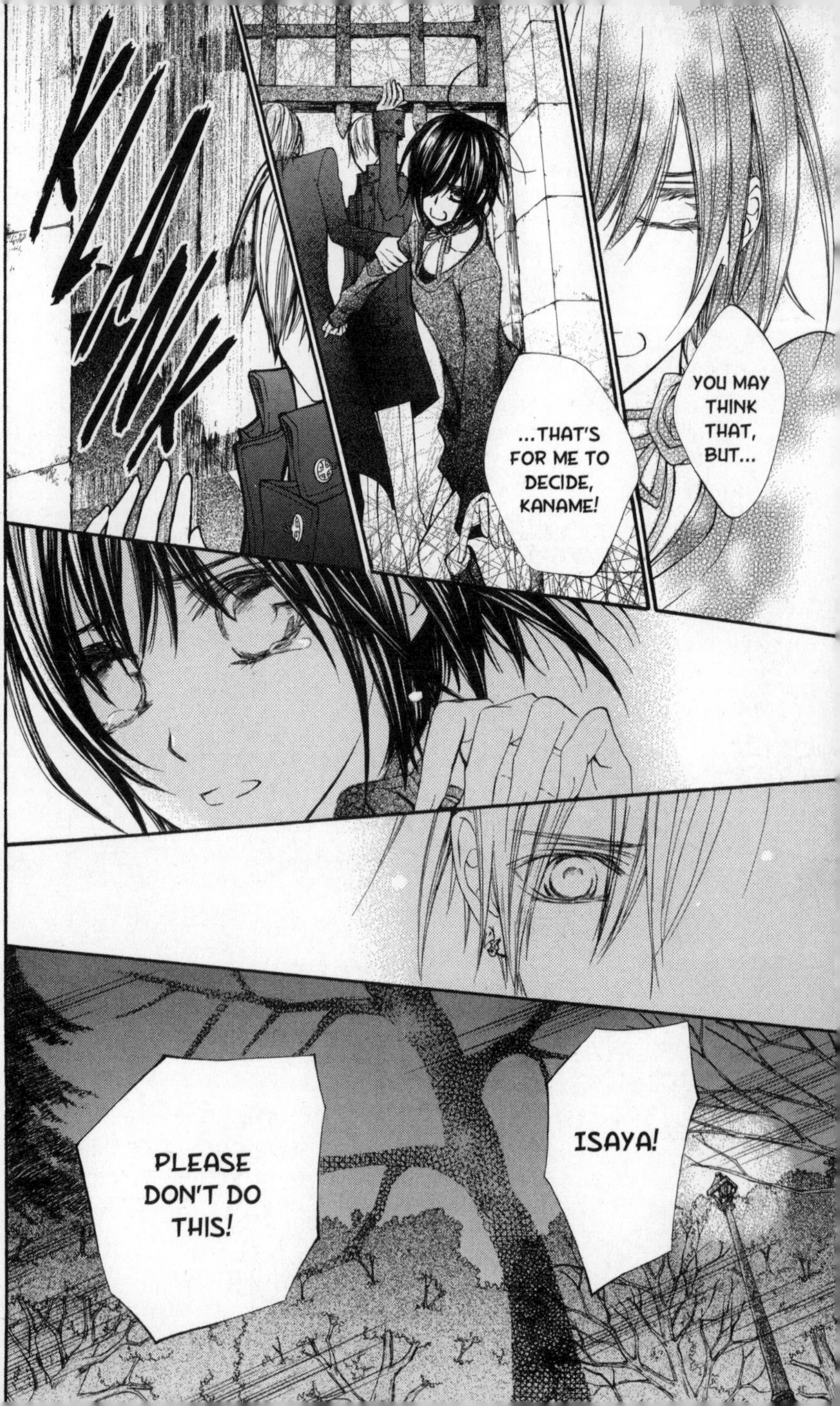
YOU MAY THINK THAT, BUT...
...THAT'S FOR ME TO DECIDE, KANAME!
KLANK
ISAYA!
PLEASE DON'T DO THIS!

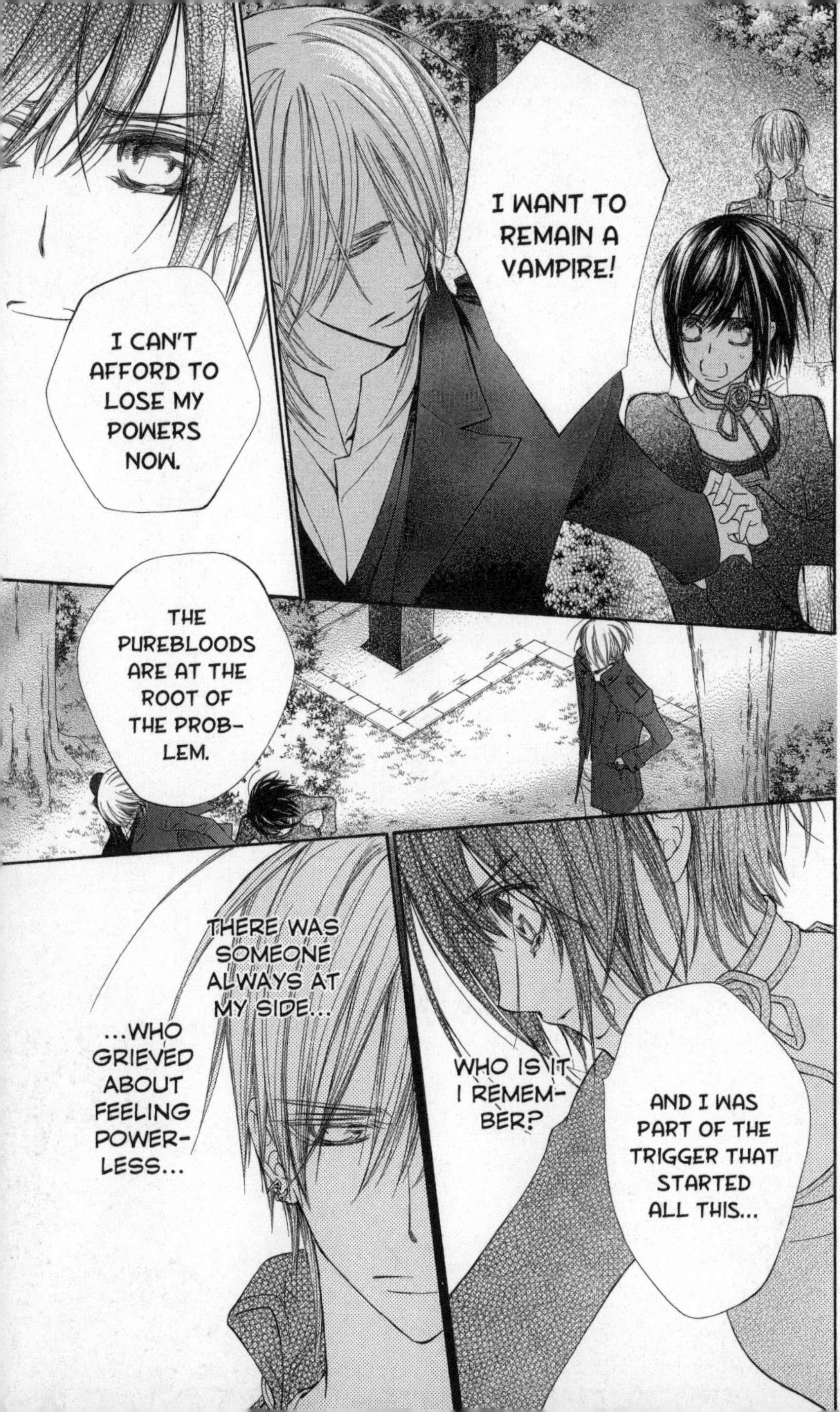
I WANT TO REMAIN A VAMPIRE!
I CAN'T AFFORD TO LOSE MY POWERS NOW.
THE PUREBLOODS ARE AT THE ROOT OF THE PROB-LEM.
AND I WAS PART OF THE TRIGGER THAT STARTED ALL THIS...
WHO IS IT I REMEM-BER?
THERE WAS SOMEONE ALWAYS AT MY SIDE...
...WHO GRIEVED ABOUT FEELING POWER-LESS...

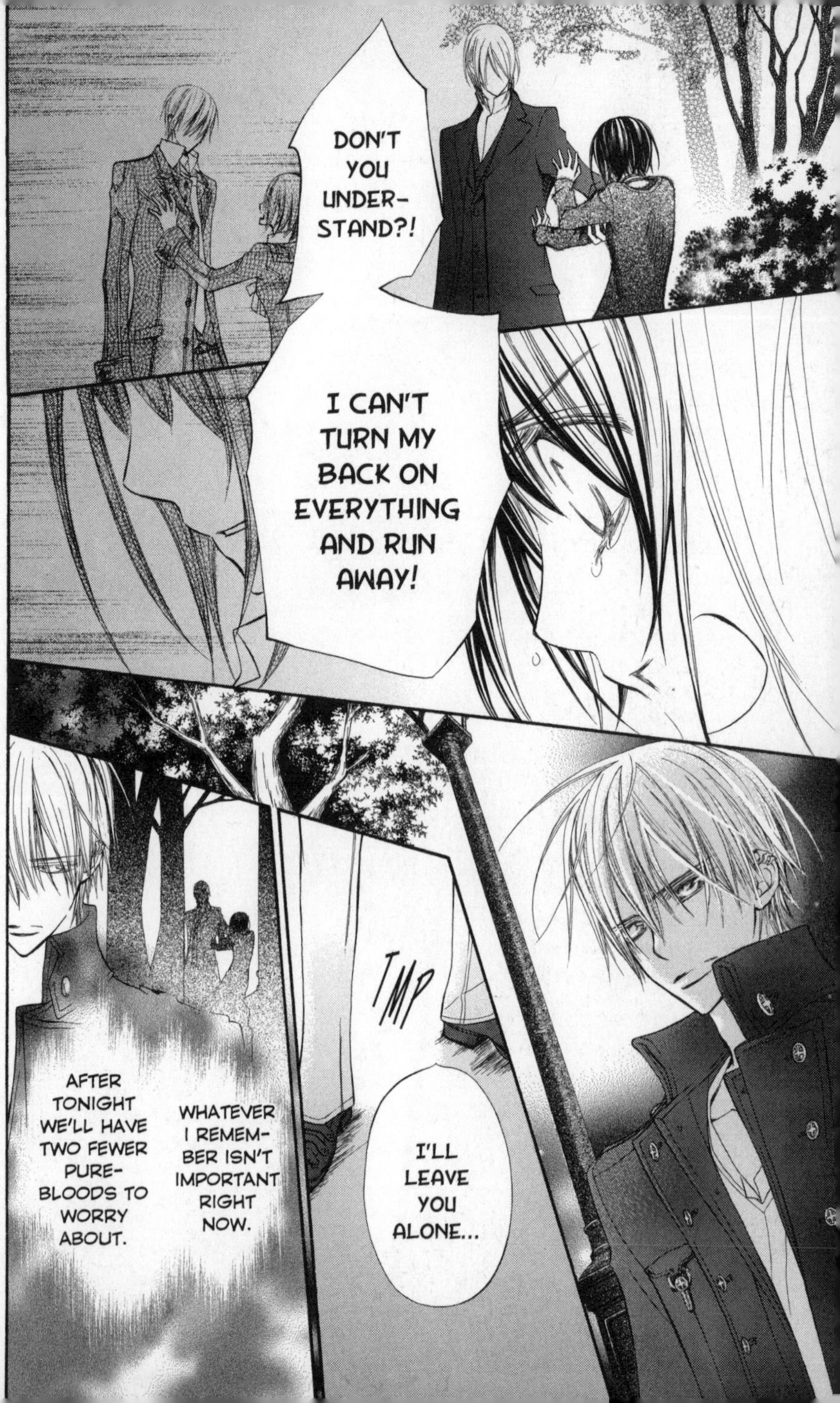
DON'T YOU UNDER-STAND?!
I CAN'T TURN MY BACK ON EVERYTHING AND RUN AWAY!
I'LL LEAVE YOU ALONE...
TMP
WHATEVER I REMEMBER ISN'T IMPORTANT RIGHT NOW.
AFTER TONIGHT WE'LL HAVE TWO FEWER PURE-BLOODS TO WORRY ABOUT.

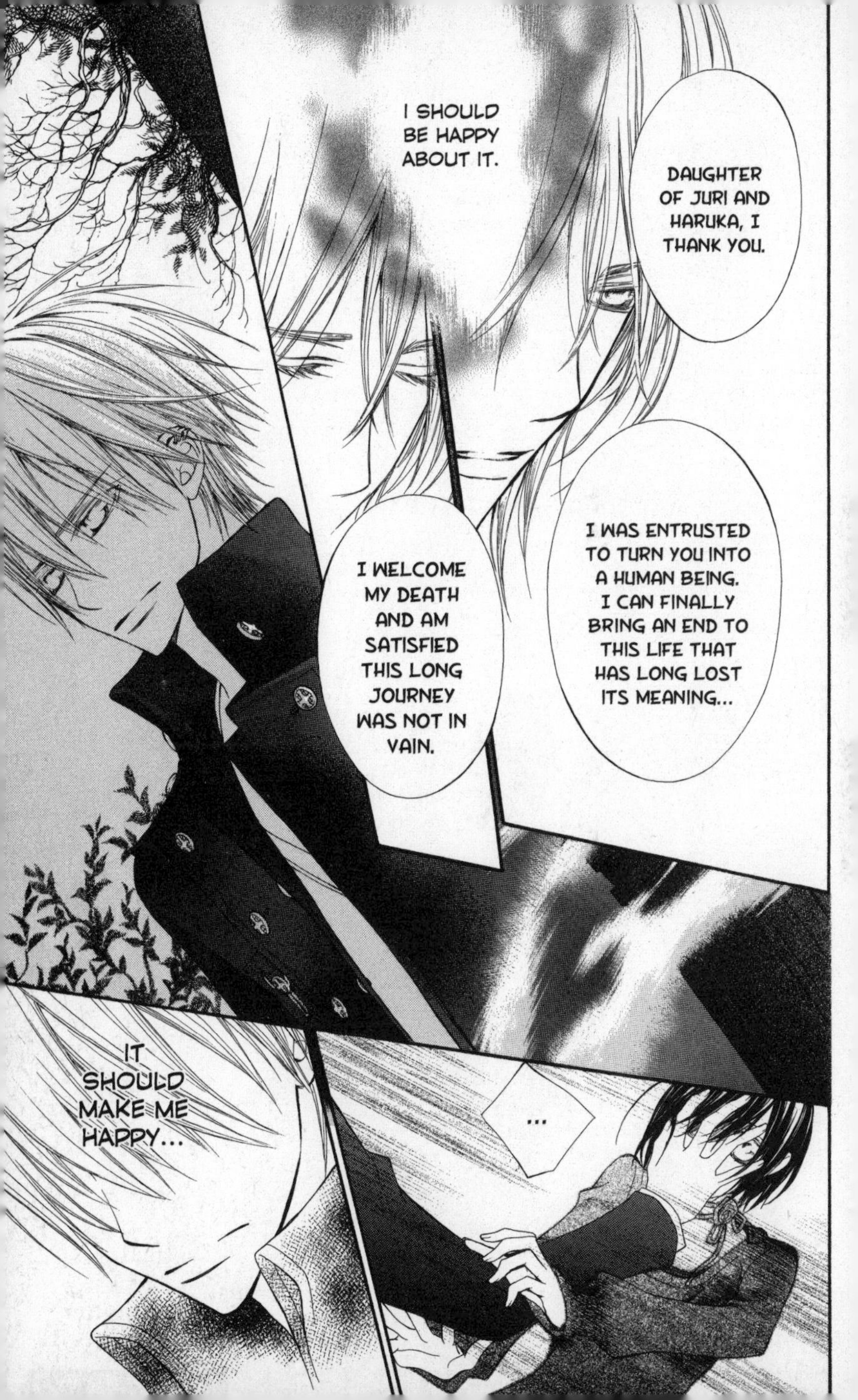
DAUGHTER OF JURI AND HARUKA, I THANK YOU.
I WAS ENTRUSTED TO TURN YOU INTO A HUMAN BEING. I CAN FINALLY BRING AN END TO THIS LIFE THAT HAS LONG LOST ITS MEANING...
I WELCOME MY DEATH AND AM SATISFIED THIS LONG JOURNEY WAS NOT IN VAIN.
I SHOULD BE HAPPY ABOUT IT.
...
IT SHOULD MAKE ME HAPPY...

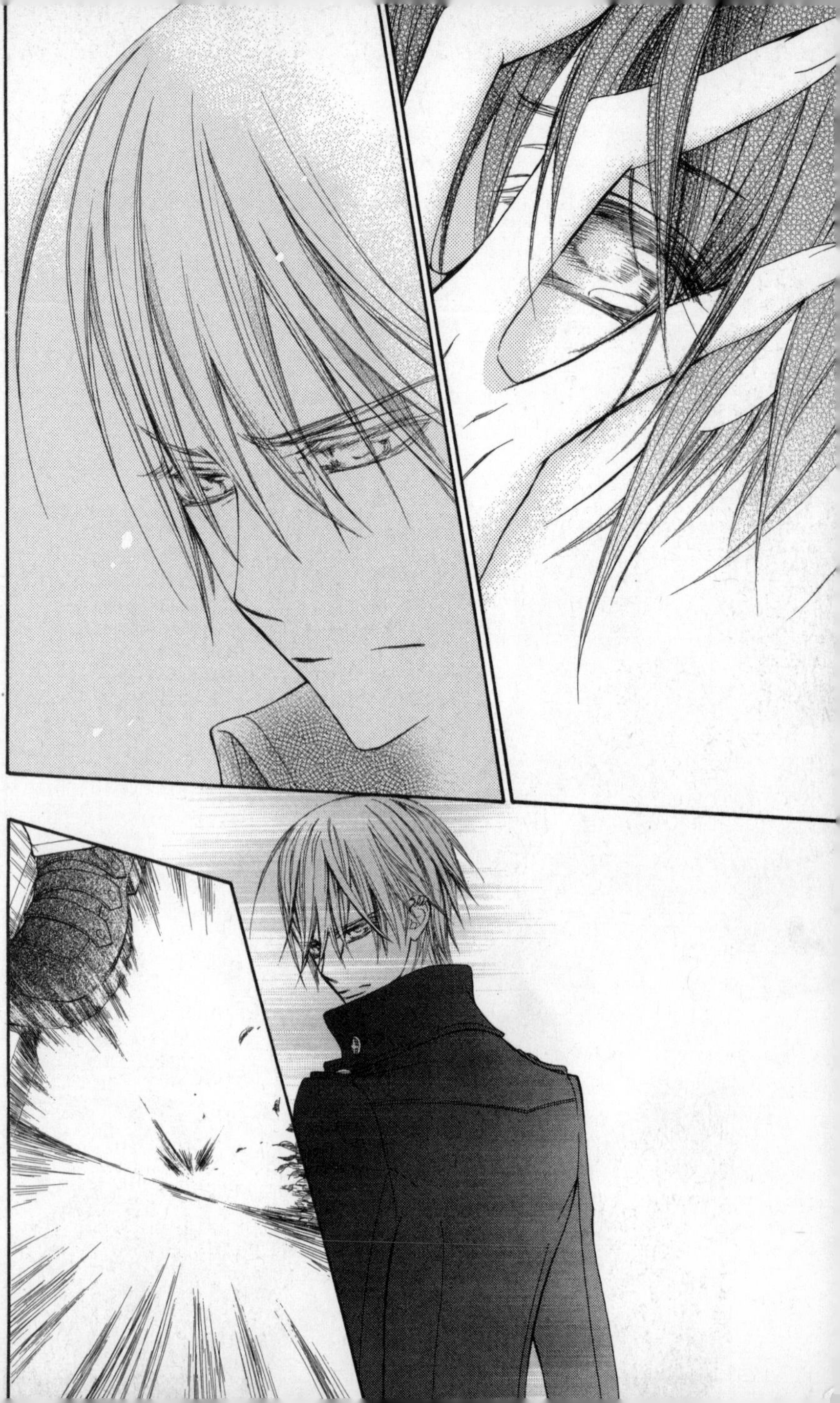

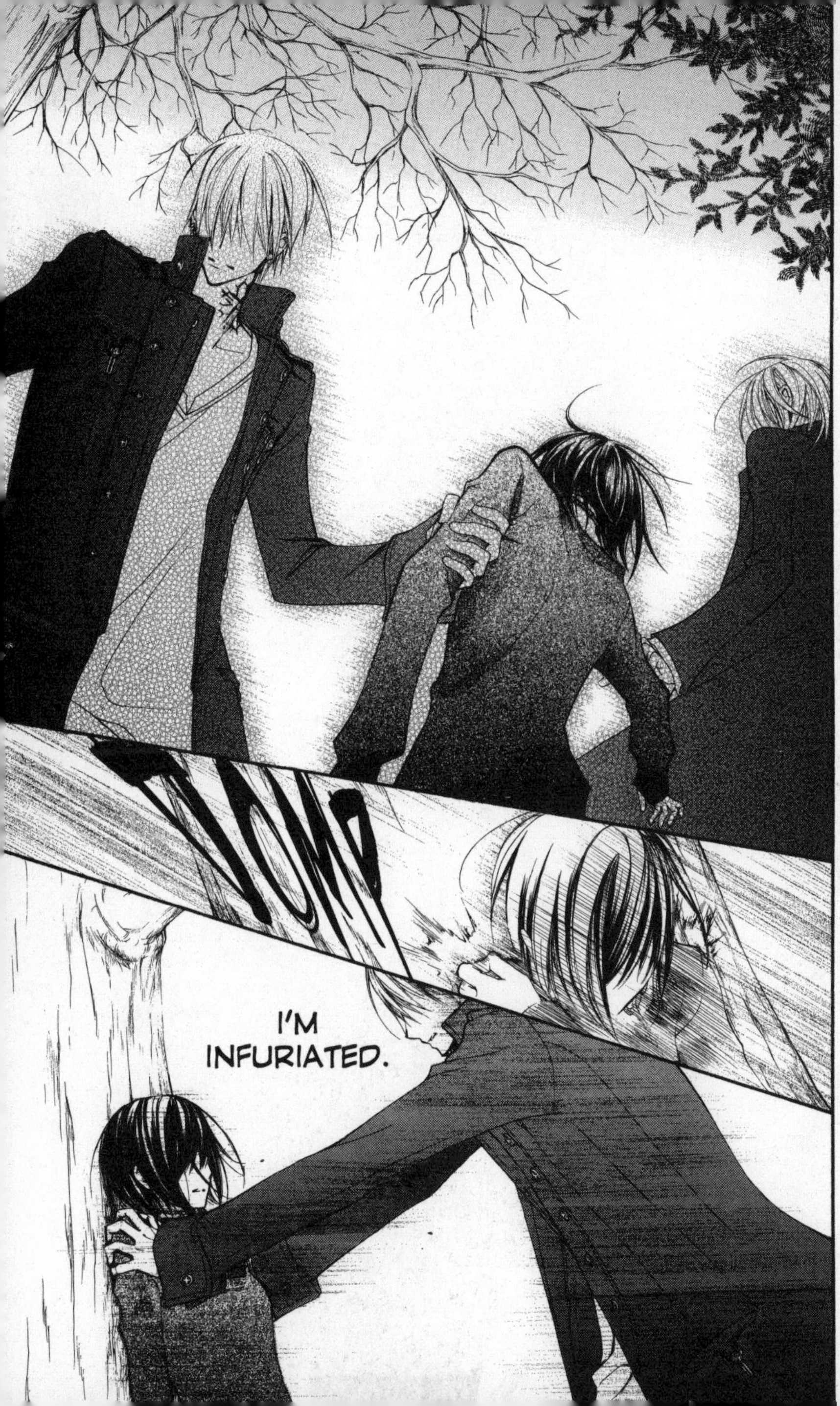
THOMP
I'M INFURIATED.

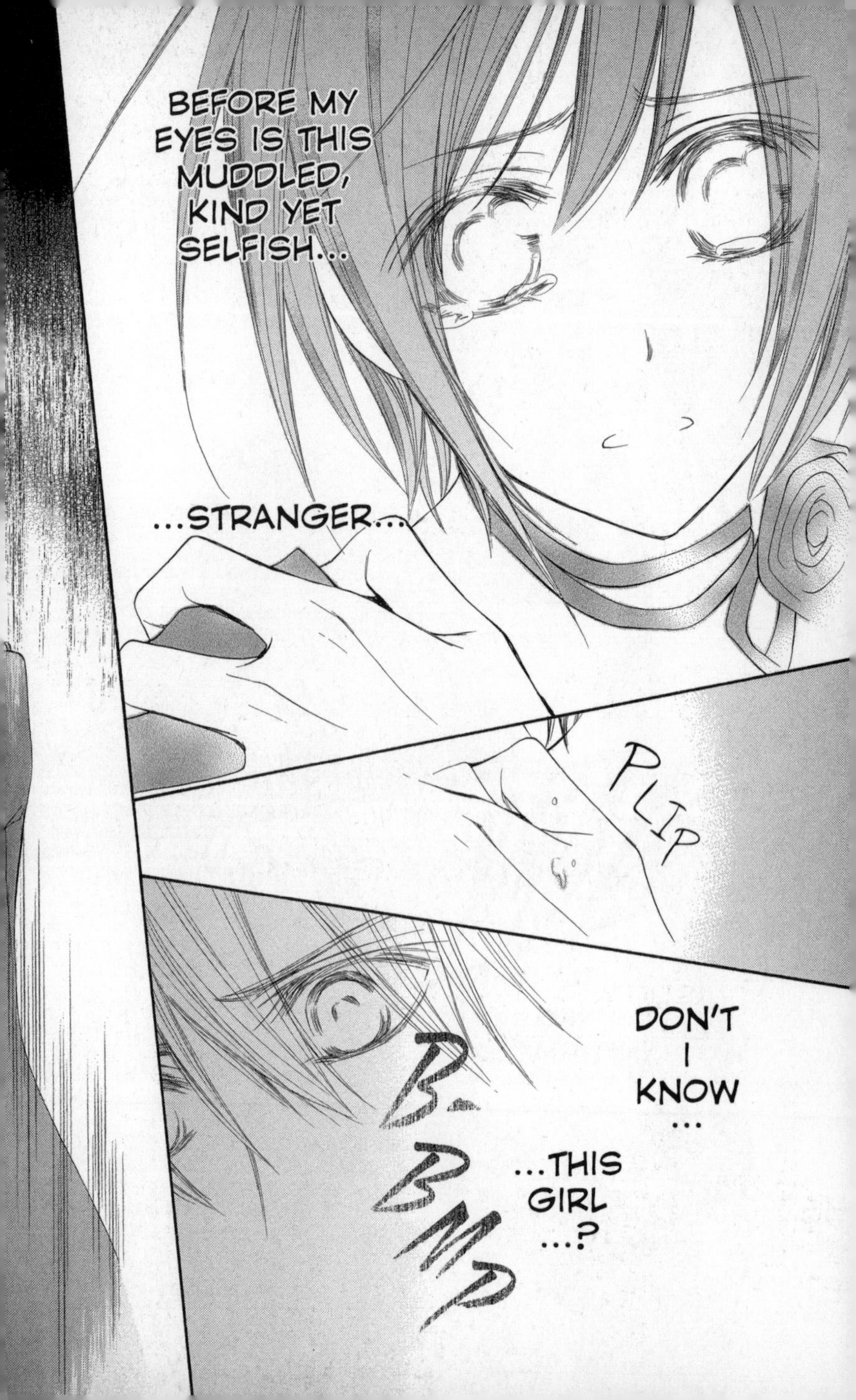
BEFORE MY EYES IS THIS MUDDLED, KIND YET SELFISH...
...STRANGER...
PLIP
DON'T I KNOW ...
...THIS GIRL ...?
BA-BMP

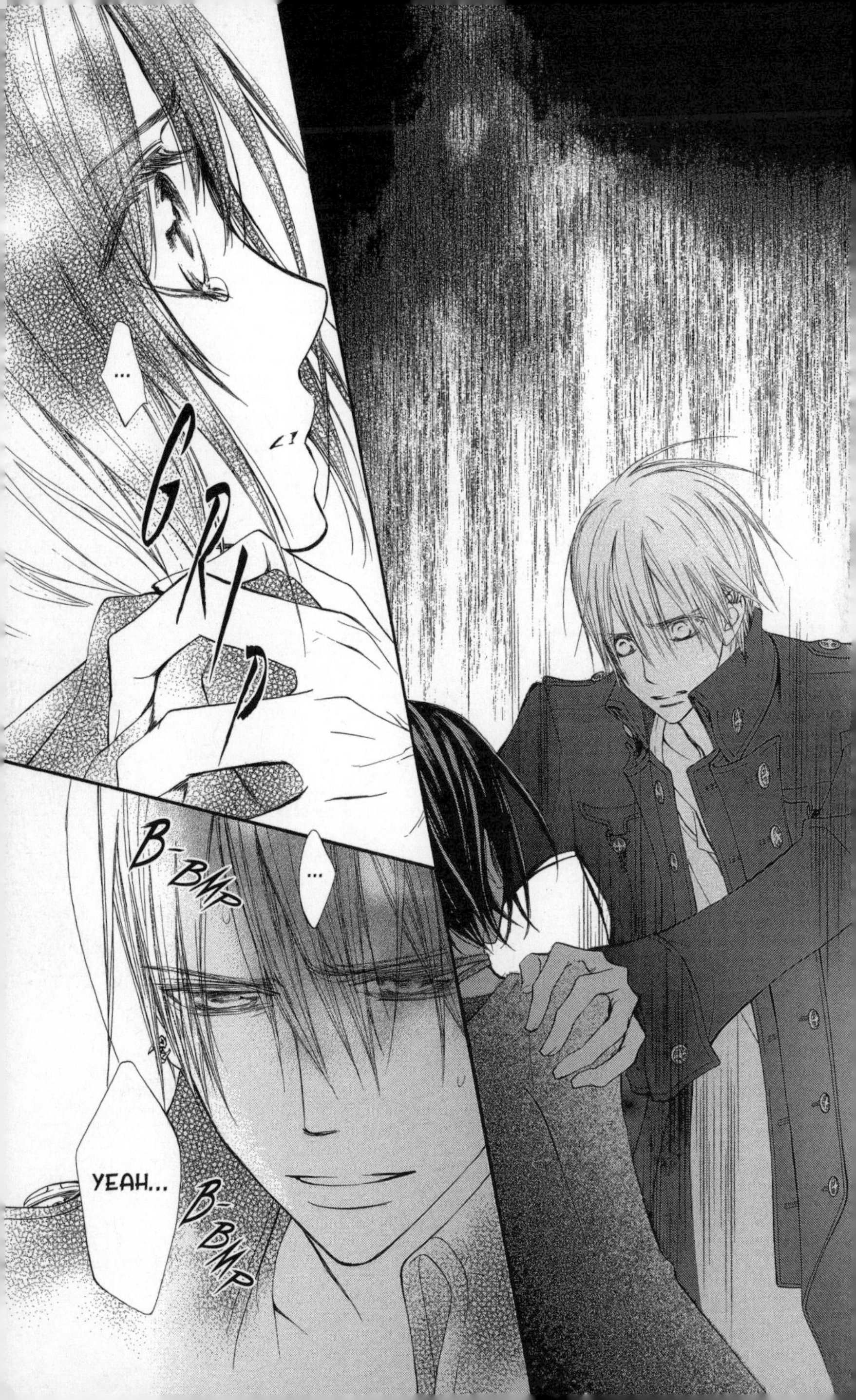
...
GRIP
B-BMP
...
YEAH...
B-BMP

YOU'RE YUKI.
YOU'RE THE GIRL I'VE ALWAYS WANTED TO PROTECT!
AND SHE'S NEVER ALLOWED ME TO.
NINETY-FIRST NIGHT/END

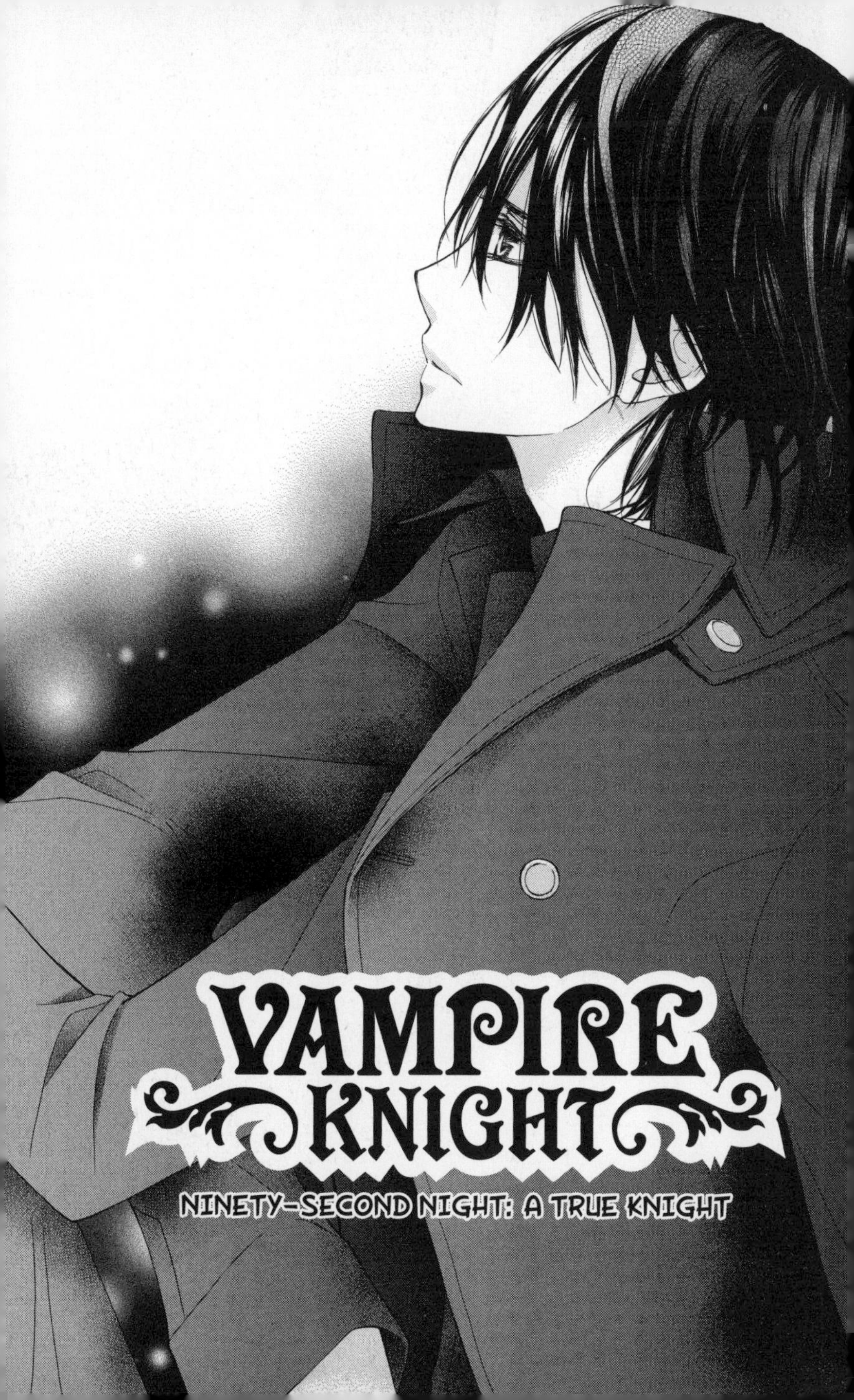
VAMPIRE KNIGHT
NINETY-SECOND NIGHT: A TRUE KNIGHT

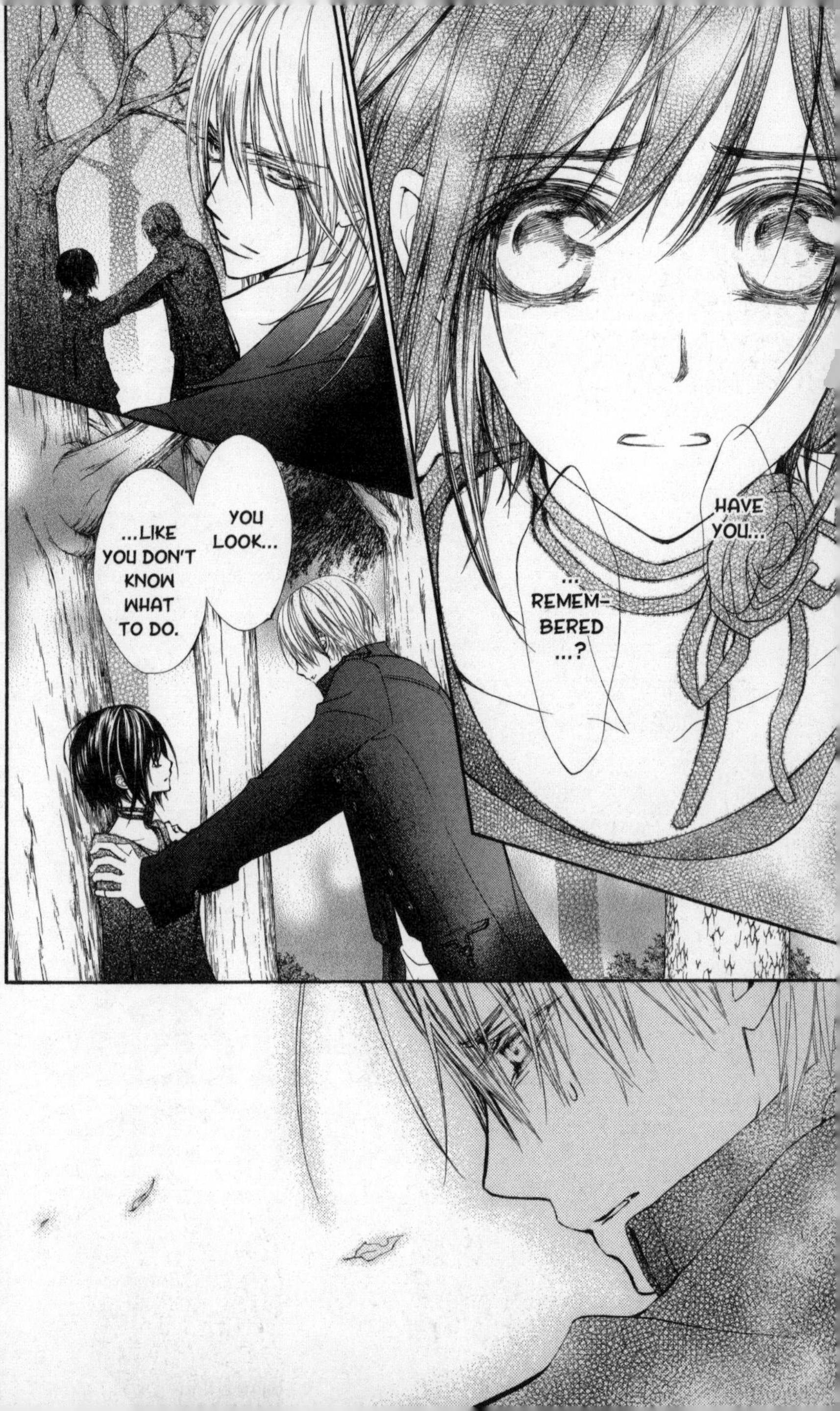
HAVE YOU...
...REMEMBERED...?
YOU LOOK...
...LIKE YOU DON'T KNOW WHAT TO DO.

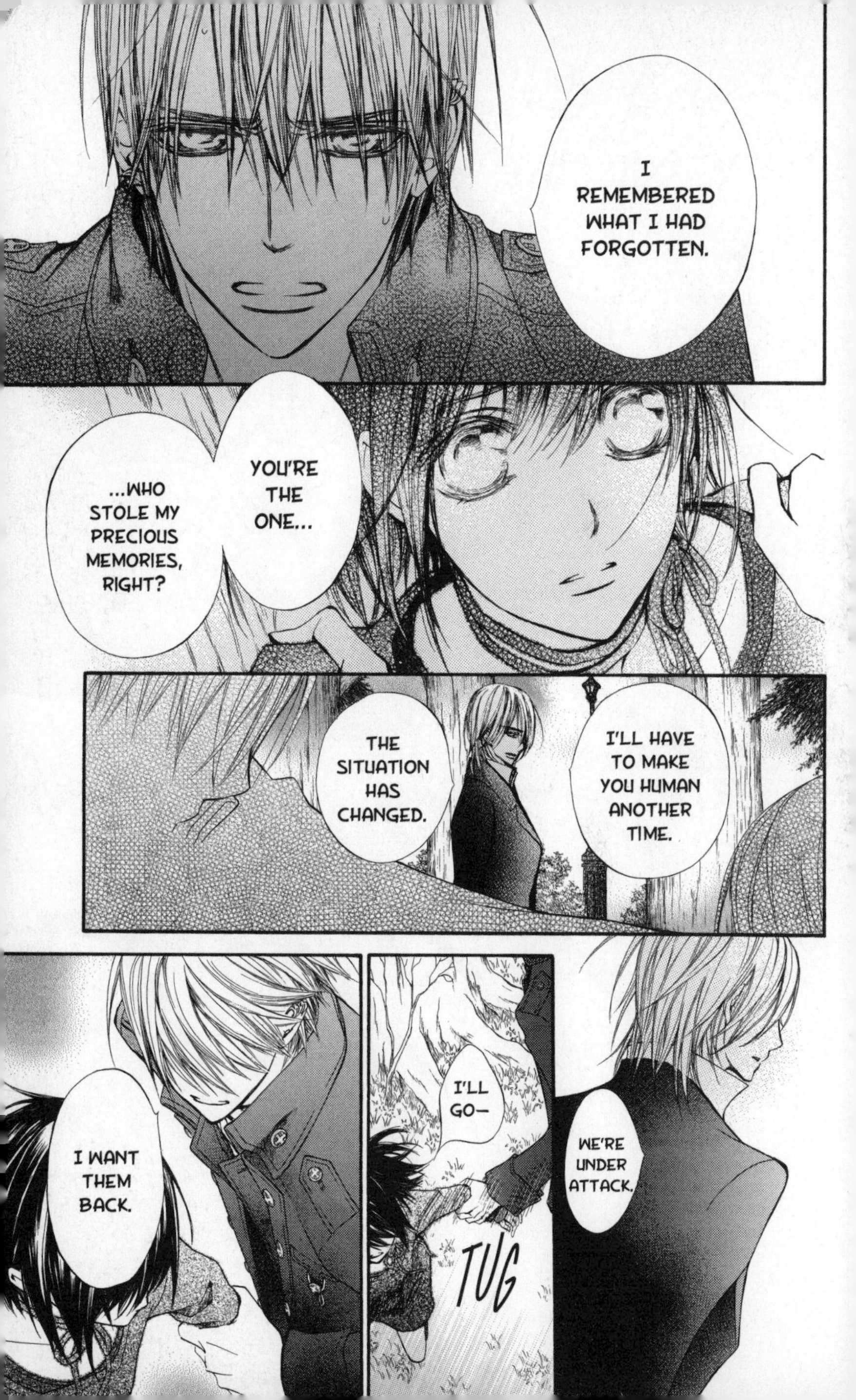
I REMEMBERED WHAT I HAD FORGOTTEN.
YOU'RE THE ONE...
...WHO STOLE MY PRECIOUS MEMORIES, RIGHT?
I'LL HAVE TO MAKE YOU HUMAN ANOTHER TIME.
THE SITUATION HAS CHANGED.
WE'RE UNDER ATTACK.
I'LL GO—
TUG
I WANT THEM BACK.

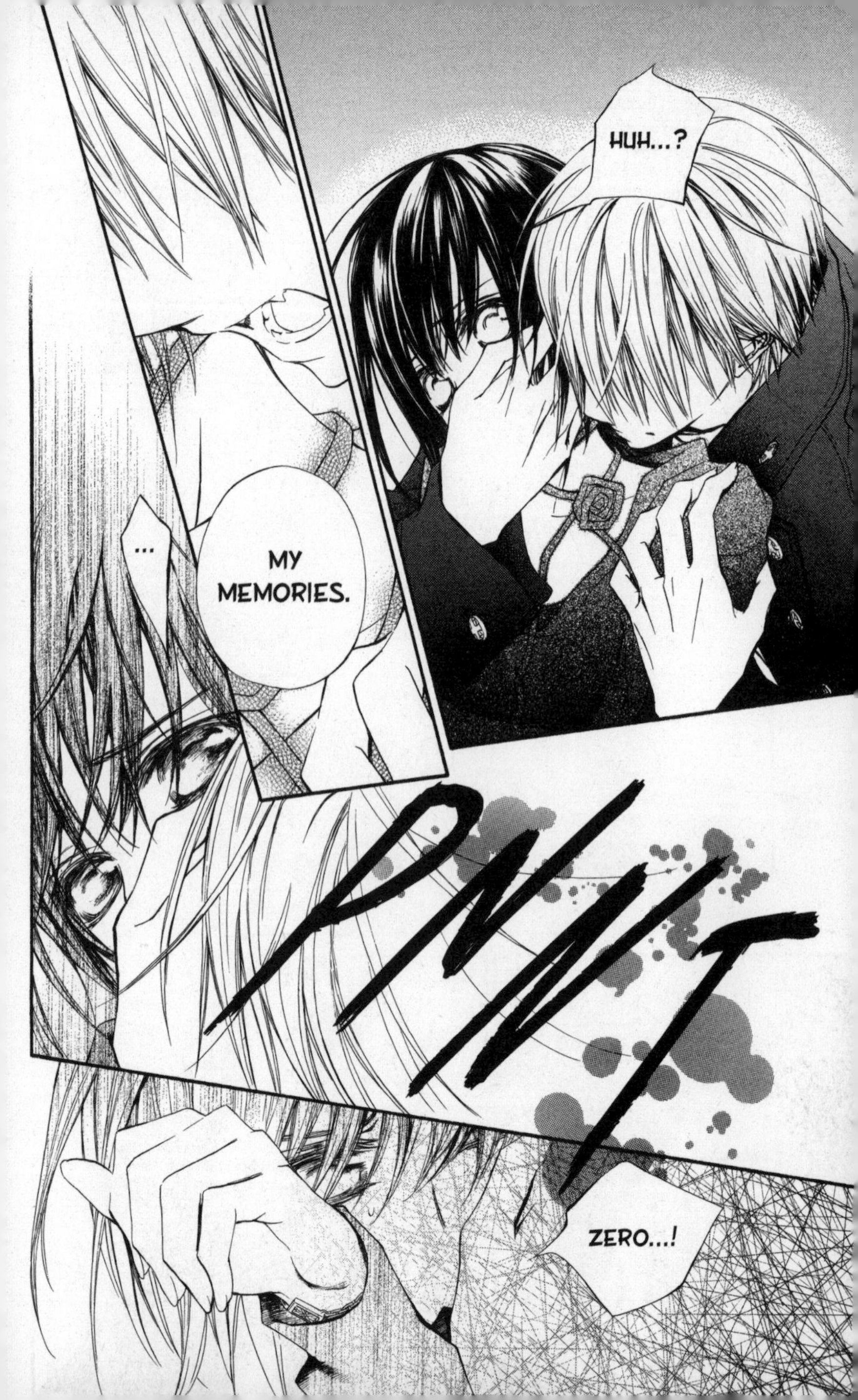
HUH...?
MY MEMORIES.
...
ZERO...!

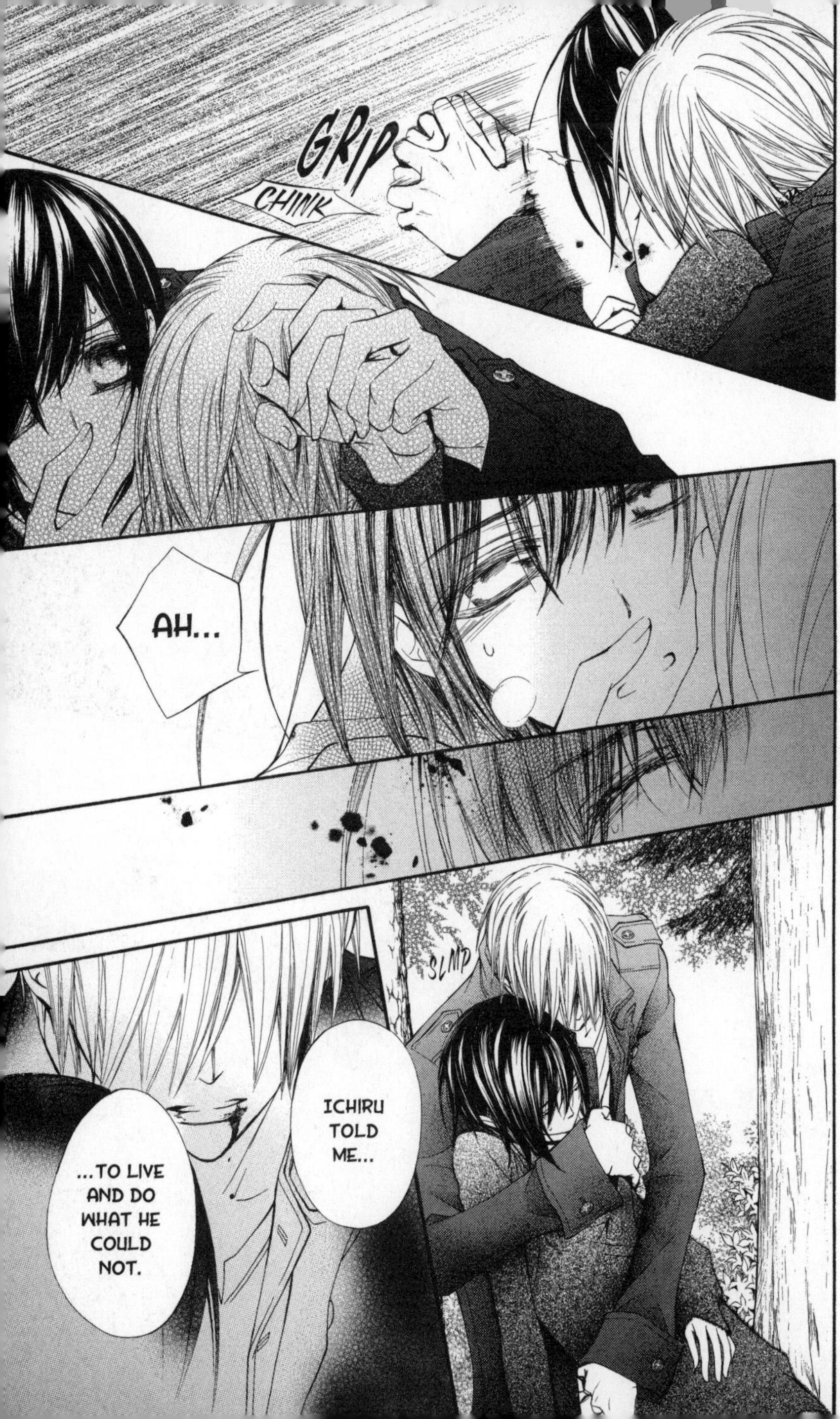
GRIP
CHINK
AH...
SLMP
ICHIRU TOLD ME...
...TO LIVE AND DO WHAT HE COULD NOT.

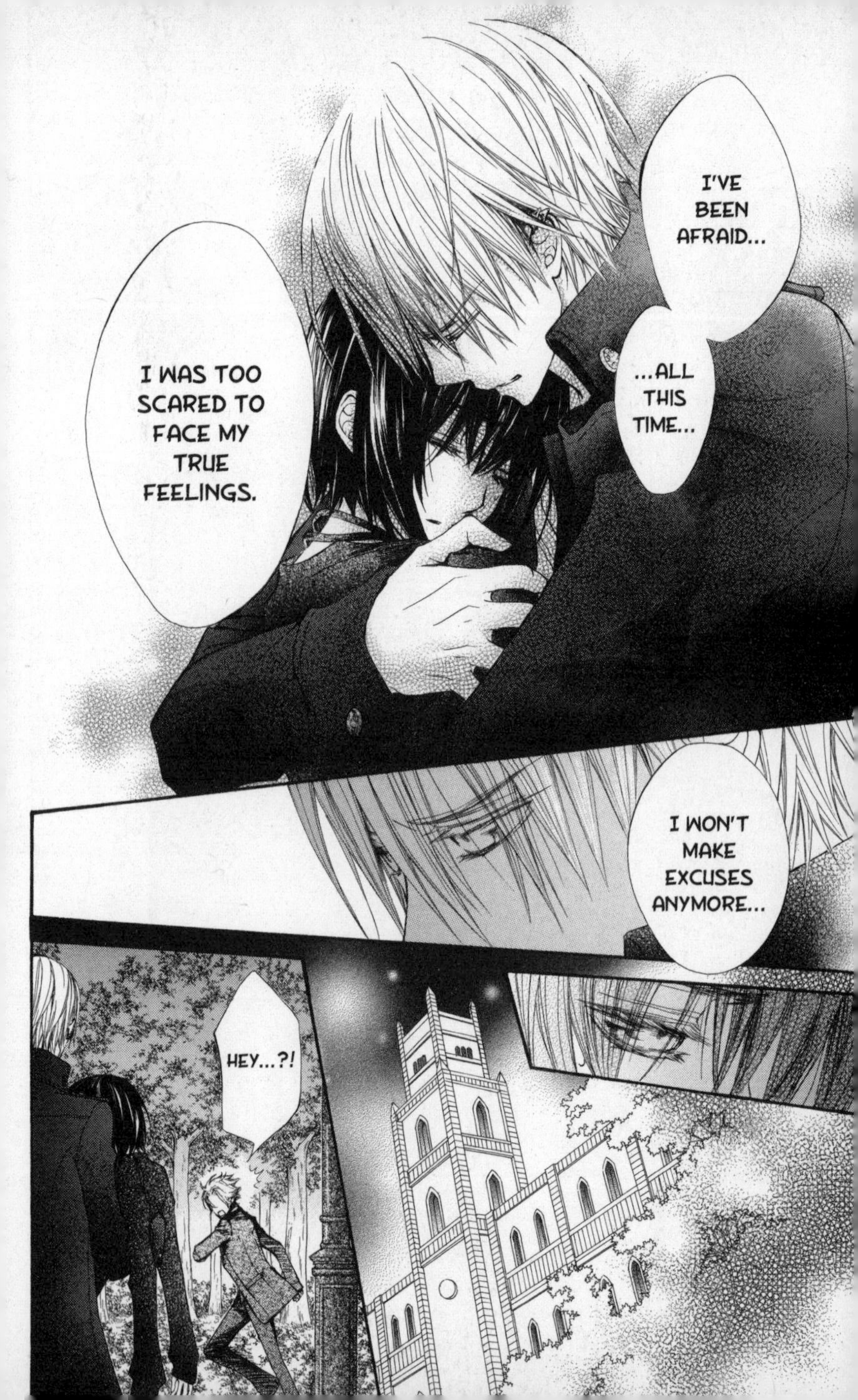
I'VE BEEN AFRAID...
...ALL THIS TIME...
I WAS TOO SCARED TO FACE MY TRUE FEELINGS.
I WON'T MAKE EXCUSES ANYMORE...
HEY...?!

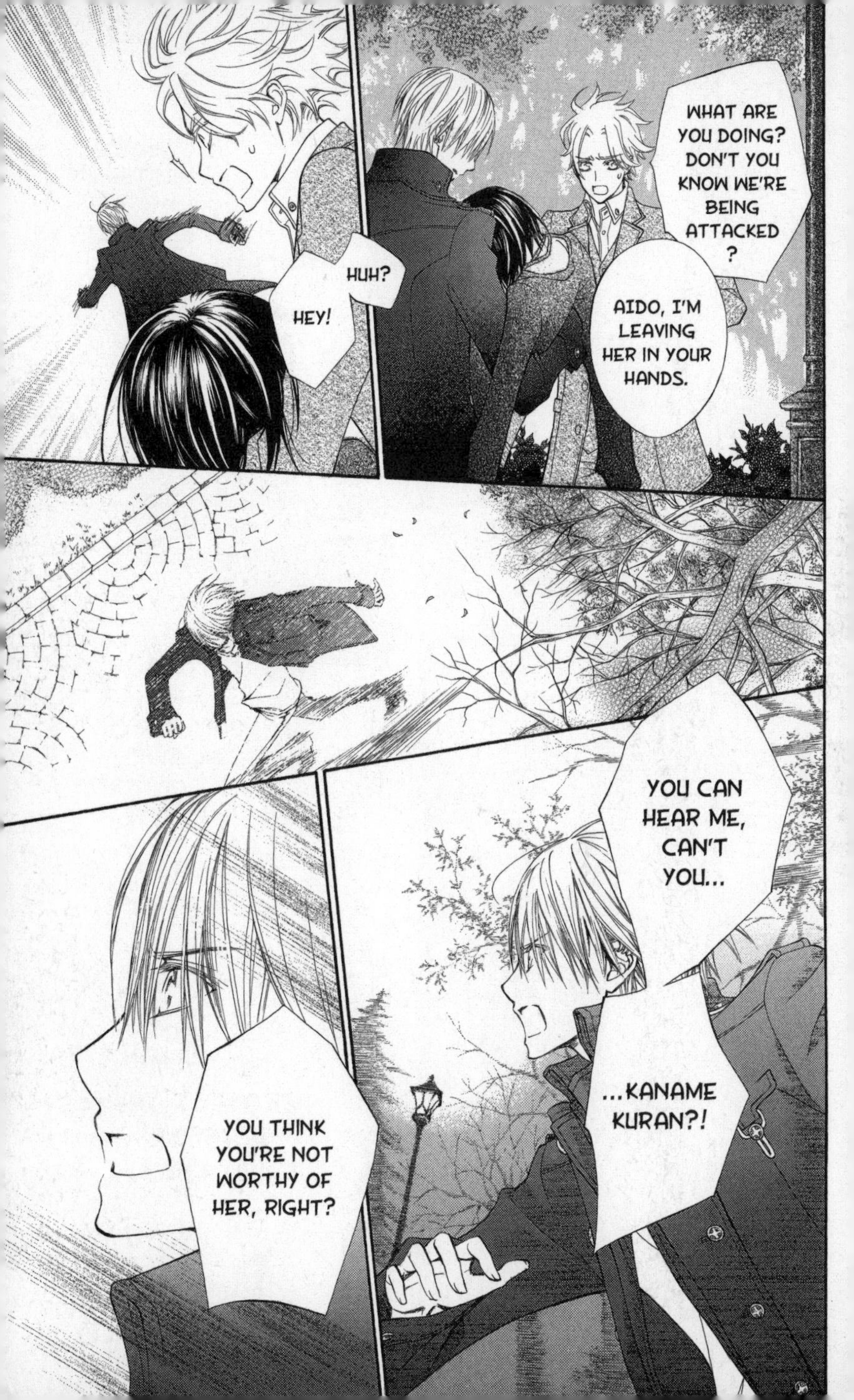
WHAT ARE YOU DOING? DON'T YOU KNOW WE'RE BEING ATTACKED?
AIDO, I'M LEAVING HER IN YOUR HANDS.
HUH?
HEY!
YOU CAN HEAR ME, CAN'T YOU...
...KANAME KURAN?!
YOU THINK YOU'RE NOT WORTHY OF HER, RIGHT?

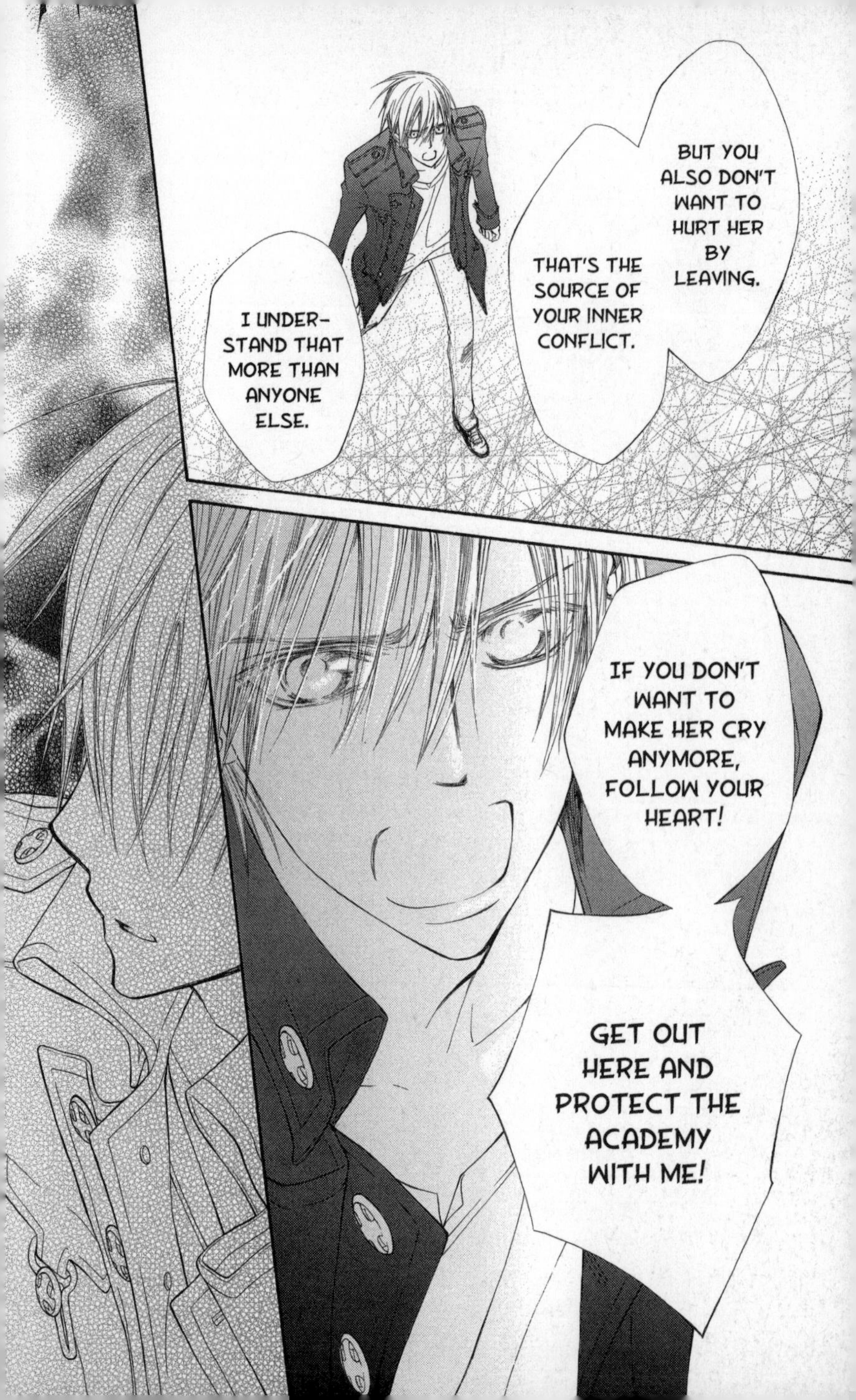
BUT YOU ALSO DON'T WANT TO HURT HER BY LEAVING.
THAT'S THE SOURCE OF YOUR INNER CONFLICT.
I UNDER-STAND THAT MORE THAN ANYONE ELSE.
IF YOU DON'T WANT TO MAKE HER CRY ANYMORE, FOLLOW YOUR HEART!
GET OUT HERE AND PROTECT THE ACADEMY WITH ME!

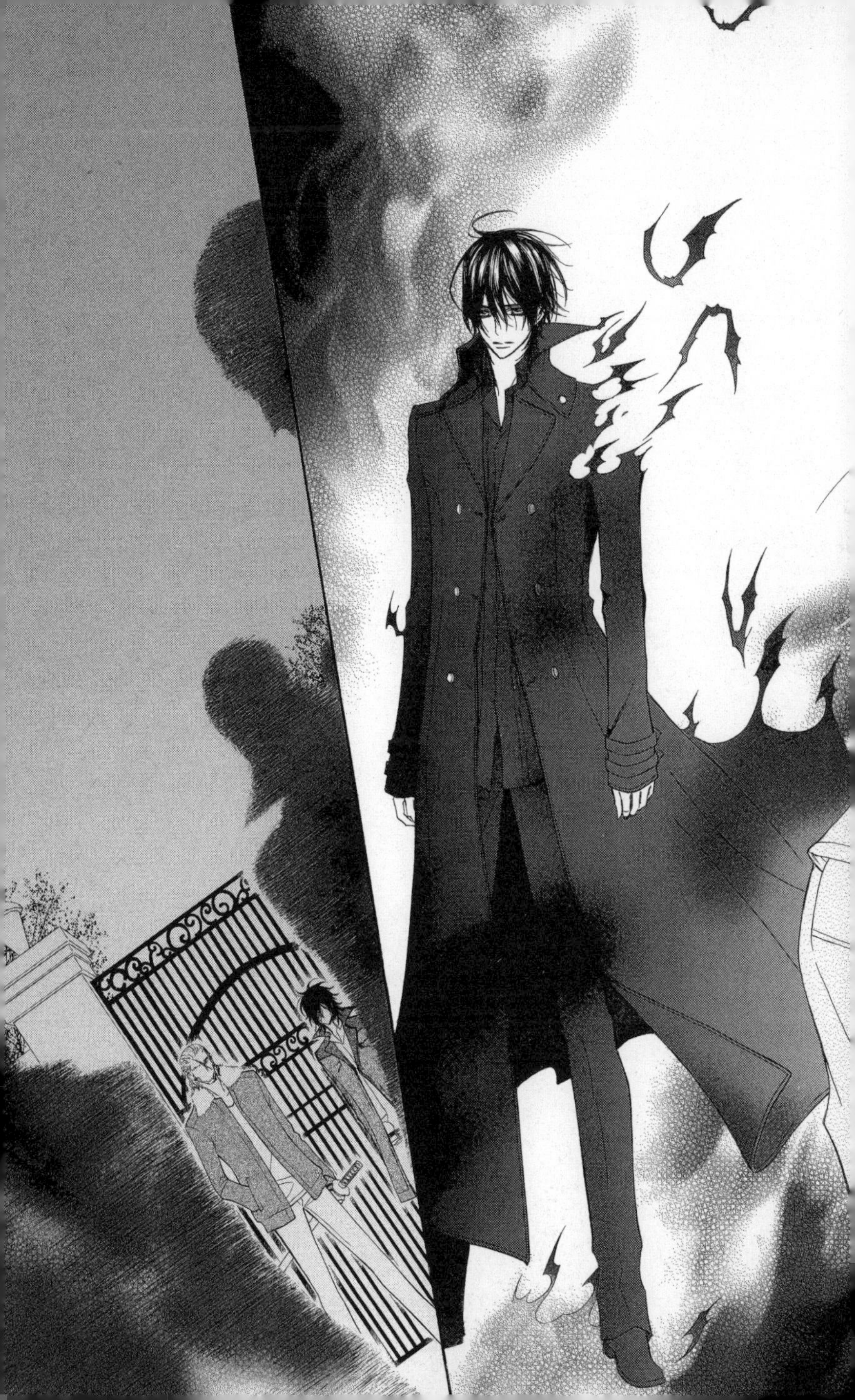

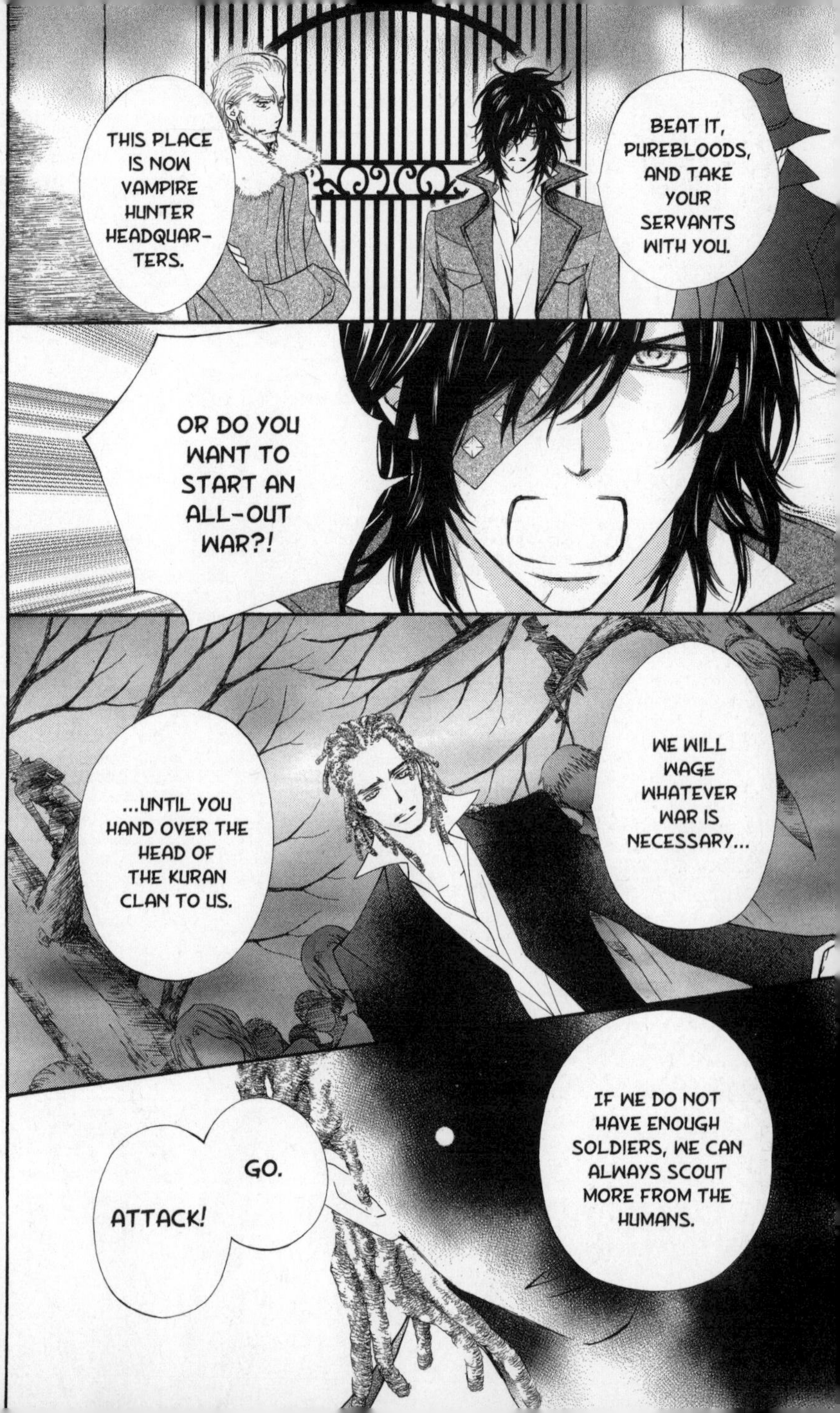
BEAT IT, PUREBLOODS, AND TAKE YOUR SERVANTS WITH YOU.
THIS PLACE IS NOW VAMPIRE HUNTER HEADQUARTERS.
OR DO YOU WANT TO START AN ALL-OUT WAR?!
WE WILL WAGE WHATEVER WAR IS NECESSARY...
...UNTIL YOU HAND OVER THE HEAD OF THE KURAN CLAN TO US.
IF WE DO NOT HAVE ENOUGH SOLDIERS, WE CAN ALWAYS SCOUT MORE FROM THE HUMANS.
GO.
ATTACK!

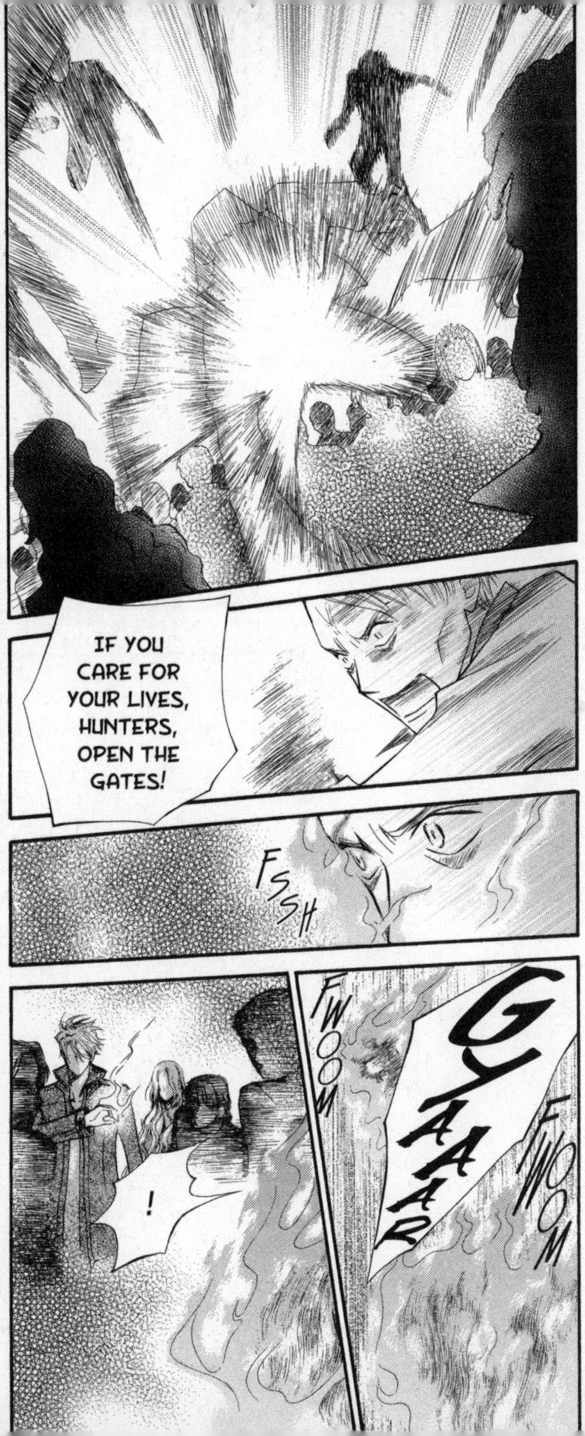
IF YOU CARE FOR YOUR LIVES, HUNTERS, OPEN THE GATES!
FSSH
GYAAAAR
FWOOOM
FWOOOM
!

III

I realized how difficult it is to have a running series in a manga magazine over these past eight and a half years. I would like to thank my mother and friends who stood beside me and supported me. And I also thank my assistants who fought alongside me on the front line...

O. Mio-sama
K. Midori-sama
I. Asami-sama
A. Ichiya-sama

And I'm grateful to my editor who worked wiith me for eight and a half years, and all the people involved for whom I caused trouble... The air carrier and the delivery company who delivered the final manuscripts by express from Sapporo to Chiyoda, Tokyo... And to every one of the readers who has purchased this series. I would not have been able to complete the series if even one of you were missing.
Thank you!!
Thank you very very much!!!

2013.
樋野まつり
Matsuri Hino

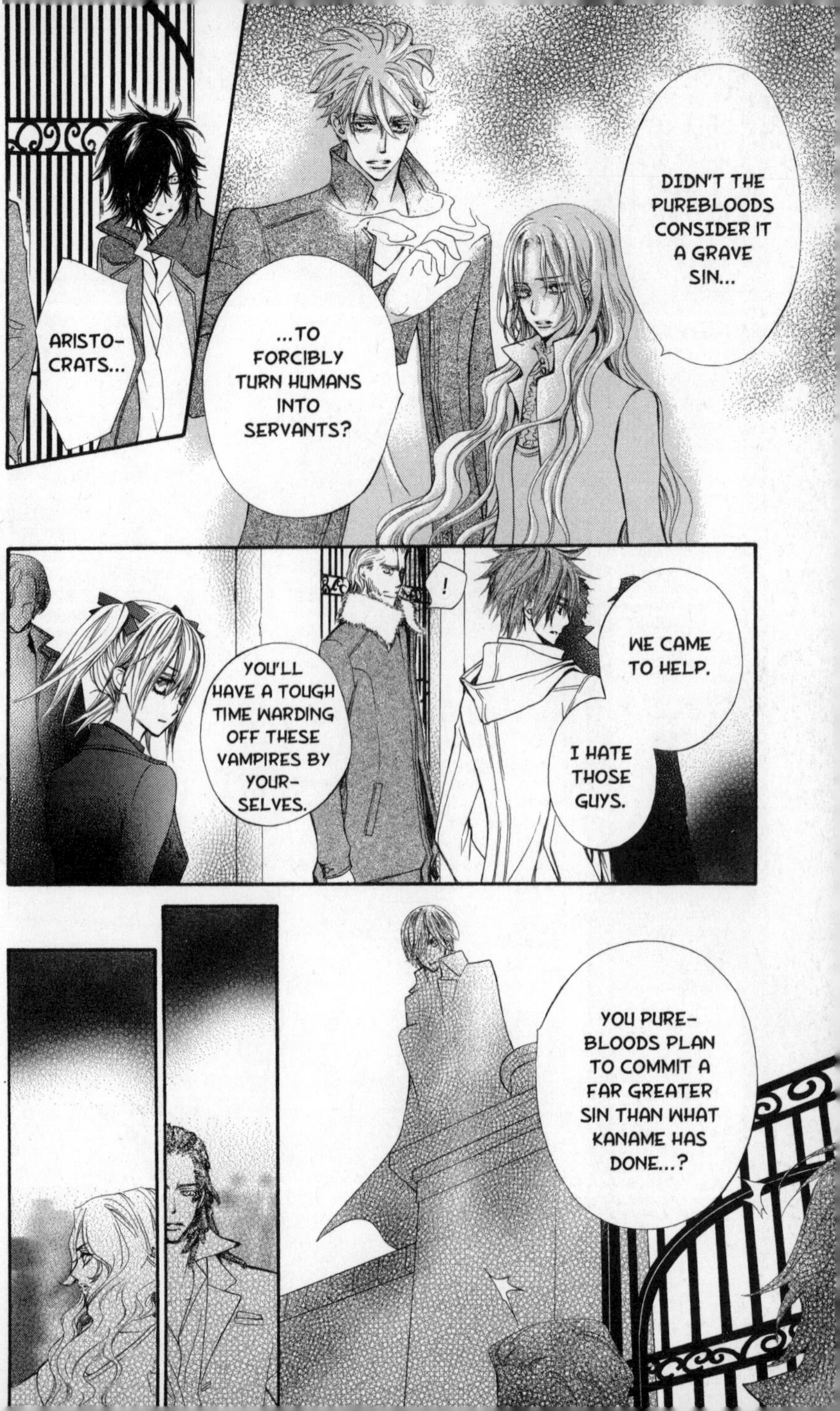
DIDN'T THE PUREBLOODS CONSIDER IT A GRAVE SIN...
...TO FORCIBLY TURN HUMANS INTO SERVANTS?
ARISTO-CRATS...
!
WE CAME TO HELP.
I HATE THOSE GUYS.
YOU'LL HAVE A TOUGH TIME WARDING OFF THESE VAMPIRES BY YOUR-SELVES.
YOU PURE-BLOODS PLAN TO COMMIT A FAR GREATER SIN THAN WHAT KANAME HAS DONE...?

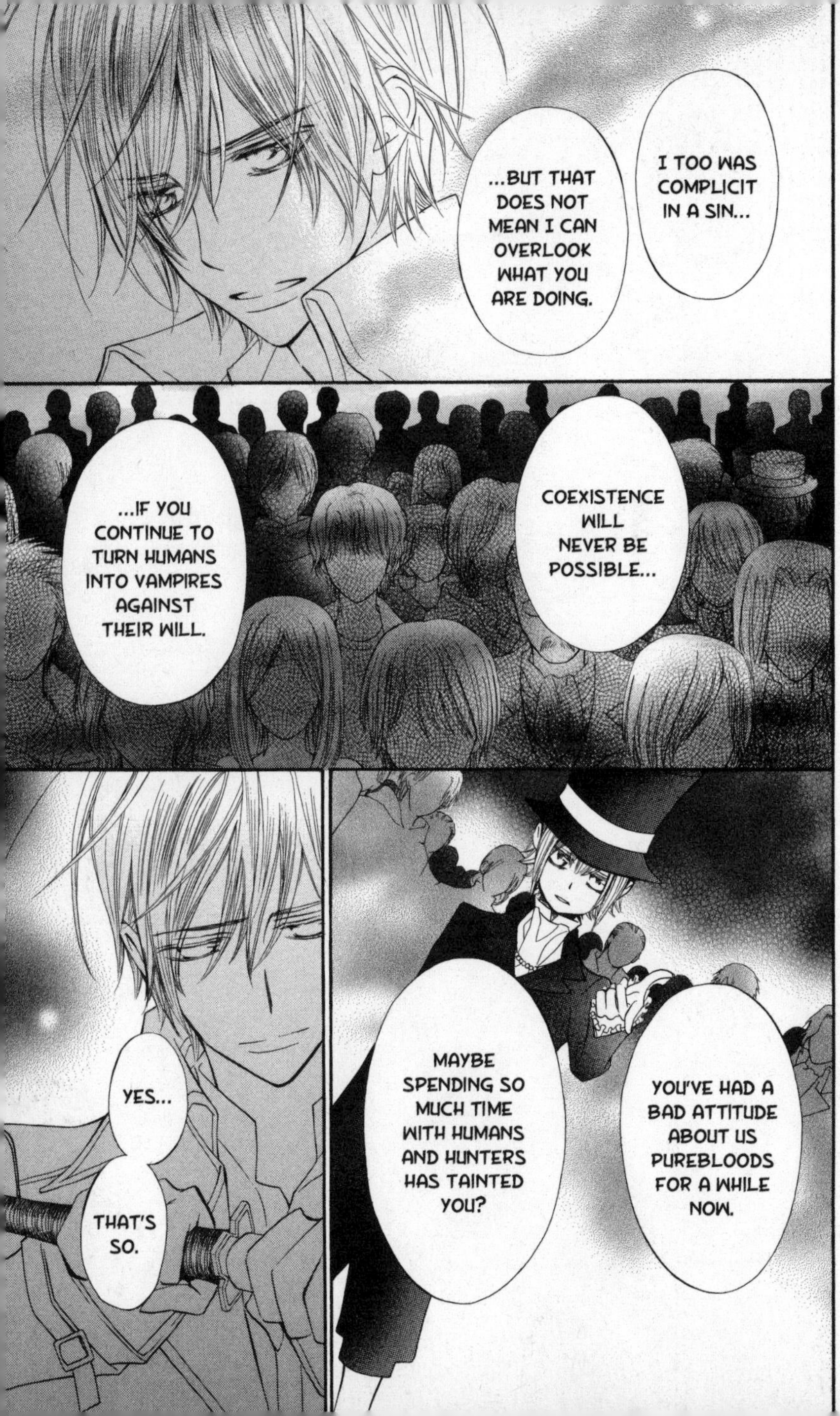
I TOO WAS COMPLICIT IN A SIN...
...BUT THAT DOES NOT MEAN I CAN OVERLOOK WHAT YOU ARE DOING.
COEXISTENCE WILL NEVER BE POSSIBLE...
...IF YOU CONTINUE TO TURN HUMANS INTO VAMPIRES AGAINST THEIR WILL.
YOU'VE HAD A BAD ATTITUDE ABOUT US PUREBLOODS FOR A WHILE NOW.
MAYBE SPENDING SO MUCH TIME WITH HUMANS AND HUNTERS HAS TAINTED YOU?
YES...
THAT'S SO.

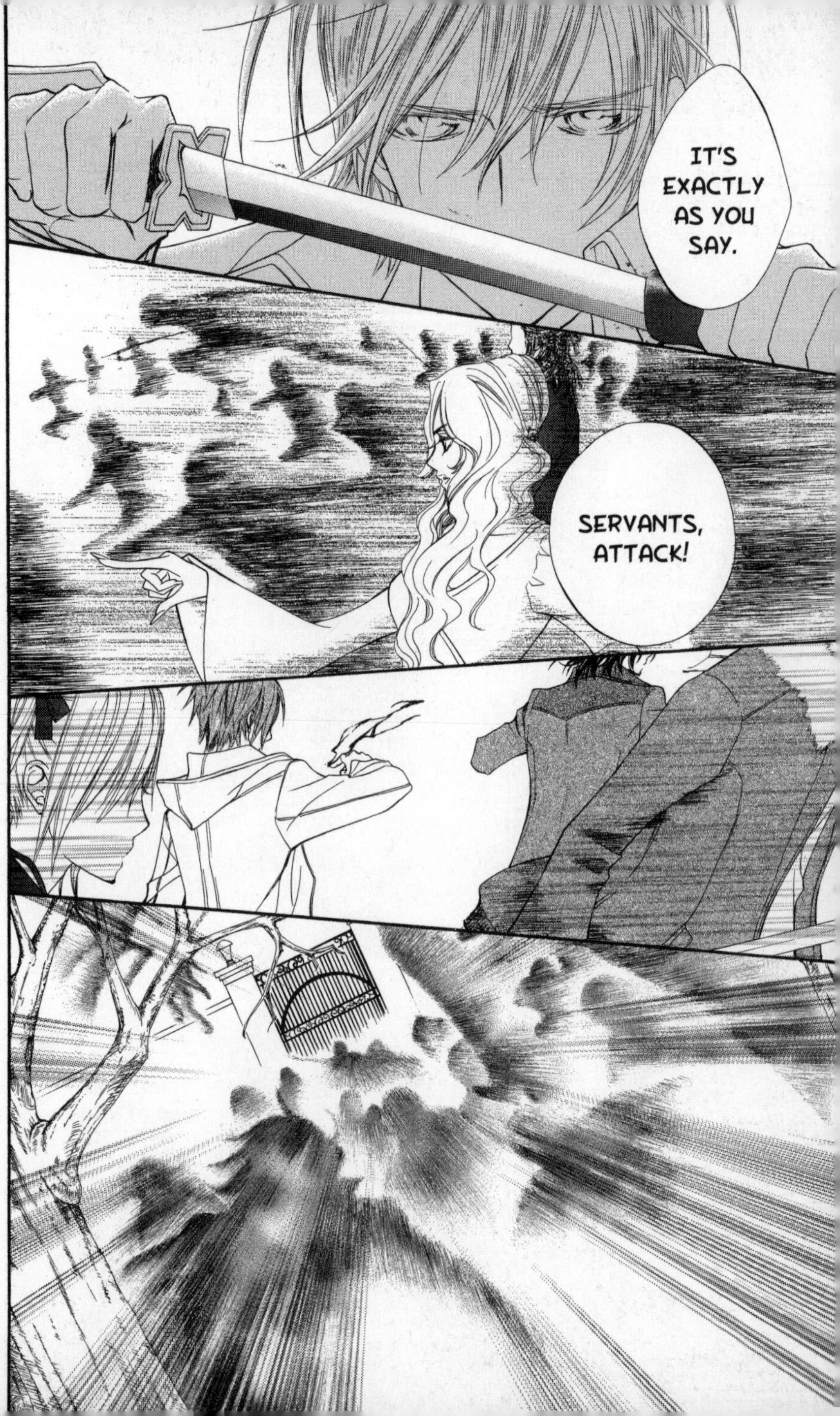
IT'S EXACTLY AS YOU SAY.
SERVANTS, ATTACK!

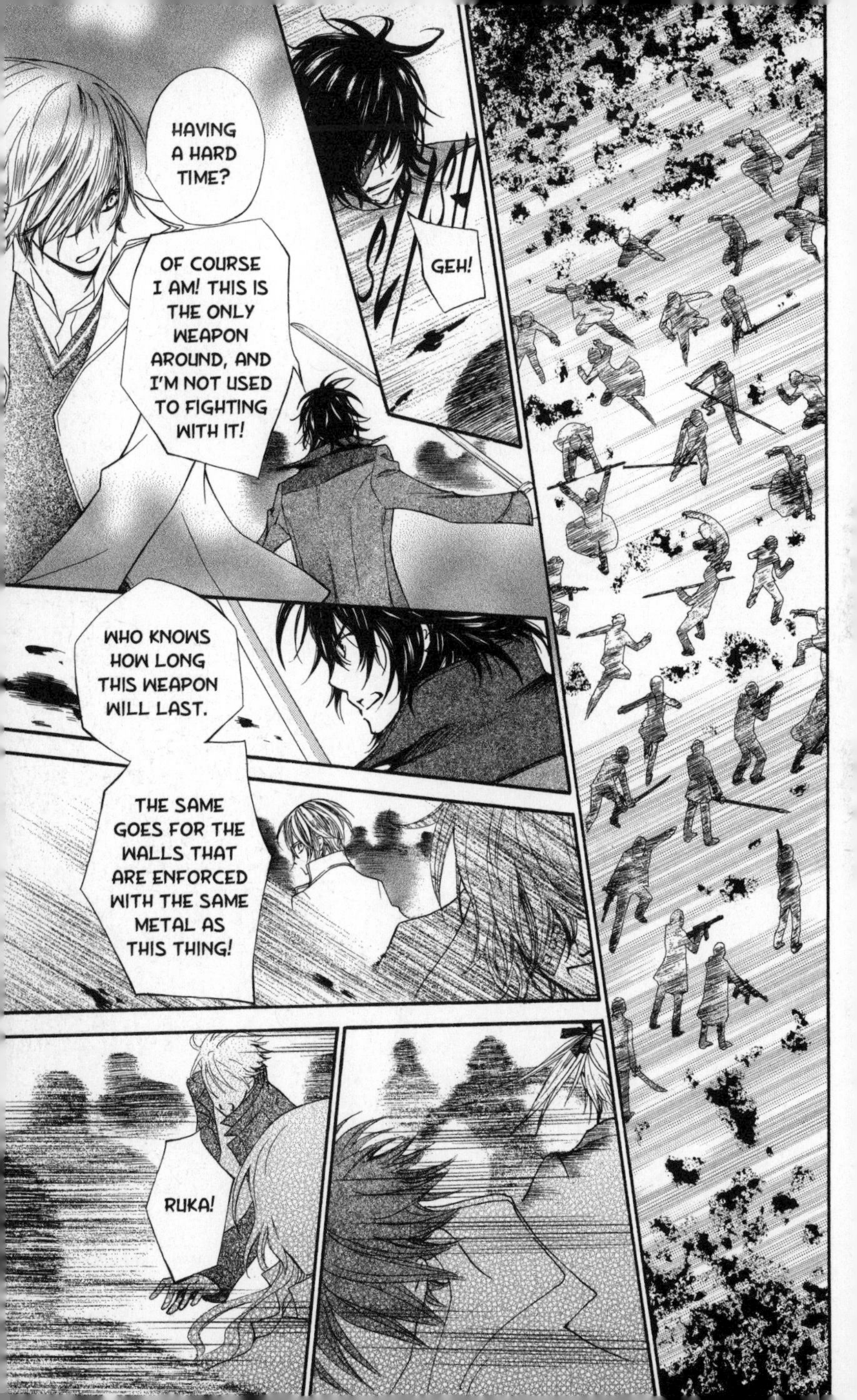
GEH!
HAVING A HARD TIME?
OF COURSE I AM! THIS IS THE ONLY WEAPON AROUND, AND I'M NOT USED TO FIGHTING WITH IT!
WHO KNOWS HOW LONG THIS WEAPON WILL LAST.
THE SAME GOES FOR THE WALLS THAT ARE ENFORCED WITH THE SAME METAL AS THIS THING!
RUKA!

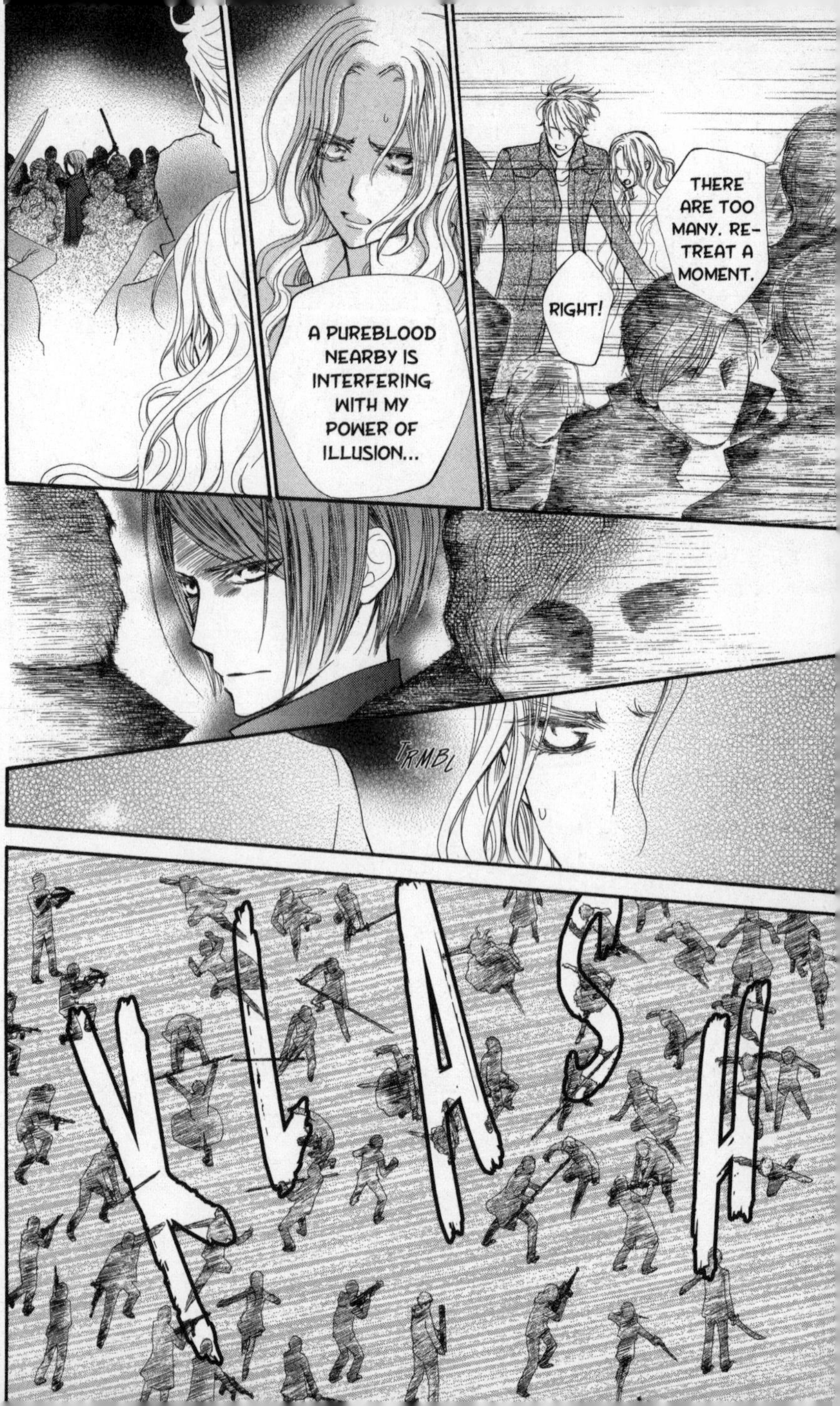
THERE ARE TOO MANY. RE-TREAT A MOMENT.
RIGHT!
A PUREBLOOD NEARBY IS INTERFERING WITH MY POWER OF ILLUSION...
TRMBL
VLASH

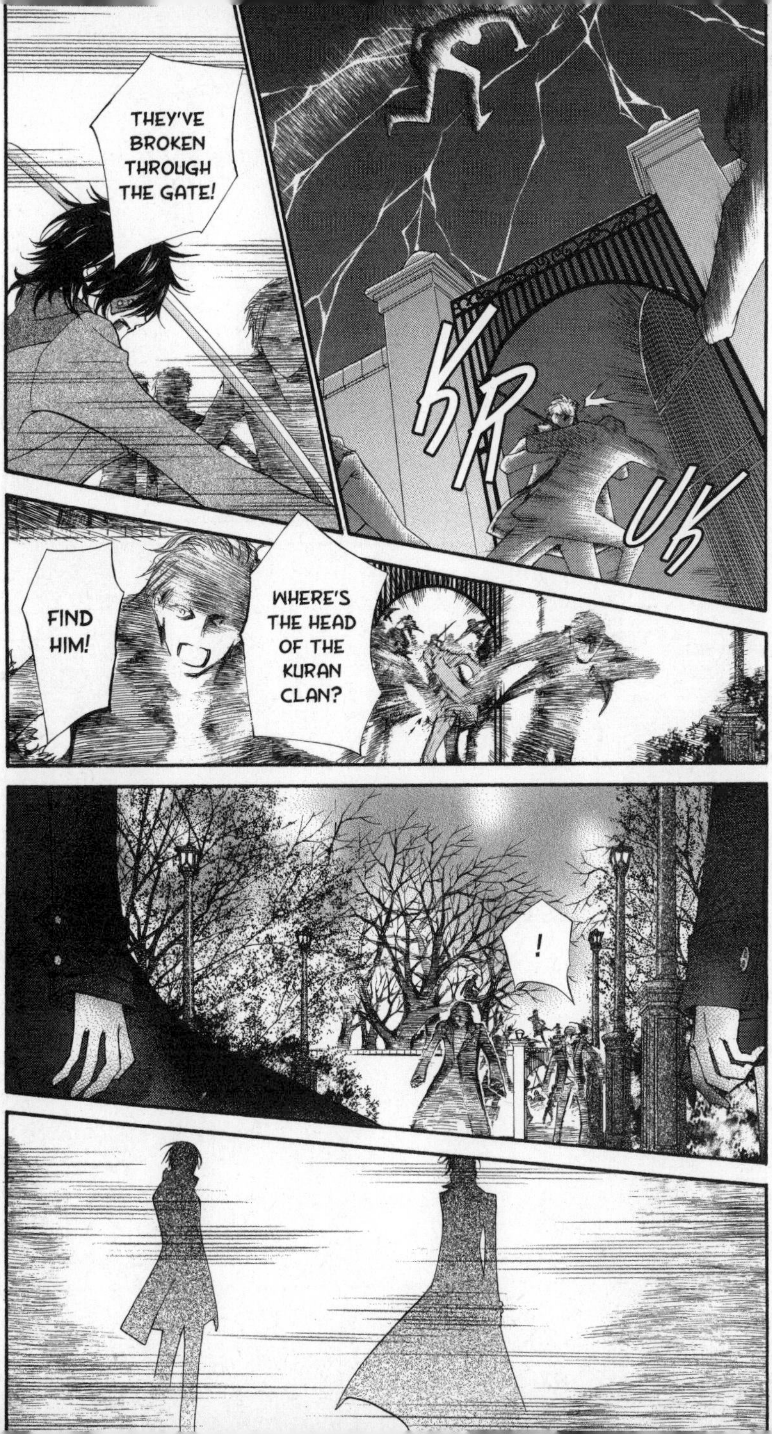
KRUK
THEY'VE BROKEN THROUGH THE GATE!
WHERE'S THE HEAD OF THE KURAN CLAN?
FIND HIM!
!

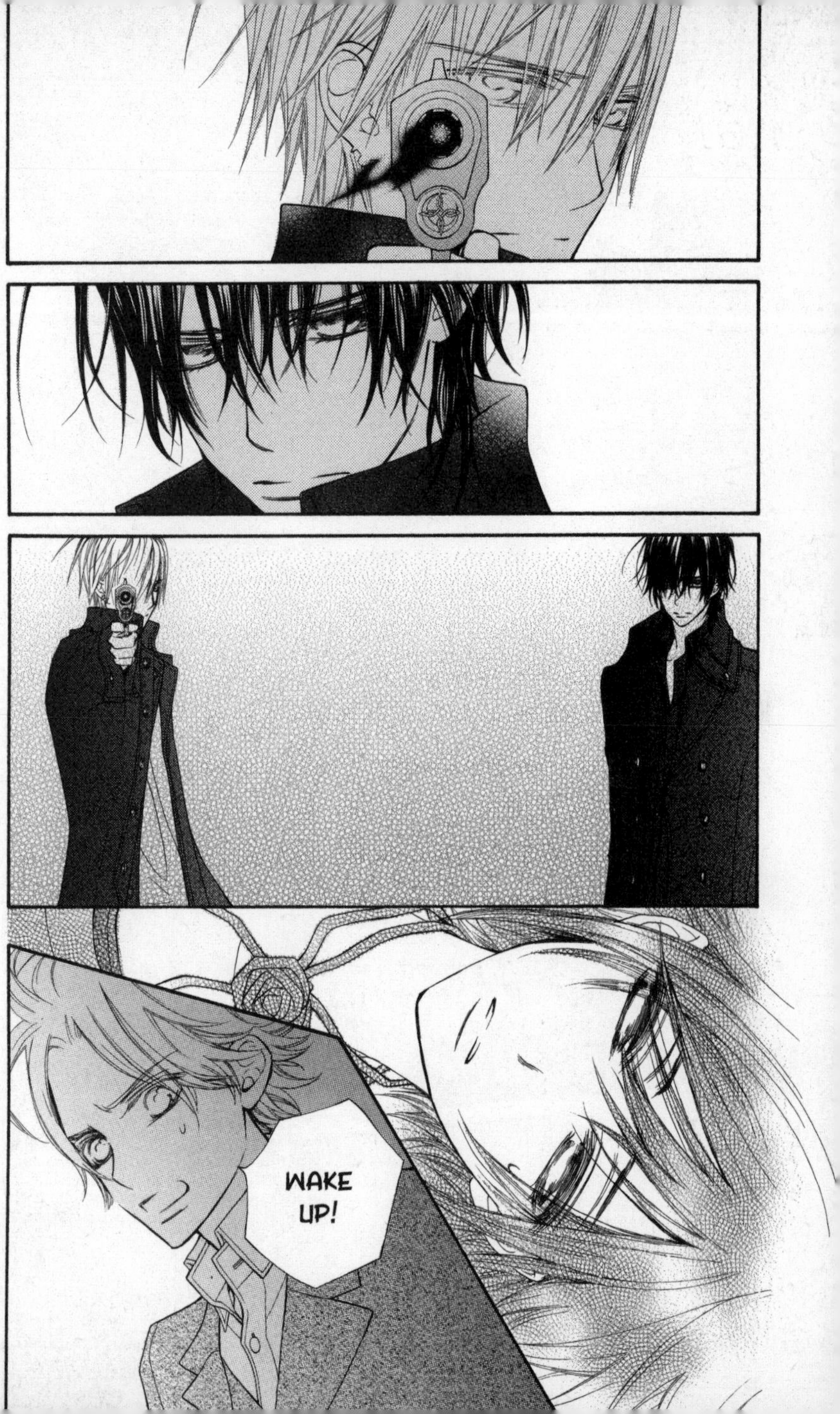
WAKE UP!

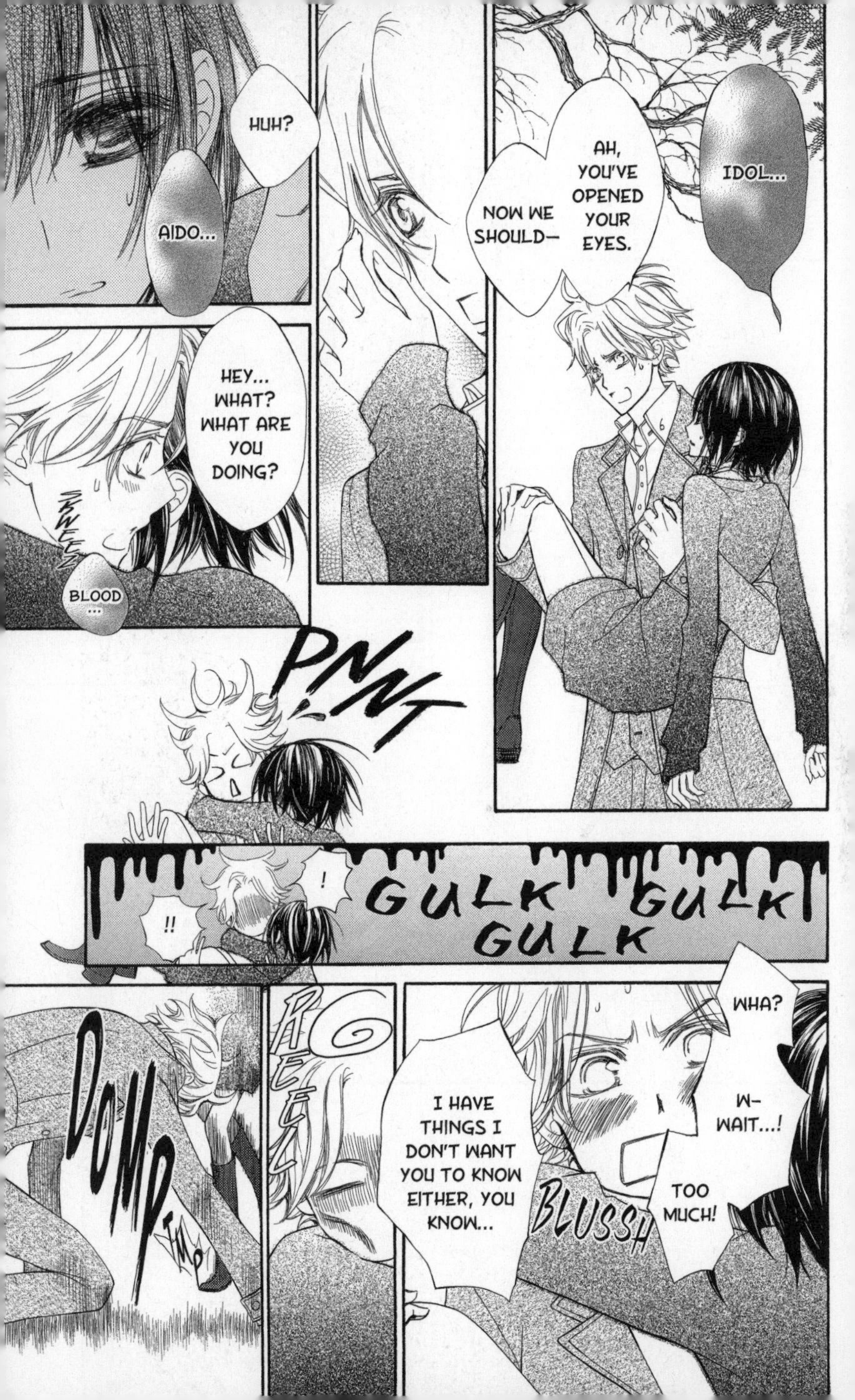
IDOL...
AH, YOU'VE OPENED YOUR EYES.
NOW WE SHOULD—
HUH?
AIDO...
HEY... WHAT? WHAT ARE YOU DOING?
SHWEEZ
BLOOD...
PNNT
!
!!
GULK GULK GULK
WHA?
W-WAIT...!
TOO MUCH!
BLUSSH
I HAVE THINGS I DON'T WANT YOU TO KNOW EITHER, YOU KNOW...
REEEL
DOMP
TMP

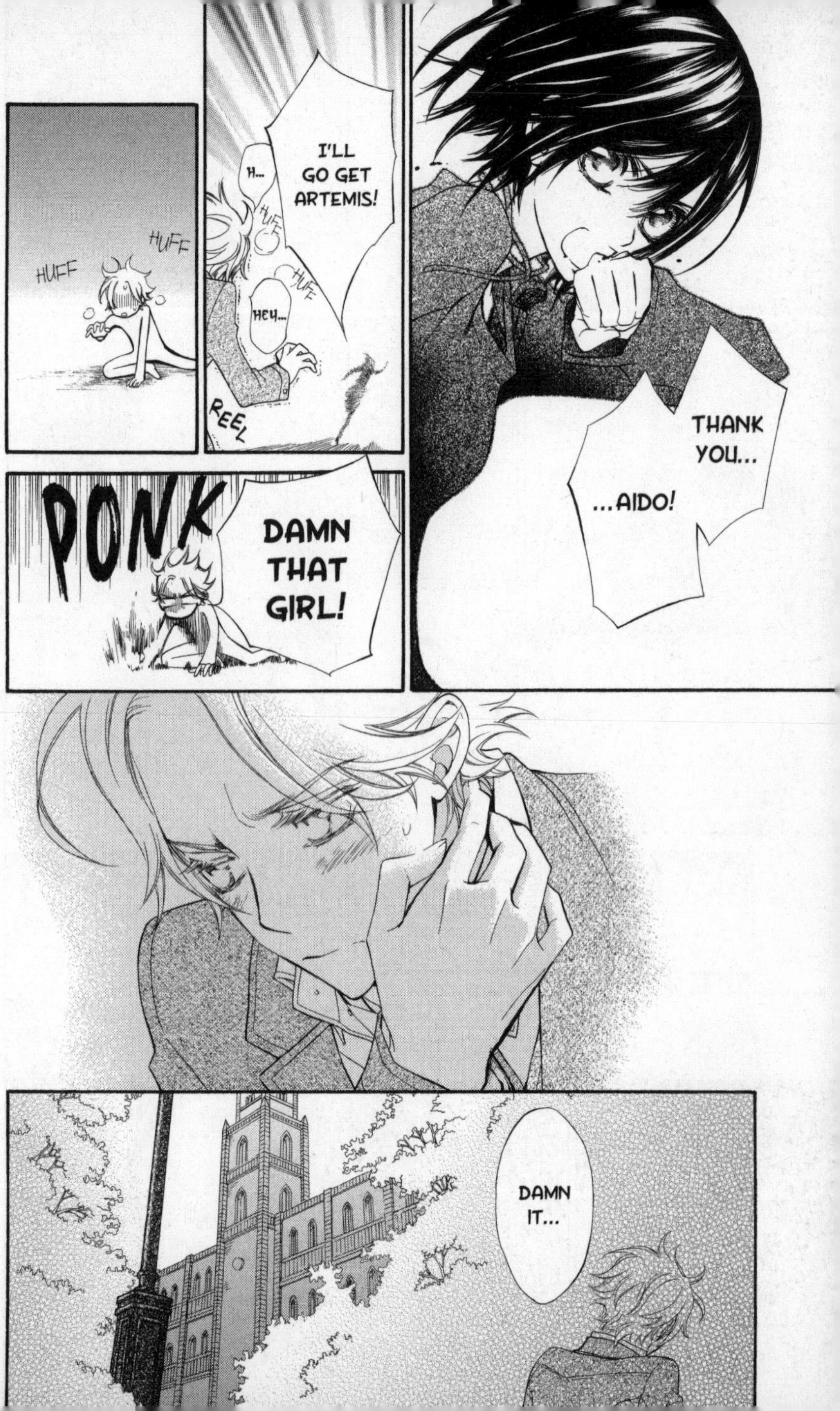
THANK YOU...
...AIDO!
I'LL GO GET ARTEMIS!
H...
HUFF
HUFF
HEY...
REEL
HUFF
HUFF
PONK
DAMN THAT GIRL!
DAMN IT...

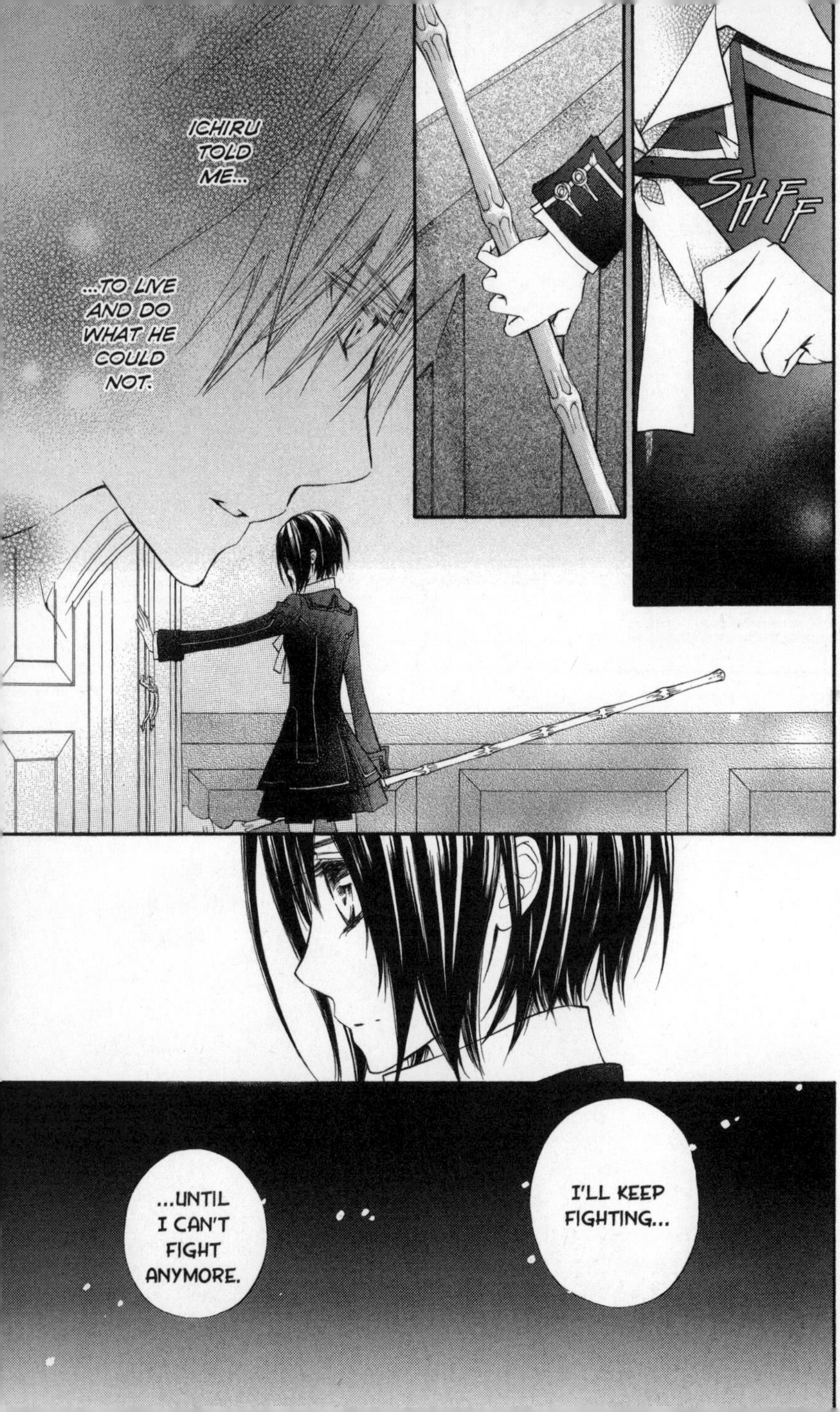
SHFF
ICHIRU TOLD ME...
...TO LIVE AND DO WHAT HE COULD NOT.
I'LL KEEP FIGHTING...
...UNTIL I CAN'T FIGHT ANYMORE.

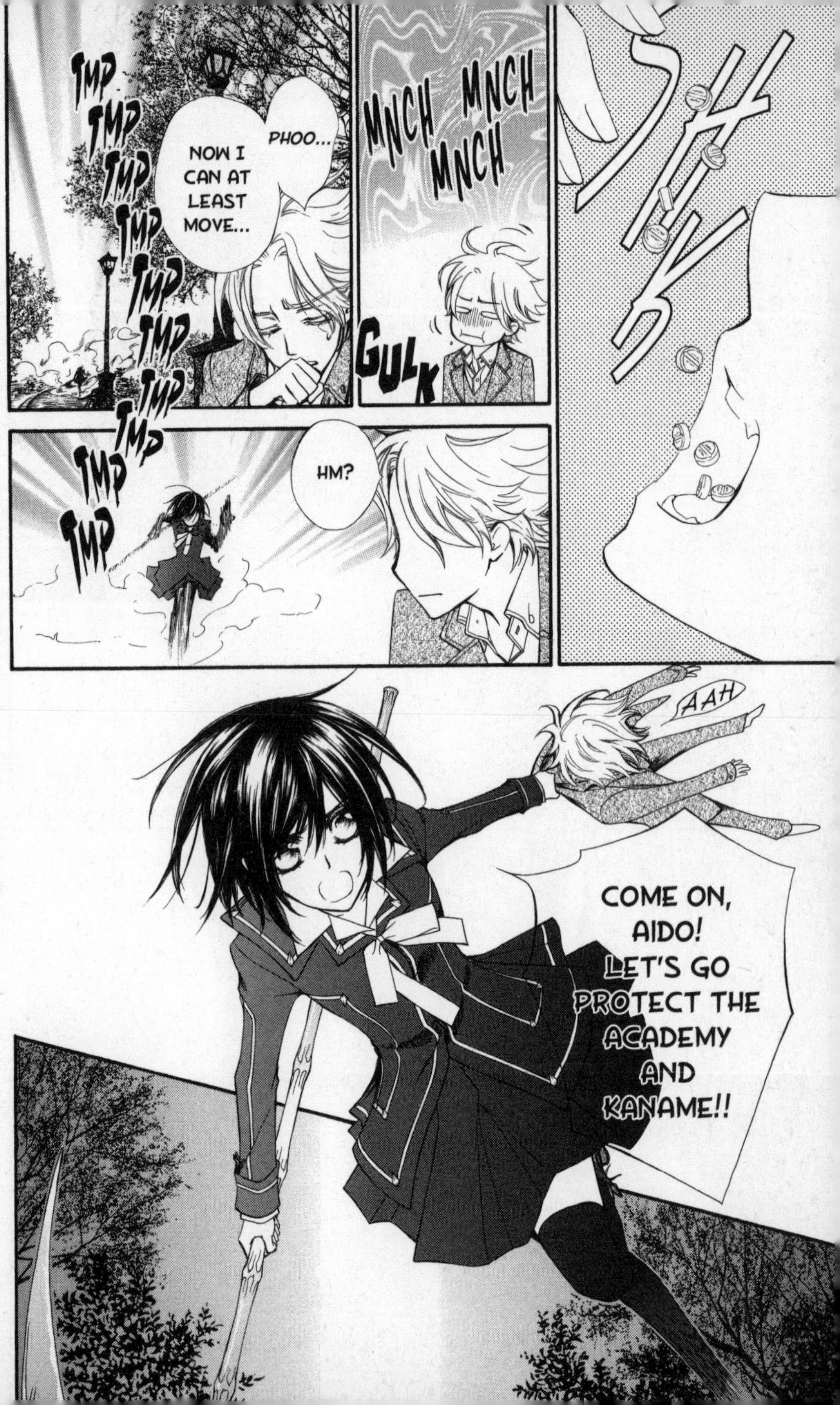
MNCH MNCH
MNCH MNCH
GULK
PHOO...
NOW I CAN AT LEAST MOVE...
TMP TMP TMP TMP TMP TMP TMP TMP TMP
HM?
TMP TMP
AAH
COME ON, AIDO! LET'S GO PROTECT THE ACADEMY AND KANAME!!

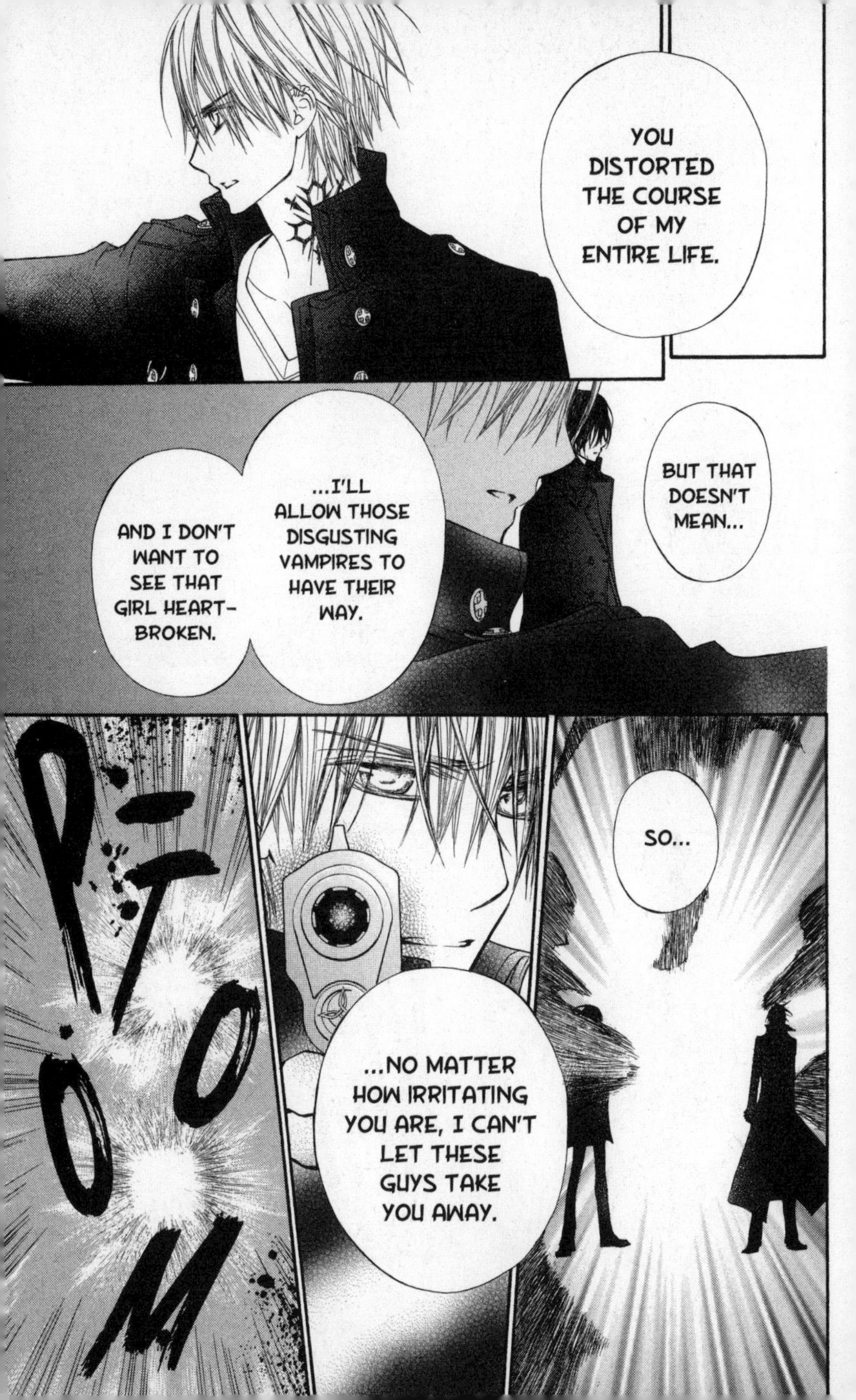
YOU DISTORTED THE COURSE OF MY ENTIRE LIFE.
BUT THAT DOESN'T MEAN...
...I'LL ALLOW THOSE DISGUSTING VAMPIRES TO HAVE THEIR WAY.
AND I DON'T WANT TO SEE THAT GIRL HEART-BROKEN.
SO...
...NO MATTER HOW IRRITATING YOU ARE, I CAN'T LET THESE GUYS TAKE YOU AWAY.
P-TOOM

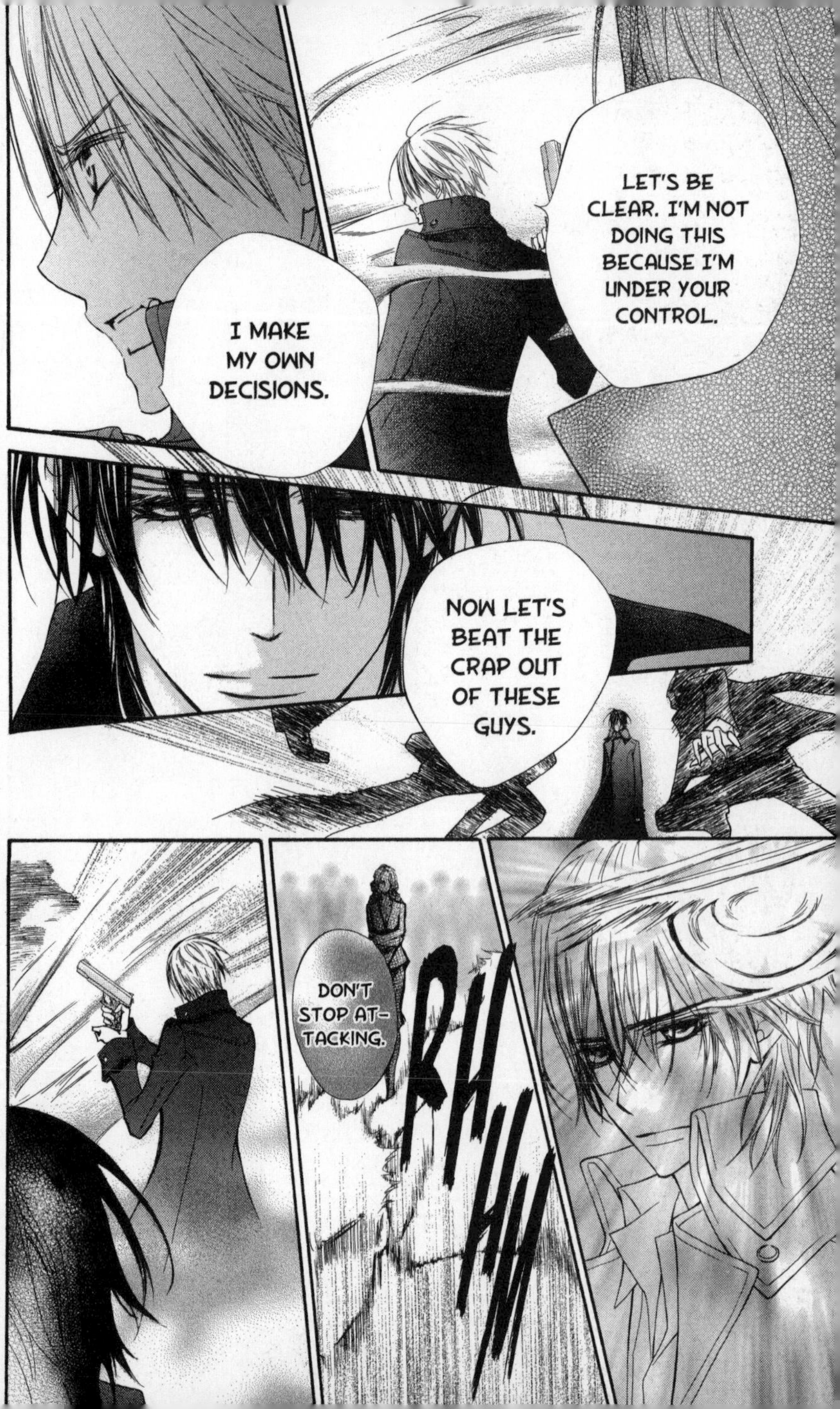
LET'S BE CLEAR. I'M NOT DOING THIS BECAUSE I'M UNDER YOUR CONTROL.
I MAKE MY OWN DECISIONS.
NOW LET'S BEAT THE CRAP OUT OF THESE GUYS.
DON'T STOP AT-TACKING.
RHHH

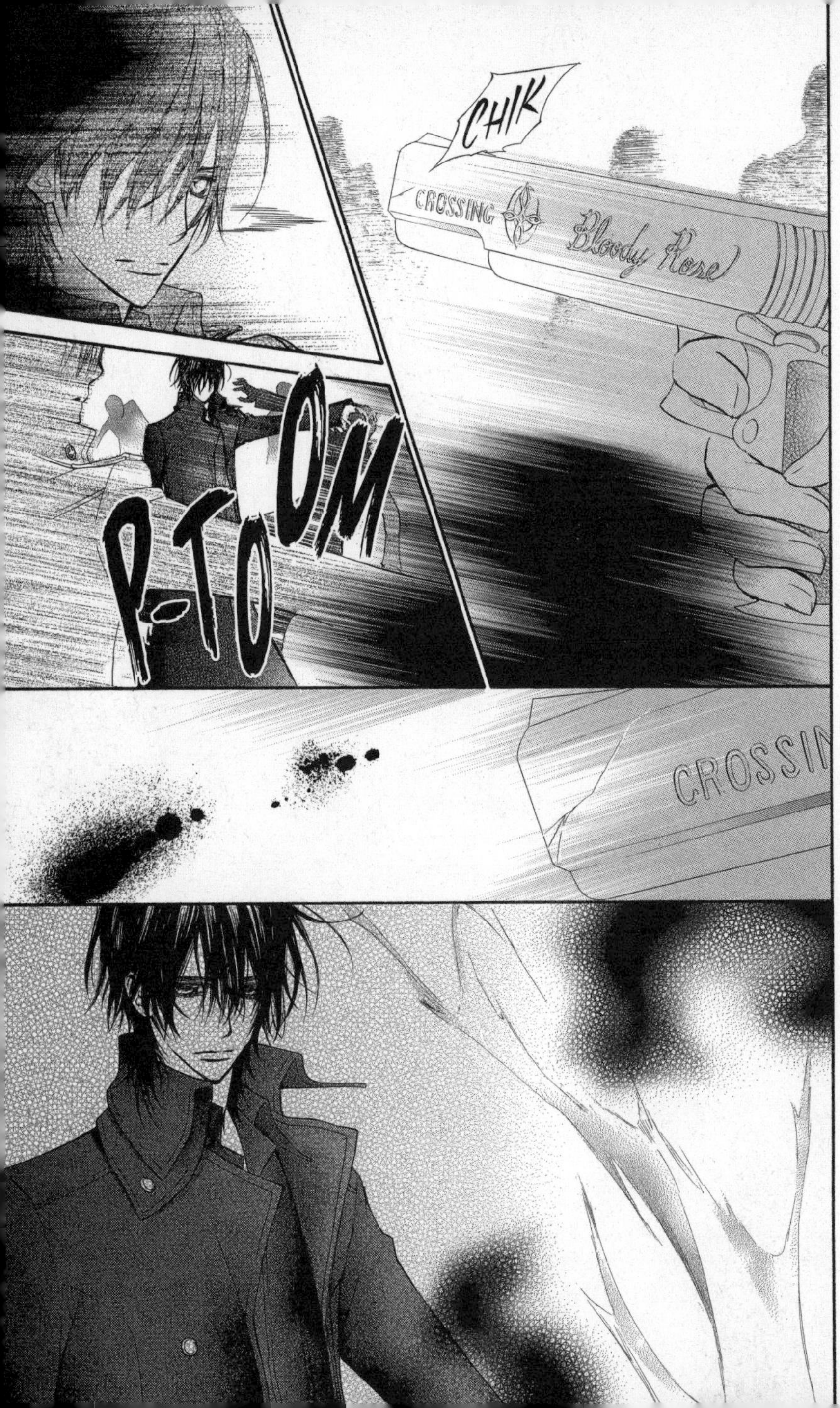
CHIK
CROSSING
Bloody Rose
P-TOOM
CROSSIN

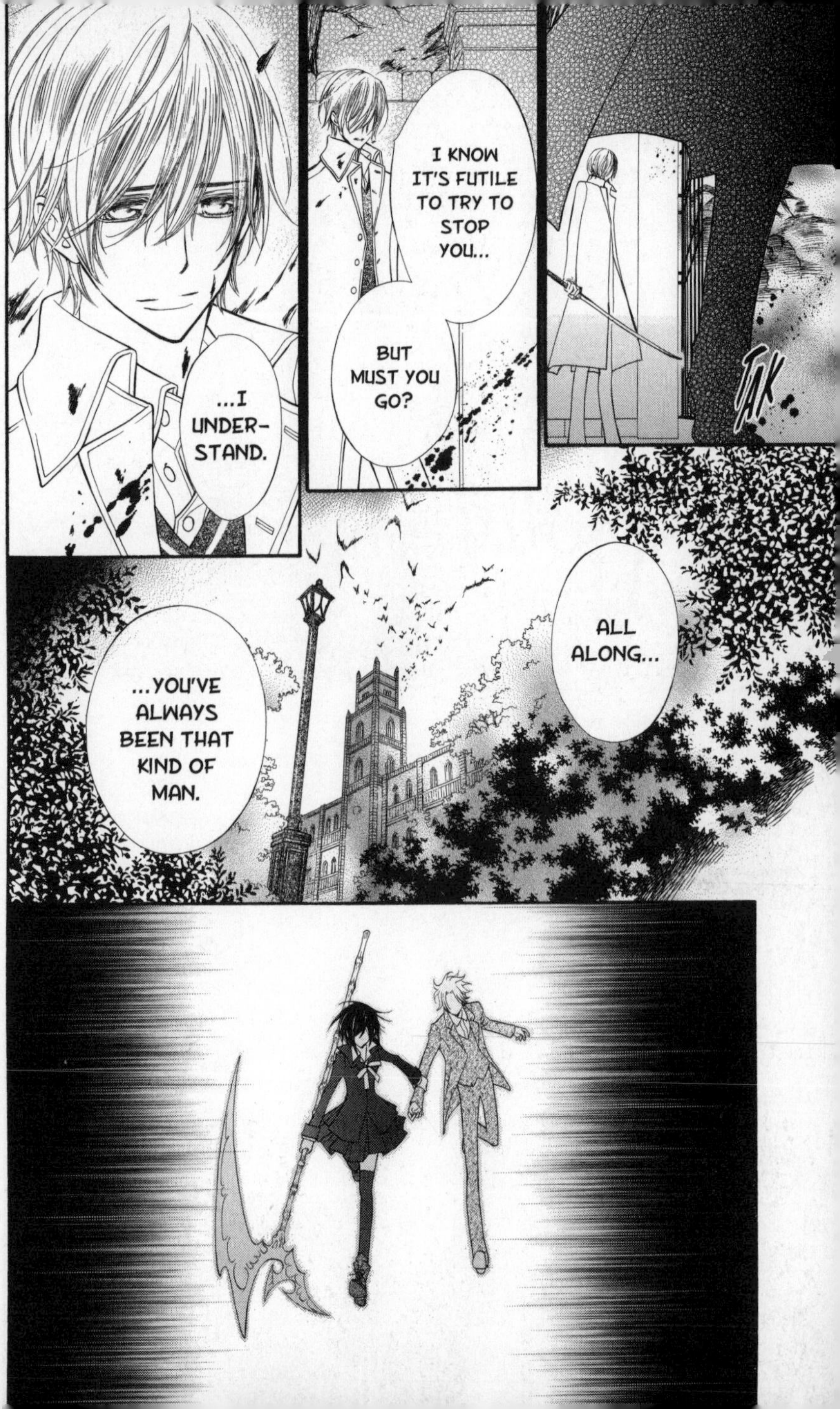
TAK
I KNOW IT'S FUTILE TO TRY TO STOP YOU...
BUT MUST YOU GO?
...I UNDER-STAND.
ALL ALONG...
...YOU'VE ALWAYS BEEN THAT KIND OF MAN.

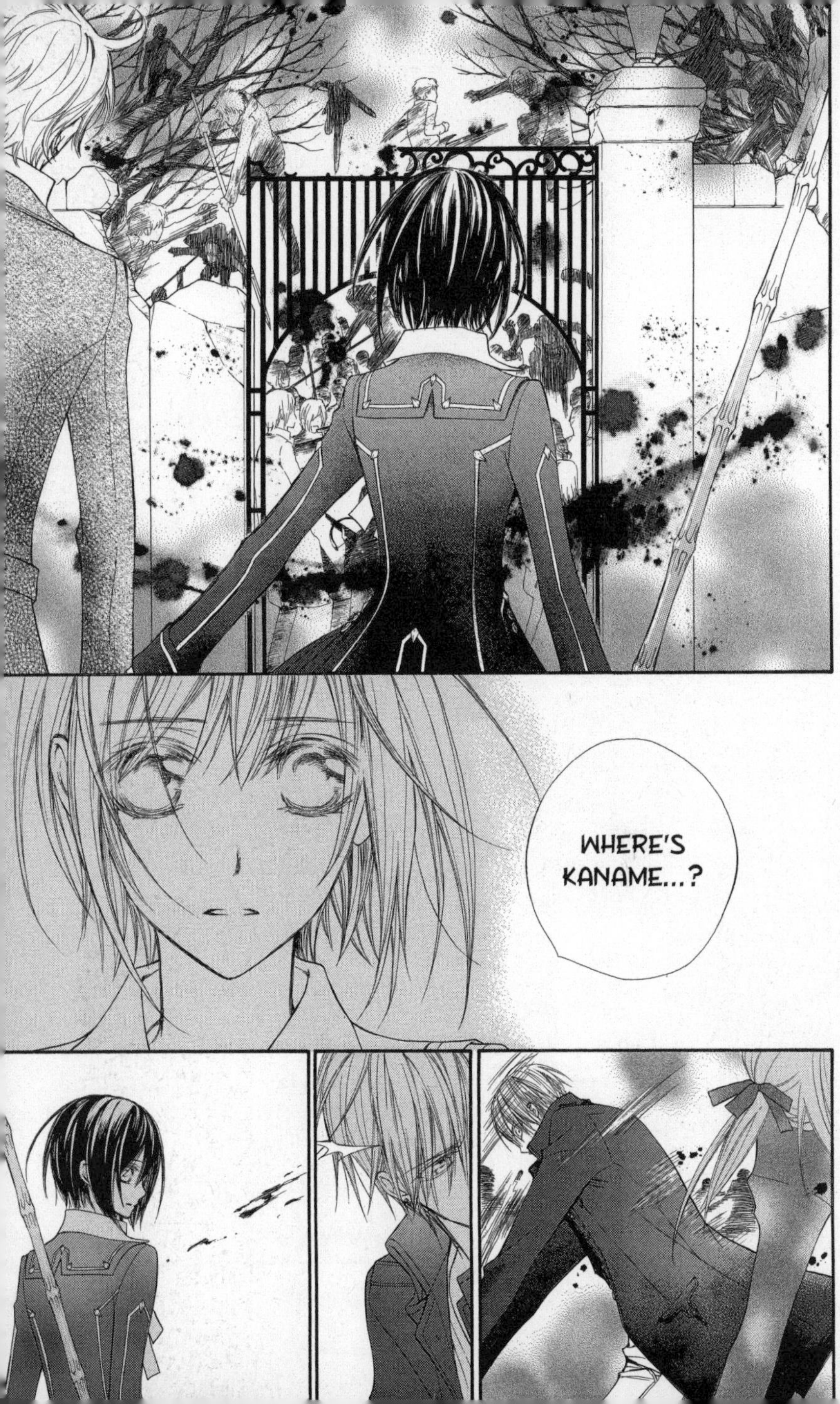
WHERE'S KANAME...?

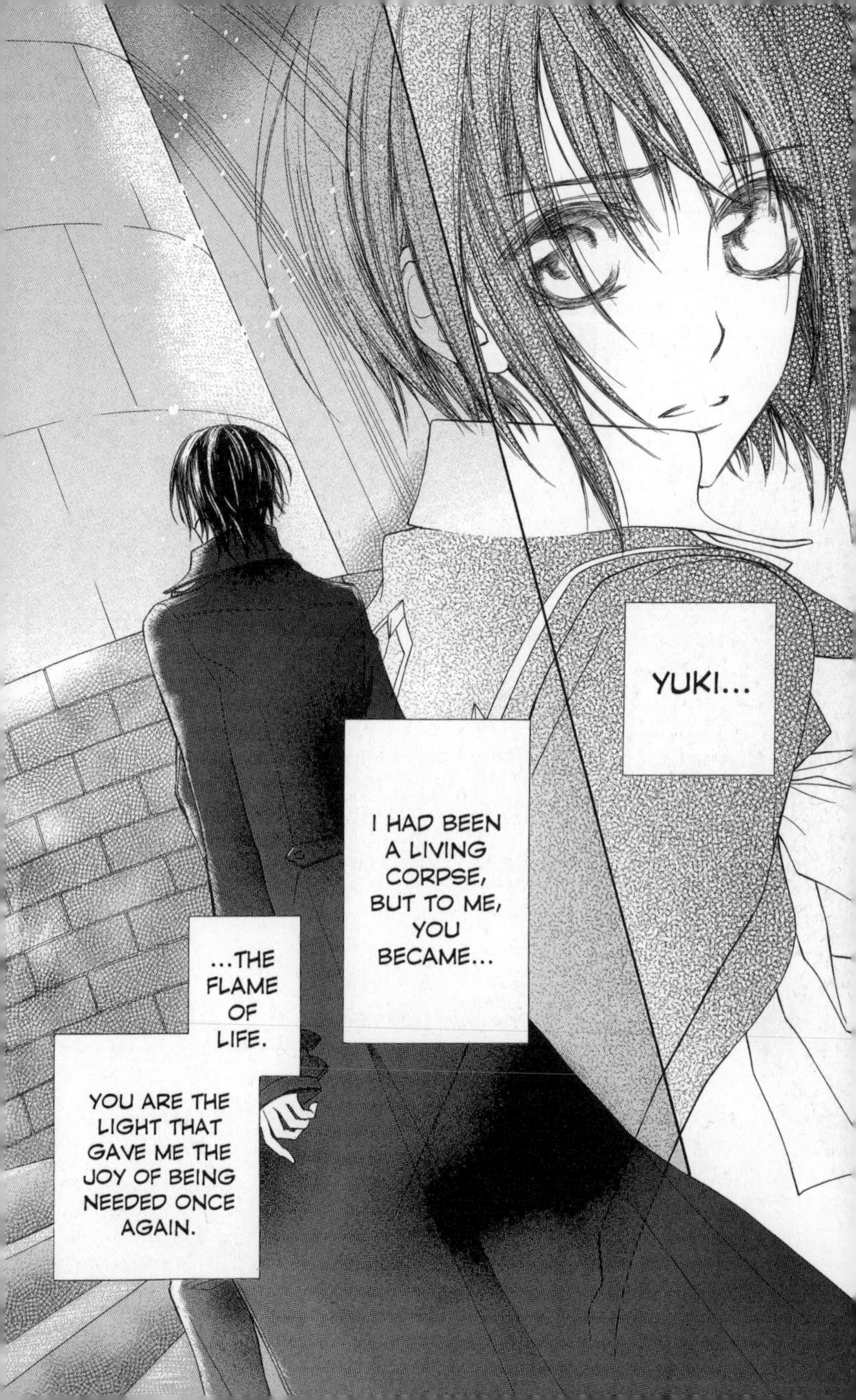
YUKI...
I HAD BEEN A LIVING CORPSE, BUT TO ME, YOU BECAME...
...THE FLAME OF LIFE.
YOU ARE THE LIGHT THAT GAVE ME THE JOY OF BEING NEEDED ONCE AGAIN.

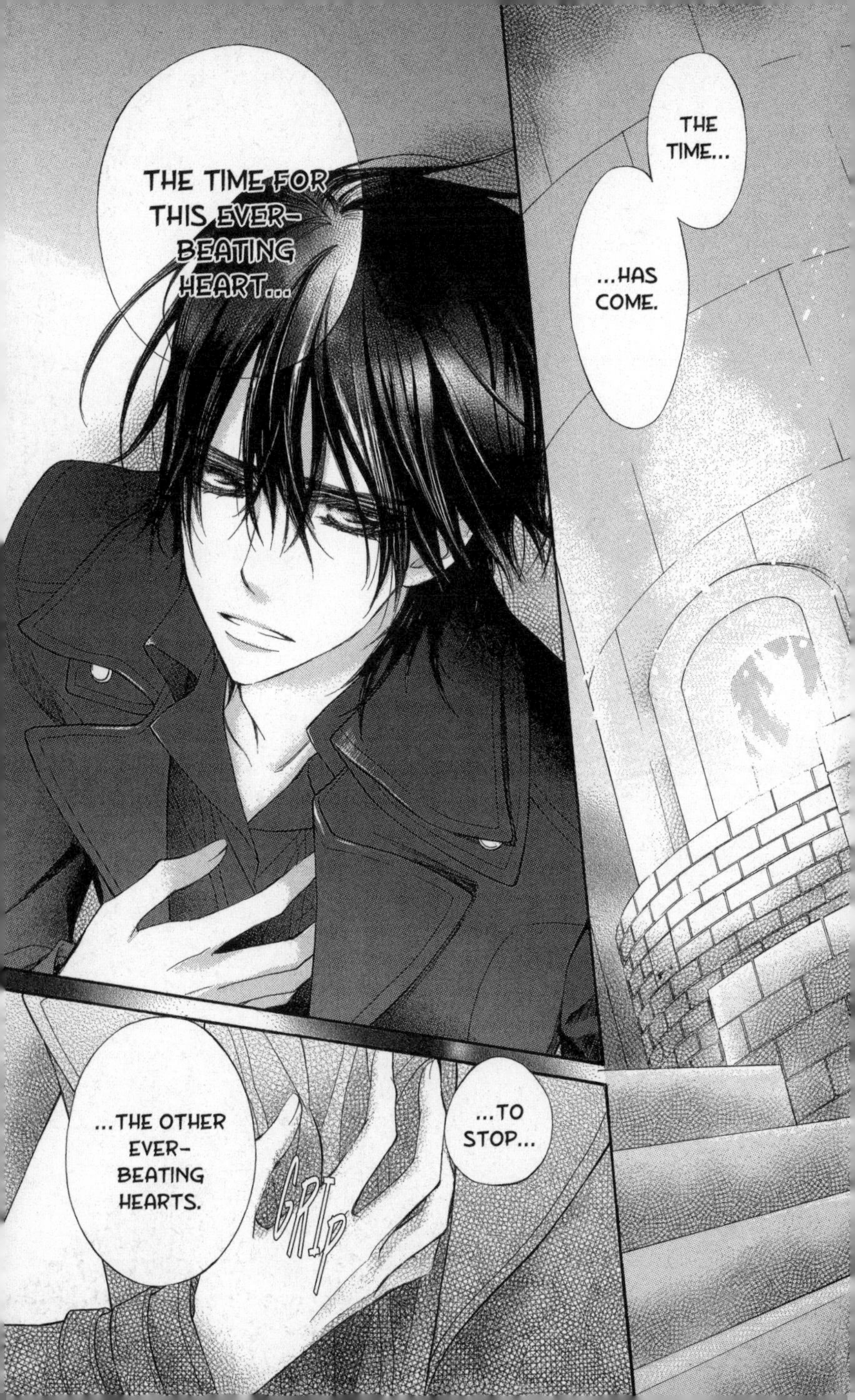
THE TIME...
...HAS COME.
THE TIME FOR THIS EVER-BEATING HEART...
...TO STOP...
...THE OTHER EVER-BEATING HEARTS.
GRIP

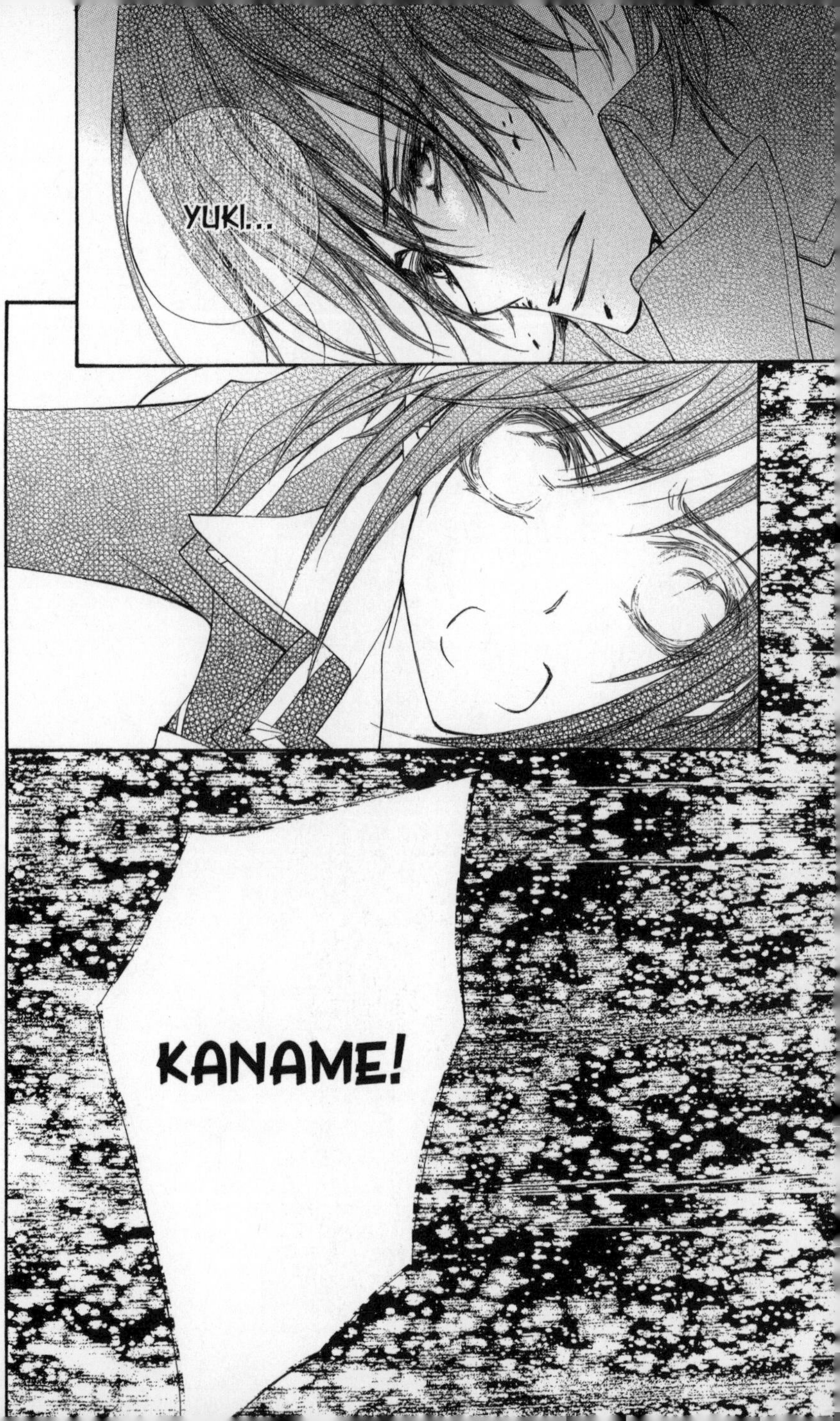
YUKI...
KANAME!

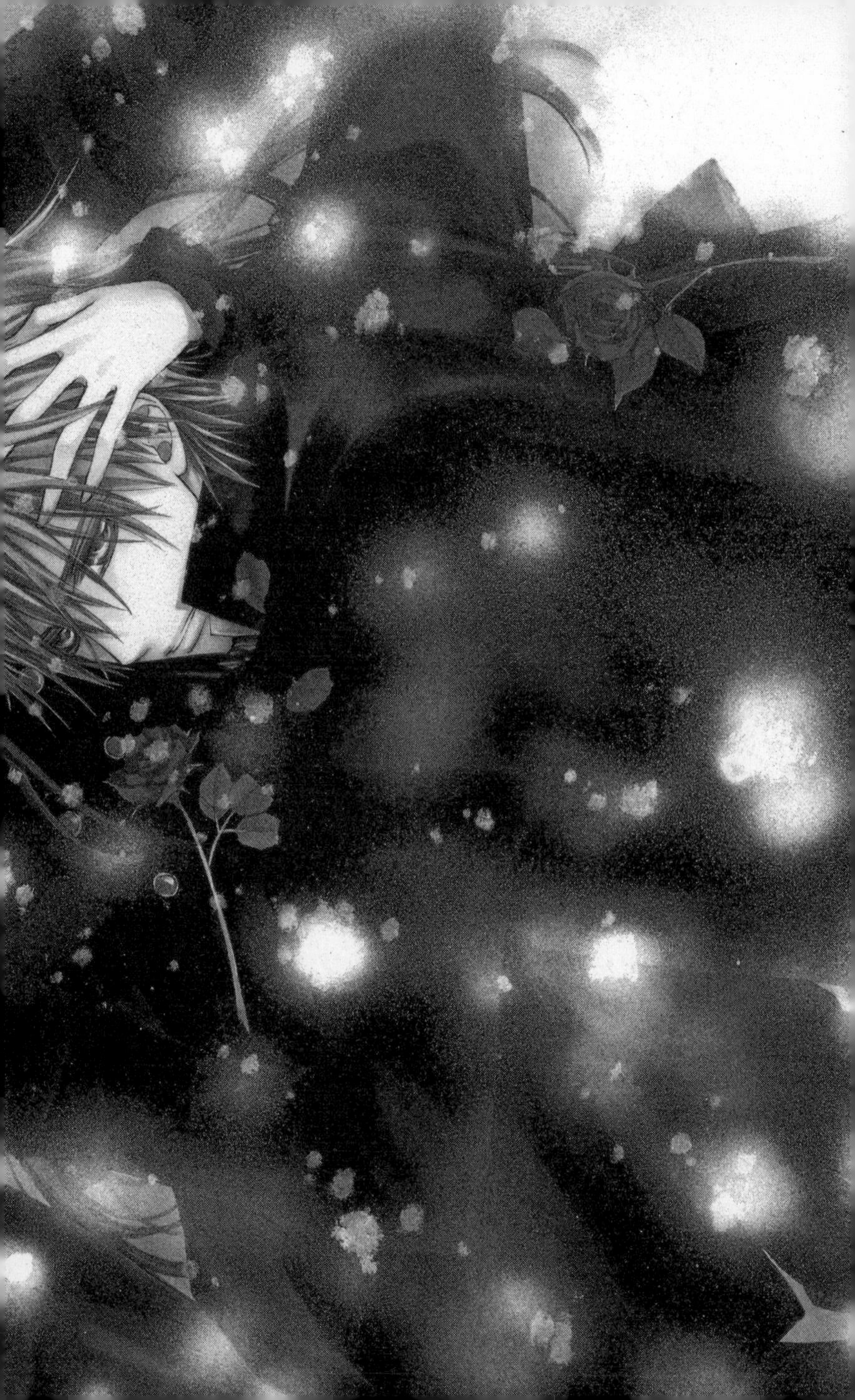

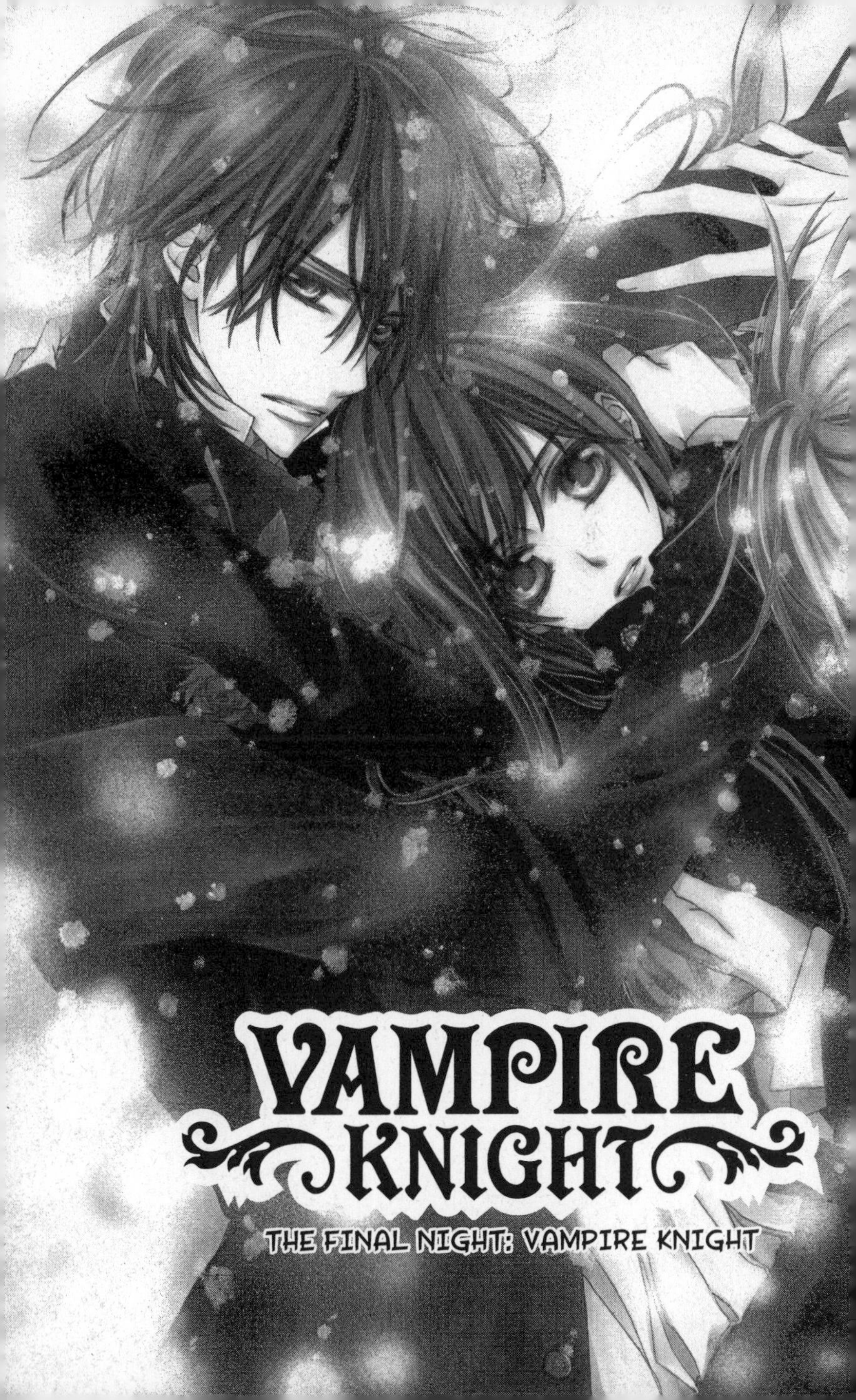
VAMPIRE KNIGHT
THE FINAL NIGHT: VAMPIRE KNIGHT

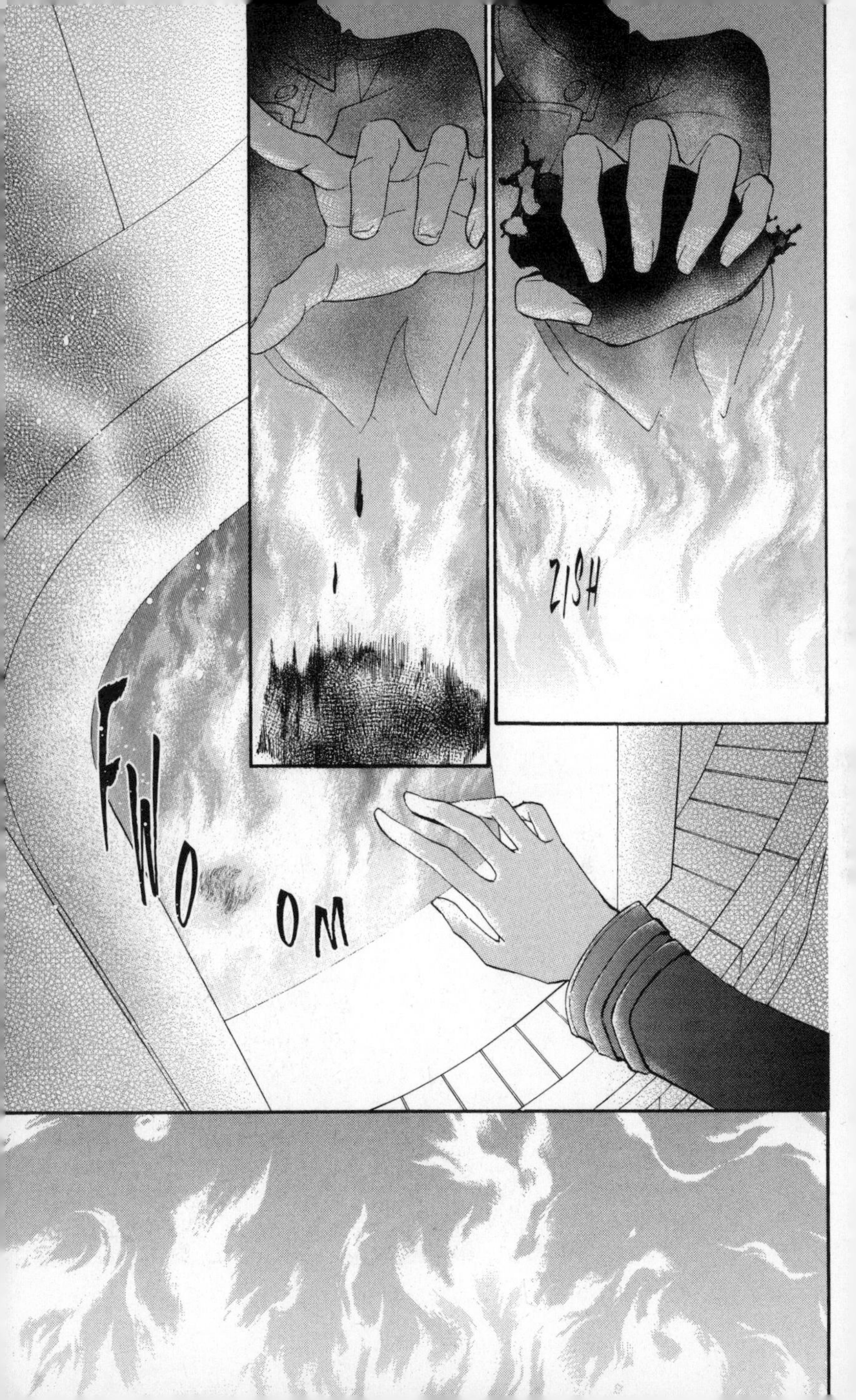
ZISH
FWOOM

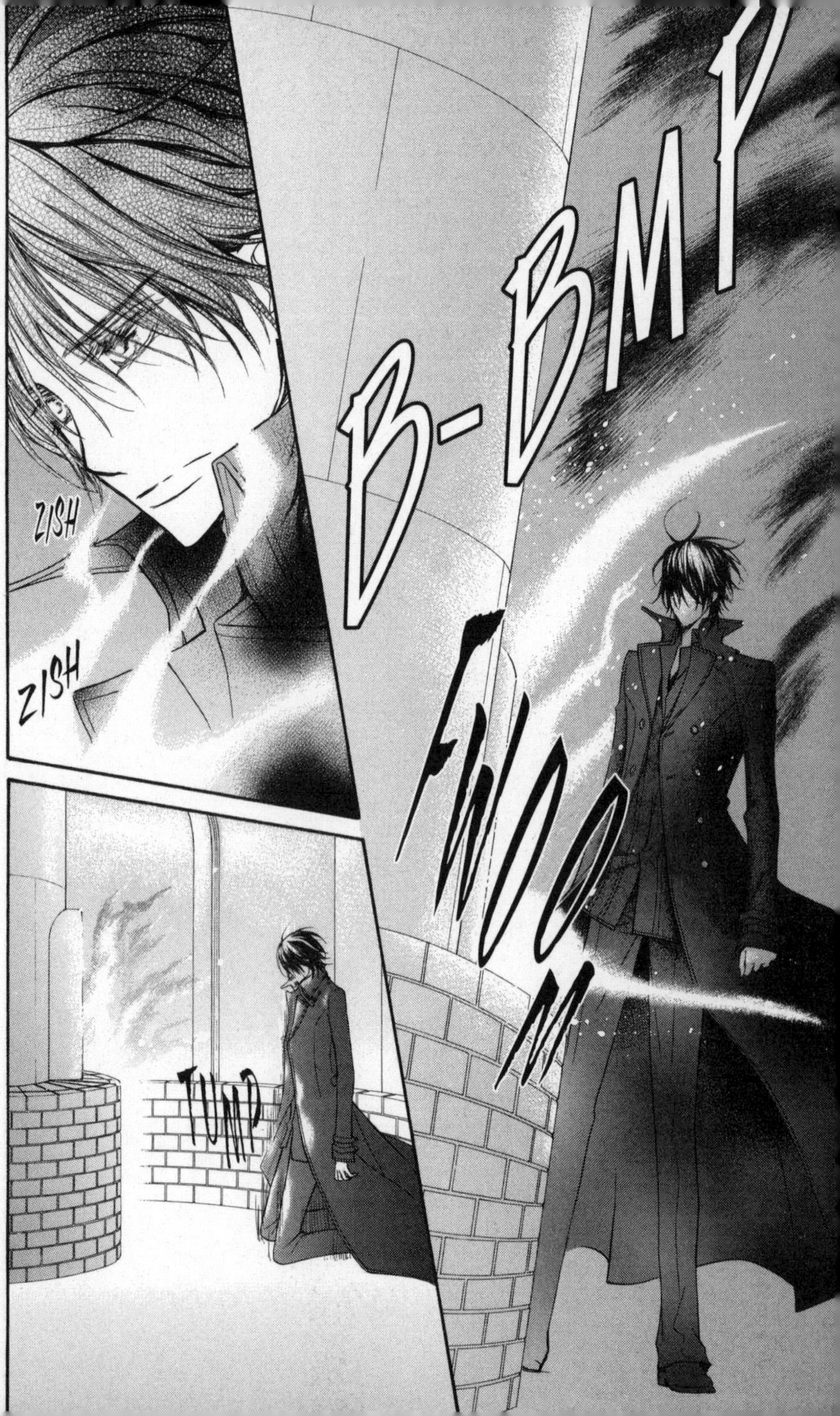
B-BMP
FWOOM
ZISH
ZISH
TUMP

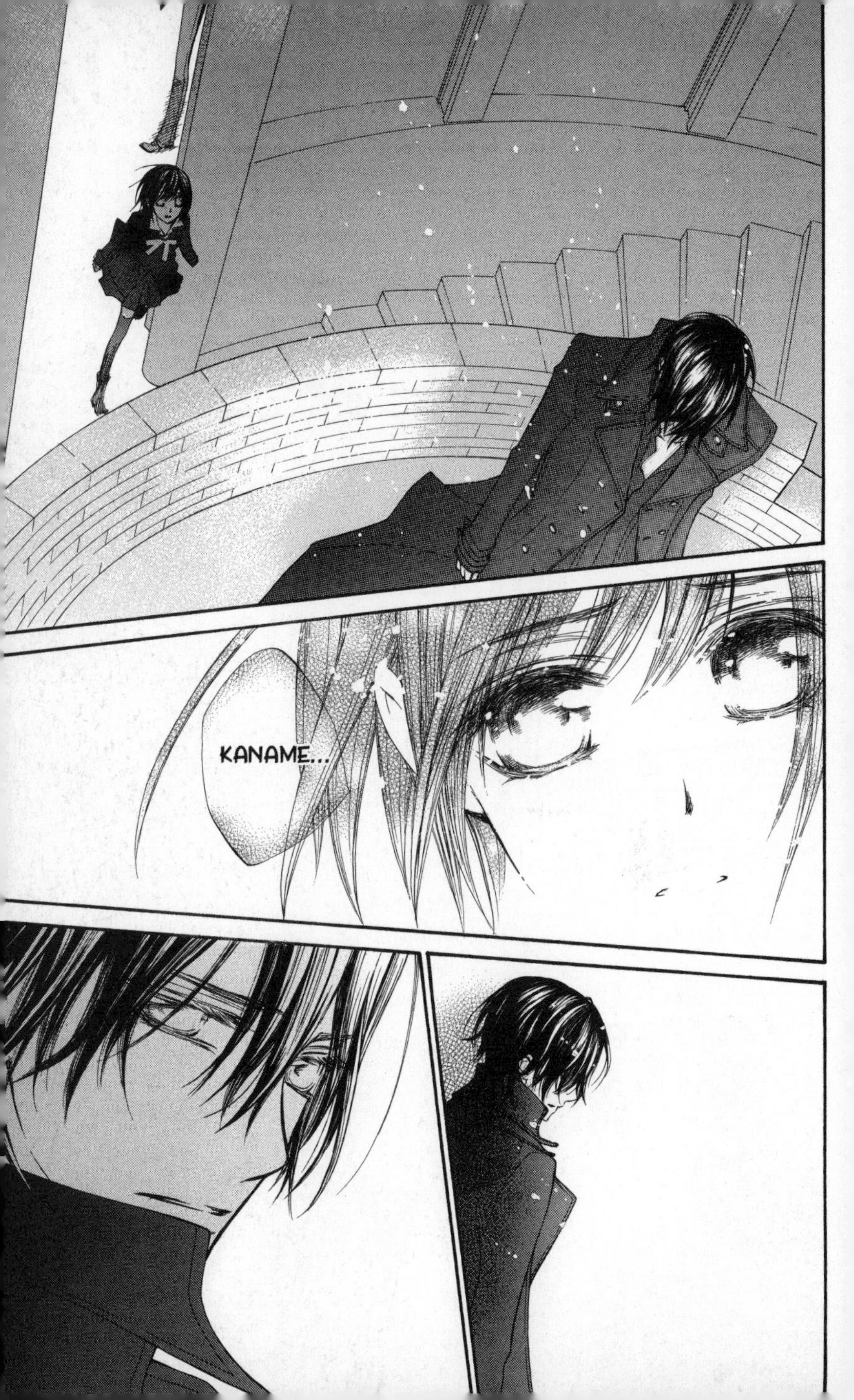
KANAME...

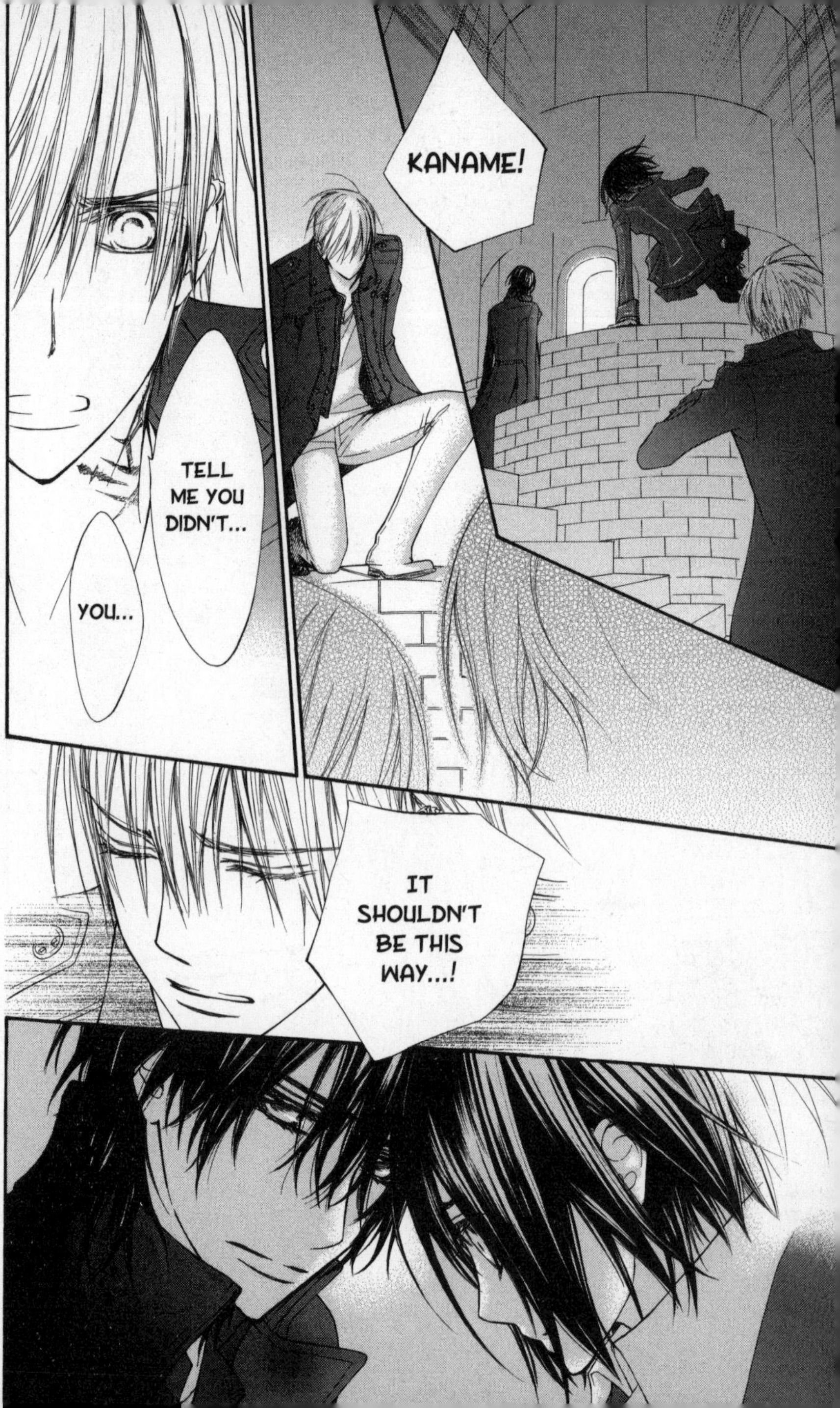
KANAME!
TELL ME YOU DIDN'T...
YOU...
IT SHOULDN'T BE THIS WAY...!

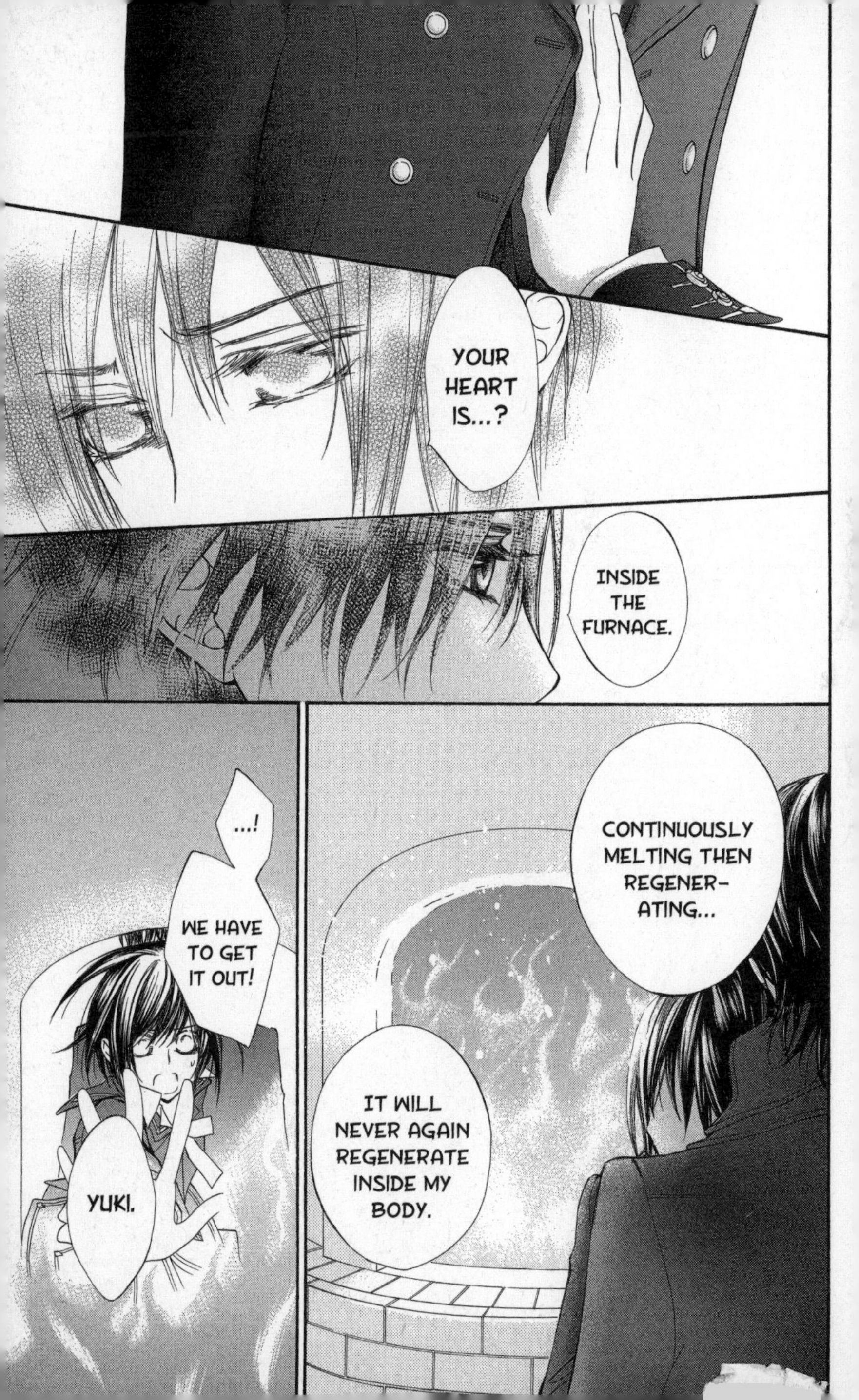
YOUR HEART IS...?
INSIDE THE FURNACE.
CONTINUOUSLY MELTING THEN REGENER-ATING...
IT WILL NEVER AGAIN REGENERATE INSIDE MY BODY.
...!
WE HAVE TO GET IT OUT!
YUKI.

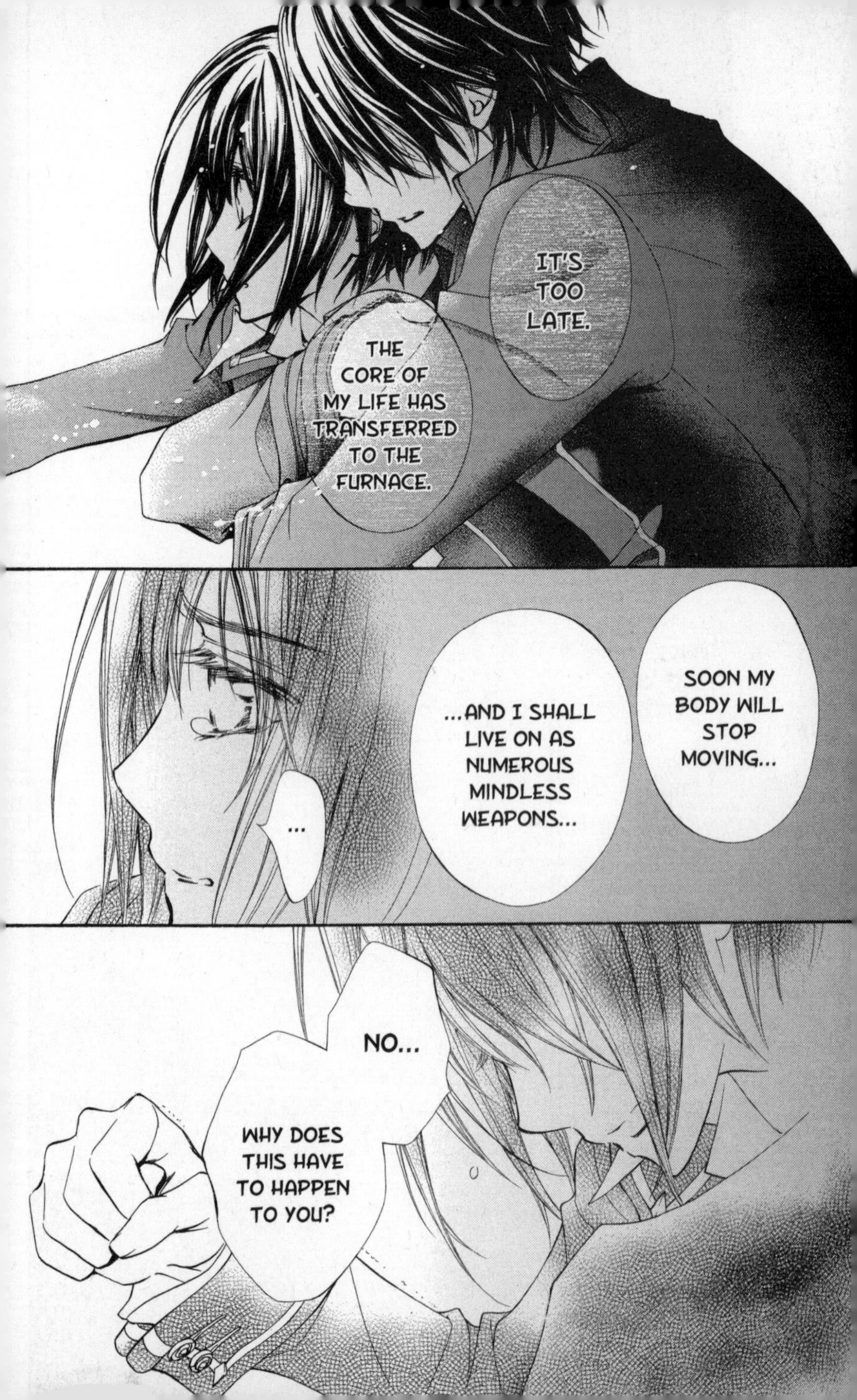
IT'S TOO LATE.
THE CORE OF MY LIFE HAS TRANSFERRED TO THE FURNACE.
SOON MY BODY WILL STOP MOVING...
...AND I SHALL LIVE ON AS NUMEROUS MINDLESS WEAPONS...
...
NO...
WHY DOES THIS HAVE TO HAPPEN TO YOU?

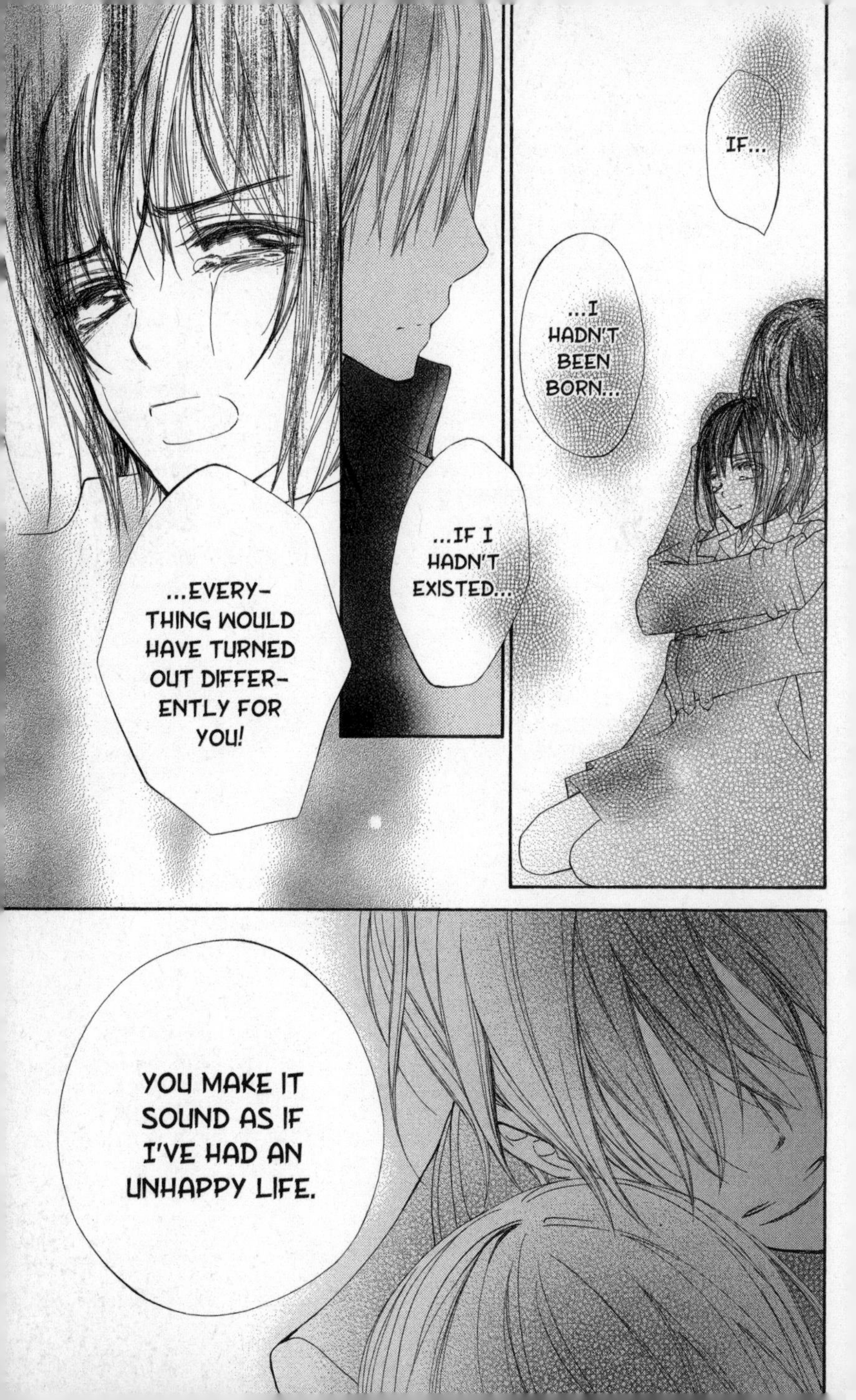
IF...
...I HADN'T BEEN BORN...
...IF I HADN'T EXISTED...
...EVERY-THING WOULD HAVE TURNED OUT DIFFER-ENTLY FOR YOU!
YOU MAKE IT SOUND AS IF I'VE HAD AN UNHAPPY LIFE.

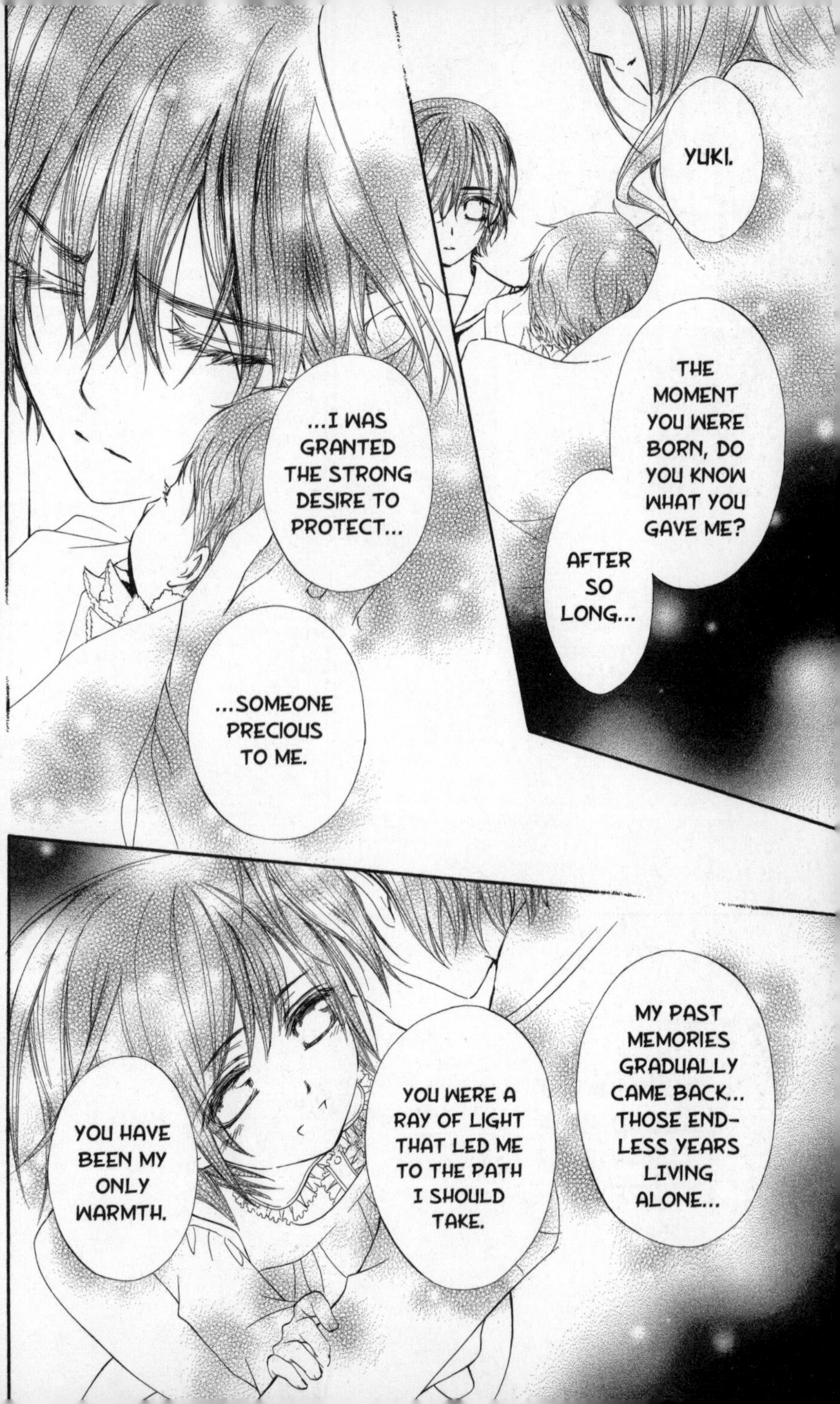
YUKI.
THE MOMENT YOU WERE BORN, DO YOU KNOW WHAT YOU GAVE ME?
AFTER SO LONG...
...I WAS GRANTED THE STRONG DESIRE TO PROTECT...
...SOMEONE PRECIOUS TO ME.
MY PAST MEMORIES GRADUALLY CAME BACK... THOSE END-LESS YEARS LIVING ALONE...
YOU WERE A RAY OF LIGHT THAT LED ME TO THE PATH I SHOULD TAKE.
YOU HAVE BEEN MY ONLY WARMTH.

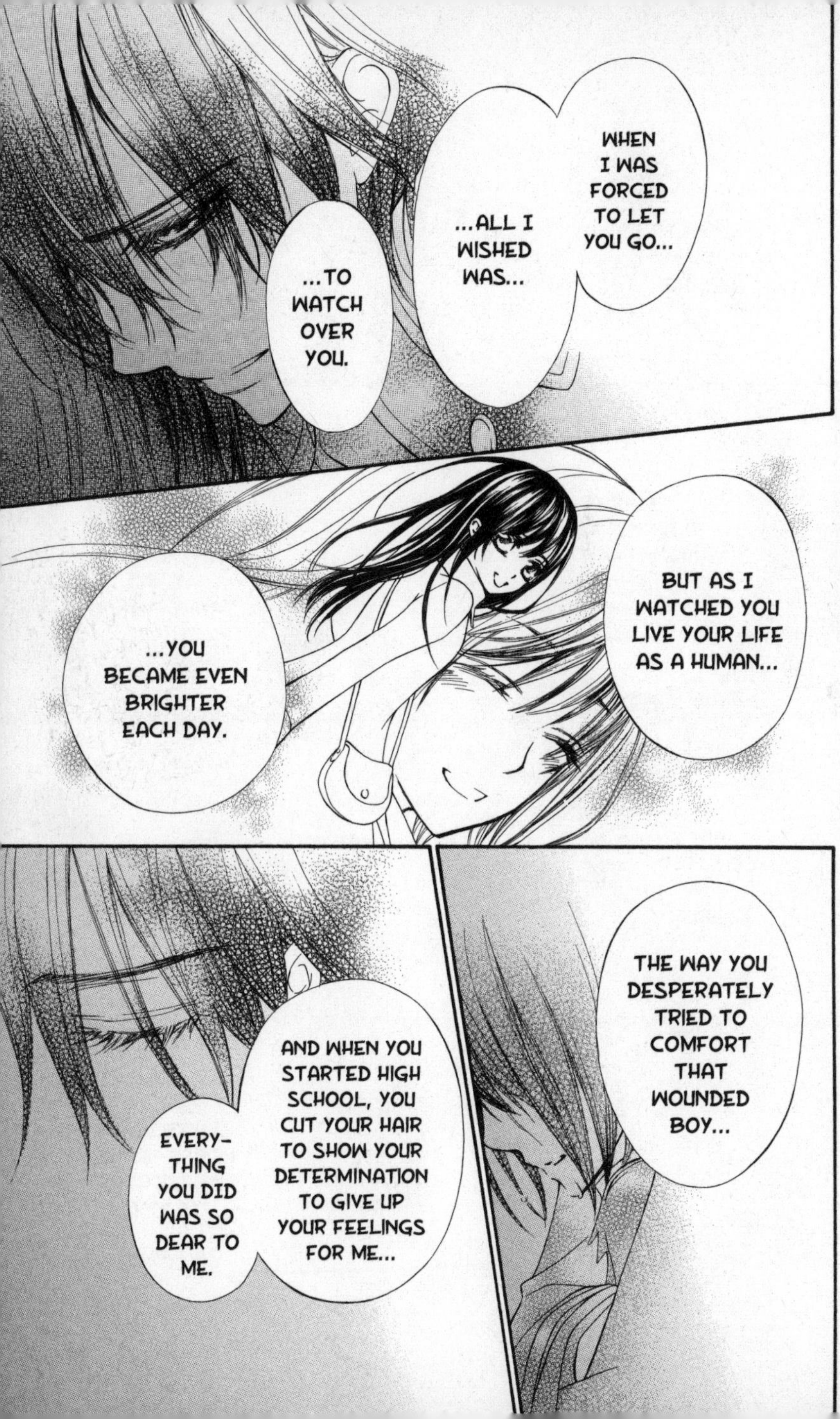
WHEN I WAS FORCED TO LET YOU GO...
...ALL I WISHED WAS...
...TO WATCH OVER YOU.
BUT AS I WATCHED YOU LIVE YOUR LIFE AS A HUMAN...
...YOU BECAME EVEN BRIGHTER EACH DAY.
THE WAY YOU DESPERATELY TRIED TO COMFORT THAT WOUNDED BOY...
AND WHEN YOU STARTED HIGH SCHOOL, YOU CUT YOUR HAIR TO SHOW YOUR DETERMINATION TO GIVE UP YOUR FEELINGS FOR ME...
EVERY-THING YOU DID WAS SO DEAR TO ME.

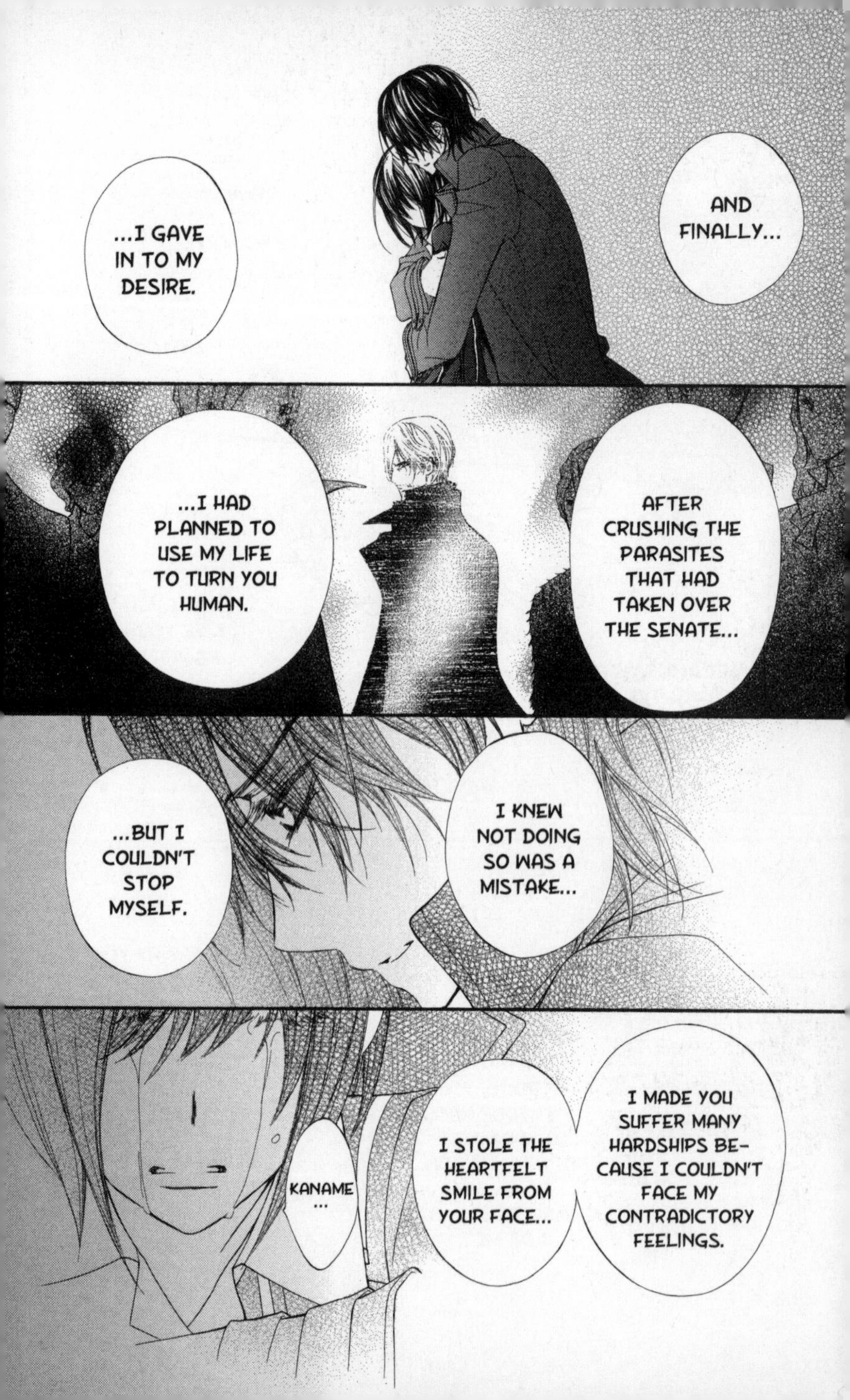
AND FINALLY...
...I GAVE IN TO MY DESIRE.
AFTER CRUSHING THE PARASITES THAT HAD TAKEN OVER THE SENATE...
...I HAD PLANNED TO USE MY LIFE TO TURN YOU HUMAN.
I KNEW NOT DOING SO WAS A MISTAKE...
...BUT I COULDN'T STOP MYSELF.
I MADE YOU SUFFER MANY HARDSHIPS BE-CAUSE I COULDN'T FACE MY CONTRADICTORY FEELINGS.
I STOLE THE HEARTFELT SMILE FROM YOUR FACE...
KANAME ...

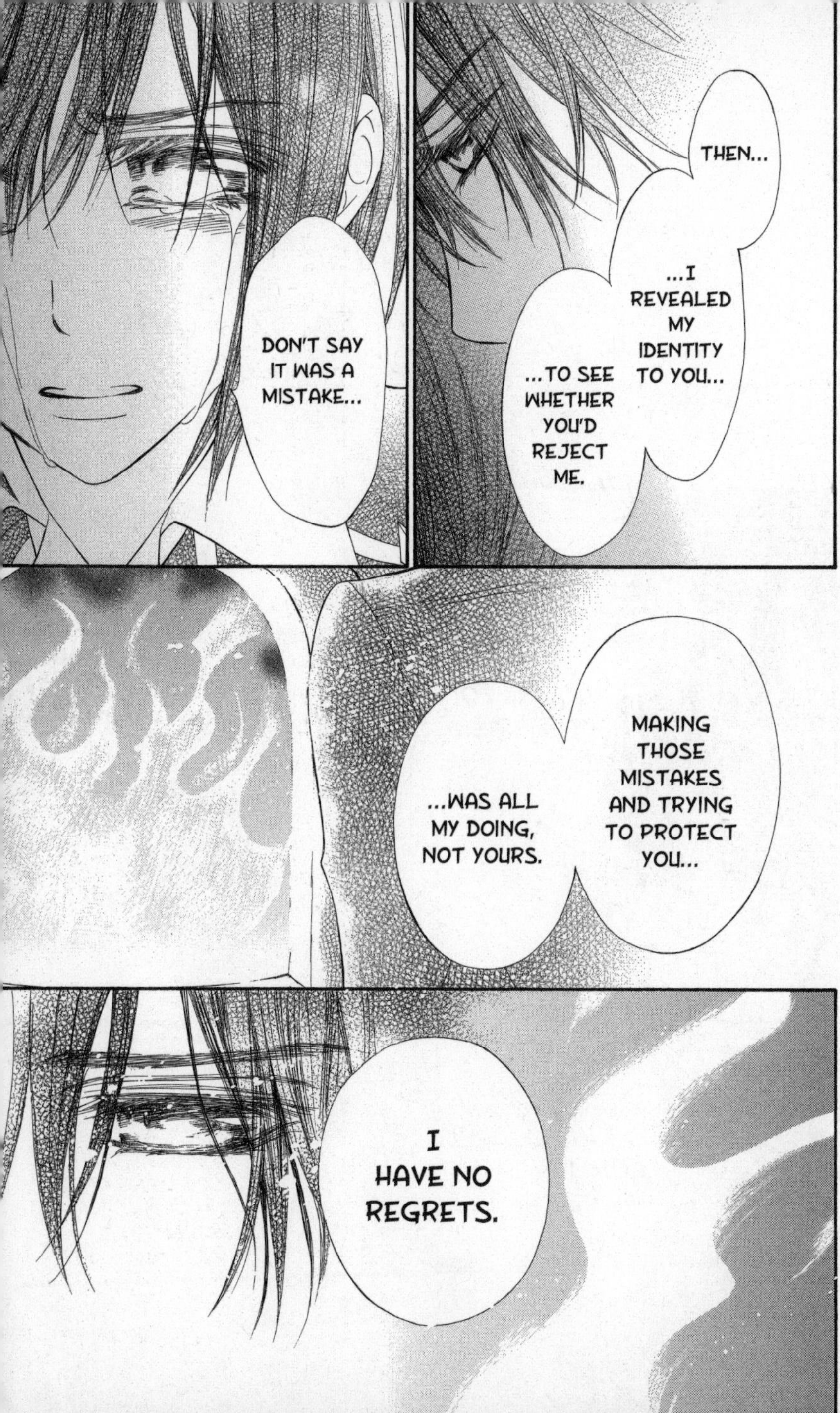
THEN...
...I REVEALED MY IDENTITY TO YOU...
...TO SEE WHETHER YOU'D REJECT ME.
DON'T SAY IT WAS A MISTAKE...
MAKING THOSE MISTAKES AND TRYING TO PROTECT YOU...
...WAS ALL MY DOING, NOT YOURS.
I HAVE NO REGRETS.

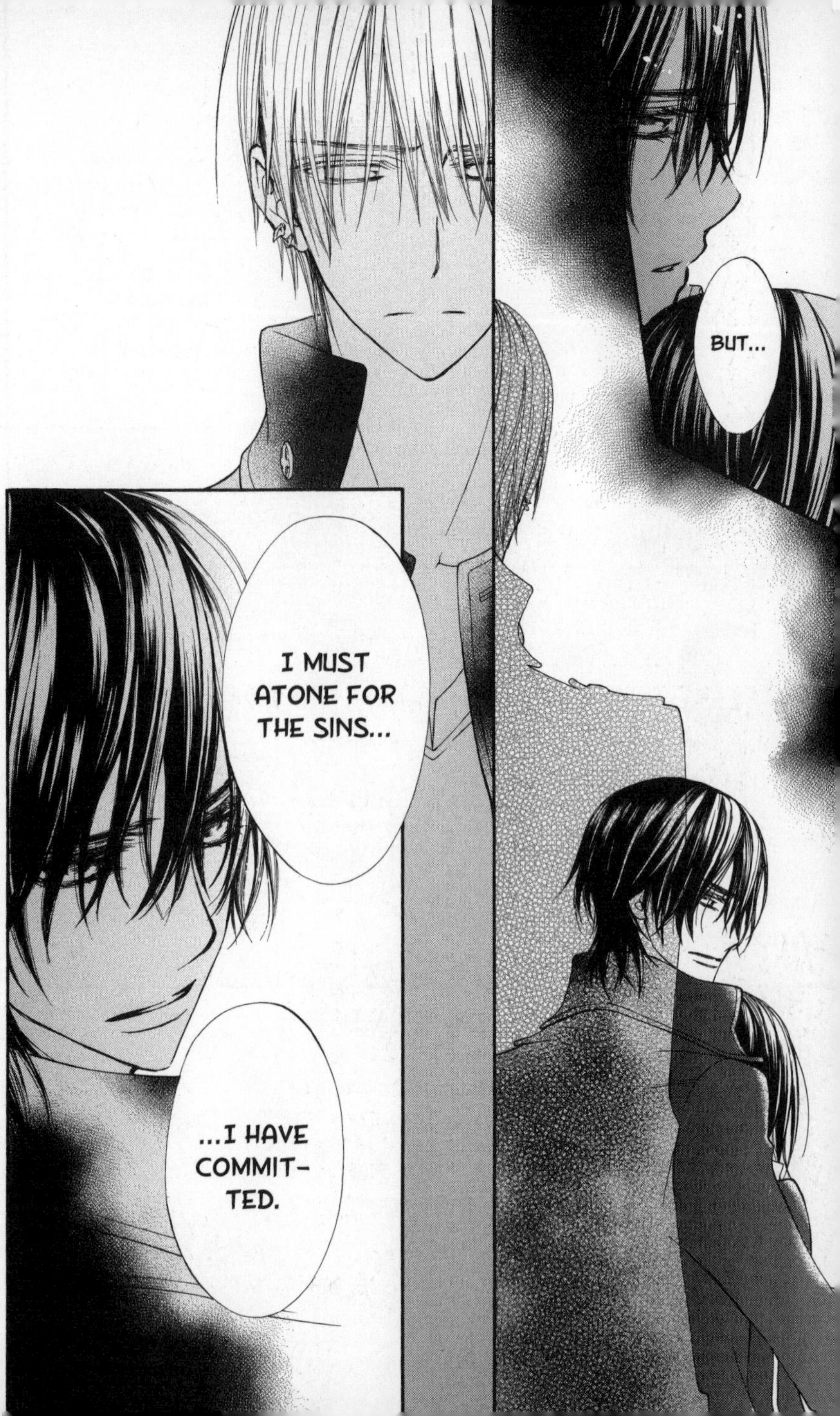
BUT...
I MUST ATONE FOR THE SINS...
...I HAVE COMMIT-TED.

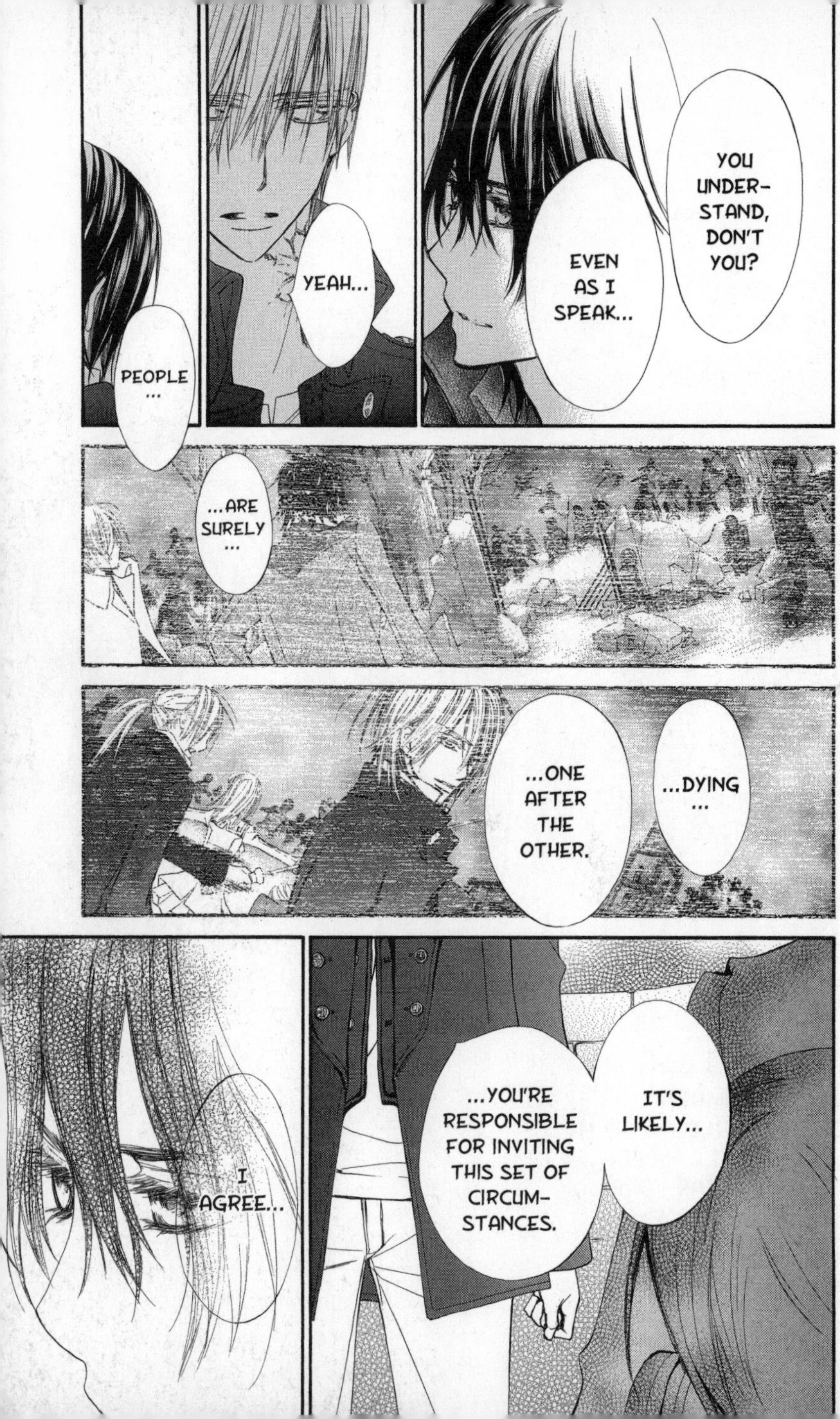
YOU UNDER-STAND, DON'T YOU?
EVEN AS I SPEAK...
YEAH...
PEOPLE ...
...ARE SURELY ...
...DYING ...
...ONE AFTER THE OTHER.
IT'S LIKELY...
...YOU'RE RESPONSIBLE FOR INVITING THIS SET OF CIRCUM-STANCES.
I AGREE...

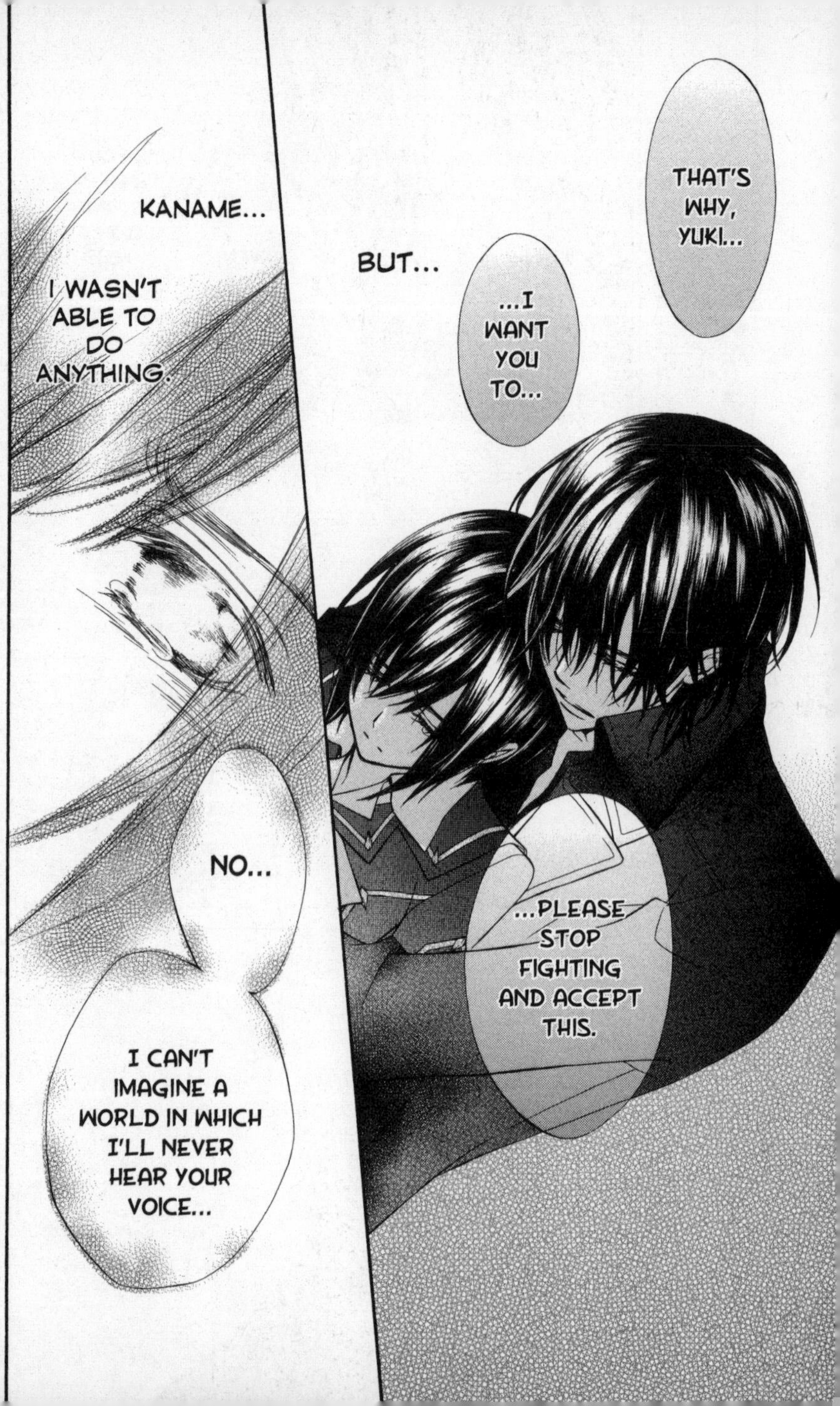
THAT'S WHY, YUKI...
...I WANT YOU TO...
BUT...
...PLEASE STOP FIGHTING AND ACCEPT THIS.
KANAME...
I WASN'T ABLE TO DO ANYTHING.
NO...
I CAN'T IMAGINE A WORLD IN WHICH I'LL NEVER HEAR YOUR VOICE...

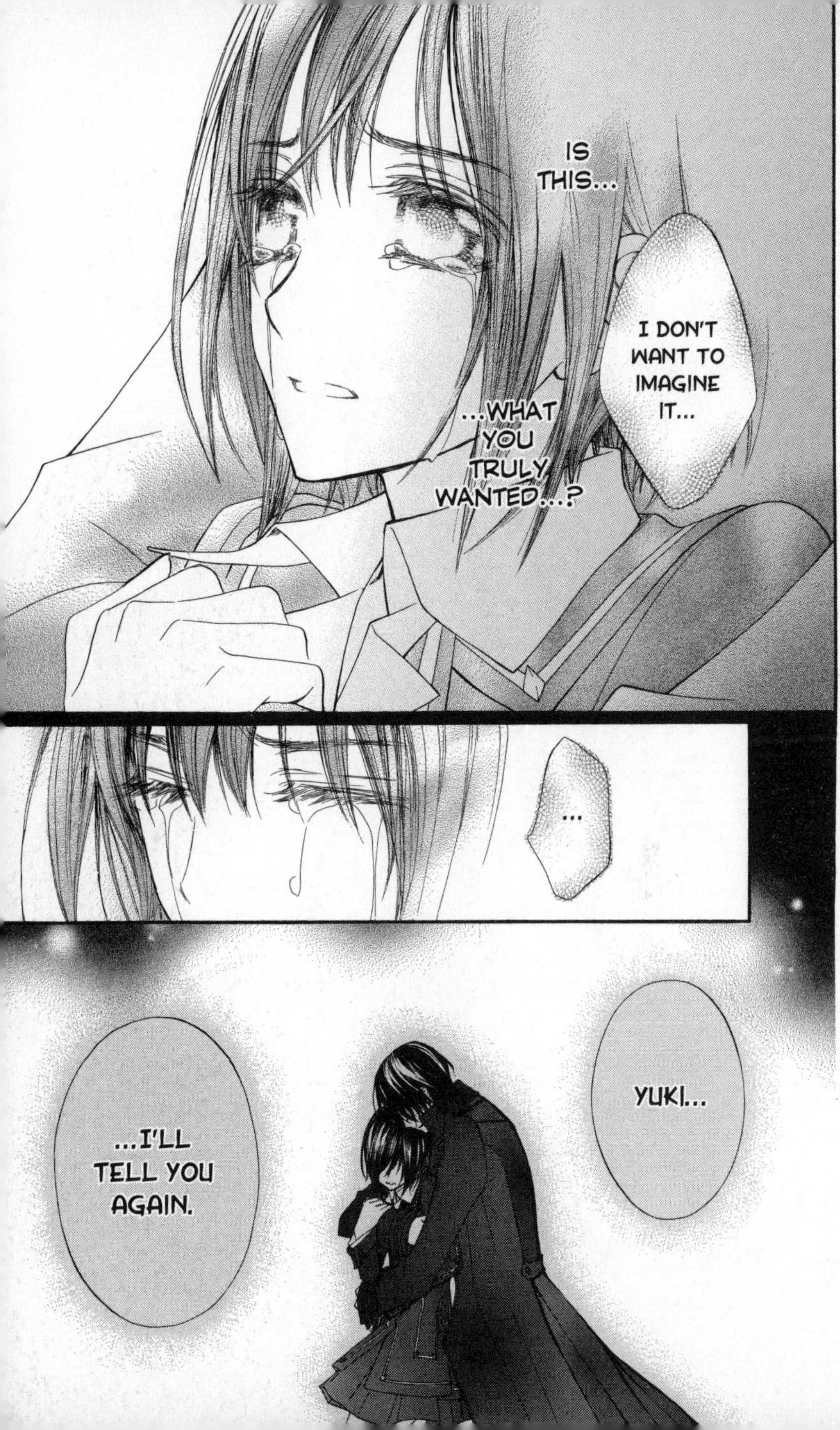
IS THIS...
I DON'T WANT TO IMAGINE IT...
...WHAT YOU TRULY WANTED...?
...
YUKI...
...I'LL TELL YOU AGAIN.

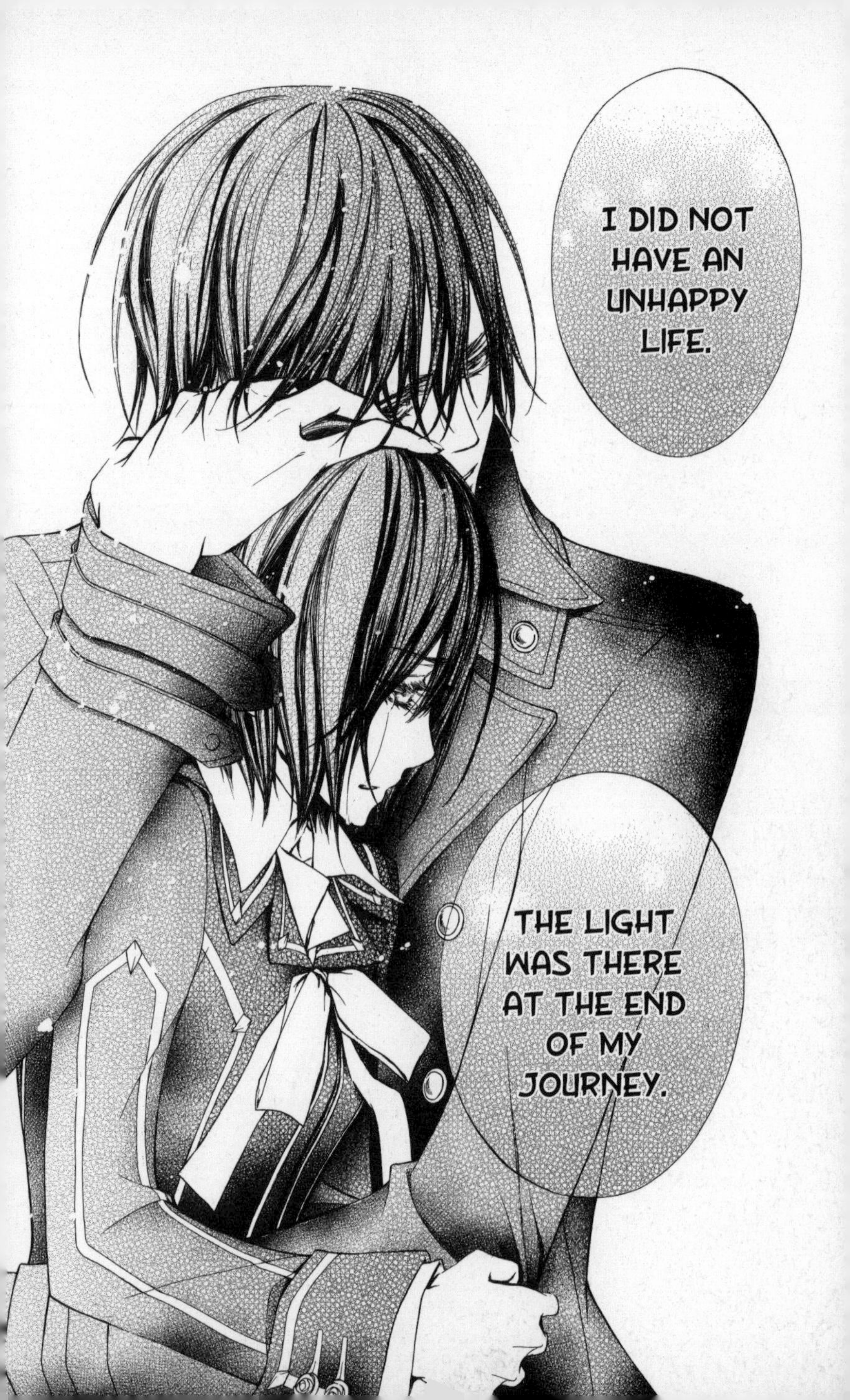
I DID NOT HAVE AN UNHAPPY LIFE.
THE LIGHT WAS THERE AT THE END OF MY JOURNEY.

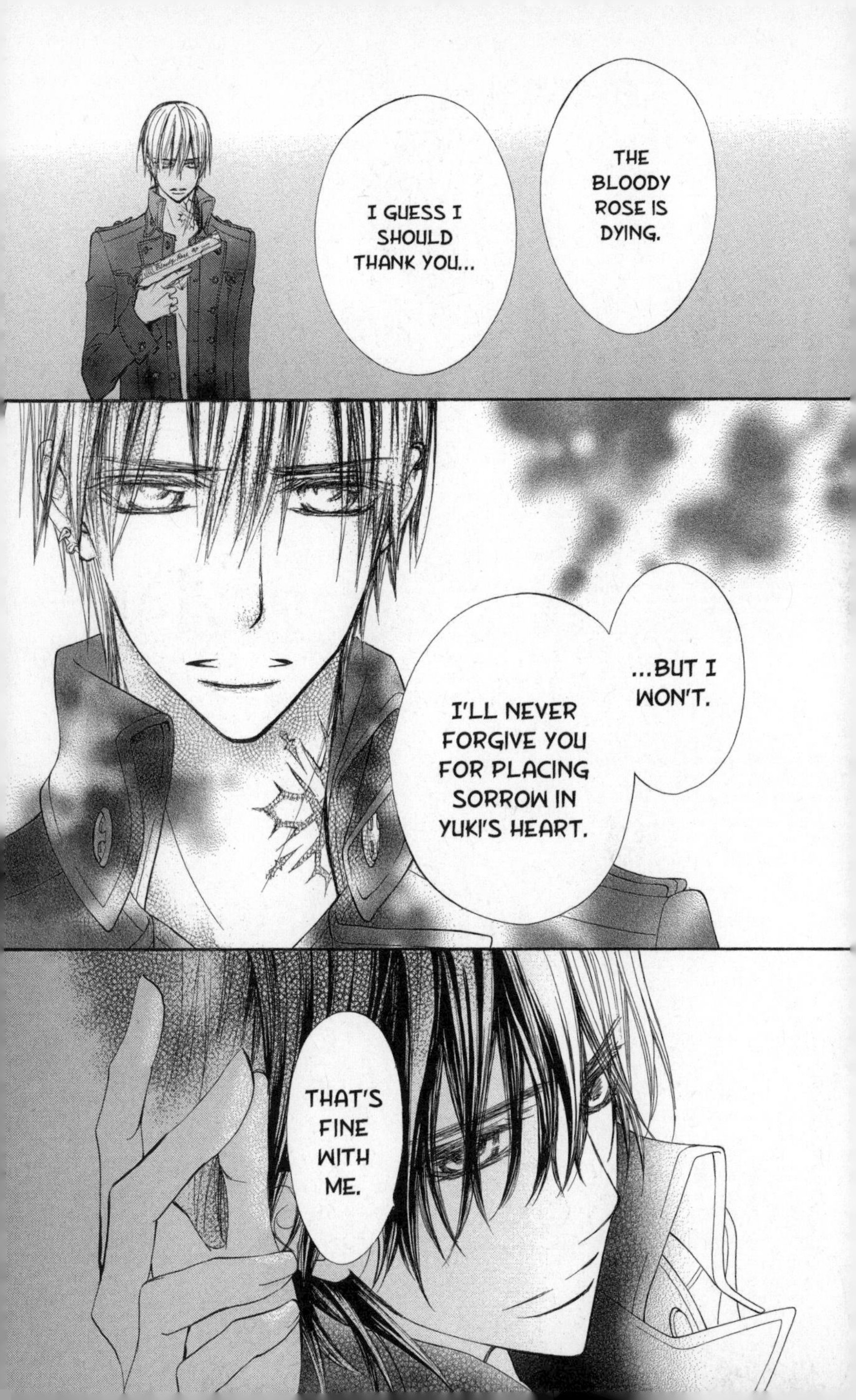
THE BLOODY ROSE IS DYING.
I GUESS I SHOULD THANK YOU...
...BUT I WON'T.
I'LL NEVER FORGIVE YOU FOR PLACING SORROW IN YUKI'S HEART.
THAT'S FINE WITH ME.

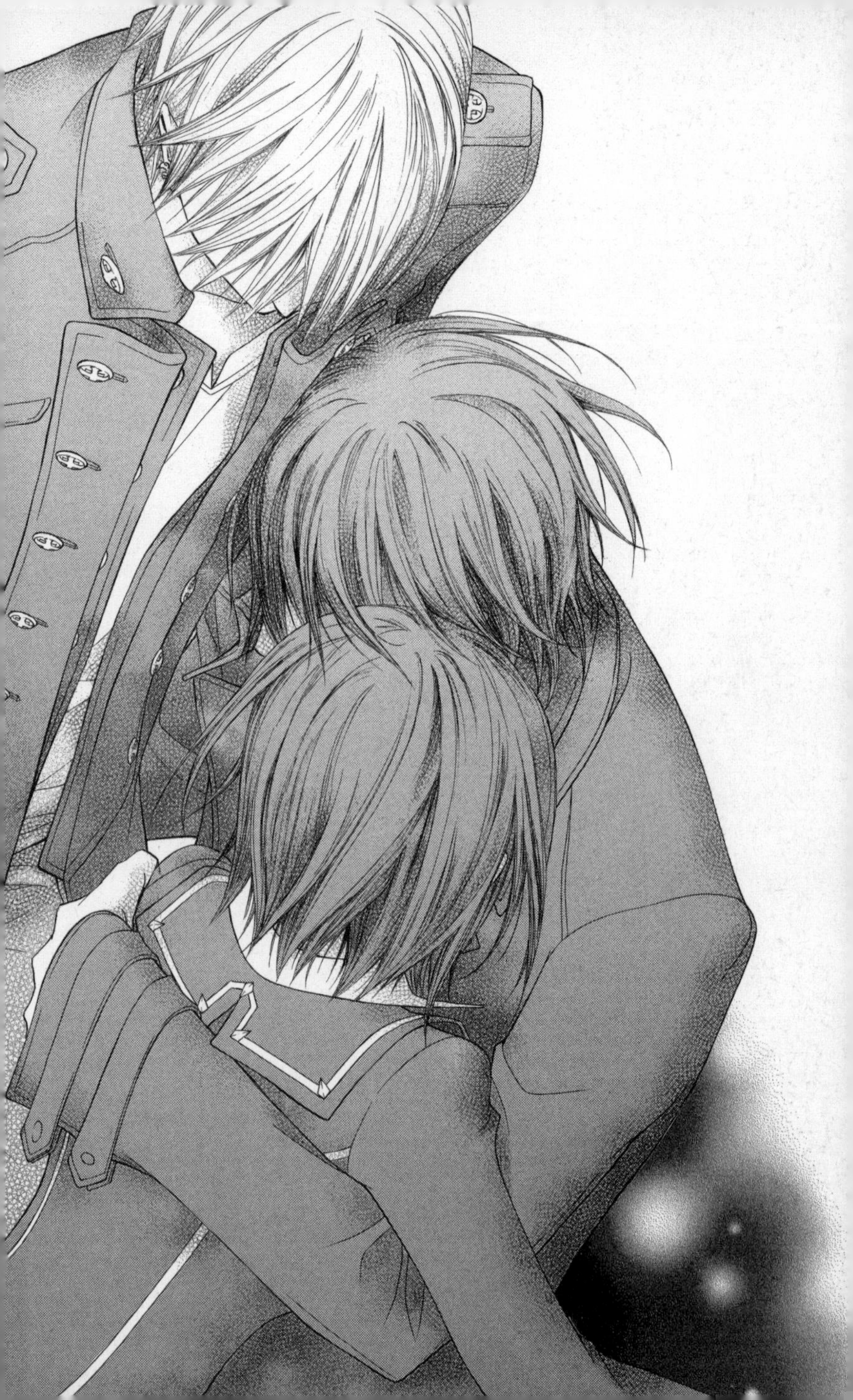

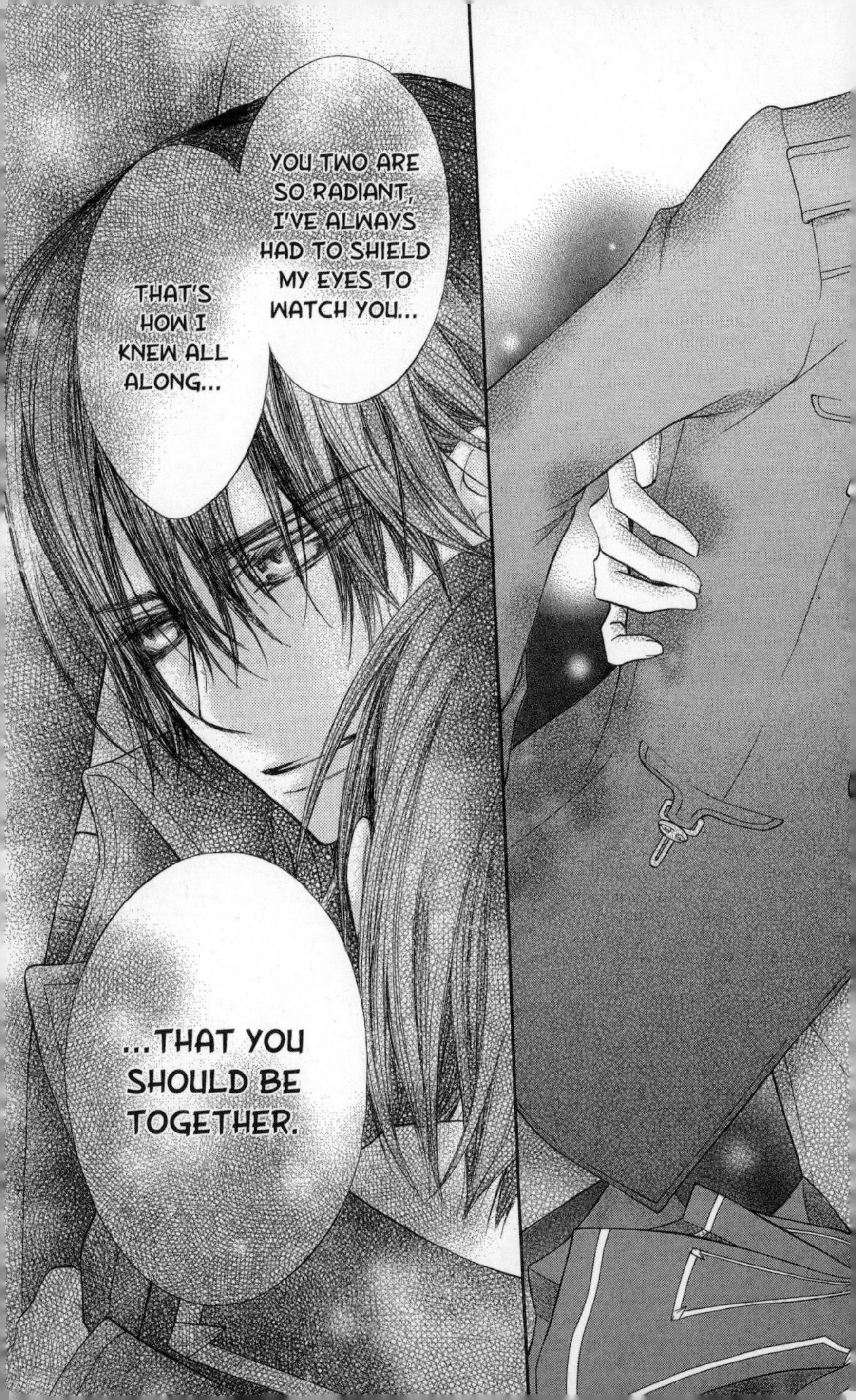
YOU TWO ARE SO RADIANT, I'VE ALWAYS HAD TO SHIELD MY EYES TO WATCH YOU...
THAT'S HOW I KNEW ALL ALONG...
...THAT YOU SHOULD BE TOGETHER.

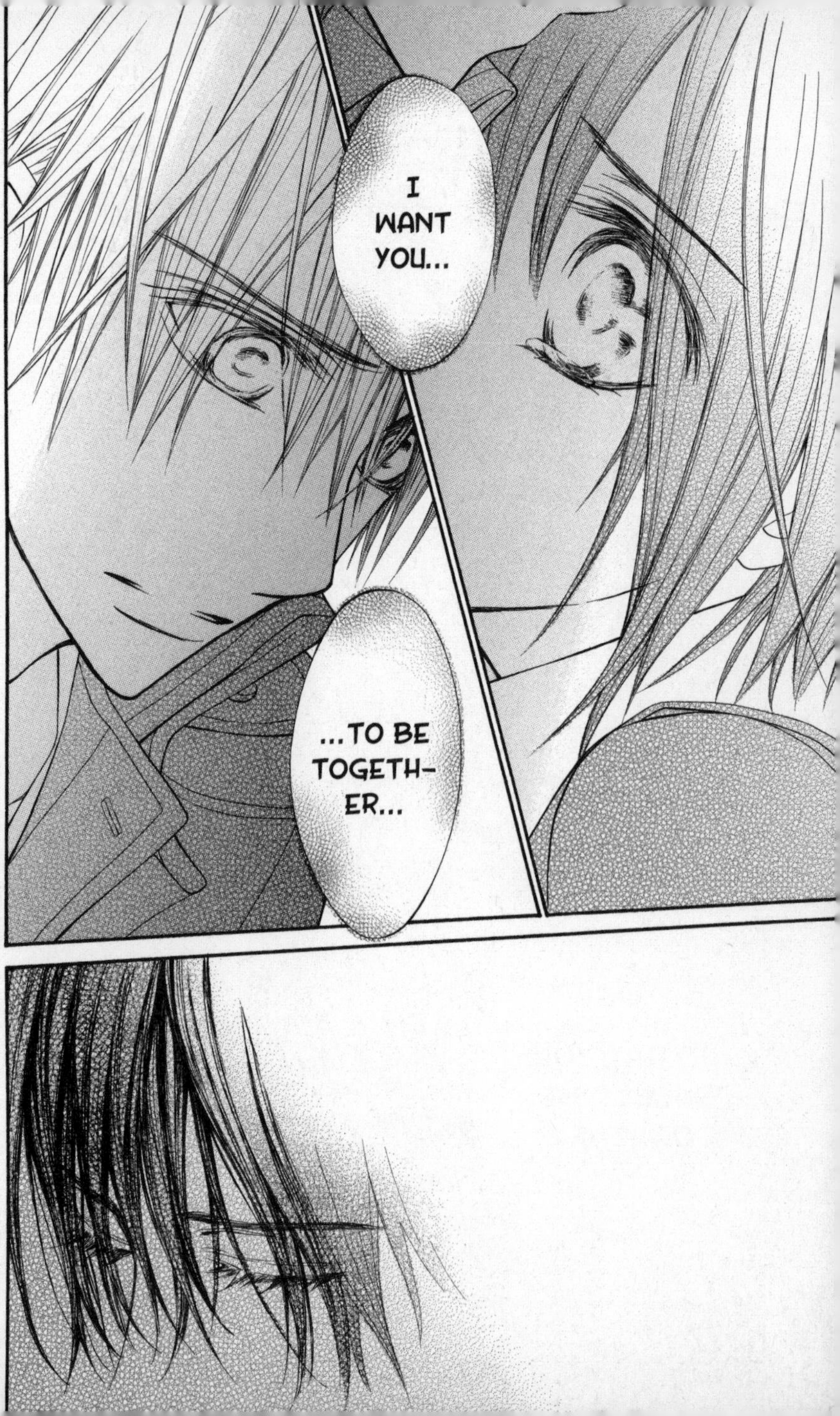
I WANT YOU...
...TO BE TOGETH-ER...

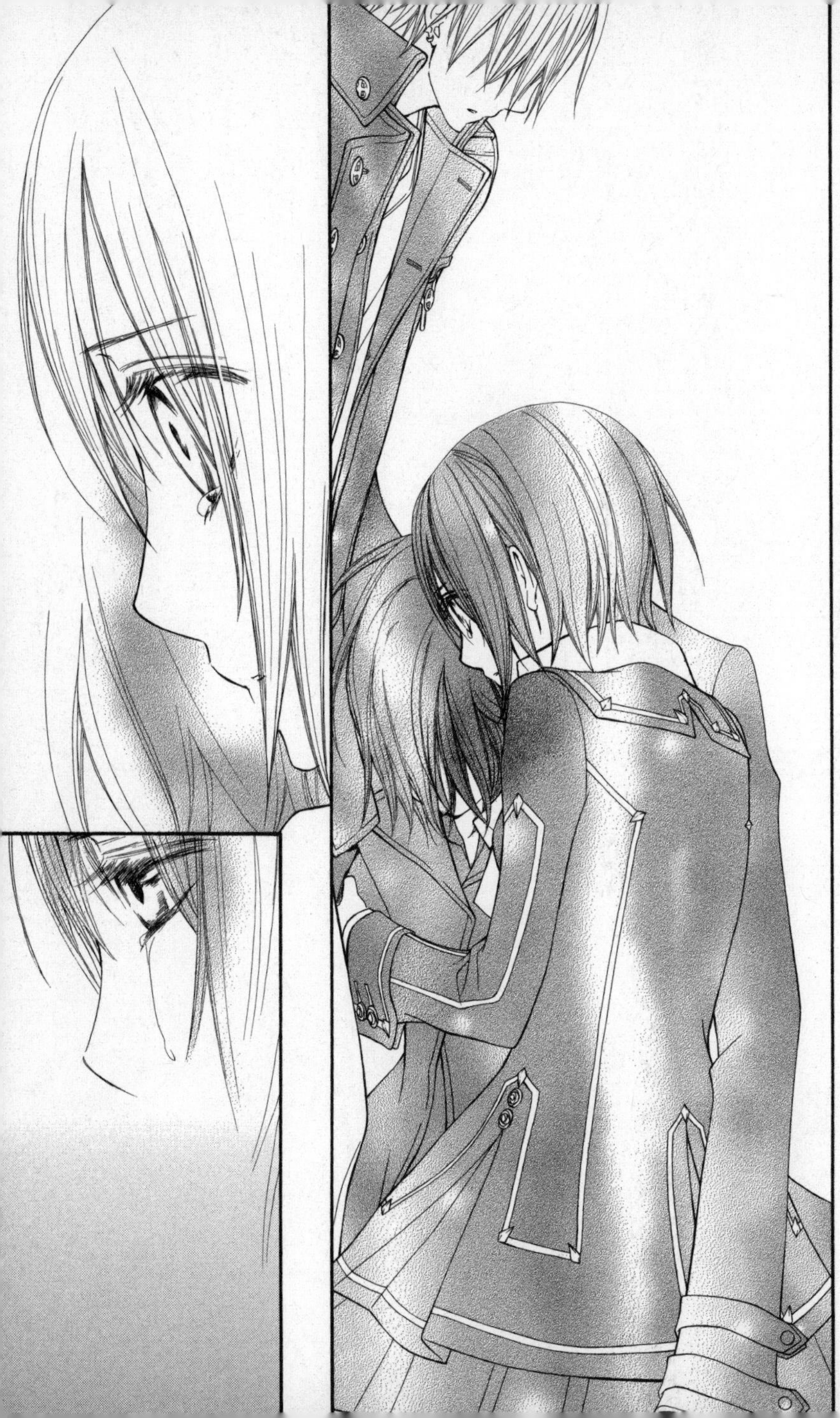

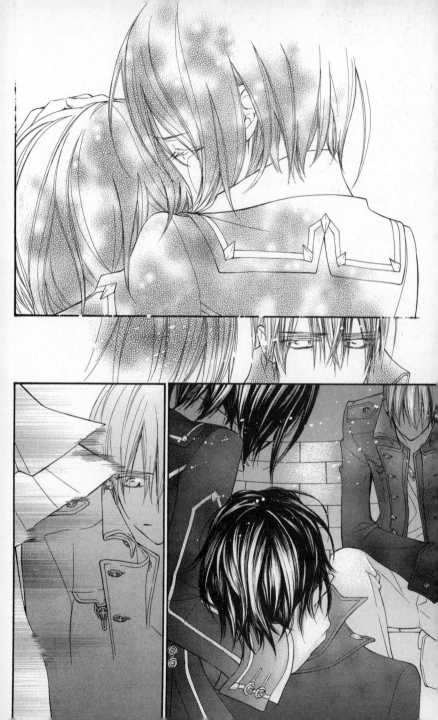

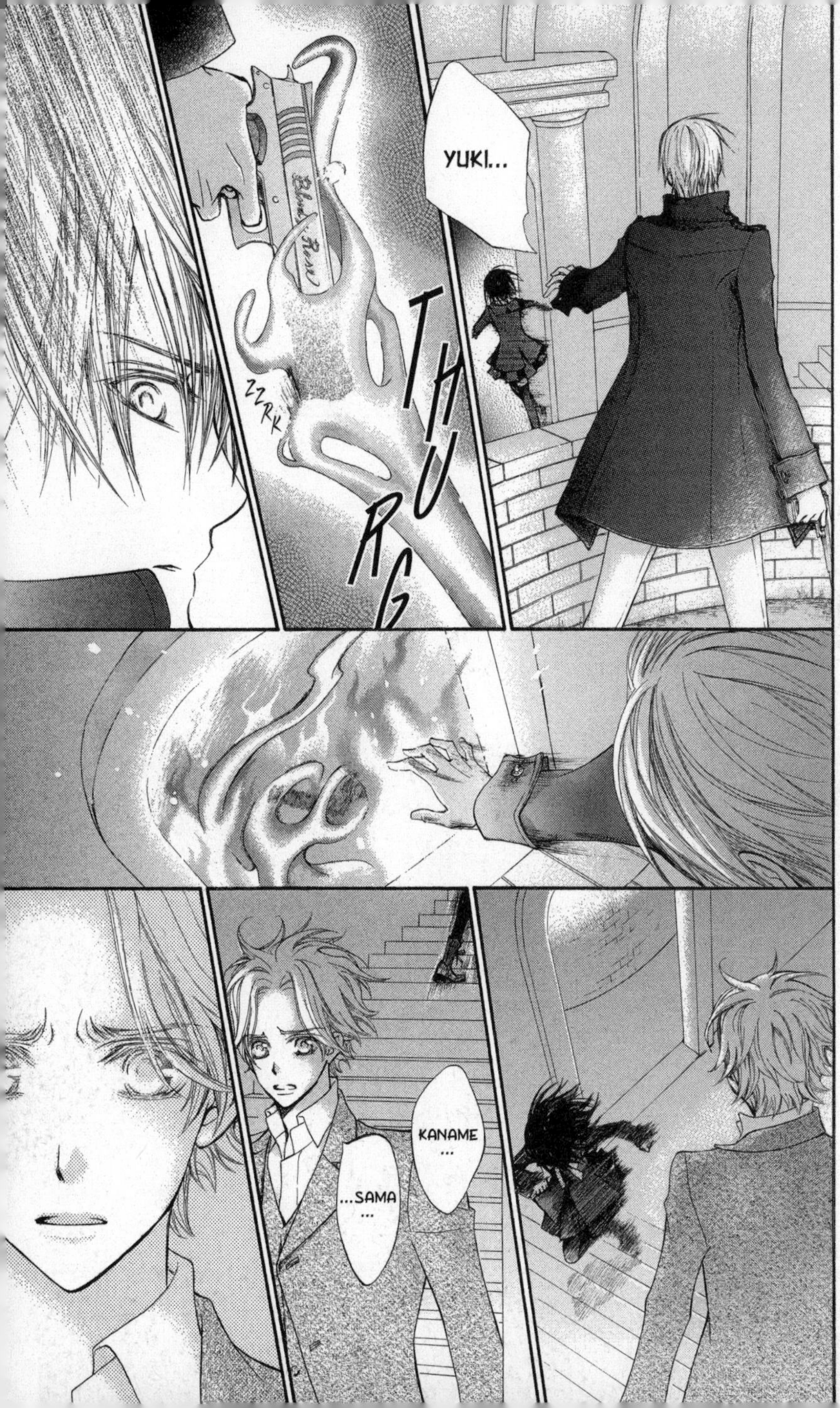
YUKI...
THURG
ZZRK
KANAME ...
...SAMA ...

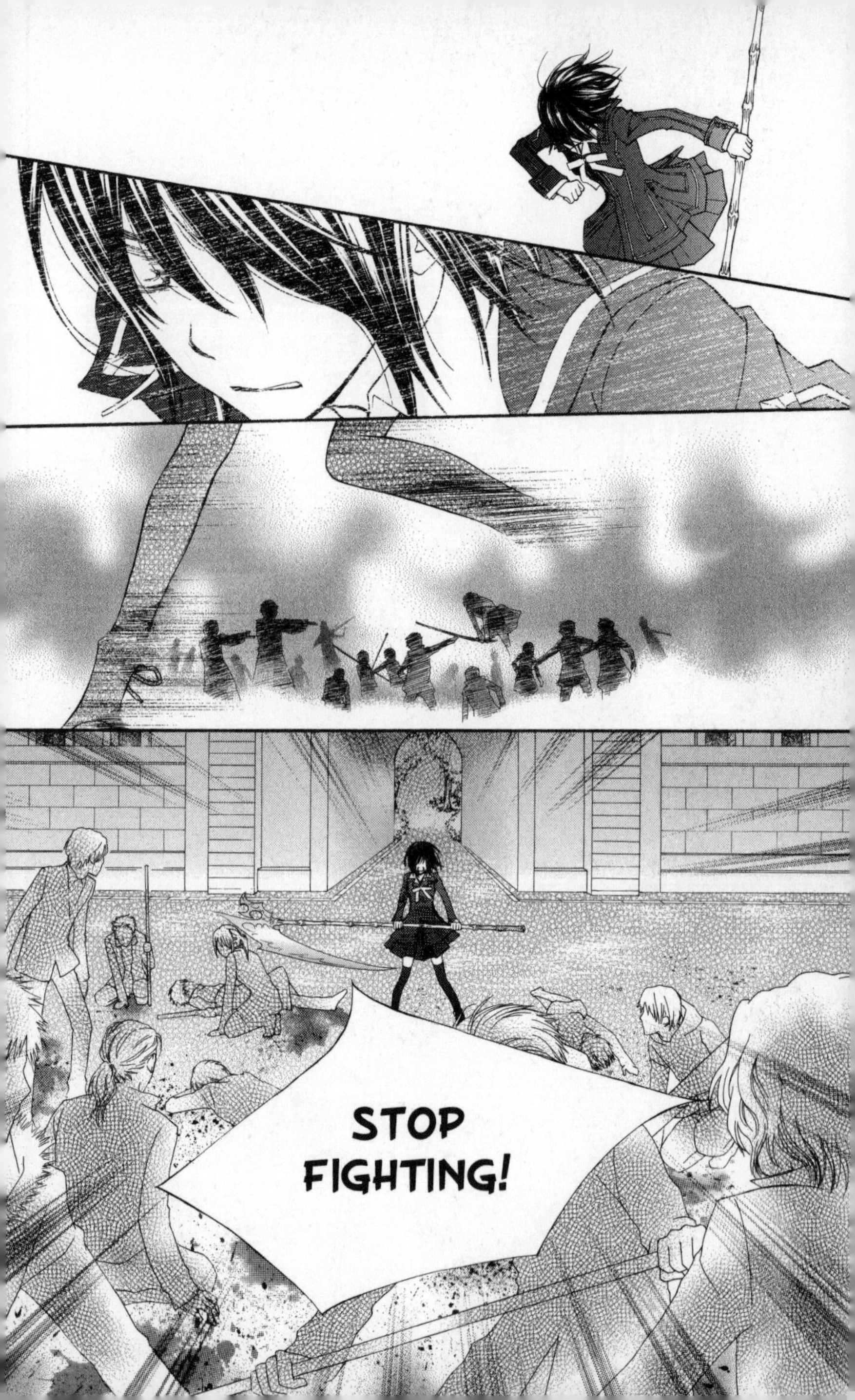
STOP FIGHTING!

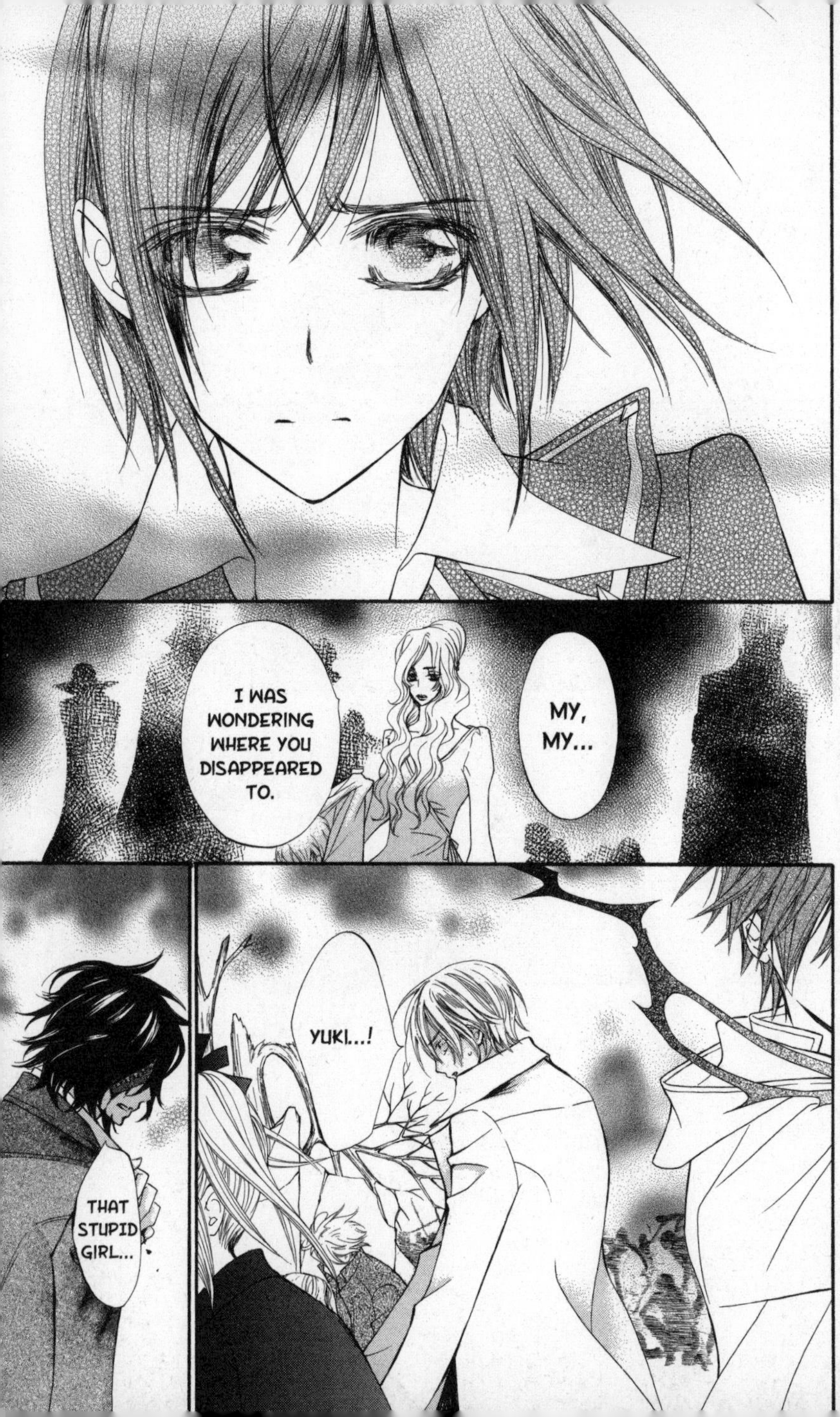

MY, MY...
I WAS WONDERING WHERE YOU DISAPPEARED TO.
YUKI...!
THAT STUPID GIRL...

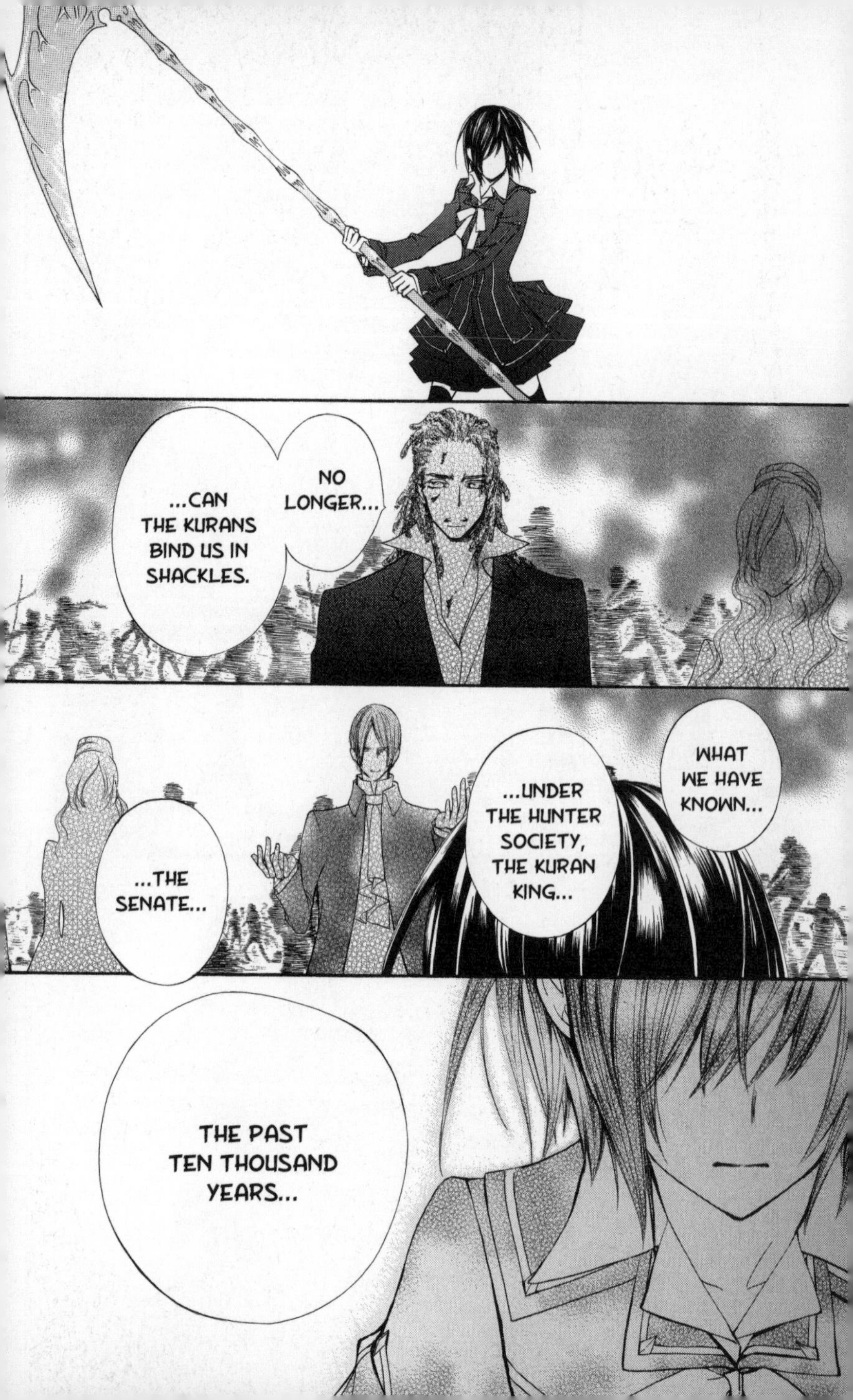
NO LONGER...
...CAN THE KURANS BIND US IN SHACKLES.
WHAT WE HAVE KNOWN...
...UNDER THE HUNTER SOCIETY, THE KURAN KING...
...THE SENATE...
THE PAST TEN THOUSAND YEARS...

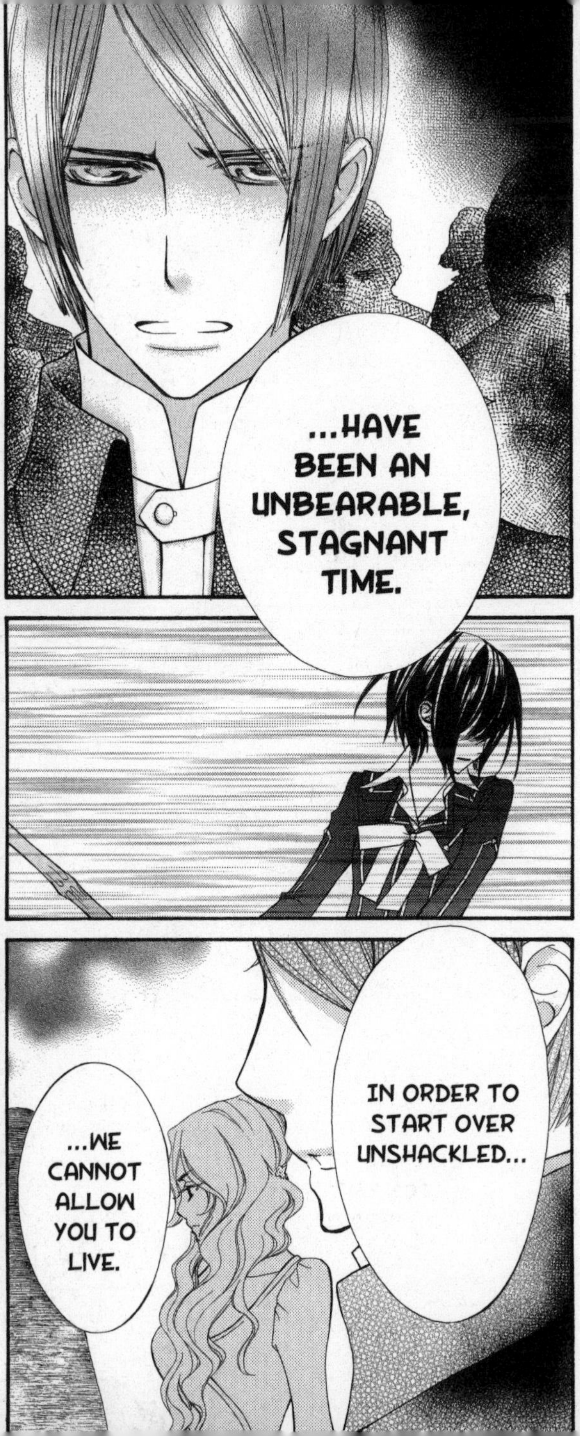
...HAVE BEEN AN UNBEARABLE, STAGNANT TIME.
IN ORDER TO START OVER UNSHACKLED...
...WE CANNOT ALLOW YOU TO LIVE.

IV

One last note.

To tell you the truth, there weren't enough pages in this volume to add a bonus story after the final chapter. (I wanted to...3) But in exchange, I was given the opportunity to draw the cover illustration and write a forty-page manga for *LaLa Fantasy*, which will come out in Japan three days after this volume is published. I hope you will enjoy that story together with this final volume and the third Vampire Knight novel.

[The novel, *Vampire Knight: Fleeting Dreams*, will be published by Shojo Beat in December 2014. The forty-page manga will be released digitally in the same month on vizmanga.com. —Ed.]

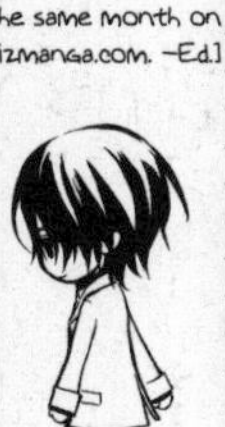

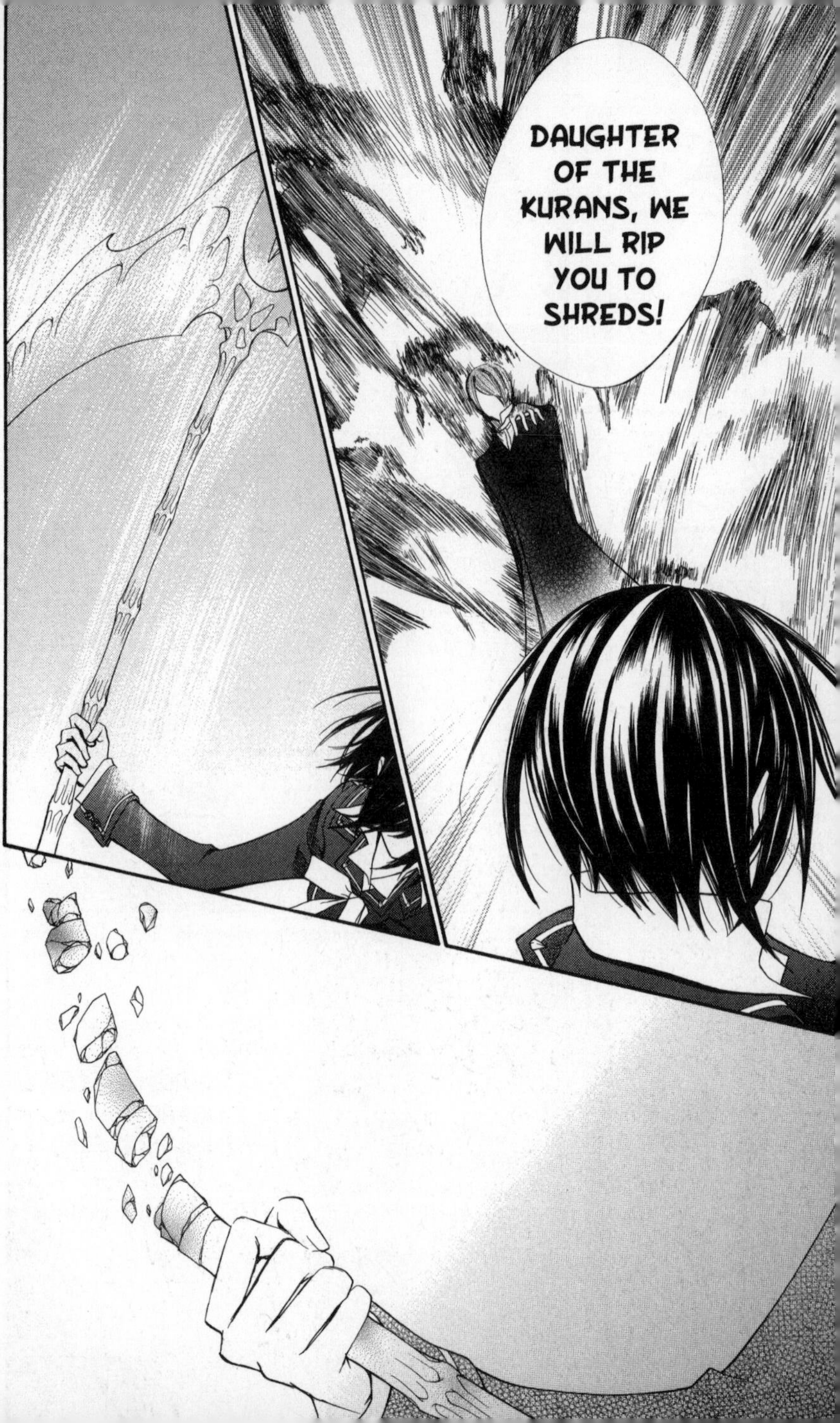
DAUGHTER OF THE KURANS, WE WILL RIP YOU TO SHREDS!

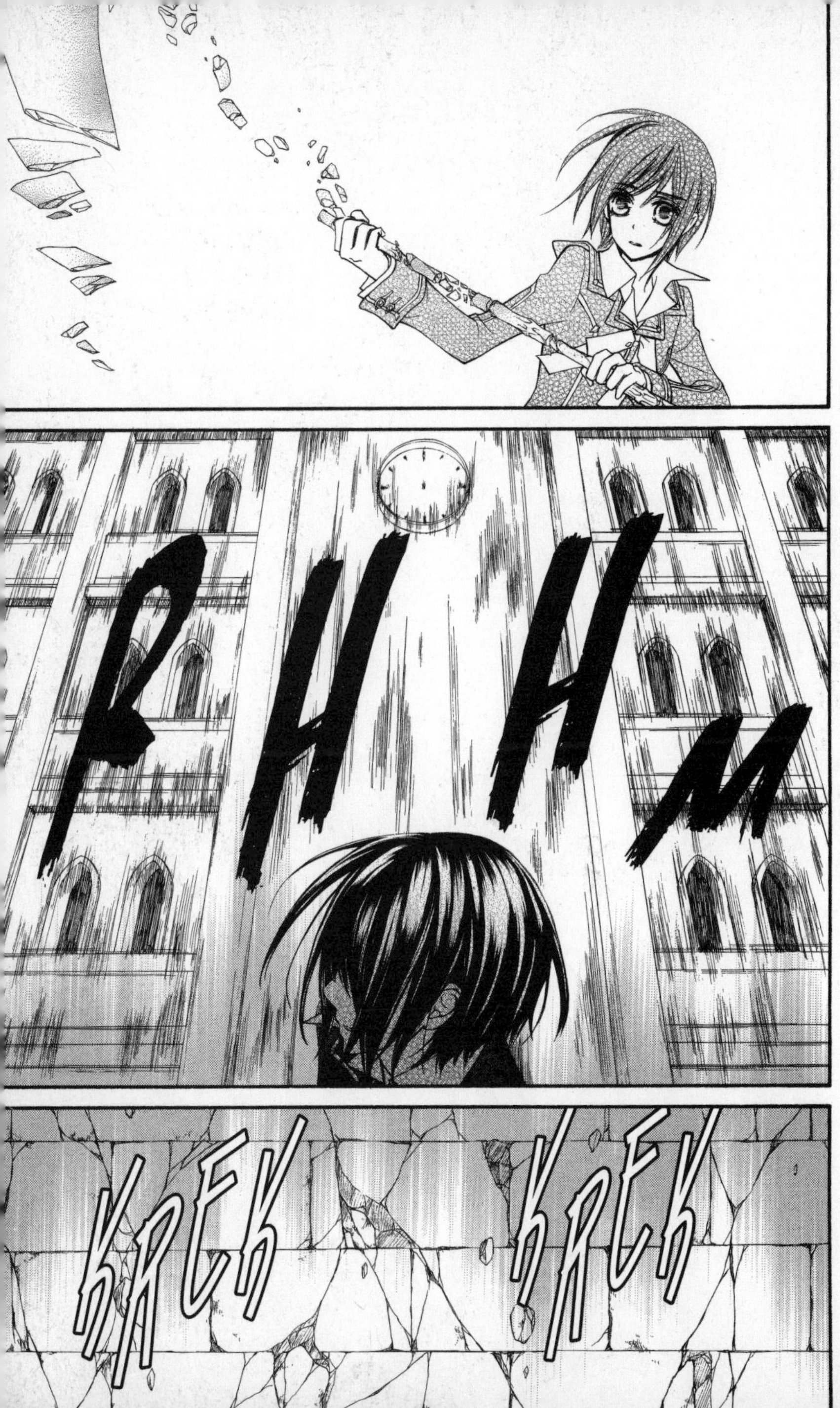
RHHM
KREK KREK

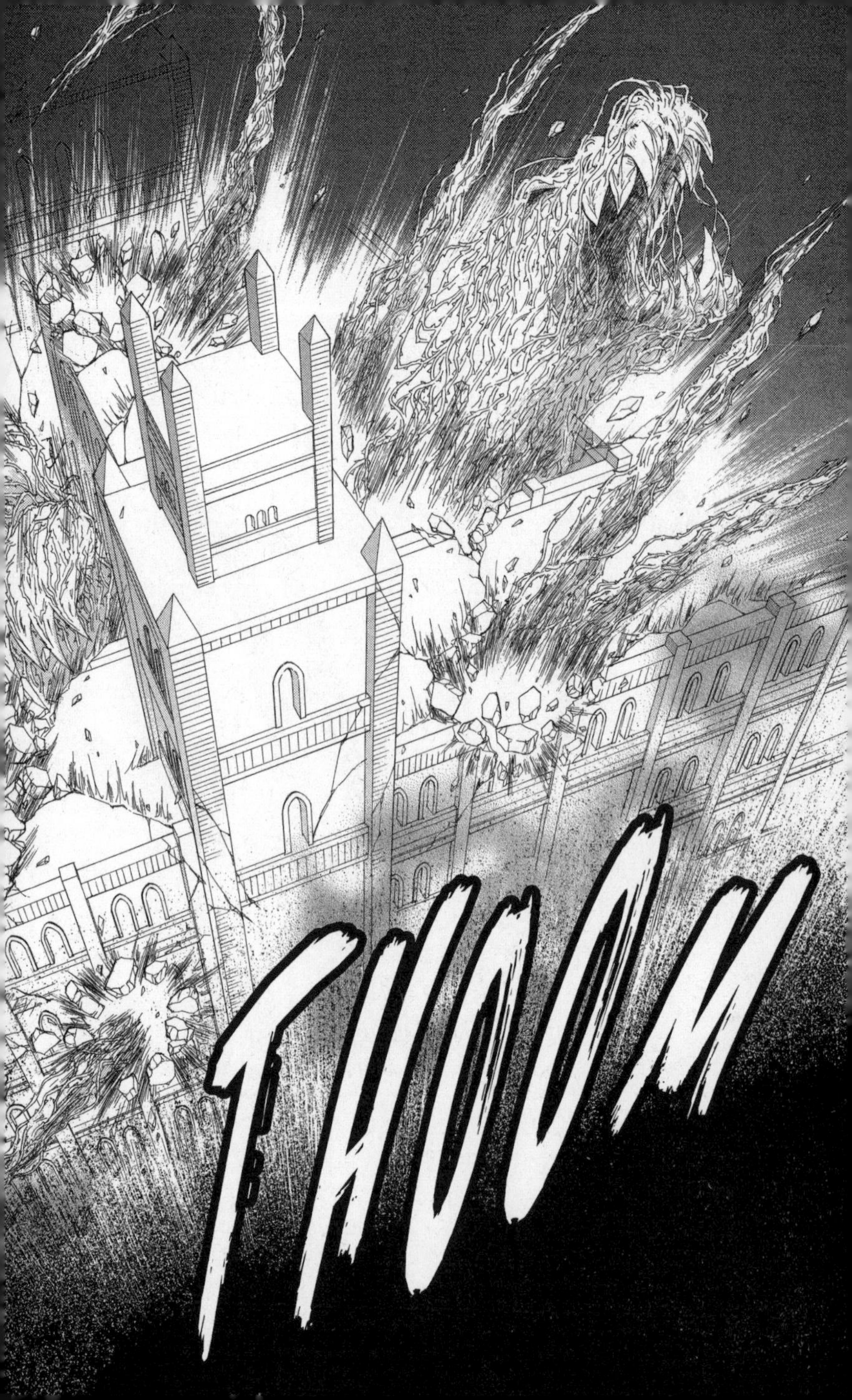
THOOM

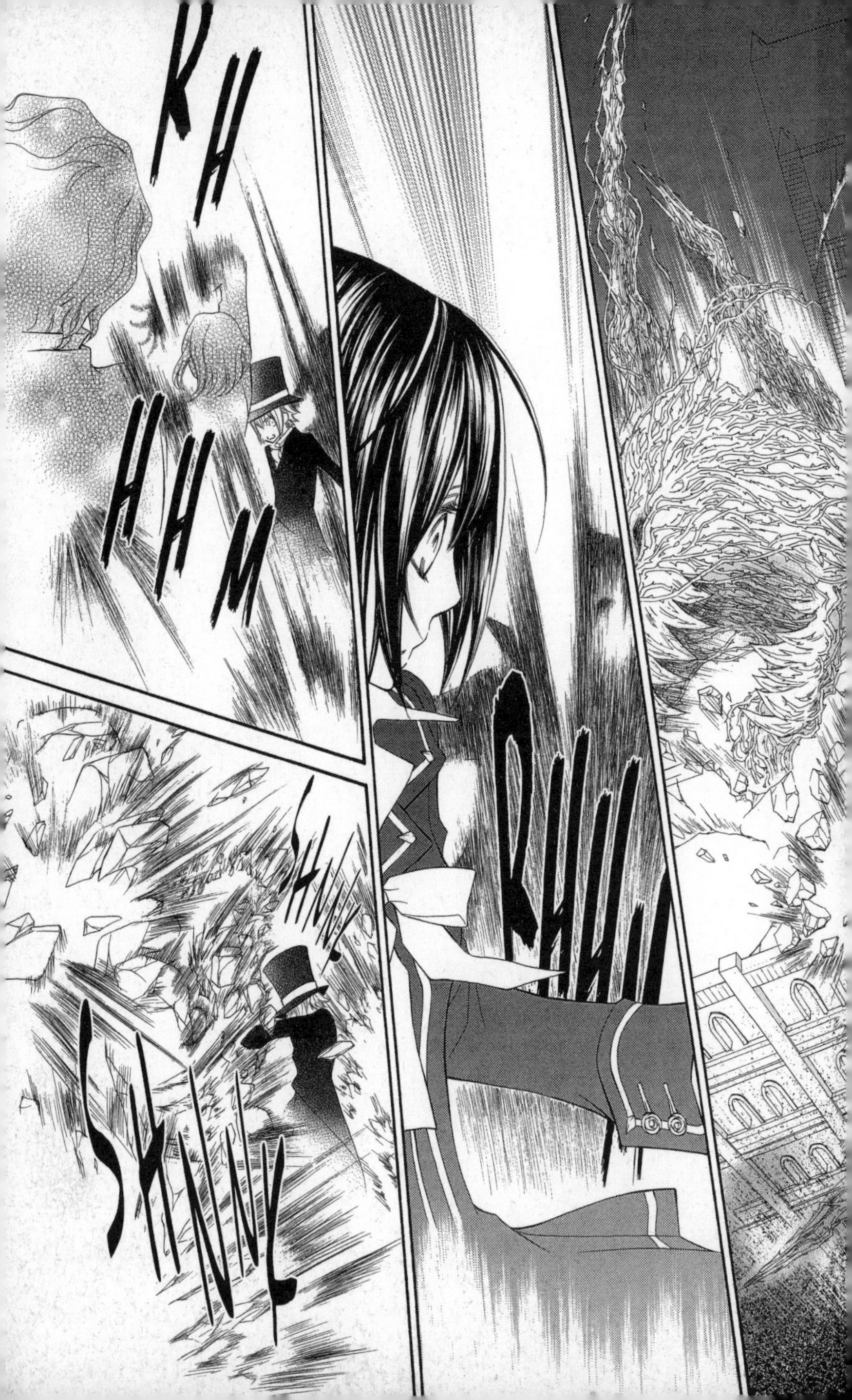
KHHHM
SHNN
SHNNN

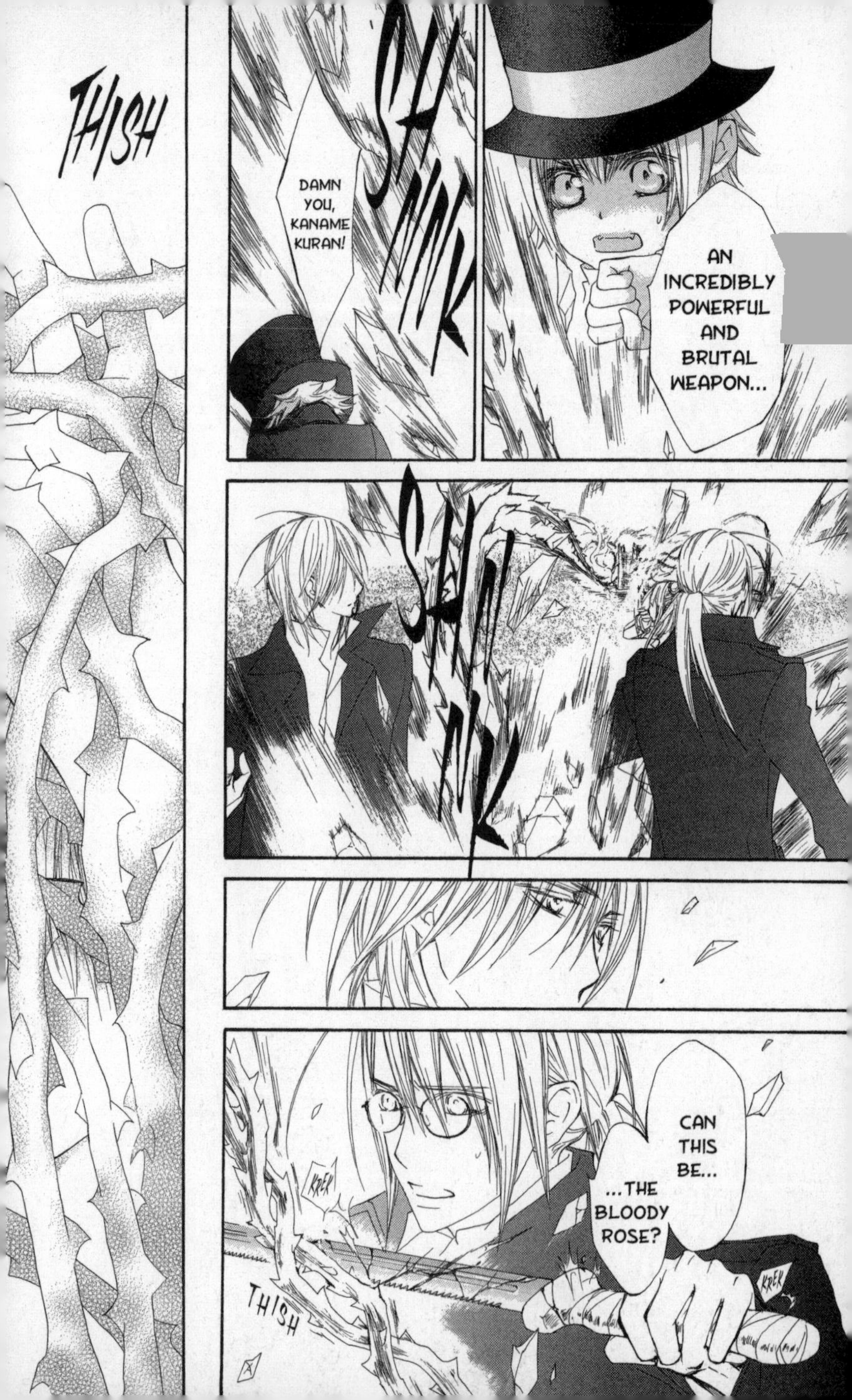

AN INCREDIBLY POWERFUL AND BRUTAL WEAPON...
SHANK
DAMN YOU, KANAME KURAN!
SHANK
CAN THIS BE...
...THE BLOODY ROSE?
KREK
KREK
THISH
THISH

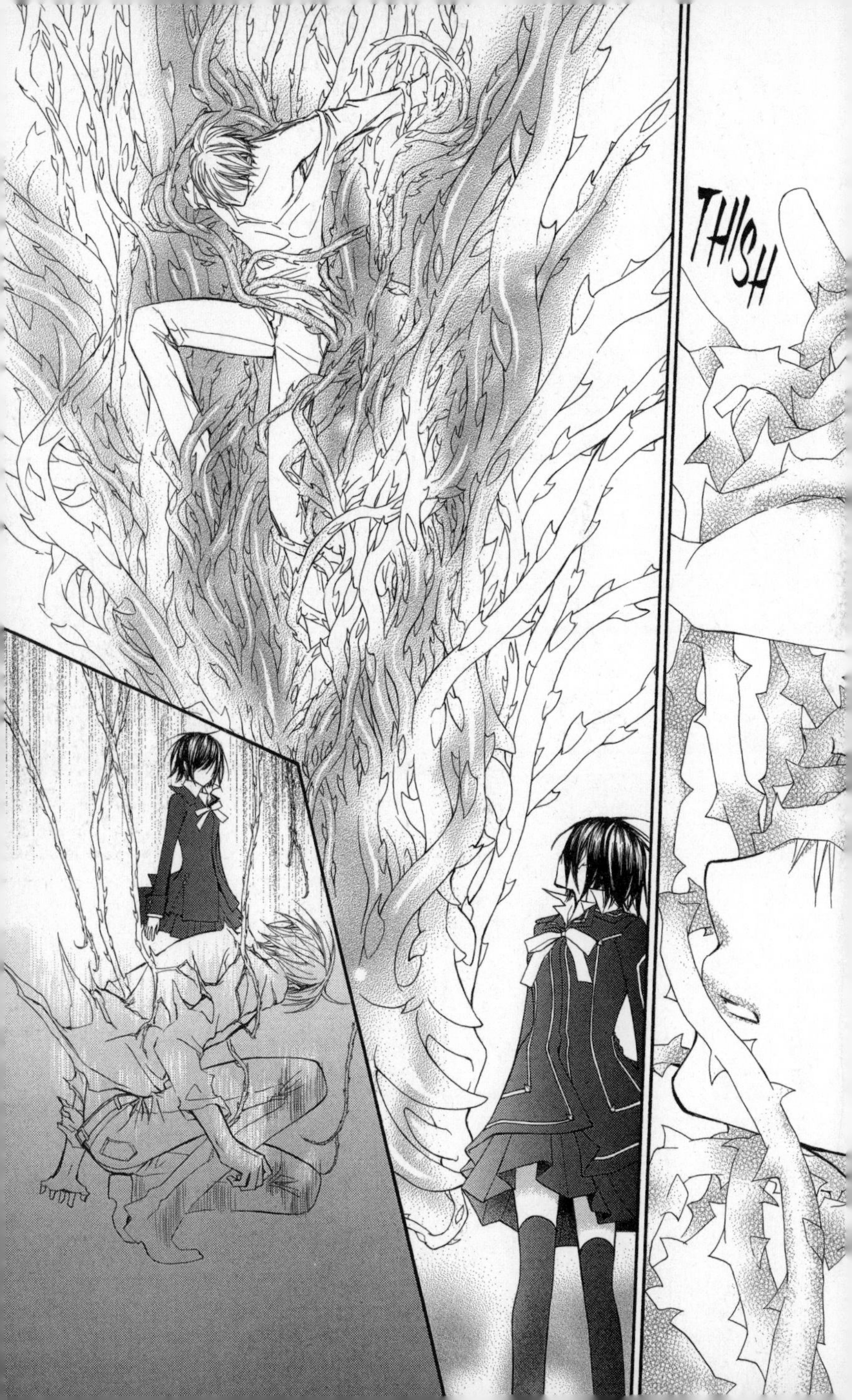
THISH

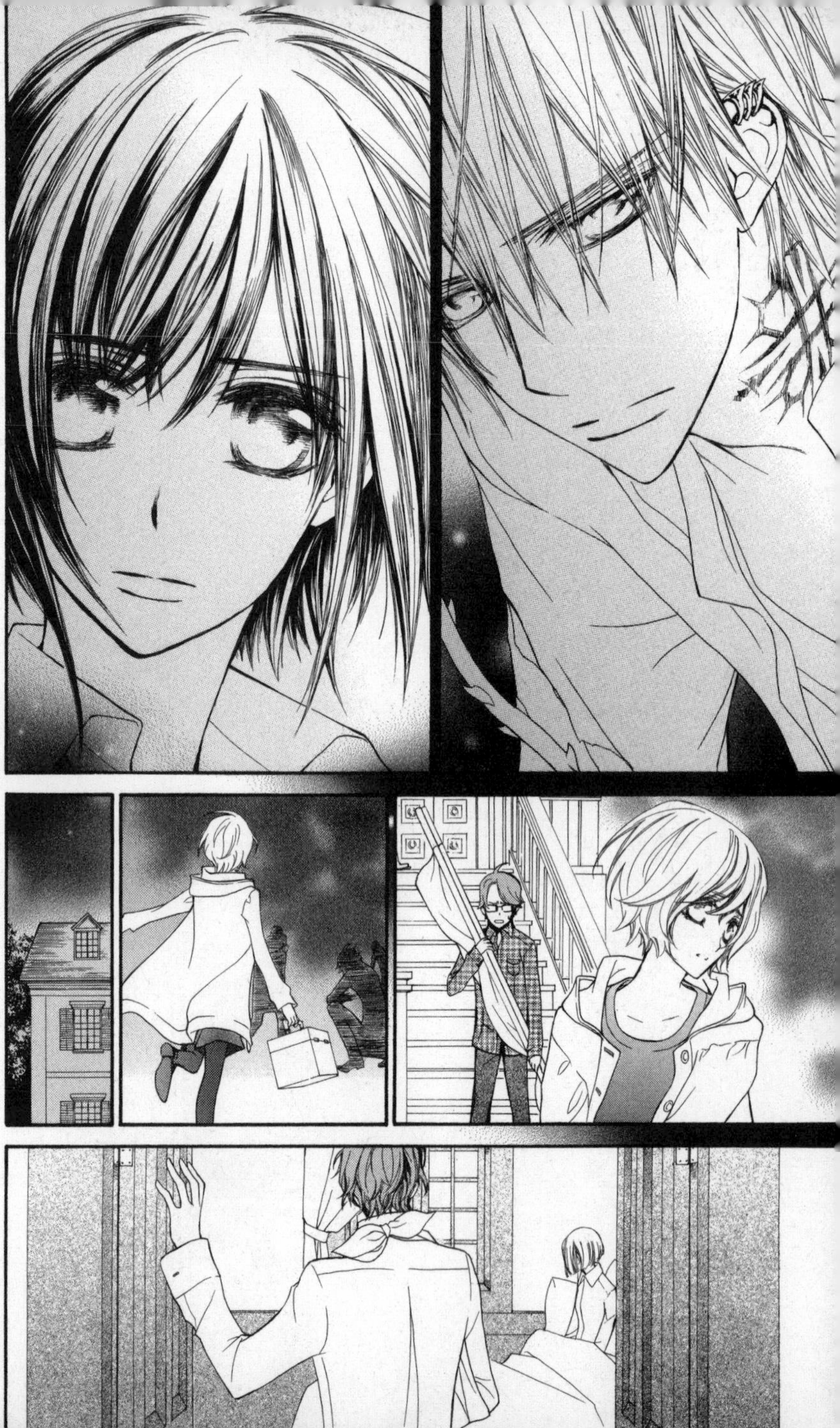

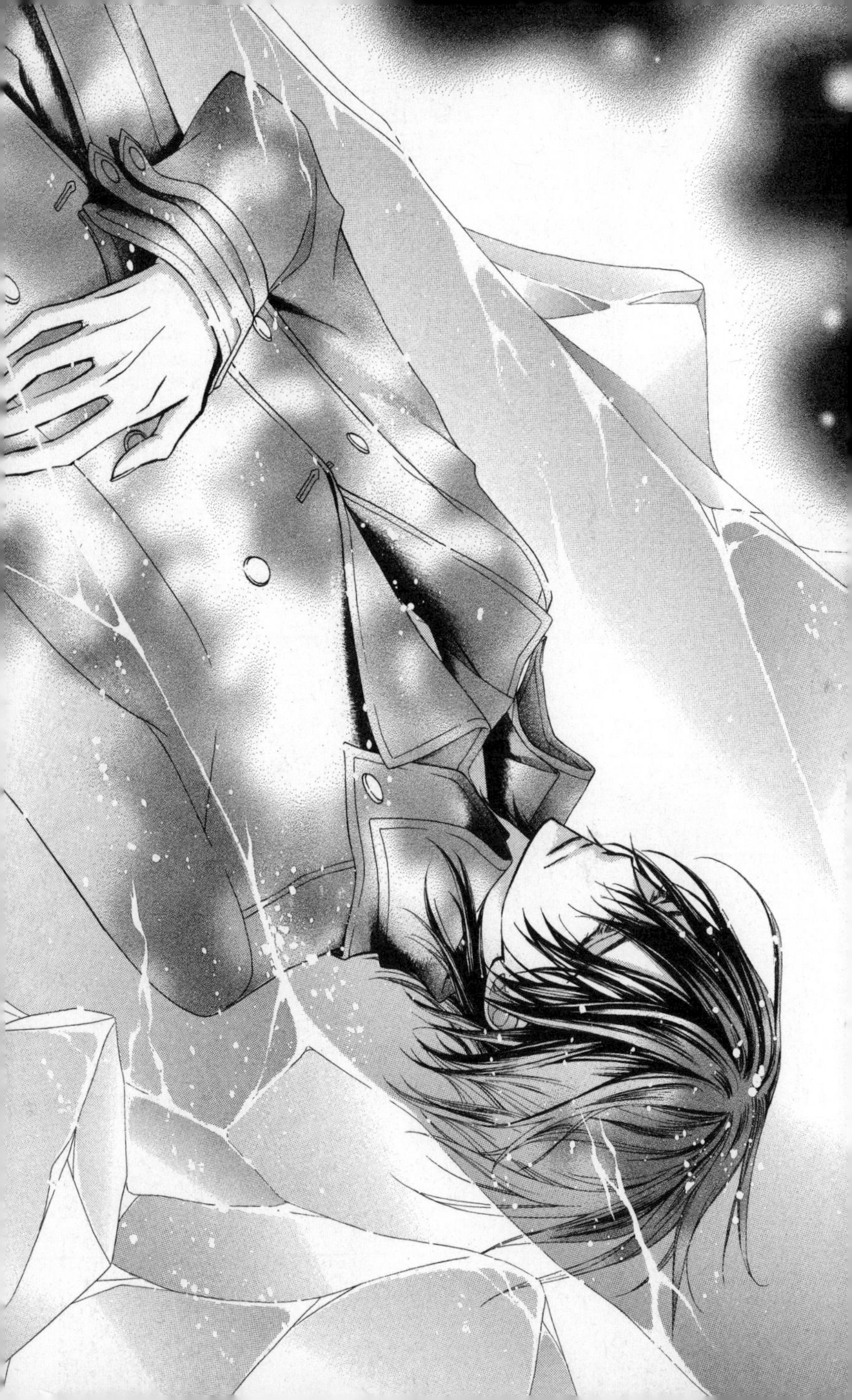

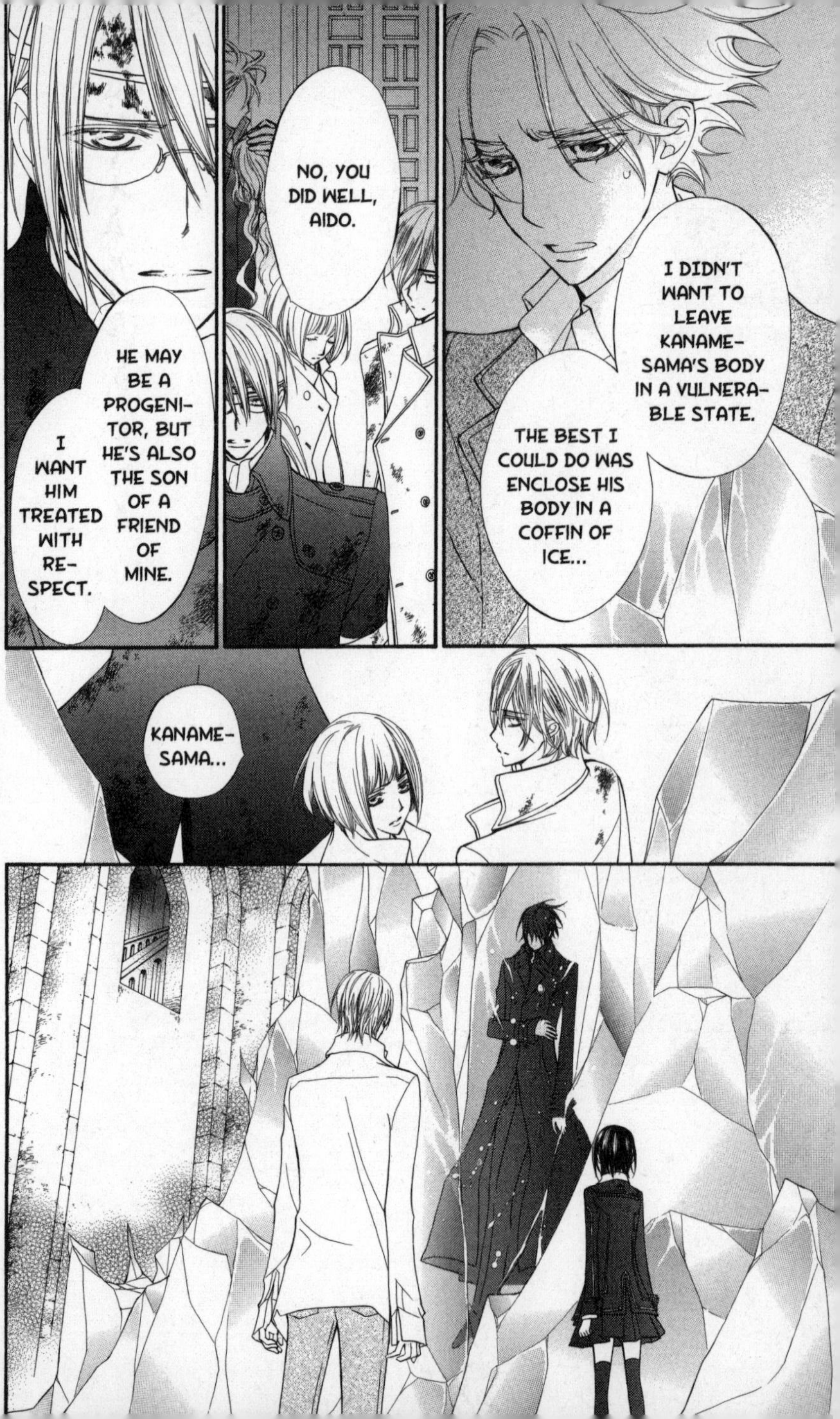
I DIDN'T WANT TO LEAVE KANAME-SAMA'S BODY IN A VULNERA-BLE STATE.
THE BEST I COULD DO WAS ENCLOSE HIS BODY IN A COFFIN OF ICE...
NO, YOU DID WELL, AIDO.
HE MAY BE A PROGENI-TOR, BUT HE'S ALSO THE SON OF A FRIEND OF MINE.
I WANT HIM TREATED WITH RE-SPECT.
KANAME-SAMA...

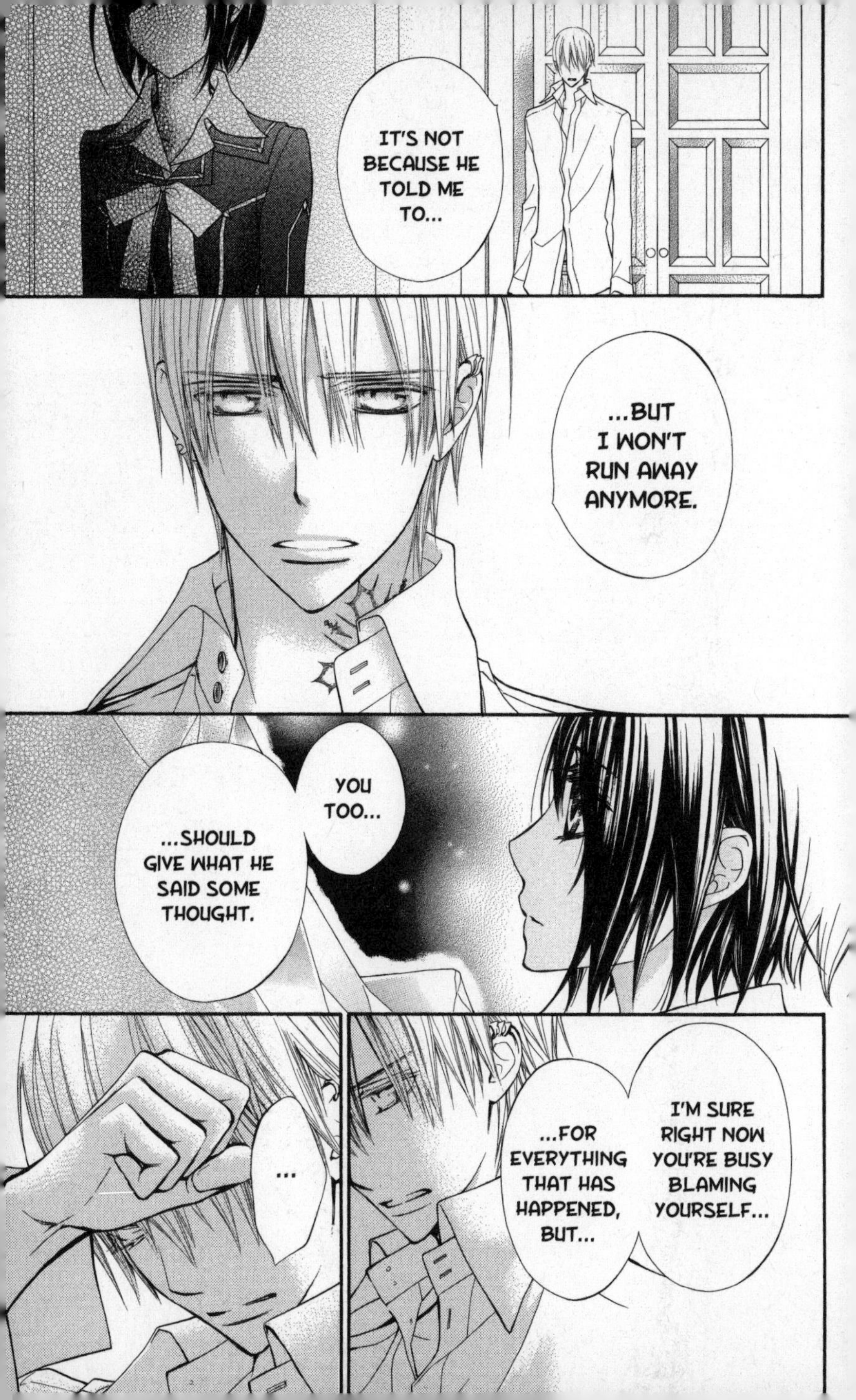
IT'S NOT BECAUSE HE TOLD ME TO...
...BUT I WON'T RUN AWAY ANYMORE.
YOU TOO...
...SHOULD GIVE WHAT HE SAID SOME THOUGHT.
I'M SURE RIGHT NOW YOU'RE BUSY BLAMING YOURSELF...
...FOR EVERYTHING THAT HAS HAPPENED, BUT...
...

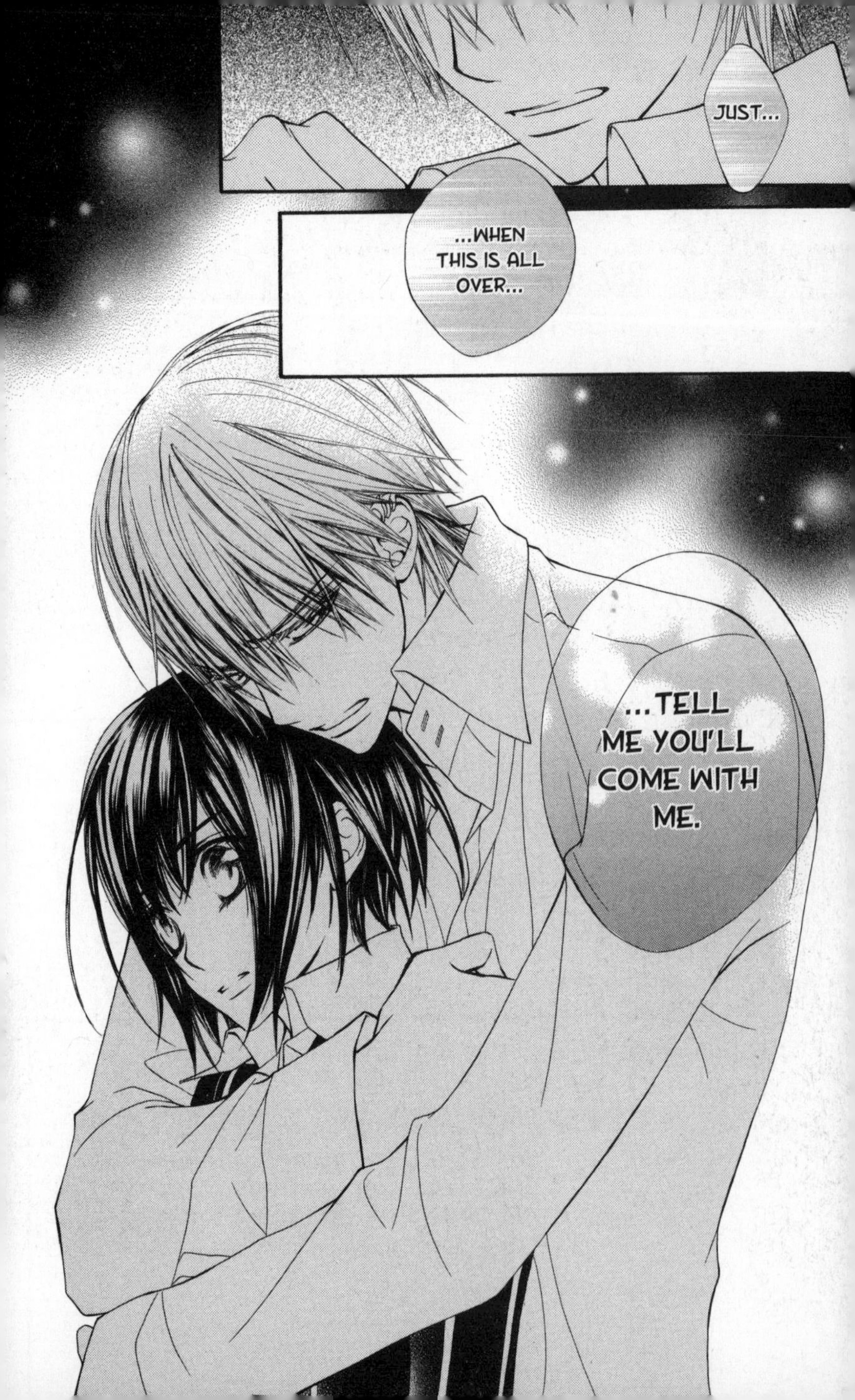
JUST...
...WHEN THIS IS ALL OVER...
...TELL ME YOU'LL COME WITH ME.

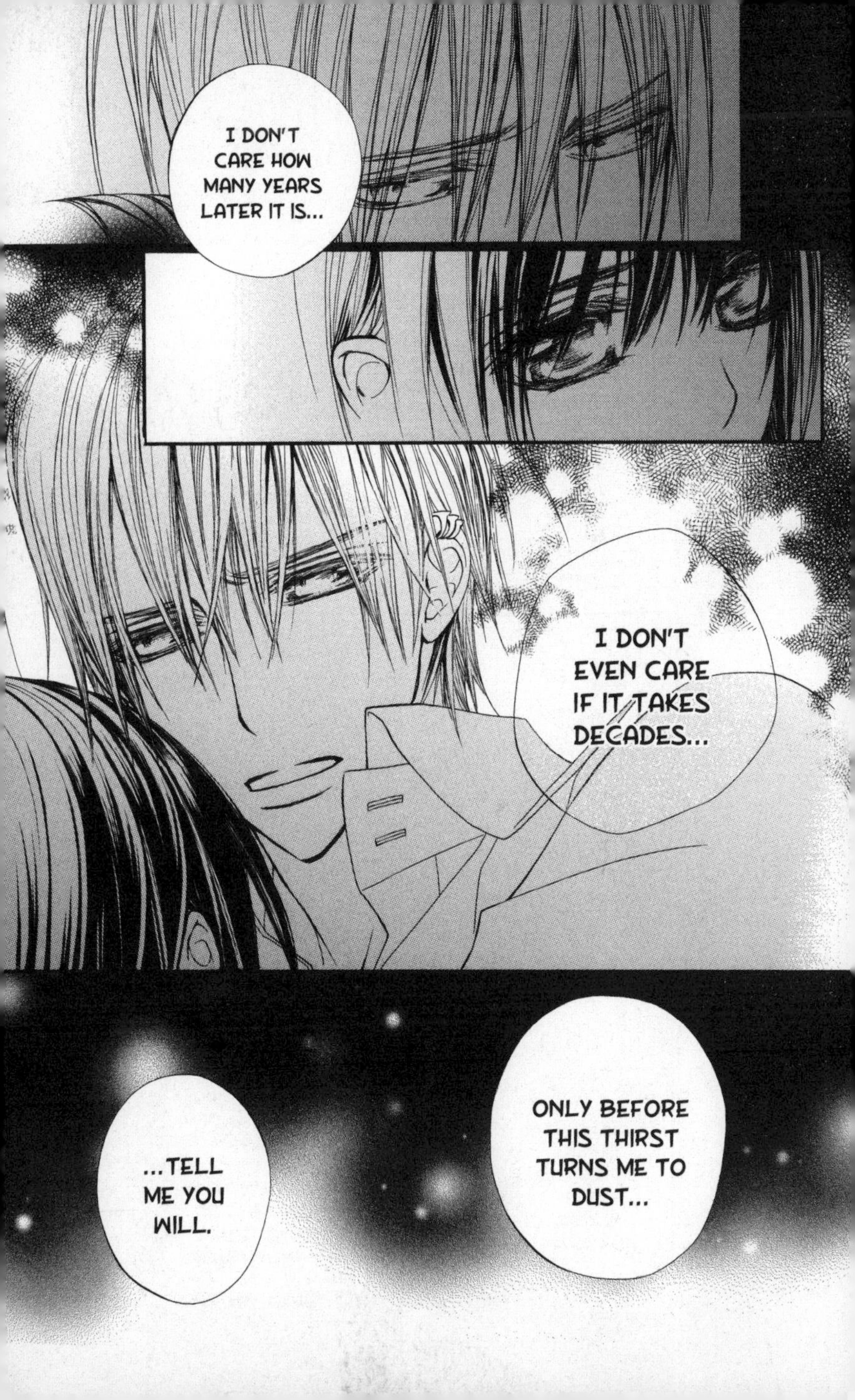
I DON'T CARE HOW MANY YEARS LATER IT IS...
I DON'T EVEN CARE IF IT TAKES DECADES...
ONLY BEFORE THIS THIRST TURNS ME TO DUST...
...TELL ME YOU WILL.

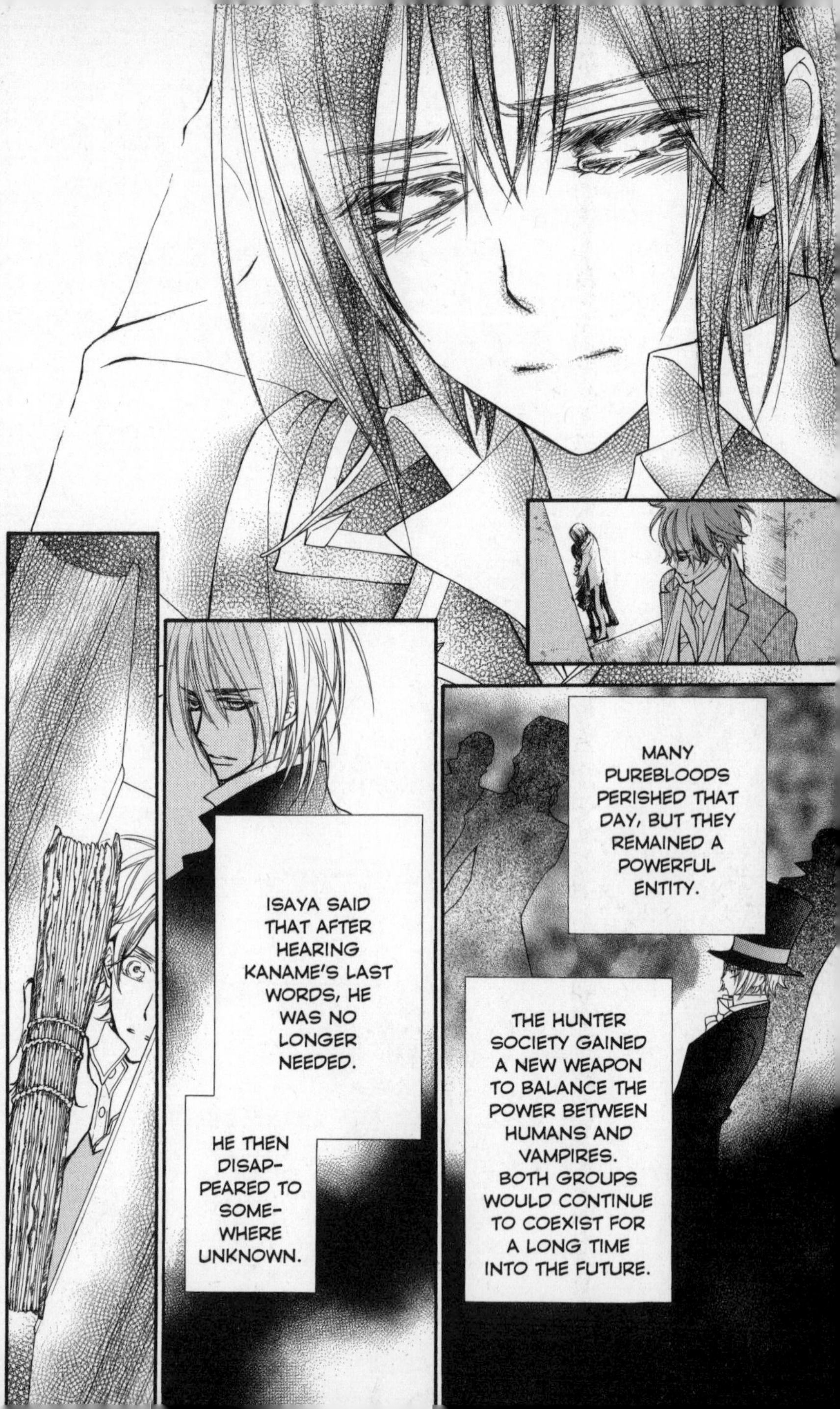
MANY PUREBLOODS PERISHED THAT DAY, BUT THEY REMAINED A POWERFUL ENTITY.
THE HUNTER SOCIETY GAINED A NEW WEAPON TO BALANCE THE POWER BETWEEN HUMANS AND VAMPIRES. BOTH GROUPS WOULD CONTINUE TO COEXIST FOR A LONG TIME INTO THE FUTURE.
ISAYA SAID THAT AFTER HEARING KANAME'S LAST WORDS, HE WAS NO LONGER NEEDED.
HE THEN DISAP-PEARED TO SOME-WHERE UNKNOWN.

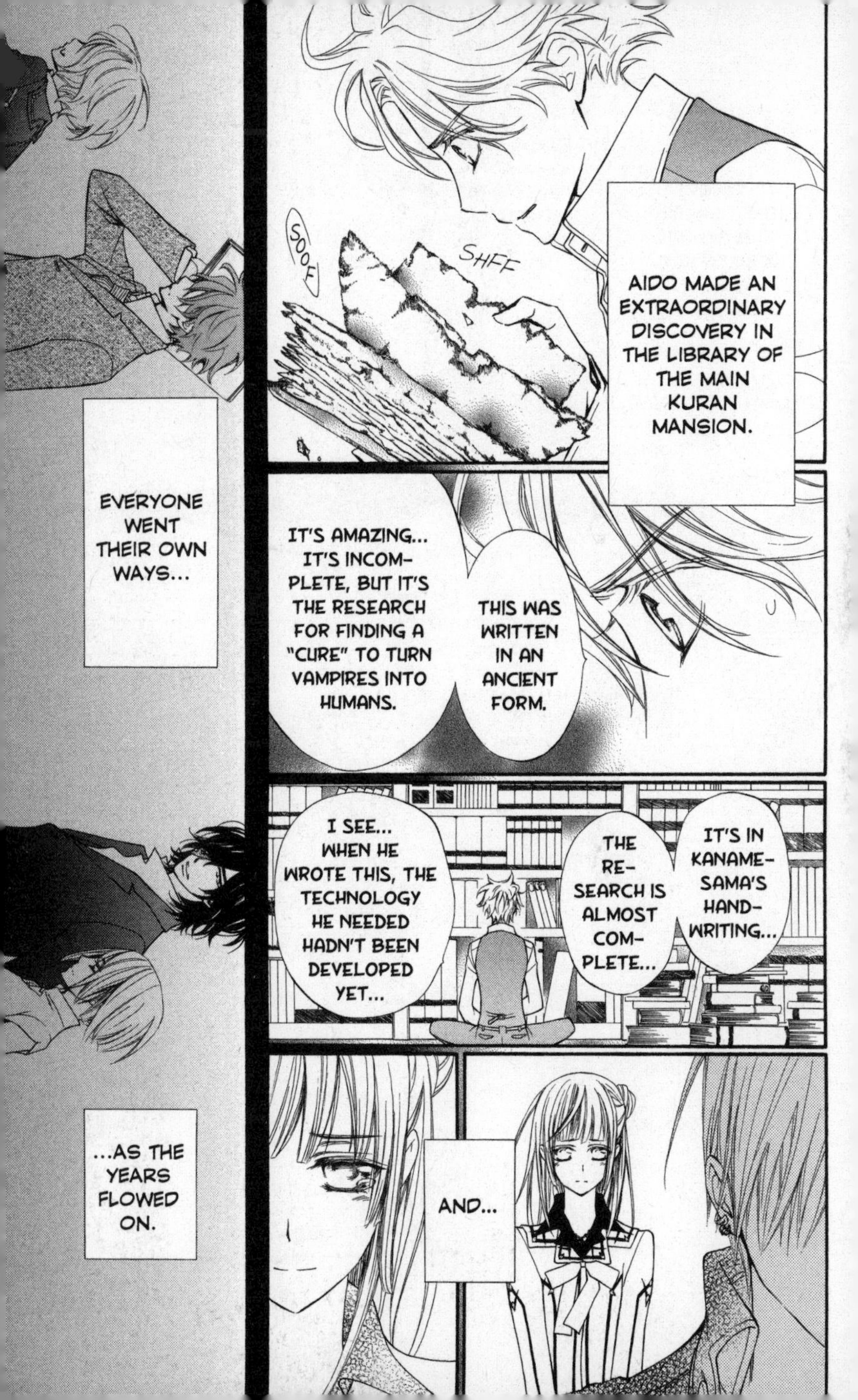
AIDO MADE AN EXTRAORDINARY DISCOVERY IN THE LIBRARY OF THE MAIN KURAN MANSION.
SHFF
SOOOF
THIS WAS WRITTEN IN AN ANCIENT FORM.
IT'S AMAZING... IT'S INCOMPLETE, BUT IT'S THE RESEARCH FOR FINDING A "CURE" TO TURN VAMPIRES INTO HUMANS.
IT'S IN KANAME-SAMA'S HANDWRITING...
THE RESEARCH IS ALMOST COMPLETE...
I SEE... WHEN HE WROTE THIS, THE TECHNOLOGY HE NEEDED HADN'T BEEN DEVELOPED YET...
AND...
EVERYONE WENT THEIR OWN WAYS...
...AS THE YEARS FLOWED ON.

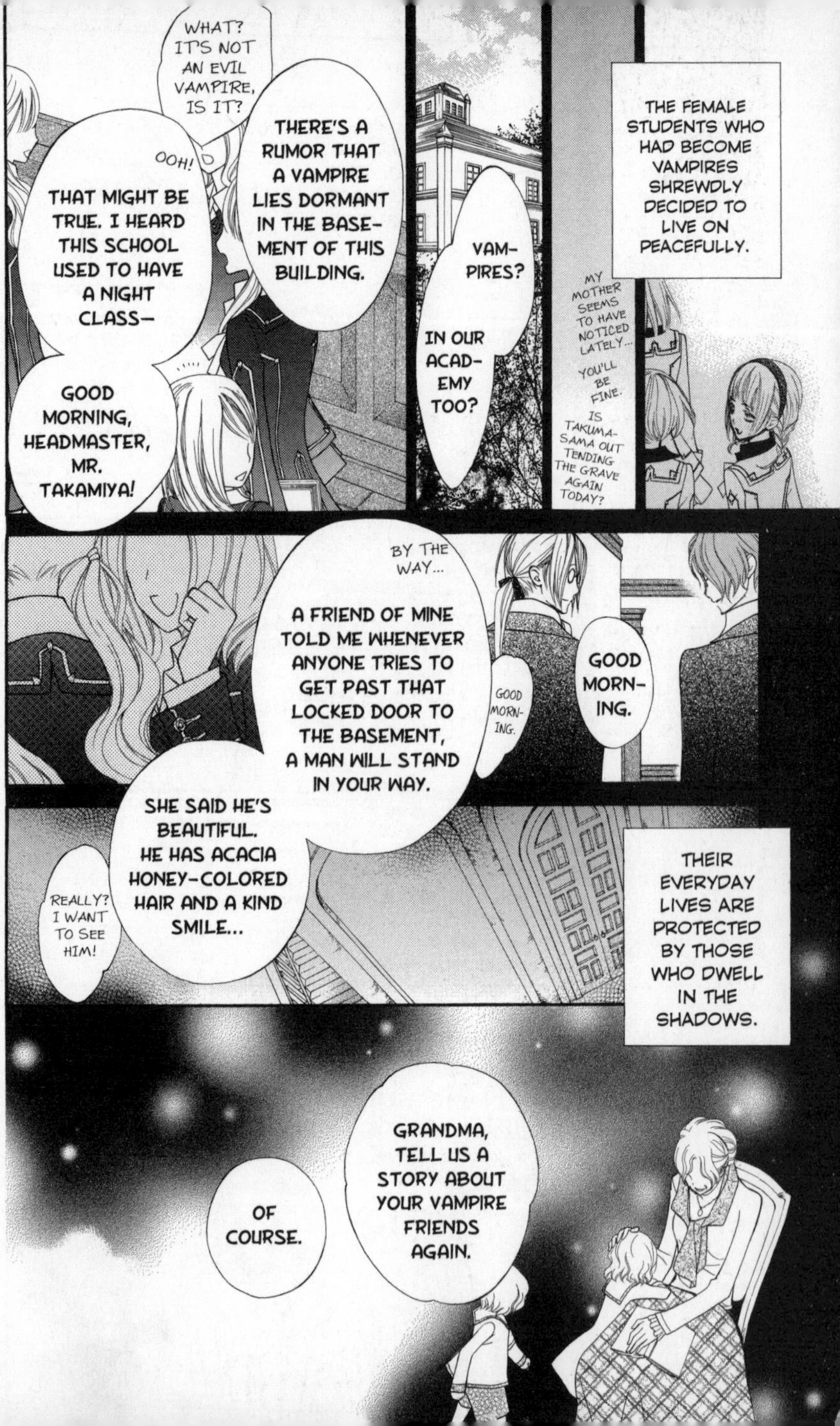
THE FEMALE STUDENTS WHO HAD BECOME VAMPIRES SHREWDLY DECIDED TO LIVE ON PEACEFULLY.
MY MOTHER SEEMS TO HAVE NOTICED LATELY...
YOU'LL BE FINE.
IS TAKUMA-SAMA OUT TENDING THE GRAVE AGAIN TODAY?
VAMPIRES?
IN OUR ACADEMY TOO?
WHAT? IT'S NOT AN EVIL VAMPIRE, IS IT?
THERE'S A RUMOR THAT A VAMPIRE LIES DORMANT IN THE BASEMENT OF THIS BUILDING.
OOH!
THAT MIGHT BE TRUE. I HEARD THIS SCHOOL USED TO HAVE A NIGHT CLASS—
GOOD MORNING, HEADMASTER, MR. TAKAMIYA!
GOOD MORNING.
GOOD MORNING.
BY THE WAY...
A FRIEND OF MINE TOLD ME WHENEVER ANYONE TRIES TO GET PAST THAT LOCKED DOOR TO THE BASEMENT, A MAN WILL STAND IN YOUR WAY.
THEIR EVERYDAY LIVES ARE PROTECTED BY THOSE WHO DWELL IN THE SHADOWS.
SHE SAID HE'S BEAUTIFUL. HE HAS ACACIA HONEY-COLORED HAIR AND A KIND SMILE...
REALLY? I WANT TO SEE HIM!
GRANDMA, TELL US A STORY ABOUT YOUR VAMPIRE FRIENDS AGAIN.
OF COURSE.

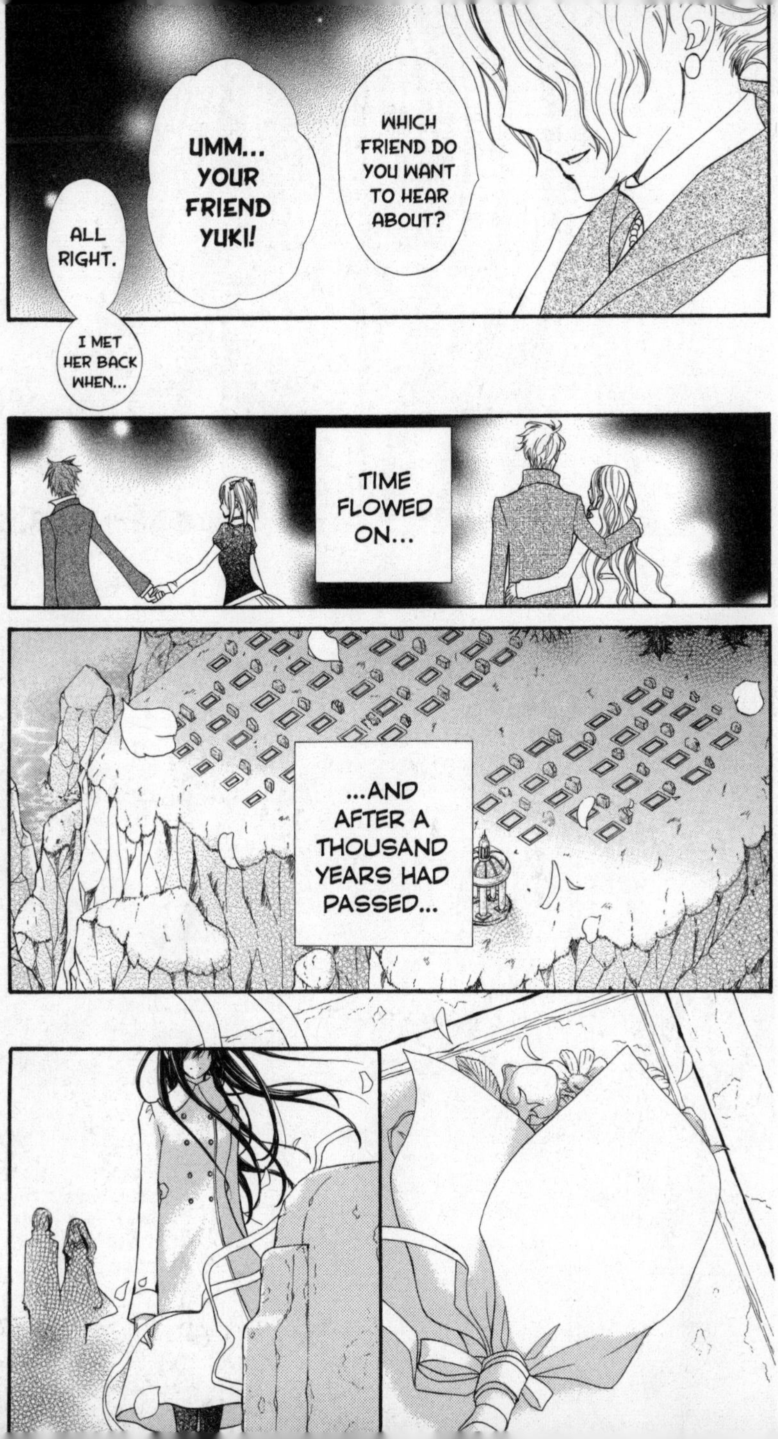
WHICH FRIEND DO YOU WANT TO HEAR ABOUT?
UMM... YOUR FRIEND YUKI!
ALL RIGHT.
I MET HER BACK WHEN...
TIME FLOWED ON...
...AND AFTER A THOUSAND YEARS HAD PASSED...

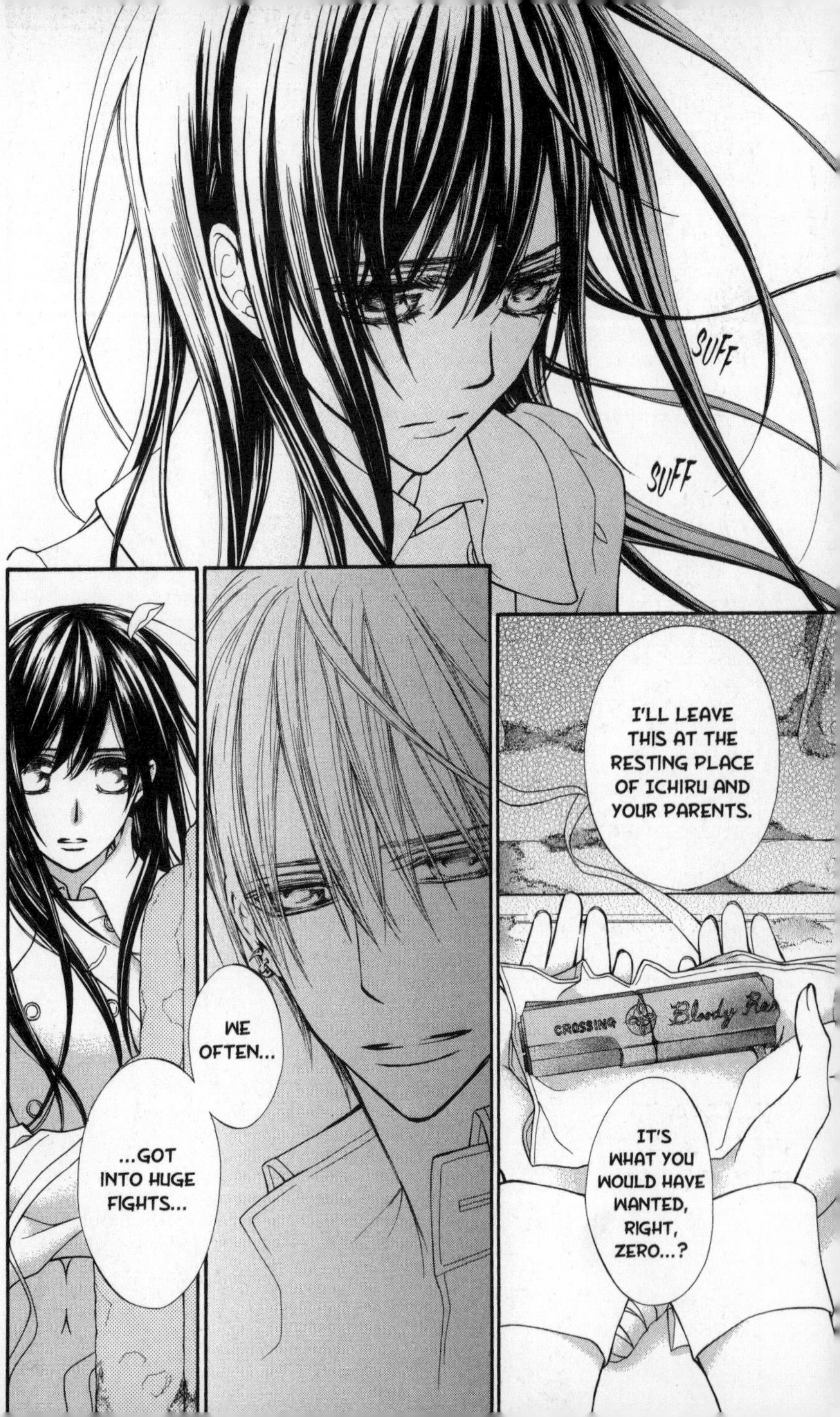
SUFF
SUFF
I'LL LEAVE THIS AT THE RESTING PLACE OF ICHIRU AND YOUR PARENTS.
CROSSING
IT'S WHAT YOU WOULD HAVE WANTED, RIGHT, ZERO...?
WE OFTEN...
...GOT INTO HUGE FIGHTS...

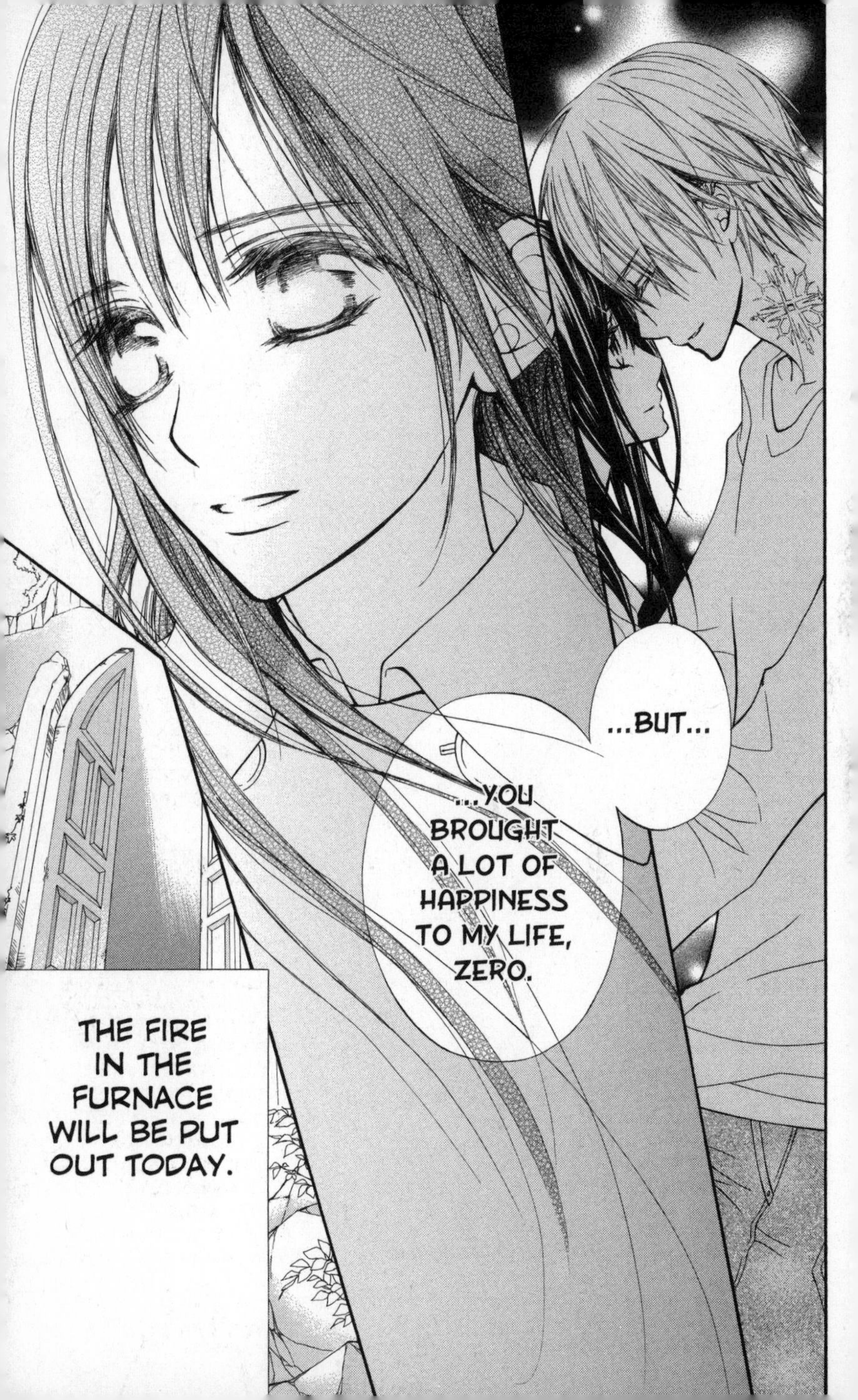
...BUT...
...YOU BROUGHT A LOT OF HAPPINESS TO MY LIFE, ZERO.
THE FIRE IN THE FURNACE WILL BE PUT OUT TODAY.

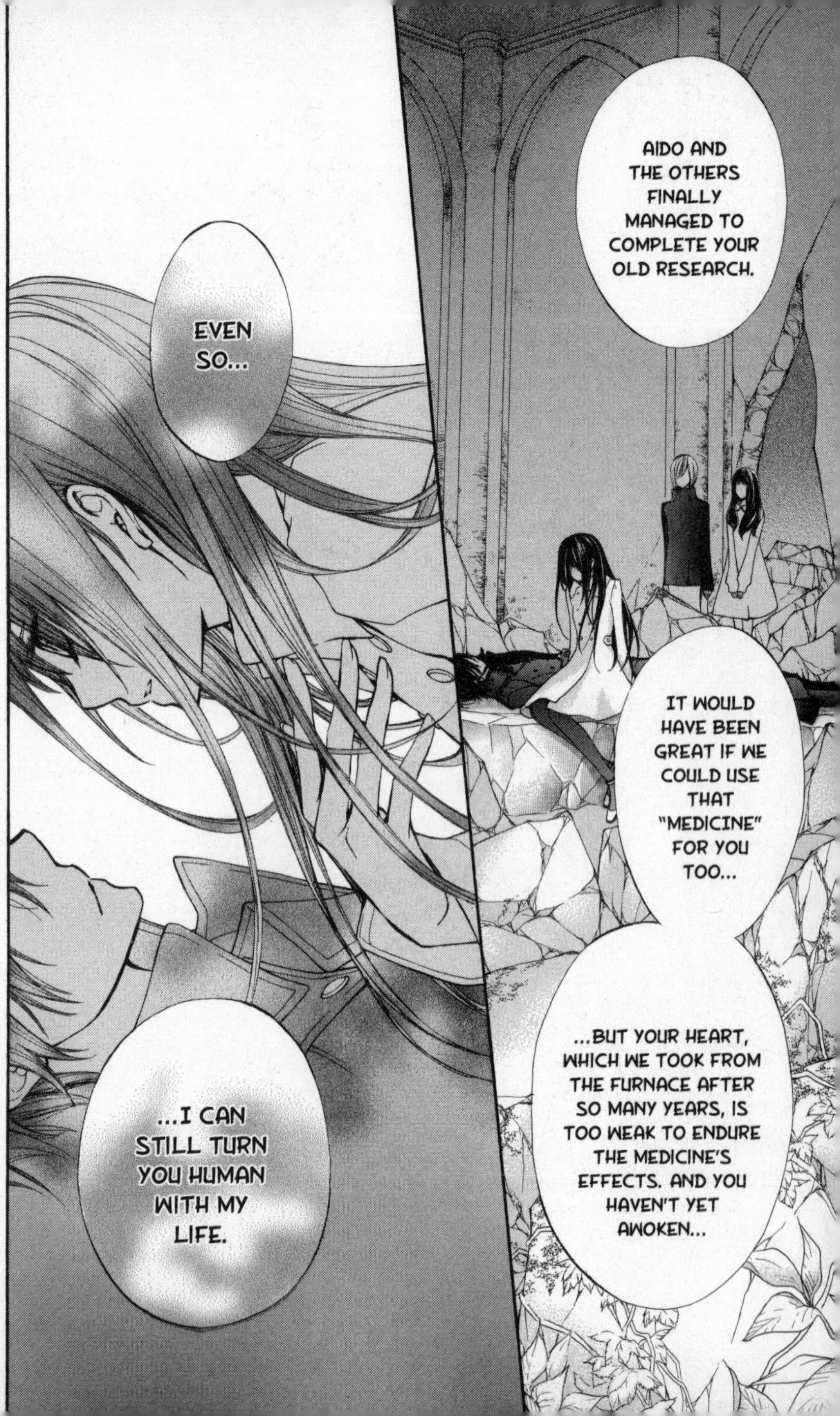
AIDO AND THE OTHERS FINALLY MANAGED TO COMPLETE YOUR OLD RESEARCH.
IT WOULD HAVE BEEN GREAT IF WE COULD USE THAT "MEDICINE" FOR YOU TOO...
...BUT YOUR HEART, WHICH WE TOOK FROM THE FURNACE AFTER SO MANY YEARS, IS TOO WEAK TO ENDURE THE MEDICINE'S EFFECTS. AND YOU HAVEN'T YET AWOKEN...
EVEN SO...
...I CAN STILL TURN YOU HUMAN WITH MY LIFE.

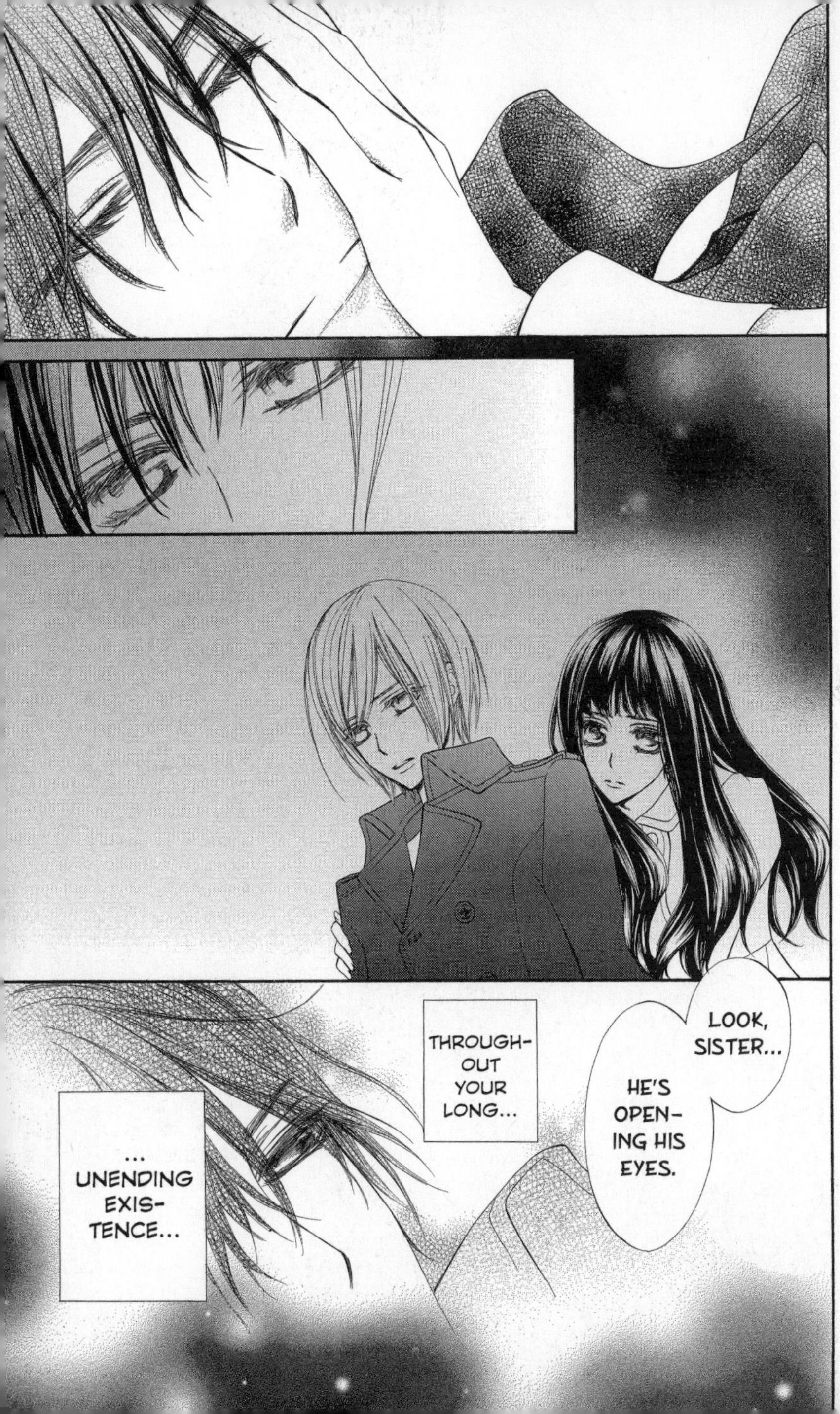
LOOK, SISTER... HE'S OPEN-ING HIS EYES.
THROUGH-OUT YOUR LONG...
... UNENDING EXIS-TENCE...

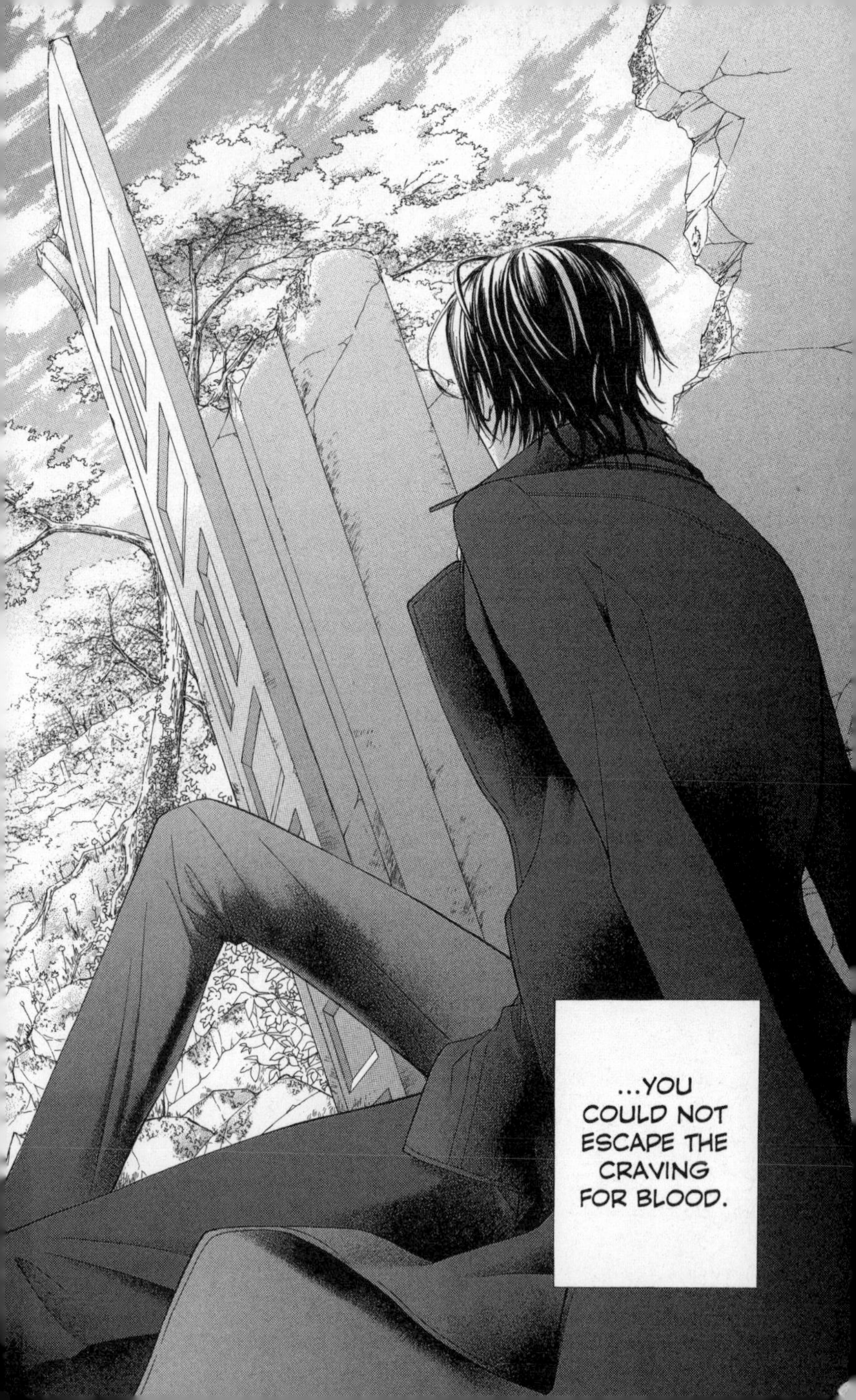
...YOU COULD NOT ESCAPE THE CRAVING FOR BLOOD.

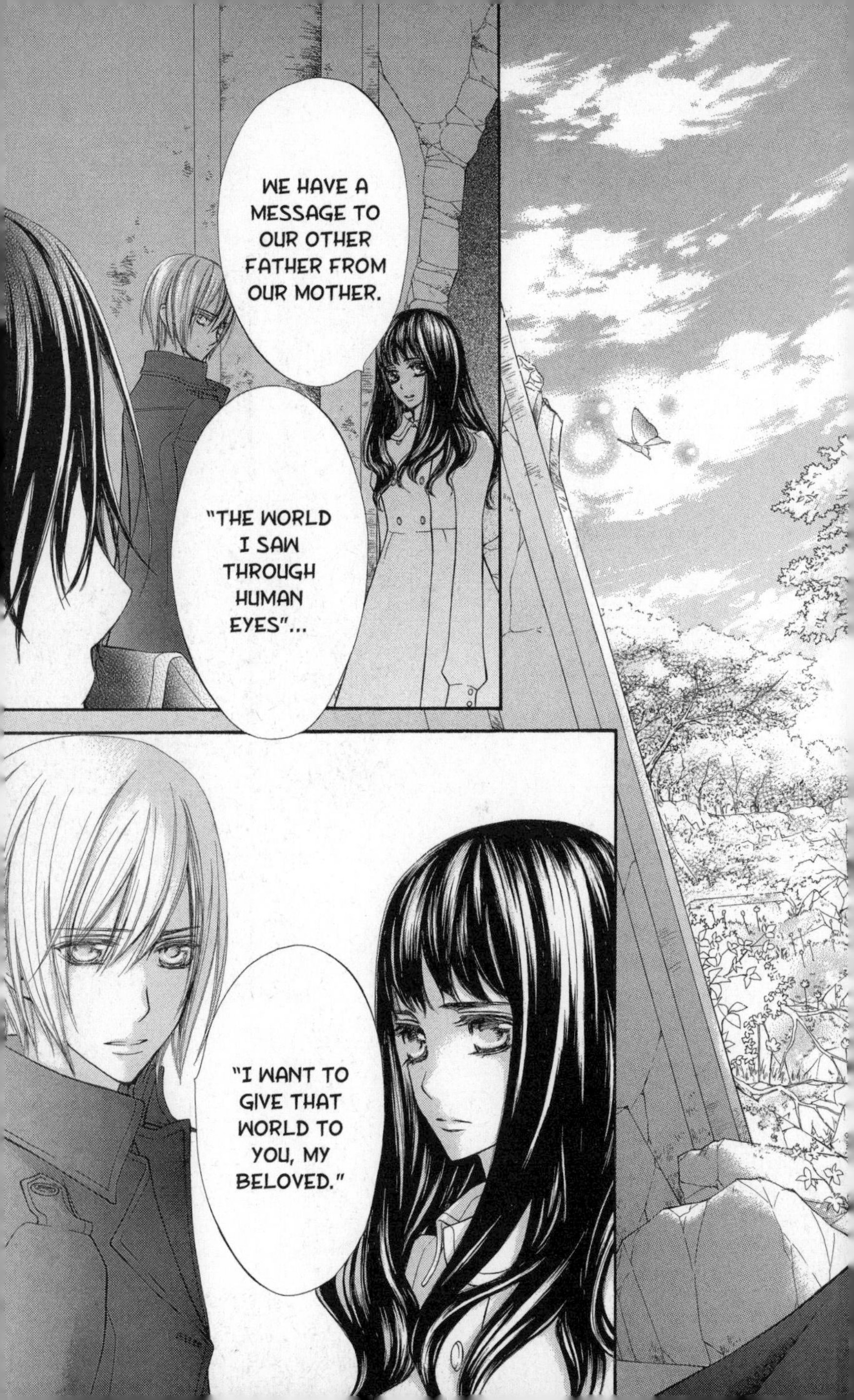
WE HAVE A MESSAGE TO OUR OTHER FATHER FROM OUR MOTHER.
"THE WORLD I SAW THROUGH HUMAN EYES"...
"I WANT TO GIVE THAT WORLD TO YOU, MY BELOVED."

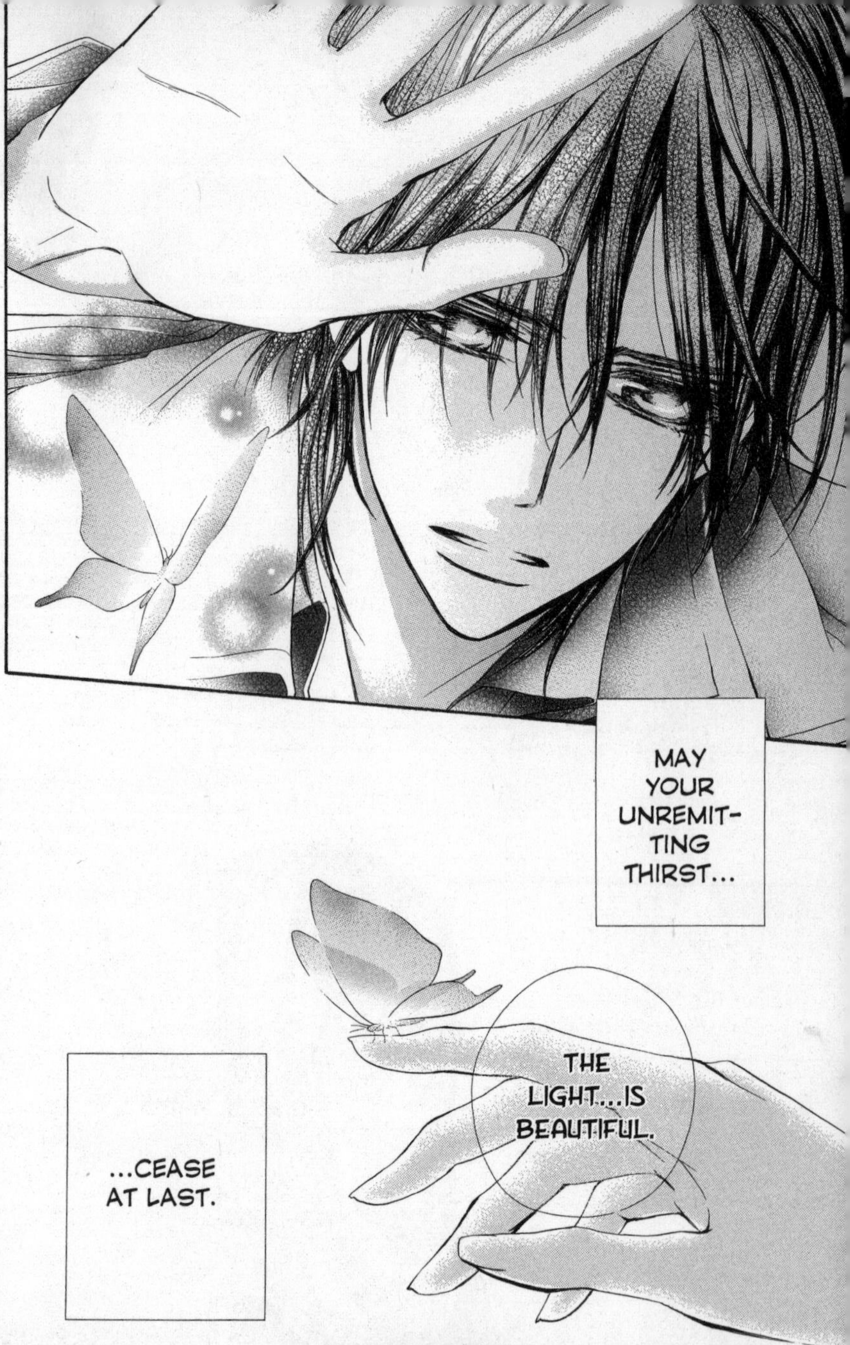
MAY YOUR UNREMIT-TING THIRST...
THE LIGHT...IS BEAUTIFUL.
...CEASE AT LAST.

VAMPIRE KNIGHT/END

EDITOR'S NOTES

Characters

Matsuri Hino puts careful thought into the names of her characters in *Vampire Knight*. Below is the collection of characters throughout the manga. Each character's name is presented family name first, per the kanji reading.

黒主優姫

Cross Yuki

Yuki's last name, *Kurosu*, is the Japanese pronunciation of the English word "cross." However, the kanji has a different meaning—*kuro* means "black" and *su* means "master." Her first name is a combination of *yuu*, meaning "tender" or "kind," and *ki*, meaning "princess."

錐生零

Kiryu Zero

Zero's first name is the kanji for *rei*, meaning "zero." In his last name, *Kiryu*, the *ki* means "auger" or "drill," and the *ryu* means "life."

玖蘭枢

Kuran Kaname

Kaname means "hinge" or "door." The kanji for his last name is a combination of the old-fashioned way of writing *ku*, meaning "nine," and *ran*, meaning "orchid": "nine orchids."

藍堂英

Aido Hanabusa

Hanabusa means "petals of a flower." *Aido* means "indigo temple." In Japanese, the pronunciation of *Aido* is very close to the pronunciation of the English word *idol*.

架院暁

Kain Akatsuki

Akatsuki means "dawn" or "daybreak." In *Kain*, *ka* is a base or support, while *in* denotes a building that has high fences around it, such as a temple or school.

早園瑠佳

Souen Ruka

In *Ruka*, the *ru* means "lapis lazuli" while the *ka* means "good-looking" or "beautiful." The *sou* in Ruka's surname, *Souen*, means "early," but this kanji also has an obscure meaning of "strong fragrance." The *en* means "garden."

一条拓麻

Ichijo Takuma

Ichijo can mean a "ray" or "streak." The kanji for *Takuma* is a combination of *taku*, meaning "to cultivate" and *ma*, which is the kanji for *asa*, meaning "hemp" or "flax," a plant with blue flowers.

支葵千里

Shiki Senri

Shiki's last name is a combination of *shi*, meaning "to support" and *ki*, meaning "mallow"—a flowering plant with pink or white blossoms. The *ri* in *Senri* is a traditional Japanese unit of measure for distance, and one *ri* is about 2.44 miles. *Senri* means "1,000 *ri*."

夜刈十牙

Yagari Toga

Yagari is a combination of *ya*, meaning "night," and *gari*, meaning "to harvest." *Toga* means "ten fangs."

一条麻遠, 一翁

Ichijo Asato, aka "Ichio"

Ichijo can mean a "ray" or "streak." Asato's first name is comprised of *asa*, meaning "hemp" or "flax," and *tou*, meaning "far off." His nickname is *ichi*, or "one," combined with *ou*, which can be used as an honorific when referring to an older man.

若葉沙頼

Wakaba Sayori

Yori's full name is Sayori Wakaba. *Wakaba* means "young leaves." Her given name, *Sayori*, is a combination of *sa*, meaning "sand," and *yori*, meaning "trust."

星煉

Seiren

Sei means "star" and *ren* means "to smelt" or "refine." *Ren* is also the same kanji used in *rengoku*, or "purgatory."

遠矢莉磨

Toya Rima

Toya means a "far-reaching arrow." Rima's first name is a combination of *ri*, or "jasmine," and *ma*, which signifies enhancement by wearing away, such as by polishing or scouring.

紅まり亜

Kurenai Maria

Kurenai means "crimson." The kanji for the last *a* in Maria's first name is the same that is used in "Asia."

錐生壱縷

Kiryu Ichiru

Ichi is the old-fashioned way of writing "one," and *ru* means "thread."

緋桜閑, 狂咲姫

Hio Shizuka, Kuruizaki-hime

Shizuka means "calm and quiet." In Shizuka's family name, *hi* is "scarlet," and *ou* is "cherry blossoms." Shizuka Hio is also referred to as the "Kuruizaki-hime." *Kuruizaki* means "flowers blooming out of season," and *hime* means "princess."

藍堂月子

Aido Tsukiko

Aido means "indigo temple." *Tsukiko* means "moon child."

白蕗更

Shirabuki Sara

Shira is "white," and *buki* is "butterbur," a plant with white flowers. *Sara* means "renew."

黒主灰閻

Cross Kaien

Cross, or *Kurosu*, means "black master." Kaien is a combination of *kai*, meaning "ashes," and *en*, meaning "village gate." The kanji for *en* is also used for Enma, the ruler of the Underworld in Buddhist mythology.

玖蘭李土

Kuran Rido

Kuran means "nine orchids." In *Rido*, *ri* means "plum" and *do* means "earth."

玖蘭樹里

Kuran Juri

Kuran means "nine orchids." In her first name, *ju* means "tree" and a *ri* is a traditional Japanese unit of measure for distance. The kanji for *ri* is the same as in Senri's name.

玖蘭悠

Kuran Haruka

Kuran means "nine orchids." *Haruka* means "distant" or "remote."

鷹宮海斗

Takamiya Kaito

Taka means "hawk" and *miya* means "imperial palace" or "shrine." *Kai* is "sea" and *to* means "to measure" or "grid."

菖藤依砂也

Shoto Isaya

Sho means "Siberian Iris" and *to* is "wisteria." The *I* in *Isaya* means "to rely on," while the *sa* means "sand." *Ya* is a suffix used for emphasis.

橙茉

Toma

In the family name *Toma*, *to* means "seville orange" and *ma* means "jasmine flower."

藍堂永路

Aido Nagamichi

The name *Nagamichi* is a combination of *naga*, which means "long" or "eternal," and *michi*, which is the kanji for "road" or "path." *Aido* means "indigo temple."

縹木

Hanadagi

In this family name, *hanada* means "bright light blue" and *gi* means "tree."

影山霞

Kageyama Kasumi

In the Class Rep's family name, *kage* means "shadow," and *yama* means "mountain." His first name, Kasumi, means "haze" or "mist."

Terms

-sama: The suffix *sama* is used in formal address for someone who ranks higher in the social hierarchy. The vampires call their leader "Kaname-sama" only when they are among their own kind.

Matsuri Hino burst onto the manga scene with her series *Kono Yume ga Sametara* (When This Dream Is Over), which was published in *LaLa DX* magazine. Hino was a manga artist a mere nine months after she decided to become one.

With the success of her popular series *Captive Hearts* and *MeruPuri*, Hino has established herself as a major player in the world of shojo manga.

Hino enjoys creative activities and has commented that she would have been either an architect or an apprentice to traditional Japanese craft masters if she had not become a manga artist.

VAMPIRE KNIGHT
Vol. 19
Shojo Beat Edition

STORY AND ART BY
MATSURI HINO

Adaptation/Nancy Thistlethwaite
Translation/Tetsuichiro Miyaki
Touch-up Art & Lettering/Inori Fukuda Trant
Graphic Design/Amy Martin
Editor/Nancy Thistlethwaite

Vampire Knight by Matsuri Hino © Matsuri Hino 2013. All rights reserved.
First published in Japan in 2013 by HAKUSENSHA, Inc., Tokyo. English
language translation rights arranged with HAKUSENSHA, Inc., Tokyo.

The stories, characters and incidents mentioned in this publication are
entirely fictional.

No portion of this book may be reproduced or transmitted in any form or by
any means without written permission from the copyright holders.

Printed in the U.S.A.

Published by VIZ Media, LLC
P.O. Box 77010
San Francisco, CA 94107

10 9 8 7 6 5 4 3 2 1
First printing, October 2014

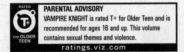

www.viz.com

www.shojobeat.com

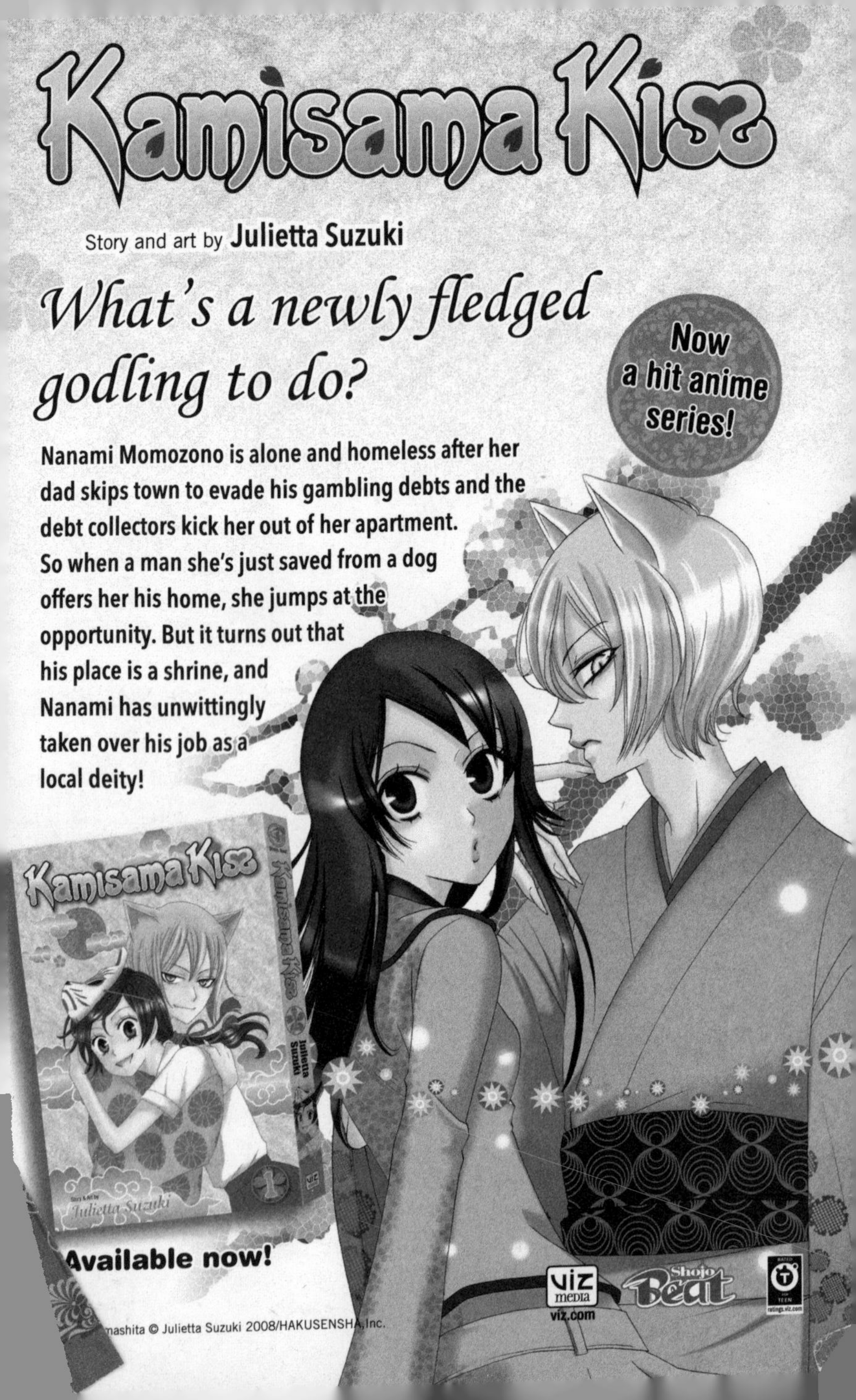
Kamisama Kiss
Story and art by Julietta Suzuki
What's a newly fledged godling to do?
Now a hit anime series!
Nanami Momozono is alone and homeless after her dad skips town to evade his gambling debts and the debt collectors kick her out of her apartment. So when a man she's just saved from a dog offers her his home, she jumps at the opportunity. But it turns out that his place is a shrine, and Nanami has unwittingly taken over his job as a local deity!
Kamisama Kiss
Kamisama Kiss
Julietta Suzuki
1
Story & Art by Julietta Suzuki
Available now!
VIZ media
viz.com
Shojo Beat
RATED T FOR TEEN
ratings.viz.com
mashita © Julietta Suzuki 2008/HAKUSENSHA, Inc.

SURPRISE!

You may be reading the wrong way!

It's true: In keeping with the original Japanese comic format, this book reads from right to left—so action, sound effects, and word balloons are completely reversed. This preserves the orientation of the original artwork—plus, it's fun! Check out the diagram shown here to get the hang of things, and then turn to the other side of the book to get started!

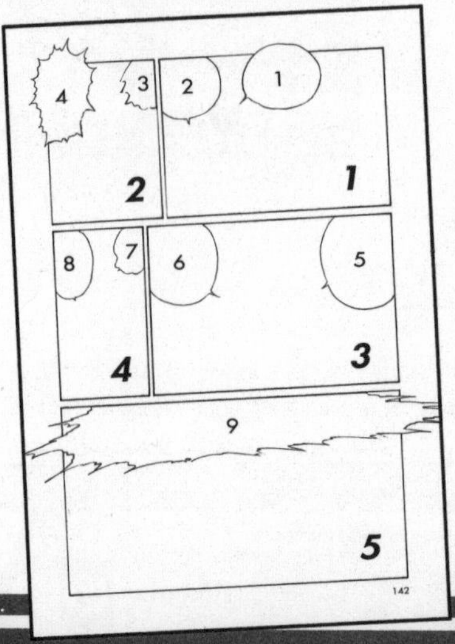

1
1
2
3
4
2
5
6
3
7
8
4
9
5
142

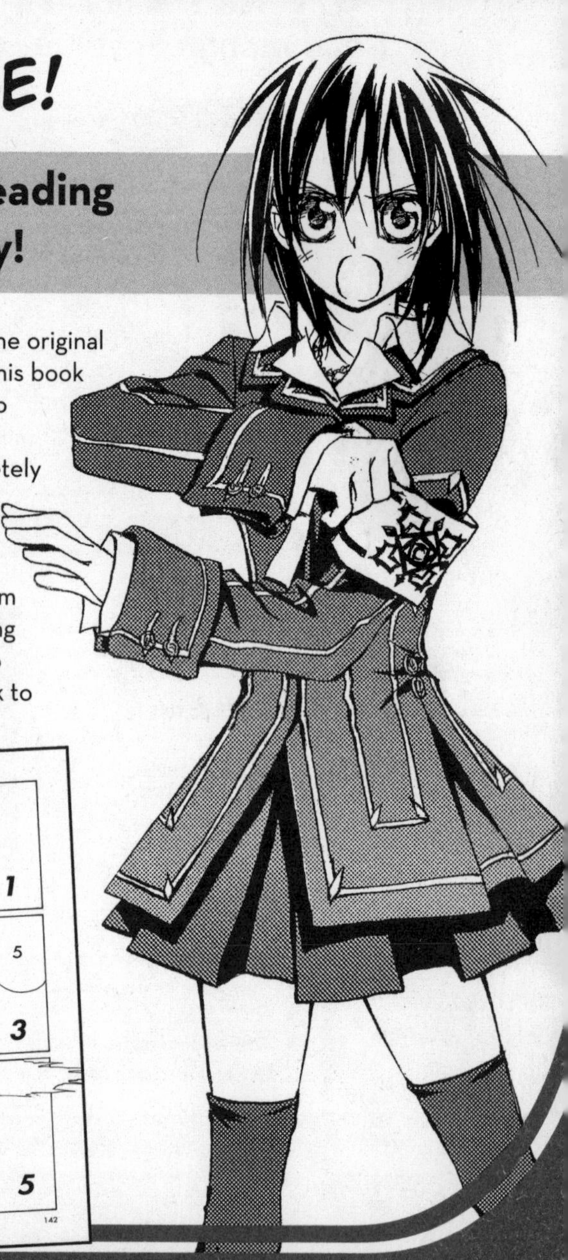

UQ HOLDER!

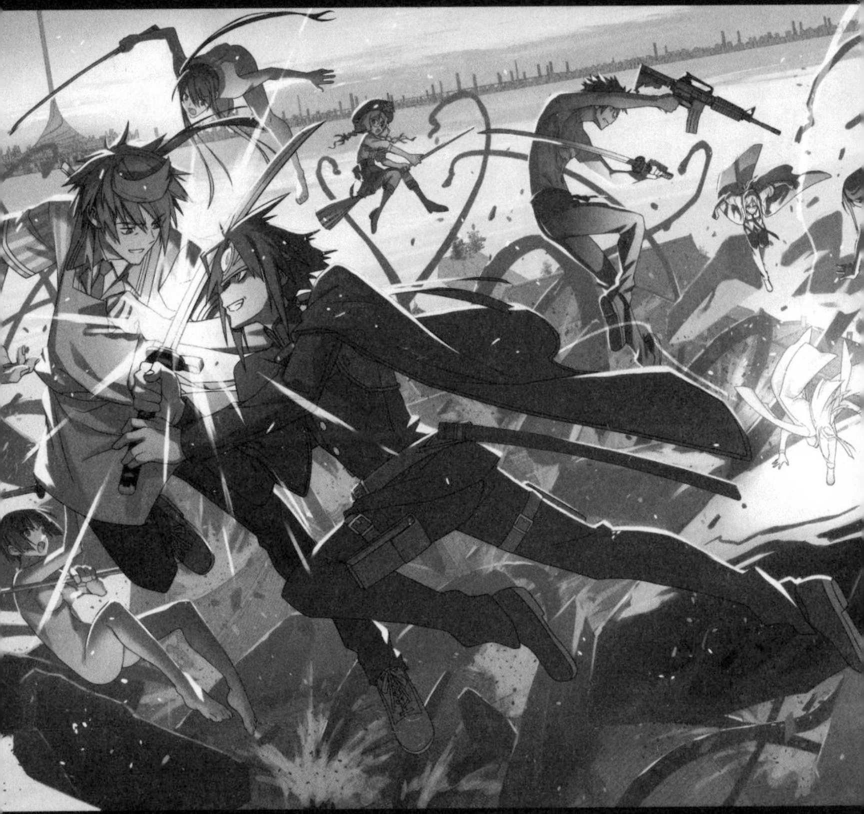

KEN AKAMATSU

vol. 21

CHARACTERS

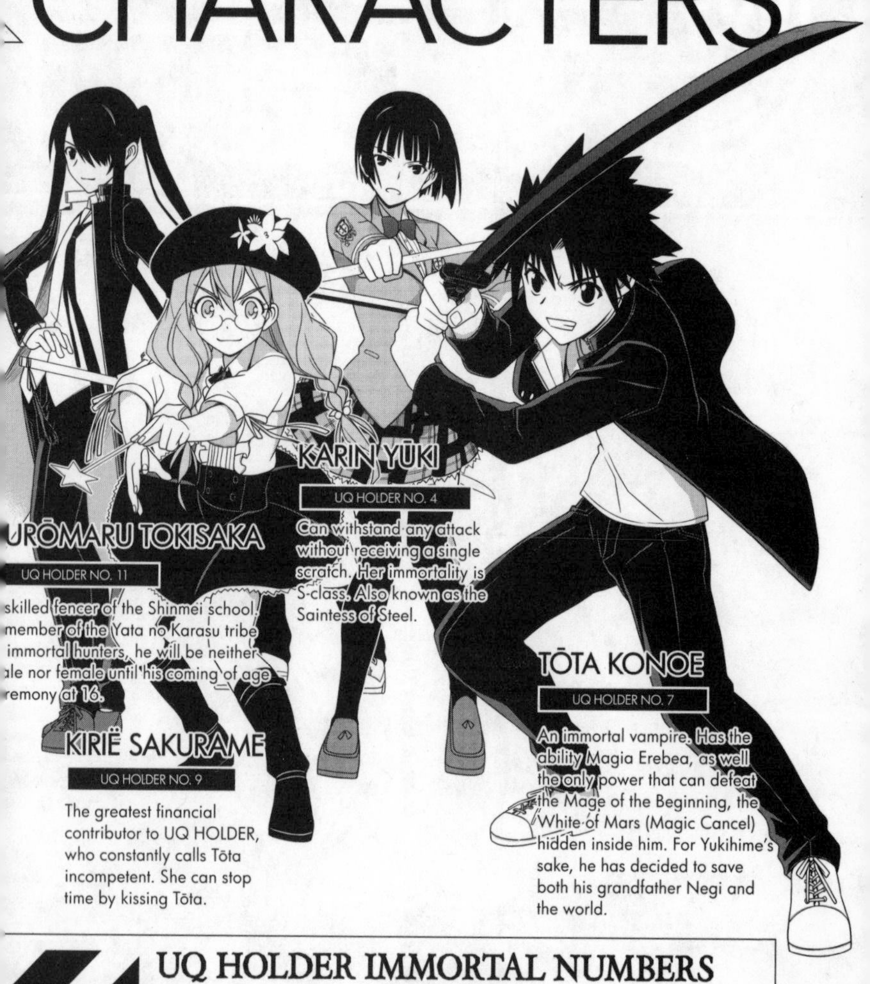

URŌMARU TOKISAKA

UQ HOLDER NO. 11

skilled fencer of the Shinmei school. member of the Yata no Karasu tribe immortal hunters, he will be neither ale nor female until his coming of age remony at 16.

KARIN YŪKI

UQ HOLDER NO. 4

Can withstand any attack without receiving a single scratch. Her immortality is S-class. Also known as the Saintess of Steel.

KIRIË SAKURAME

UQ HOLDER NO. 9

The greatest financial contributor to UQ HOLDER, who constantly calls Tōta incompetent. She can stop time by kissing Tōta.

TŌTA KONOE

UQ HOLDER NO. 7

An immortal vampire. Has the ability Magia Erebea, as well the only power that can defeat the Mage of the Beginning, the White of Mars (Magic Cancel) hidden inside him. For Yukihime's sake, he has decided to save both his grandfather Negi and the world.

UQ HOLDER IMMORTAL NUMBERS

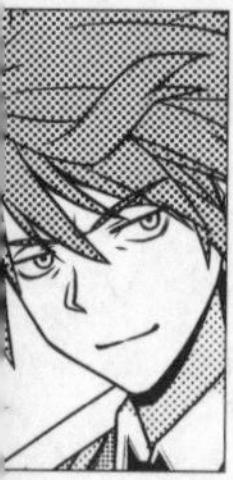

JINBEI SHISHIDO

UQ HOLDER NO. 2

UQ HOLDER's oldest member. Became an immortal in the middle ages, when he ate mermaid flesh in the Muromachi Period. Has the "Switcheroo" skill that switches the locations of physical objects.

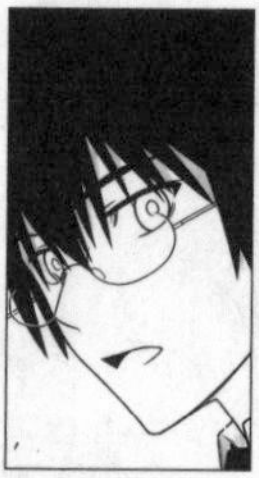

GENGORŌ MAKABE

UQ HOLDER NO. 6

Manages the business side of UQ HOLDER's hideout and inn. He has a skill known as "Multiple Lives," so when he dies, another Gengorō appears.

倣 UQ HOLDER!...

Ken Akamatsu Presents

BA'AL
A High Daylight Walker. The archenemy Eva once fought in the battle against the Magical World.

EVANGELINE (YUKIHIME)
The female leader of UQ HOLDER and a 700-year-old vampire. Her past self met Tōta in a rift in time-space, and that encounter gave hope to her bleak immortal existence.

DANA
A High Daylight Walker. Tōta's master, also known as the Witch of the Rift.

SEPT SHICHIJŪRŌ NANAO

`UQ HOLDER NO. 3`

One of the creator Ba'al's followers.

JŪZŌ SHISHIMI

`UQ HOLDER NO. 5`

The Numbers' top sword master. He is being manipulated by Ba'al.

NIKITIS LAPS

`UQ HOLDER NO. 8`

A High Daylight Walker. He drew out Tōta's true power, but the true meaning behind that is unknown.

IKKŪ AMEYA

`UQ HOLDER NO. 10`

After falling into a coma at age 13 and lying in a hospital bed for 72 years, he became a full-body cyborg at age 85. He's very good with his hands. ♡

SANTA SASAKI

`UQ HOLDER NO. 12`

A revenant brought back to life through necromancy. He has multiple abilities, including flight, intangibility, possession, telekinesis, etc.

THE STORY SO FAR

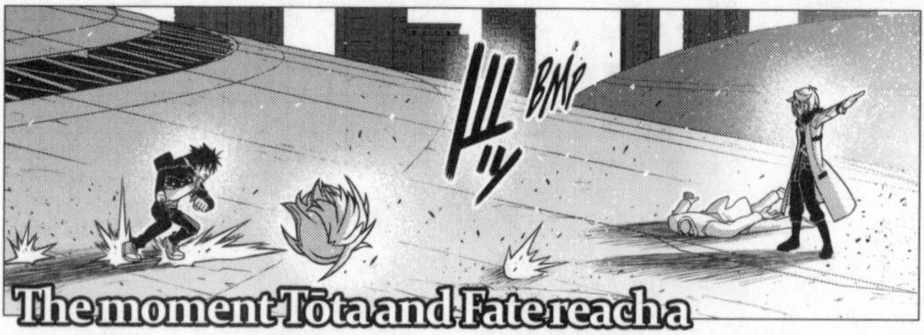
BMP
The moment Tōta and Fate reach a compromise, Nikitis attacks them!!

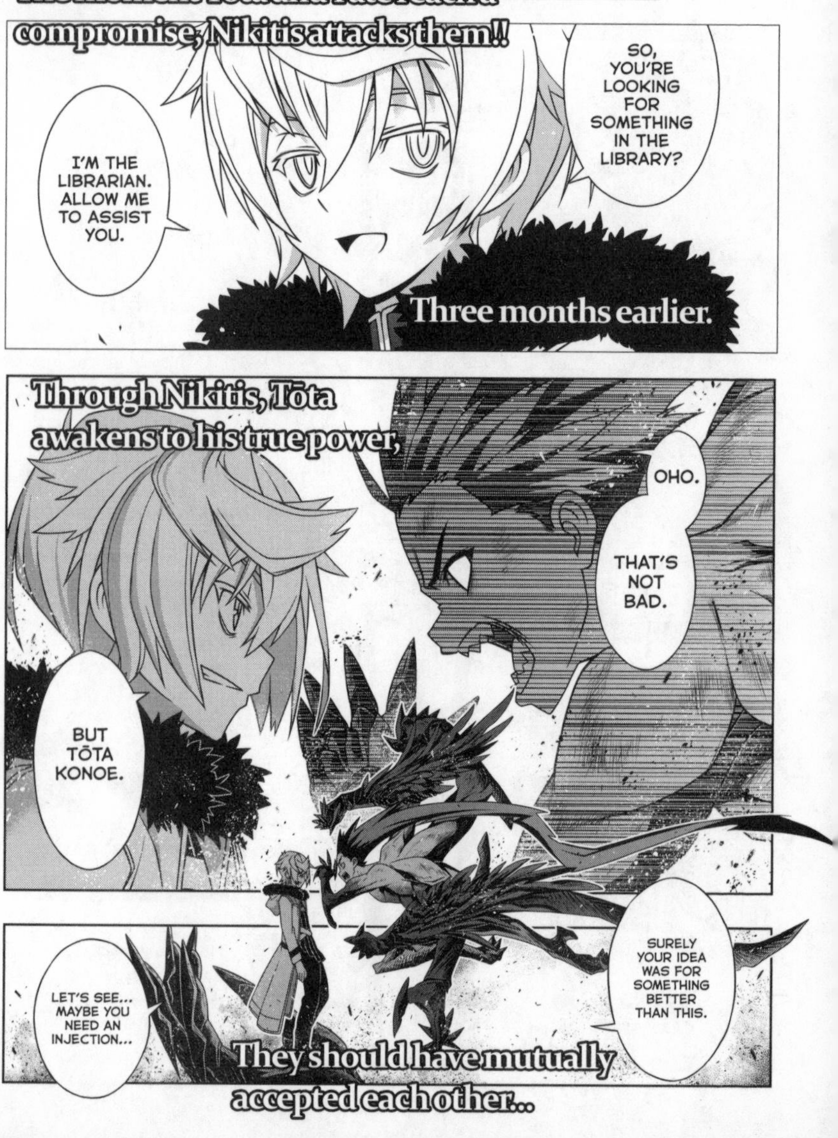
SO, YOU'RE LOOKING FOR SOMETHING IN THE LIBRARY?
I'M THE LIBRARIAN. ALLOW ME TO ASSIST YOU.
Three months earlier.
Through Nikitis, Tōta awakens to his true power,
OHO.
THAT'S NOT BAD.
BUT TŌTA KONOE.
SURELY YOUR IDEA WAS FOR SOMETHING BETTER THAN THIS.
LET'S SEE... MAYBE YOU NEED AN INJECTION...
They should have mutually accepted each other...

At the same time,
ドシャ
SKRSSH
the Numbers' strongest duo assault the UQ HOLDER base!
...I WOULD CUT DOWN THE GODS.
EN GARDE.
Manipulated as an enemy, Jūzō Shishimi and his sword that reached the gods' domain...
...annihilate UQ HOLDER!!

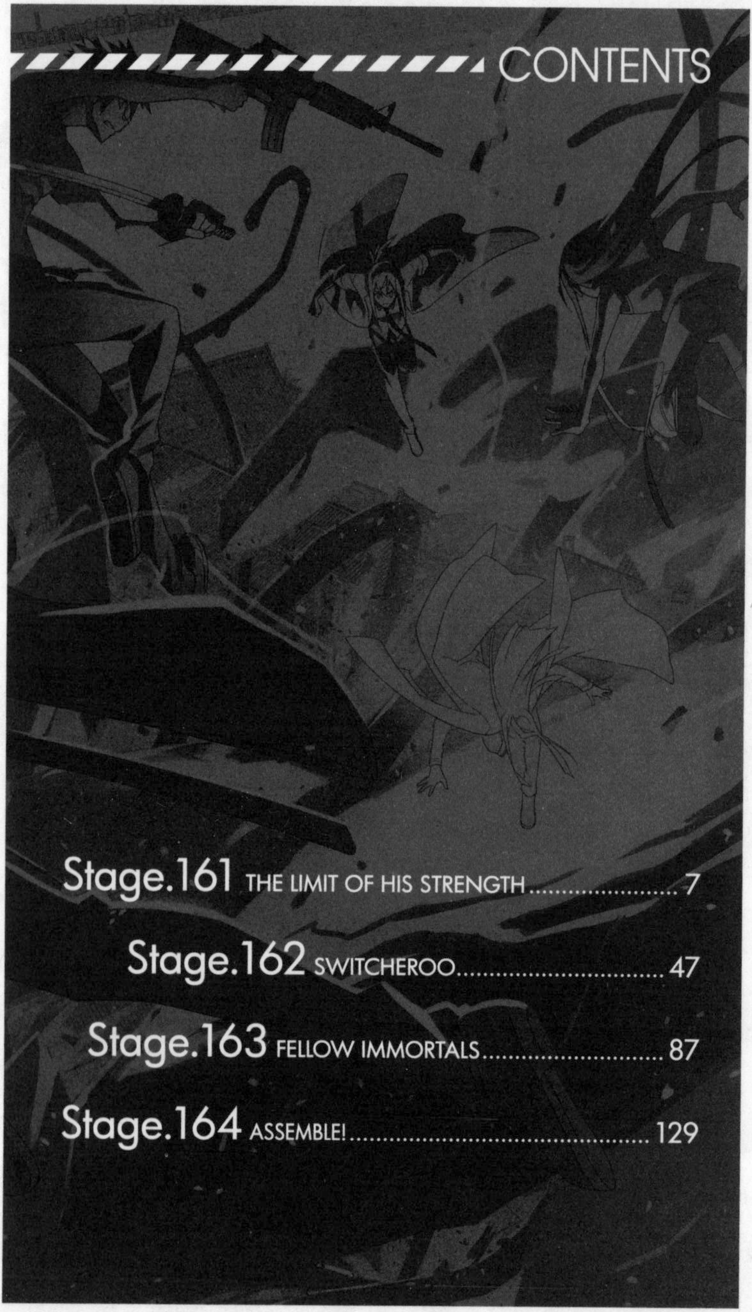

CONTENTS

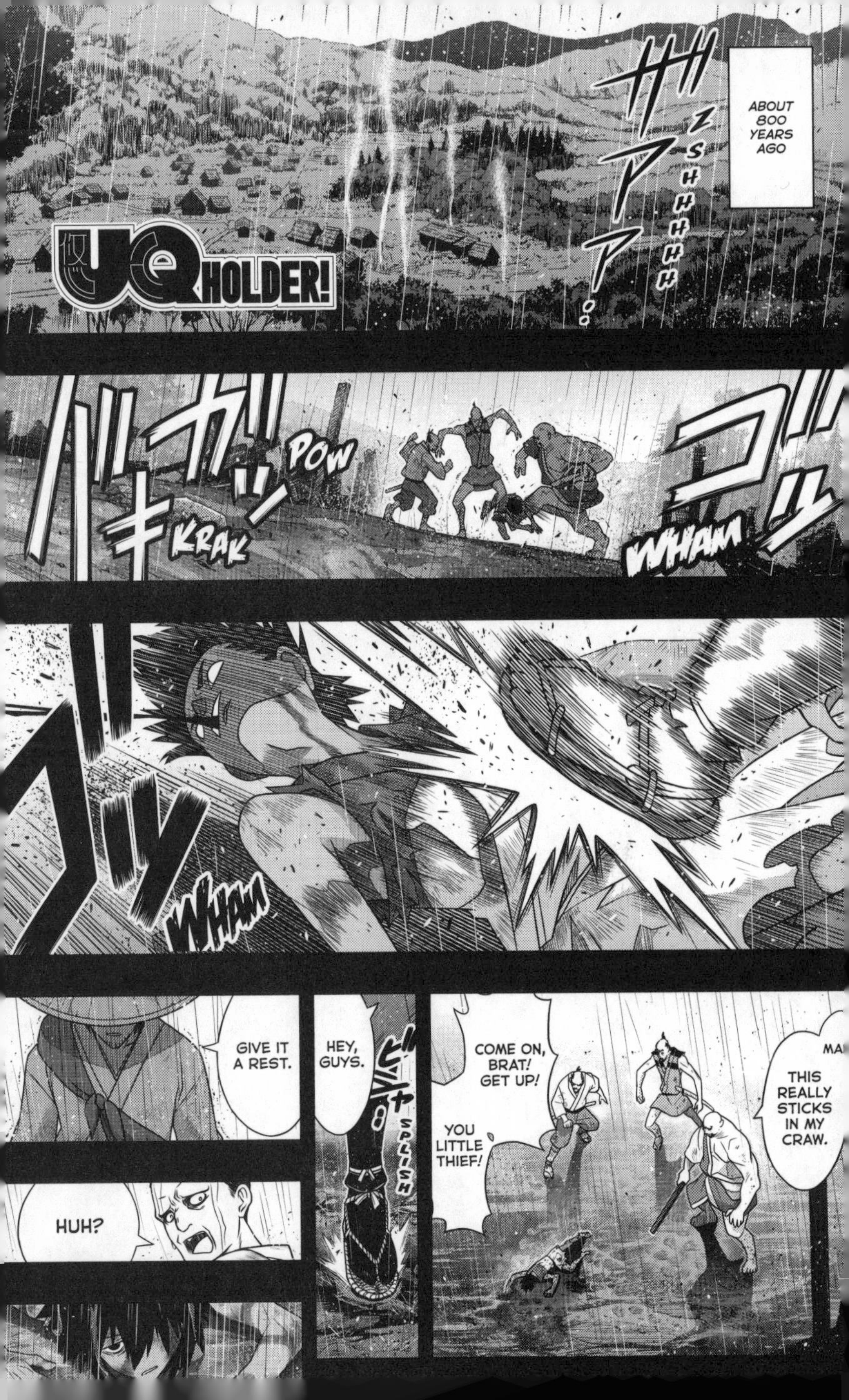

ABOUT 800 YEARS AGO
ZSHHHHHHH
UQ HOLDER!
WHAM
POW
KRAK
WHAM
MA
THIS REALLY STICKS IN MY CRAW.
COME ON, BRAT! GET UP!
YOU LITTLE THIEF!
HEY, GUYS.
SPLISH
GIVE IT A REST.
HUH?

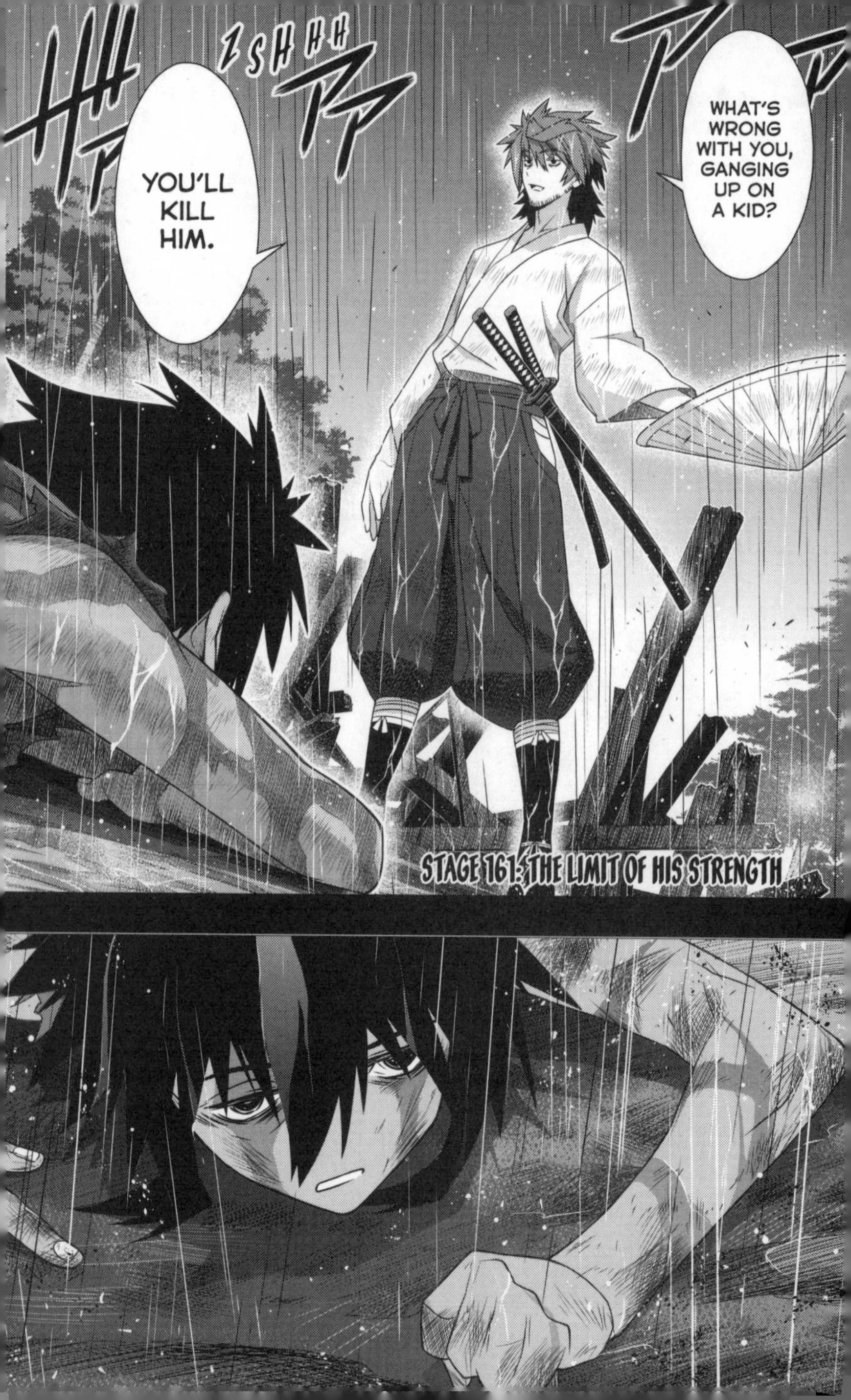
WHAT'S WRONG WITH YOU, GANGING UP ON A KID?
YOU'LL KILL HIM.
ZSHHH
STAGE 161: THE LIMIT OF HIS STRENGTH

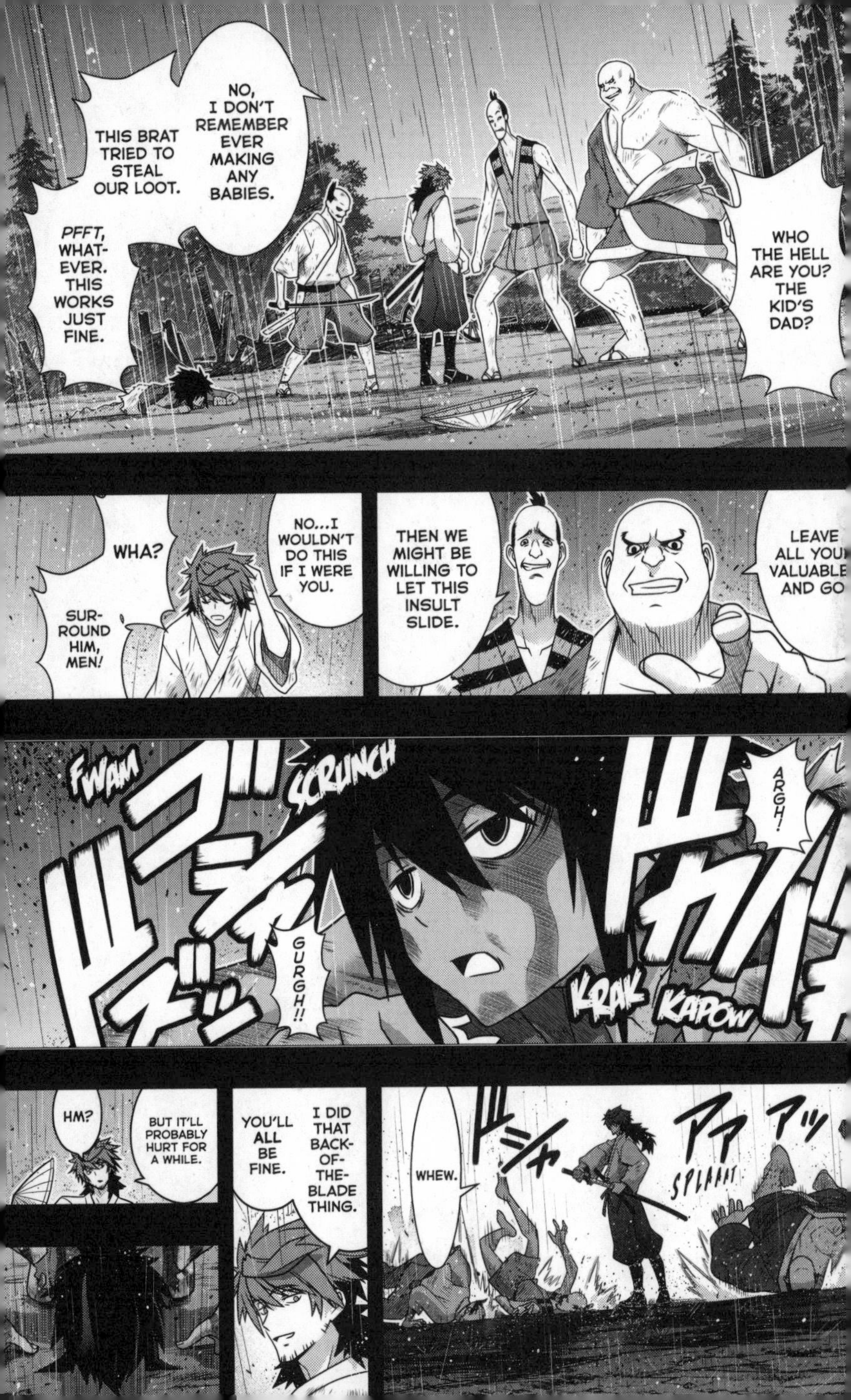

WHO THE HELL ARE YOU? THE KID'S DAD?
NO, I DON'T REMEMBER EVER MAKING ANY BABIES.
THIS BRAT TRIED TO STEAL OUR LOOT.
PFFT, WHATEVER. THIS WORKS JUST FINE.
LEAVE ALL YOU VALUABLE AND GO
THEN WE MIGHT BE WILLING TO LET THIS INSULT SLIDE.
NO...I WOULDN'T DO THIS IF I WERE YOU.
WHA?
SURROUND HIM, MEN!
ARGH!
KAPOW
KRAK
GURGH!!
SCRUNCH
FWAM
SPLAAAT
WHEW.
I DID THAT BACK-OF-THE-BLADE THING.
YOU'LL ALL BE FINE.
BUT IT'LL PROBABLY HURT FOR A WHILE.
HM?

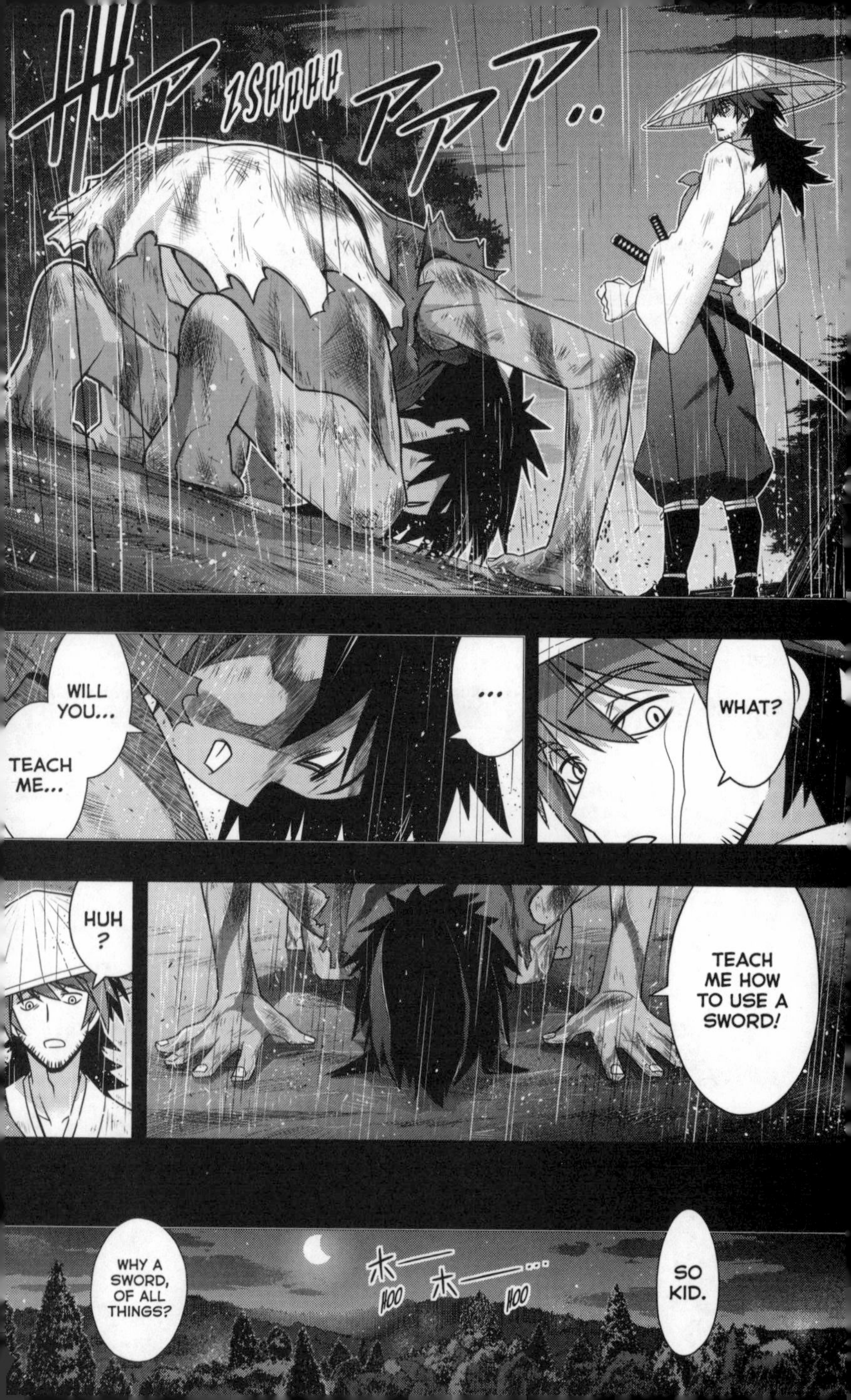
ザァ
ZSHHHH
ァァ..
WHAT?
...
WILL YOU...
TEACH ME...
TEACH ME HOW TO USE A SWORD!
HUH?
SO KID.
ホー ホー..
HOO HOO
WHY A SWORD, OF ALL THINGS?

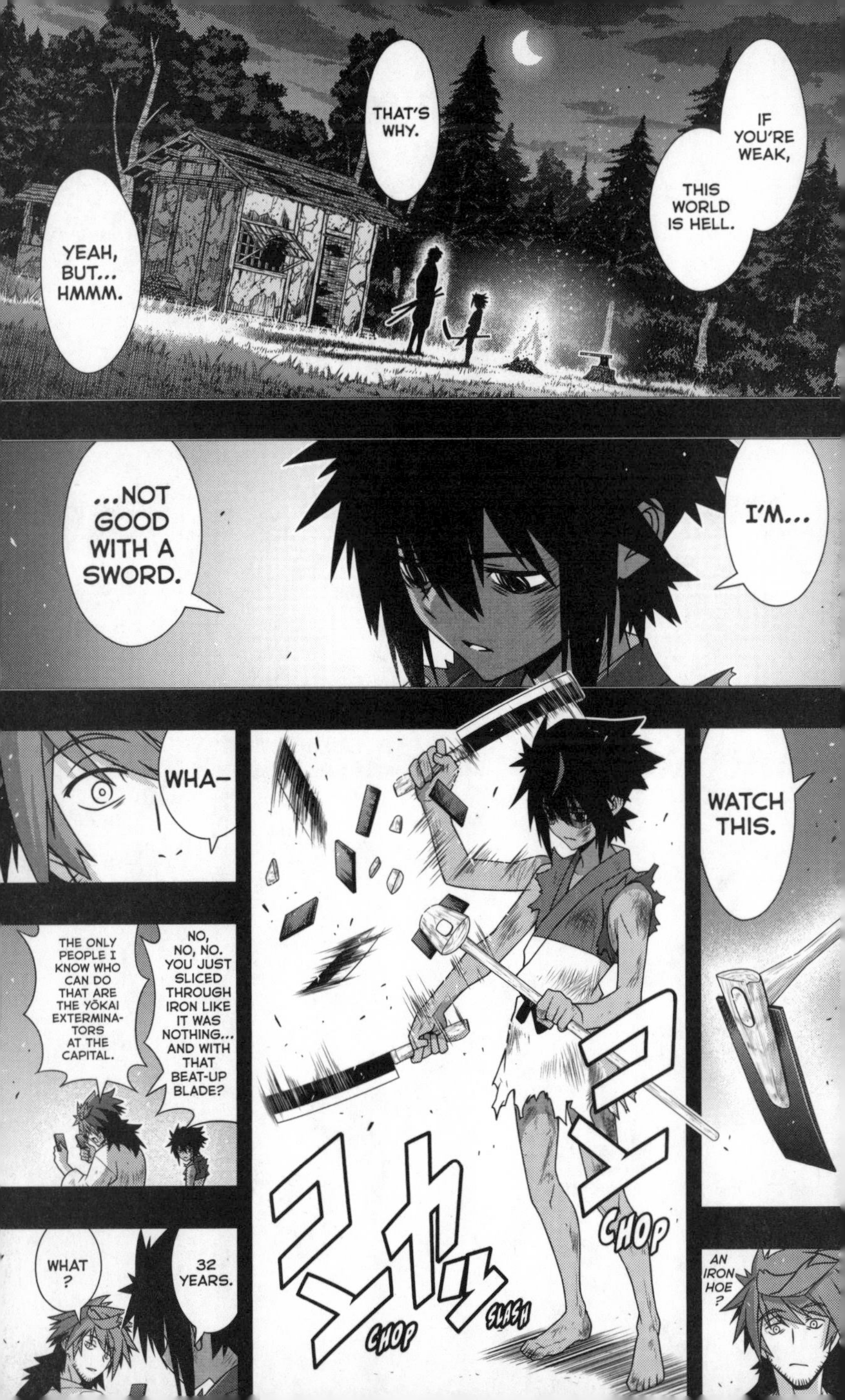
IF YOU'RE WEAK,
THIS WORLD IS HELL.
THAT'S WHY.
YEAH, BUT... HMMM.
I'M...
...NOT GOOD WITH A SWORD.
WATCH THIS.
AN IRON HOE ?
CHOP
SLASH
CHOP
WHA-
NO, NO, NO. YOU JUST SLICED THROUGH IRON LIKE IT WAS NOTHING... AND WITH THAT BEAT-UP BLADE?
THE ONLY PEOPLE I KNOW WHO CAN DO THAT ARE THE YŌKAI EXTERMINATORS AT THE CAPITAL.
32 YEARS.
WHAT ?

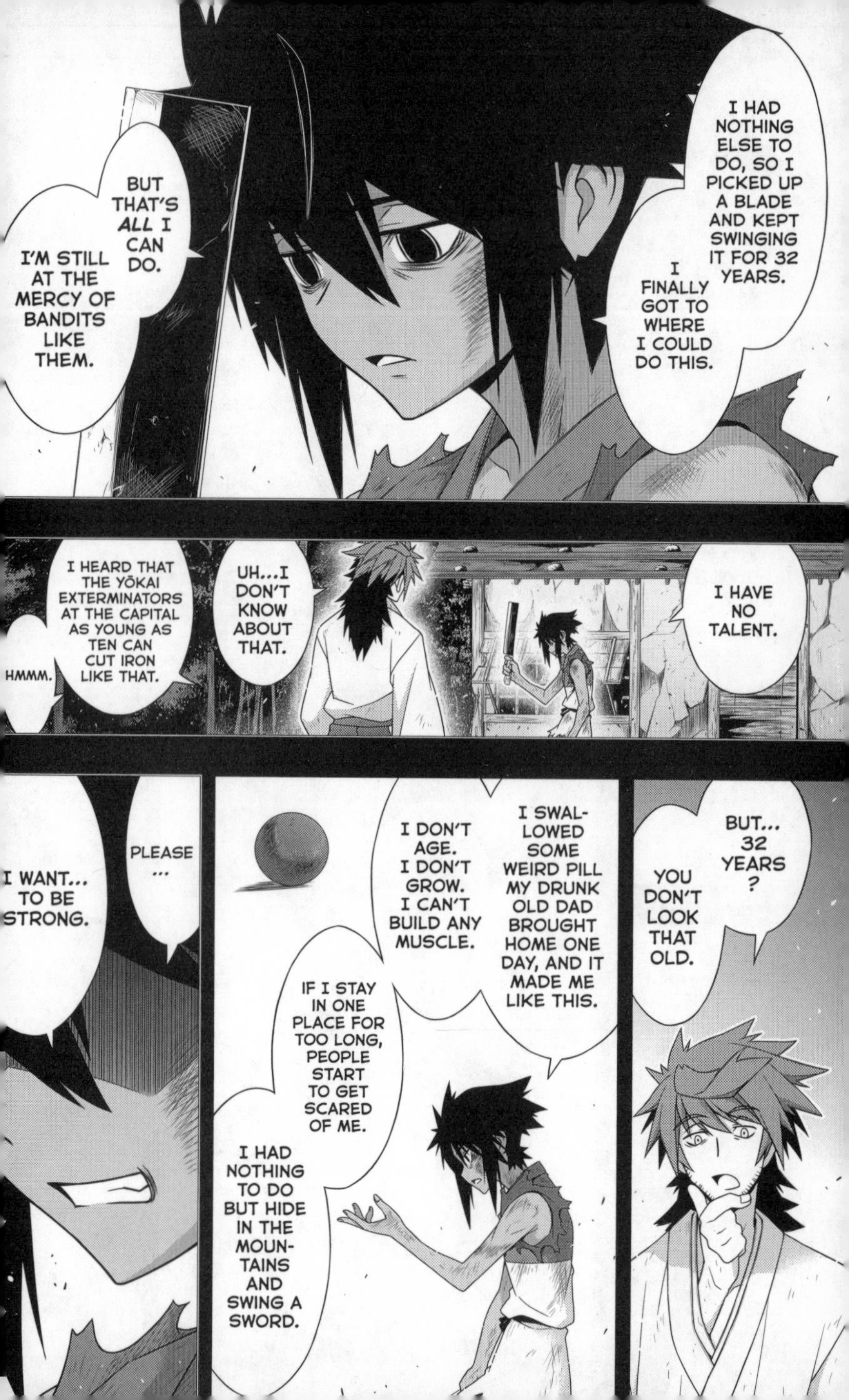
I HAD NOTHING ELSE TO DO, SO I PICKED UP A BLADE AND KEPT SWINGING IT FOR 32 YEARS.
I FINALLY GOT TO WHERE I COULD DO THIS.
BUT THAT'S *ALL* I CAN DO.
I'M STILL AT THE MERCY OF BANDITS LIKE THEM.
I HAVE NO TALENT.
UH...I DON'T KNOW ABOUT THAT.
I HEARD THAT THE YŌKAI EXTERMINATORS AT THE CAPITAL AS YOUNG AS TEN CAN CUT IRON LIKE THAT.
HMMM.
BUT... 32 YEARS?
YOU DON'T LOOK THAT OLD.
I SWAL-LOWED SOME WEIRD PILL MY DRUNK OLD DAD BROUGHT HOME ONE DAY, AND IT MADE ME LIKE THIS.
I DON'T AGE. I DON'T GROW. I CAN'T BUILD ANY MUSCLE.
IF I STAY IN ONE PLACE FOR TOO LONG, PEOPLE START TO GET SCARED OF ME.
I HAD NOTHING TO DO BUT HIDE IN THE MOUN-TAINS AND SWING A SWORD.
PLEASE ...
I WANT... TO BE STRONG.

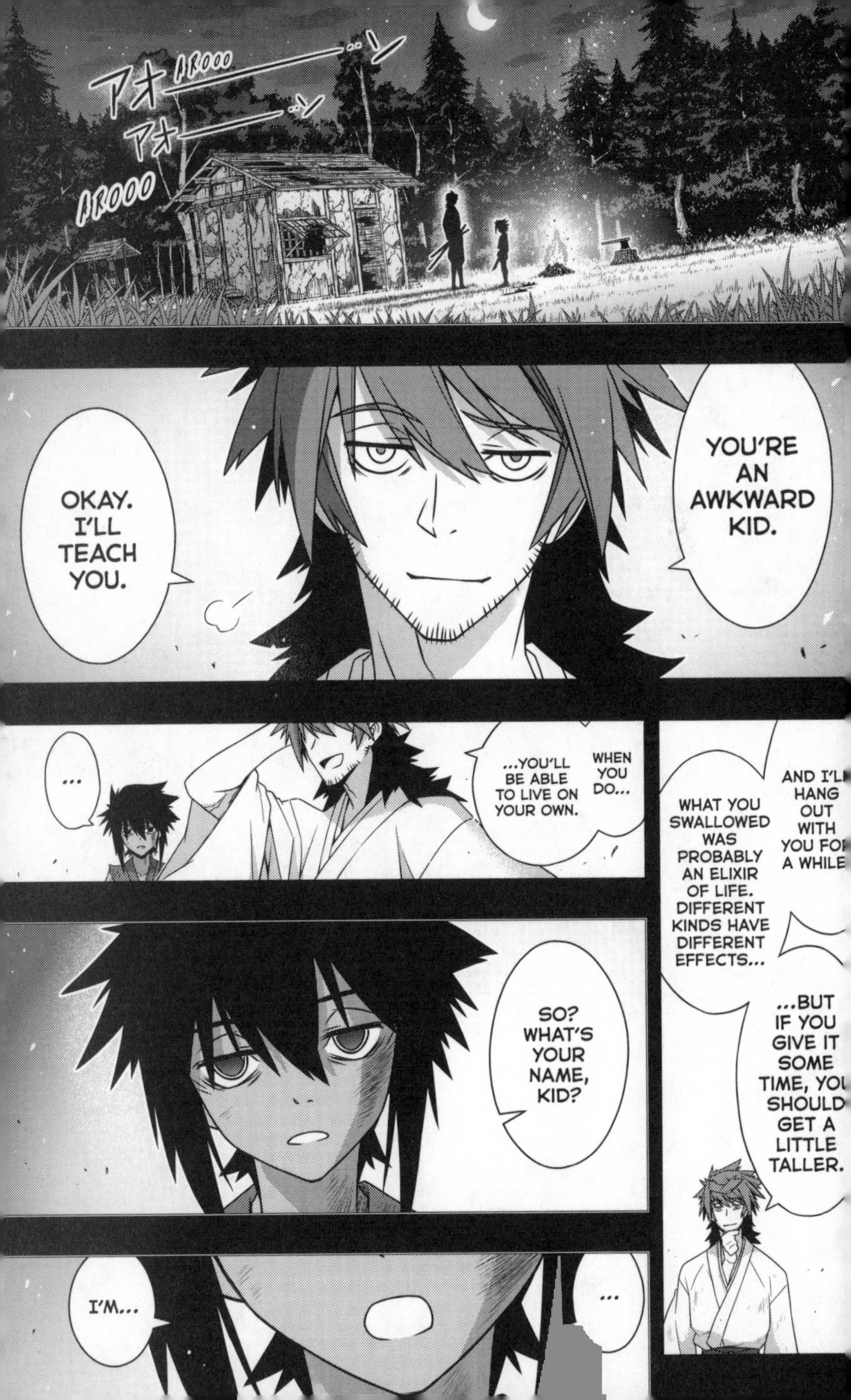

アオーーーン AROOO
アオーーーン AROOO
YOU'RE AN AWKWARD KID.
OKAY. I'LL TEACH YOU.
AND I'L HANG OUT WITH YOU FO A WHILE
WHAT YOU SWALLOWED WAS PROBABLY AN ELIXIR OF LIFE. DIFFERENT KINDS HAVE DIFFERENT EFFECTS...
...BUT IF YOU GIVE IT SOME TIME, YOU SHOULD GET A LITTLE TALLER.
WHEN YOU DO...
...YOU'LL BE ABLE TO LIVE ON YOUR OWN.
...
SO? WHAT'S YOUR NAME, KID?
...
I'M...

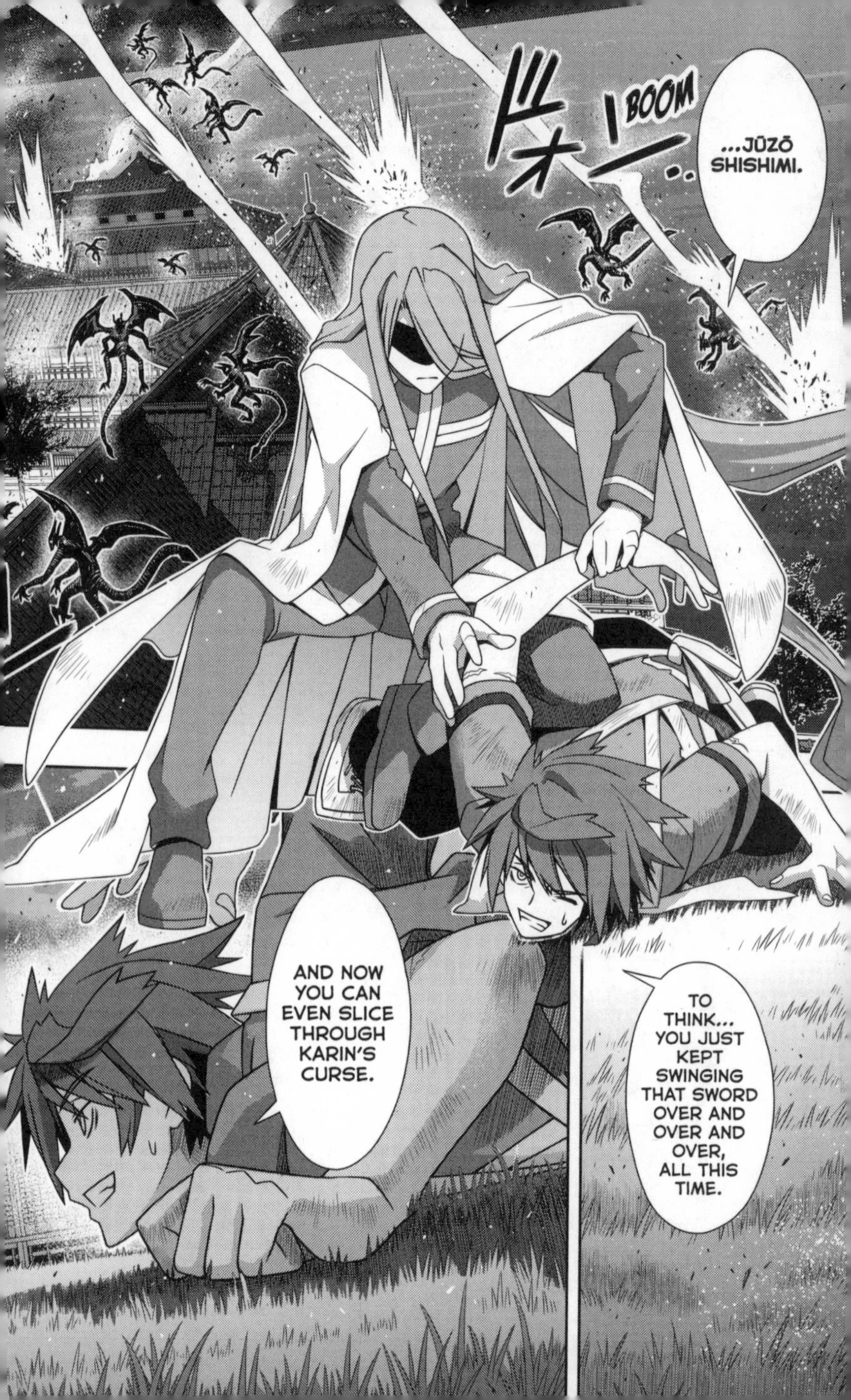
ドォー
BOOM
...JŪZŌ SHISHIMI.
TO THINK... YOU JUST KEPT SWINGING THAT SWORD OVER AND OVER AND OVER, ALL THIS TIME.
AND NOW YOU CAN EVEN SLICE THROUGH KARIN'S CURSE.

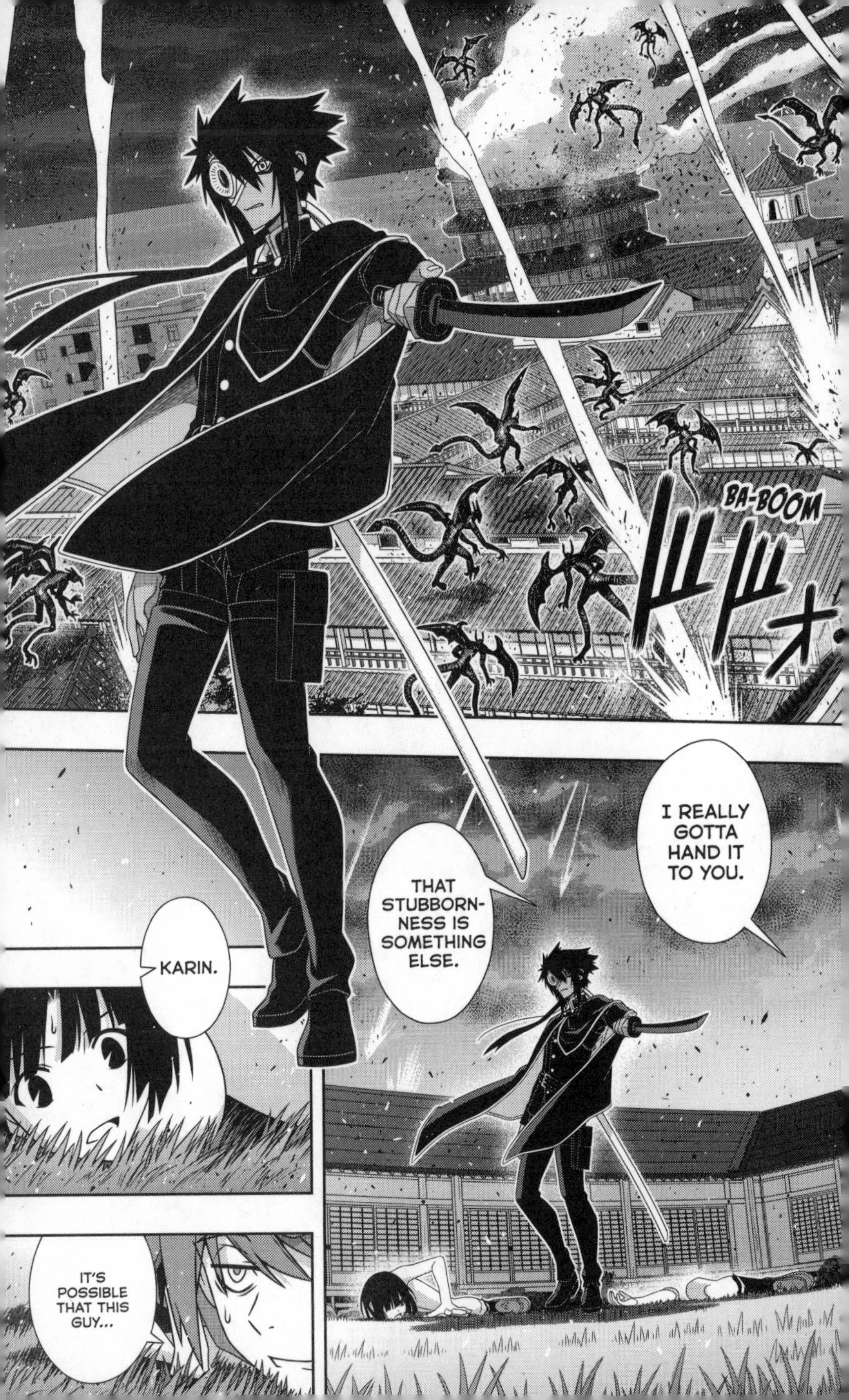
BA-BOOM
I REALLY GOTTA HAND IT TO YOU.
THAT STUBBORN-NESS IS SOMETHING ELSE.
KARIN.
IT'S POSSIBLE THAT THIS GUY...

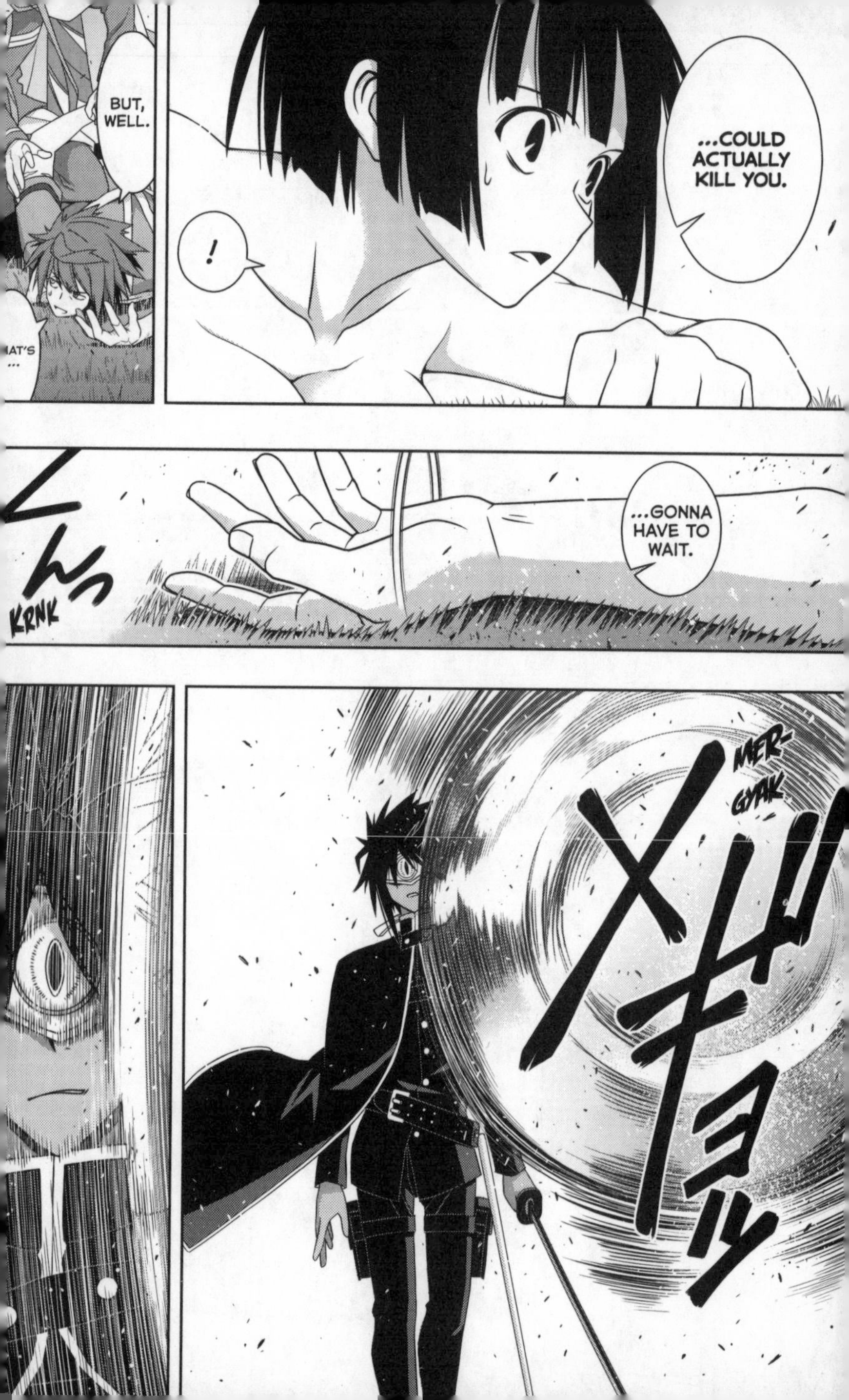
...COULD ACTUALLY KILL YOU.
!
BUT, WELL.
AT'S ...
...GONNA HAVE TO WAIT.
KRNK
MER-GYAK

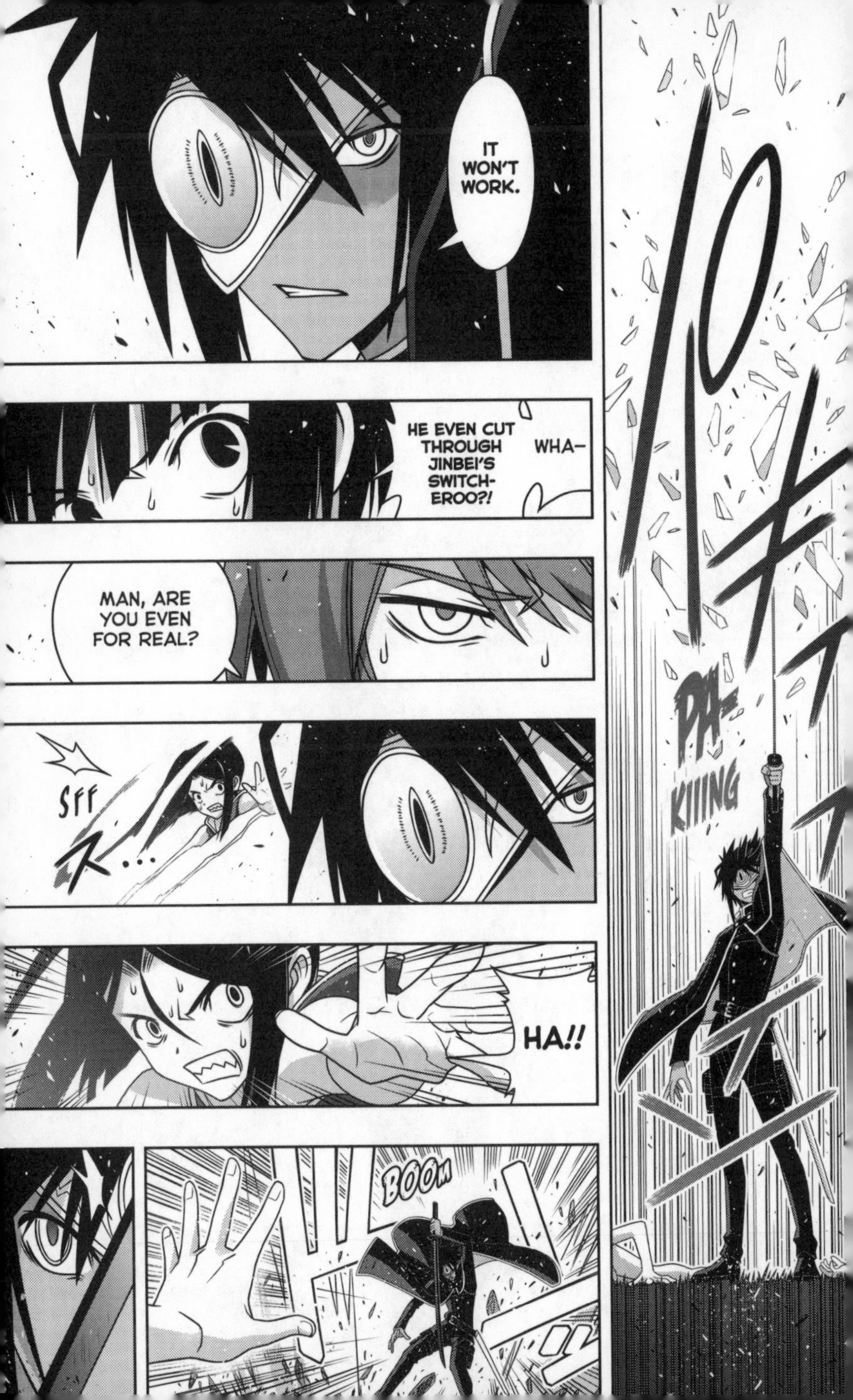
PA-
KIIING
IT WON'T WORK.
WHA—
HE EVEN CUT THROUGH JINBEI'S SWITCH-EROO?!
MAN, ARE YOU EVEN FOR REAL?
SFF
...
HA!!
BOOM

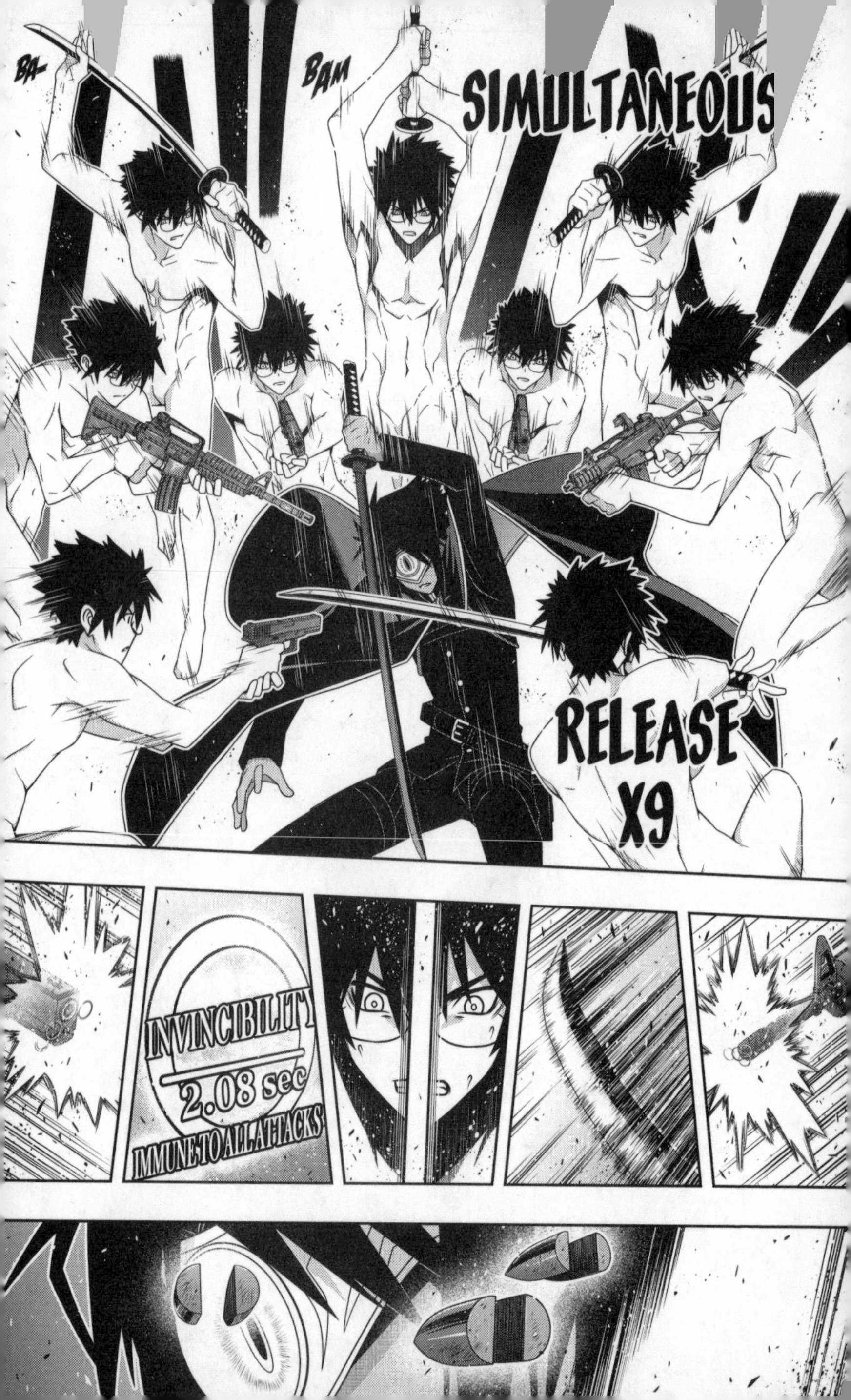
SIMULTANEOUS
BAM
BA-
RELEASE X9
INVINCIBILITY
2.08 sec
IMMUNE TO ALL ATTACKS

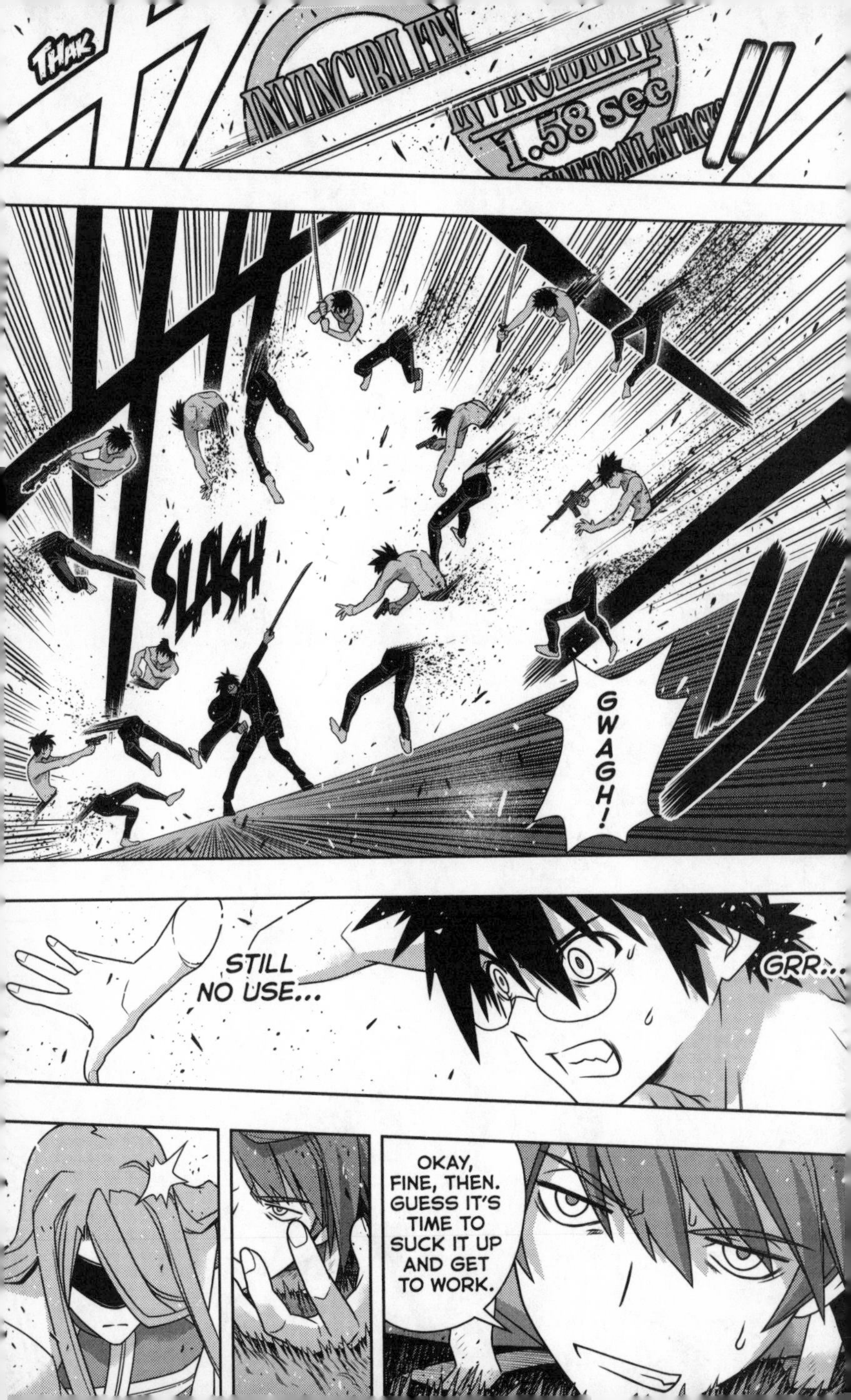
1.58 sec
THAK
SLASH
GWAGH!
GRR...
STILL NO USE...
OKAY, FINE, THEN. GUESS IT'S TIME TO SUCK IT UP AND GET TO WORK.

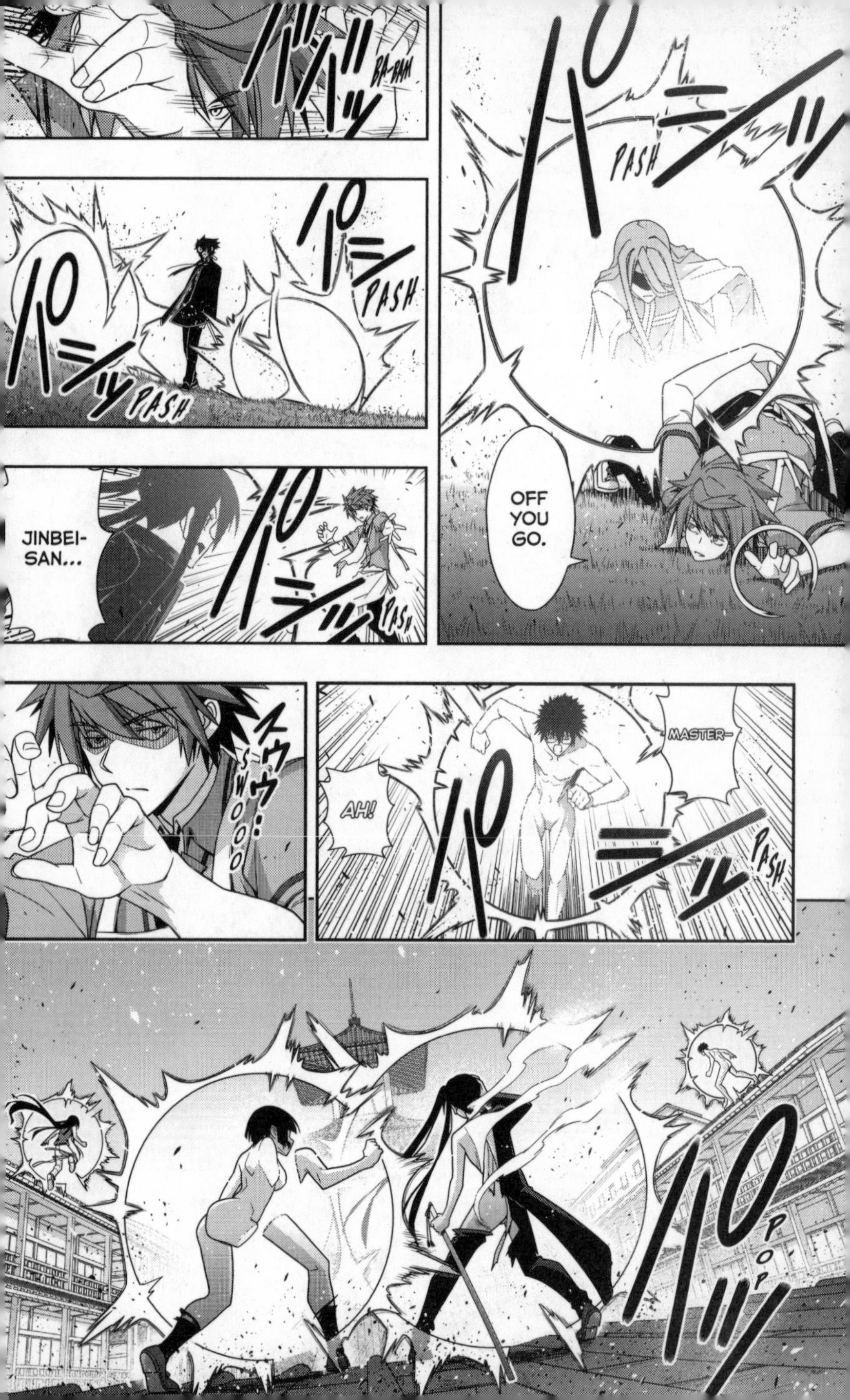
PASH
OFF YOU GO.
BA-BAM
PASH
PASH
PASH
JINBEI-SAN...
MASTER-
PASH
AH!
SWOOOO
POP

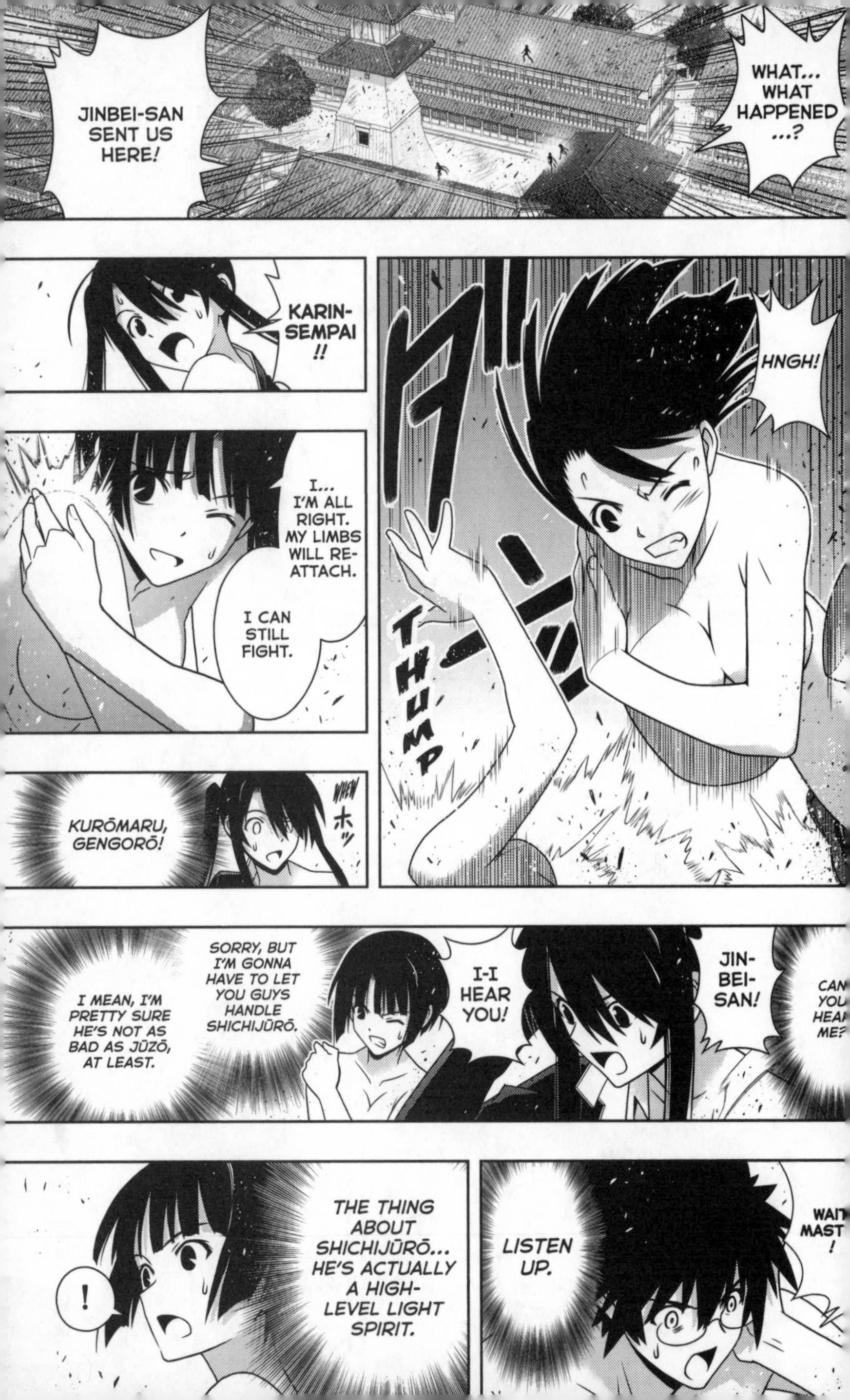
WHAT... WHAT HAPPENED ...?
JINBEI-SAN SENT US HERE!
HNGH!
THUMP
KARIN-SEMPAI !!
I... I'M ALL RIGHT. MY LIMBS WILL RE-ATTACH.
I CAN STILL FIGHT.
WHEN
ホッ
KURŌMARU, GENGORŌ!
CAN YOU HEA ME?
JIN-BEI-SAN!
I-I HEAR YOU!
SORRY, BUT I'M GONNA HAVE TO LET YOU GUYS HANDLE SHICHIJŪRŌ.
I MEAN, I'M PRETTY SURE HE'S NOT AS BAD AS JŪZŌ, AT LEAST.
WAI MAST !
LISTEN UP.
THE THING ABOUT SHICHIJŪRŌ... HE'S ACTUALLY A HIGH-LEVEL LIGHT SPIRIT.
!

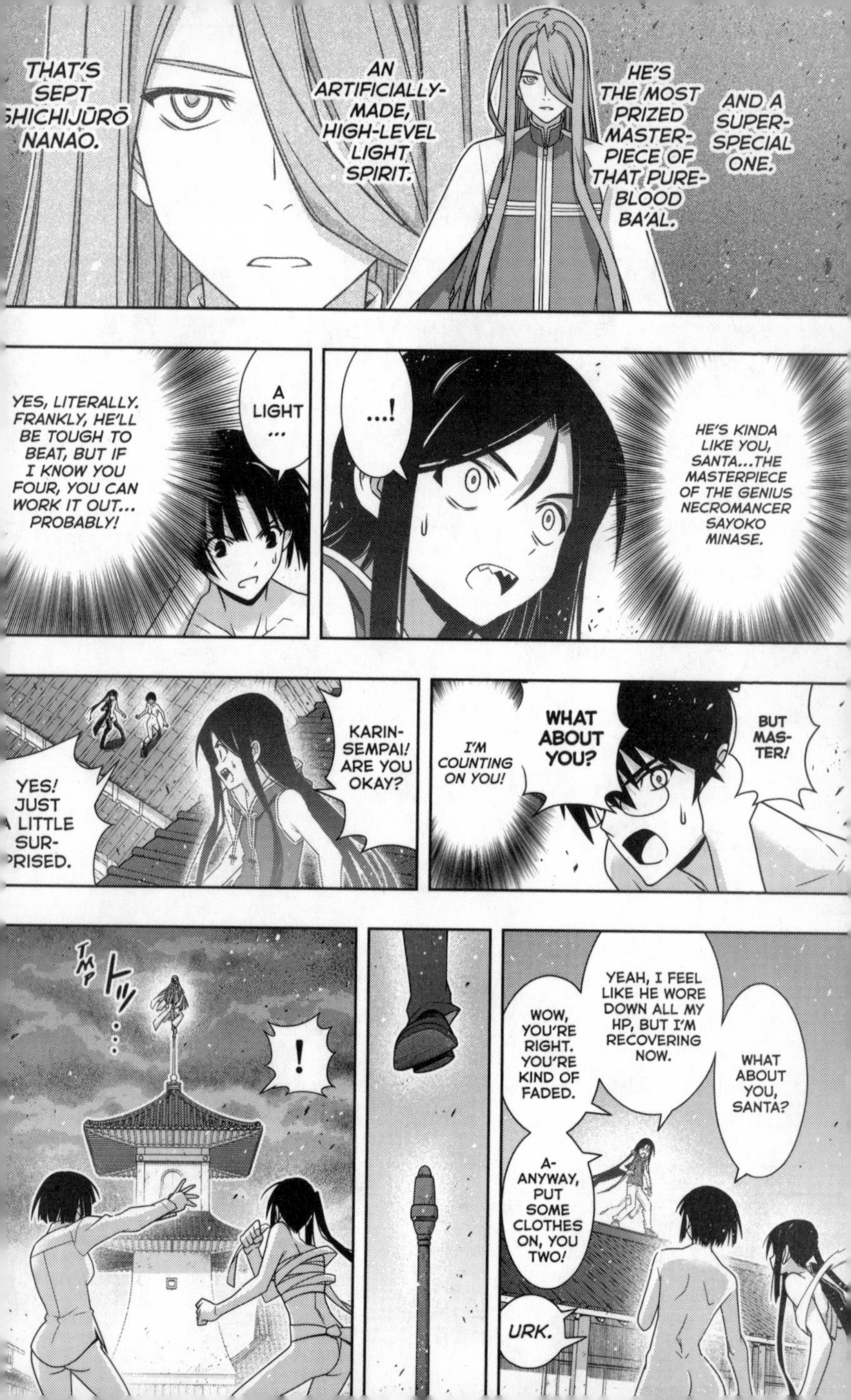
THAT'S SEPT SHICHIJŪRŌ NANAO.
AN ARTIFICIALLY-MADE, HIGH-LEVEL LIGHT SPIRIT.
HE'S THE MOST PRIZED MASTERPIECE OF THAT PUREBLOOD BA'AL.
AND A SUPER-SPECIAL ONE.
HE'S KINDA LIKE YOU, SANTA...THE MASTERPIECE OF THE GENIUS NECROMANCER SAYOKO MINASE.
...!
A LIGHT ...
YES, LITERALLY. FRANKLY, HE'LL BE TOUGH TO BEAT, BUT IF I KNOW YOU FOUR, YOU CAN WORK IT OUT... PROBABLY!
BUT MASTER!
WHAT ABOUT YOU?
I'M COUNTING ON YOU!
KARIN-SEMPAI! ARE YOU OKAY?
YES! JUST A LITTLE SURPRISED.
WHAT ABOUT YOU, SANTA?
YEAH, I FEEL LIKE HE WORE DOWN ALL MY HP, BUT I'M RECOVERING NOW.
WOW, YOU'RE RIGHT. YOU'RE KIND OF FADED.
A-ANYWAY, PUT SOME CLOTHES ON, YOU TWO!
URK.
!
TMP トッ...

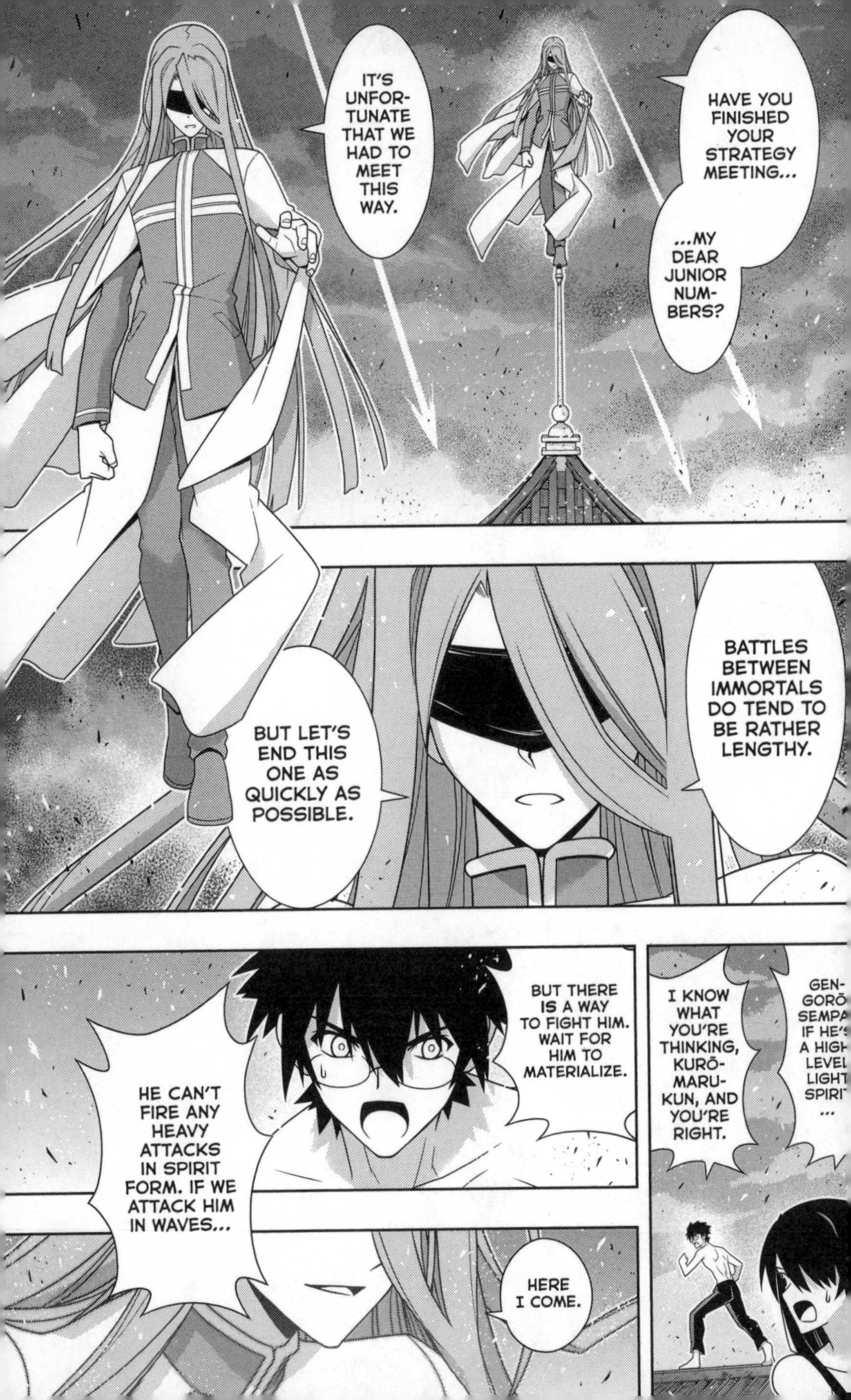
HAVE YOU FINISHED YOUR STRATEGY MEETING...
...MY DEAR JUNIOR NUMBERS?
IT'S UNFORTUNATE THAT WE HAD TO MEET THIS WAY.
BATTLES BETWEEN IMMORTALS DO TEND TO BE RATHER LENGTHY.
BUT LET'S END THIS ONE AS QUICKLY AS POSSIBLE.
GEN-GORŌ SEMPA IF HE'S A HIGH LEVEL LIGHT SPIRIT ...
I KNOW WHAT YOU'RE THINKING, KURŌMARU-KUN, AND YOU'RE RIGHT.
BUT THERE IS A WAY TO FIGHT HIM. WAIT FOR HIM TO MATERIALIZE.
HE CAN'T FIRE ANY HEAVY ATTACKS IN SPIRIT FORM. IF WE ATTACK HIM IN WAVES...
HERE I COME.

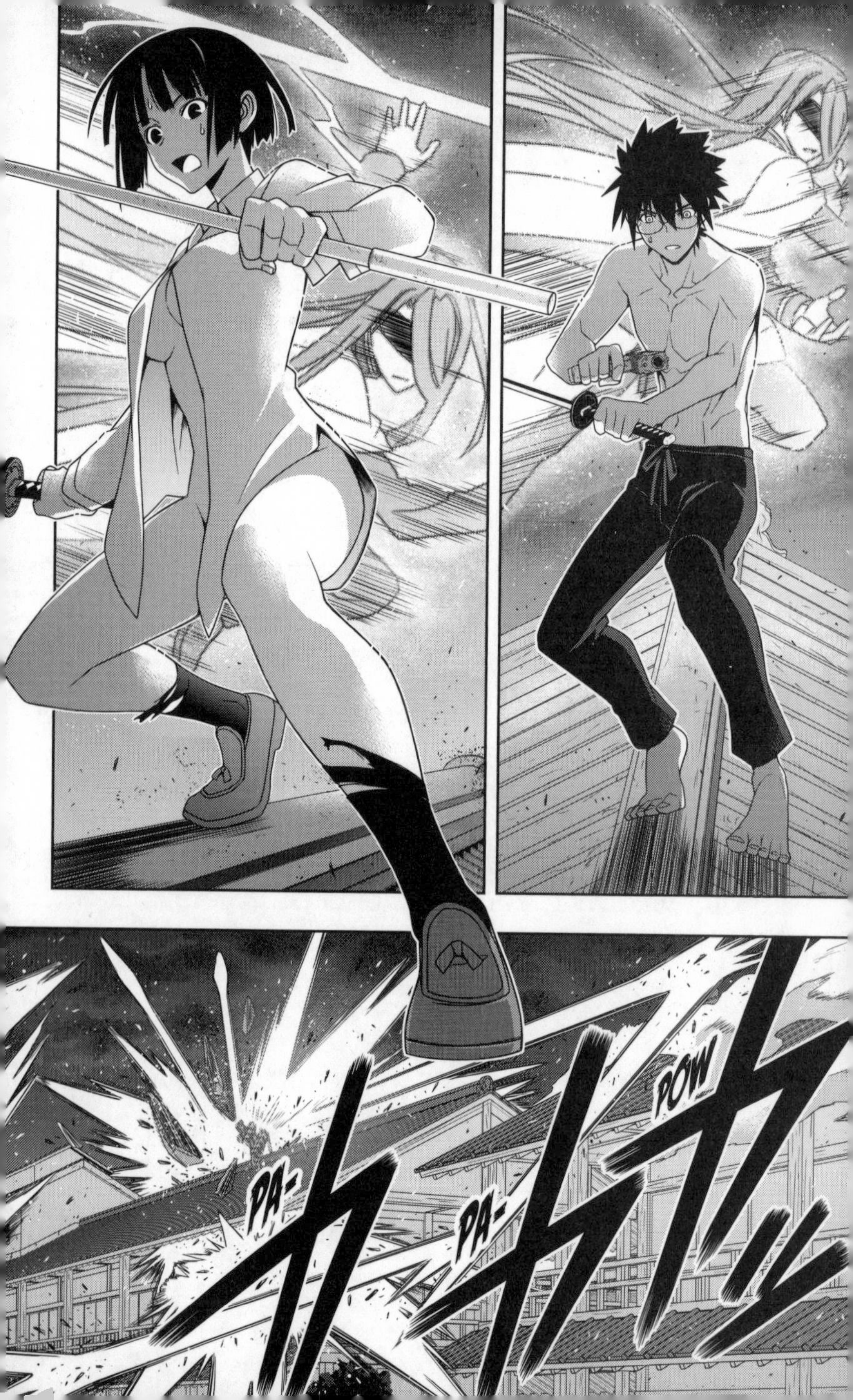
POW
PA-
PA-

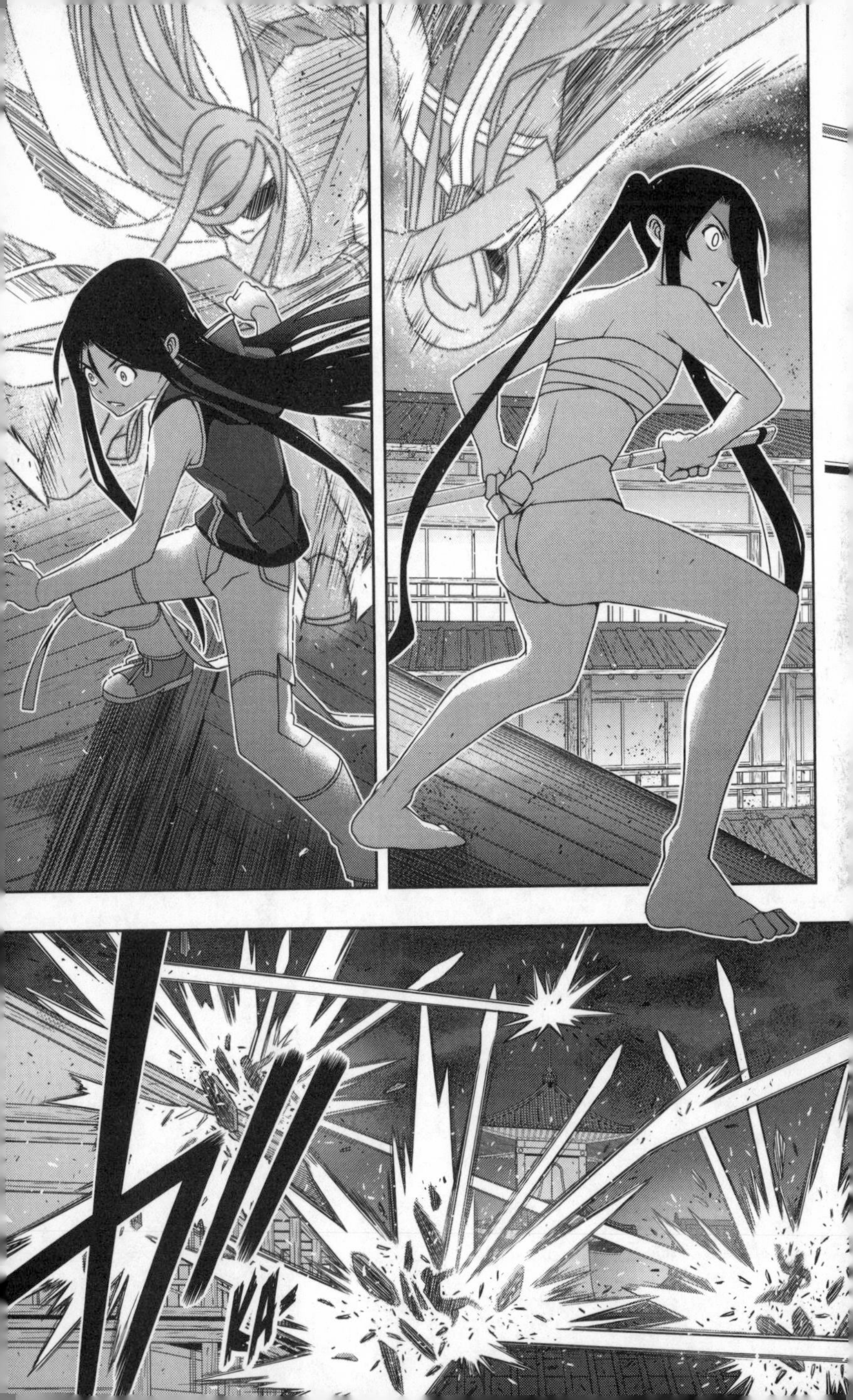
KA-

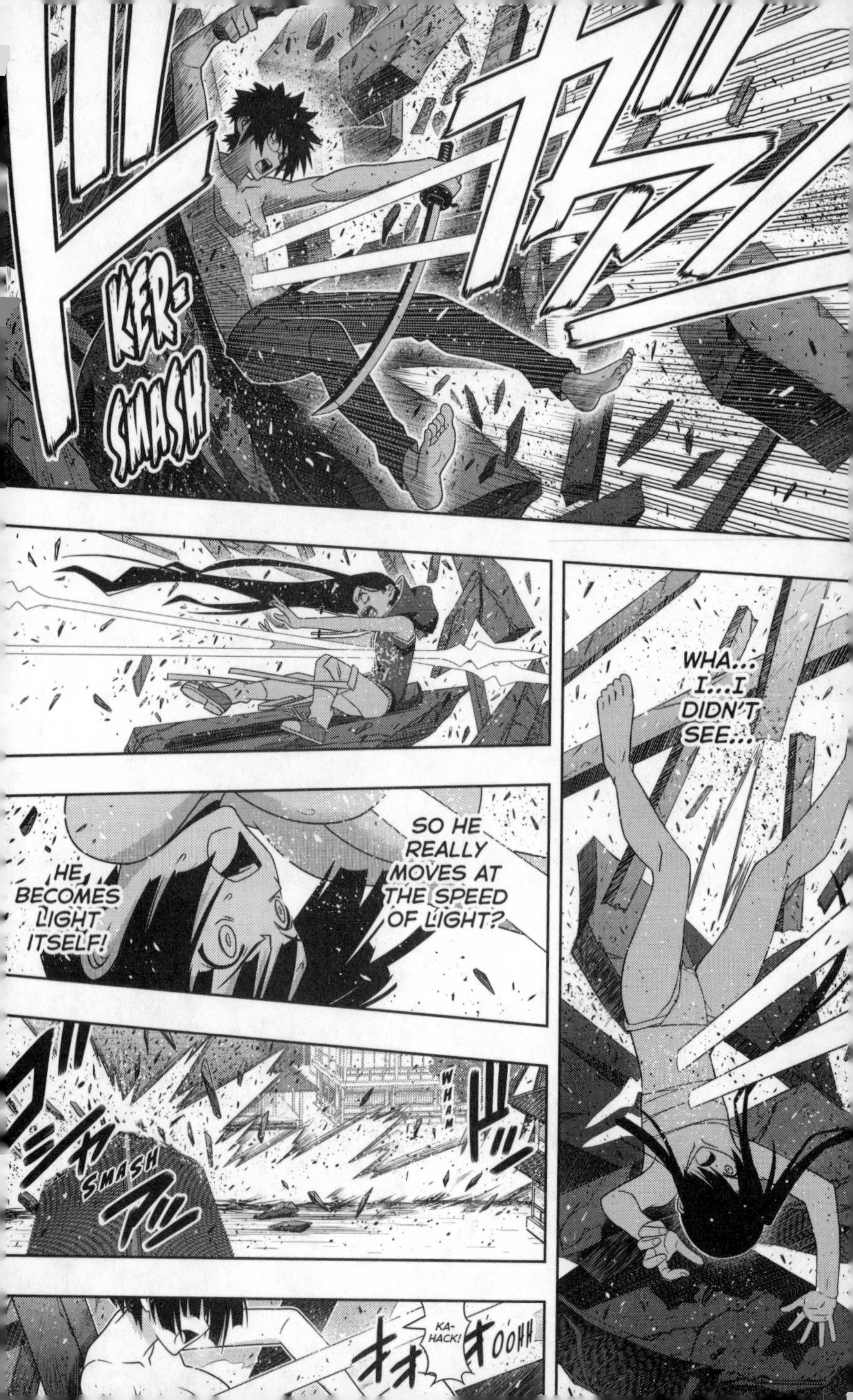

KER-SMASH
WHA... I...I DIDN'T SEE...
SO HE REALLY MOVES AT THE SPEED OF LIGHT?
HE BECOMES LIGHT ITSELF!
WHAM
SMASH
KA-HACK!
OOHH

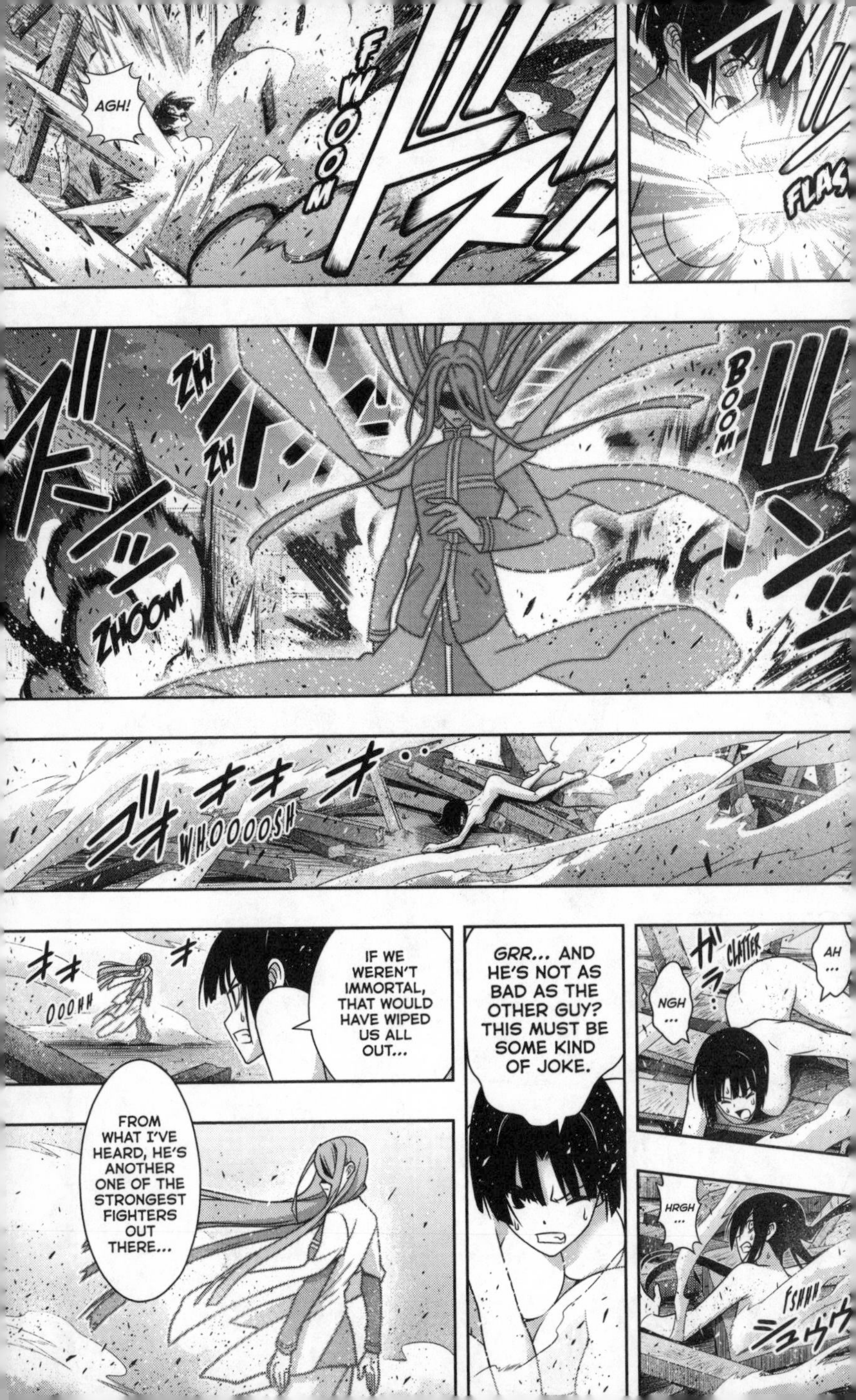
FLAS
FWOOOM
AGH!
BOOM
ZH
ZH
ZHOOM
WHOOOOSH
AH ...
CLATTER
NGH ...
HRGH ...
FSHHH
GRR... AND HE'S NOT AS BAD AS THE OTHER GUY? THIS MUST BE SOME KIND OF JOKE.
IF WE WEREN'T IMMORTAL, THAT WOULD HAVE WIPED US ALL OUT...
OOOHH
FROM WHAT I'VE HEARD, HE'S ANOTHER ONE OF THE STRONGEST FIGHTERS OUT THERE...

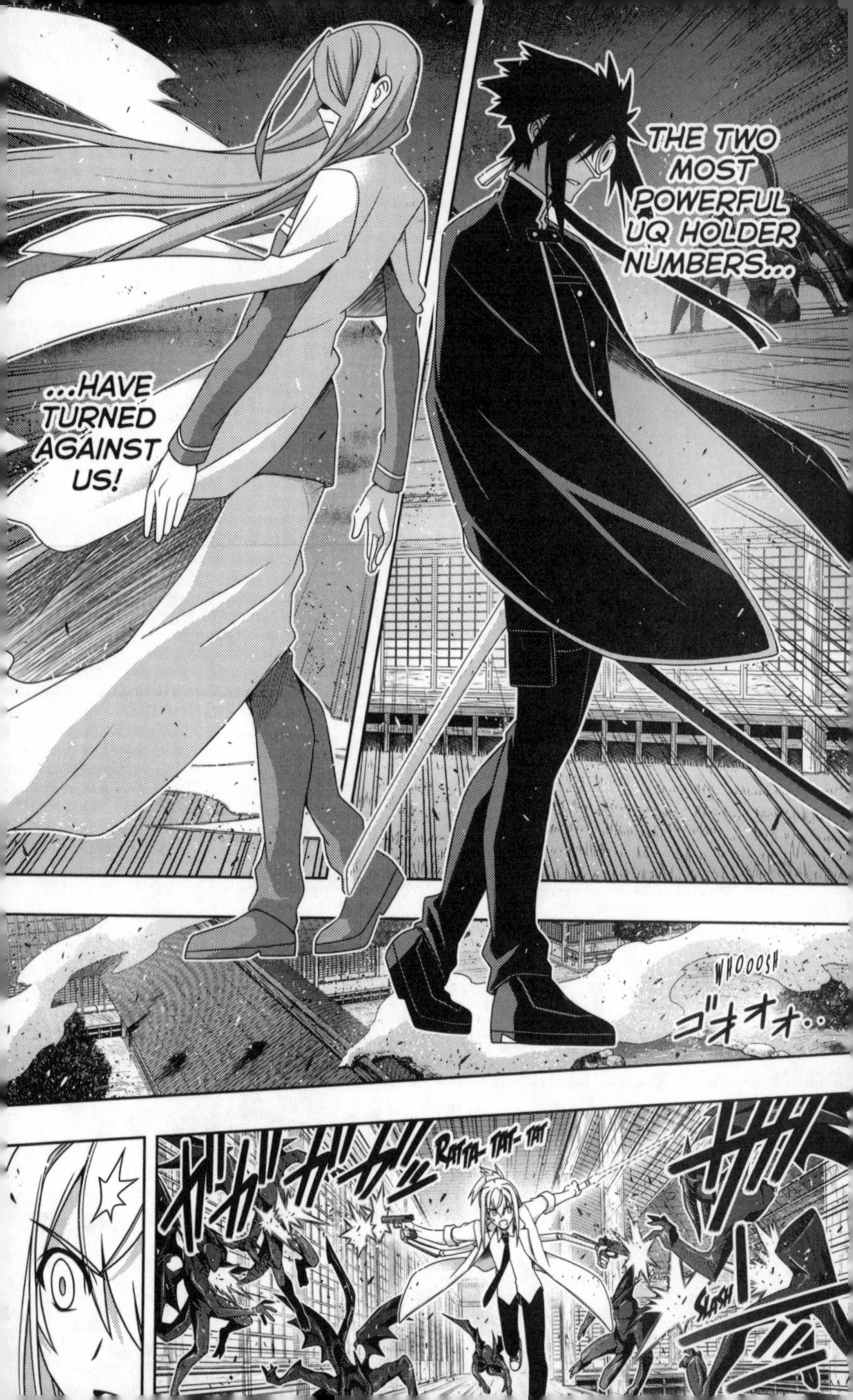
THE TWO MOST POWERFUL UQ HOLDER NUMBERS...
...HAVE TURNED AGAINST US!
WHOOOSH
ゴオオオ..
RATTA-TAT-TAT
SLASH

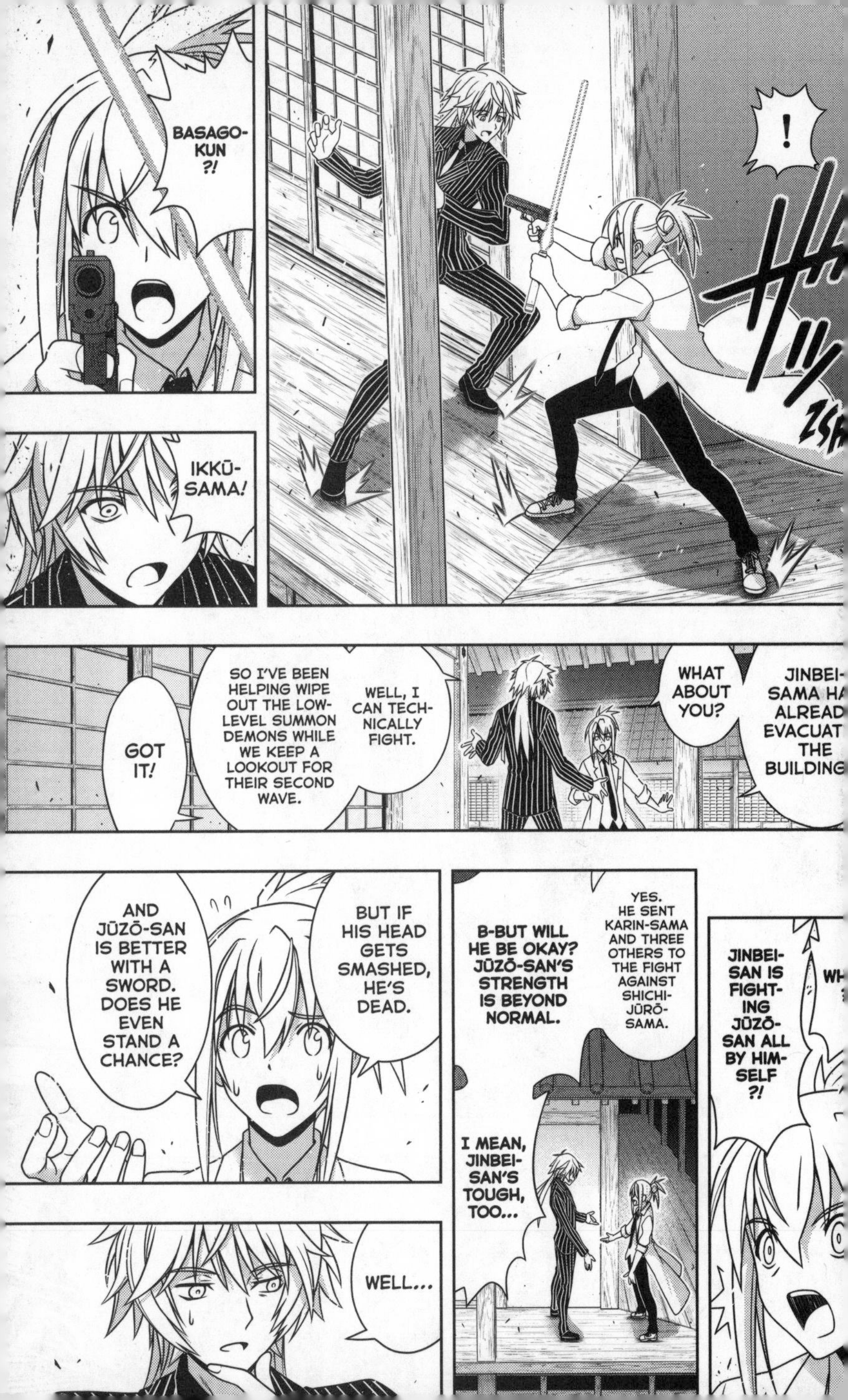
!
ZSH
BASAGO-KUN?!
IKKŪ-SAMA!
JINBEI-SAMA HA ALREAD EVACUAT THE BUILDING
WHAT ABOUT YOU?
WELL, I CAN TECHNICALLY FIGHT.
SO I'VE BEEN HELPING WIPE OUT THE LOW-LEVEL SUMMON DEMONS WHILE WE KEEP A LOOKOUT FOR THEIR SECOND WAVE.
GOT IT!
WH
JINBEI-SAN IS FIGHTING JŪZŌ-SAN ALL BY HIMSELF?!
YES. HE SENT KARIN-SAMA AND THREE OTHERS TO THE FIGHT AGAINST SHICHIJŪRŌ-SAMA.
B-BUT WILL HE BE OKAY? JŪZŌ-SAN'S STRENGTH IS BEYOND NORMAL.
I MEAN, JINBEI-SAN'S TOUGH, TOO...
BUT IF HIS HEAD GETS SMASHED, HE'S DEAD.
AND JŪZŌ-SAN IS BETTER WITH A SWORD. DOES HE EVEN STAND A CHANCE?
WELL...

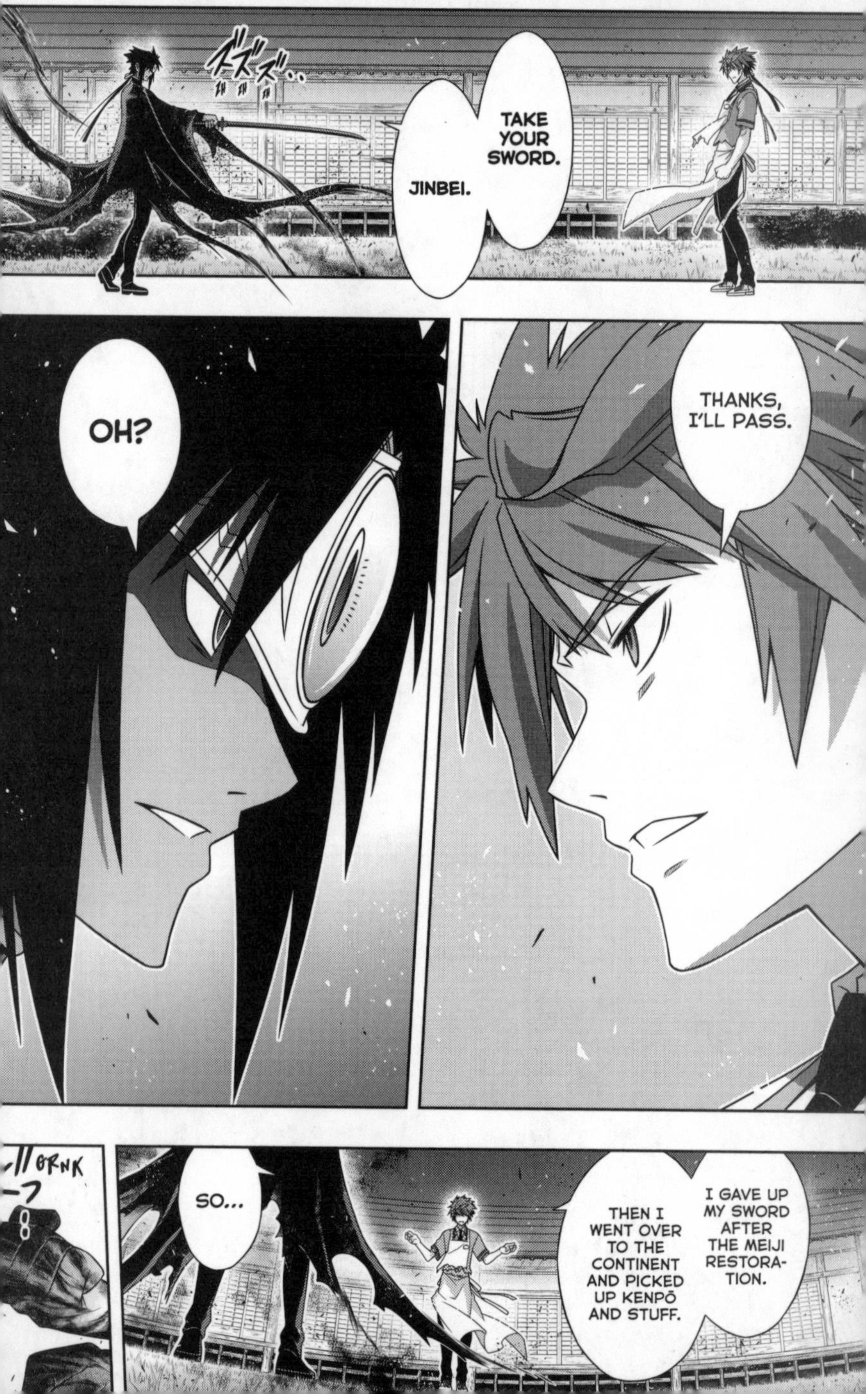

TAKE YOUR SWORD.
JINBEI.
ズズズ…
THANKS, I'LL PASS.
OH?
I GAVE UP MY SWORD AFTER THE MEIJI RESTORA-TION.
THEN I WENT OVER TO THE CONTINENT AND PICKED UP KENPŌ AND STUFF.
SO...

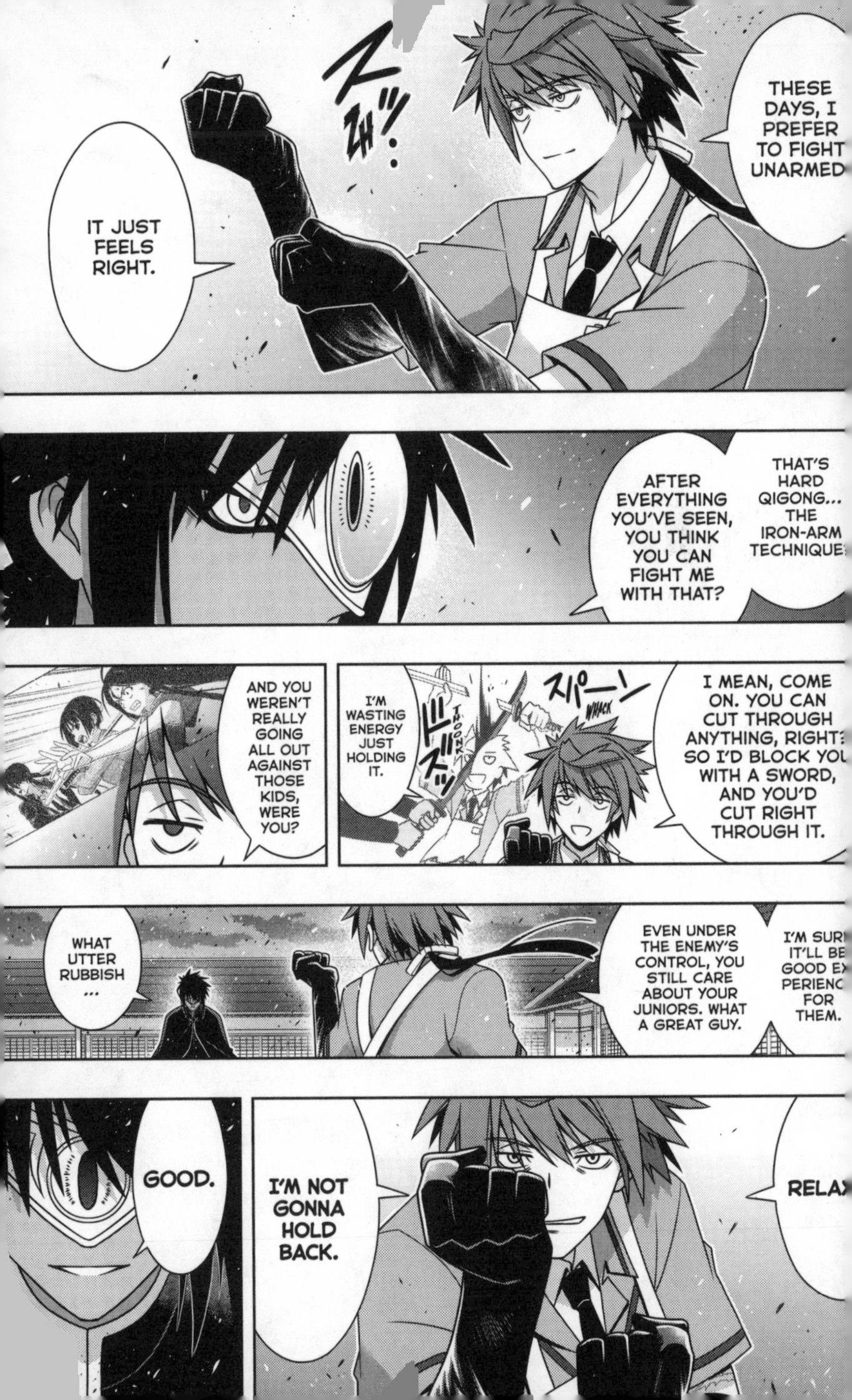

THESE DAYS, I PREFER TO FIGHT UNARMED
IT JUST FEELS RIGHT.
THAT'S HARD QIGONG... THE IRON-ARM TECHNIQUE
AFTER EVERYTHING YOU'VE SEEN, YOU THINK YOU CAN FIGHT ME WITH THAT?
I MEAN, COME ON. YOU CAN CUT THROUGH ANYTHING, RIGHT? SO I'D BLOCK YOU WITH A SWORD, AND YOU'D CUT RIGHT THROUGH IT.
スパーン
WHACK
ドドズッ
THOONK
I'M WASTING ENERGY JUST HOLDING IT.
AND YOU WEREN'T REALLY GOING ALL OUT AGAINST THOSE KIDS, WERE YOU?
I'M SUR IT'LL BE GOOD EX PERIENC FOR THEM.
EVEN UNDER THE ENEMY'S CONTROL, YOU STILL CARE ABOUT YOUR JUNIORS. WHAT A GREAT GUY.
WHAT UTTER RUBBISH...
RELA
I'M NOT GONNA HOLD BACK.
GOOD.

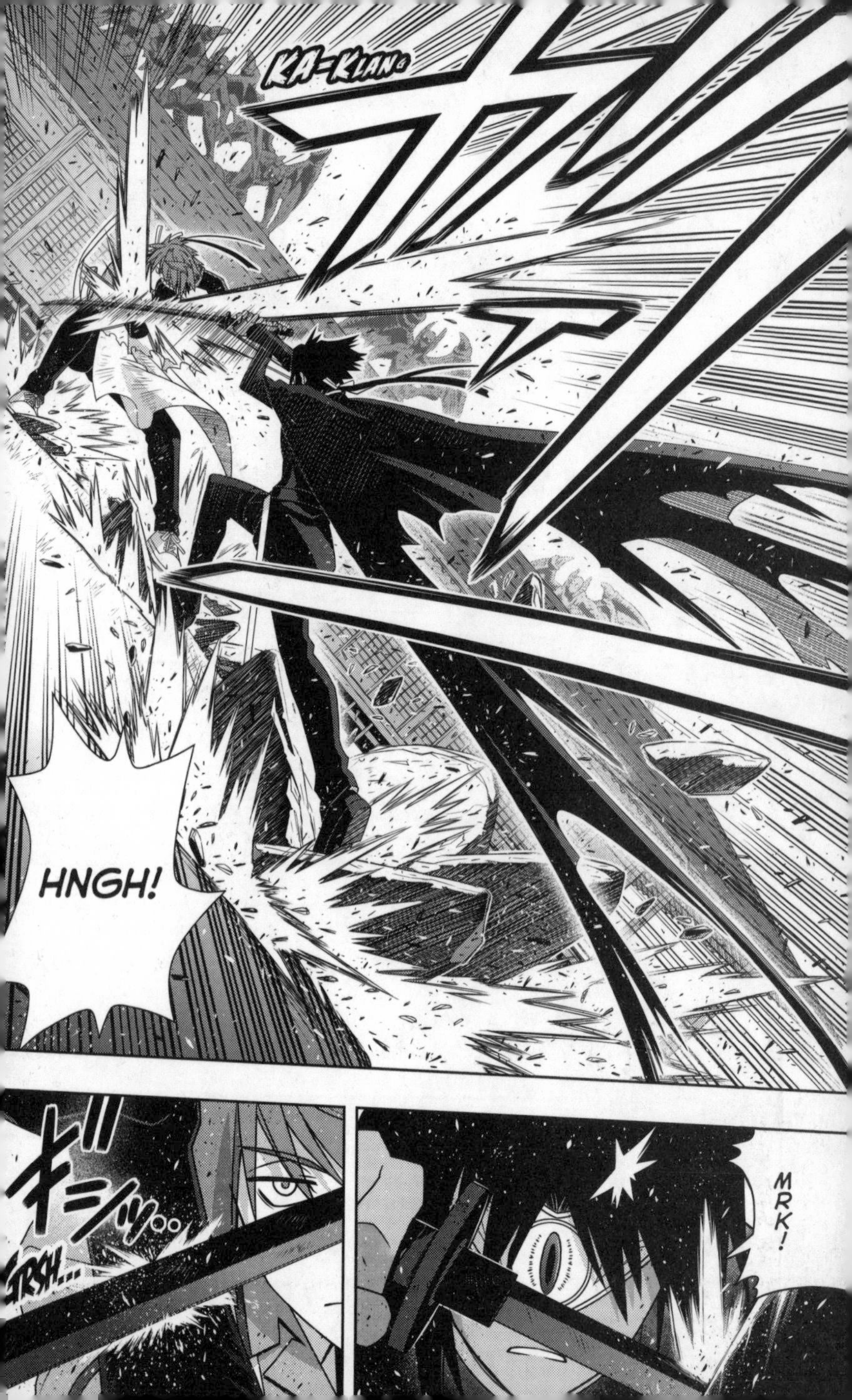
KA-KLANG
HNGH!
MRK!
RSH...

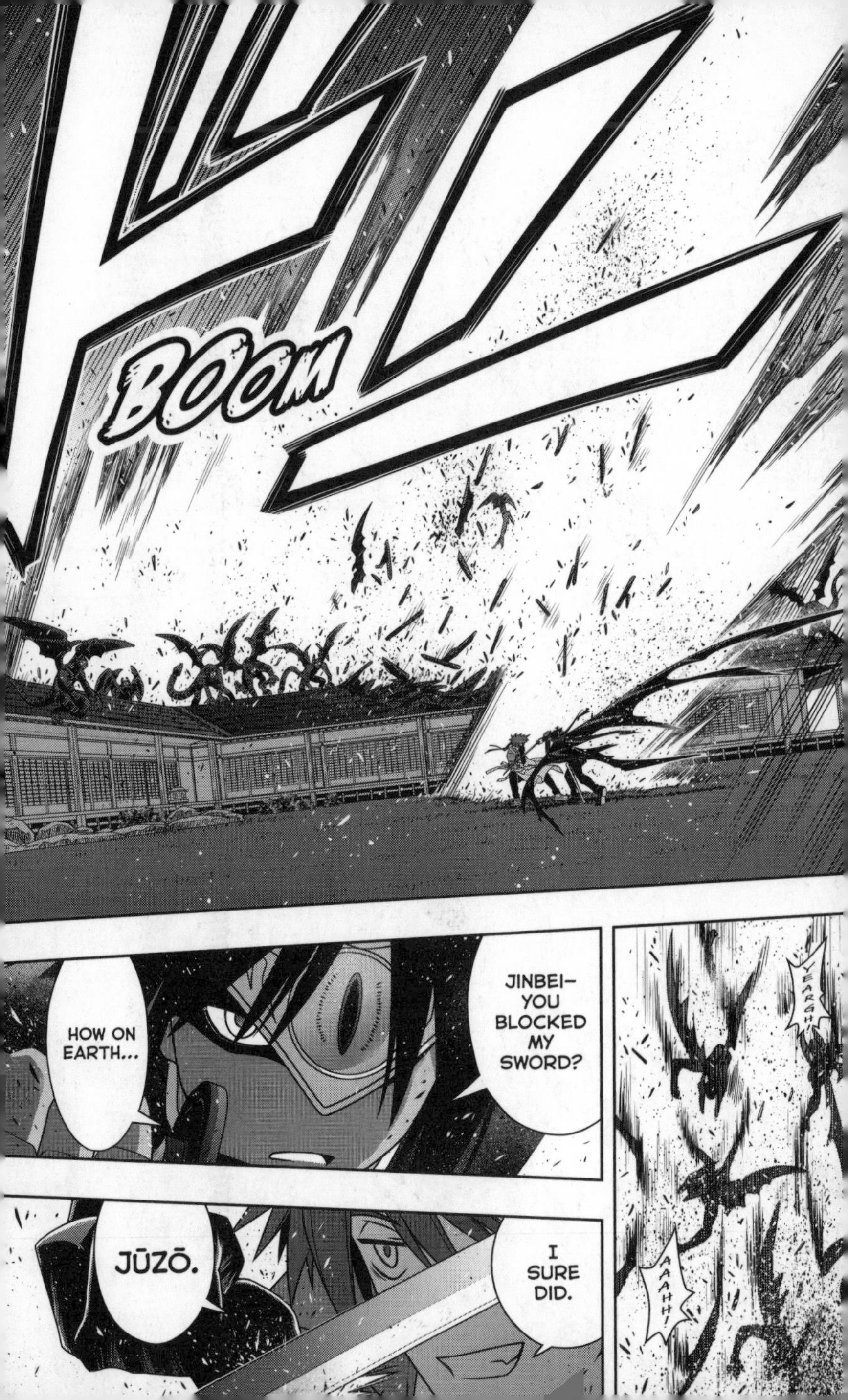
BOOM
YEARGH!
AAAHH!
JINBEI—YOU BLOCKED MY SWORD?
HOW ON EARTH...
I SURE DID.
JŪZŌ.

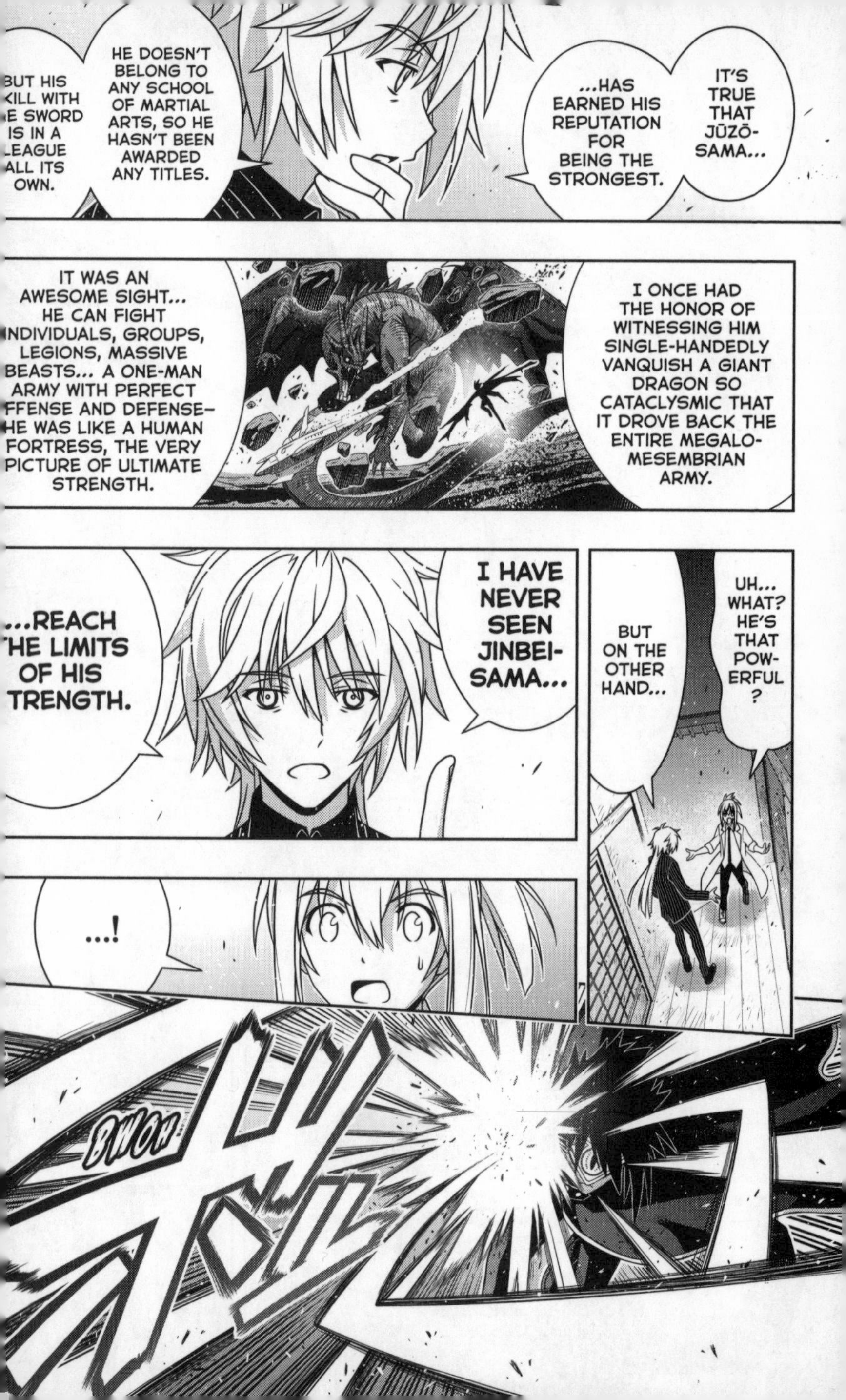
IT'S TRUE THAT JŪZŌ-SAMA...
...HAS EARNED HIS REPUTATION FOR BEING THE STRONGEST.
HE DOESN'T BELONG TO ANY SCHOOL OF MARTIAL ARTS, SO HE HASN'T BEEN AWARDED ANY TITLES.
BUT HIS KILL WITH E SWORD IS IN A EAGUE ALL ITS OWN.
I ONCE HAD THE HONOR OF WITNESSING HIM SINGLE-HANDEDLY VANQUISH A GIANT DRAGON SO CATACLYSMIC THAT IT DROVE BACK THE ENTIRE MEGALO-MESEMBRIAN ARMY.
IT WAS AN AWESOME SIGHT... HE CAN FIGHT NDIVIDUALS, GROUPS, LEGIONS, MASSIVE BEASTS... A ONE-MAN ARMY WITH PERFECT FFENSE AND DEFENSE– HE WAS LIKE A HUMAN FORTRESS, THE VERY PICTURE OF ULTIMATE STRENGTH.
UH... WHAT? HE'S THAT POW-ERFUL?
BUT ON THE OTHER HAND...
I HAVE NEVER SEEN JINBEI-SAMA...
...REACH HE LIMITS OF HIS TRENGTH.
...!
BWOH

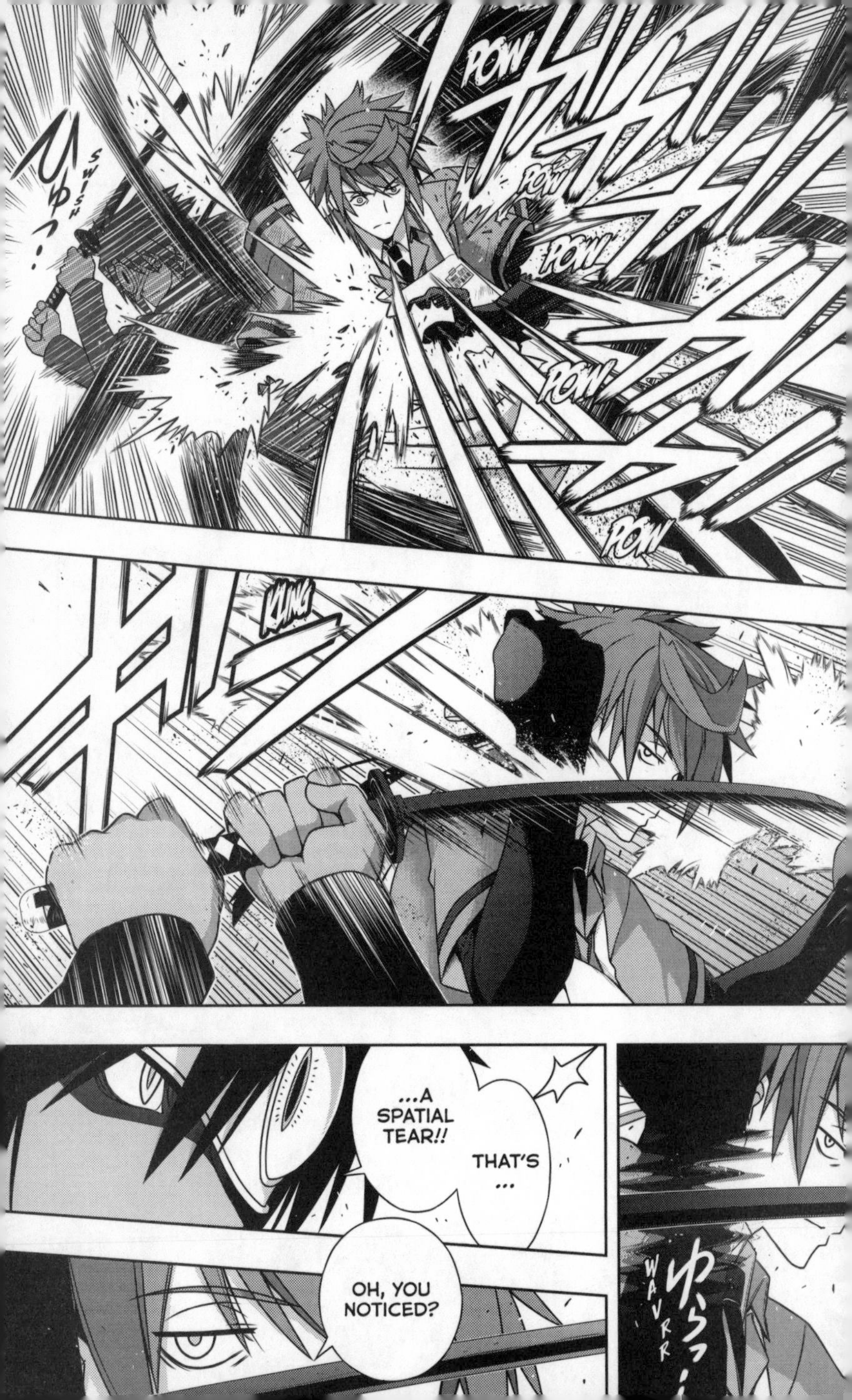
POW
POW
POW
POW
POW
ひゅっ!!
SWISH
KLING
ゆらっ!!
WAVRR
THAT'S...
...A SPATIAL TEAR!!
OH, YOU NOTICED?

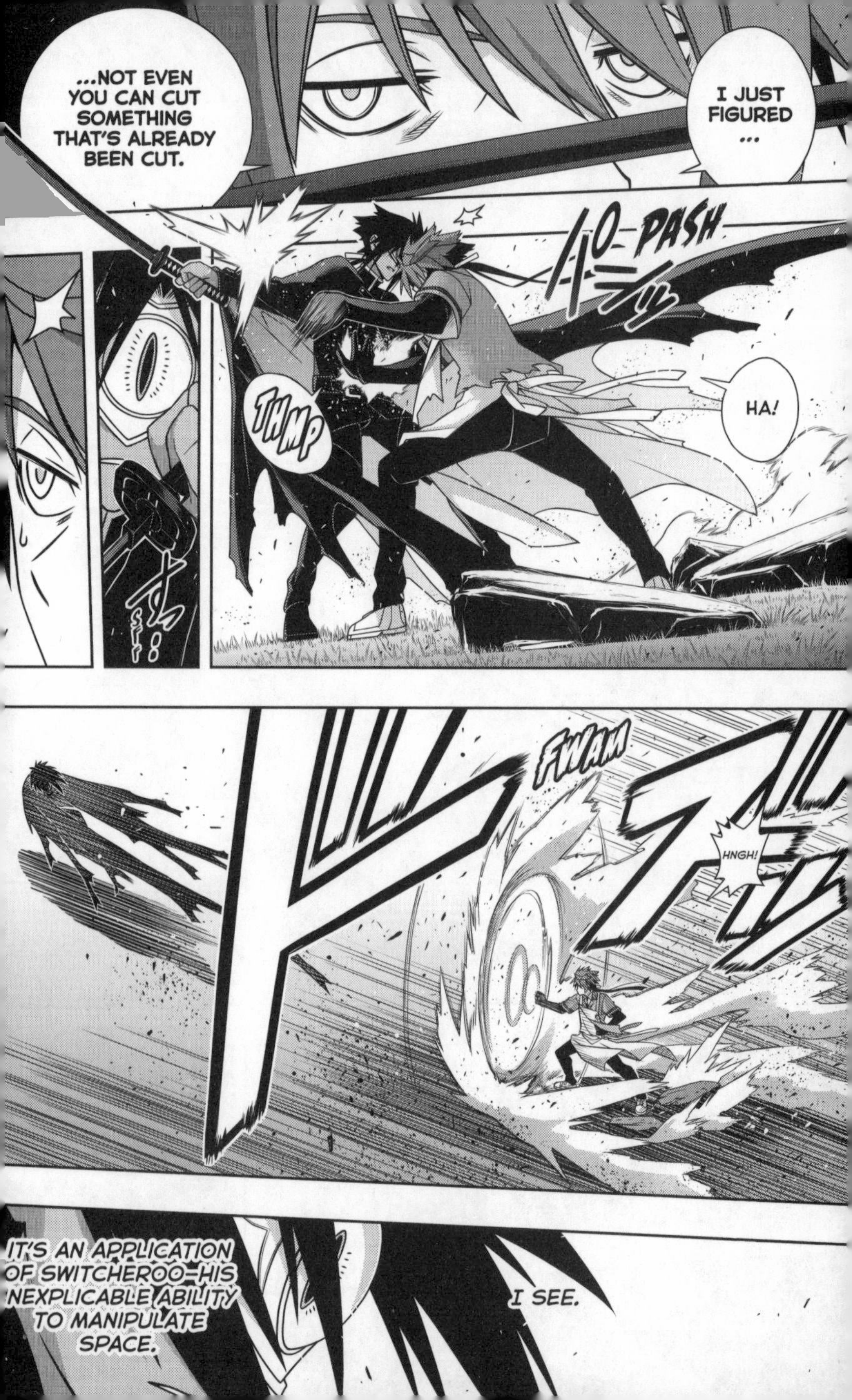

I JUST FIGURED ...
...NOT EVEN YOU CAN CUT SOMETHING THAT'S ALREADY BEEN CUT.
O-PASH
HA!
THMP
FWAM
HNGH!
I SEE.
IT'S AN APPLICATION OF SWITCHEROO—HIS NEXPLICABLE ABILITY TO MANIPULATE SPACE.

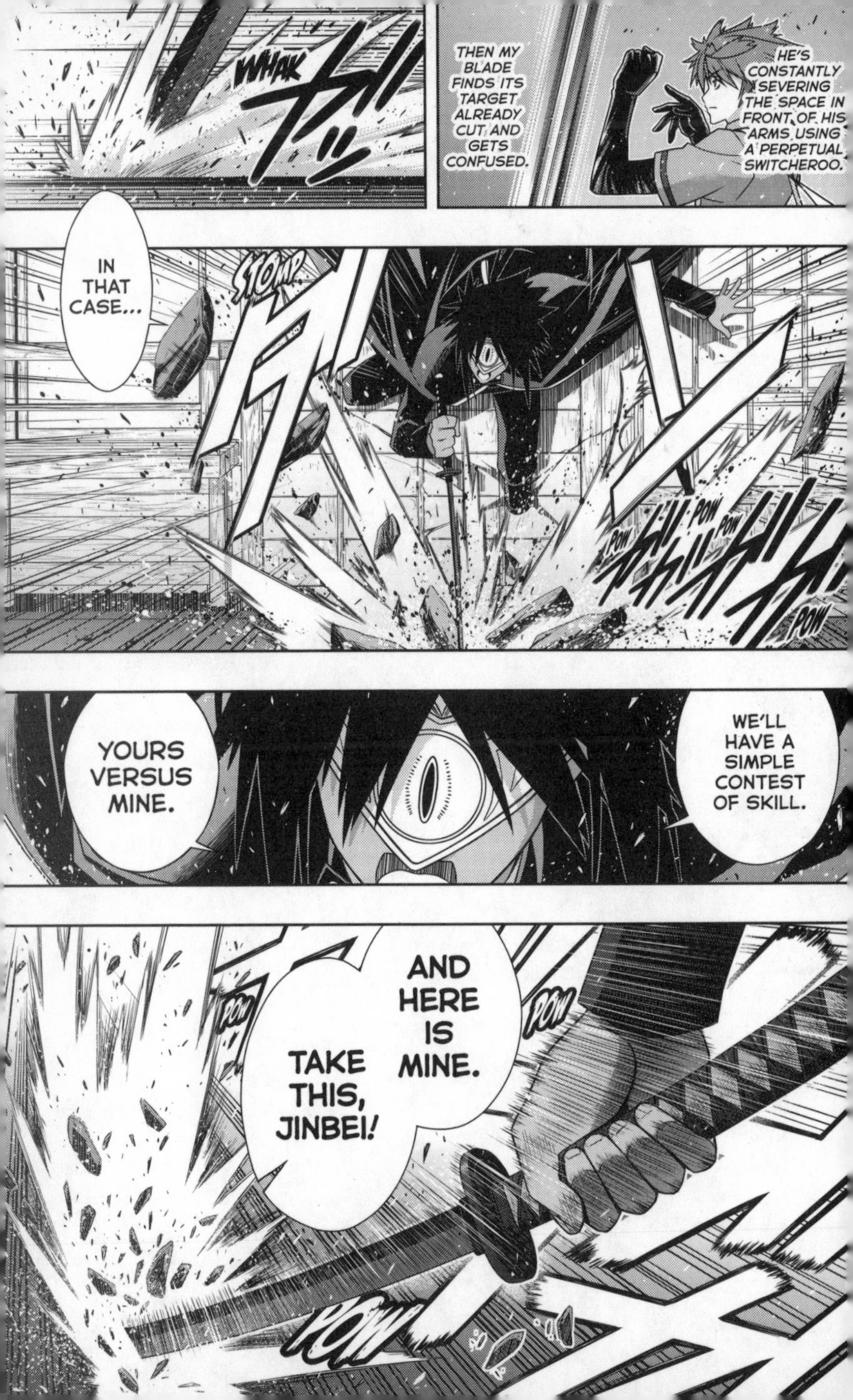
HE'S CONSTANTLY SEVERING THE SPACE IN FRONT OF HIS ARMS USING A PERPETUAL SWITCHEROO.
THEN MY BLADE FINDS ITS TARGET ALREADY CUT AND GETS CONFUSED.
WHAK
IN THAT CASE...
STOMP
POW
POW
POW
POW
WE'LL HAVE A SIMPLE CONTEST OF SKILL.
YOURS VERSUS MINE.
POW
AND HERE IS MINE.
TAKE THIS, JINBEI!
POW
POW

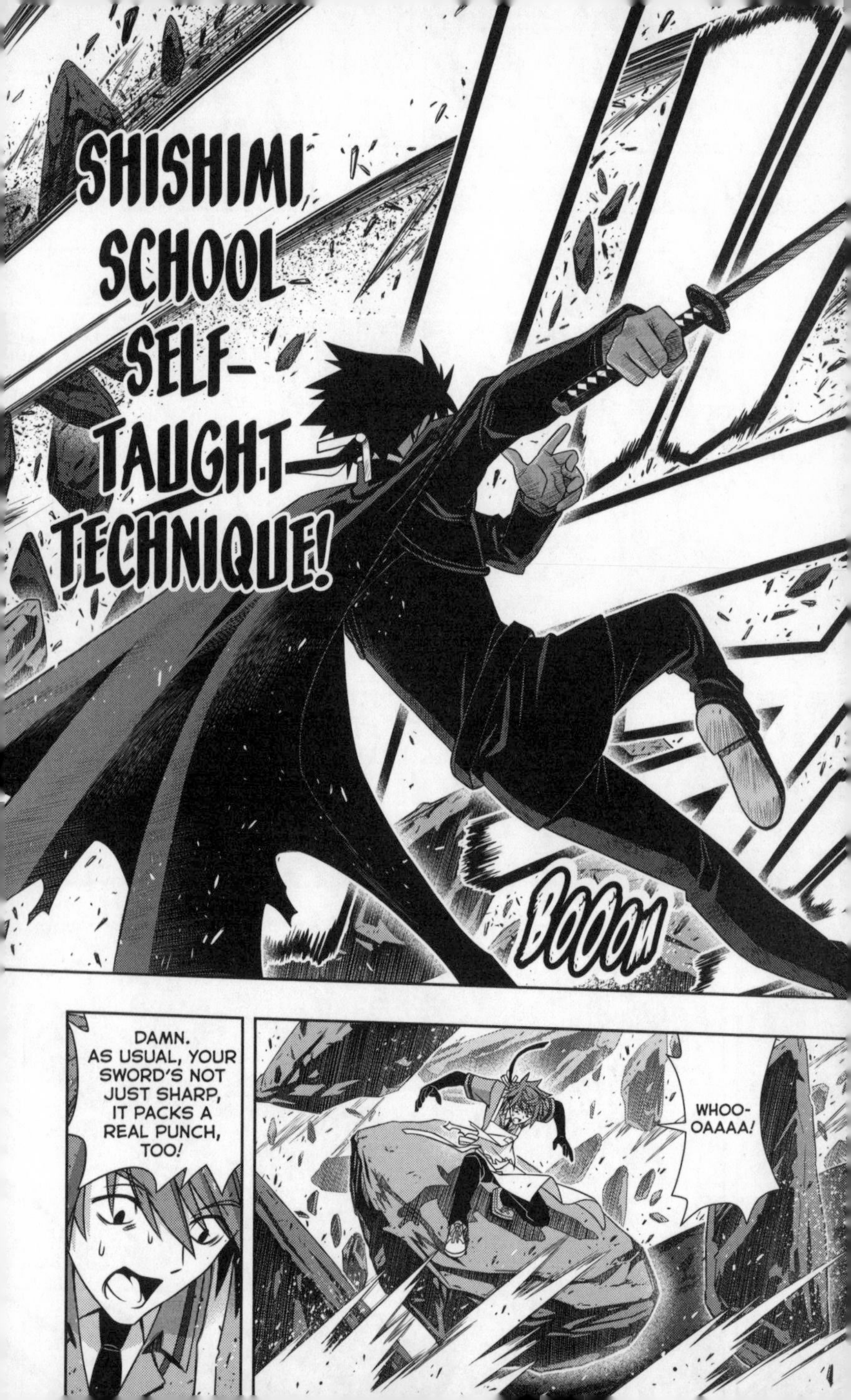
SHISHIMI SCHOOL SELF-TAUGHT TECHNIQUE!
BOOOM
WHOO-OAAAA!
DAMN. AS USUAL, YOUR SWORD'S NOT JUST SHARP, IT PACKS A REAL PUNCH, TOO!

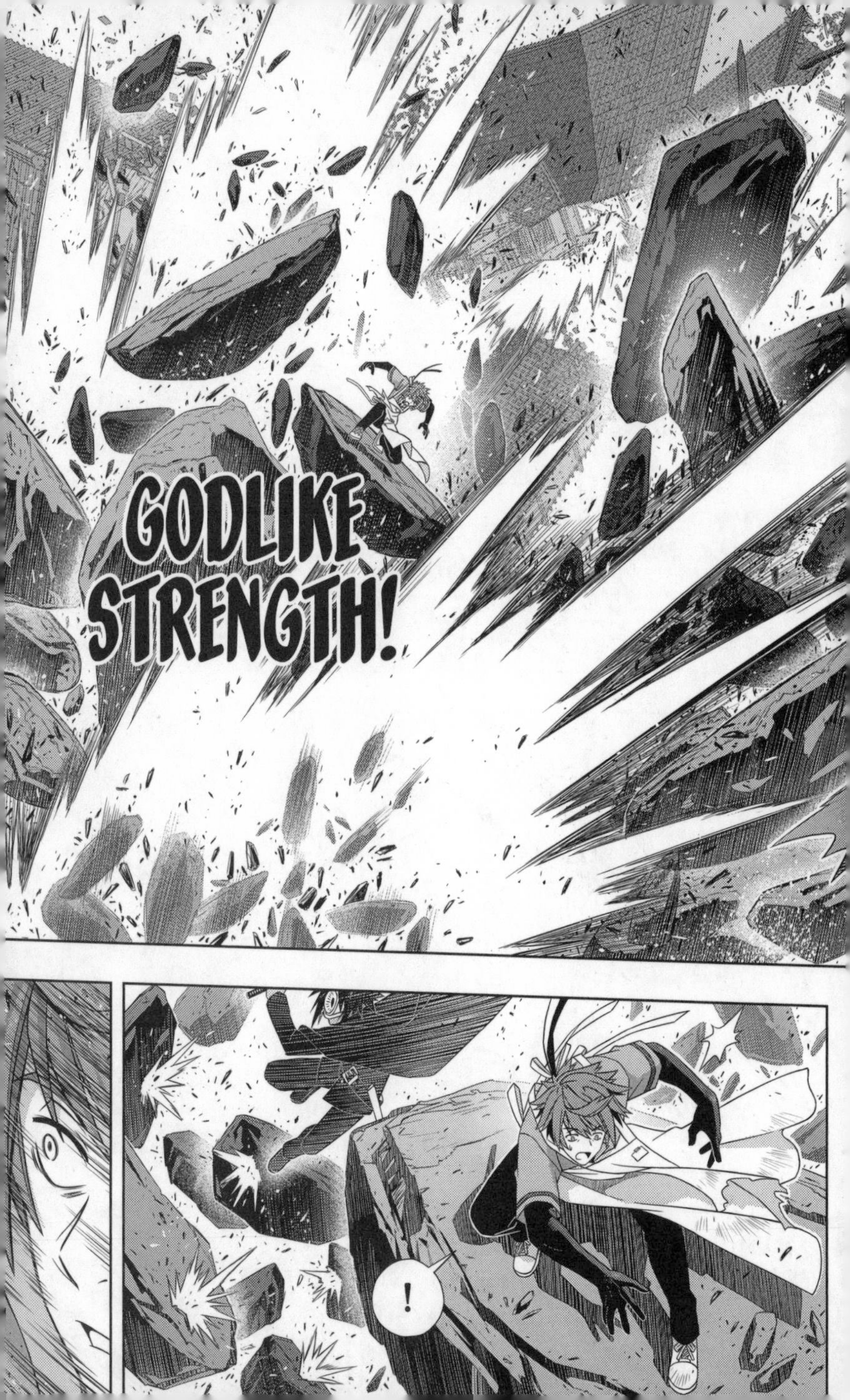
GODLIKE STRENGTH!
!

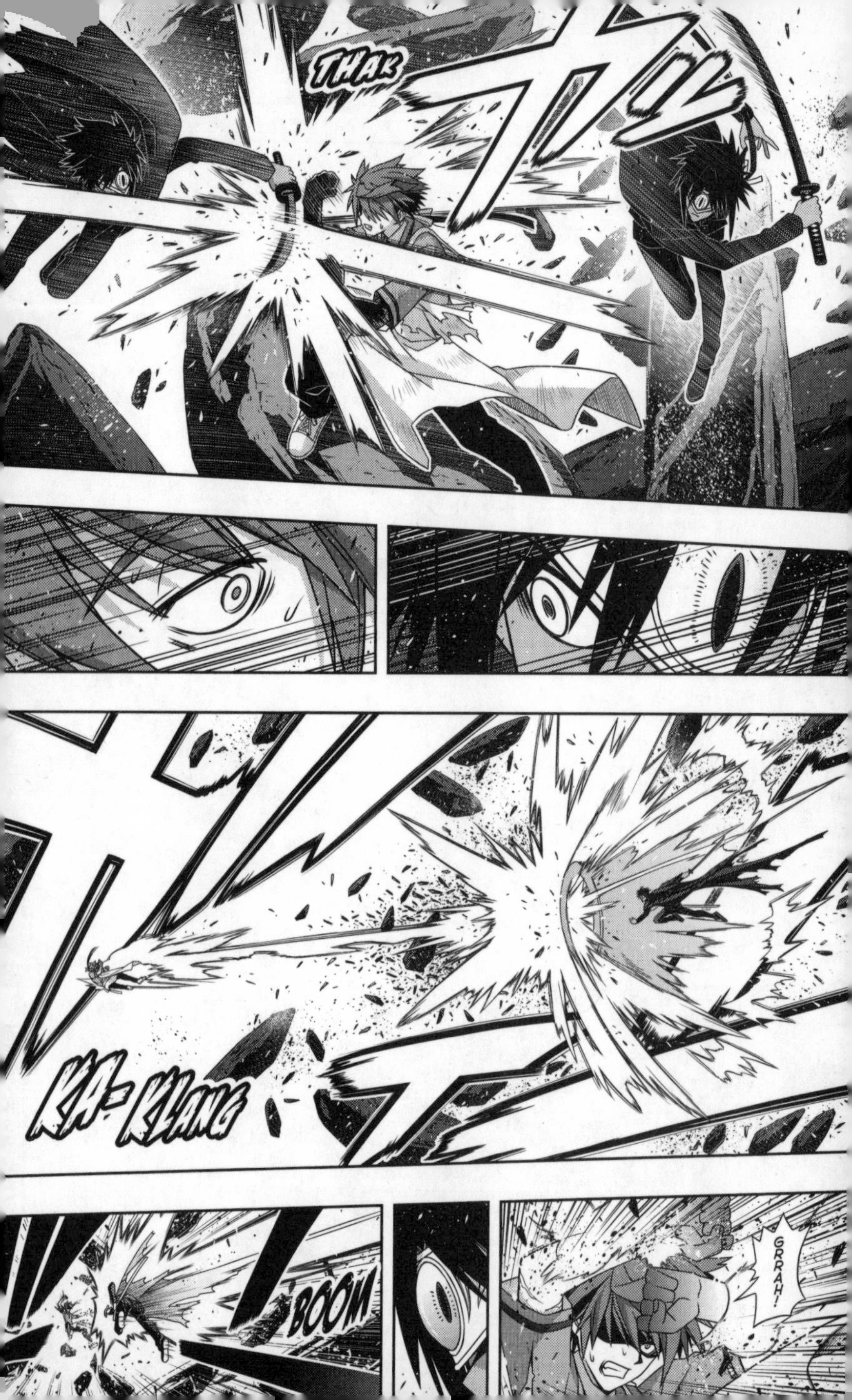
THAK
KA-KLANG
GRRAH!
BOOM

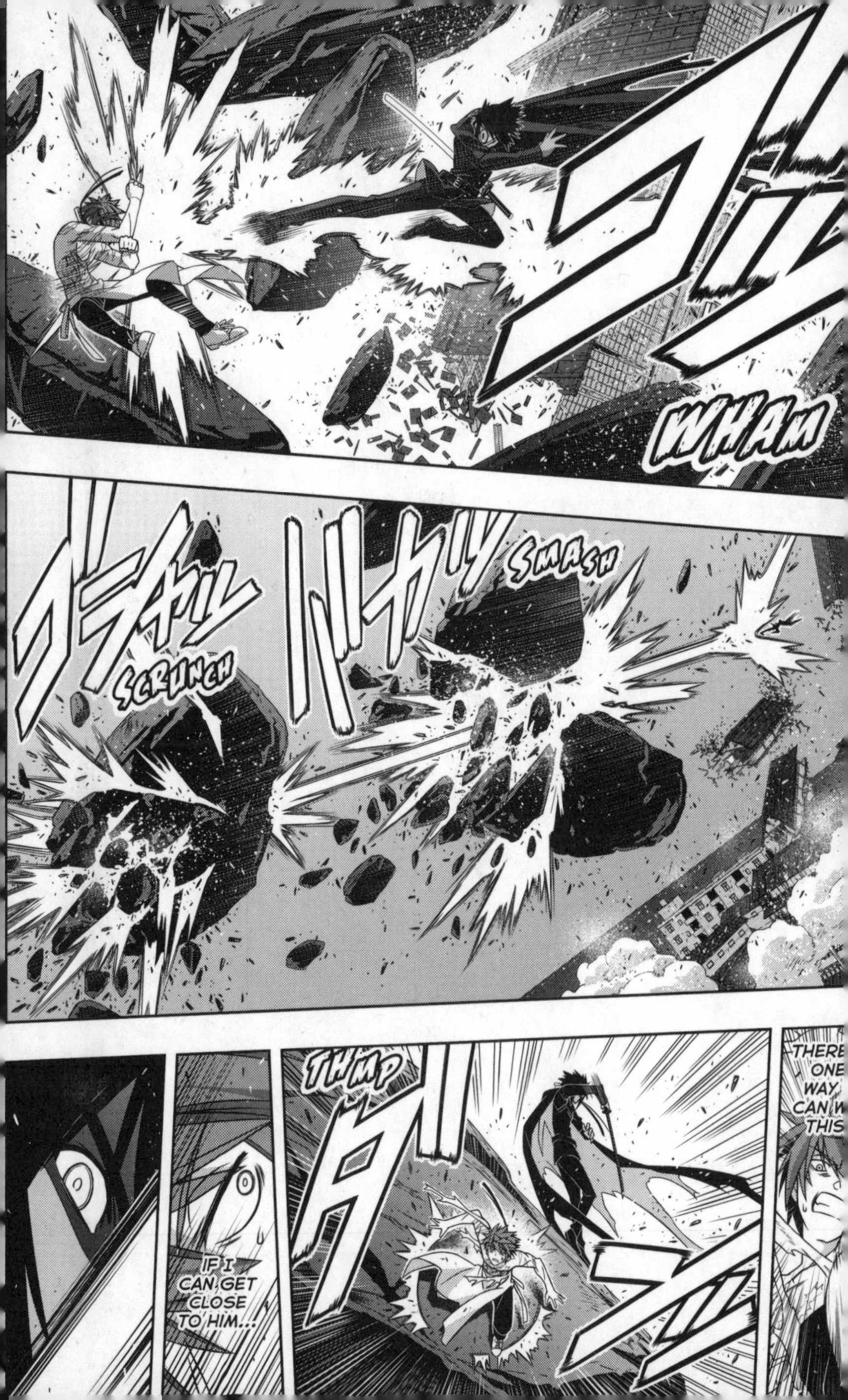
WHAM
SMASH
SCRUNCH
THERE ONE WAY CAN W THIS
THMP
IF I CAN GET CLOSE TO HIM...

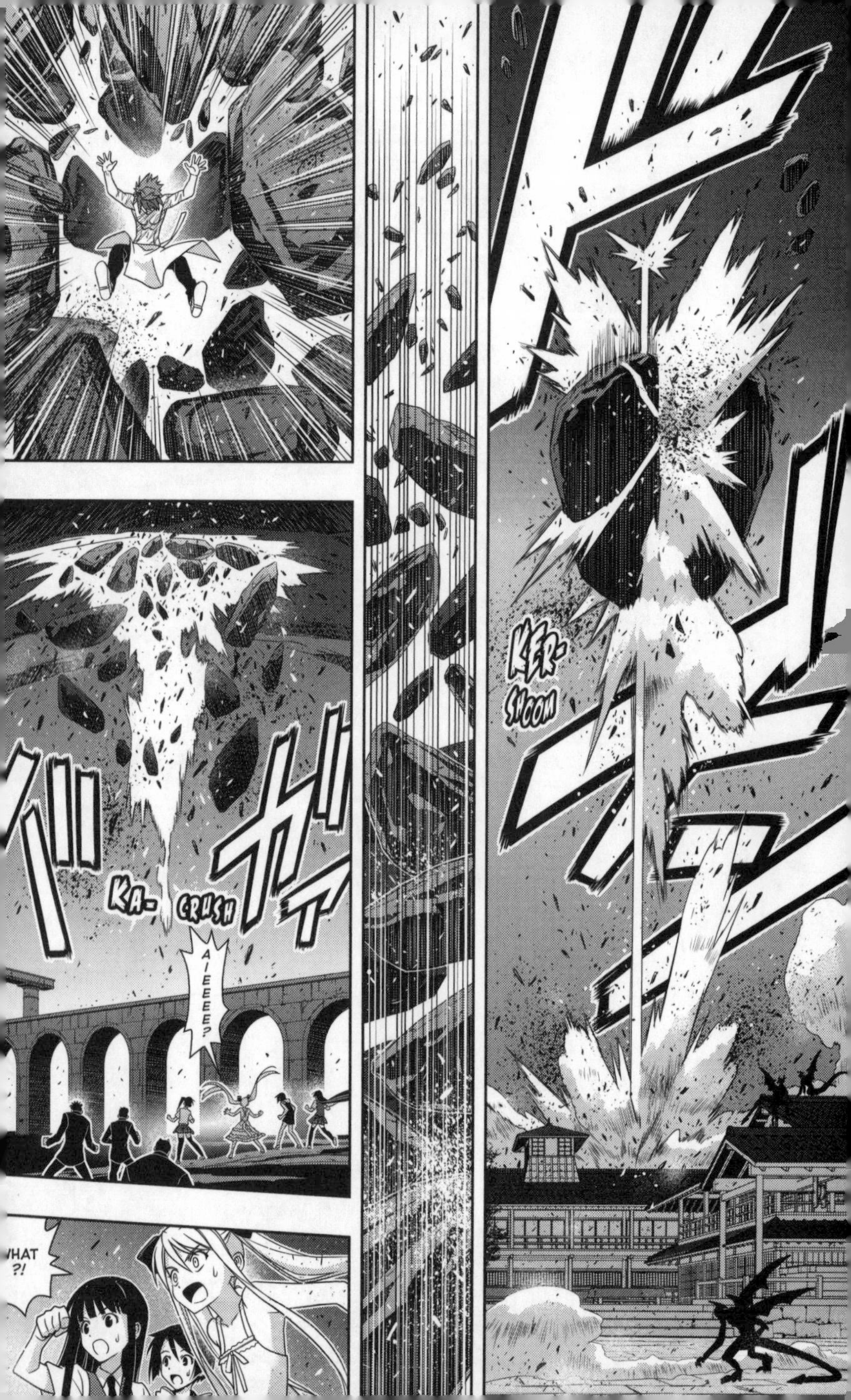
KER-SHOOM
KA- CRUSH
AIEEEEE?!
WHAT ?!

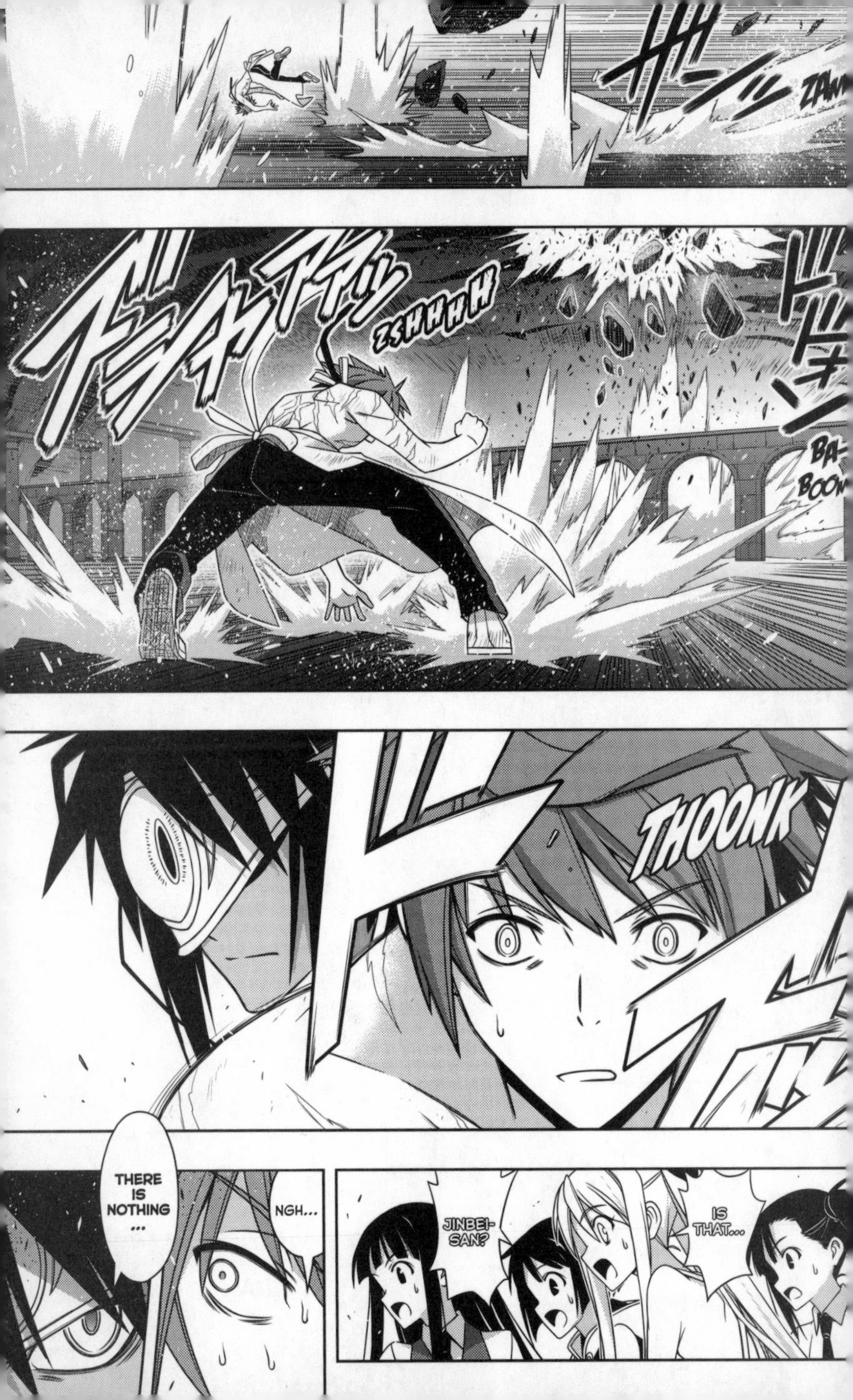
ZAN
BA-BOOM
ZSHHHHH
THOONK
IS THAT...
JINBEI-SAN?
NGH...
THERE IS NOTHING ...

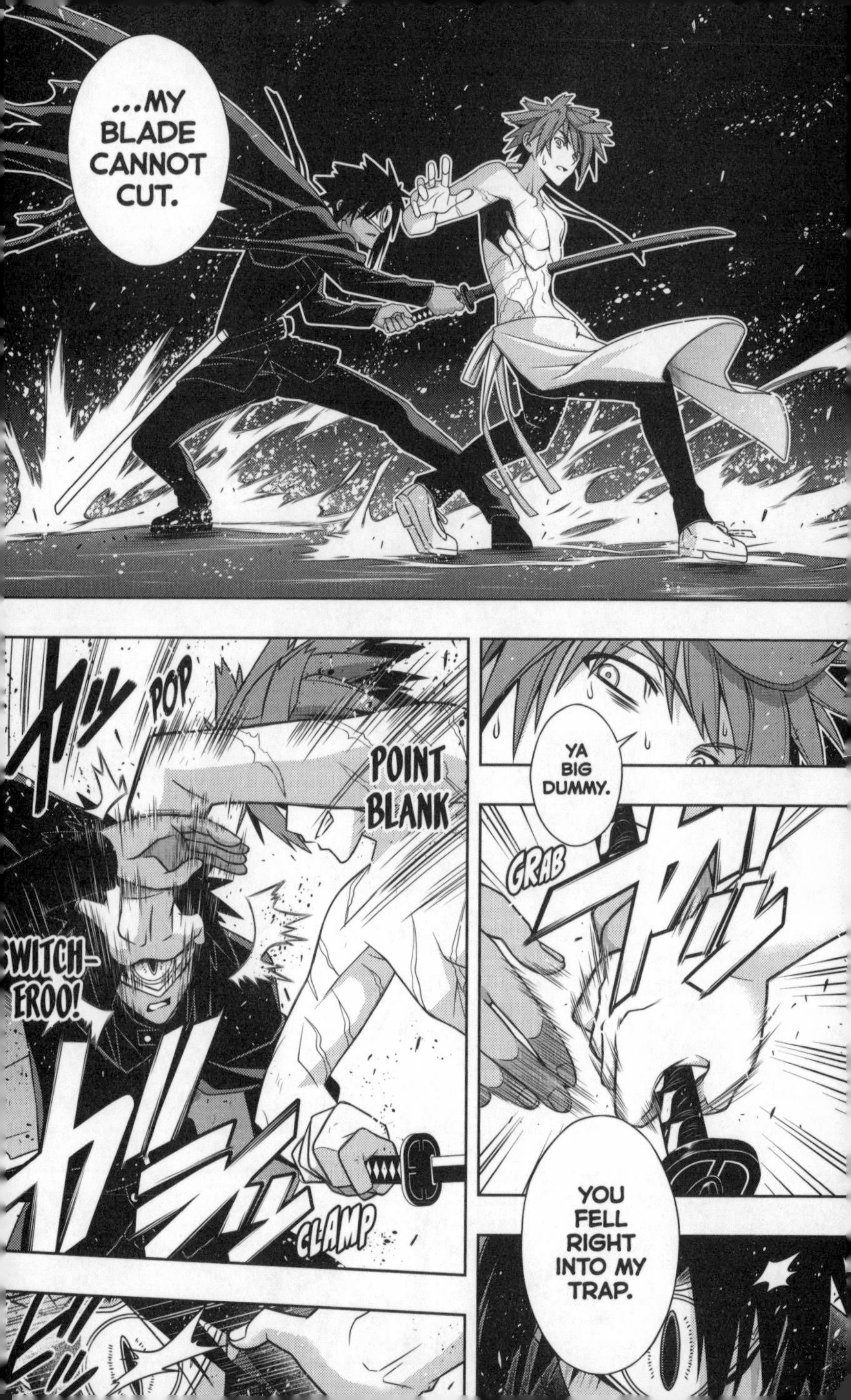
...MY BLADE CANNOT CUT.
YA BIG DUMMY.
GRAB
YOU FELL RIGHT INTO MY TRAP.
POP
POINT BLANK
WITCH-EROO!
CLAMP

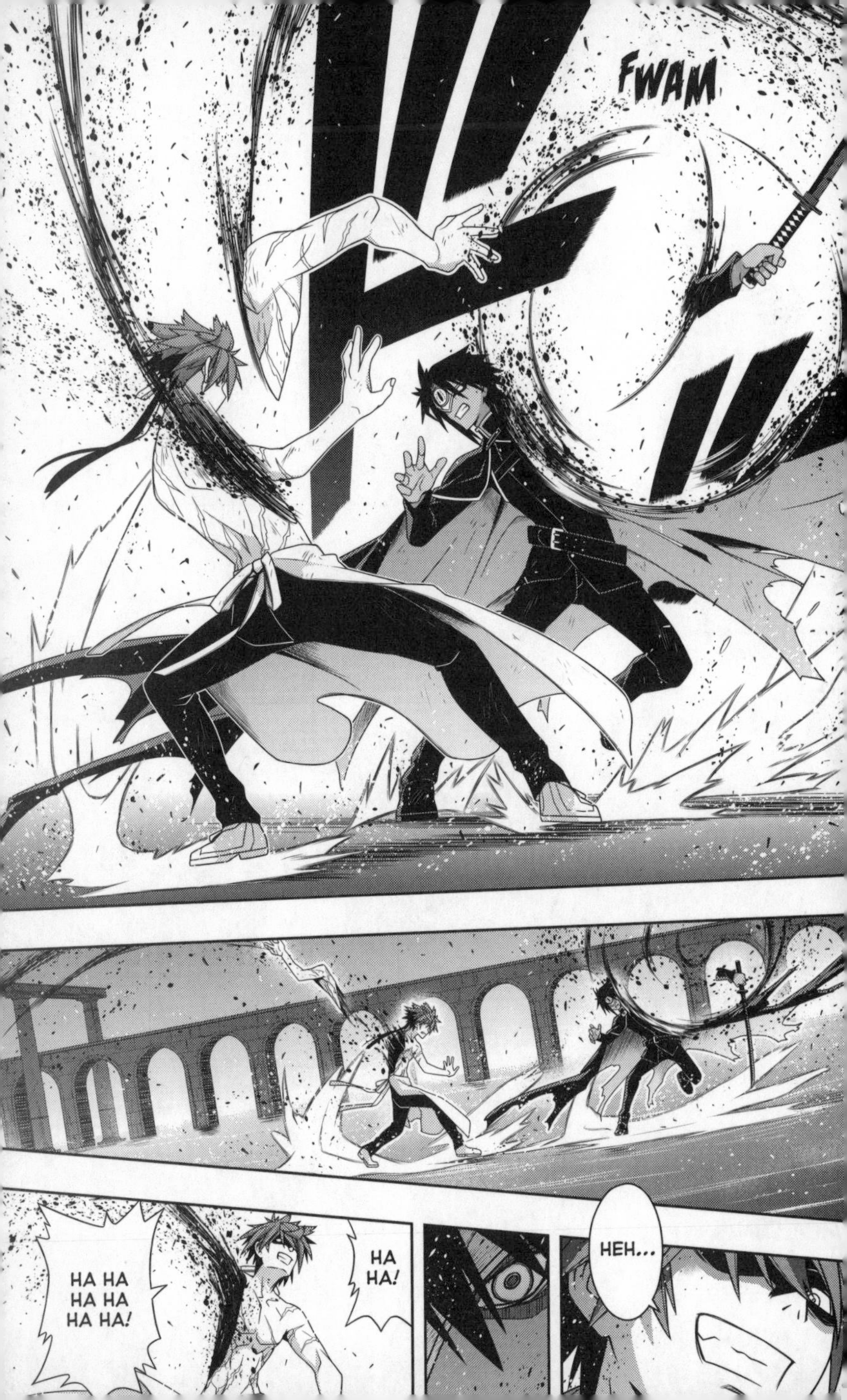
FWAM
HEH...
HA HA!
HA HA HA HA HA HA!

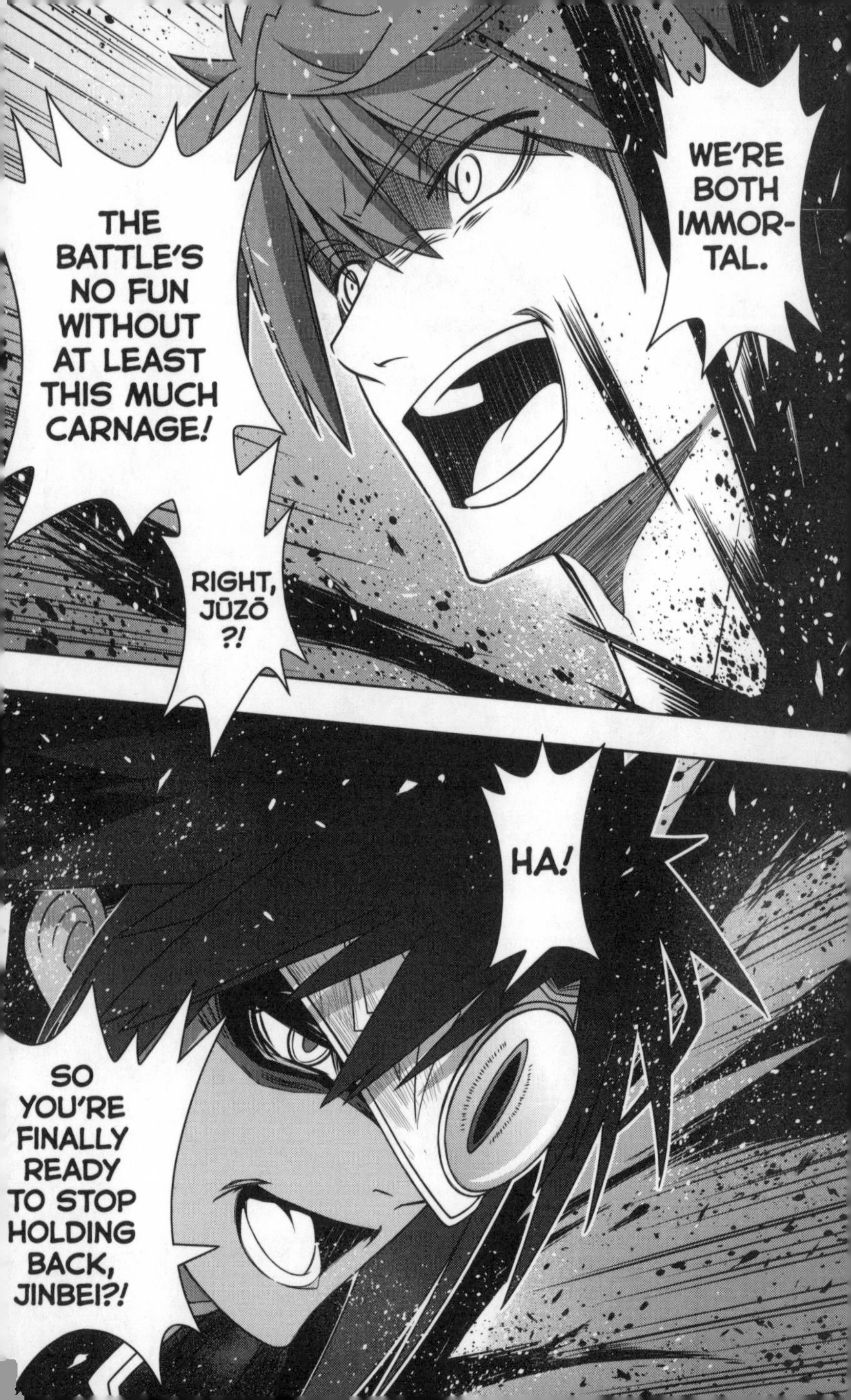
WE'RE BOTH IMMOR-TAL.
THE BATTLE'S NO FUN WITHOUT AT LEAST THIS MUCH CARNAGE!
RIGHT, JŪZŌ ?!
HA!
SO YOU'RE FINALLY READY TO STOP HOLDING BACK, JINBEI?!

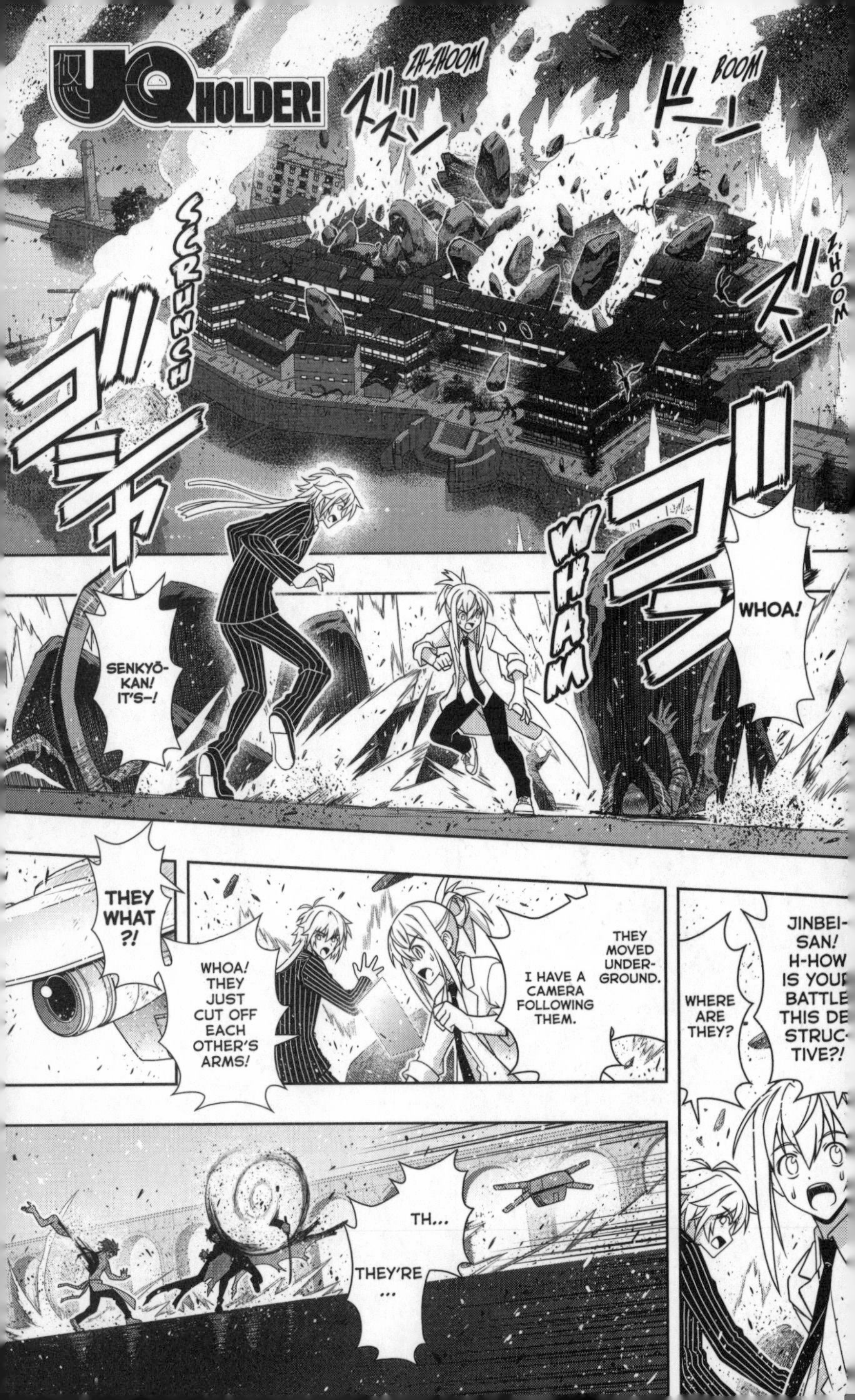
UQ HOLDER!
ZH-ZHOOM
BOOM
ZHOOM
SCRUNCH
WHAM
WHOA!
SENKYŌ-KAN! IT'S–!
JINBEI-SAN! H-HOW IS YOUR BATTLE THIS DESTRUCTIVE?!
WHERE ARE THEY?
THEY MOVED UNDERGROUND.
I HAVE A CAMERA FOLLOWING THEM.
WHOA! THEY JUST CUT OFF EACH OTHER'S ARMS!
THEY WHAT?!
TH...
THEY'RE ...

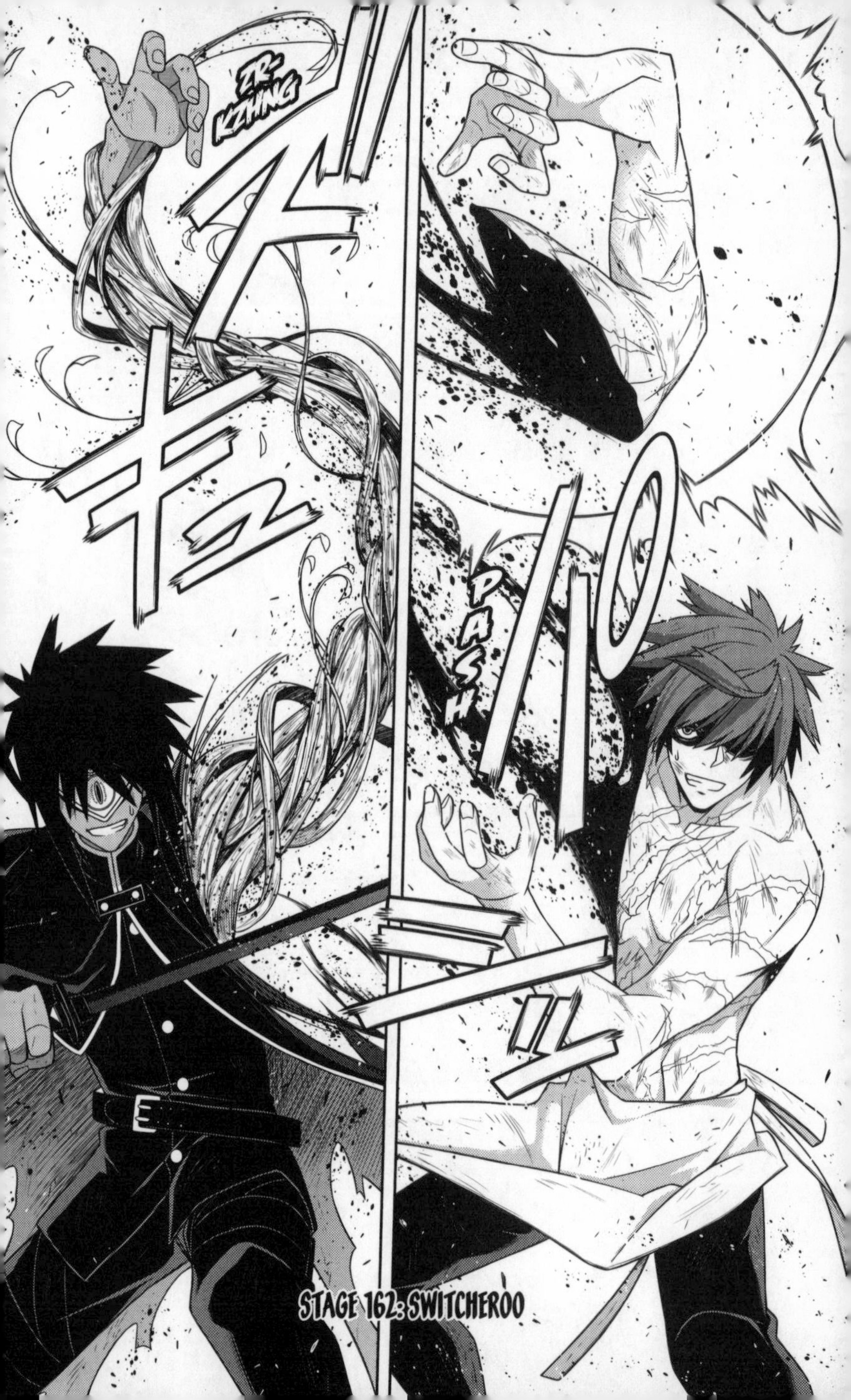
ZR-KZHING
PASH
STAGE 162: SWITCHEROO

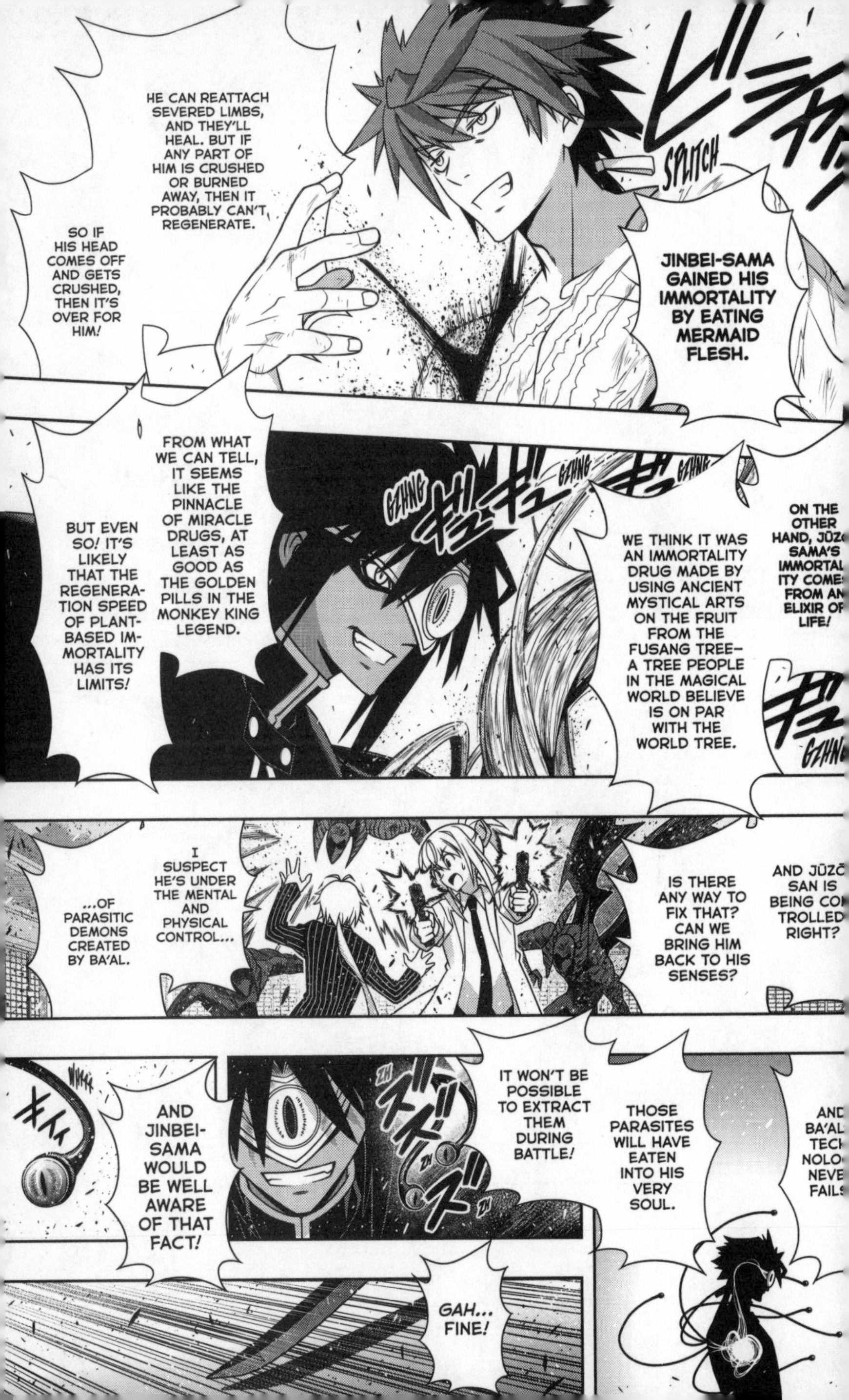
SPLITCH
JINBEI-SAMA GAINED HIS IMMORTALITY BY EATING MERMAID FLESH.
HE CAN REATTACH SEVERED LIMBS, AND THEY'LL HEAL. BUT IF ANY PART OF HIM IS CRUSHED OR BURNED AWAY, THEN IT PROBABLY CAN'T REGENERATE.
SO IF HIS HEAD COMES OFF AND GETS CRUSHED, THEN IT'S OVER FOR HIM!
GZHNG
ON THE OTHER HAND, JŪZŌ SAMA'S IMMORTAL ITY COMES FROM AN ELIXIR OF LIFE!
WE THINK IT WAS AN IMMORTALITY DRUG MADE BY USING ANCIENT MYSTICAL ARTS ON THE FRUIT FROM THE FUSANG TREE– A TREE PEOPLE IN THE MAGICAL WORLD BELIEVE IS ON PAR WITH THE WORLD TREE.
GZHNG
GZHNG
FROM WHAT WE CAN TELL, IT SEEMS LIKE THE PINNACLE OF MIRACLE DRUGS, AT LEAST AS GOOD AS THE GOLDEN PILLS IN THE MONKEY KING LEGEND.
BUT EVEN SO! IT'S LIKELY THAT THE REGENERATION SPEED OF PLANT-BASED IMMORTALITY HAS ITS LIMITS!
AND JŪZŌ SAN IS BEING CO TROLLED RIGHT?
IS THERE ANY WAY TO FIX THAT? CAN WE BRING HIM BACK TO HIS SENSES?
I SUSPECT HE'S UNDER THE MENTAL AND PHYSICAL CONTROL...
...OF PARASITIC DEMONS CREATED BY BA'AL.
AND BA'AL TECH NOLO NEVE FAILS
THOSE PARASITES WILL HAVE EATEN INTO HIS VERY SOUL.
IT WON'T BE POSSIBLE TO EXTRACT THEM DURING BATTLE!
ZH
ZH
ZH
AND JINBEI-SAMA WOULD BE WELL AWARE OF THAT FACT!
GAH... FINE!

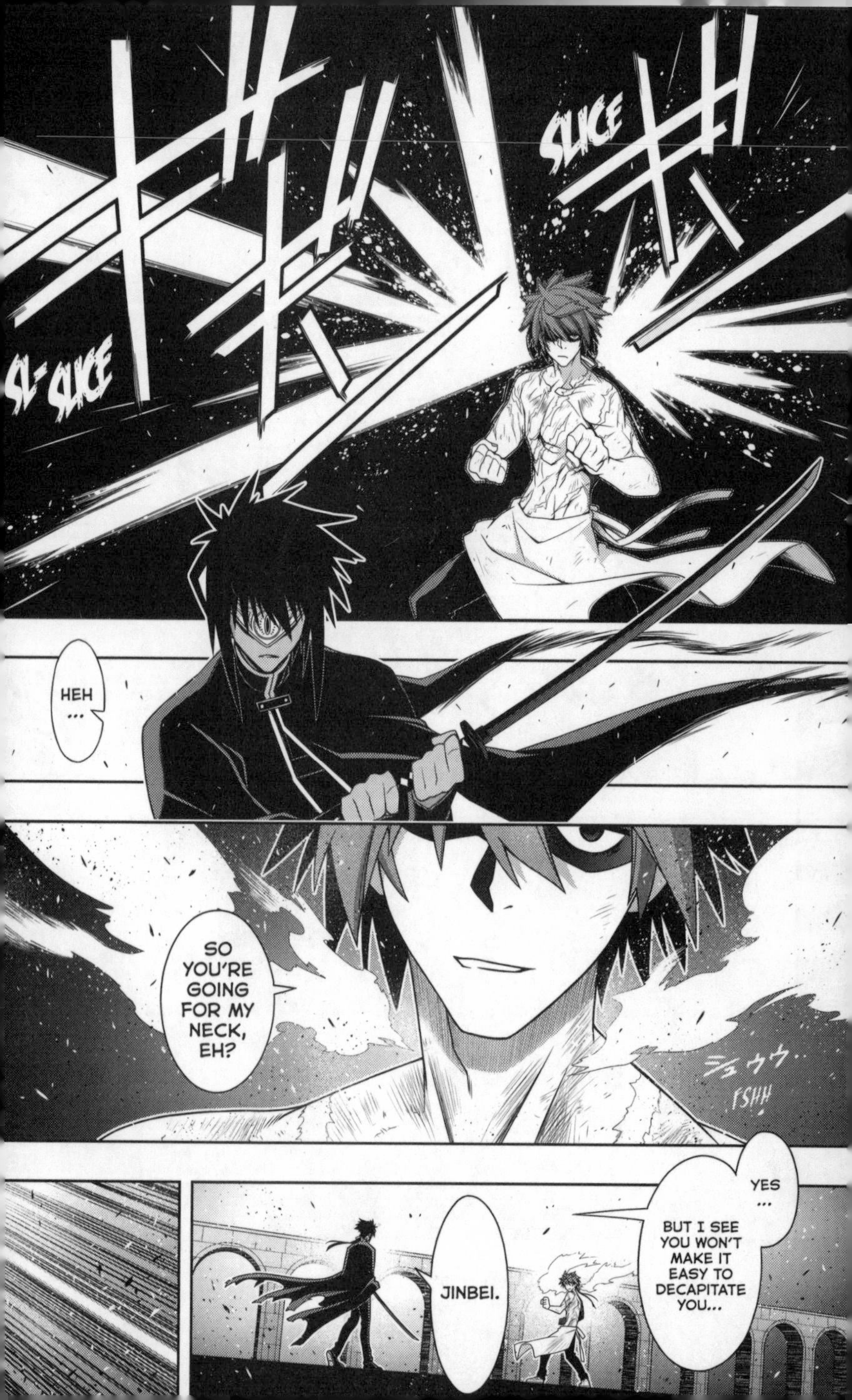
SLICE
SL-SLICE
HEH ...
SO YOU'RE GOING FOR MY NECK, EH?
シュウウ
FSHH
YES ...
BUT I SEE YOU WON'T MAKE IT EASY TO DECAPITATE YOU...
JINBEI.

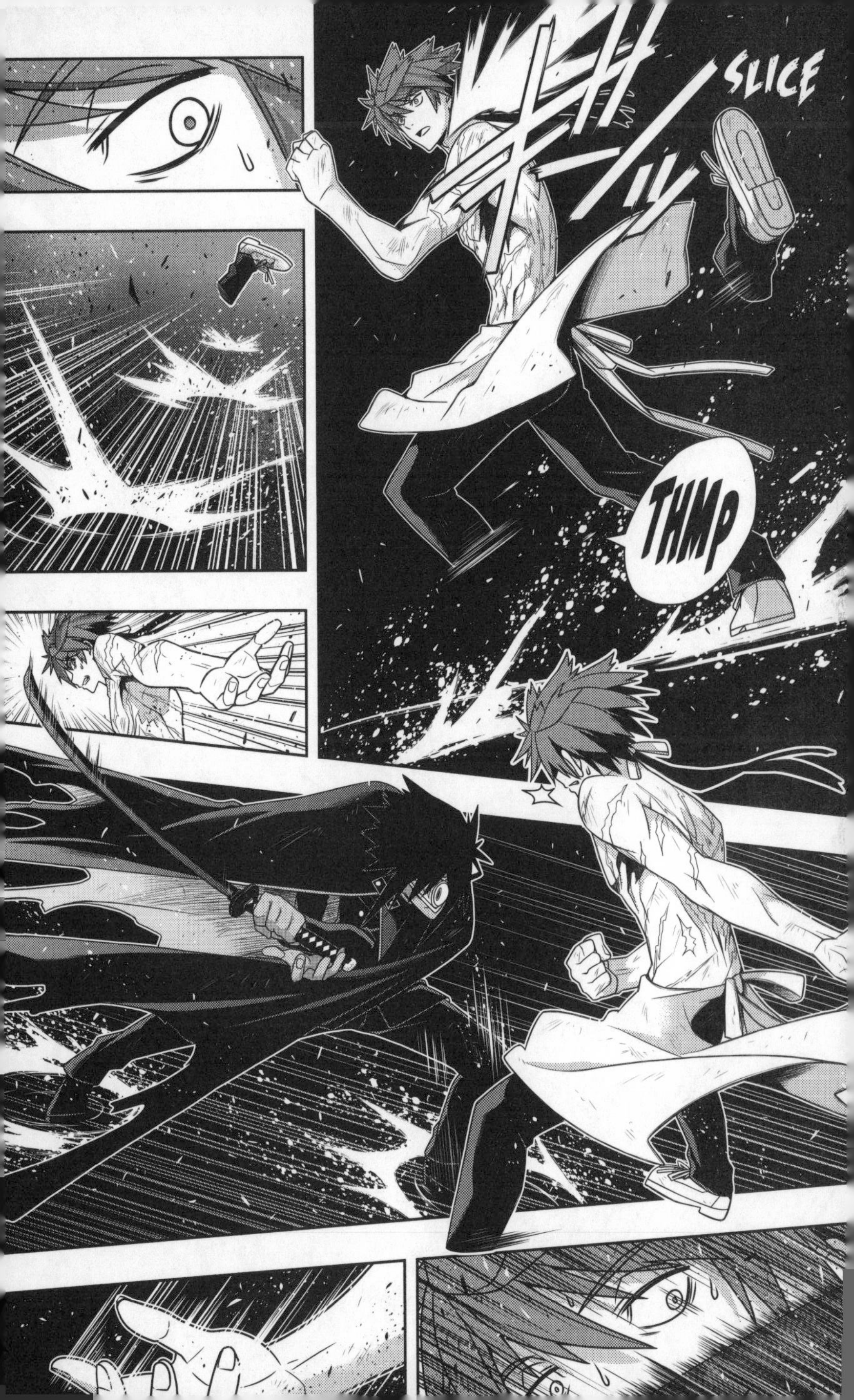
SLICE
THMP

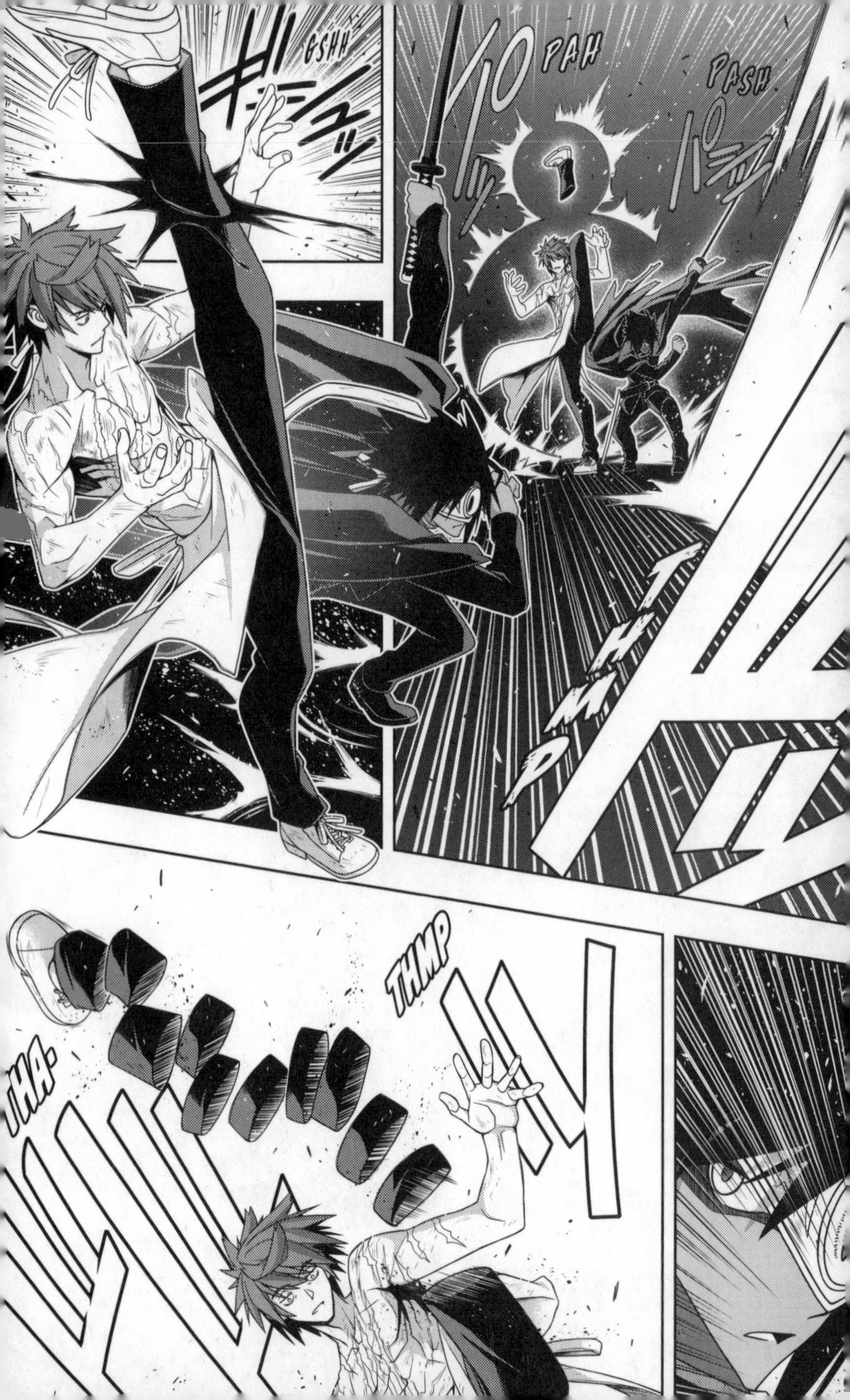
PAH
PASH
GSHH
THMP
THA-

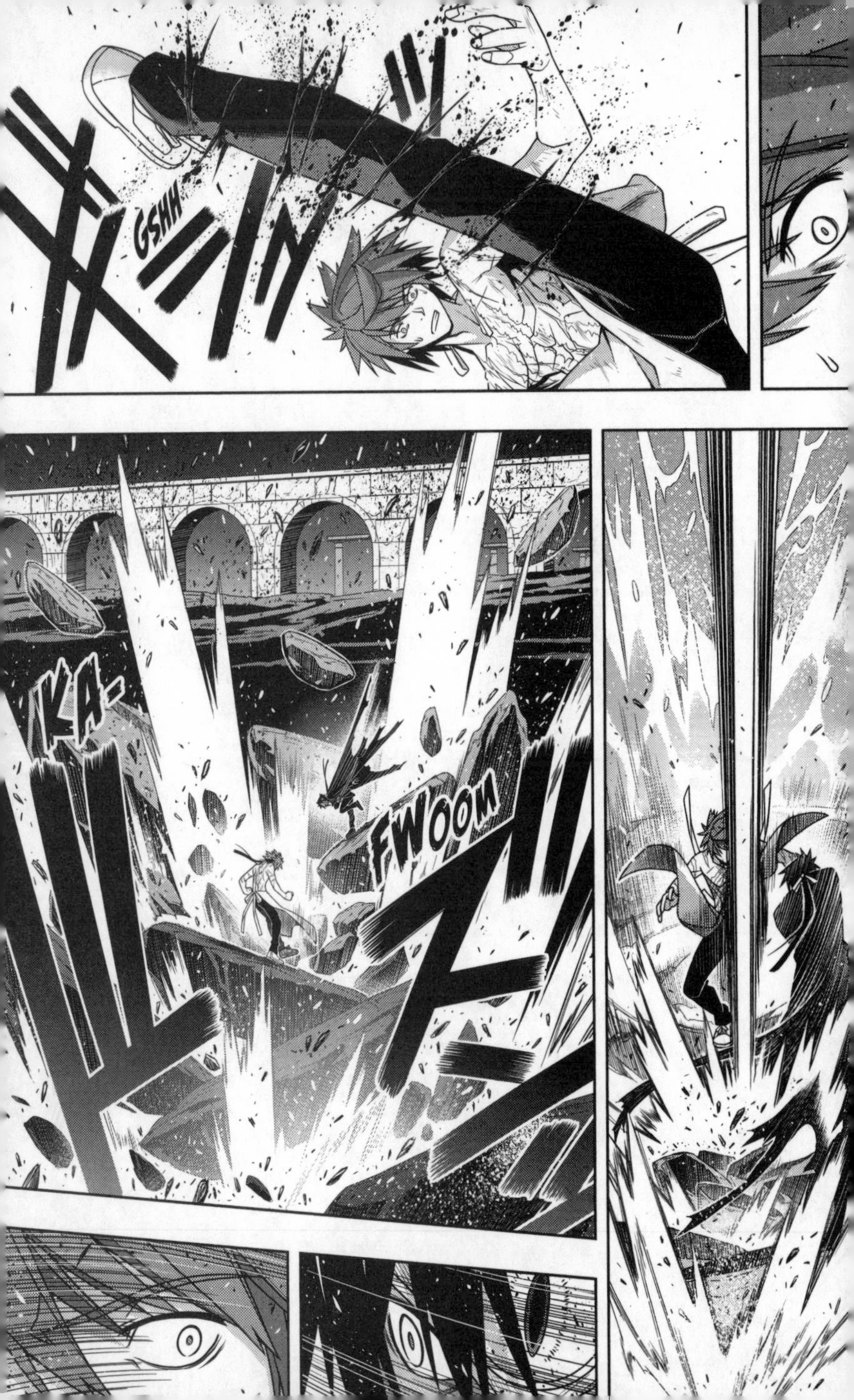
GSHH
KA-
FWOOM

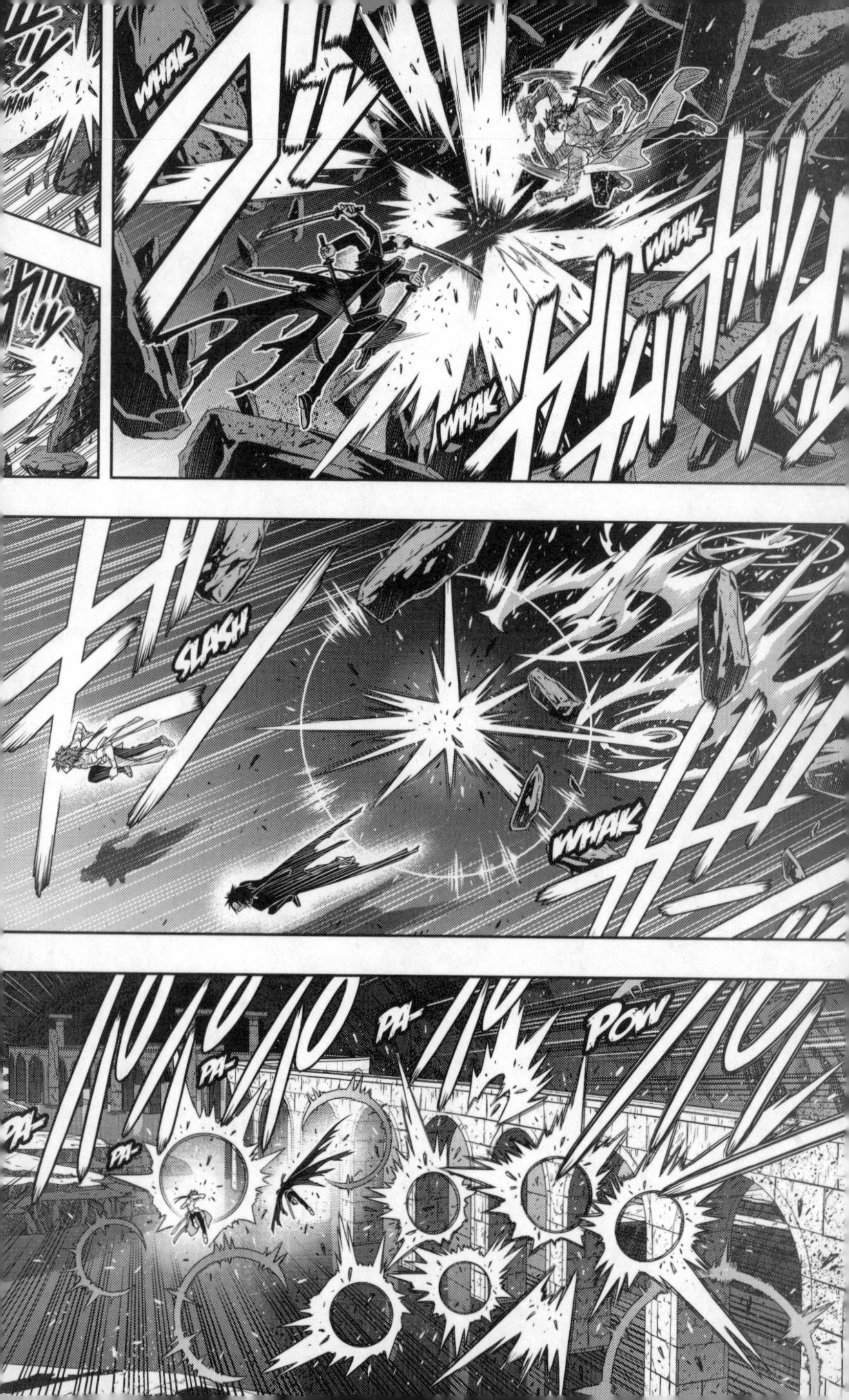
WHAK
WHAK
WHAK
WHAK
SLASH
POW
PA-
PA-
PA-
PA-

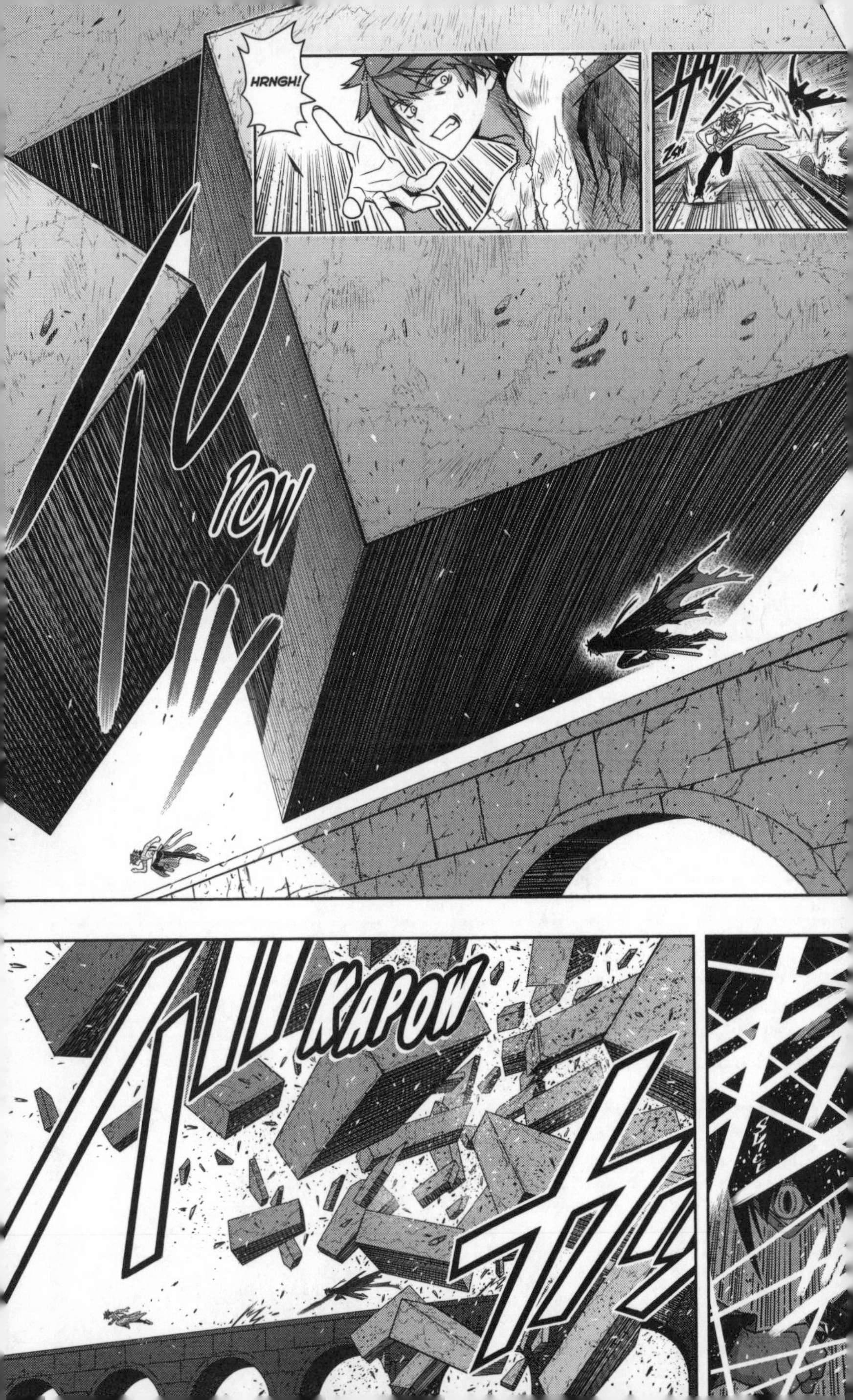
ZSH
HRNGH!
POW
KRAPOW
SLICE

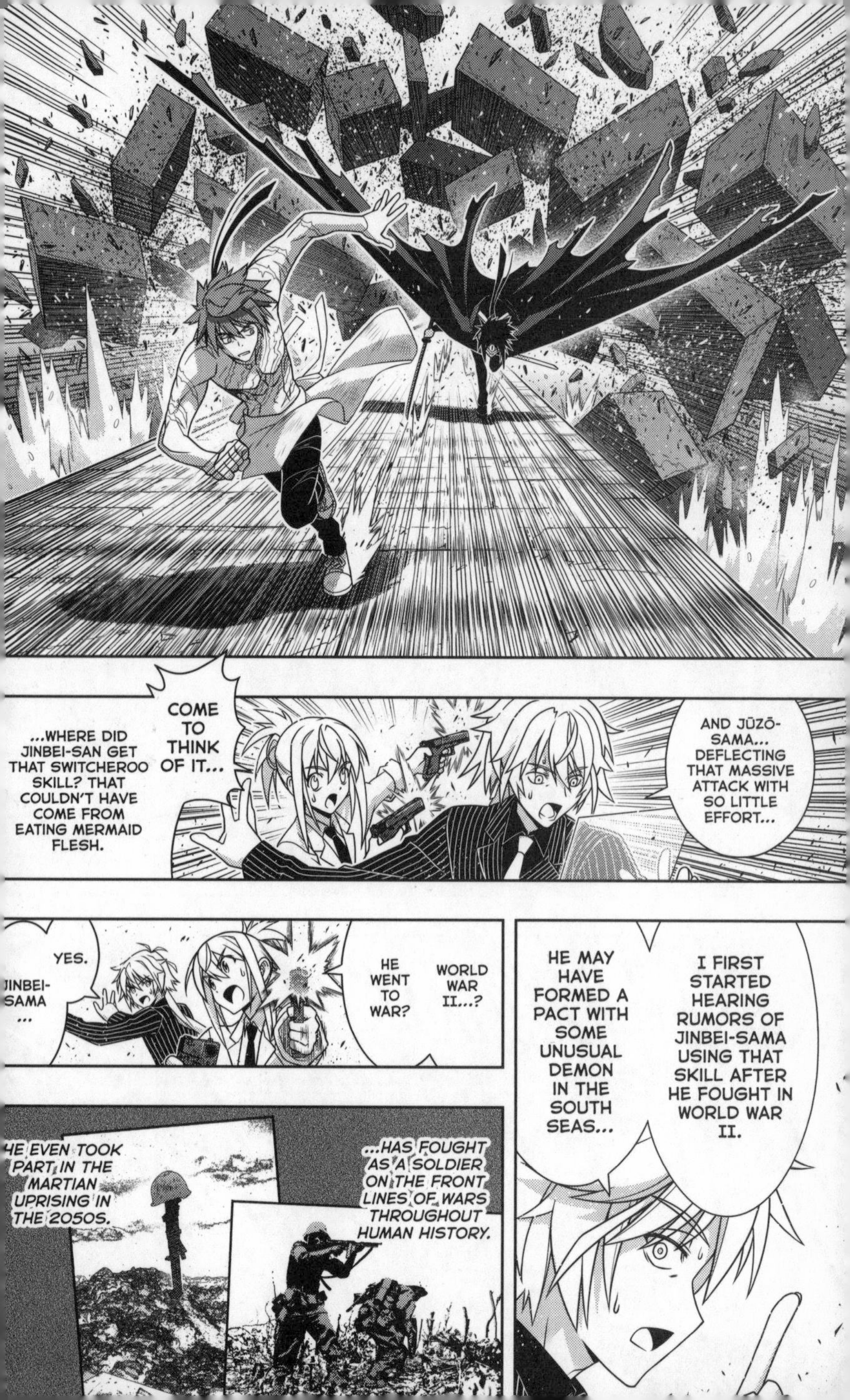
AND JŪZŌ-SAMA... DEFLECTING THAT MASSIVE ATTACK WITH SO LITTLE EFFORT...
COME TO THINK OF IT...
...WHERE DID JINBEI-SAN GET THAT SWITCHEROO SKILL? THAT COULDN'T HAVE COME FROM EATING MERMAID FLESH.
I FIRST STARTED HEARING RUMORS OF JINBEI-SAMA USING THAT SKILL AFTER HE FOUGHT IN WORLD WAR II.
HE MAY HAVE FORMED A PACT WITH SOME UNUSUAL DEMON IN THE SOUTH SEAS...
WORLD WAR II...?
HE WENT TO WAR?
YES. JINBEI-SAMA...
...HAS FOUGHT AS A SOLDIER ON THE FRONT LINES OF WARS THROUGHOUT HUMAN HISTORY.
HE EVEN TOOK PART IN THE MARTIAN UPRISING IN THE 2050S.

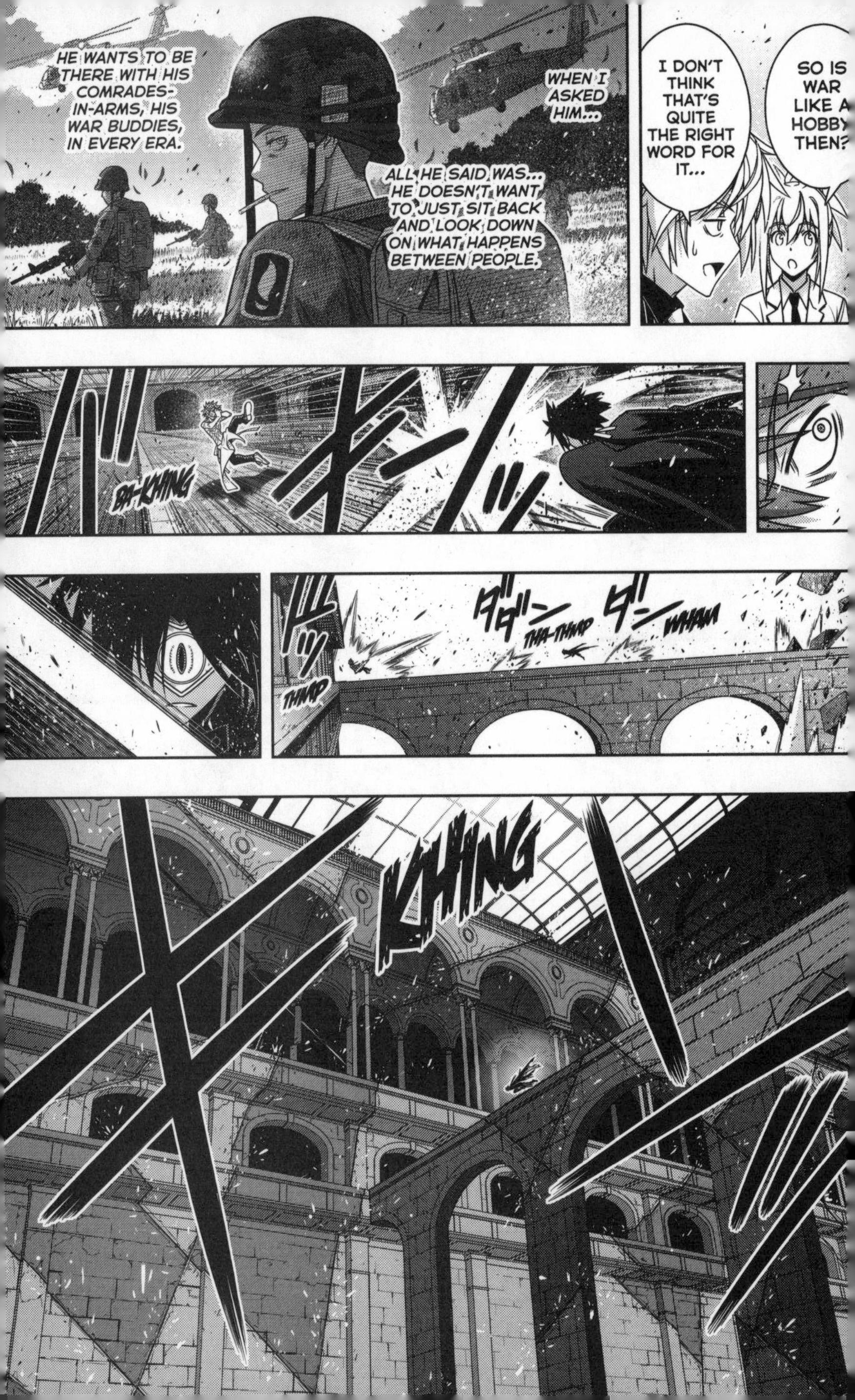
SO IS WAR LIKE A HOBBY THEN?
I DON'T THINK THAT'S QUITE THE RIGHT WORD FOR IT...
WHEN I ASKED HIM...
ALL HE SAID WAS... HE DOESN'T WANT TO JUST SIT BACK AND LOOK DOWN ON WHAT HAPPENS BETWEEN PEOPLE.
HE WANTS TO BE THERE WITH HIS COMRADES-IN-ARMS, HIS WAR BUDDIES, IN EVERY ERA.
BA-KHING
ダン
WHAM
ダダン
THA-THMP
THMP
KHING

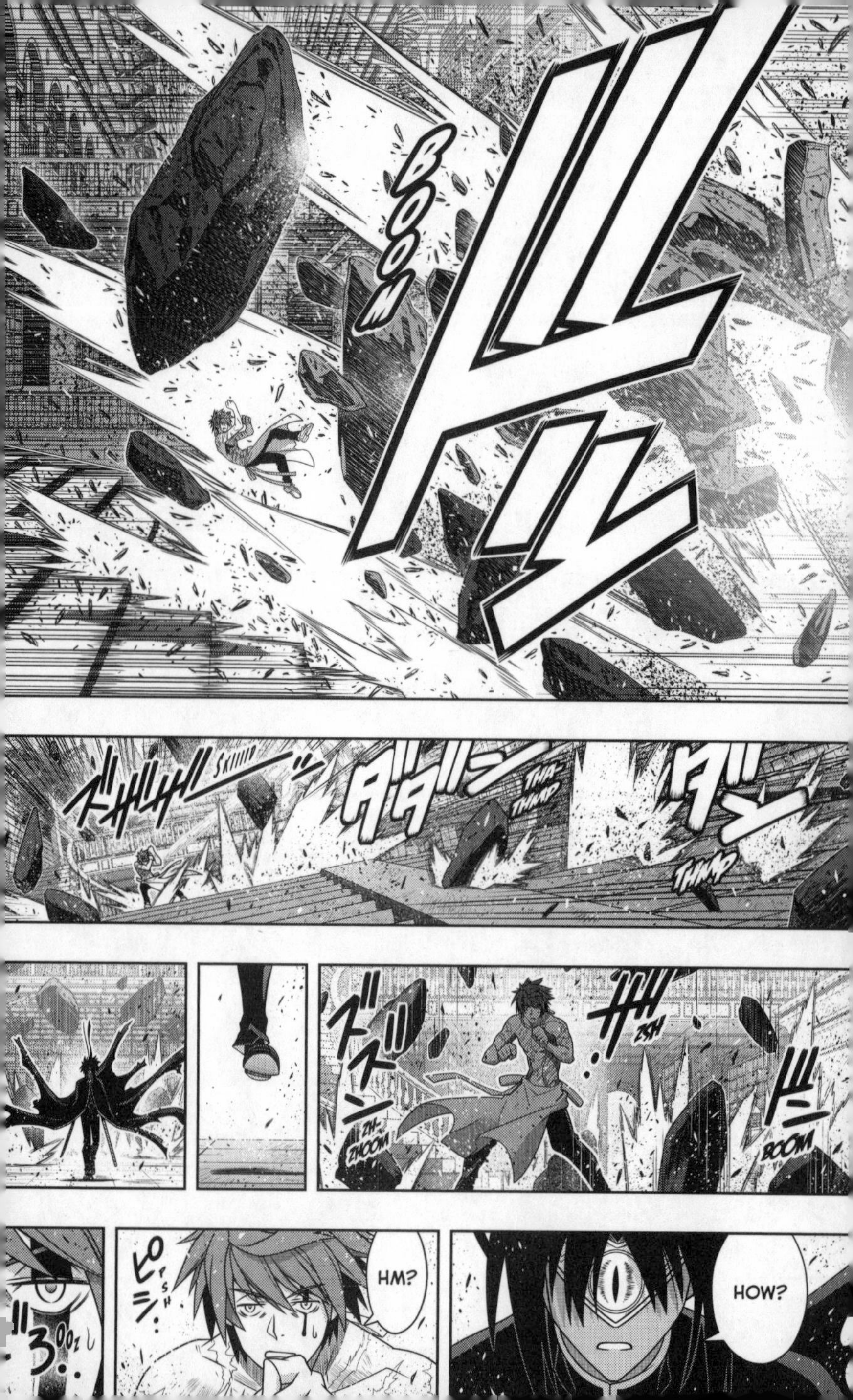
BOOOOM
THMP
THA-THMP
SKIIIID
BOOM
ZSH
ZH-ZHOOM
HOW?
HM?
PSH

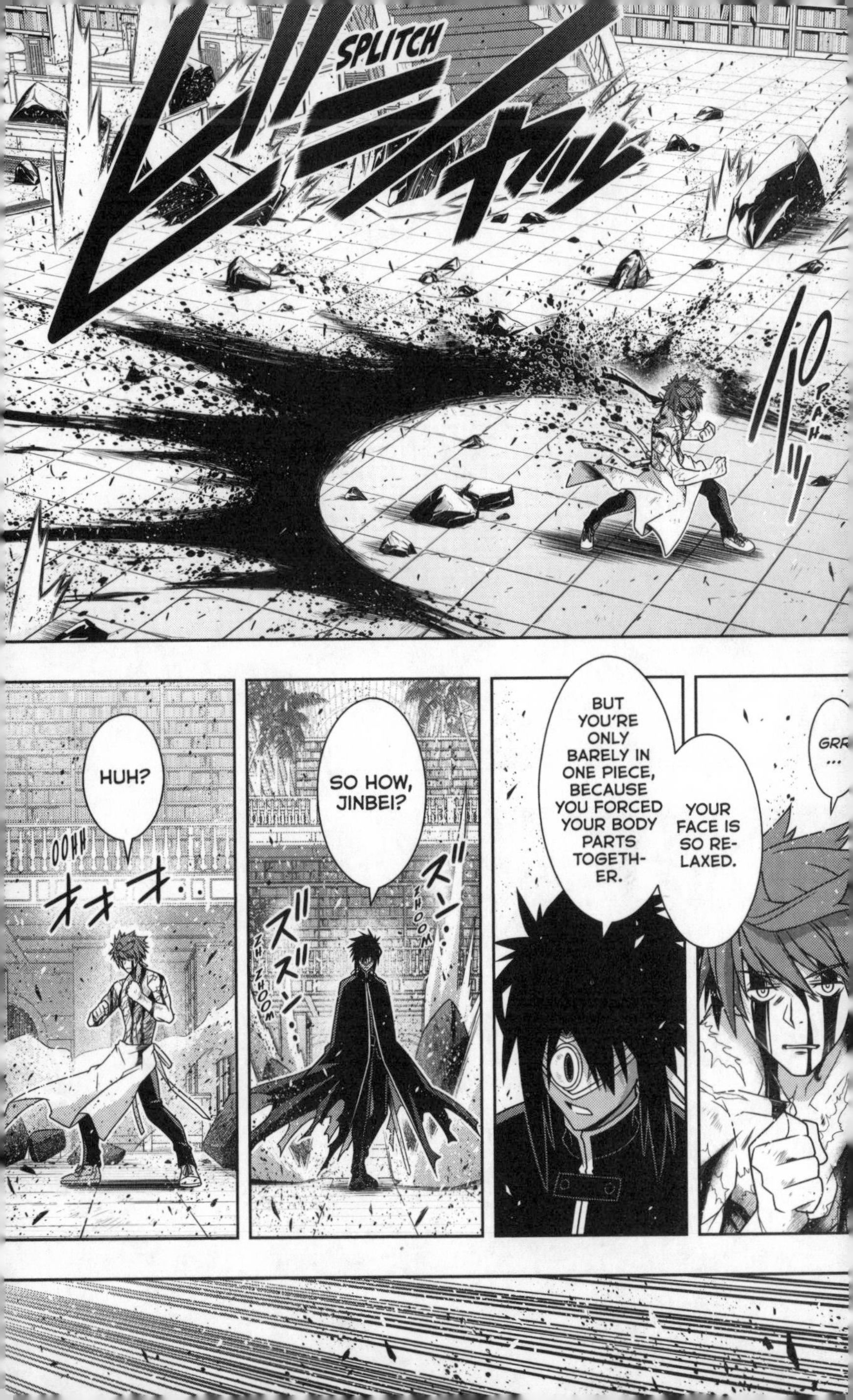
SPLITCH
PAH
GRR...
YOUR FACE IS SO RE-LAXED.
BUT YOU'RE ONLY BARELY IN ONE PIECE, BECAUSE YOU FORCED YOUR BODY PARTS TOGETH-ER.
SO HOW, JINBEI?
ZHOOM
ZHOOM
HUH?
OOHH

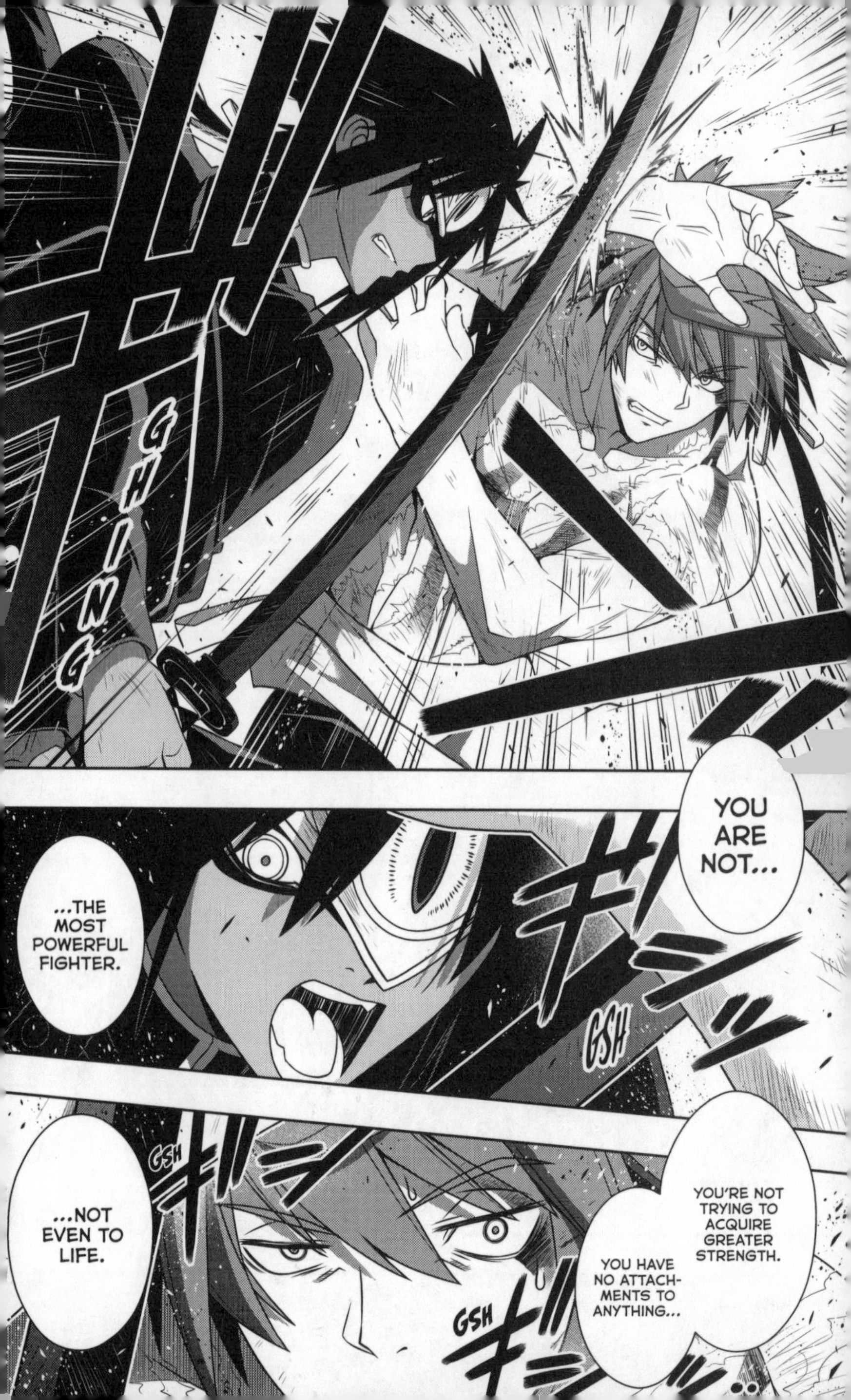
GHING
YOU ARE NOT...
...THE MOST POWERFUL FIGHTER.
GSH
YOU'RE NOT TRYING TO ACQUIRE GREATER STRENGTH.
YOU HAVE NO ATTACHMENTS TO ANYTHING...
GSH
GSH
...NOT EVEN TO LIFE.

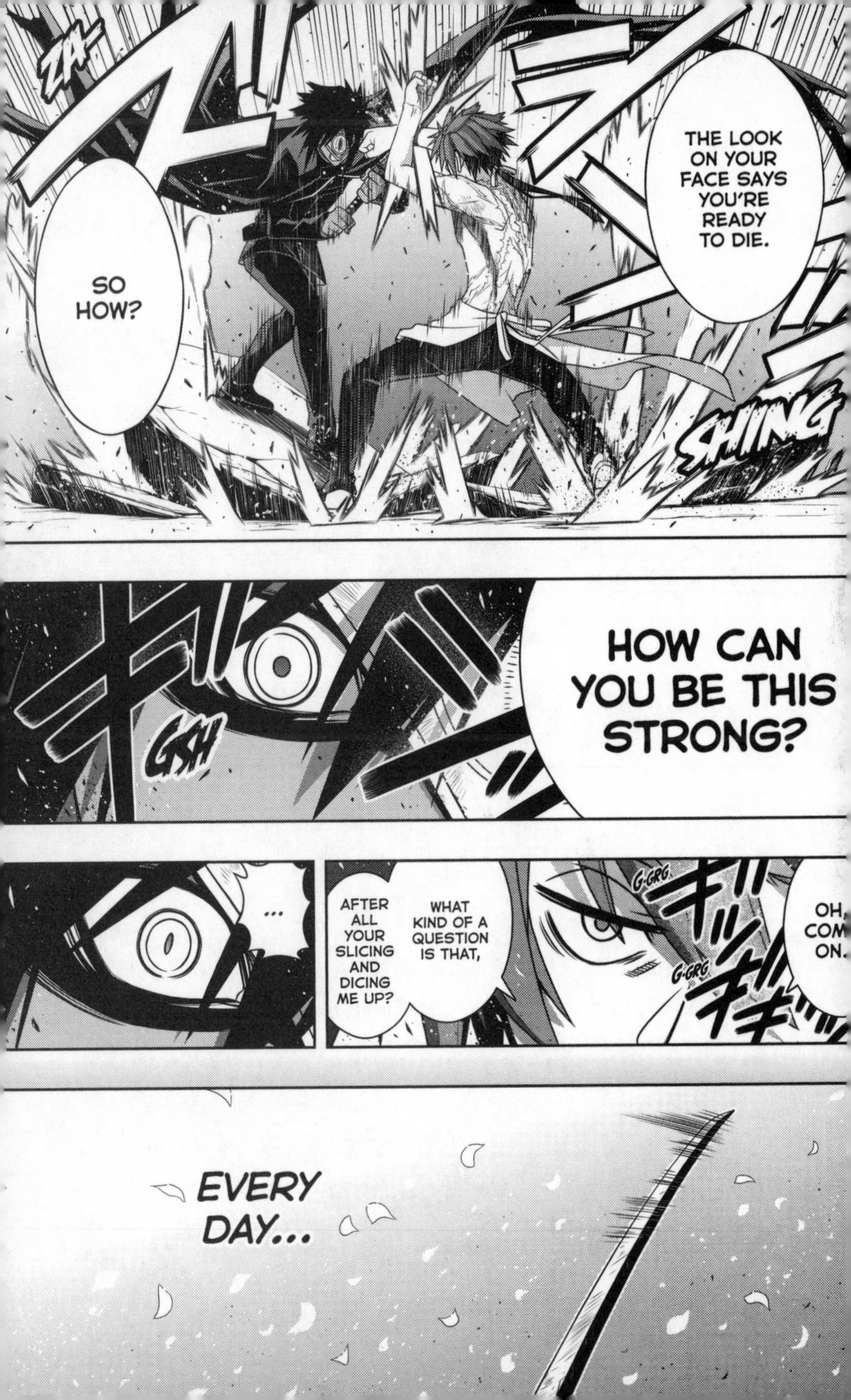
THE LOOK ON YOUR FACE SAYS YOU'RE READY TO DIE.
SO HOW?
ZA-
SHING
HOW CAN YOU BE THIS STRONG?
GISH
OH, COM ON.
G-GRG
G-GRG
WHAT KIND OF A QUESTION IS THAT,
AFTER ALL YOUR SLICING AND DICING ME UP?
...
EVERY DAY...

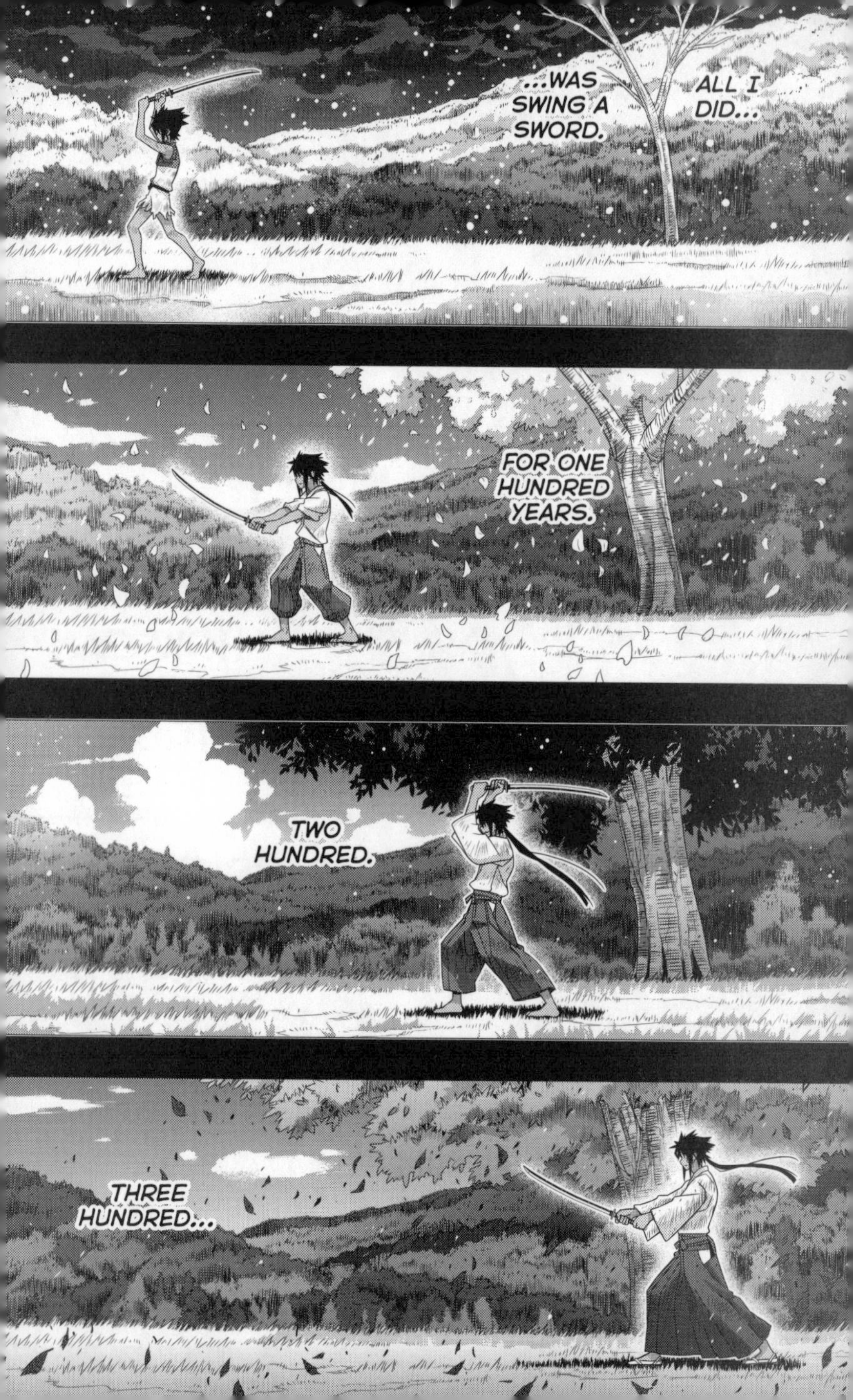
ALL I DID...
...WAS SWING A SWORD.
FOR ONE HUNDRED YEARS.
TWO HUNDRED.
THREE HUNDRED...

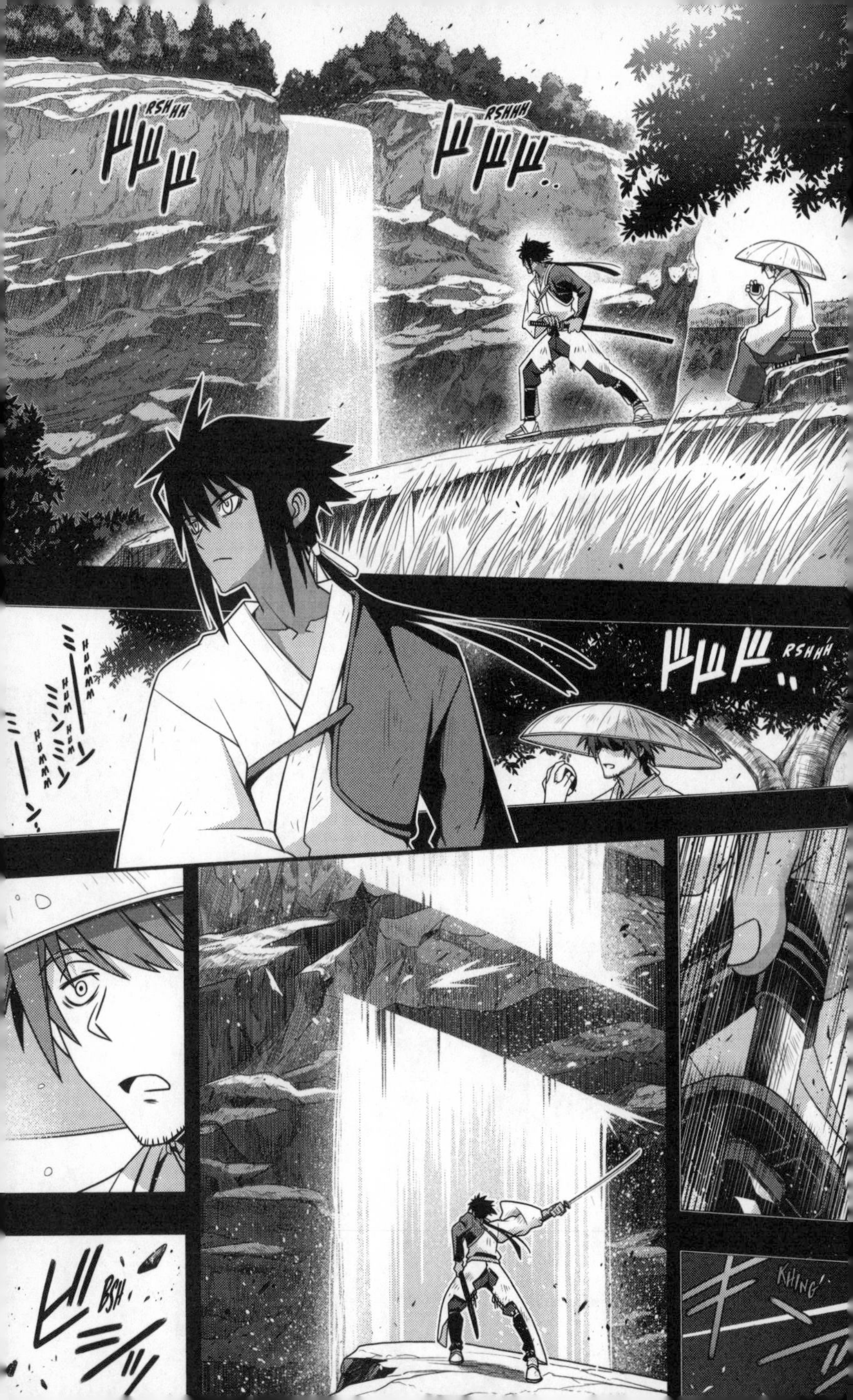
RSHHH
RSHHH
RSHHH
HUMMM
HUM HUM
HUMMM
KHING
BSH

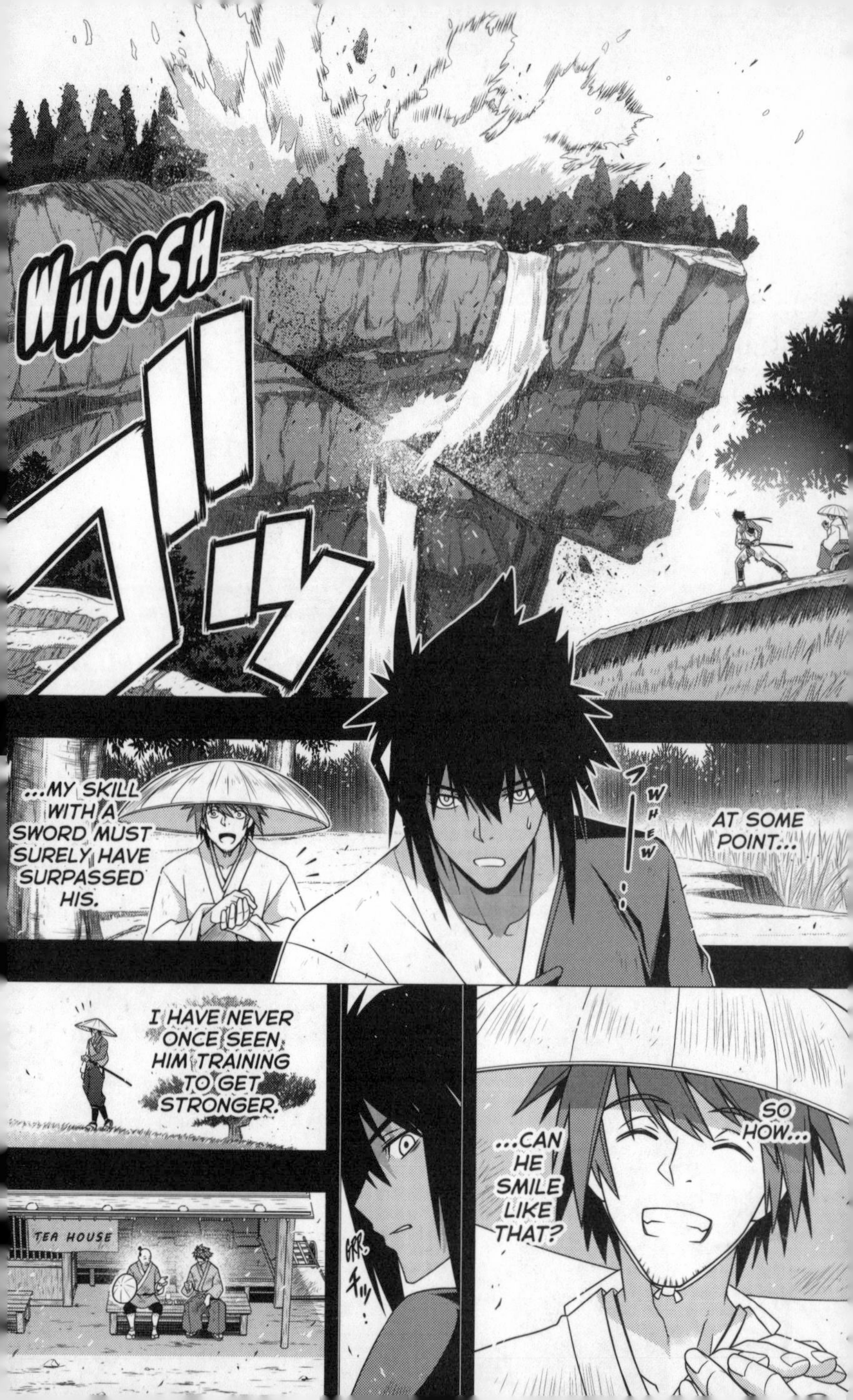
WHOOSH
ズッ
AT SOME POINT...
WHEW
...MY SKILL WITH A SWORD MUST SURELY HAVE SURPASSED HIS.
SO HOW...
...CAN HE SMILE LIKE THAT?
GRR.
チッ
I HAVE NEVER ONCE SEEN HIM TRAINING TO GET STRONGER.
TEA HOUSE

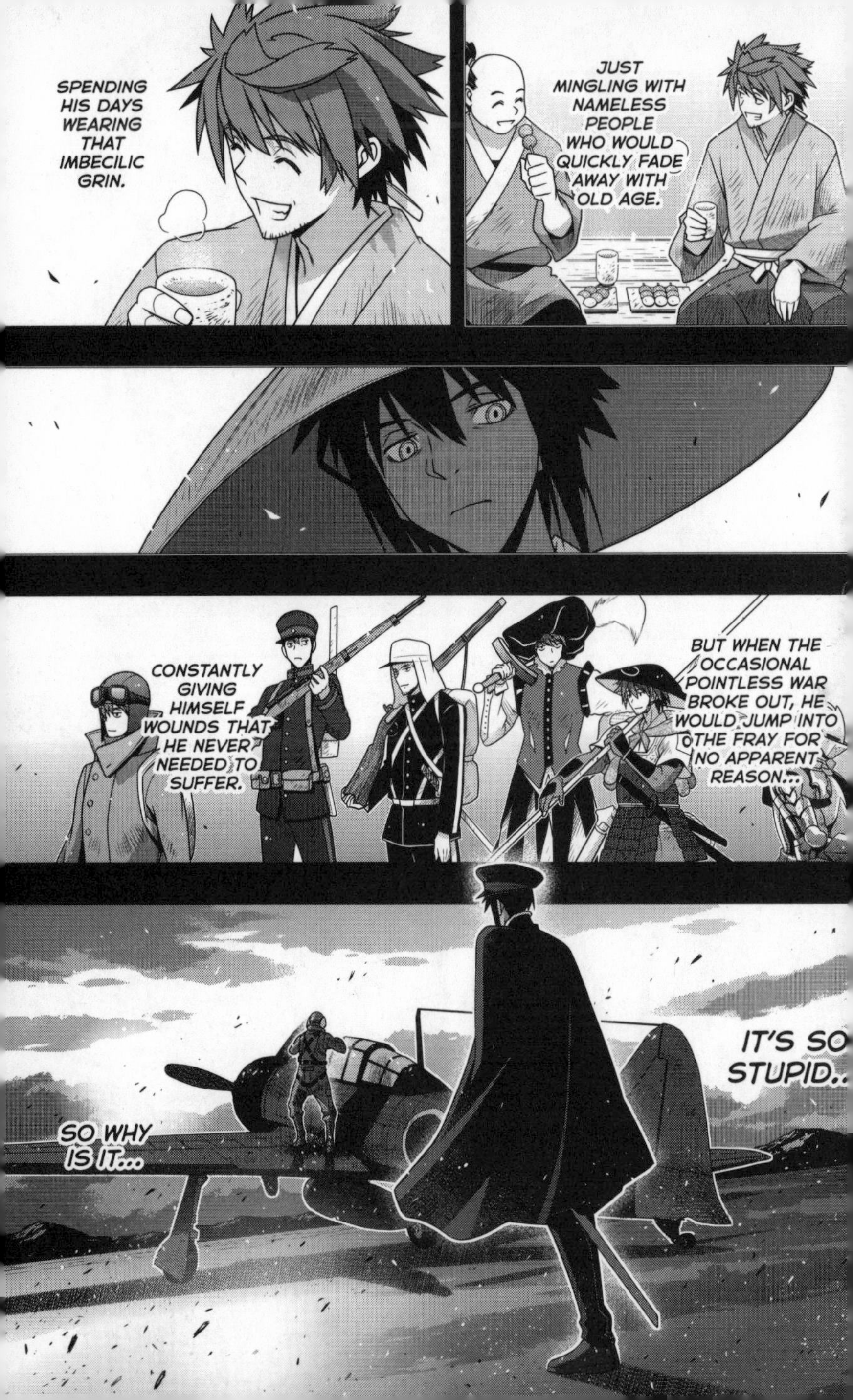
JUST MINGLING WITH NAMELESS PEOPLE WHO WOULD QUICKLY FADE AWAY WITH OLD AGE.
SPENDING HIS DAYS WEARING THAT IMBECILIC GRIN.
BUT WHEN THE OCCASIONAL POINTLESS WAR BROKE OUT, HE WOULD JUMP INTO THE FRAY FOR NO APPARENT REASON...
CONSTANTLY GIVING HIMSELF WOUNDS THAT HE NEVER NEEDED TO SUFFER.
IT'S SO STUPID...
SO WHY IS IT...

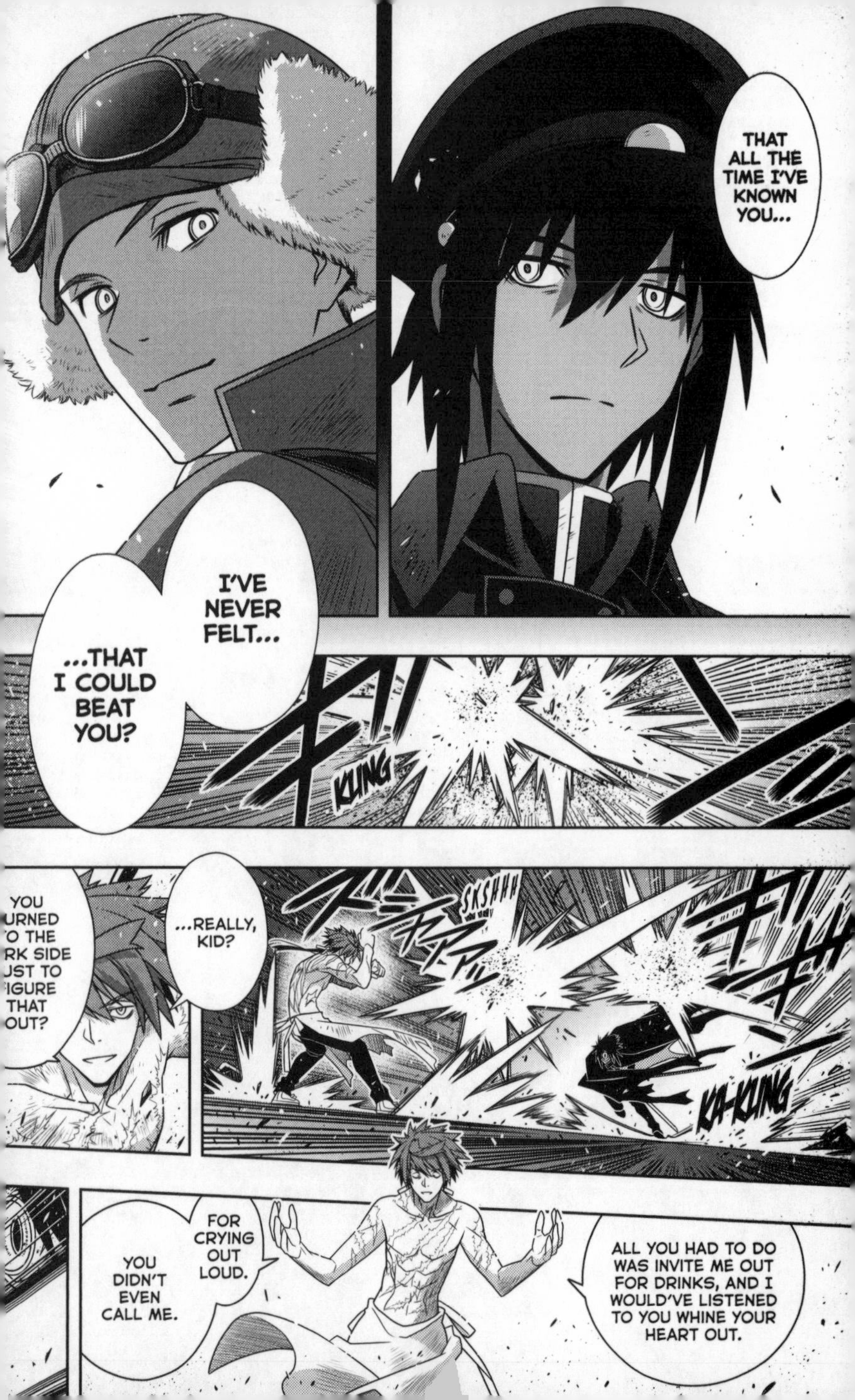
THAT ALL THE TIME I'VE KNOWN YOU...
I'VE NEVER FELT...
...THAT I COULD BEAT YOU?
KUNG
SKSHHH
...REALLY, KID?
KA-KUNG
YOU URNED O THE RK SIDE UST TO IGURE THAT OUT?
ALL YOU HAD TO DO WAS INVITE ME OUT FOR DRINKS, AND I WOULD'VE LISTENED TO YOU WHINE YOUR HEART OUT.
FOR CRYING OUT LOUD.
YOU DIDN'T EVEN CALL ME.

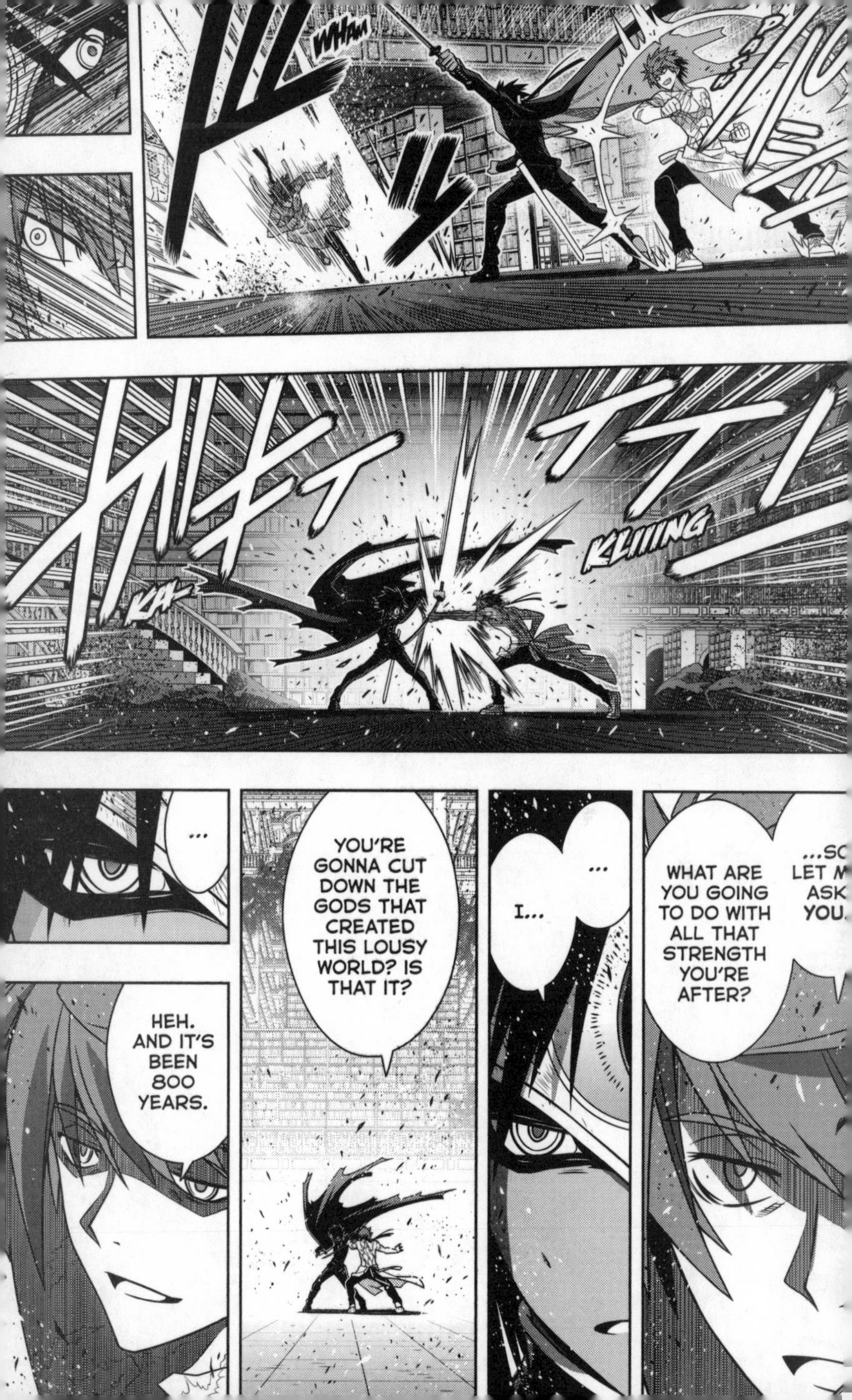
PASH
WHAM
KA-
KLIIIING
...SO LET M ASK YOU.
WHAT ARE YOU GOING TO DO WITH ALL THAT STRENGTH YOU'RE AFTER?
...
I...
YOU'RE GONNA CUT DOWN THE GODS THAT CREATED THIS LOUSY WORLD? IS THAT IT?
...
HEH. AND IT'S BEEN 800 YEARS.

YOU ONLY SAY THAT...

...BECAUSE WHAT YOU REALLY WANT IS TO AVENGE YOUR FAMILY,

AND YOU COULDN'T GET THAT EVEN WITH ALL YOUR NEWFOUND STRENGTH.

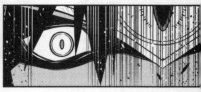

WHAM

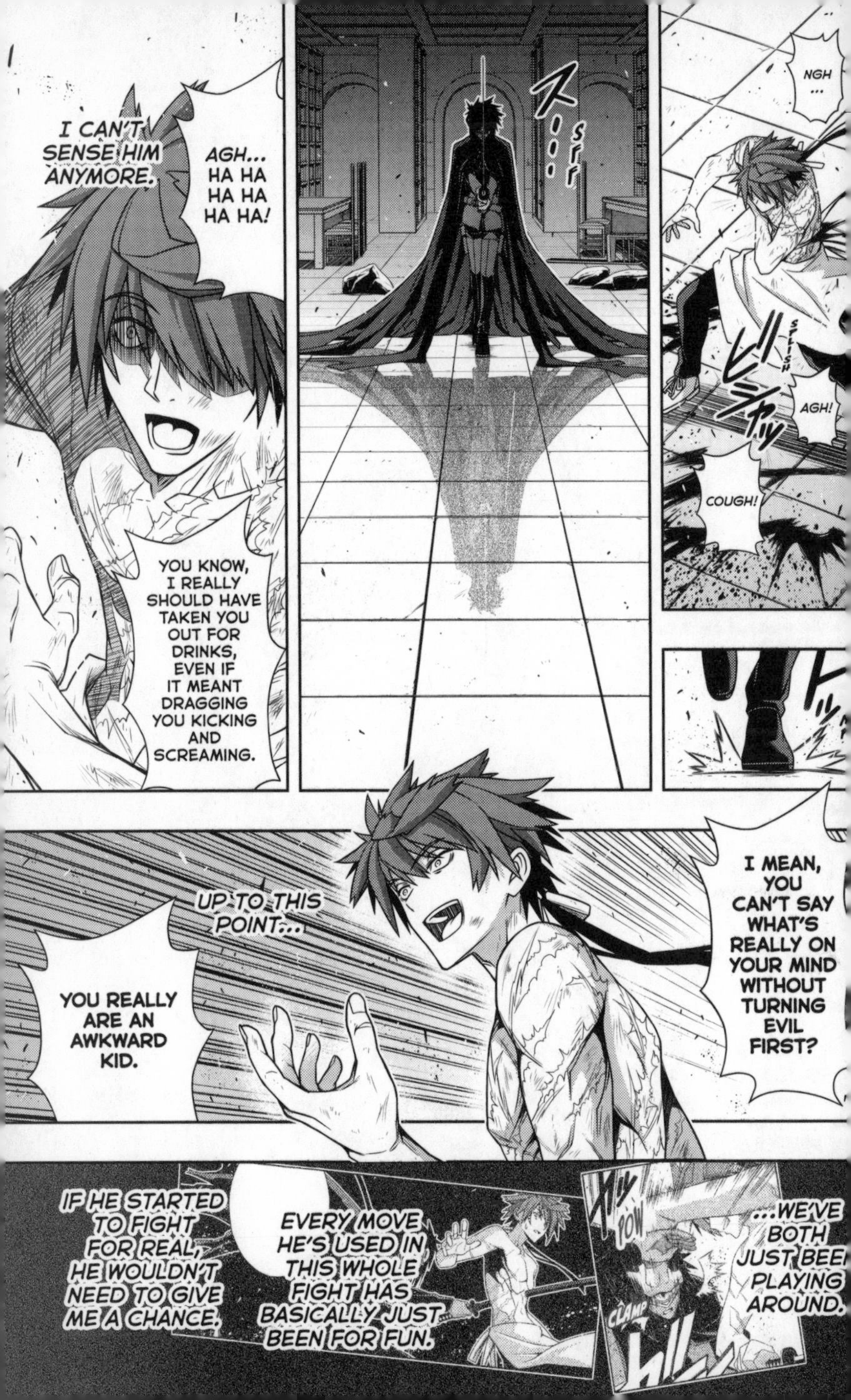
NGH...
SPLISH
AGH!
COUGH!
SRR
AGH... HA HA HA HA HA HA!
I CAN'T SENSE HIM ANYMORE.
YOU KNOW, I REALLY SHOULD HAVE TAKEN YOU OUT FOR DRINKS, EVEN IF IT MEANT DRAGGING YOU KICKING AND SCREAMING.
I MEAN, YOU CAN'T SAY WHAT'S REALLY ON YOUR MIND WITHOUT TURNING EVIL FIRST?
UP TO THIS POINT...
YOU REALLY ARE AN AWKWARD KID.
...WE'VE BOTH JUST BEE PLAYING AROUND.
POW
CLAMP
EVERY MOVE HE'S USED IN THIS WHOLE FIGHT HAS BASICALLY JUST BEEN FOR FUN.
IF HE STARTED TO FIGHT FOR REAL, HE WOULDN'T NEED TO GIVE ME A CHANCE.

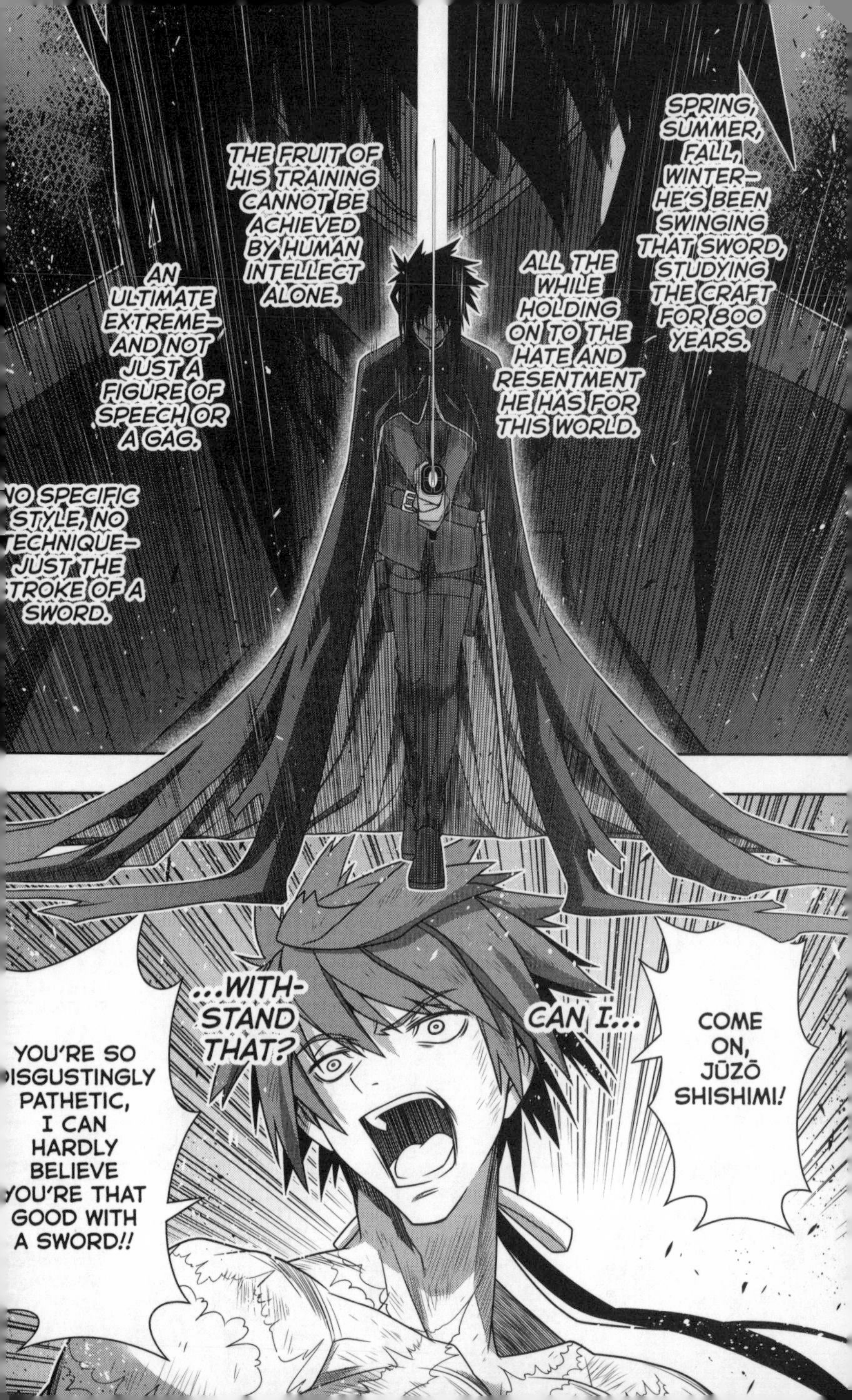
SPRING, SUMMER, FALL, WINTER— HE'S BEEN SWINGING THAT SWORD, STUDYING THE CRAFT FOR 800 YEARS.
ALL THE WHILE HOLDING ON TO THE HATE AND RESENTMENT HE HAS FOR THIS WORLD.
THE FRUIT OF HIS TRAINING CANNOT BE ACHIEVED BY HUMAN INTELLECT ALONE.
AN ULTIMATE EXTREME— AND NOT JUST A FIGURE OF SPEECH OR A GAG.
NO SPECIFIC STYLE, NO TECHNIQUE— JUST THE STROKE OF A SWORD.
COME ON, JŪZŌ SHISHIMI!
CAN I...
...WITH-STAND THAT?
YOU'RE SO DISGUSTINGLY PATHETIC, I CAN HARDLY BELIEVE YOU'RE THAT GOOD WITH A SWORD!!

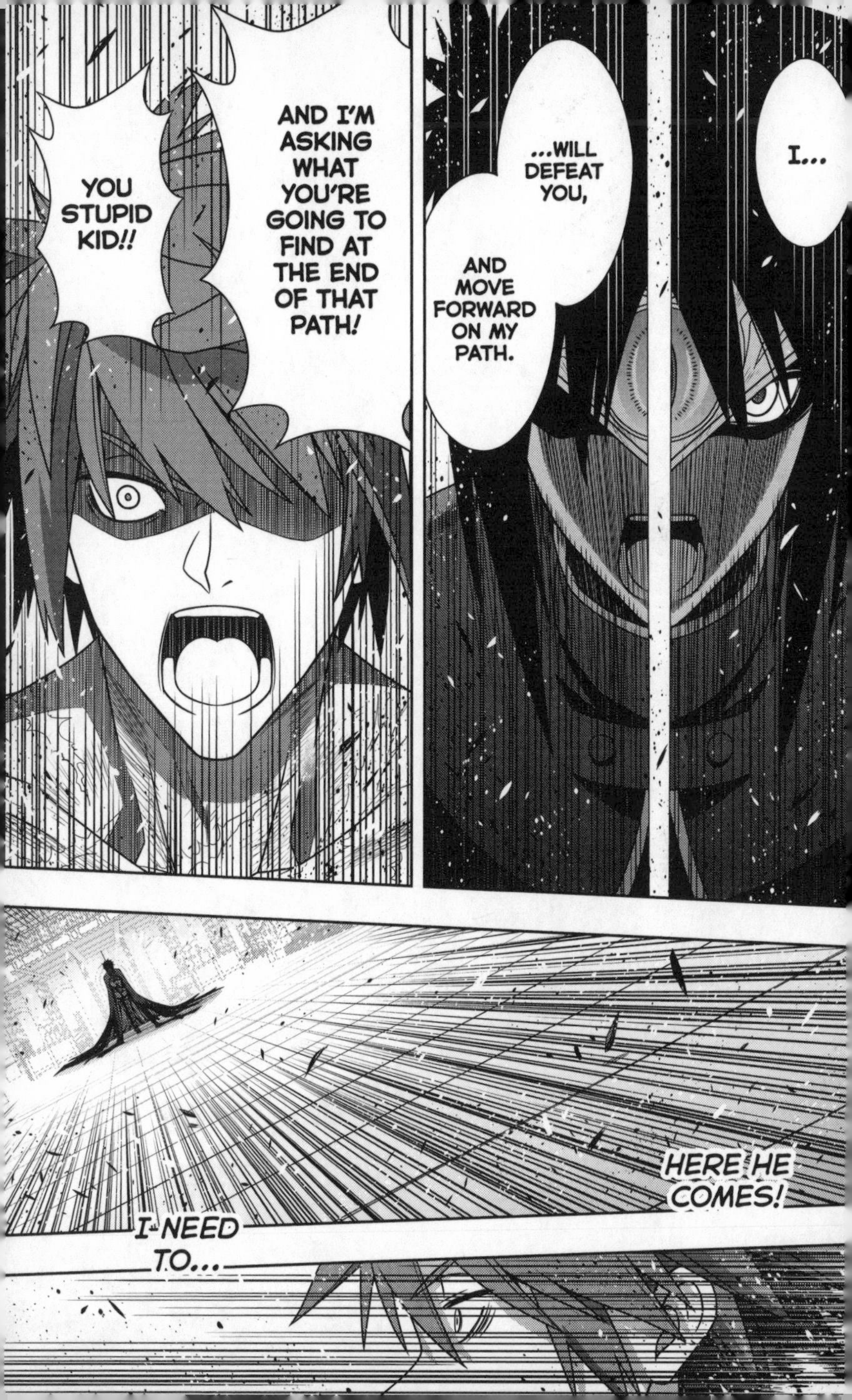
I...
...WILL DEFEAT YOU,
AND MOVE FORWARD ON MY PATH.
AND I'M ASKING WHAT YOU'RE GOING TO FIND AT THE END OF THAT PATH!
YOU STUPID KID!!
HERE HE COMES!
I NEED TO...

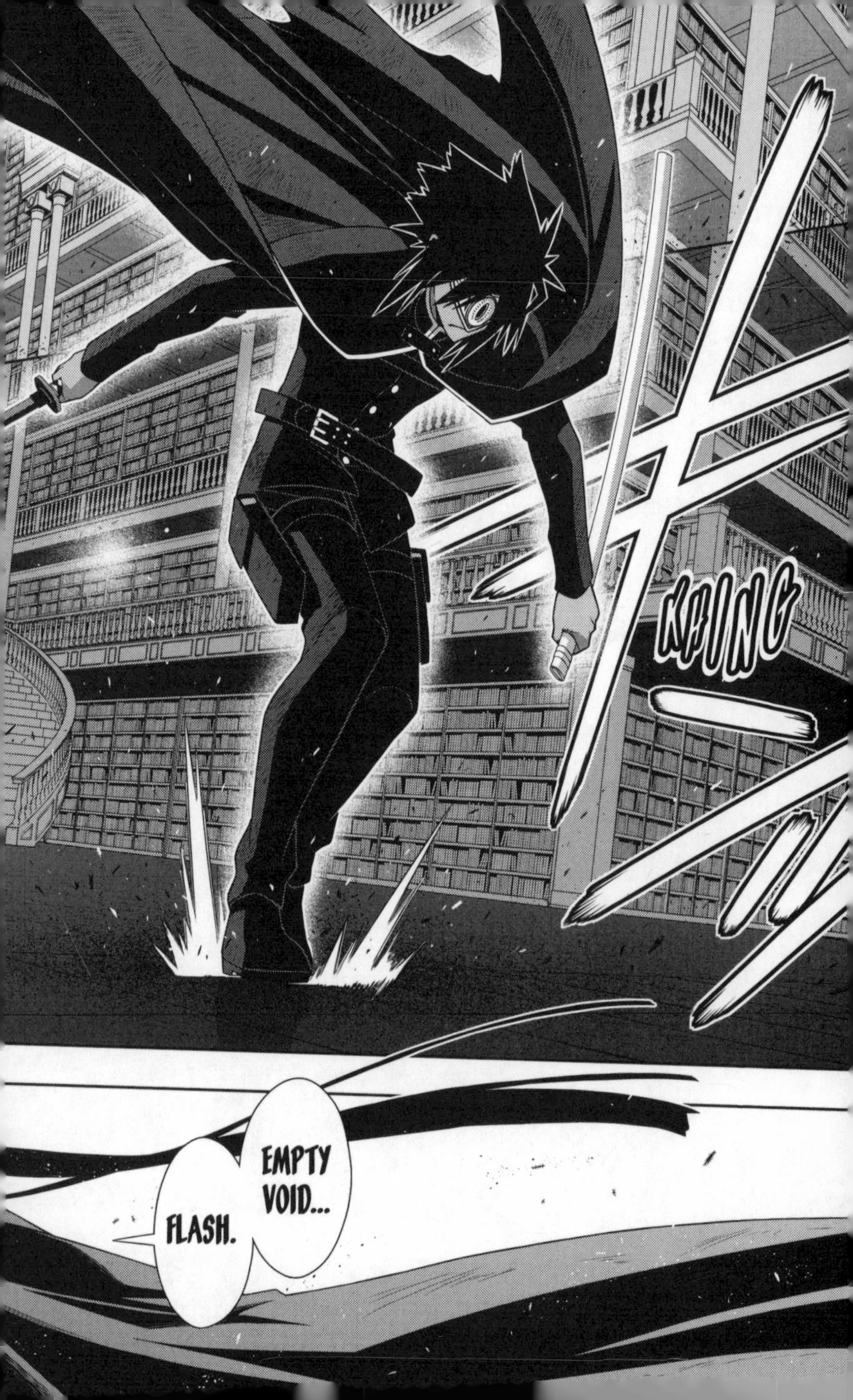
KCHING
EMPTY VOID...
FLASH.

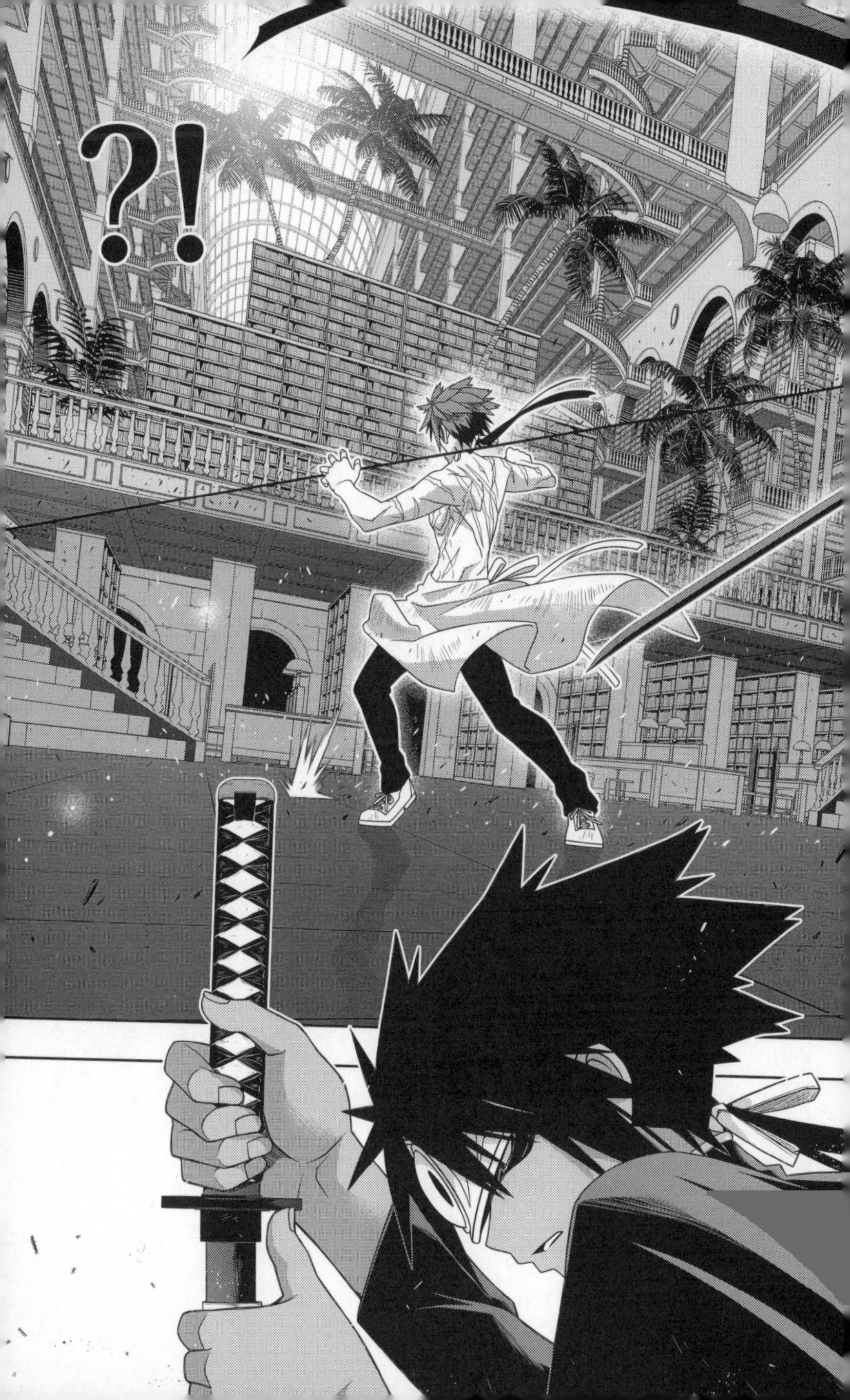
?!

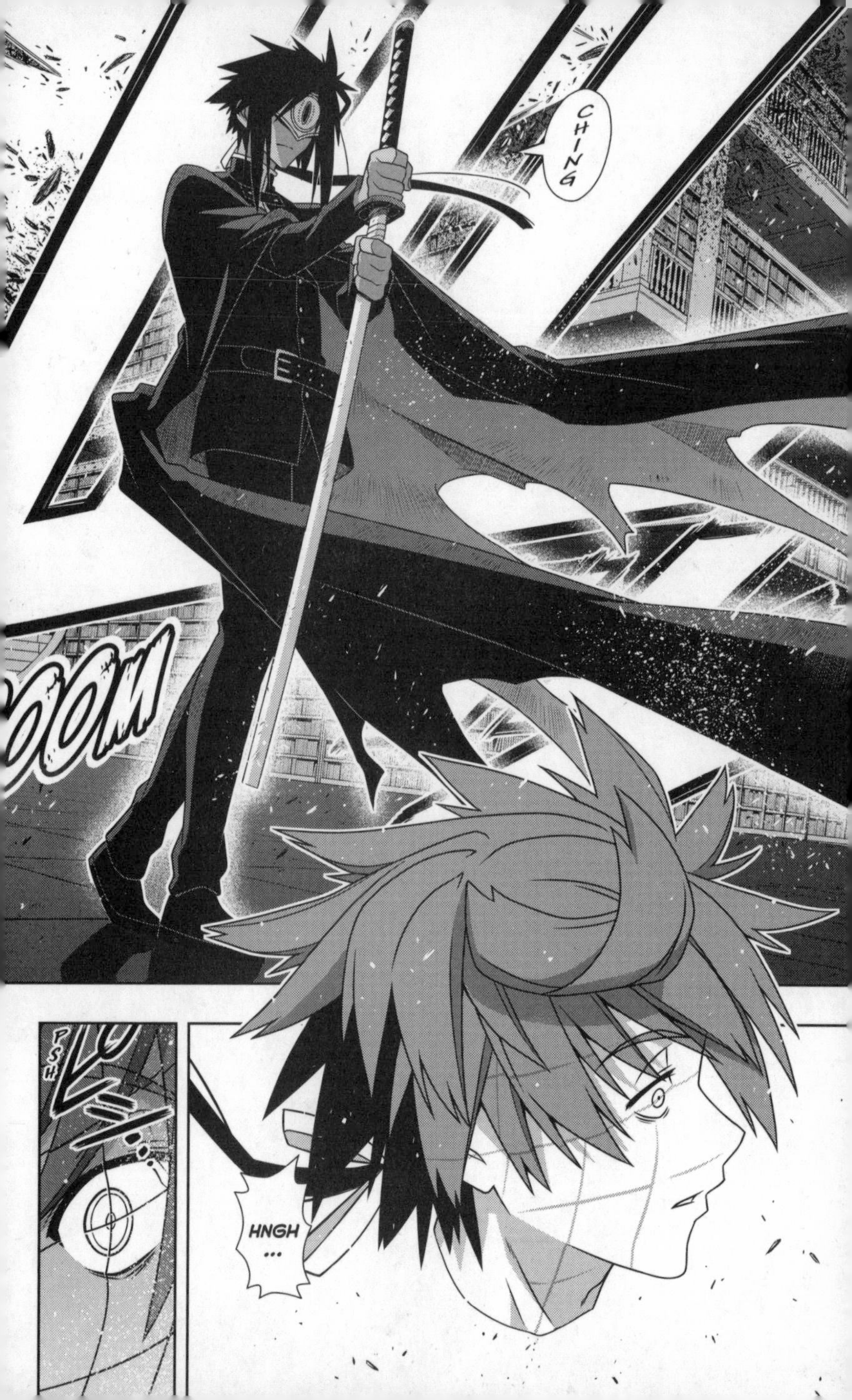
CHING
HNGH ...
PSH

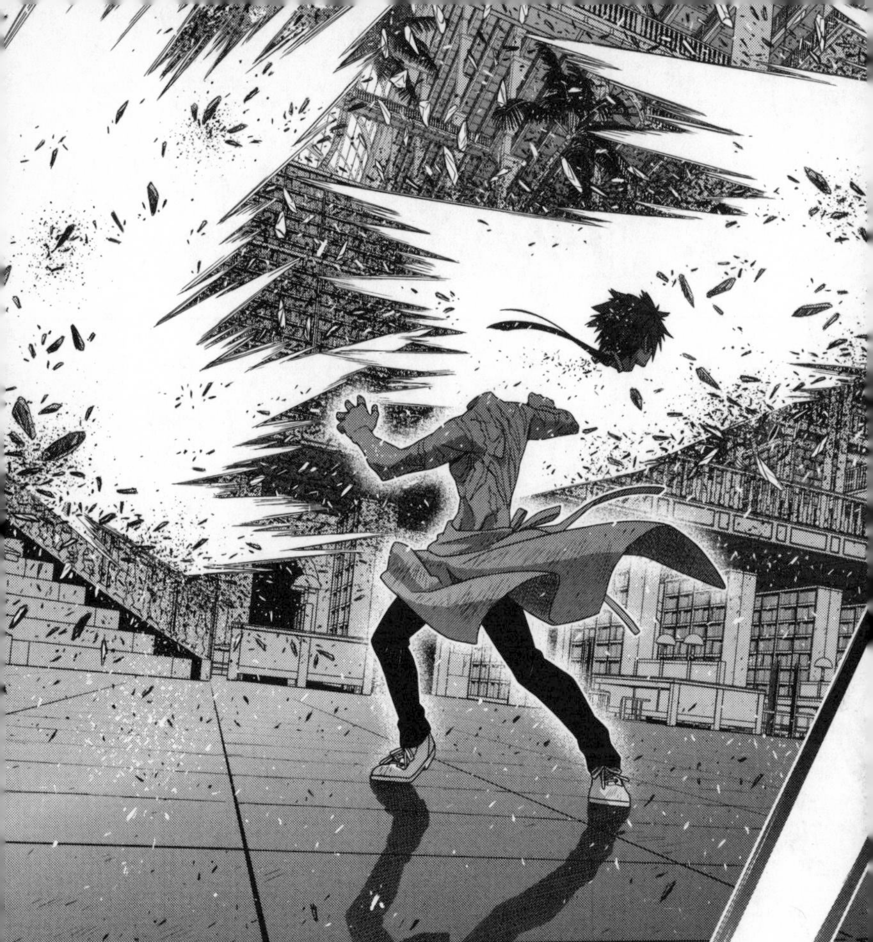
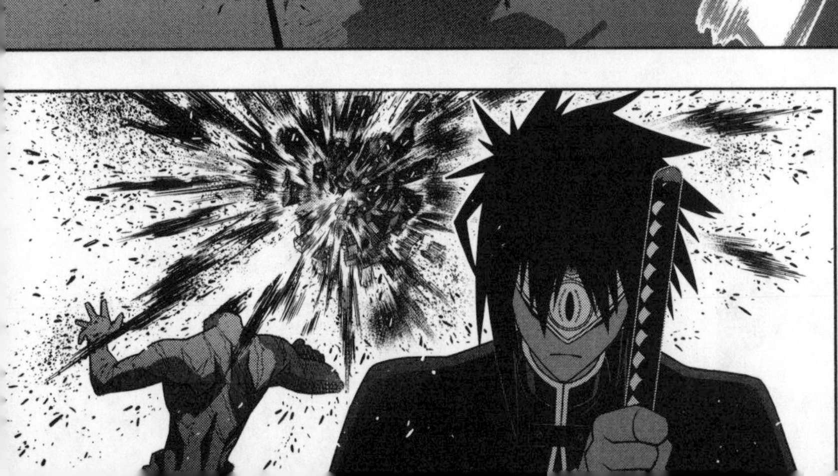

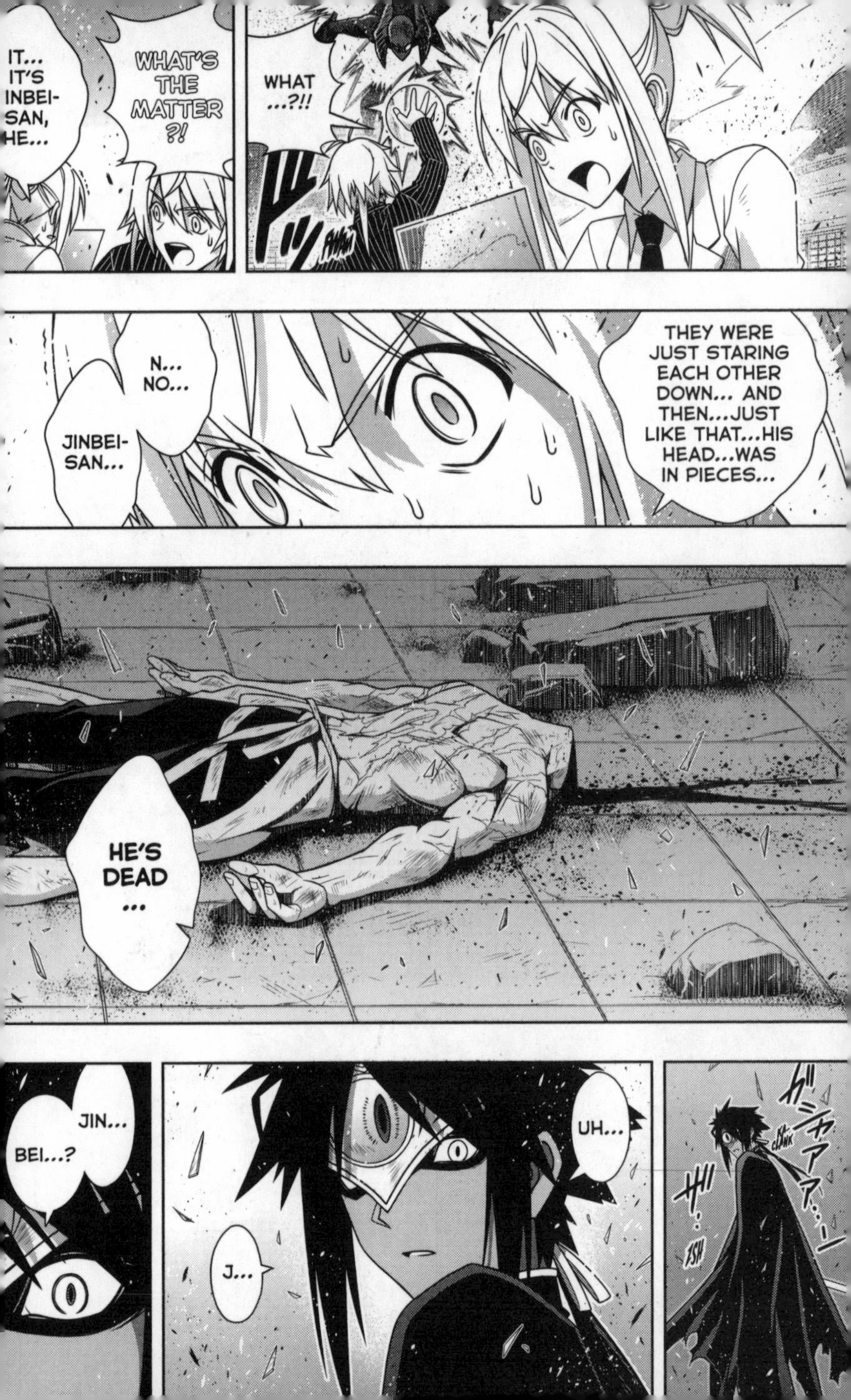
WHAT ...?!!
WHAT'S THE MATTER ?!
IT... IT'S INBEI-SAN, HE...
THEY WERE JUST STARING EACH OTHER DOWN... AND THEN...JUST LIKE THAT...HIS HEAD...WAS IN PIECES...
N... NO...
JINBEI-SAN...
HE'S DEAD ...
KA-CLANK
ISH
UH...
J...
JIN... BEI...?

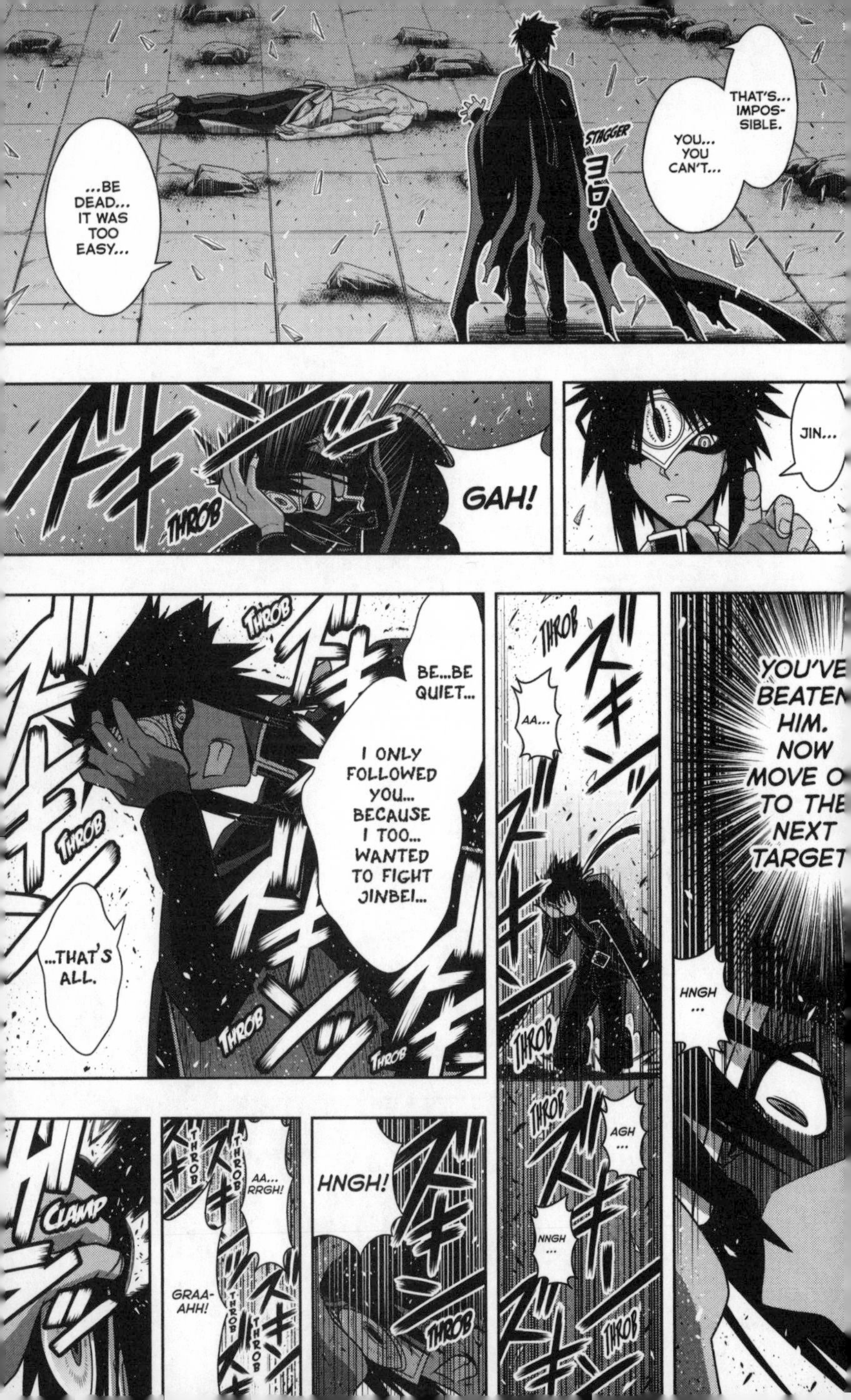
THAT'S... IMPOSSIBLE.
YOU... YOU CAN'T...
STAGGER
...BE DEAD... IT WAS TOO EASY...
JIN...
GAH!
THROB
YOU'VE BEATEN HIM. NOW MOVE O TO THE NEXT TARGET
HNGH ...
THROB
AA...
THROB
AGH ...
NNGH ...
THROB
THROB
THROB
BE...BE QUIET...
I ONLY FOLLOWED YOU... BECAUSE I TOO... WANTED TO FIGHT JINBEI...
THROB
...THAT'S ALL.
THROB
THROB
HNGH!
THROB
AA... RRGH!
THROB
THROB
GRAA-AHH!
CLAMP

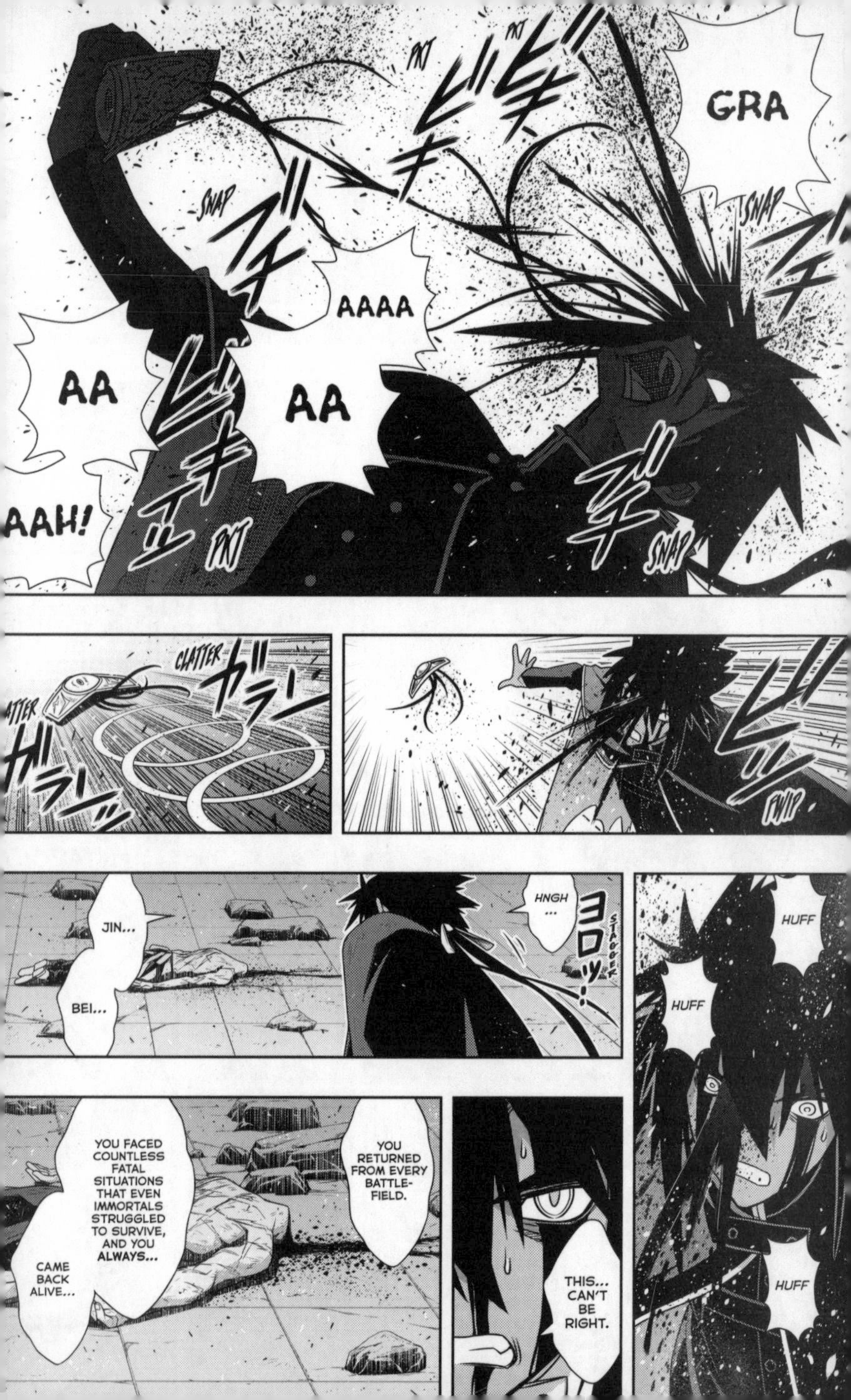
GRA
SNAP
SNAP
PKT
PKT
SNAP
AAAA
AA
AA
AAH!
PKT
FWIP
CLATTER
HUFF
HUFF
HUFF
HNGH...
STAGGER
JIN...
BEI...
THIS... CAN'T BE RIGHT.
YOU RETURNED FROM EVERY BATTLE-FIELD.
YOU FACED COUNTLESS FATAL SITUATIONS THAT EVEN IMMORTALS STRUGGLED TO SURVIVE, AND YOU ALWAYS...
CAME BACK ALIVE...

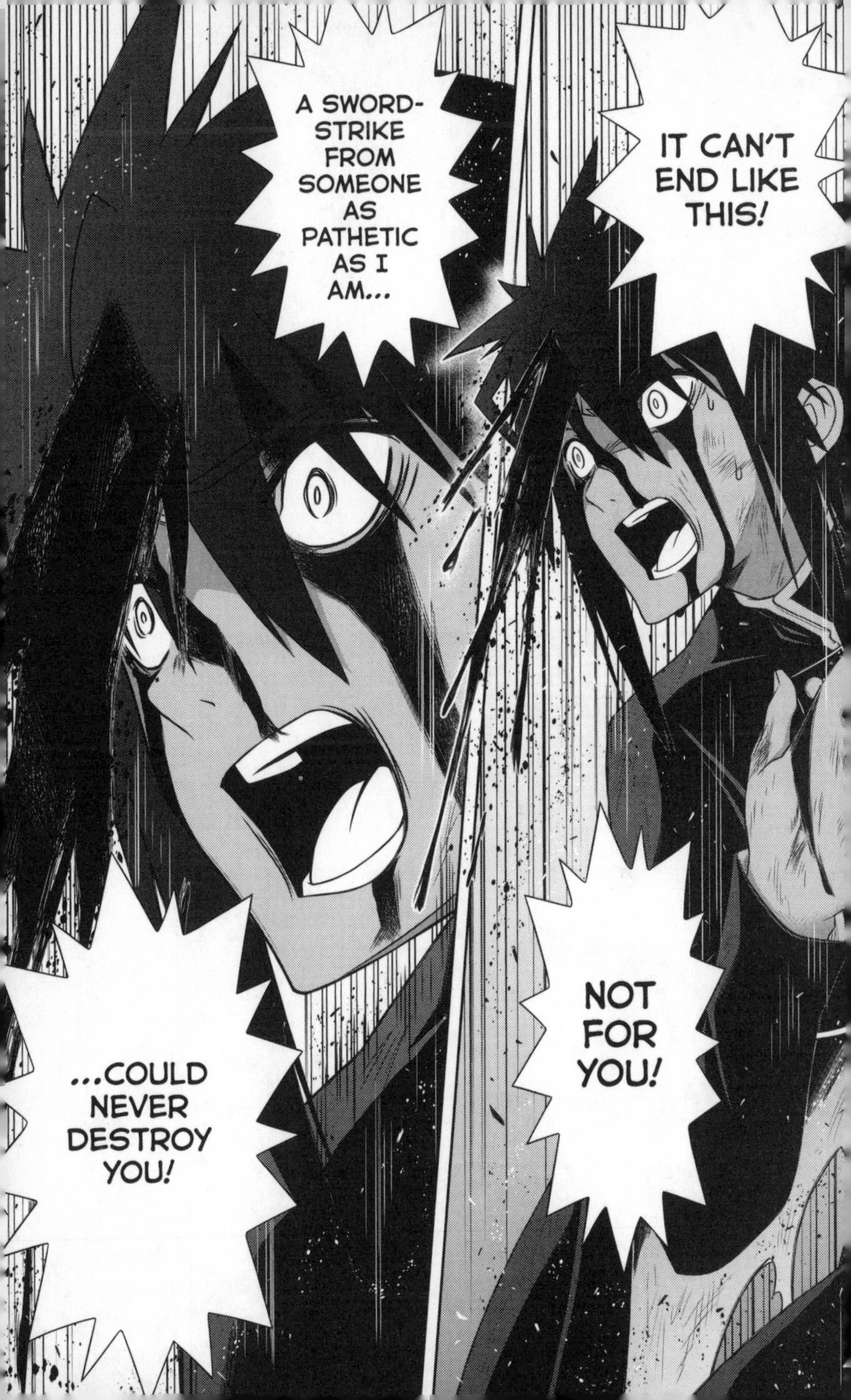
IT CAN'T END LIKE THIS!
NOT FOR YOU!
A SWORD-STRIKE FROM SOMEONE AS PATHETIC AS I AM...
...COULD NEVER DESTROY YOU!

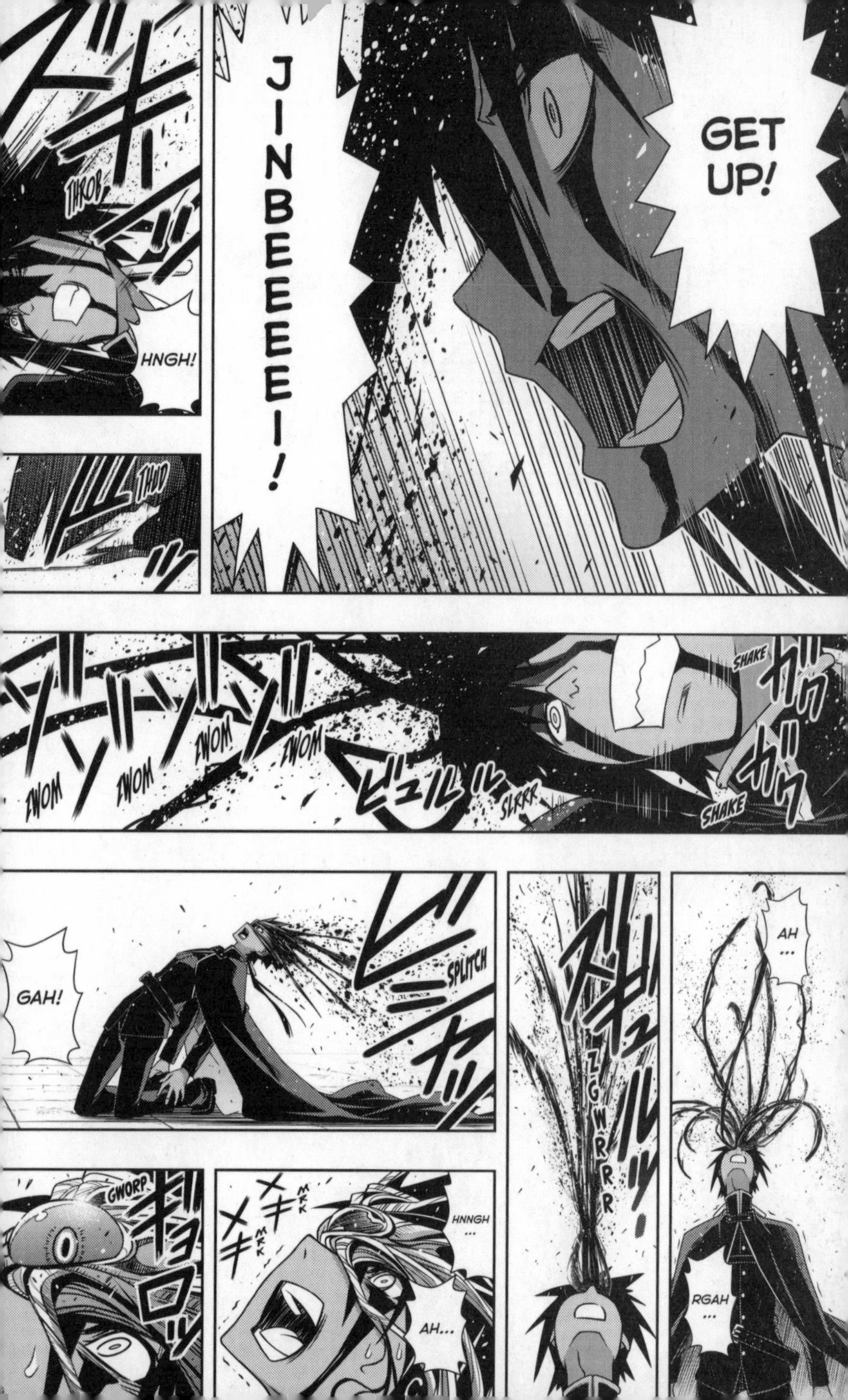
GET UP!
JINBEEEEEI!
THROB
HNGH!
THUD
SHAKE
SHAKE
SLRRR
ZWOM
ZWOM
ZWOM
ZWOM
AH ...
RGAH ...
ZGWRRRR
SPLITCH
GAH!
HNNGH ...
MRK
MRK
AH...
GWORP

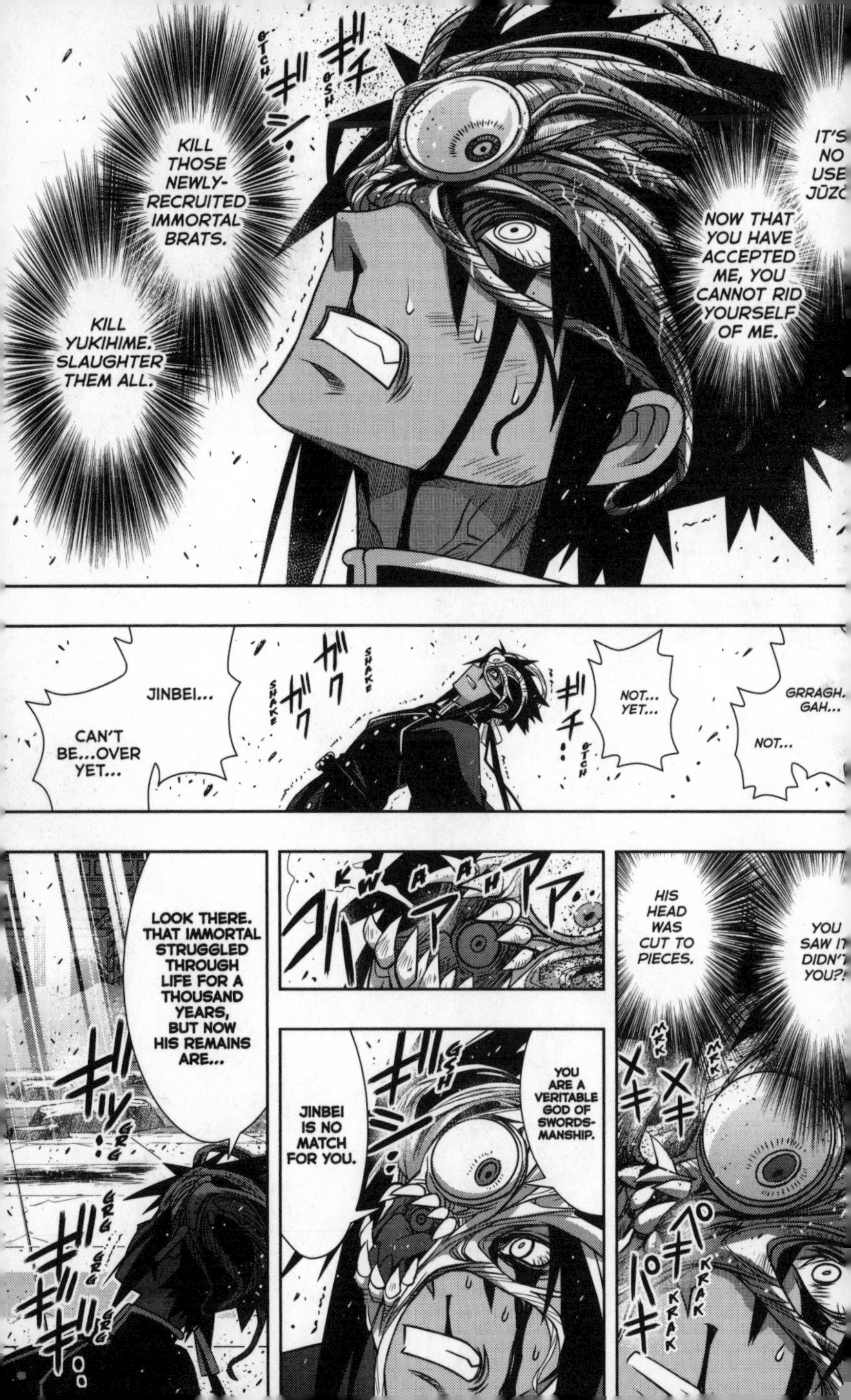

IT'S NO USE JŪZO
NOW THAT YOU HAVE ACCEPTED ME, YOU CANNOT RID YOURSELF OF ME.
GSH
GOTCH
KILL THOSE NEWLY-RECRUITED IMMORTAL BRATS.
KILL YUKIHIME. SLAUGHTER THEM ALL.
GRRAGH. GAH...
NOT...
NOT... YET...
GOTCH
SHAKE
SHAKE
JINBEI...
CAN'T BE...OVER YET...
YOU SAW IT, DIDN'T YOU?!
HIS HEAD WAS CUT TO PIECES.
MRK
MRK
KRAK
KRAK
KRAK
KWAAH
YOU ARE A VERITABLE GOD OF SWORDS-MANSHIP.
JINBEI IS NO MATCH FOR YOU.
GSH
LOOK THERE. THAT IMMORTAL STRUGGLED THROUGH LIFE FOR A THOUSAND YEARS, BUT NOW HIS REMAINS ARE...
GRG
GRG
GRG
GRG

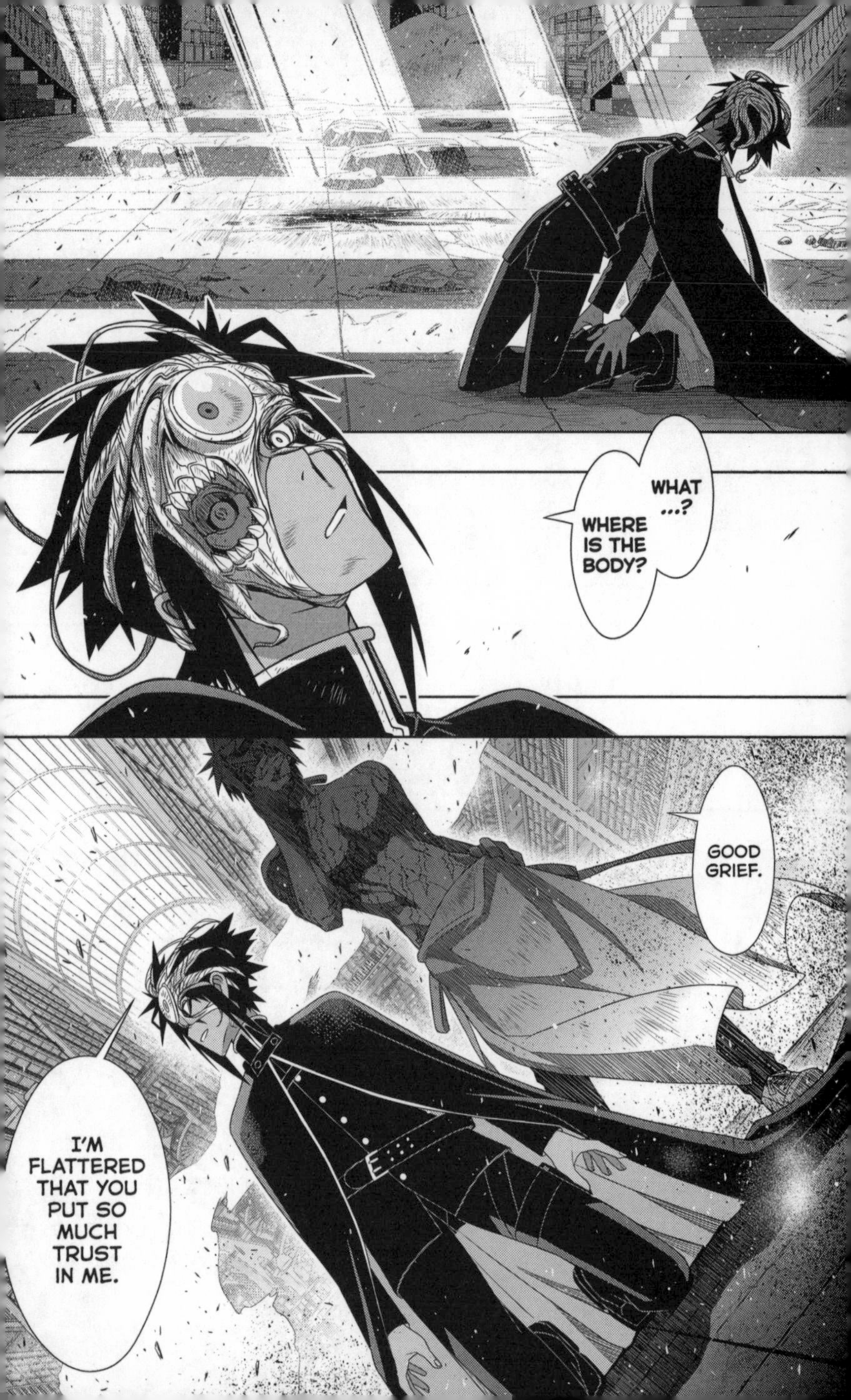
WHAT ...? WHERE IS THE BODY?
GOOD GRIEF.
I'M FLATTERED THAT YOU PUT SO MUCH TRUST IN ME.

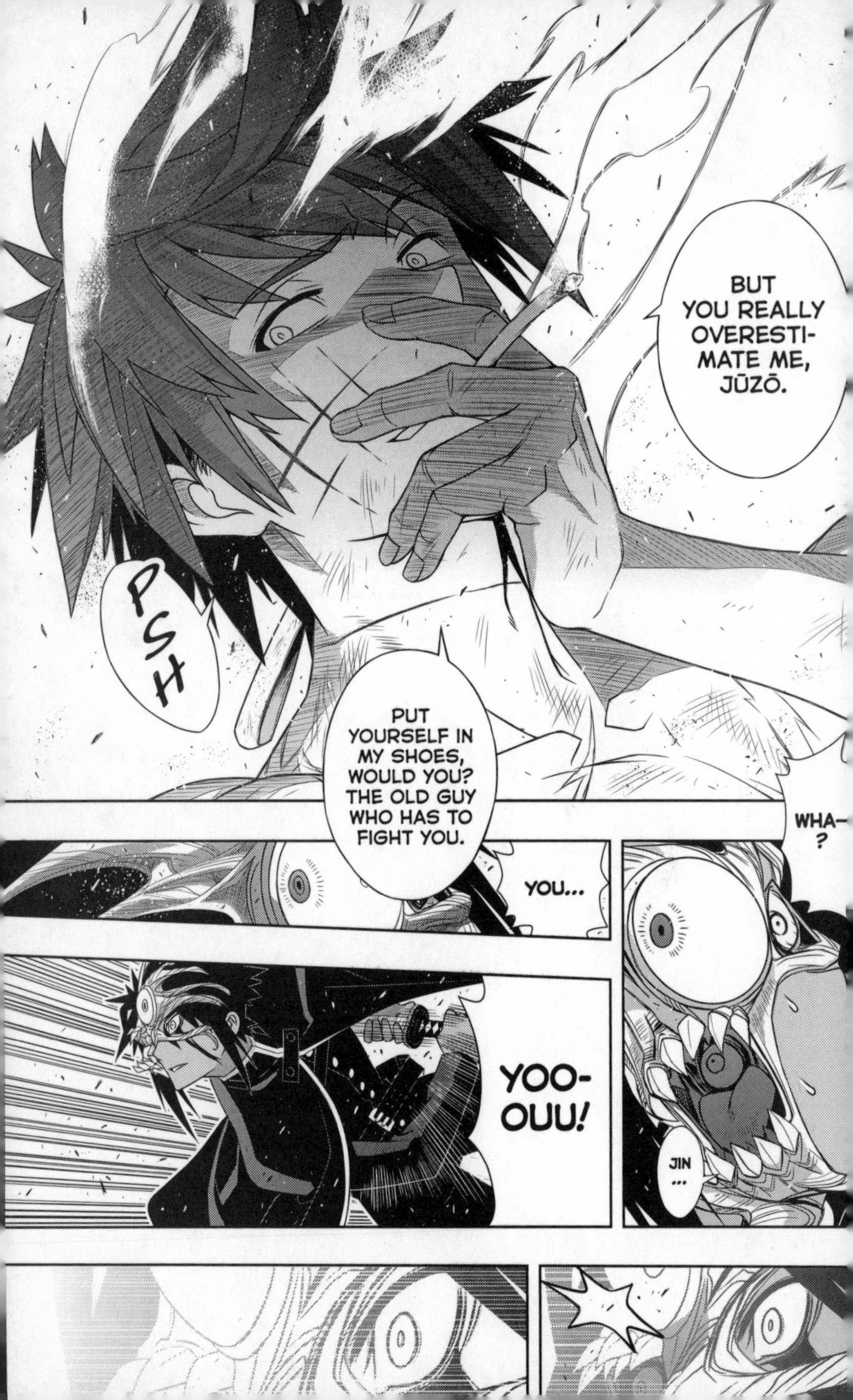
BUT YOU REALLY OVERESTIMATE ME, JŪZŌ.
PSH
PUT YOURSELF IN MY SHOES, WOULD YOU? THE OLD GUY WHO HAS TO FIGHT YOU.
WHA—?
JIN...
YOU...
YOO-OUU!

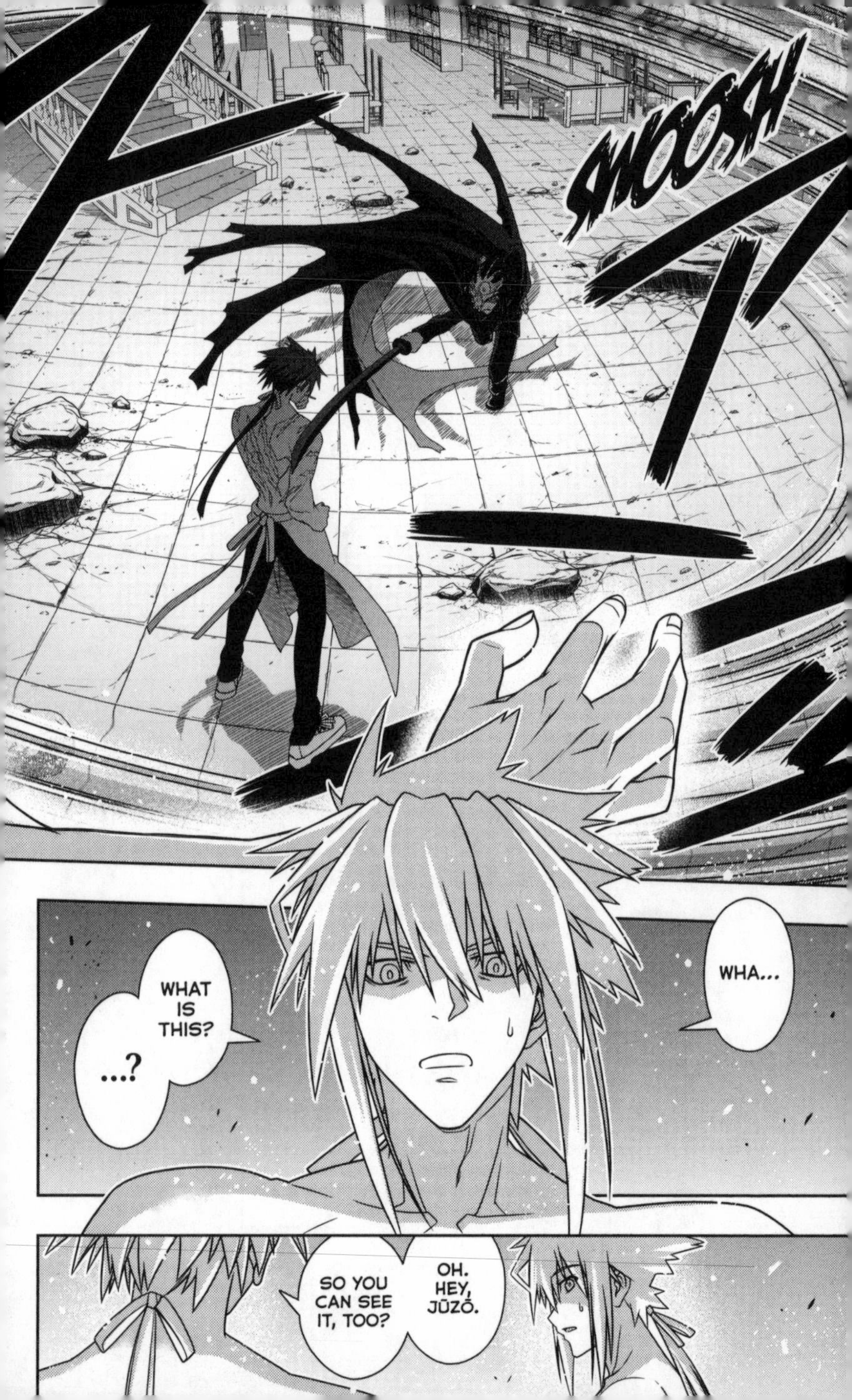
SWOOAH
WHA...
WHAT IS THIS?
...?
OH. HEY, JŪZŌ.
SO YOU CAN SEE IT, TOO?

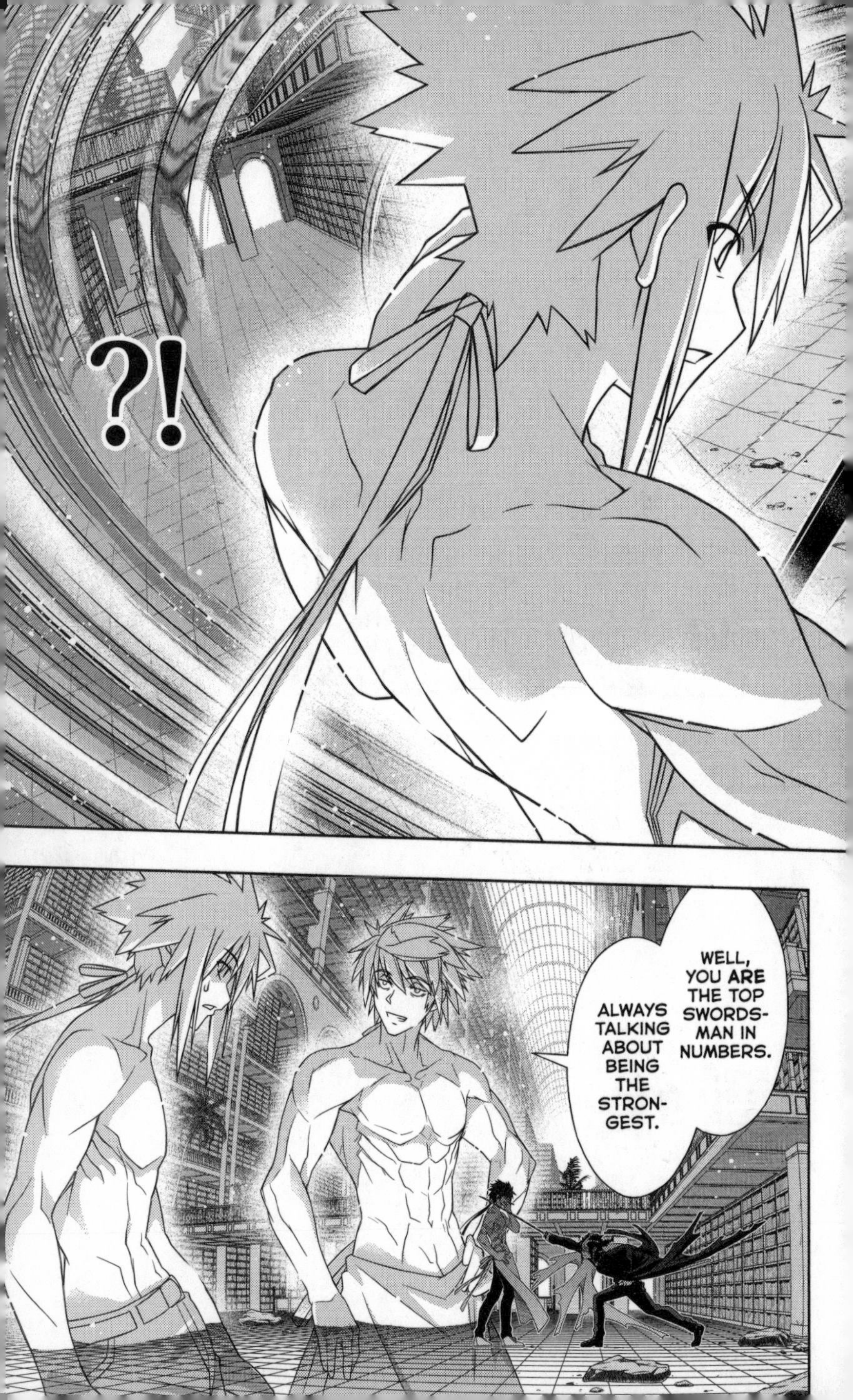
?!
WELL, YOU **ARE** THE TOP SWORDS-MAN IN NUMBERS.
ALWAYS TALKING ABOUT BEING THE STRON-GEST.

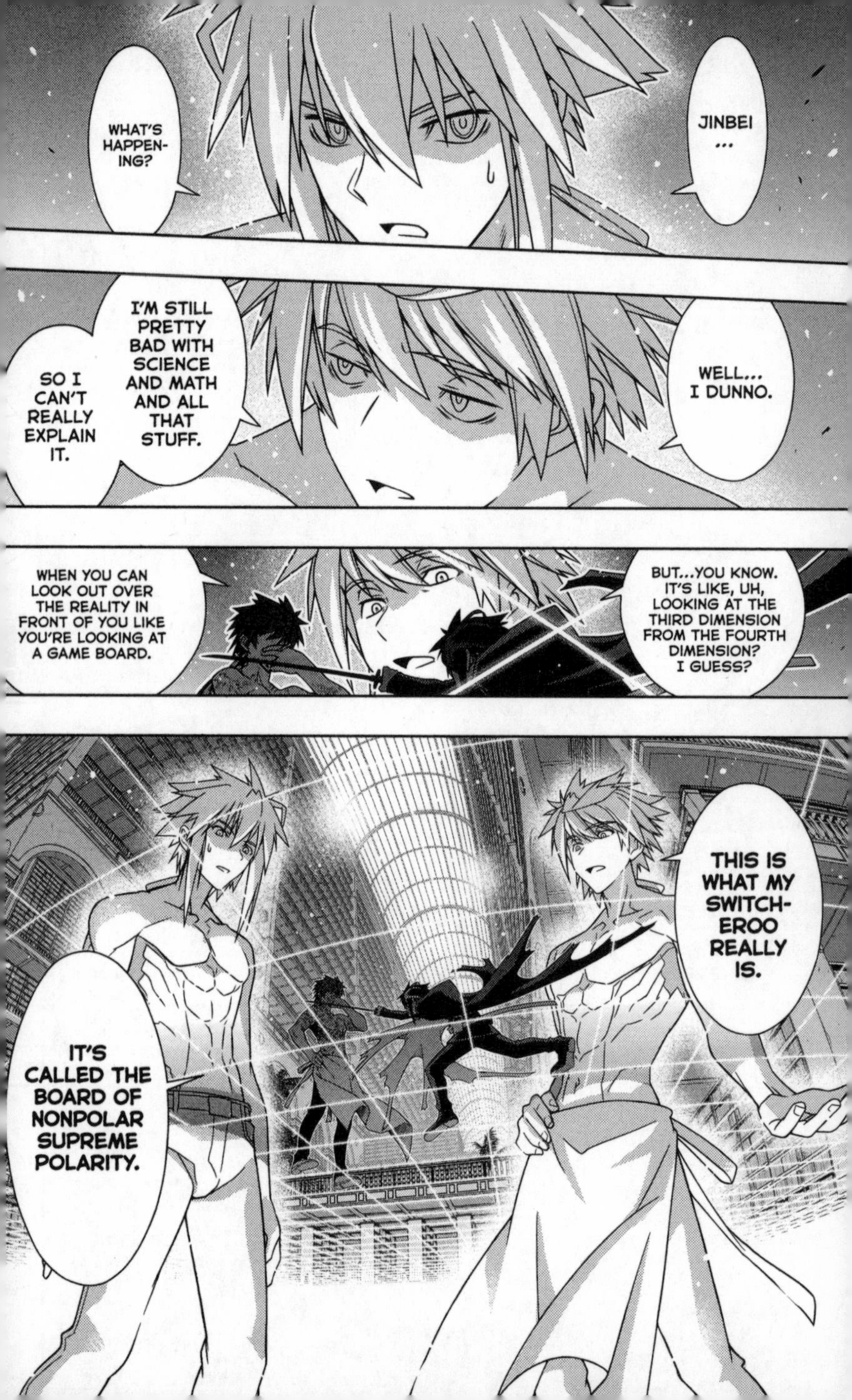
JINBEI ...
WHAT'S HAPPEN-ING?
WELL... I DUNNO.
I'M STILL PRETTY BAD WITH SCIENCE AND MATH AND ALL THAT STUFF.
SO I CAN'T REALLY EXPLAIN IT.
BUT...YOU KNOW. IT'S LIKE, UH, LOOKING AT THE THIRD DIMENSION FROM THE FOURTH DIMENSION? I GUESS?
WHEN YOU CAN LOOK OUT OVER THE REALITY IN FRONT OF YOU LIKE YOU'RE LOOKING AT A GAME BOARD.
THIS IS WHAT MY SWITCH-EROO REALLY IS.
IT'S CALLED THE BOARD OF NONPOLAR SUPREME POLARITY.

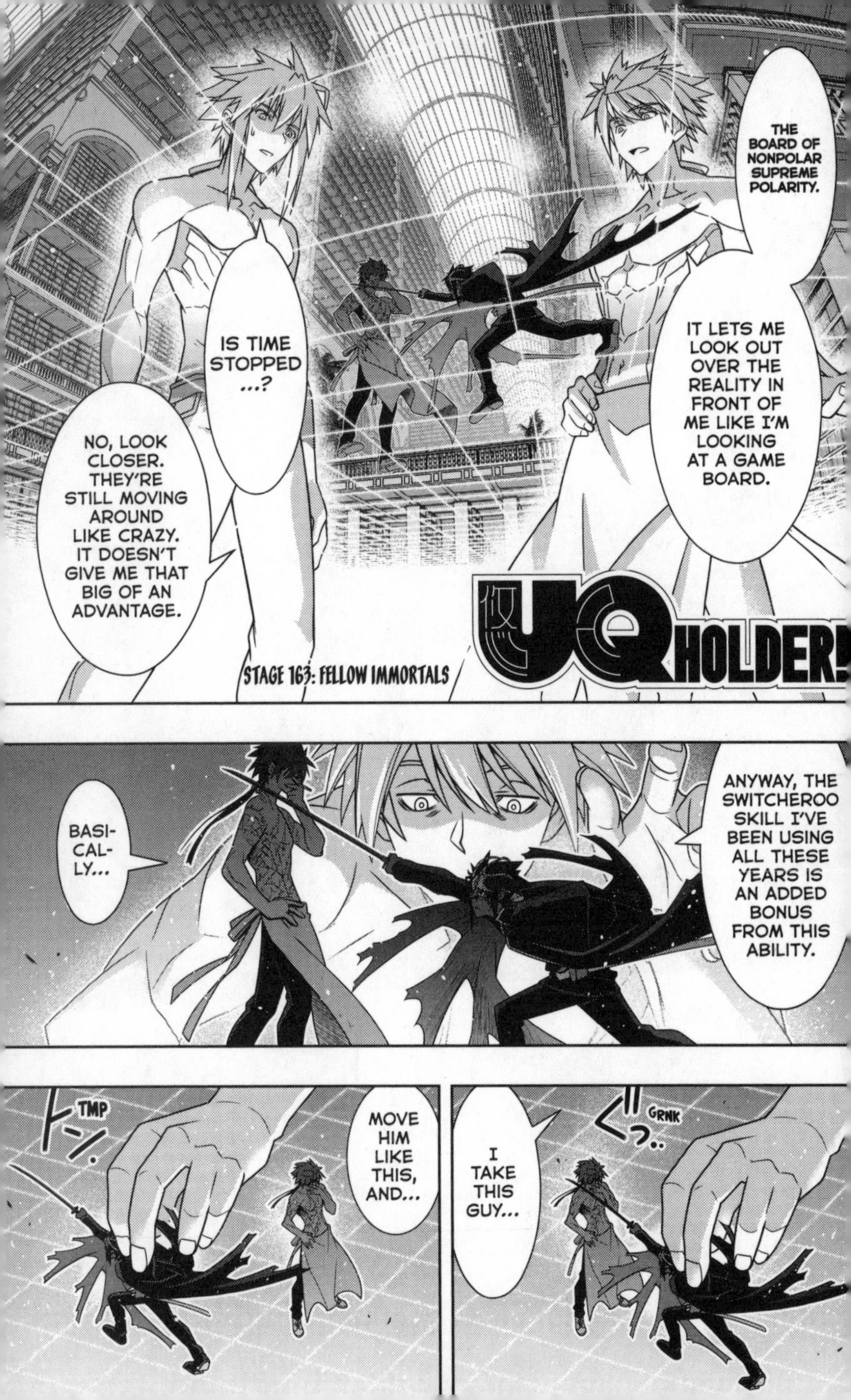
THE BOARD OF NONPOLAR SUPREME POLARITY.
IT LETS ME LOOK OUT OVER THE REALITY IN FRONT OF ME LIKE I'M LOOKING AT A GAME BOARD.
IS TIME STOPPED ...?
NO, LOOK CLOSER. THEY'RE STILL MOVING AROUND LIKE CRAZY. IT DOESN'T GIVE ME THAT BIG OF AN ADVANTAGE.
UQ HOLDER!
STAGE 163: FELLOW IMMORTALS
ANYWAY, THE SWITCHEROO SKILL I'VE BEEN USING ALL THESE YEARS IS AN ADDED BONUS FROM THIS ABILITY.
BASI-CAL-LY...
GRNK
I TAKE THIS GUY...
MOVE HIM LIKE THIS, AND...
TMP

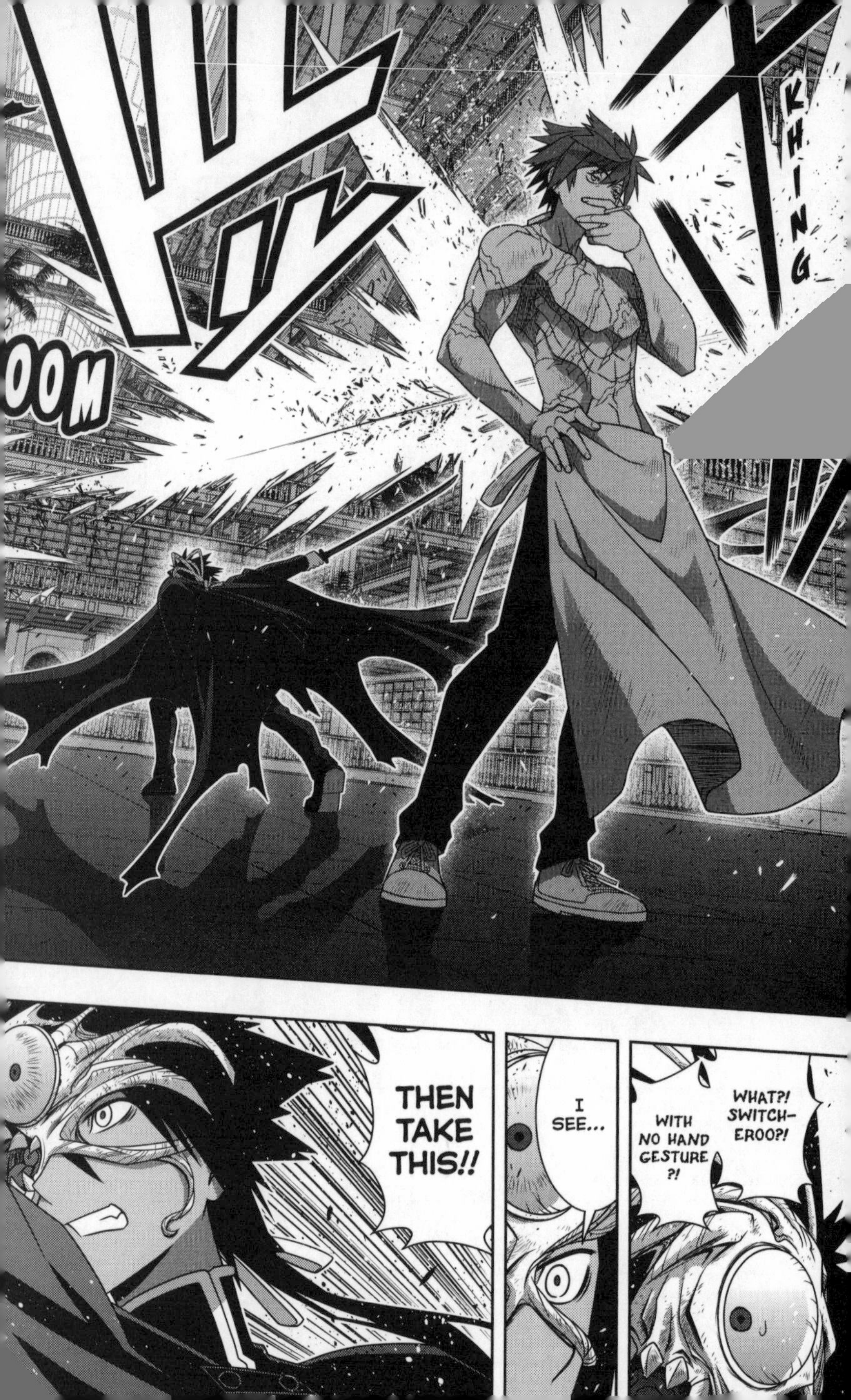
KHING
OOM
WHAT?! SWITCH-EROO?!
WITH NO HAND GESTURE ?!
I SEE...
THEN TAKE THIS!!

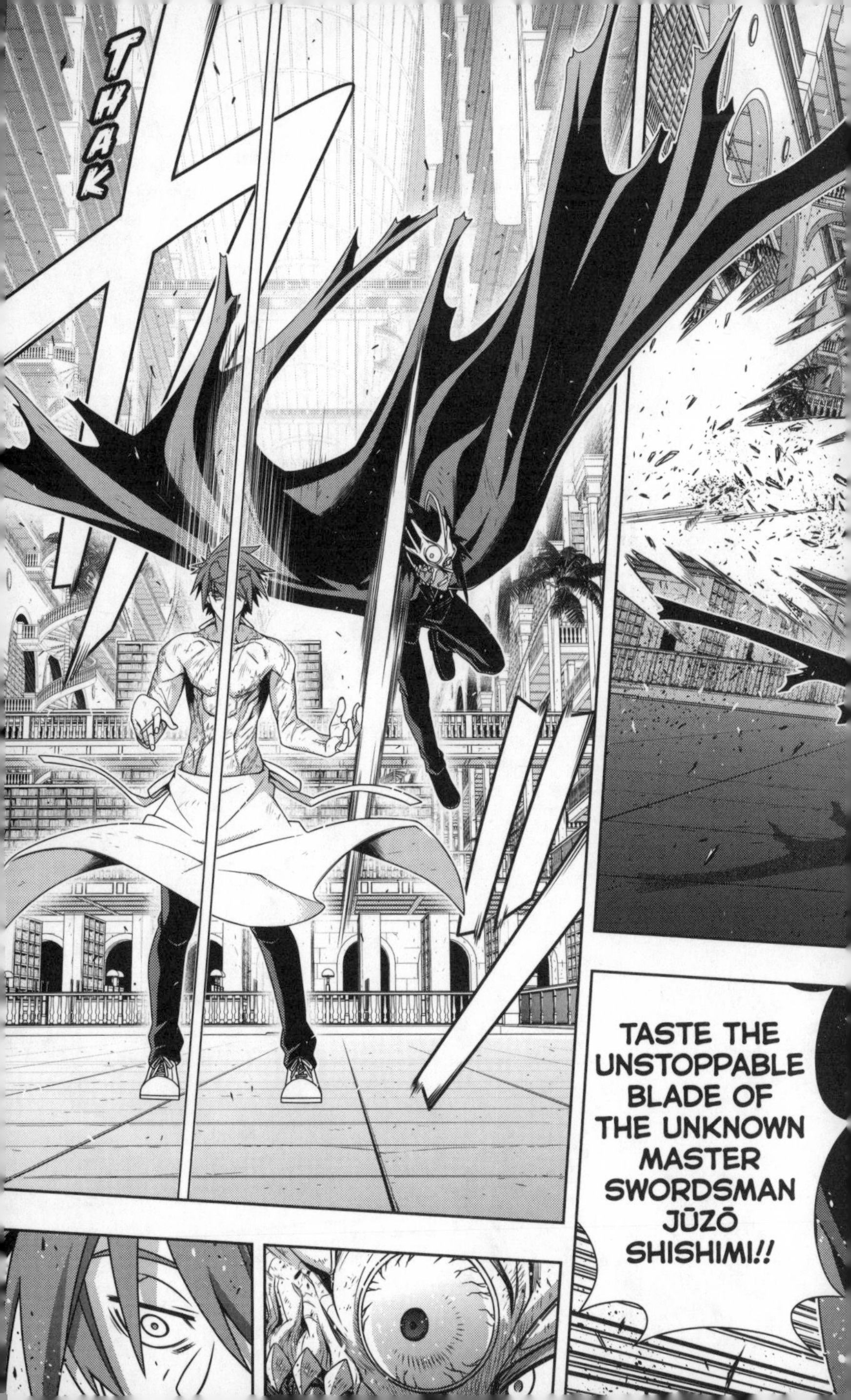
THAK
TASTE THE UNSTOPPABLE BLADE OF THE UNKNOWN MASTER SWORDSMAN JŪZŌ SHISHIMI!!

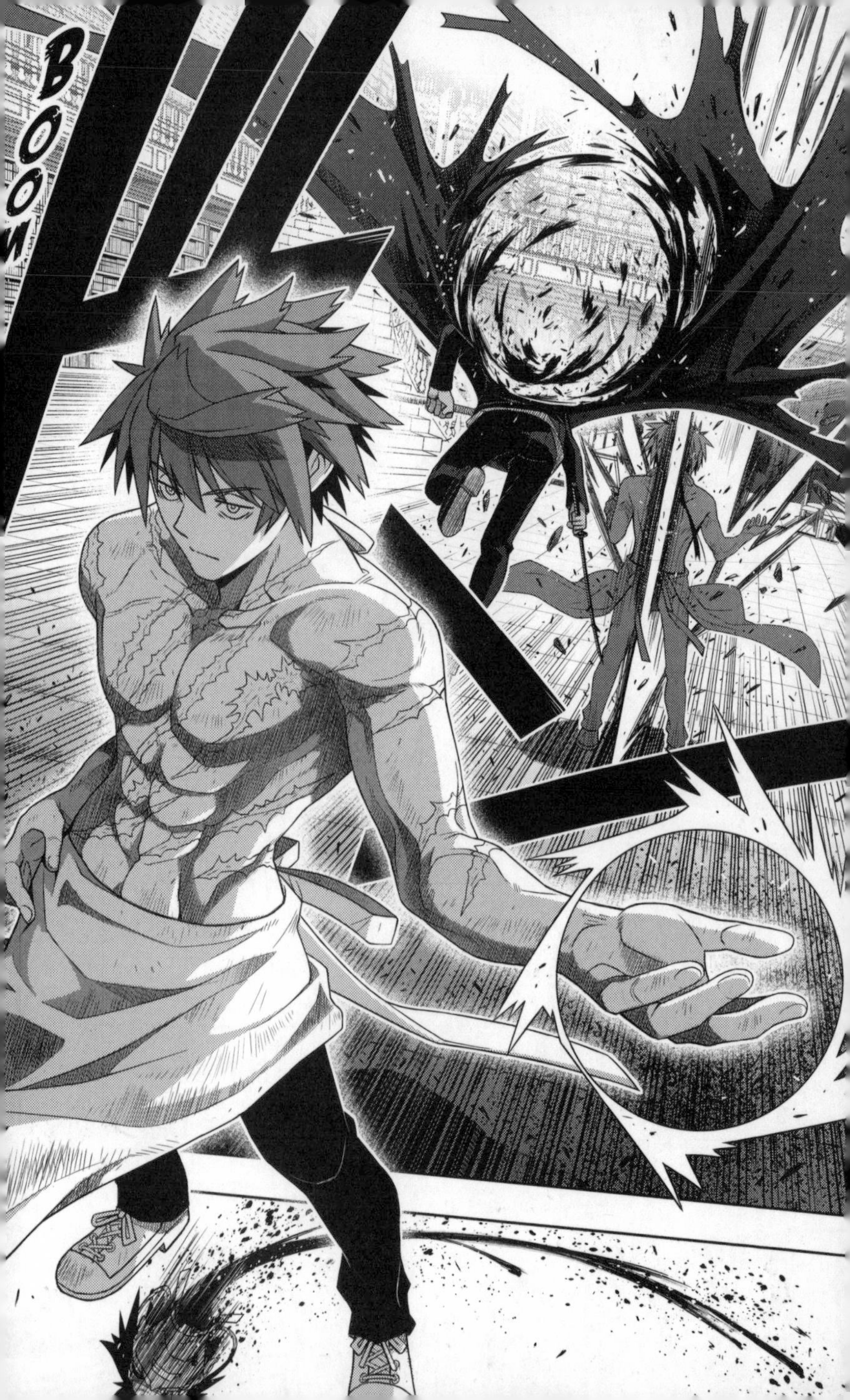
BOOOM

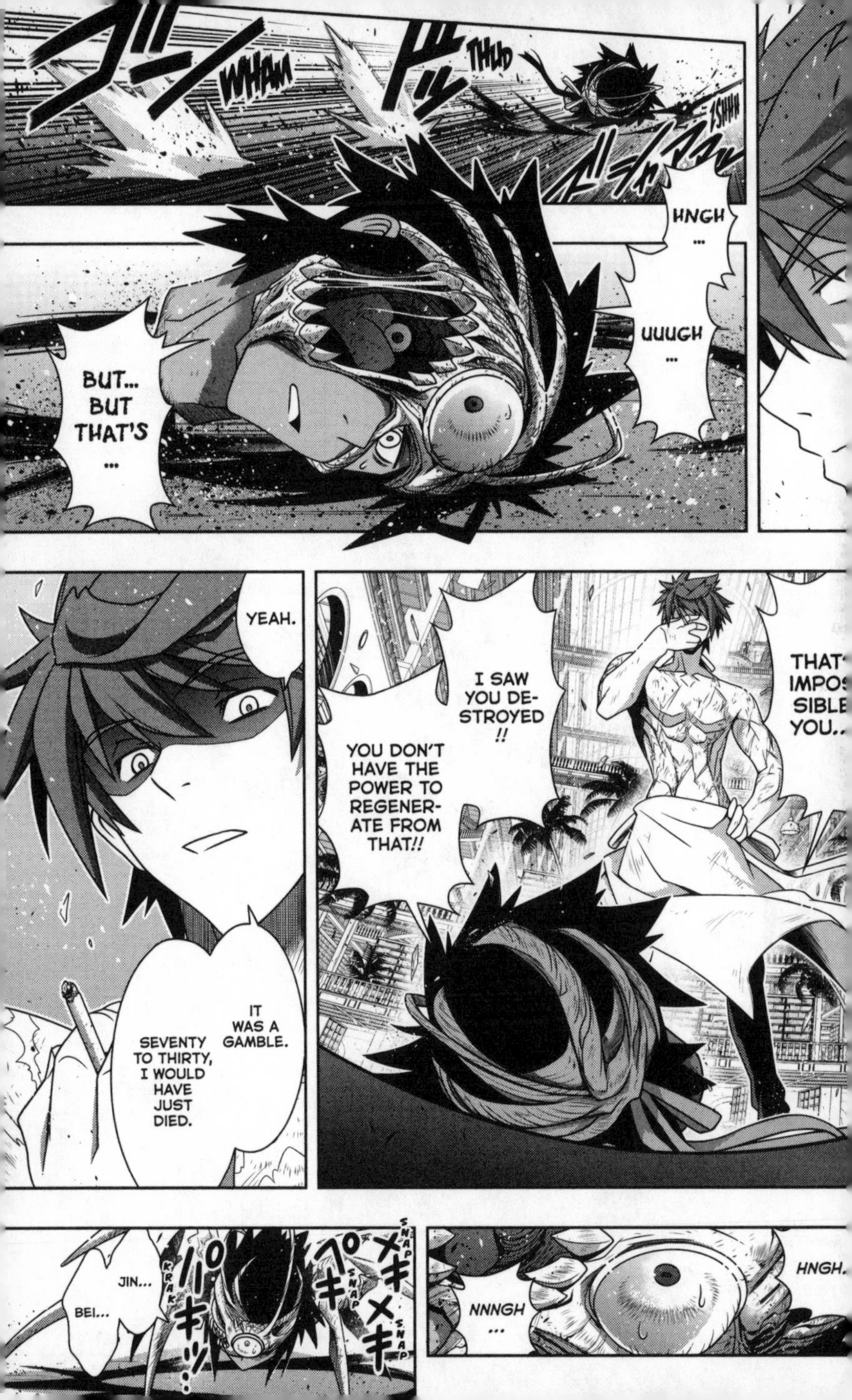
WHAM
THUD
SHHH
HNGH...
UUUGH...
BUT... BUT THAT'S...
THAT' IMPOS SIBLE YOU..
I SAW YOU DE-STROYED!!
YOU DON'T HAVE THE POWER TO REGENER-ATE FROM THAT!!
YEAH.
IT WAS A GAMBLE.
SEVENTY TO THIRTY, I WOULD HAVE JUST DIED.
HNGH.
NNNGH...
SNAP
SNAP
SNAP
KRAK
JIN...
BEI...

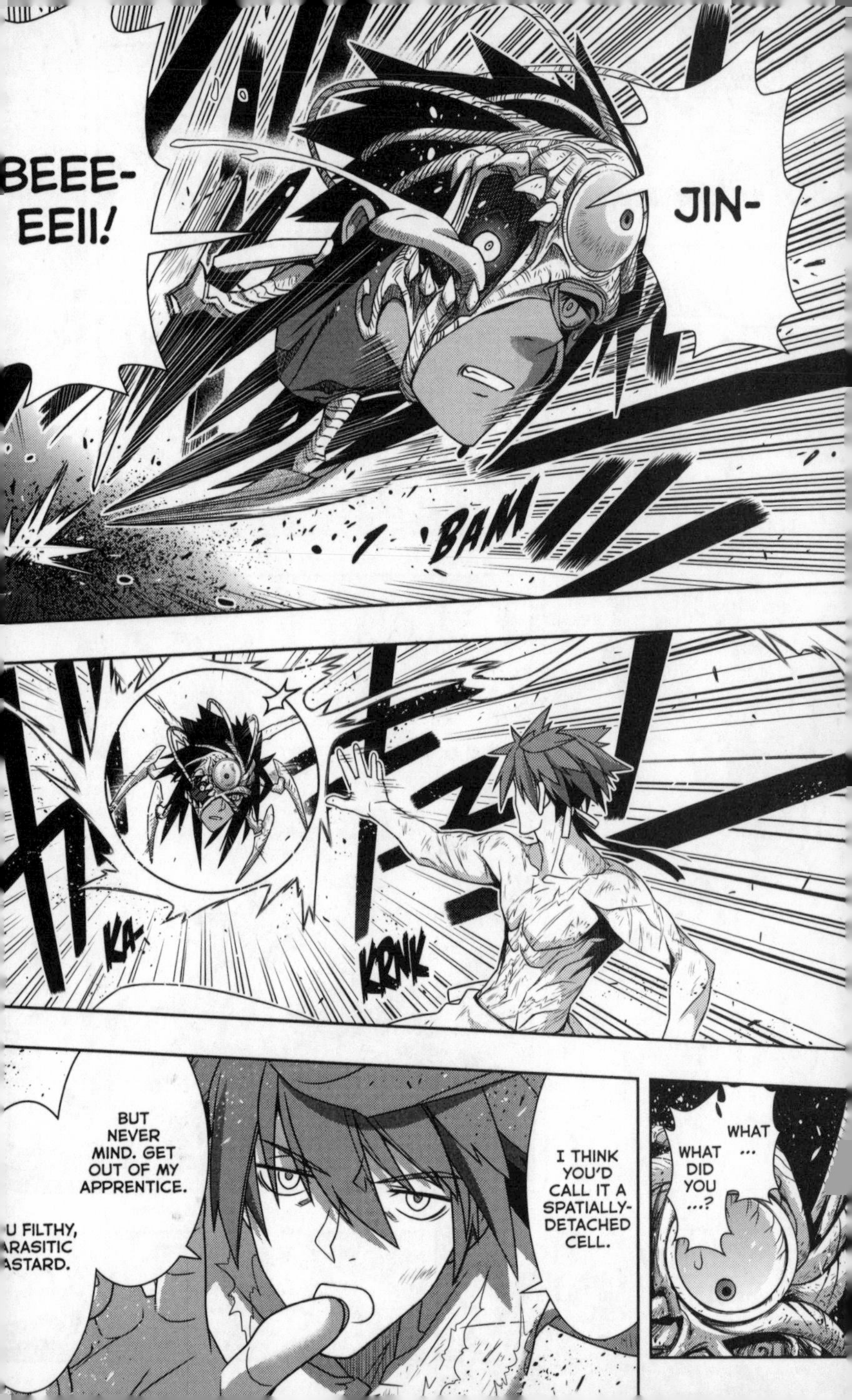
JIN-
BEEEE-EEII!
BAM
KA-
KRNK
WHAT ...
WHAT DID YOU ...?
I THINK YOU'D CALL IT A SPATIALLY-DETACHED CELL.
BUT NEVER MIND. GET OUT OF MY APPRENTICE.
U FILTHY, ARASITIC ASTARD.

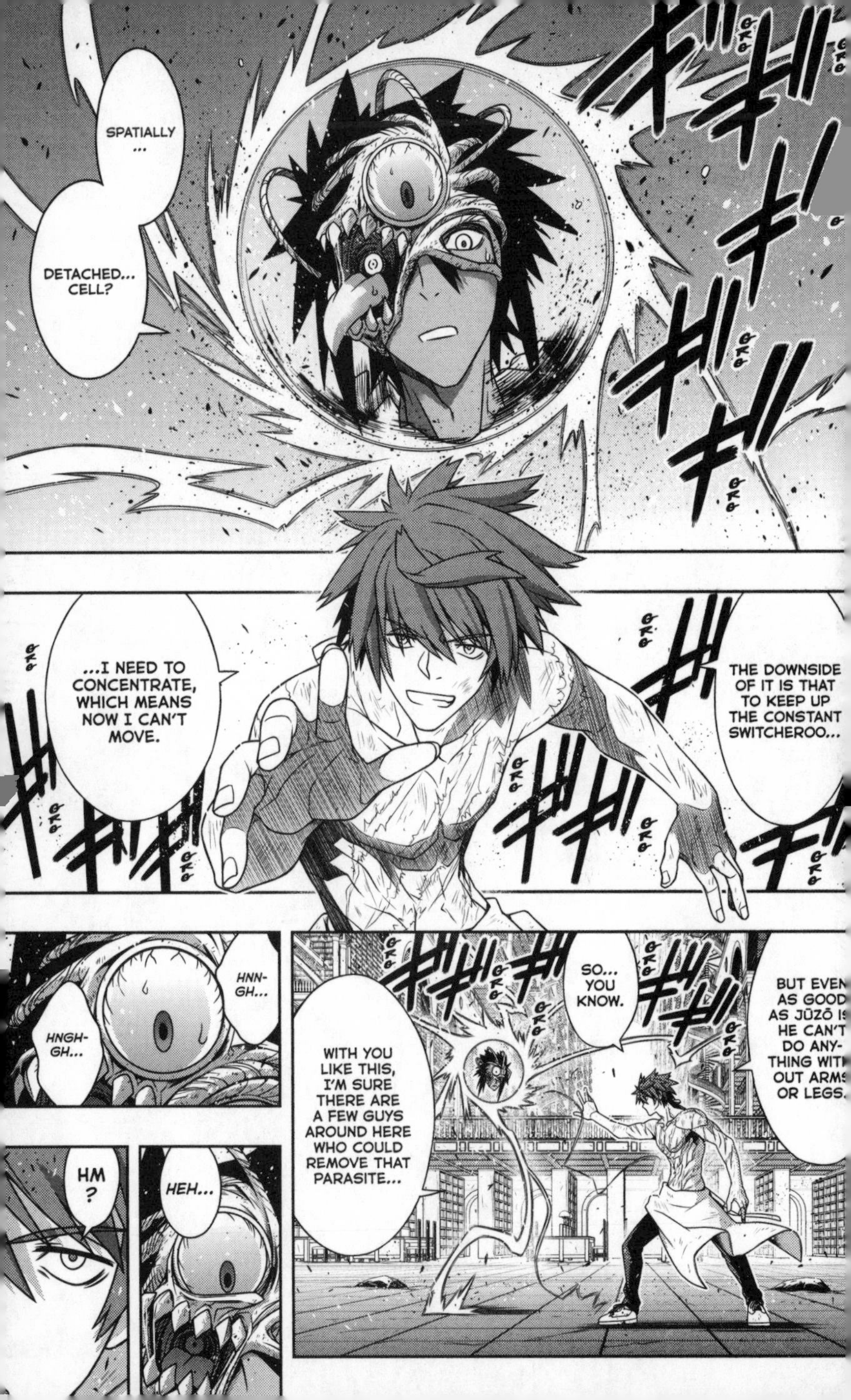
GRO
SPATIALLY...
DETACHED... CELL?
GRO
THE DOWNSIDE OF IT IS THAT TO KEEP UP THE CONSTANT SWITCHEROO...
...I NEED TO CONCENTRATE, WHICH MEANS NOW I CAN'T MOVE.
GRO
BUT EVEN AS GOOD AS JŪZŌ IS HE CAN'T DO ANY-THING WITHOUT ARMS OR LEGS.
SO... YOU KNOW.
WITH YOU LIKE THIS, I'M SURE THERE ARE A FEW GUYS AROUND HERE WHO COULD REMOVE THAT PARASITE...
HNN-GH...
HNGH-GH...
HEH...
HM?

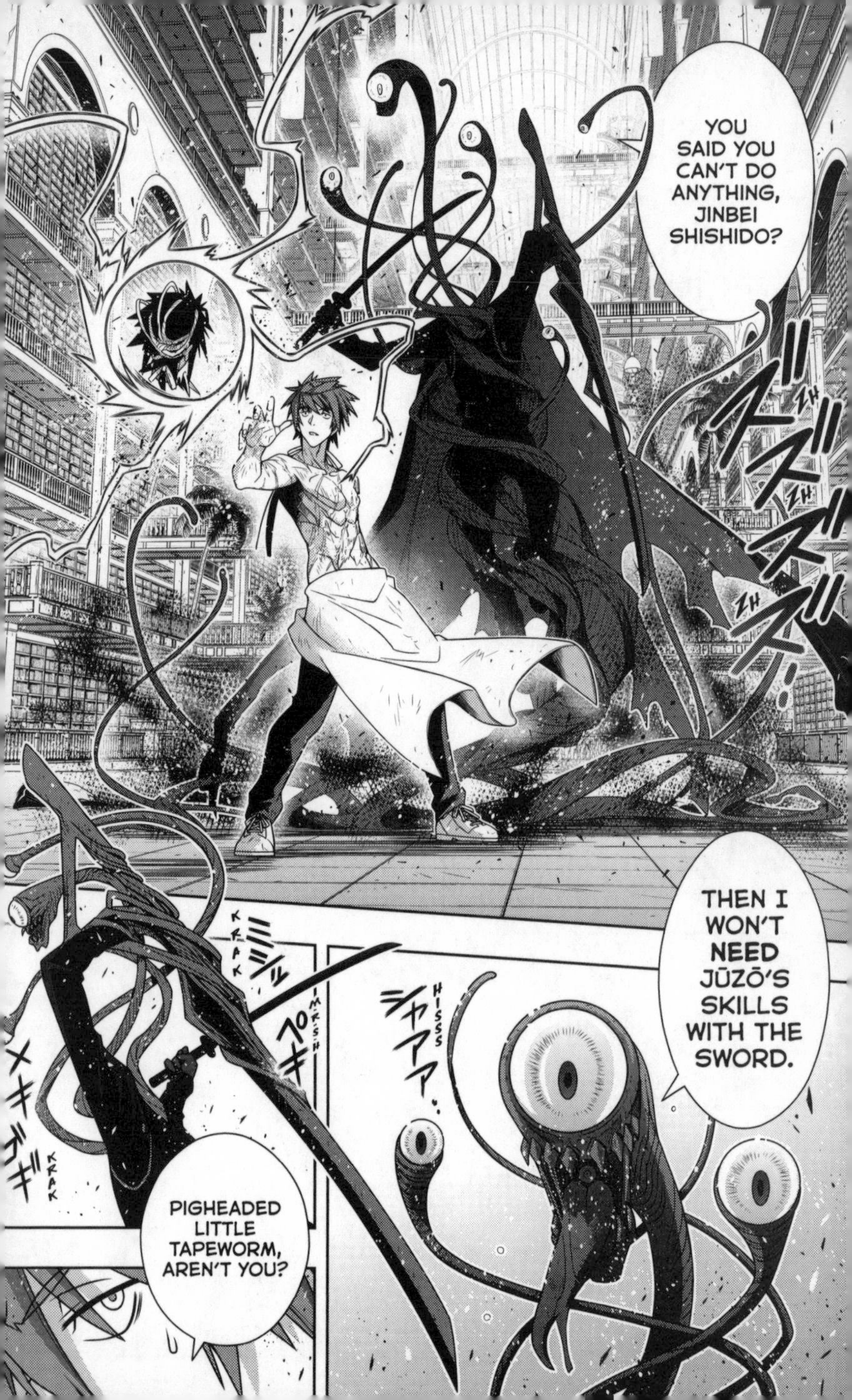
YOU SAID YOU CAN'T DO ANYTHING, JINBEI SHISHIDO?
ZH
ZH
ZH
THEN I WON'T NEED JŪZŌ'S SKILLS WITH THE SWORD.
HISSS
KRAK
MRSH
KRAK
PIGHEADED LITTLE TAPEWORM, AREN'T YOU?

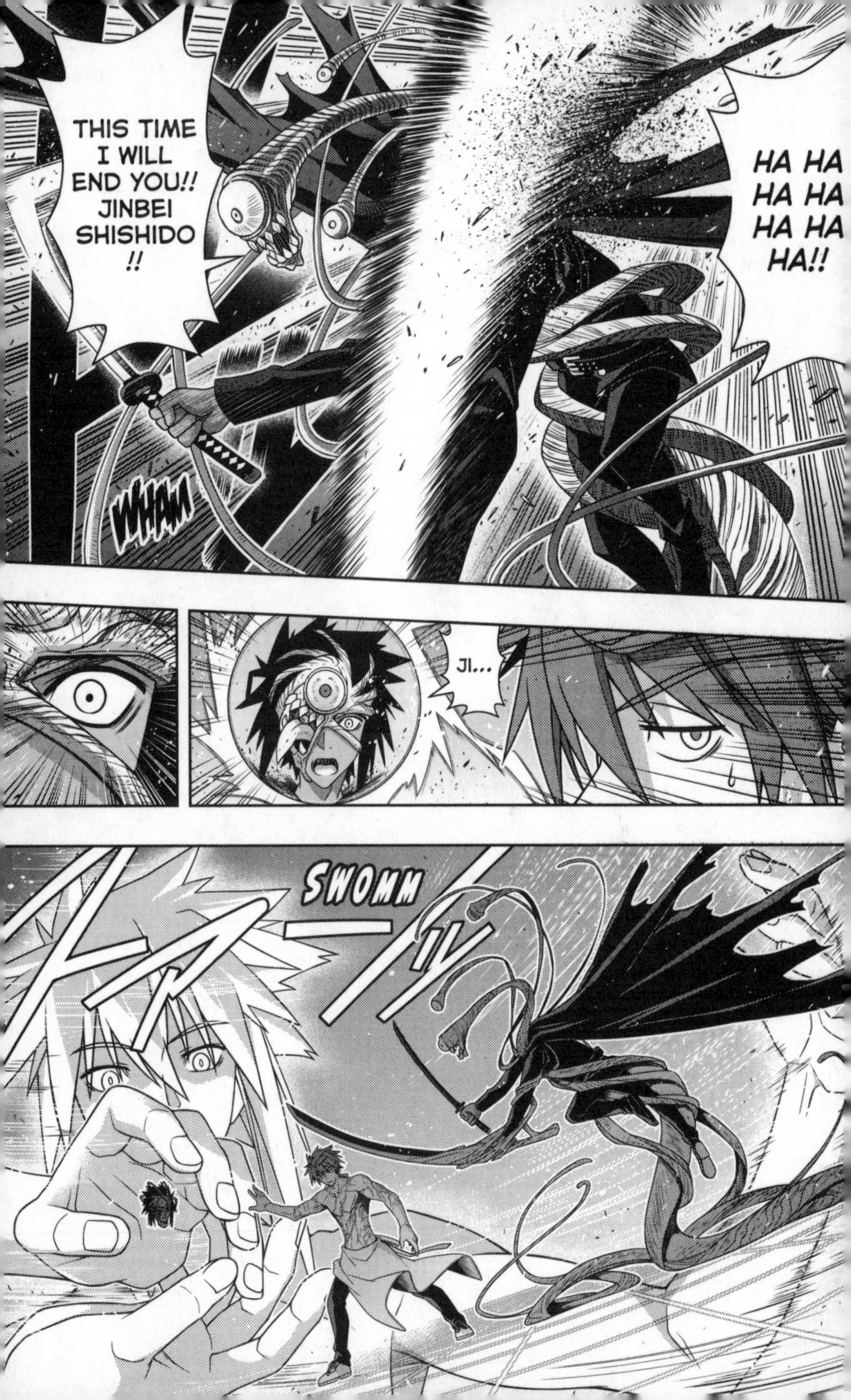
HA HA HA HA HA HA HA!!
THIS TIME I WILL END YOU!! JINBEI SHISHIDO !!
WHAM
JI...
SWOMM

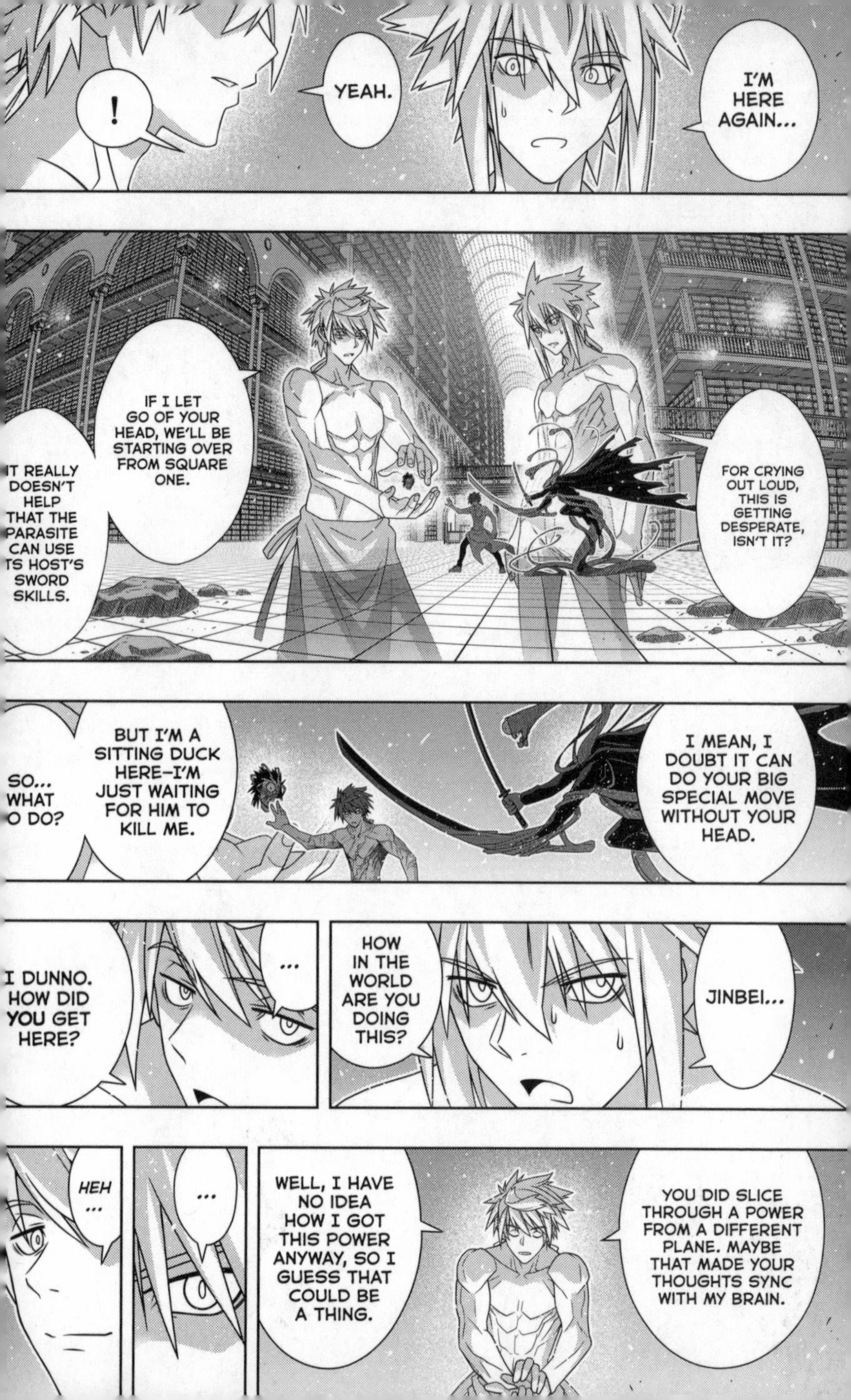
I'M HERE AGAIN...
YEAH.
!
FOR CRYING OUT LOUD, THIS IS GETTING DESPERATE, ISN'T IT?
IF I LET GO OF YOUR HEAD, WE'LL BE STARTING OVER FROM SQUARE ONE.
IT REALLY DOESN'T HELP THAT THE PARASITE CAN USE TS HOST'S SWORD SKILLS.
I MEAN, I DOUBT IT CAN DO YOUR BIG SPECIAL MOVE WITHOUT YOUR HEAD.
BUT I'M A SITTING DUCK HERE—I'M JUST WAITING FOR HIM TO KILL ME.
SO... WHAT O DO?
JINBEI...
HOW IN THE WORLD ARE YOU DOING THIS?
...
I DUNNO. HOW DID YOU GET HERE?
YOU DID SLICE THROUGH A POWER FROM A DIFFERENT PLANE. MAYBE THAT MADE YOUR THOUGHTS SYNC WITH MY BRAIN.
WELL, I HAVE NO IDEA HOW I GOT THIS POWER ANYWAY, SO I GUESS THAT COULD BE A THING.
...
HEH ...

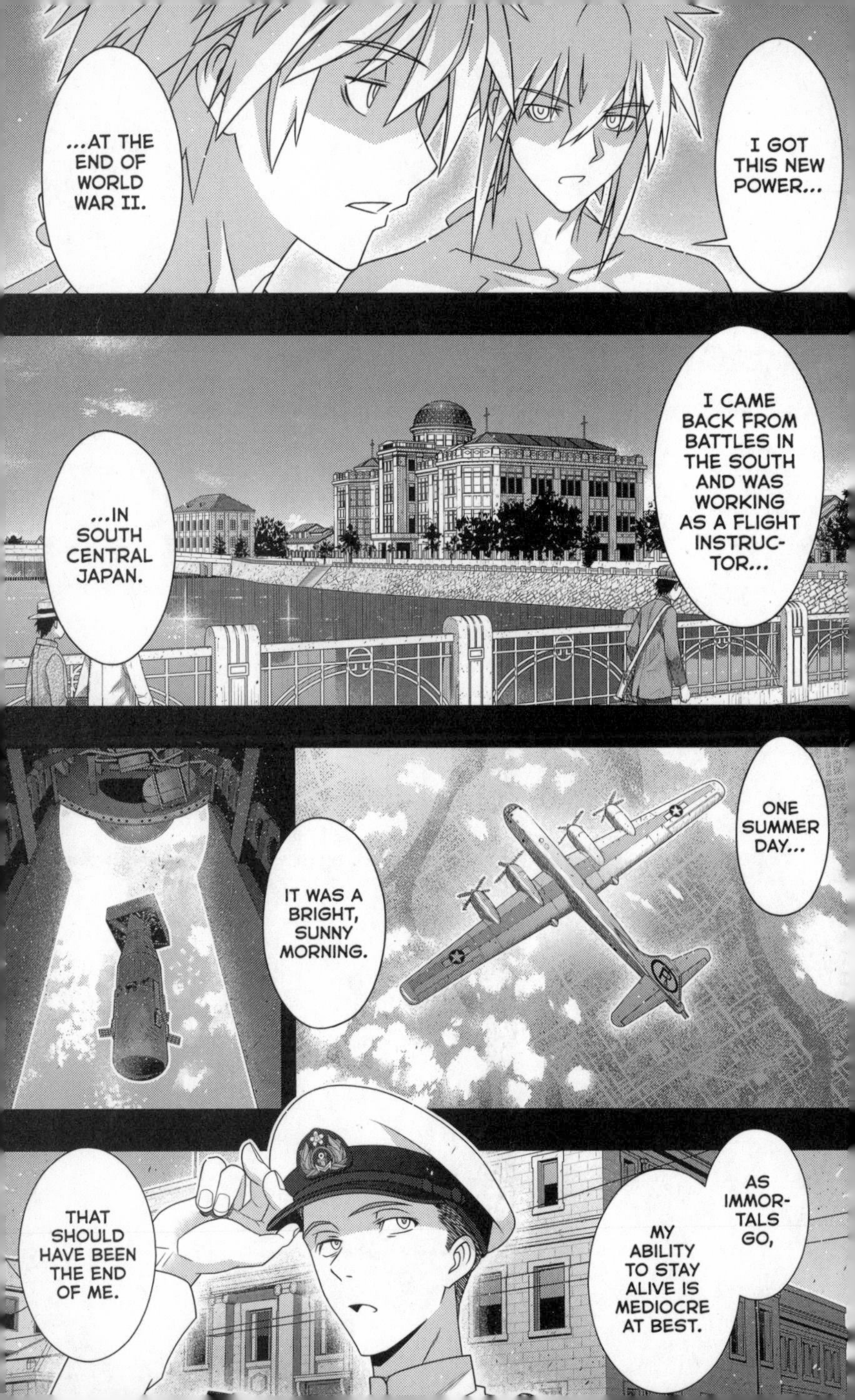
I GOT THIS NEW POWER...
...AT THE END OF WORLD WAR II.
I CAME BACK FROM BATTLES IN THE SOUTH AND WAS WORKING AS A FLIGHT INSTRUCTOR...
...IN SOUTH CENTRAL JAPAN.
ONE SUMMER DAY...
IT WAS A BRIGHT, SUNNY MORNING.
AS IMMORTALS GO,
MY ABILITY TO STAY ALIVE IS MEDIOCRE AT BEST.
THAT SHOULD HAVE BEEN THE END OF ME.

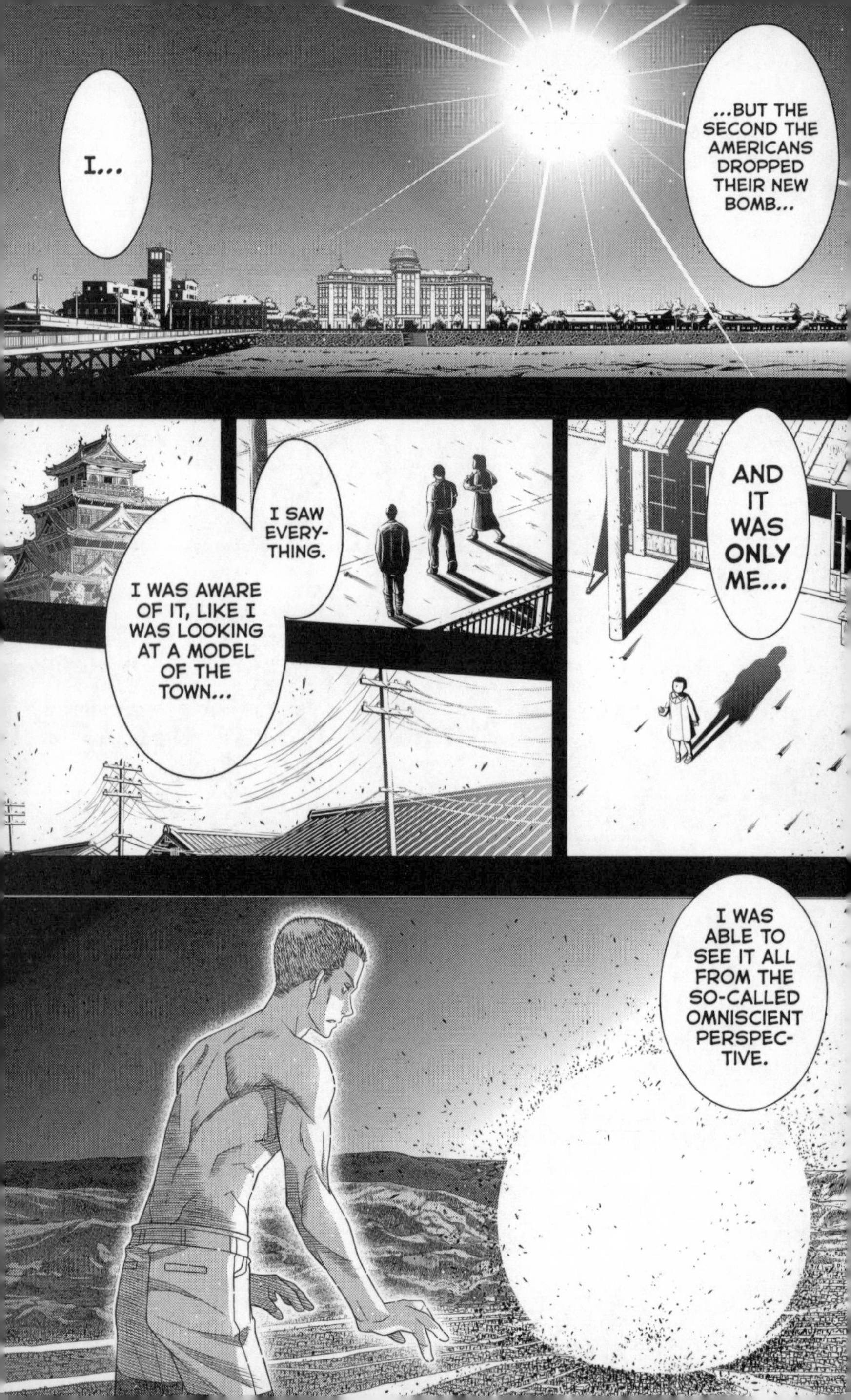
...BUT THE SECOND THE AMERICANS DROPPED THEIR NEW BOMB...
I...
AND IT WAS ONLY ME...
I SAW EVERY-THING.
I WAS AWARE OF IT, LIKE I WAS LOOKING AT A MODEL OF THE TOWN...
I WAS ABLE TO SEE IT ALL FROM THE SO-CALLED OMNISCIENT PERSPEC-TIVE.

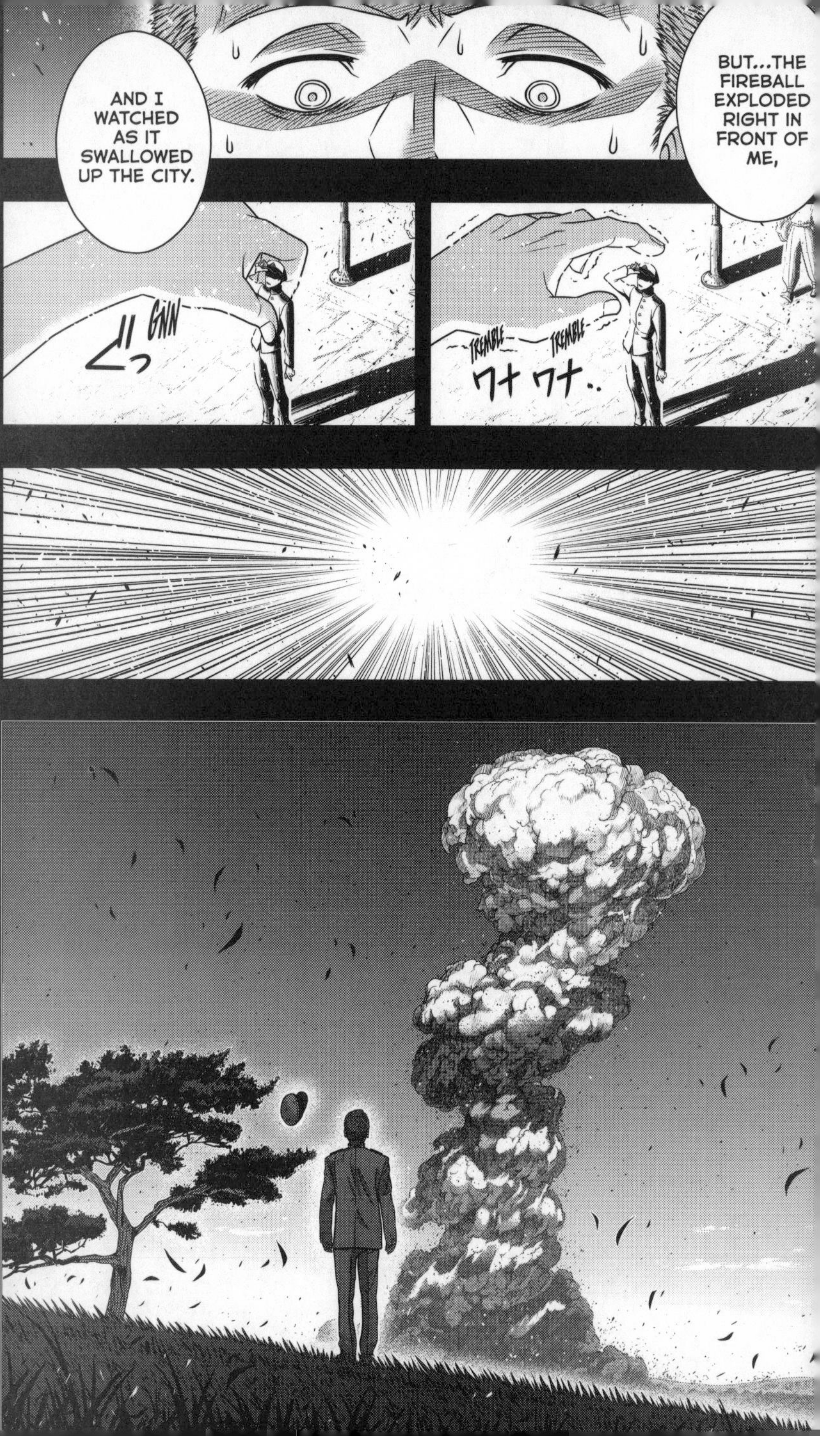
BUT...THE FIREBALL EXPLODED RIGHT IN FRONT OF ME,
AND I WATCHED AS IT SWALLOWED UP THE CITY.
TREMBLE TREMBLE
ワナ ワナ..
GNN
ぐっ

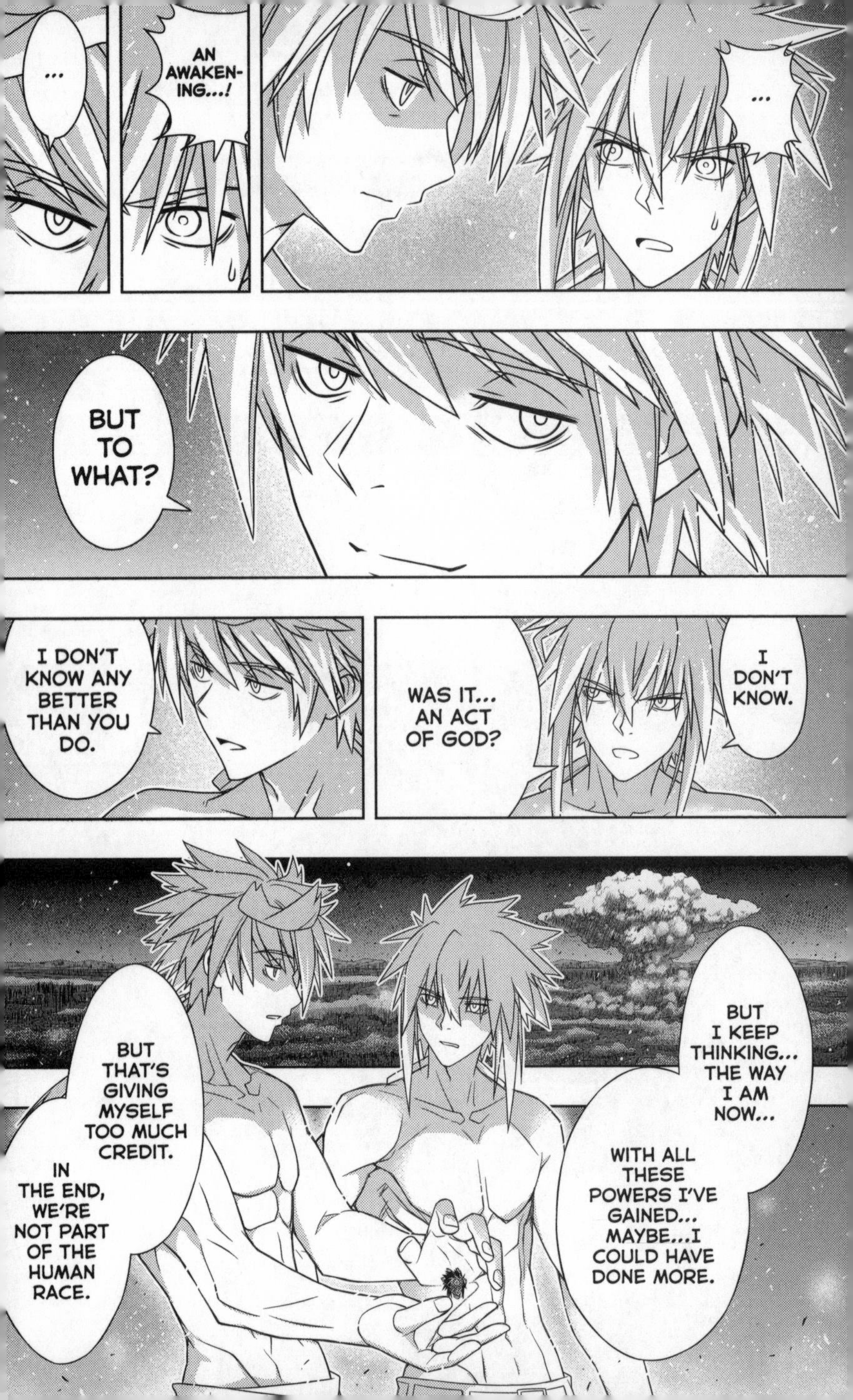
...
AN AWAKEN-ING...!
...
BUT TO WHAT?
I DON'T KNOW.
WAS IT... AN ACT OF GOD?
I DON'T KNOW ANY BETTER THAN YOU DO.
BUT I KEEP THINKING... THE WAY I AM NOW...
WITH ALL THESE POWERS I'VE GAINED... MAYBE...I COULD HAVE DONE MORE.
BUT THAT'S GIVING MYSELF TOO MUCH CREDIT.
IN THE END, WE'RE NOT PART OF THE HUMAN RACE.

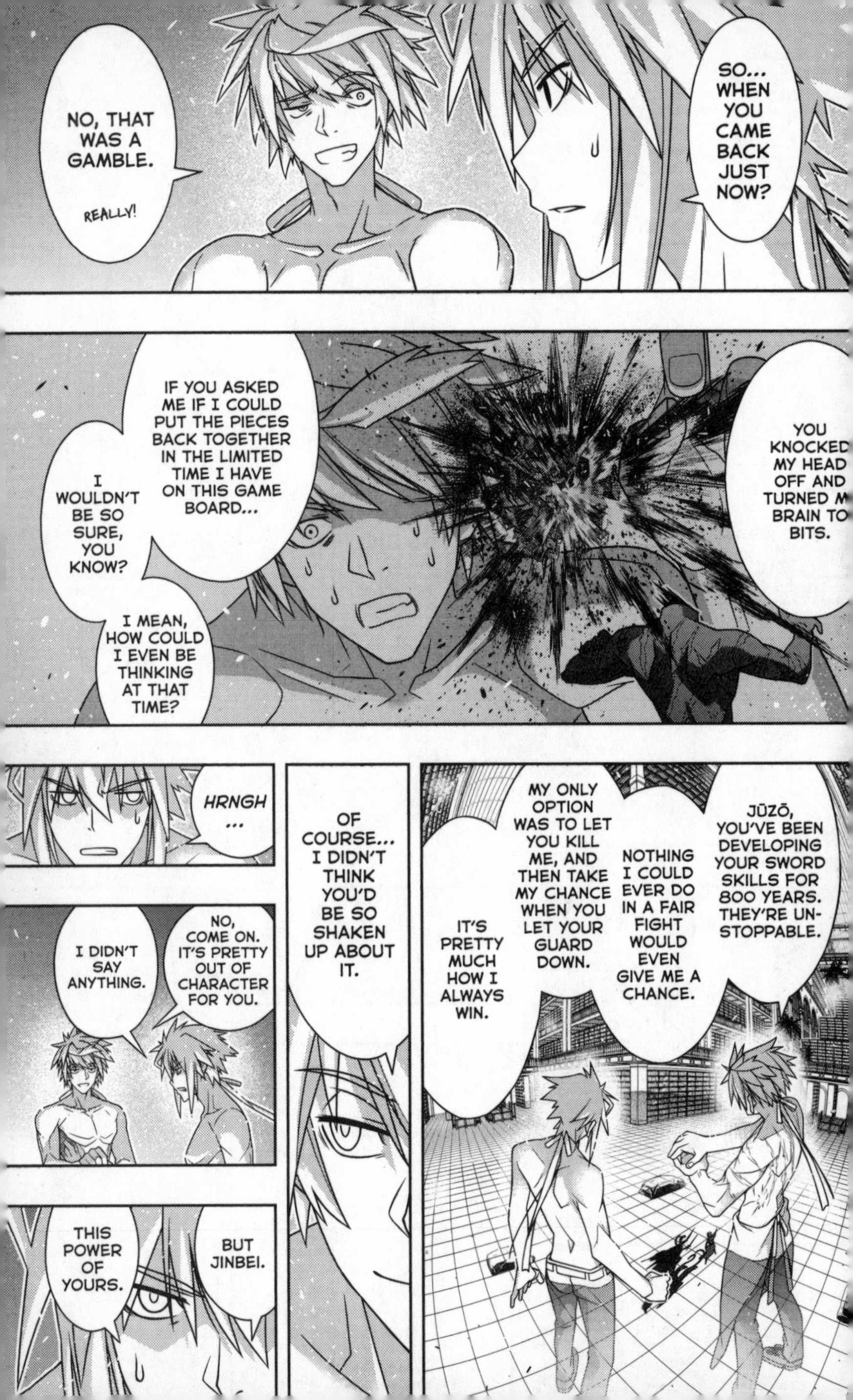
SO... WHEN YOU CAME BACK JUST NOW?
NO, THAT WAS A GAMBLE.
REALLY!
YOU KNOCKED MY HEAD OFF AND TURNED M BRAIN TO BITS.
IF YOU ASKED ME IF I COULD PUT THE PIECES BACK TOGETHER IN THE LIMITED TIME I HAVE ON THIS GAME BOARD...
I WOULDN'T BE SO SURE, YOU KNOW?
I MEAN, HOW COULD I EVEN BE THINKING AT THAT TIME?
JŪZŌ, YOU'VE BEEN DEVELOPING YOUR SWORD SKILLS FOR 800 YEARS. THEY'RE UN-STOPPABLE.
NOTHING I COULD EVER DO IN A FAIR FIGHT WOULD EVEN GIVE ME A CHANCE.
MY ONLY OPTION WAS TO LET YOU KILL ME, AND THEN TAKE MY CHANCE WHEN YOU LET YOUR GUARD DOWN.
IT'S PRETTY MUCH HOW I ALWAYS WIN.
OF COURSE... I DIDN'T THINK YOU'D BE SO SHAKEN UP ABOUT IT.
HRNGH ...
NO, COME ON. IT'S PRETTY OUT OF CHARACTER FOR YOU.
I DIDN'T SAY ANYTHING.
BUT JINBEI.
THIS POWER OF YOURS.

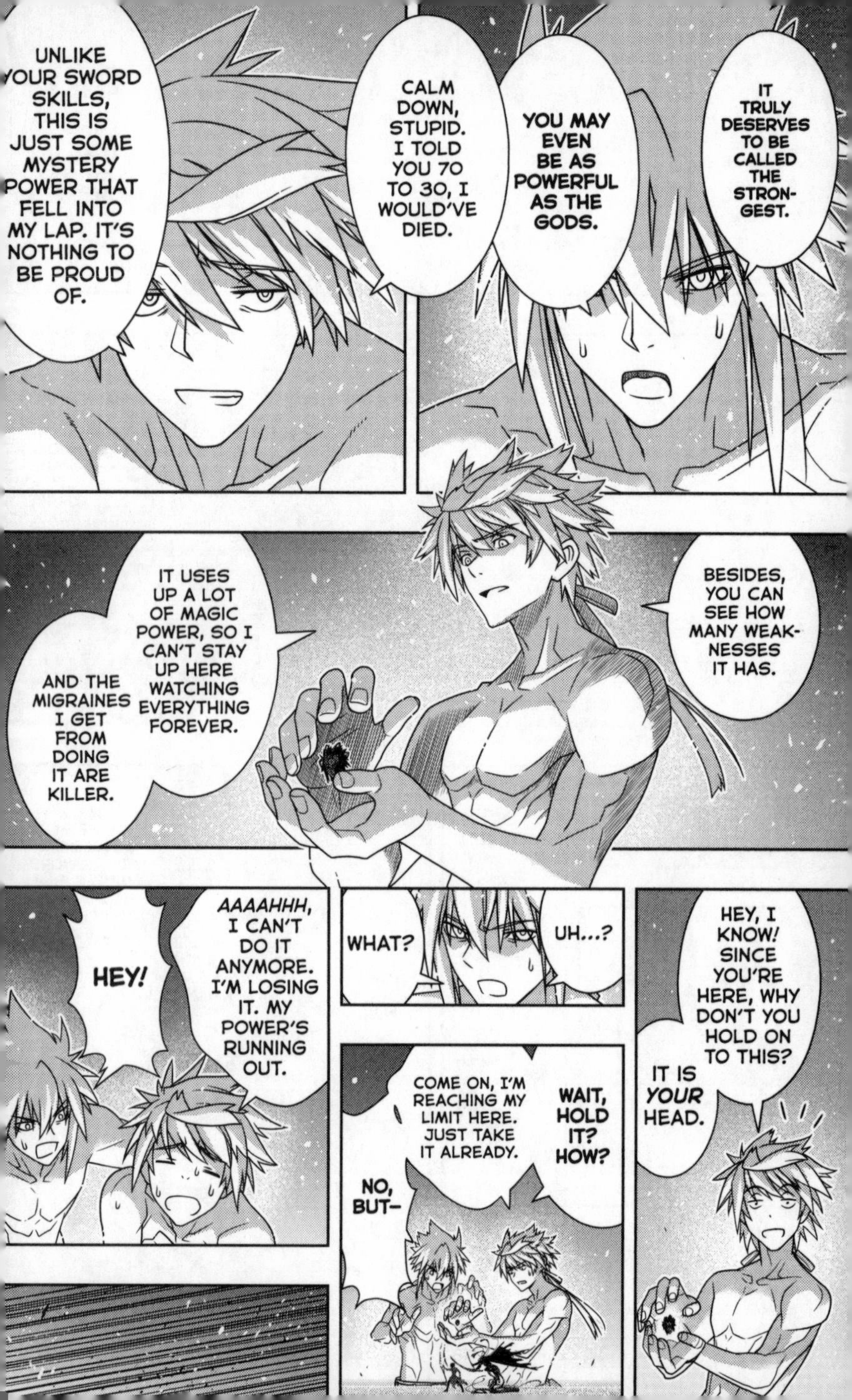
IT TRULY DESERVES TO BE CALLED THE STRONGEST.
YOU MAY EVEN BE AS POWERFUL AS THE GODS.
CALM DOWN, STUPID. I TOLD YOU 70 TO 30, I WOULD'VE DIED.
UNLIKE YOUR SWORD SKILLS, THIS IS JUST SOME MYSTERY POWER THAT FELL INTO MY LAP. IT'S NOTHING TO BE PROUD OF.
BESIDES, YOU CAN SEE HOW MANY WEAKNESSES IT HAS.
IT USES UP A LOT OF MAGIC POWER, SO I CAN'T STAY UP HERE WATCHING EVERYTHING FOREVER.
AND THE MIGRAINES I GET FROM DOING IT ARE KILLER.
HEY, I KNOW! SINCE YOU'RE HERE, WHY DON'T YOU HOLD ON TO THIS?
IT IS *YOUR* HEAD.
UH...?
WHAT?
WAIT, HOLD IT? HOW?
COME ON, I'M REACHING MY LIMIT HERE. JUST TAKE IT ALREADY.
NO, BUT–
AAAAHHH, I CAN'T DO IT ANYMORE. I'M LOSING IT. MY POWER'S RUNNING OUT.
HEY!

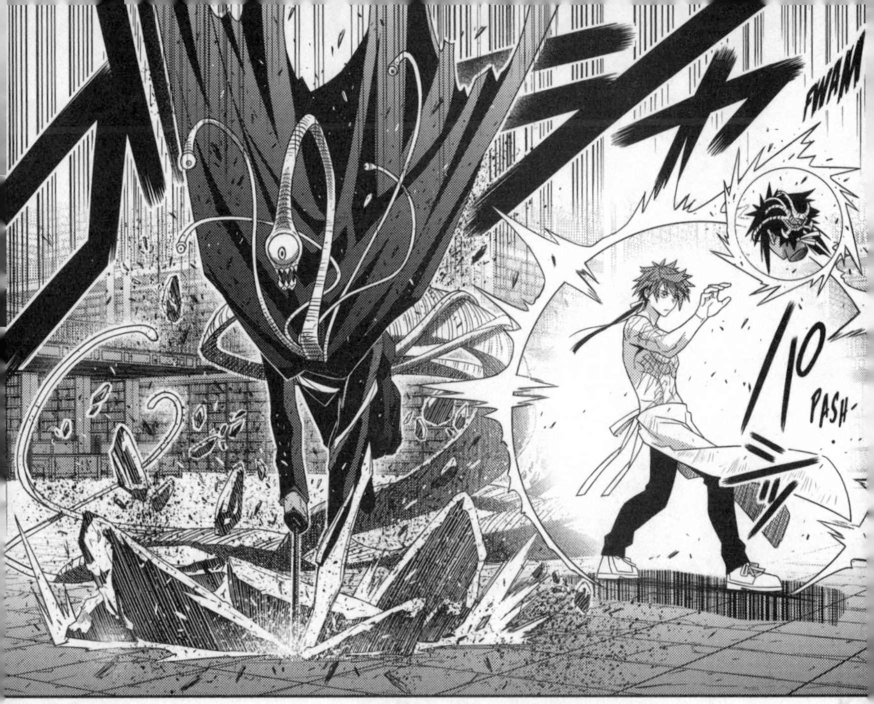
FWAM
PASH-
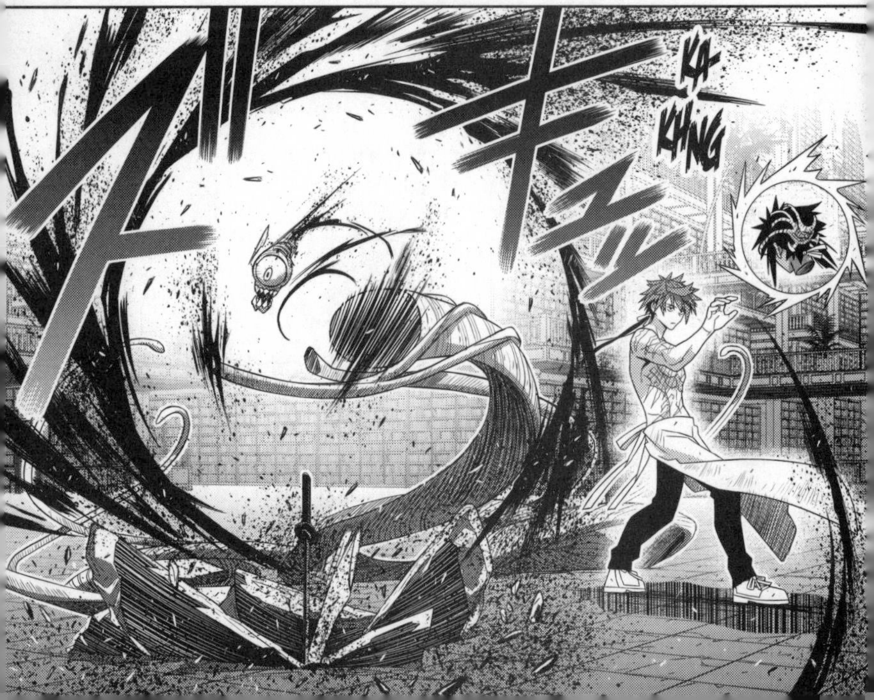
KA-KHING

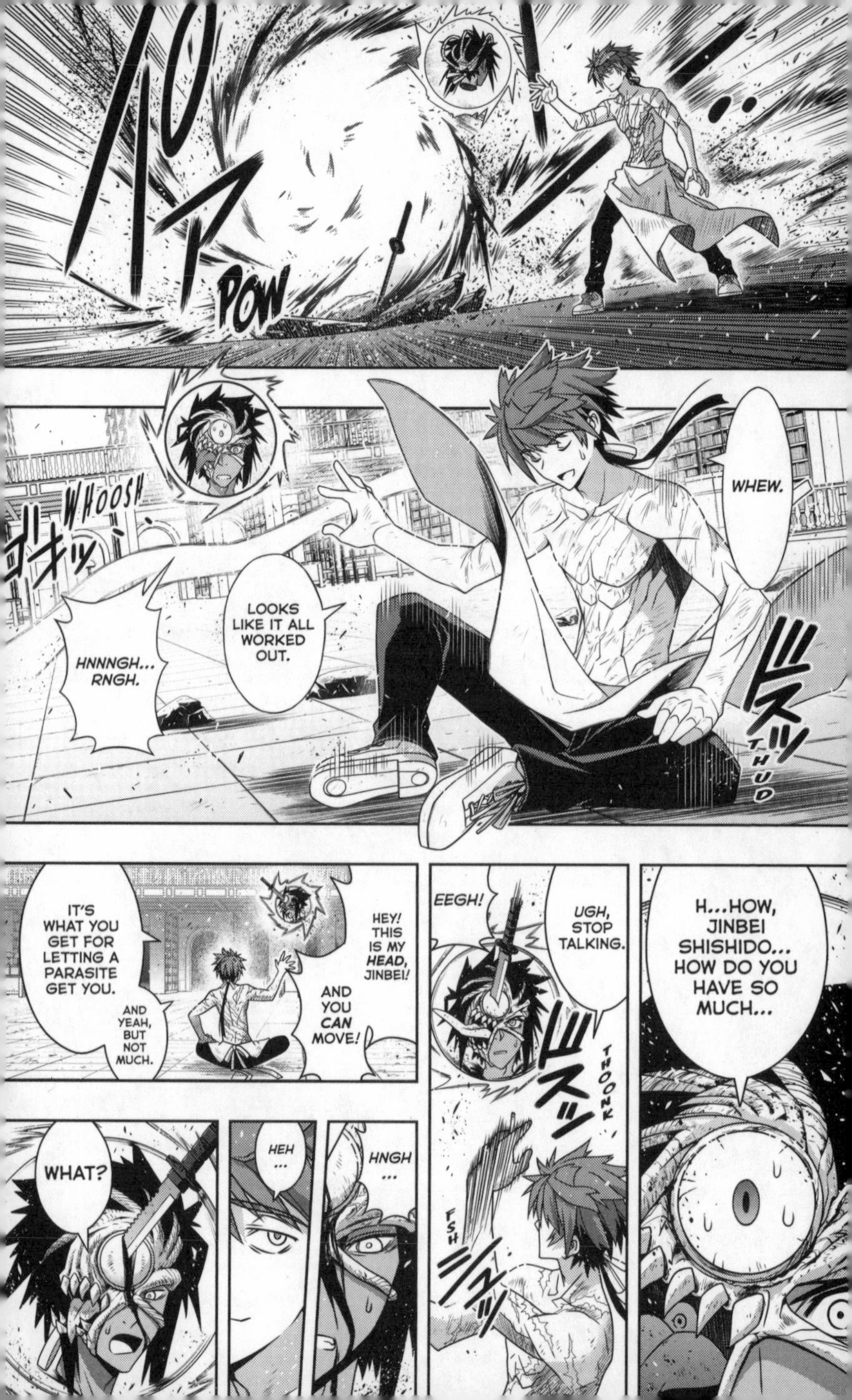
POW
WHEW.
THUD
LOOKS LIKE IT ALL WORKED OUT.
HNNNGH... RNGH.
WHOOSH
H...HOW, JINBEI SHISHIDO... HOW DO YOU HAVE SO MUCH...
UGH, STOP TALKING.
EEGH!
THOONK
FSH
HEY! THIS IS MY HEAD, JINBEI!
AND YOU CAN MOVE!
IT'S WHAT YOU GET FOR LETTING A PARASITE GET YOU.
AND YEAH, BUT NOT MUCH.
HNGH...
HEH...
WHAT?

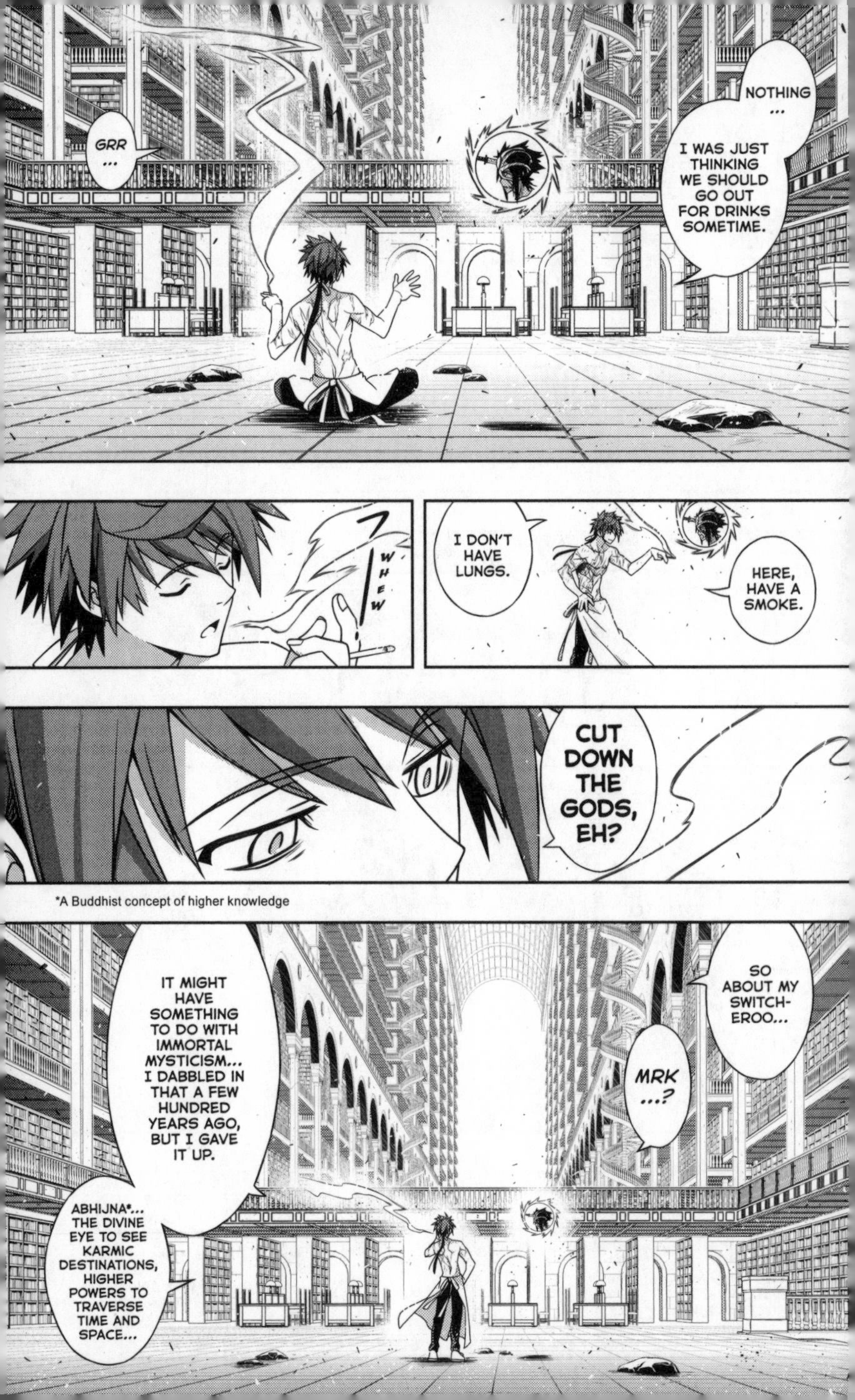
NOTHING ... I WAS JUST THINKING WE SHOULD GO OUT FOR DRINKS SOMETIME.
GRR ...
HERE, HAVE A SMOKE.
I DON'T HAVE LUNGS.
WHEW
CUT DOWN THE GODS, EH?
SO ABOUT MY SWITCH-EROO...
MRK ...?
IT MIGHT HAVE SOMETHING TO DO WITH IMMORTAL MYSTICISM... I DABBLED IN THAT A FEW HUNDRED YEARS AGO, BUT I GAVE IT UP.
ABHIJNA*... THE DIVINE EYE TO SEE KARMIC DESTINATIONS, HIGHER POWERS TO TRAVERSE TIME AND SPACE...

*A Buddhist concept of higher knowledge

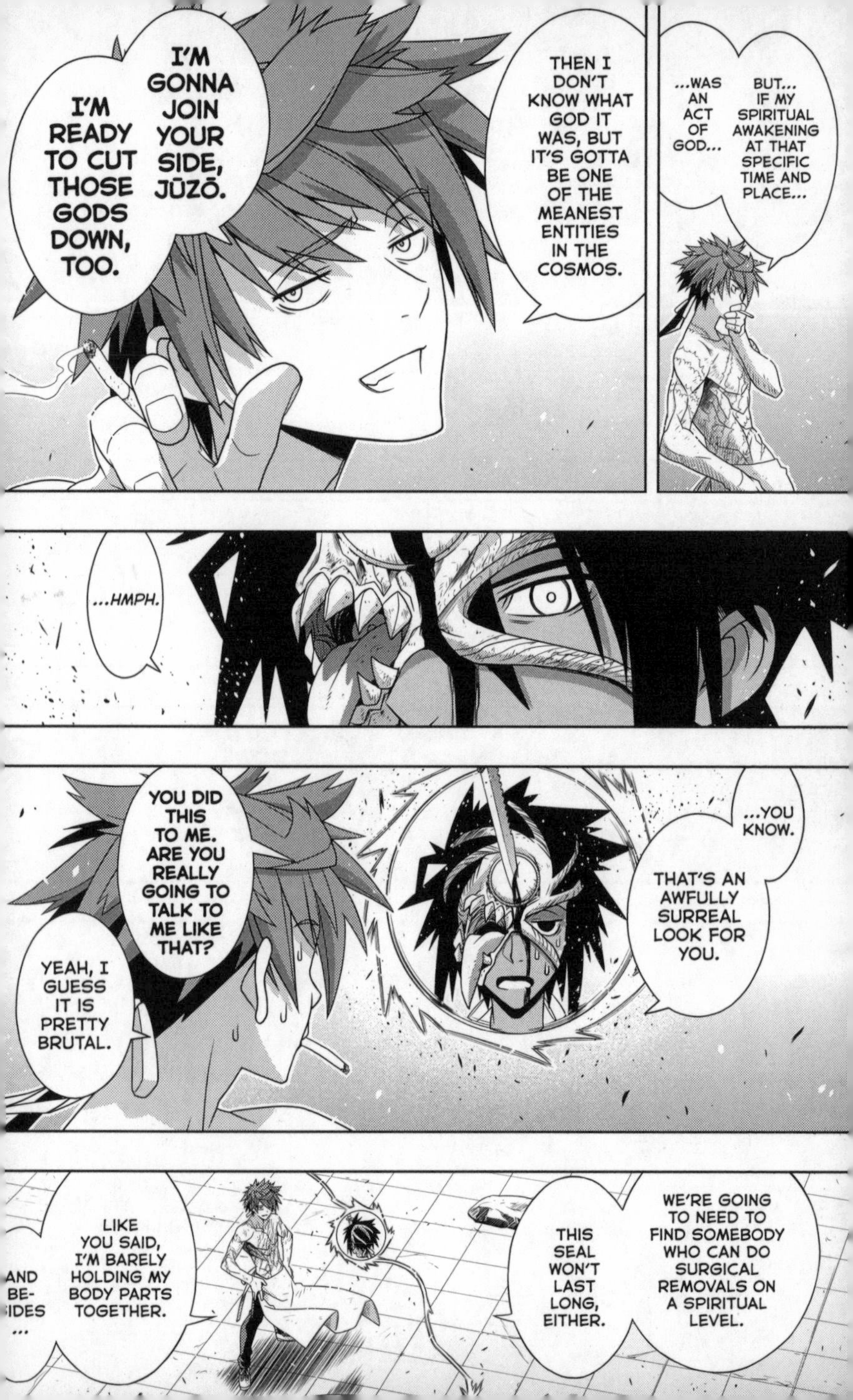
BUT... IF MY SPIRITUAL AWAKENING AT THAT SPECIFIC TIME AND PLACE...
...WAS AN ACT OF GOD...
THEN I DON'T KNOW WHAT GOD IT WAS, BUT IT'S GOTTA BE ONE OF THE MEANEST ENTITIES IN THE COSMOS.
I'M GONNA JOIN YOUR SIDE, JŪZŌ.
I'M READY TO CUT THOSE GODS DOWN, TOO.
...HMPH.
...YOU KNOW.
THAT'S AN AWFULLY SURREAL LOOK FOR YOU.
YOU DID THIS TO ME. ARE YOU REALLY GOING TO TALK TO ME LIKE THAT?
YEAH, I GUESS IT IS PRETTY BRUTAL.
WE'RE GOING TO NEED TO FIND SOMEBODY WHO CAN DO SURGICAL REMOVALS ON A SPIRITUAL LEVEL.
THIS SEAL WON'T LAST LONG, EITHER.
LIKE YOU SAID, I'M BARELY HOLDING MY BODY PARTS TOGETHER.
AND BE- SIDES ...

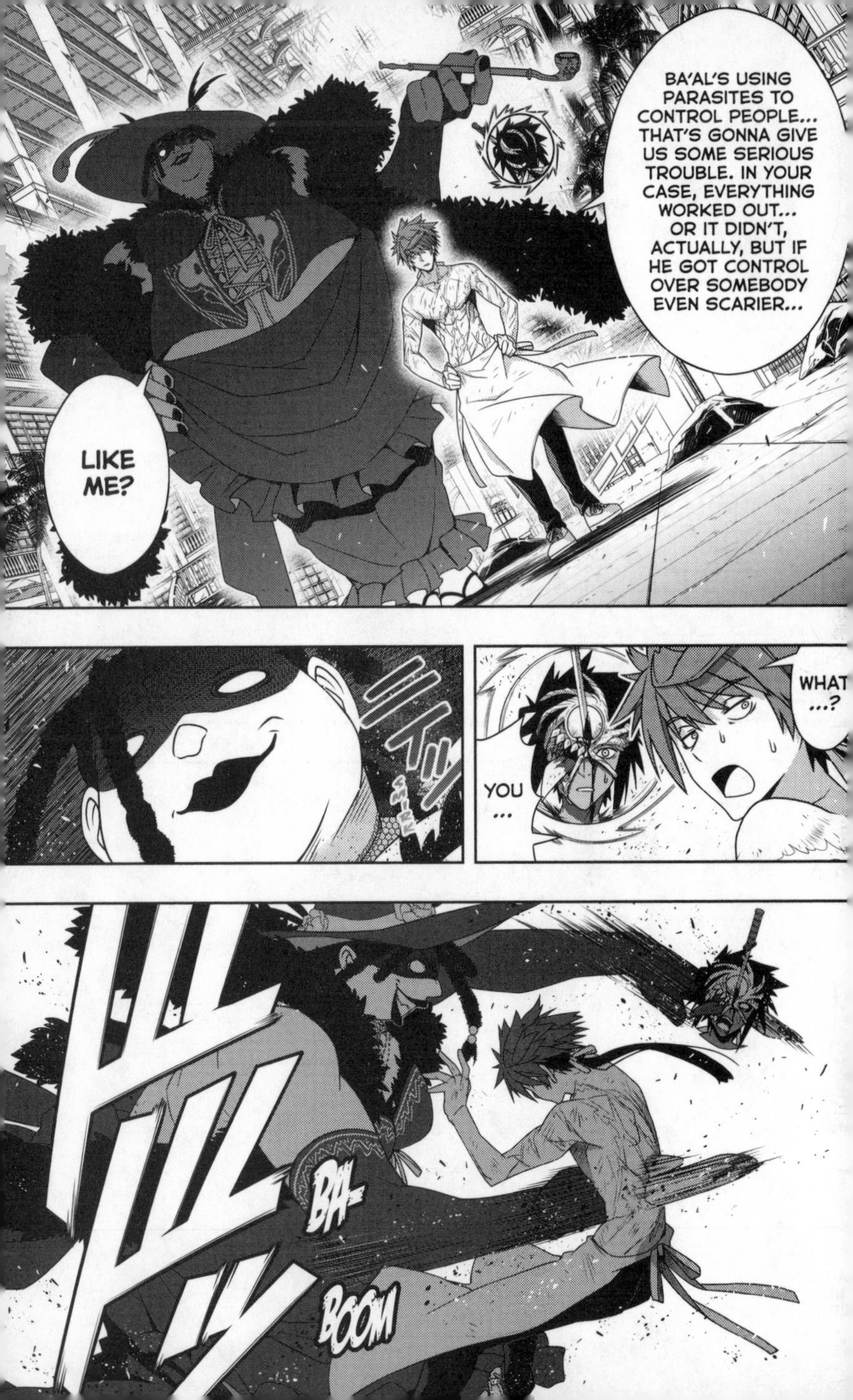
BA'AL'S USING PARASITES TO CONTROL PEOPLE... THAT'S GONNA GIVE US SOME SERIOUS TROUBLE. IN YOUR CASE, EVERYTHING WORKED OUT... OR IT DIDN'T, ACTUALLY, BUT IF HE GOT CONTROL OVER SOMEBODY EVEN SCARIER...
LIKE ME?
WHAT ...?
YOU ...
SMIRK
BA-
BOOM

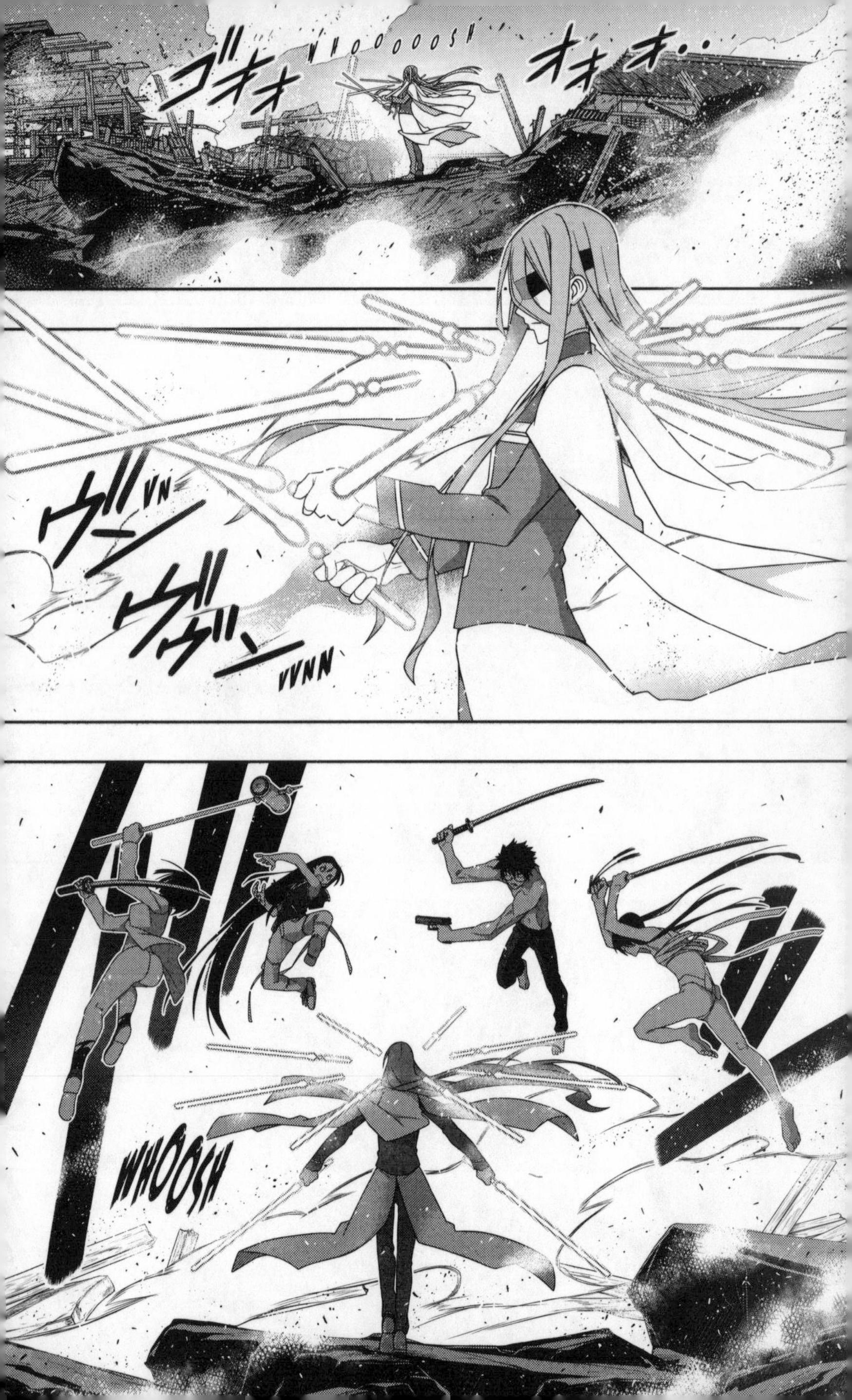

ゴオォ
WHOOOOOOSH
オォォ‥
ウーン
VN
ヴゥン
VVNN
WHOOSH

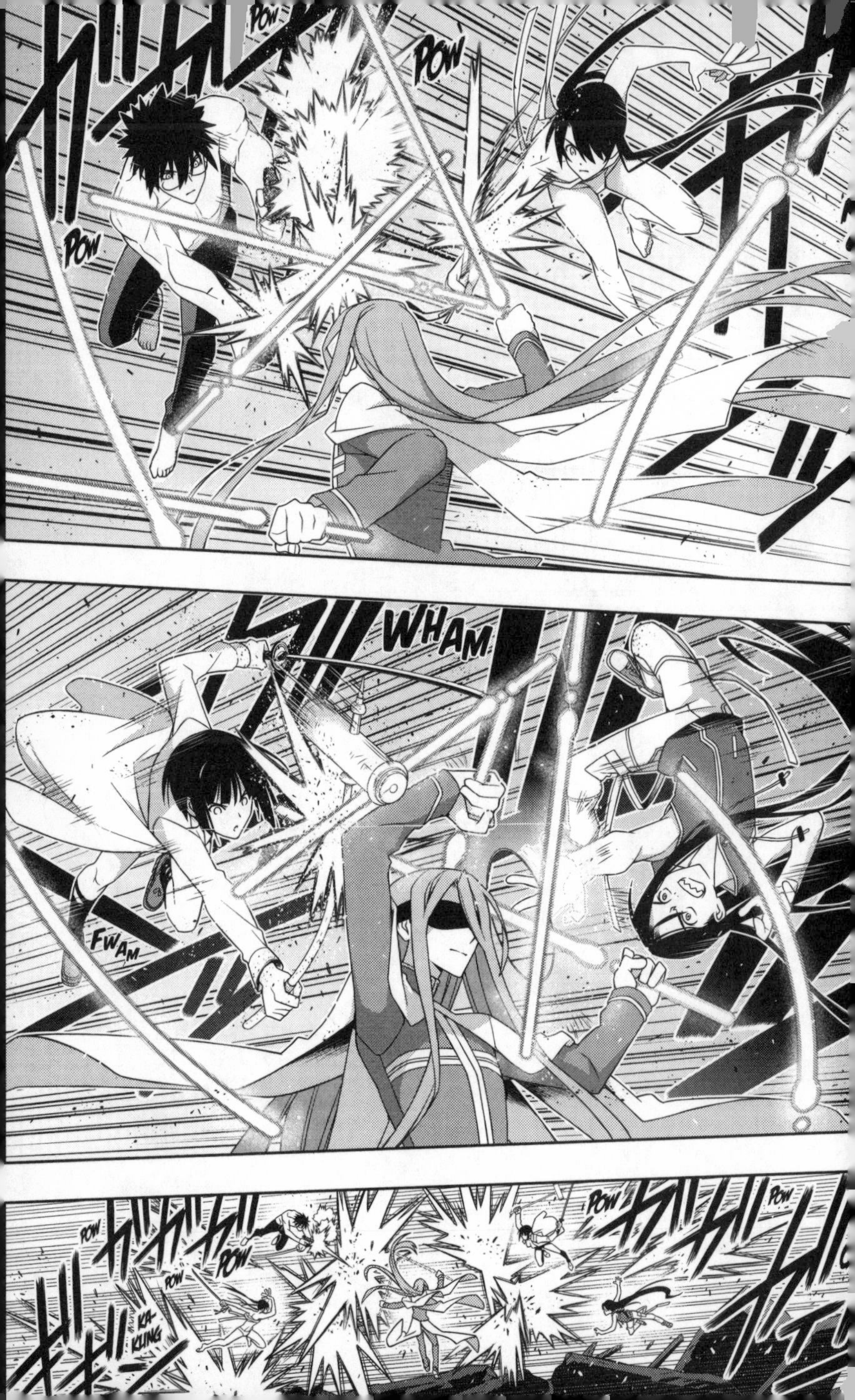
POW
POW
POW
WHAM
FWAM
POW
POW
POW
POW
POW
KA-KLING

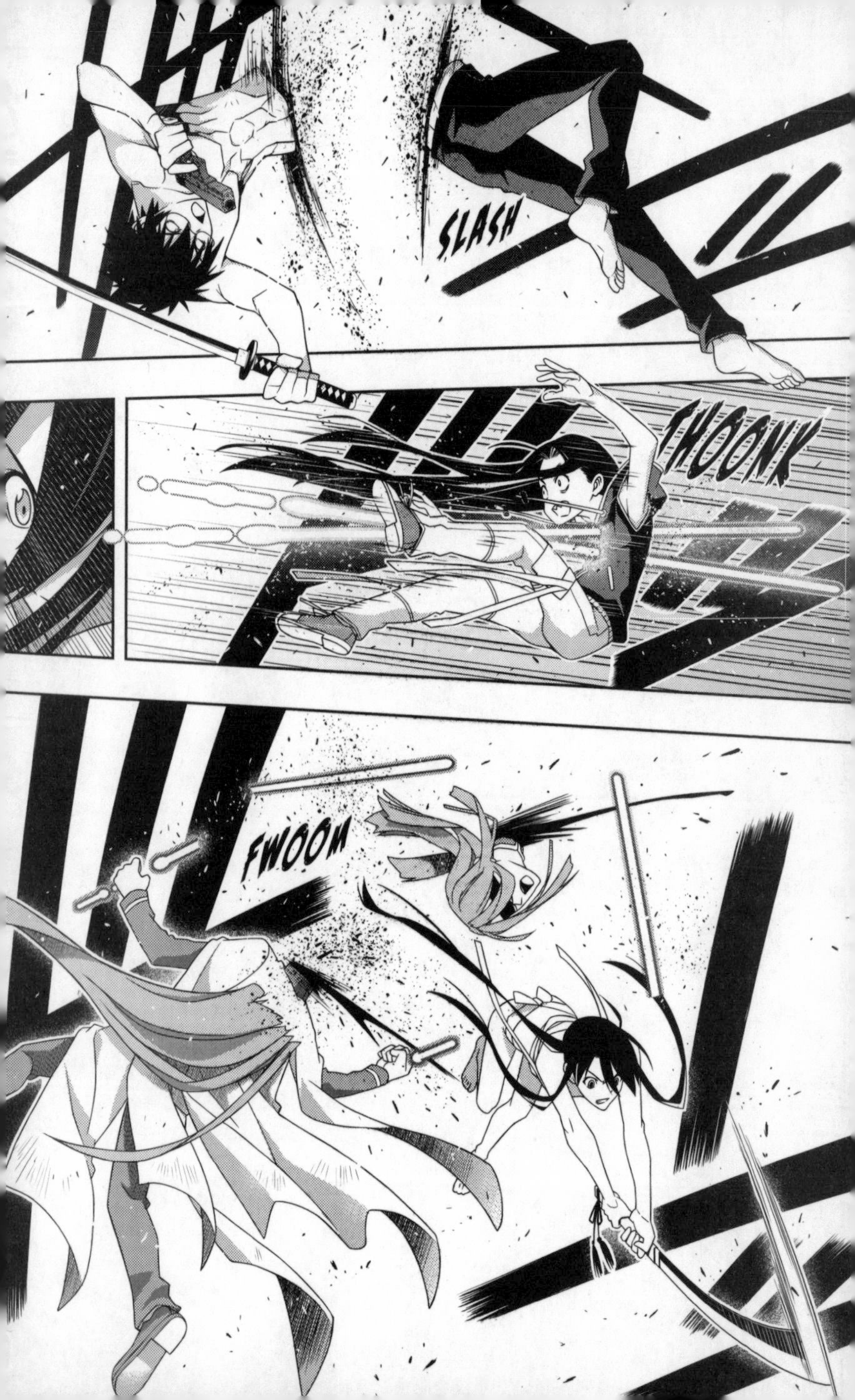
SLASH
THOONK
FWOOM

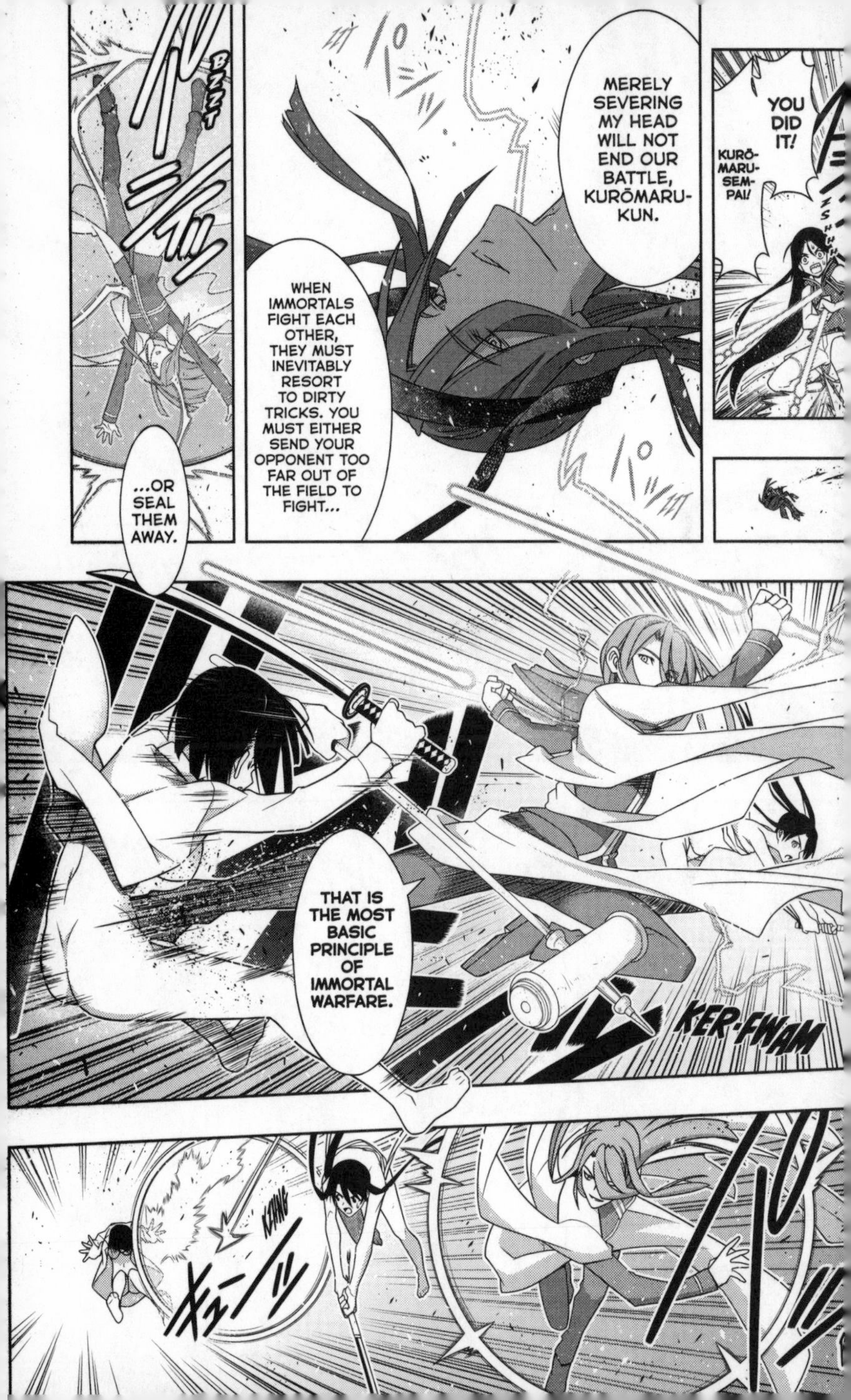
YOU DID IT!
KURŌ-MARU-SEM-PAI!
ZSHHH
MERELY SEVERING MY HEAD WILL NOT END OUR BATTLE, KURŌMARU-KUN.
WHEN IMMORTALS FIGHT EACH OTHER, THEY MUST INEVITABLY RESORT TO DIRTY TRICKS. YOU MUST EITHER SEND YOUR OPPONENT TOO FAR OUT OF THE FIELD TO FIGHT...
BZZZT
...OR SEAL THEM AWAY.
THAT IS THE MOST BASIC PRINCIPLE OF IMMORTAL WARFARE.
KER-FWAM
KSHING

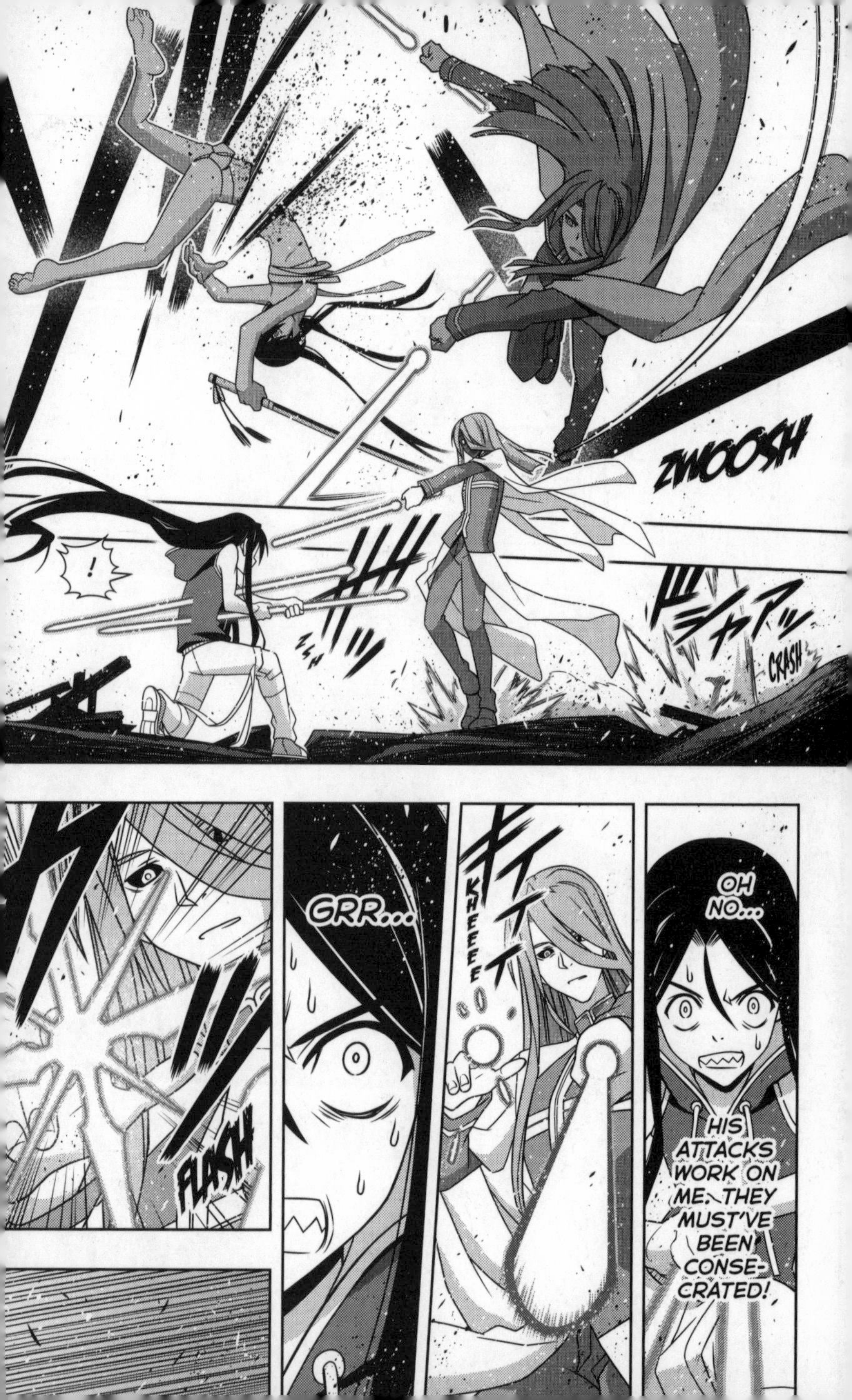
ZWOOSH
CRASH
!
OH NO...
HIS ATTACKS WORK ON ME. THEY MUST'VE BEEN CONSE-CRATED!
KHEEEE
GRR...
FLASH

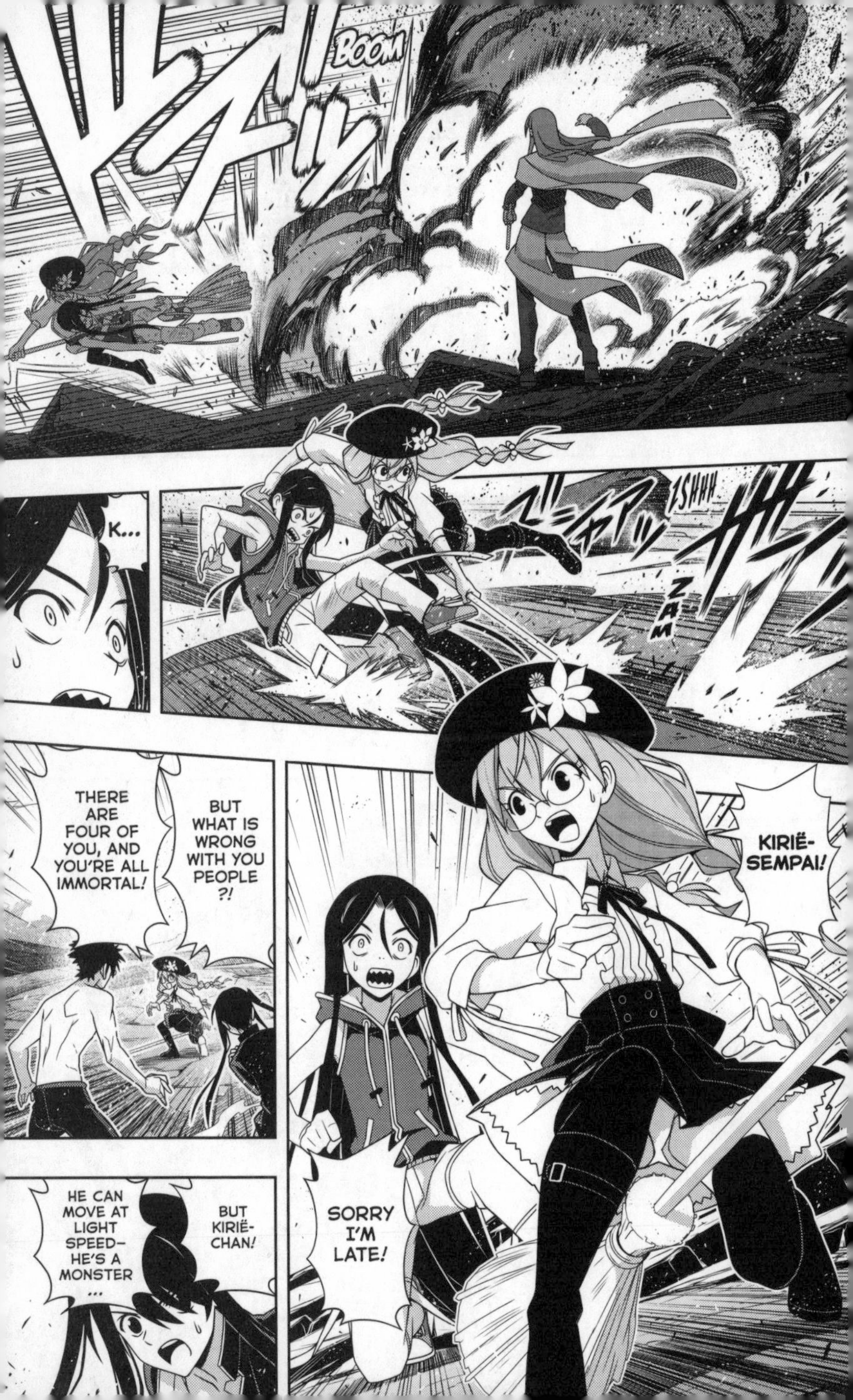
BOOM
ZSHHH
ZAM
K...
KIRIË-SEMPAI!
SORRY I'M LATE!
BUT WHAT IS WRONG WITH YOU PEOPLE?!
THERE ARE FOUR OF YOU, AND YOU'RE ALL IMMORTAL!
BUT KIRIË-CHAN!
HE CAN MOVE AT LIGHT SPEED—HE'S A MONSTER...

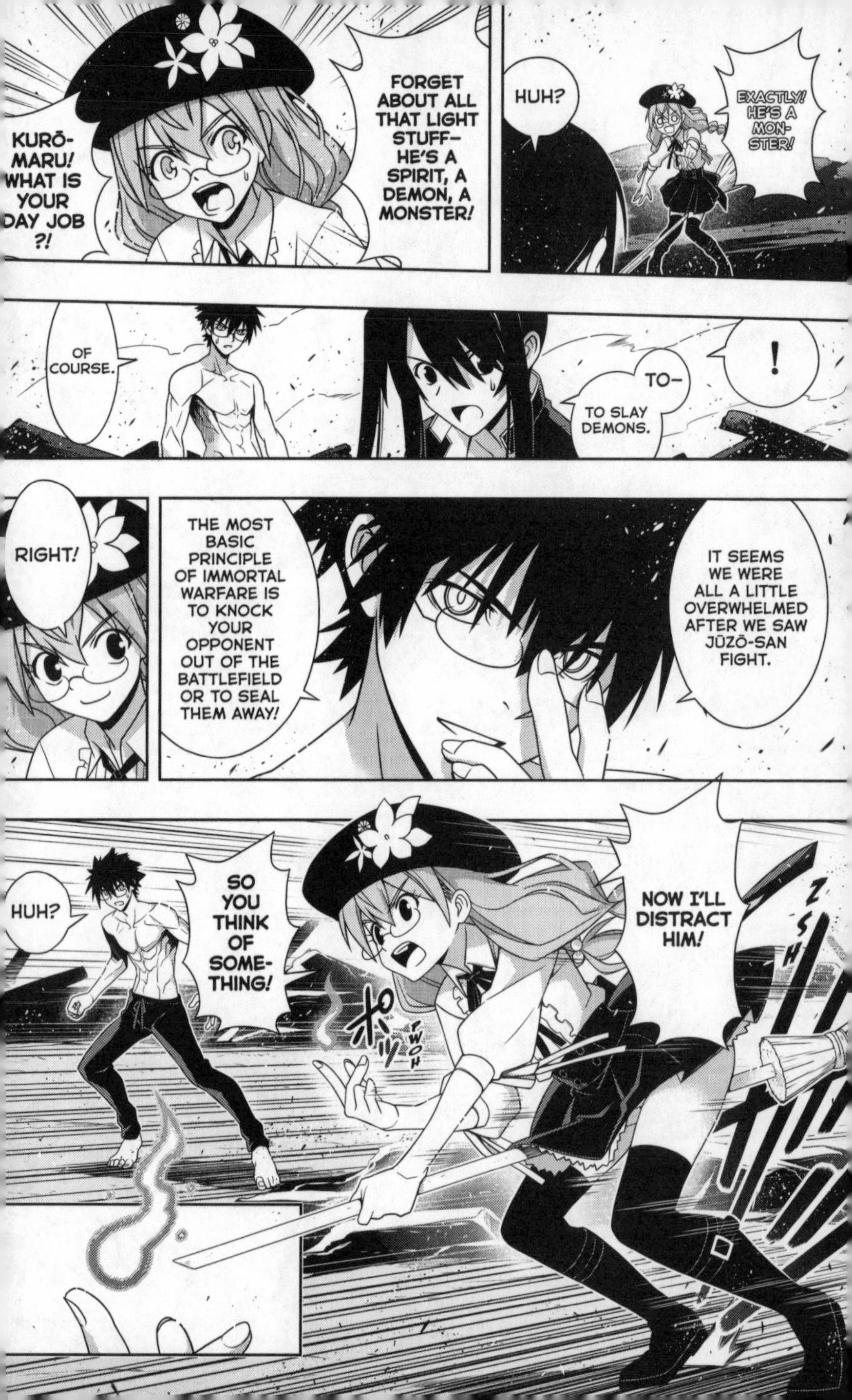
EXACTLY! HE'S A MONSTER!
HUH?
FORGET ABOUT ALL THAT LIGHT STUFF—HE'S A SPIRIT, A DEMON, A MONSTER!
KURŌ-MARU! WHAT IS YOUR DAY JOB?!
!
TO—
TO SLAY DEMONS.
OF COURSE.
IT SEEMS WE WERE ALL A LITTLE OVERWHELMED AFTER WE SAW JŪZŌ-SAN FIGHT.
THE MOST BASIC PRINCIPLE OF IMMORTAL WARFARE IS TO KNOCK YOUR OPPONENT OUT OF THE BATTLEFIELD OR TO SEAL THEM AWAY!
RIGHT!
ZSH
NOW I'LL DISTRACT HIM!
PWOH
SO YOU THINK OF SOMETHING!
HUH?

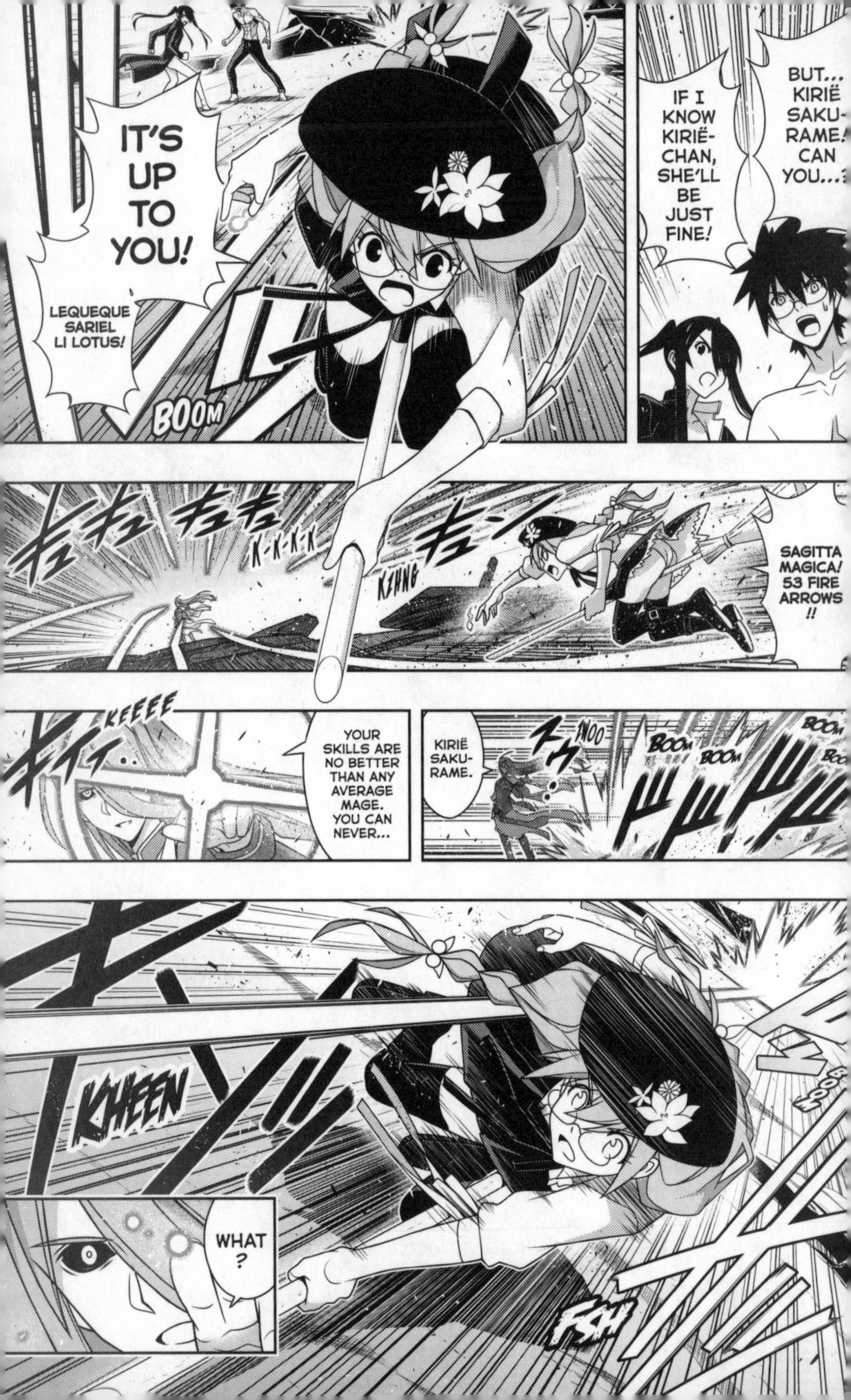

BUT... KIRIË SAKURAME! CAN YOU...!?
IF I KNOW KIRIË-CHAN, SHE'LL BE JUST FINE!
IT'S UP TO YOU!
LEQUEQUE SARIEL LI LOTUS!
BOOM
SAGITTA MAGICA! 53 FIRE ARROWS!!
KIHNG
K-K-K-K
BOOM
BOOM
BOOM
BOOM
WOO
KIRIË SAKURAME.
YOUR SKILLS ARE NO BETTER THAN ANY AVERAGE MAGE. YOU CAN NEVER...
KEEEE
BOOM
KHEEN
WHAT?
FSH

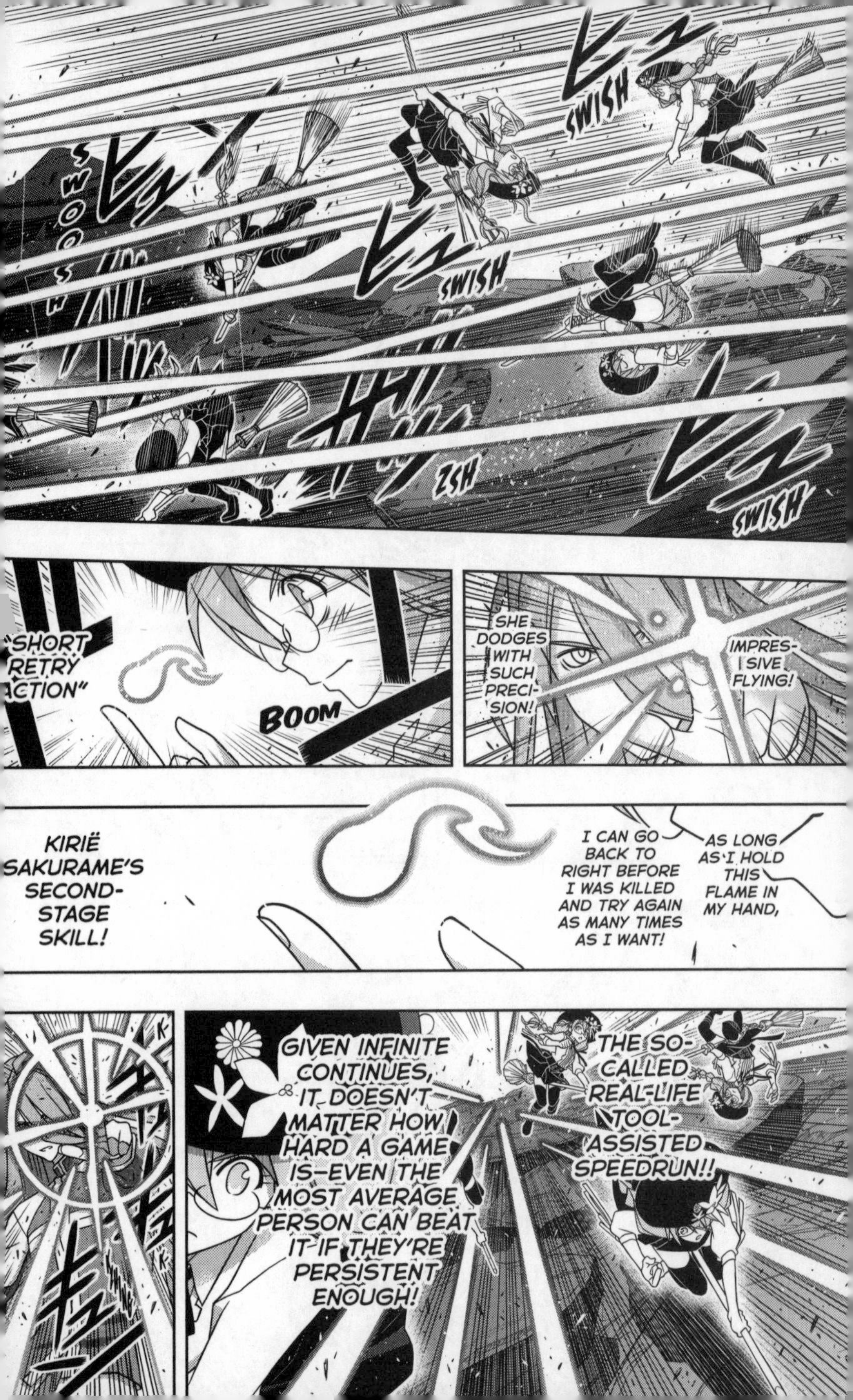
SWISH
SWISH
SWOOSH
ZSH
SWISH
IMPRESSIVE FLYING!
SHE DODGES WITH SUCH PRECISION!
BOOM
“SHORT RETRY ACTION”
AS LONG AS I HOLD THIS FLAME IN MY HAND,
I CAN GO BACK TO RIGHT BEFORE I WAS KILLED AND TRY AGAIN AS MANY TIMES AS I WANT!
KIRIË SAKURAME'S SECOND-STAGE SKILL!
THE SO-CALLED REAL-LIFE TOOL-ASSISTED SPEEDRUN!!
GIVEN INFINITE CONTINUES, IT DOESN'T MATTER HOW HARD A GAME IS—EVEN THE MOST AVERAGE PERSON CAN BEAT IT IF THEY'RE PERSISTENT ENOUGH!

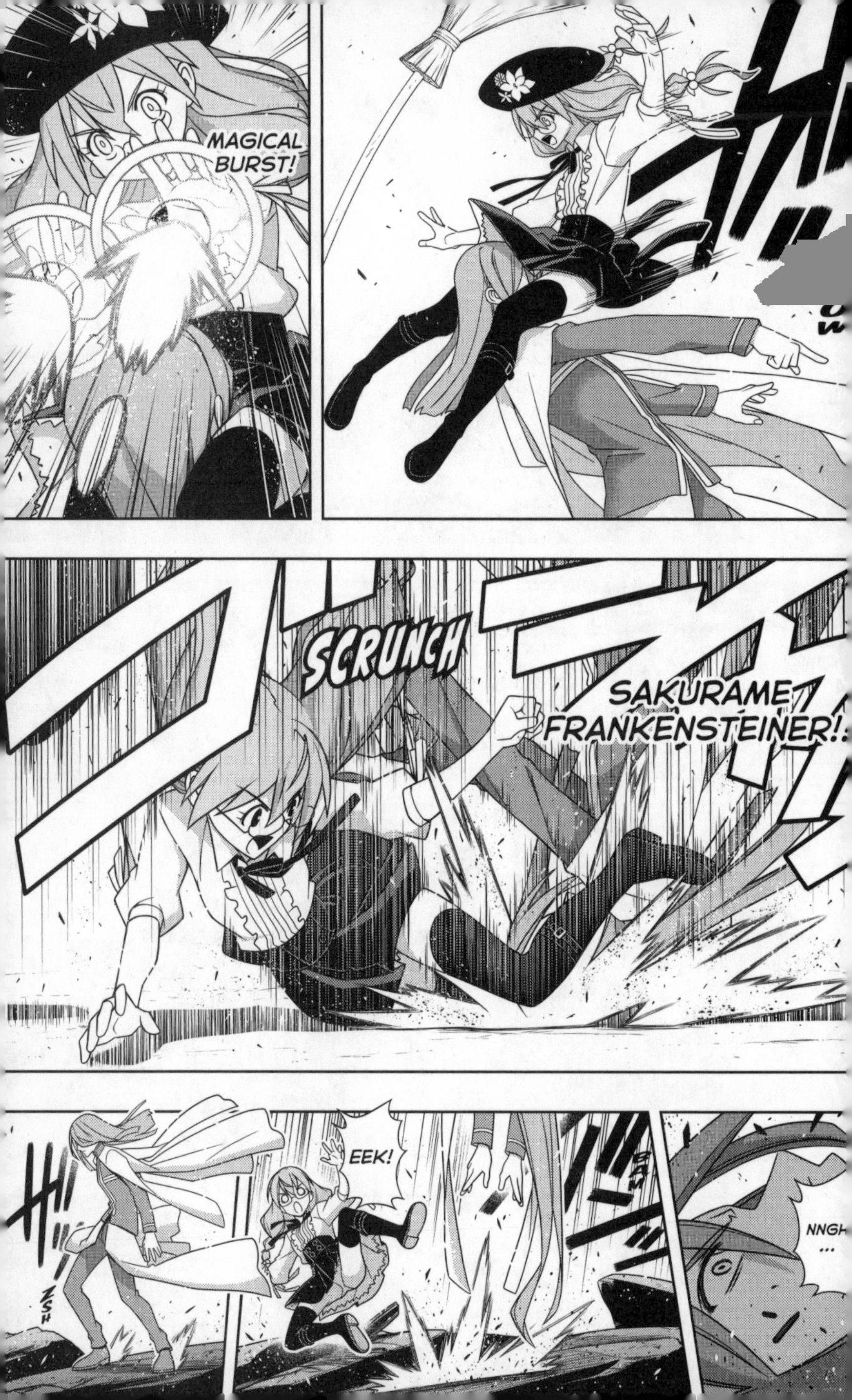
MAGICAL BURST!
SCRUNCH
SAKURAME FRANKENSTEINER!!
NNGH ...
BAM
EEK!
ZSH

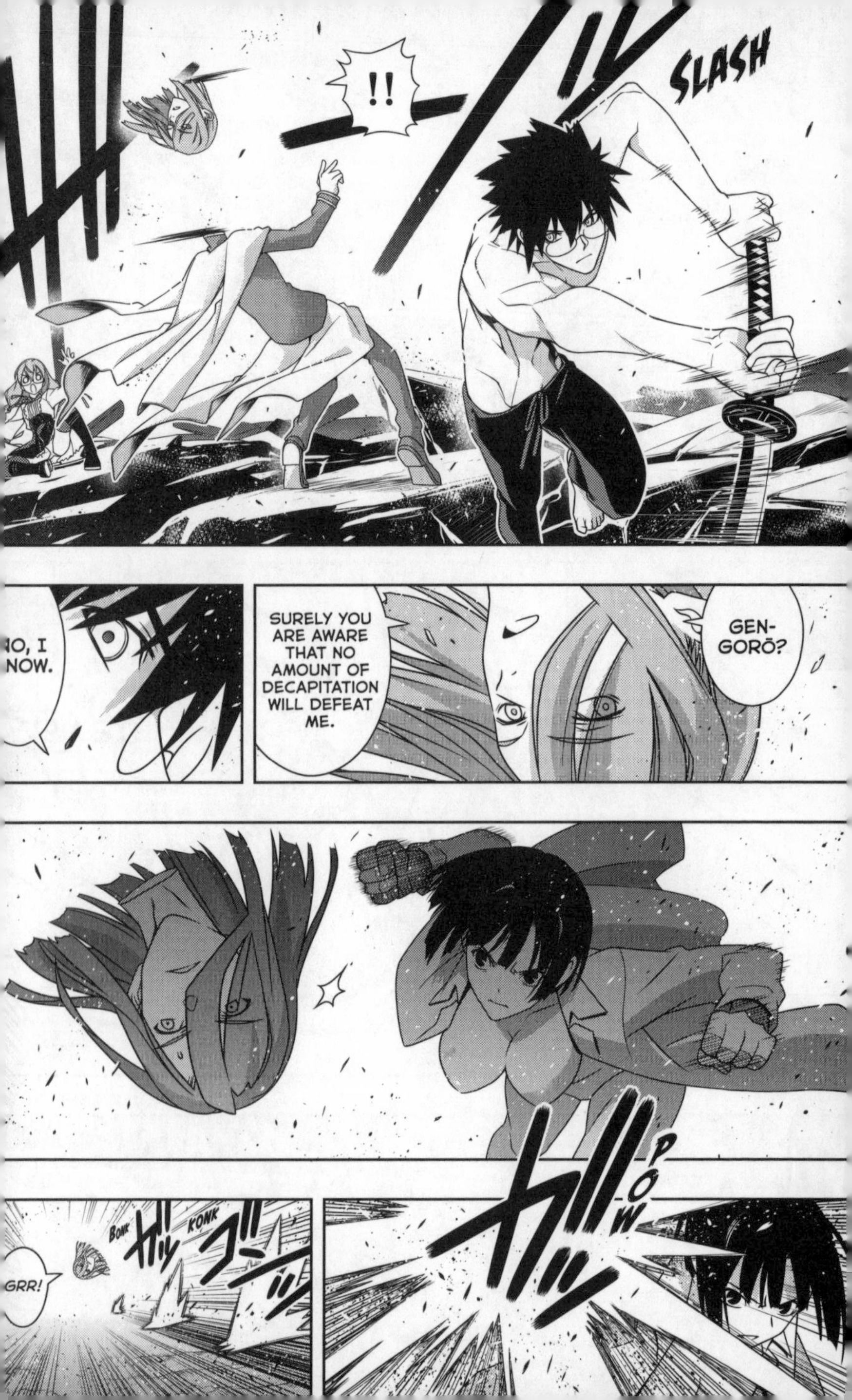
SLASH
!!
GEN-GORŌ?
SURELY YOU ARE AWARE THAT NO AMOUNT OF DECAPITATION WILL DEFEAT ME.
O, I NOW.
POW
BONK
KONK
GRR!

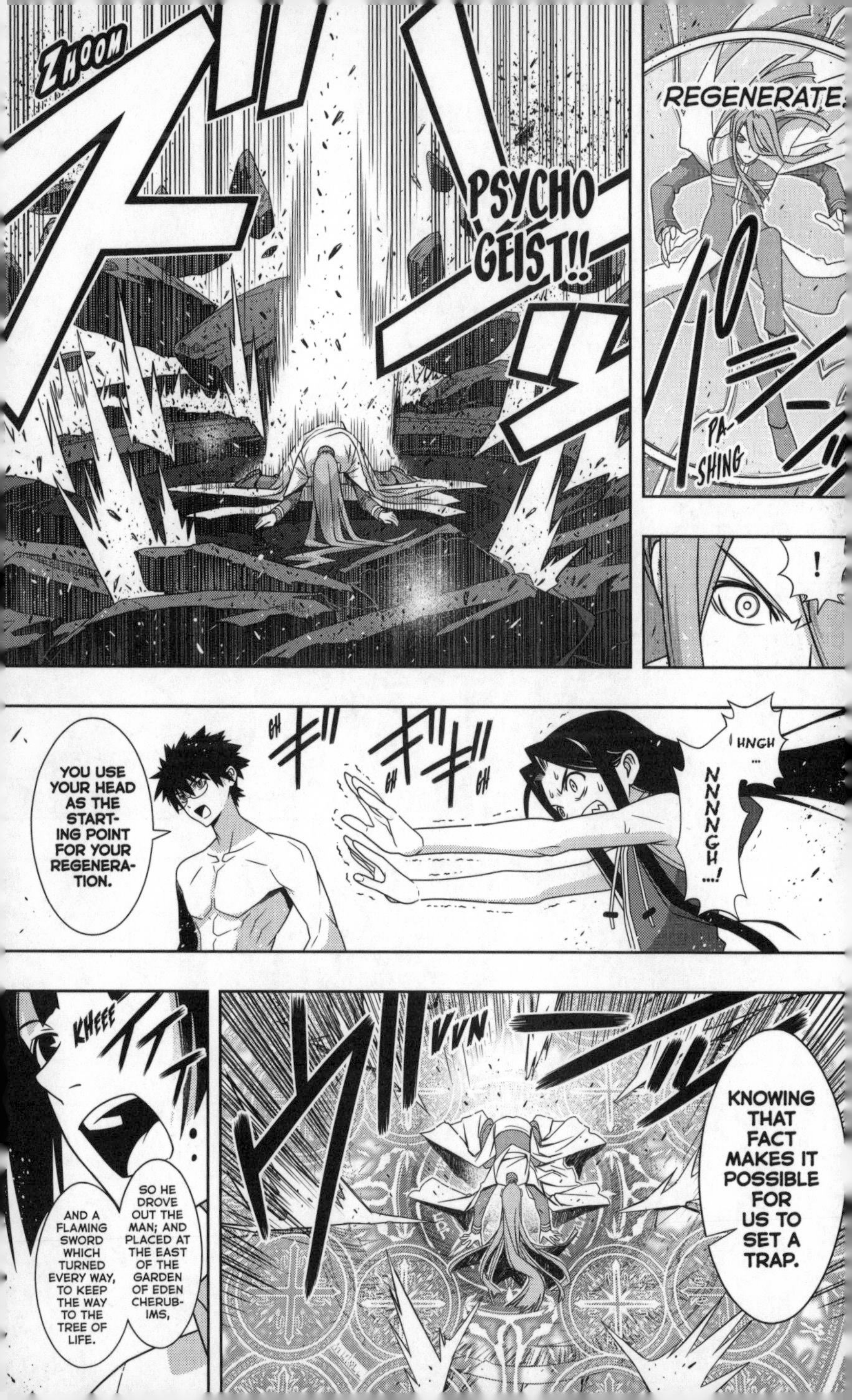
REGENERATE
PA SHING
!
ZHOOM
PSYCHO GEIST!!
HNGH... NNNNGH...!
GH GH GH
YOU USE YOUR HEAD AS THE STARTING POINT FOR YOUR REGENERATION.
KNOWING THAT FACT MAKES IT POSSIBLE FOR US TO SET A TRAP.
VVN
KHEEE
SO HE DROVE OUT THE MAN; AND PLACED AT THE EAST OF THE GARDEN OF EDEN CHERUBIMS,
AND A FLAMING SWORD WHICH TURNED EVERY WAY, TO KEEP THE WAY TO THE TREE OF LIFE.

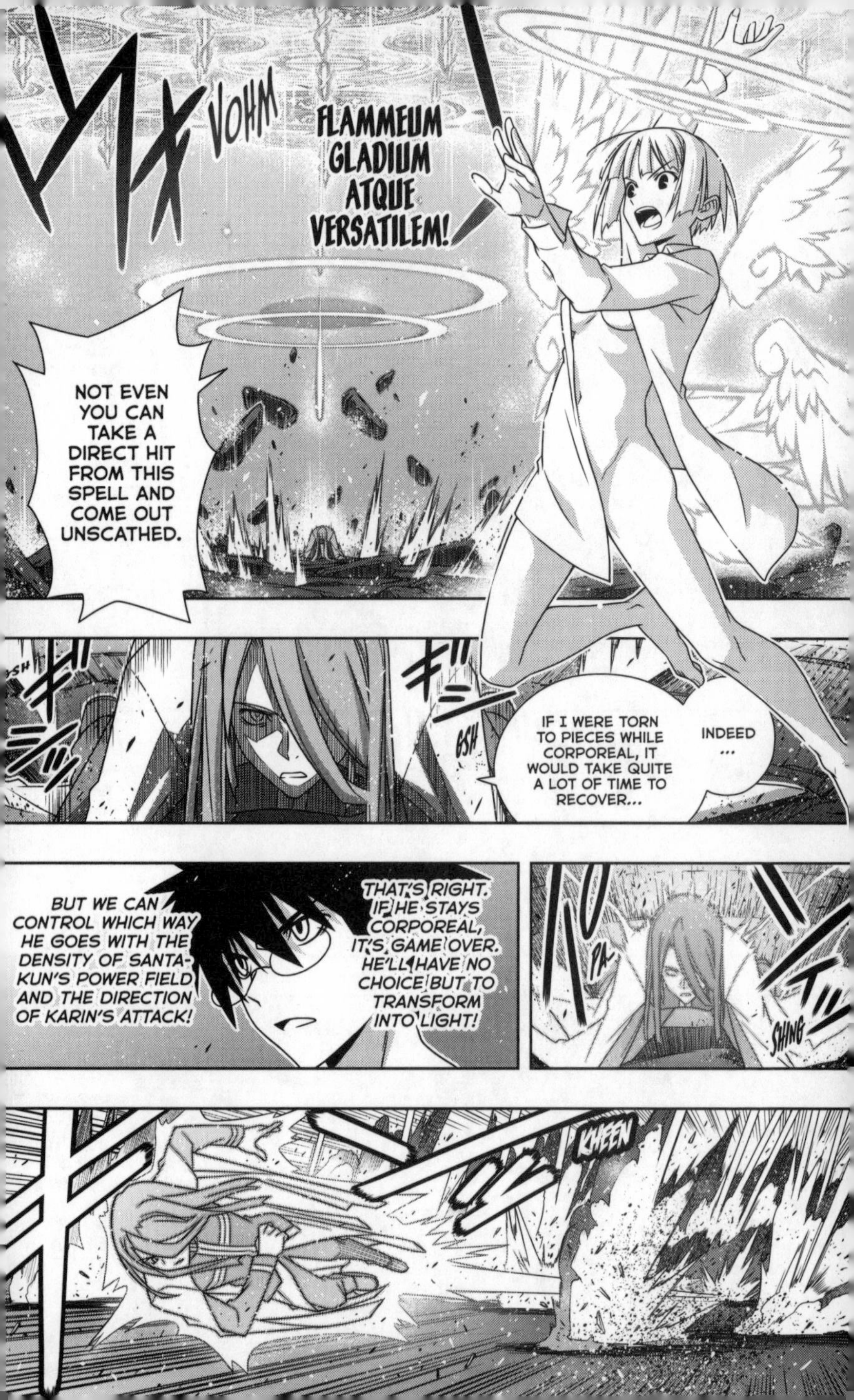
FLAMMEUM GLADIUM ATQUE VERSATILEM!
VOHM
NOT EVEN YOU CAN TAKE A DIRECT HIT FROM THIS SPELL AND COME OUT UNSCATHED.
INDEED ...
IF I WERE TORN TO PIECES WHILE CORPOREAL, IT WOULD TAKE QUITE A LOT OF TIME TO RECOVER...
GSH
PA
SHING
THAT'S RIGHT. IF HE STAYS CORPOREAL, IT'S GAME OVER. HE'LL HAVE NO CHOICE BUT TO TRANSFORM INTO LIGHT!
BUT WE CAN CONTROL WHICH WAY HE GOES WITH THE DENSITY OF SANTA-KUN'S POWER FIELD AND THE DIRECTION OF KARIN'S ATTACK!
KHEEN

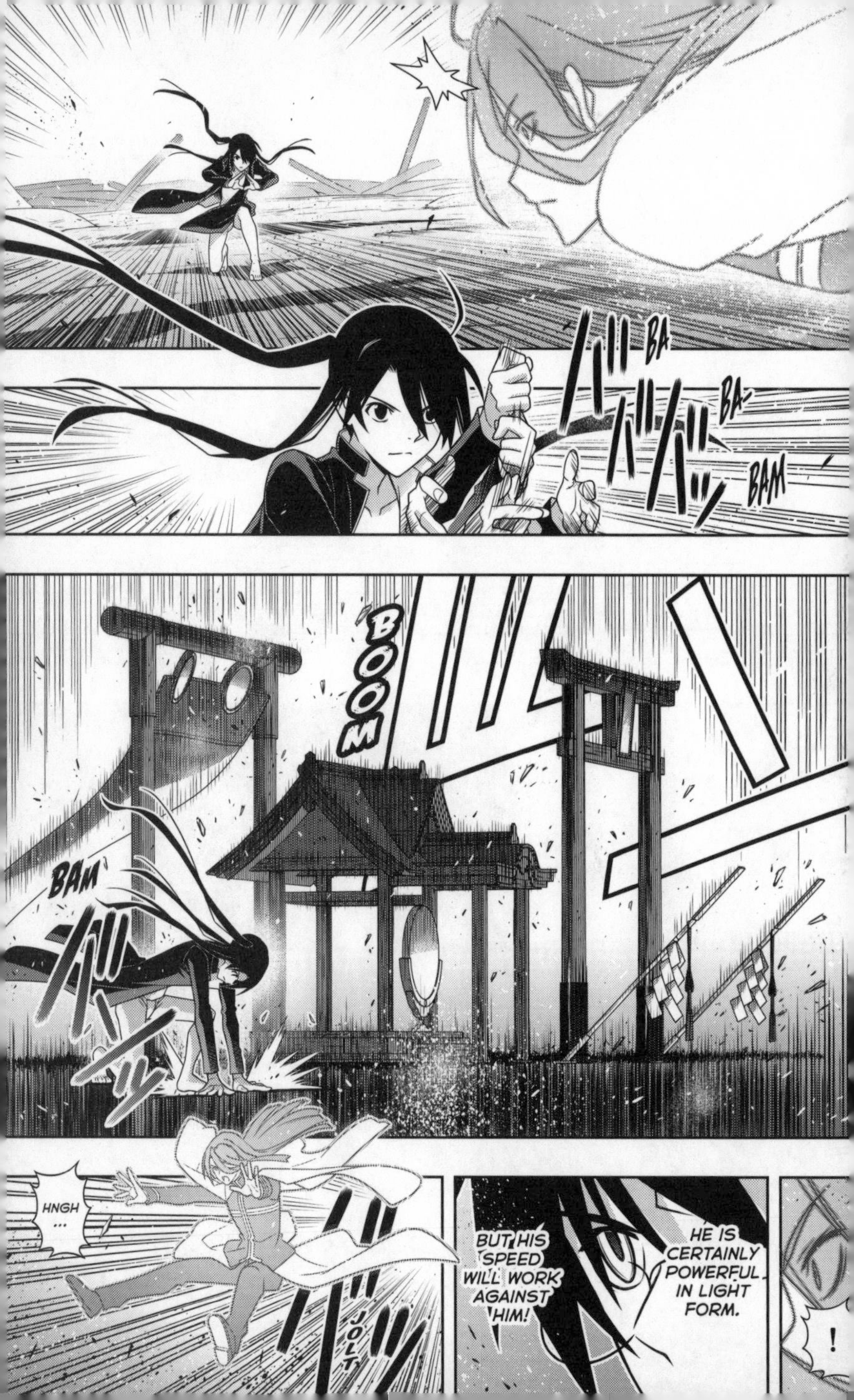
BA
BA-
BAM
BOOOM
BAM
!
HE IS CERTAINLY POWERFUL IN LIGHT FORM.
BUT HIS SPEED WILL WORK AGAINST HIM!
HNGH ...
JOLT

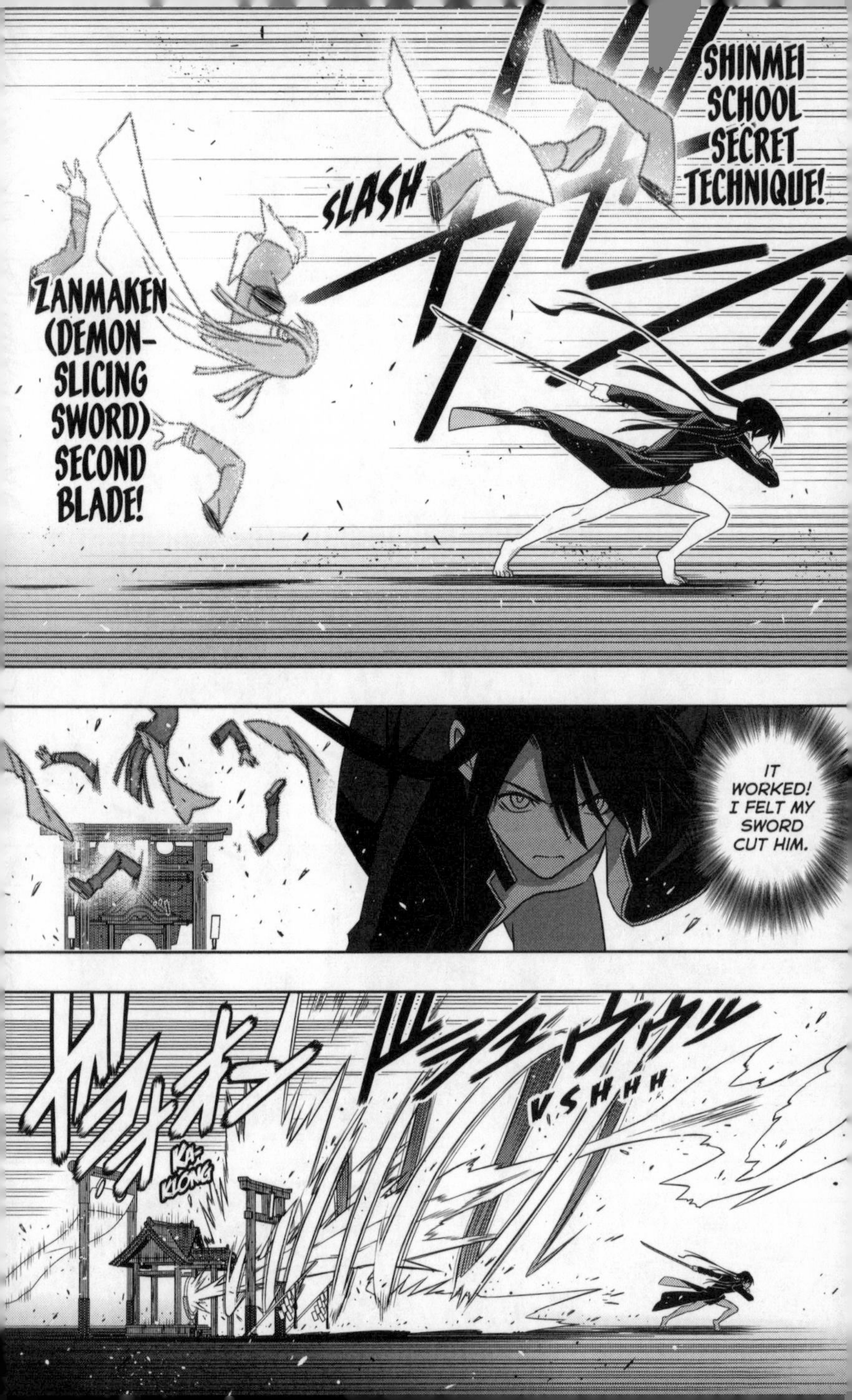
SHINMEI SCHOOL SECRET TECHNIQUE!
SLASH
ZANMAKEN (DEMON-SLICING SWORD) SECOND BLADE!
IT WORKED! I FELT MY SWORD CUT HIM.
VSHHH
KA-KLONG

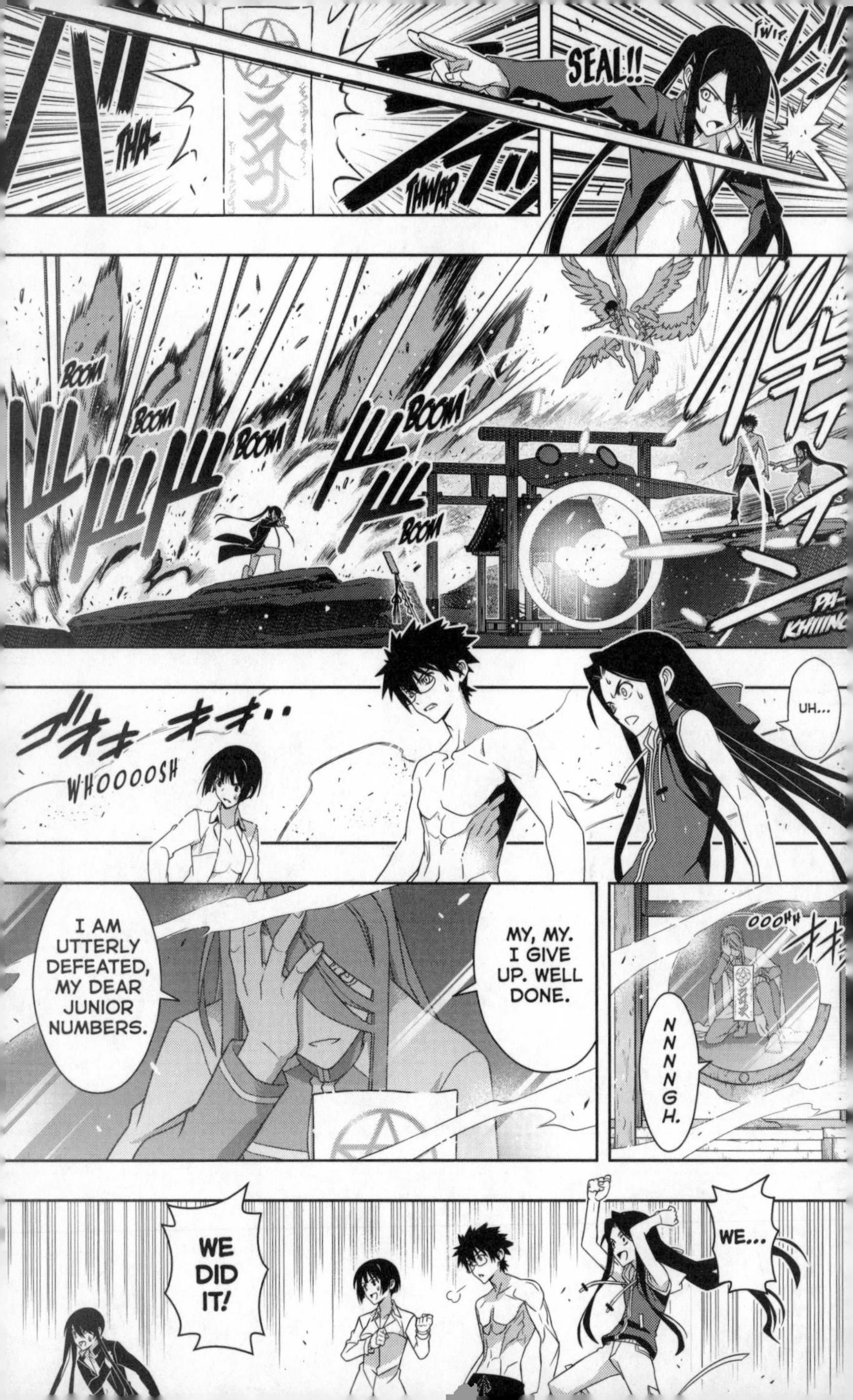
FWIT
SEAL!!
THA-
THWAP
PA-KHIIING
BOOM
BOOM
BOOM
BOOM
BOOM
UH...
WHOOOOSH
OOOHH
NNNNGH.
MY, MY. I GIVE UP. WELL DONE.
I AM UTTERLY DEFEATED, MY DEAR JUNIOR NUMBERS.
WE...
WE DID IT!

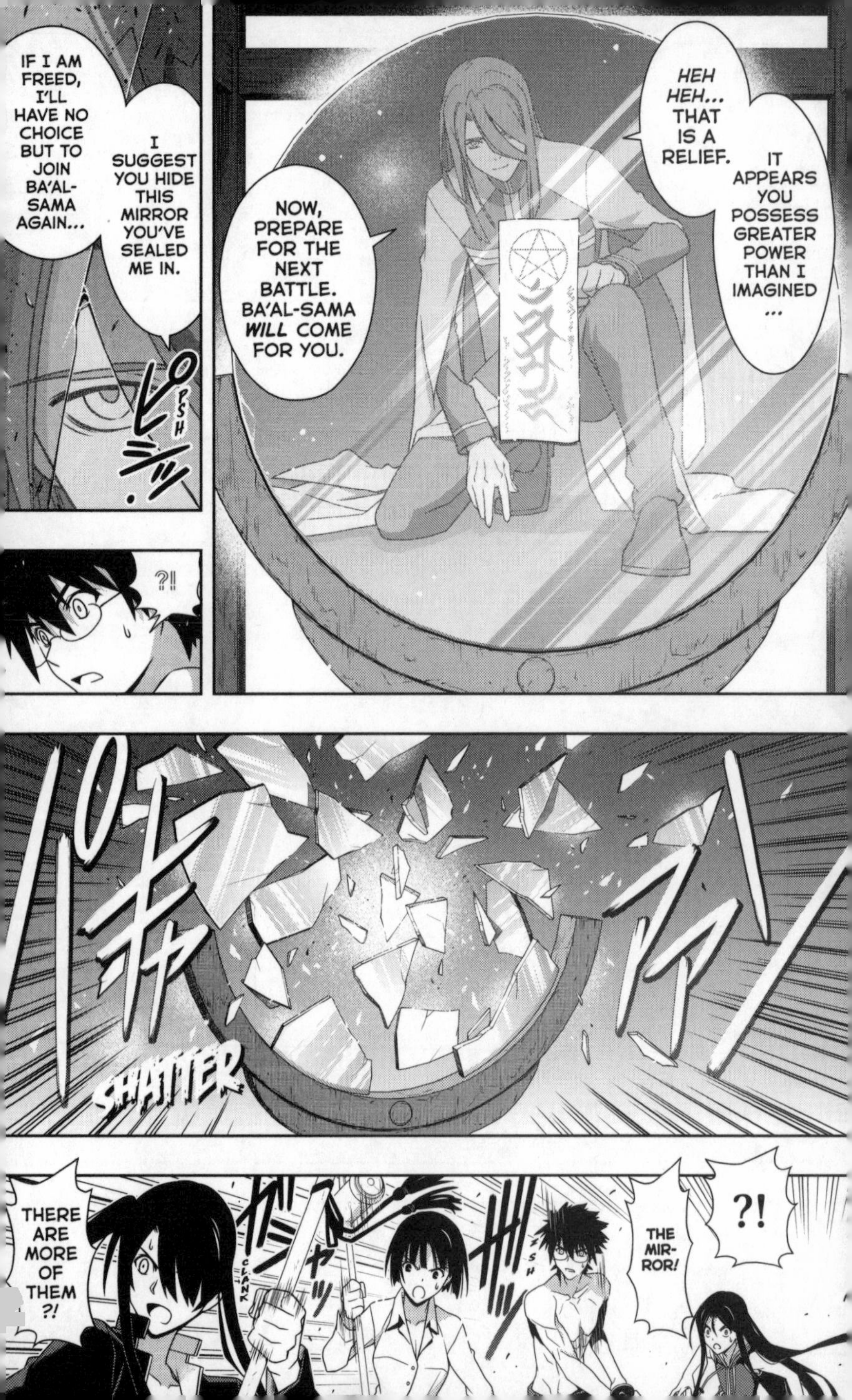
HEH HEH... THAT IS A RELIEF.
IT APPEARS YOU POSSESS GREATER POWER THAN I IMAGINED...
NOW, PREPARE FOR THE NEXT BATTLE. BA'AL-SAMA WILL COME FOR YOU.
I SUGGEST YOU HIDE THIS MIRROR YOU'VE SEALED ME IN.
IF I AM FREED, I'LL HAVE NO CHOICE BUT TO JOIN BA'AL-SAMA AGAIN...
PSH
?!!
SHATTER
?!
THE MIR-ROR!
CLANK
THERE ARE MORE OF THEM ?!

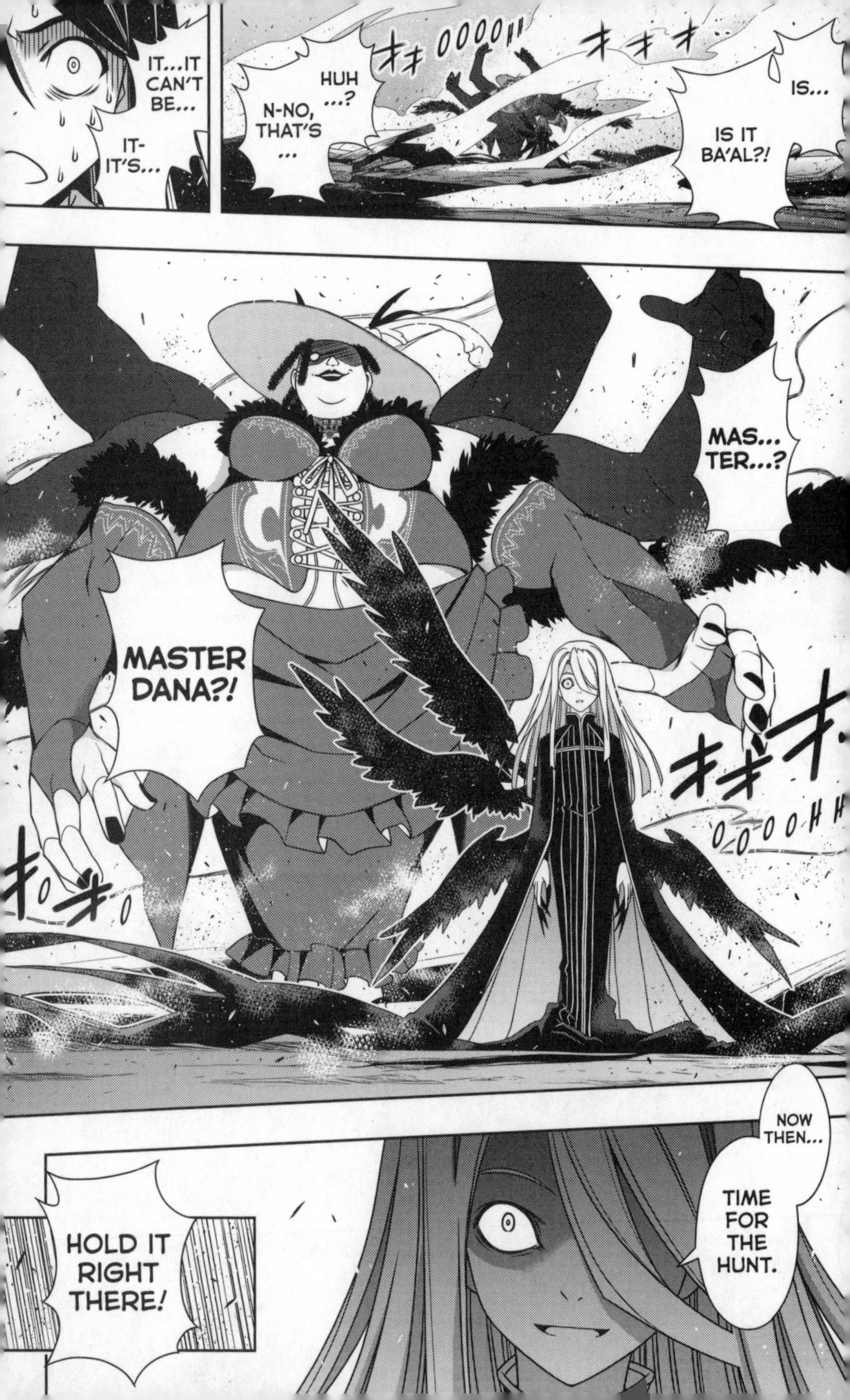
IS...
IS IT BA'AL?!
OOOO!!
HUH ...?
N-NO, THAT'S ...
IT...IT CAN'T BE...
IT- IT'S...
MAS... TER...?
OOOOOHHH
MASTER DANA?!
NOW THEN...
TIME FOR THE HUNT.
HOLD IT RIGHT THERE!

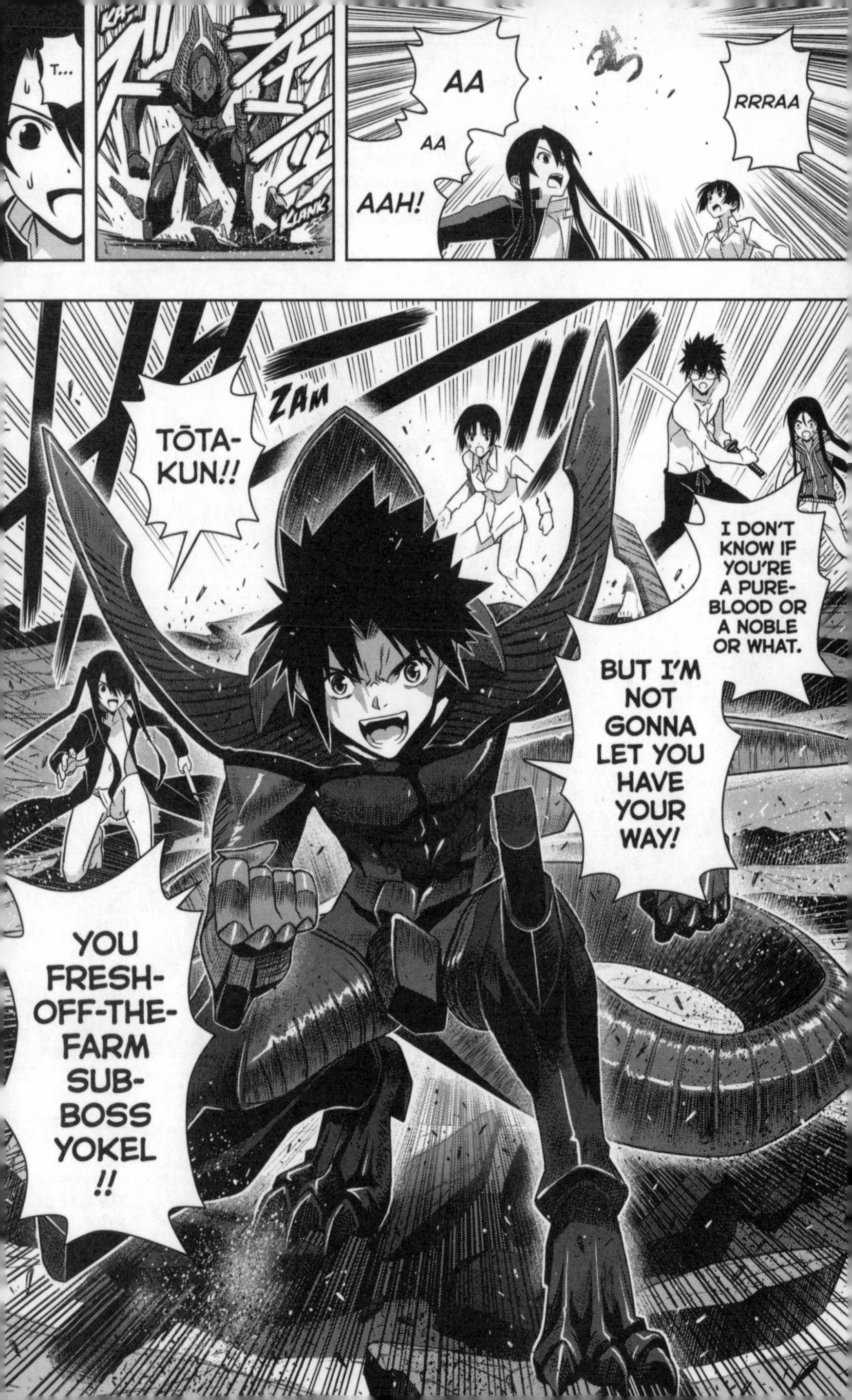
RRRAA
AA
AA
AAH!
KA-
KLANK
T...
I DON'T KNOW IF YOU'RE A PURE-BLOOD OR A NOBLE OR WHAT.
BUT I'M NOT GONNA LET YOU HAVE YOUR WAY!
ZAM
TŌTA-KUN!!
YOU FRESH-OFF-THE-FARM SUB-BOSS YOKEL!!

悠 UQ HOLDER!

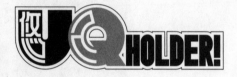

UQ HOLDER!

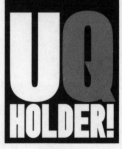

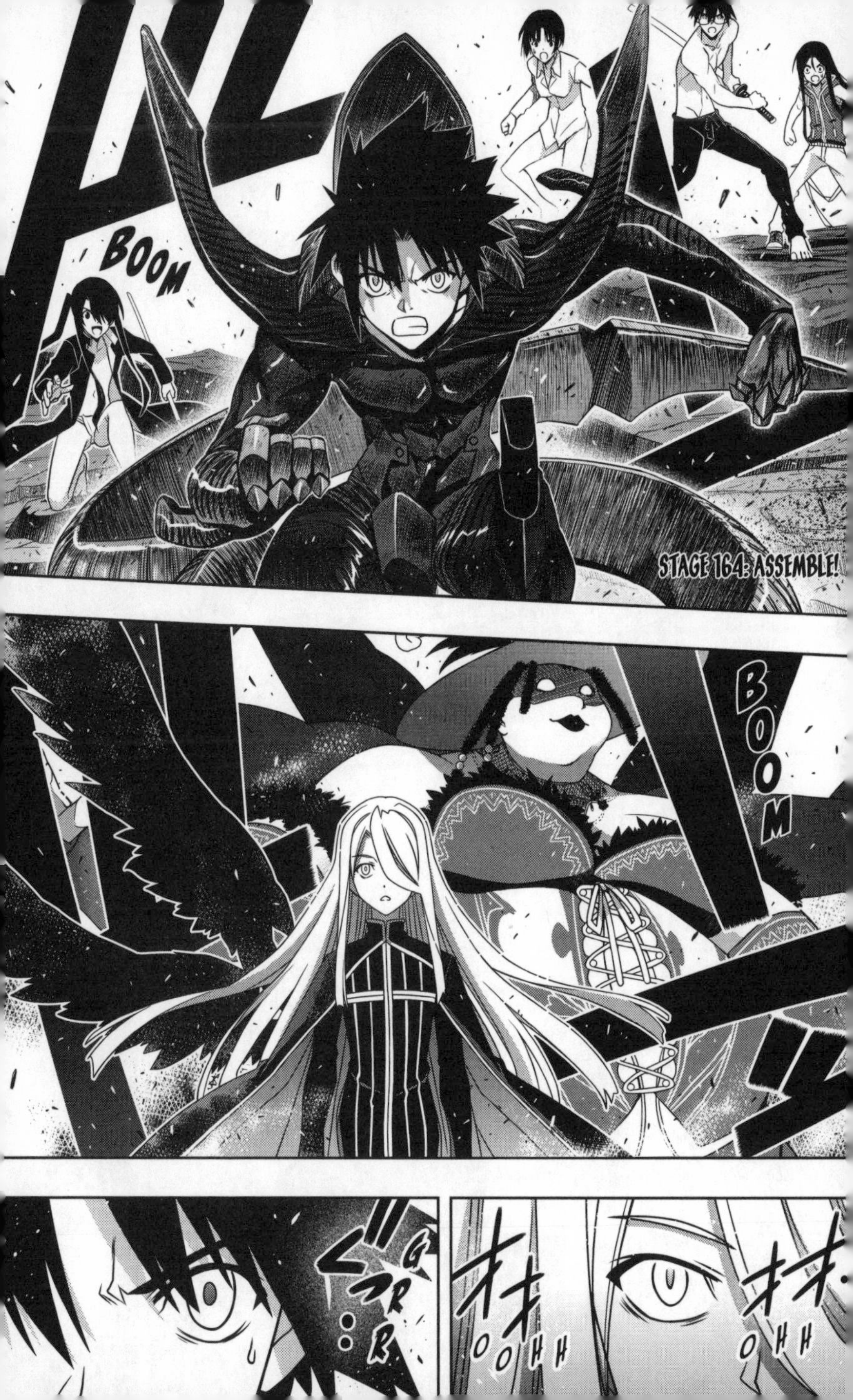
BOOM
STAGE 164: ASSEMBLE!
BOOM
OHH
OHH
GRR

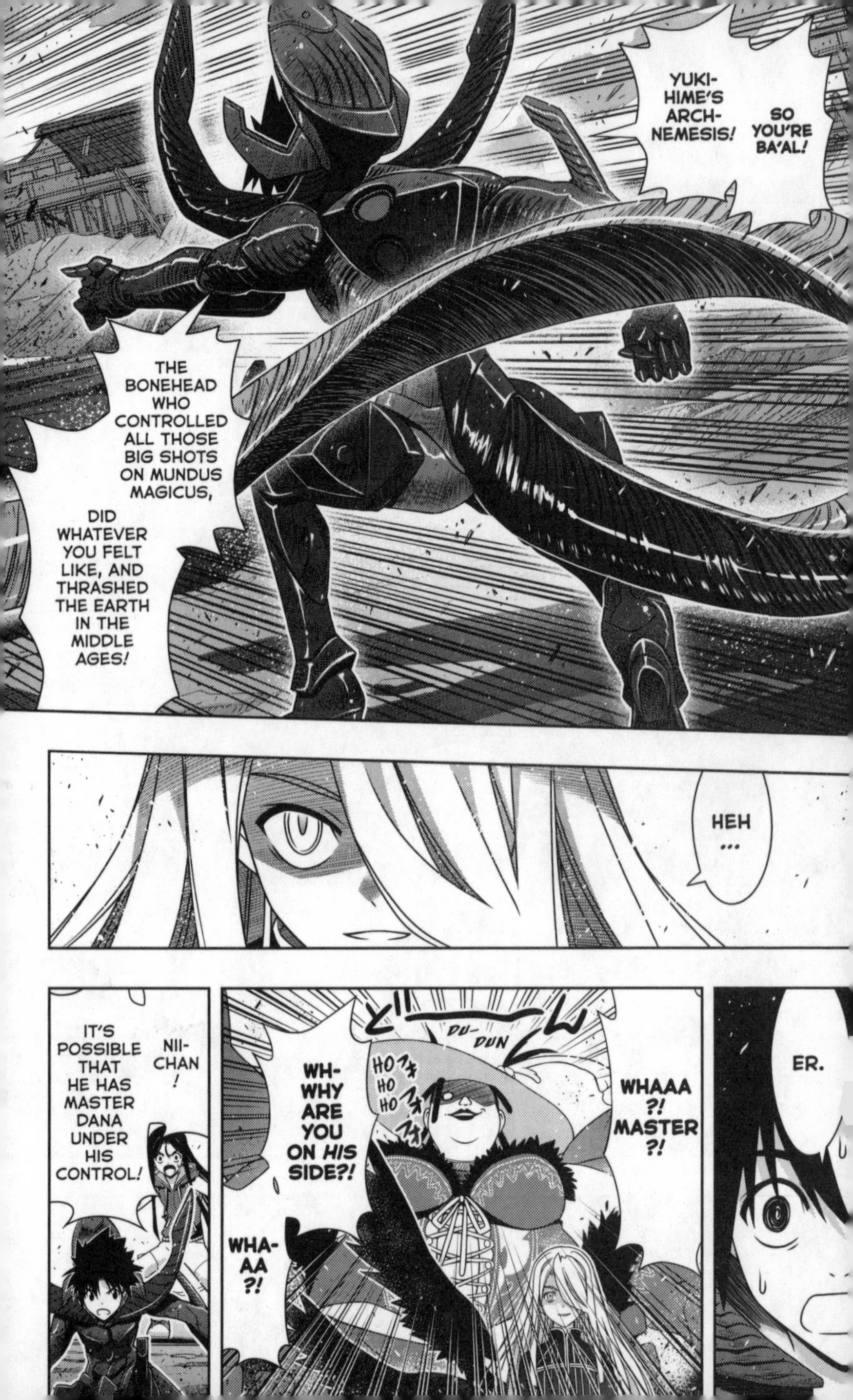
SO YOU'RE BA'AL!
YUKI-HIME'S ARCH-NEMESIS!
THE BONEHEAD WHO CONTROLLED ALL THOSE BIG SHOTS ON MUNDUS MAGICUS,
DID WHATEVER YOU FELT LIKE, AND THRASHED THE EARTH IN THE MIDDLE AGES!
HEH ...
ER.
WHAAA ?! MASTER ?!
DU-DUN
HO HO HO
WH-WHY ARE YOU ON *HIS* SIDE?!
WHAA-AA ?!
NII-CHAN!
IT'S POSSIBLE THAT HE HAS MASTER DANA UNDER HIS CONTROL!

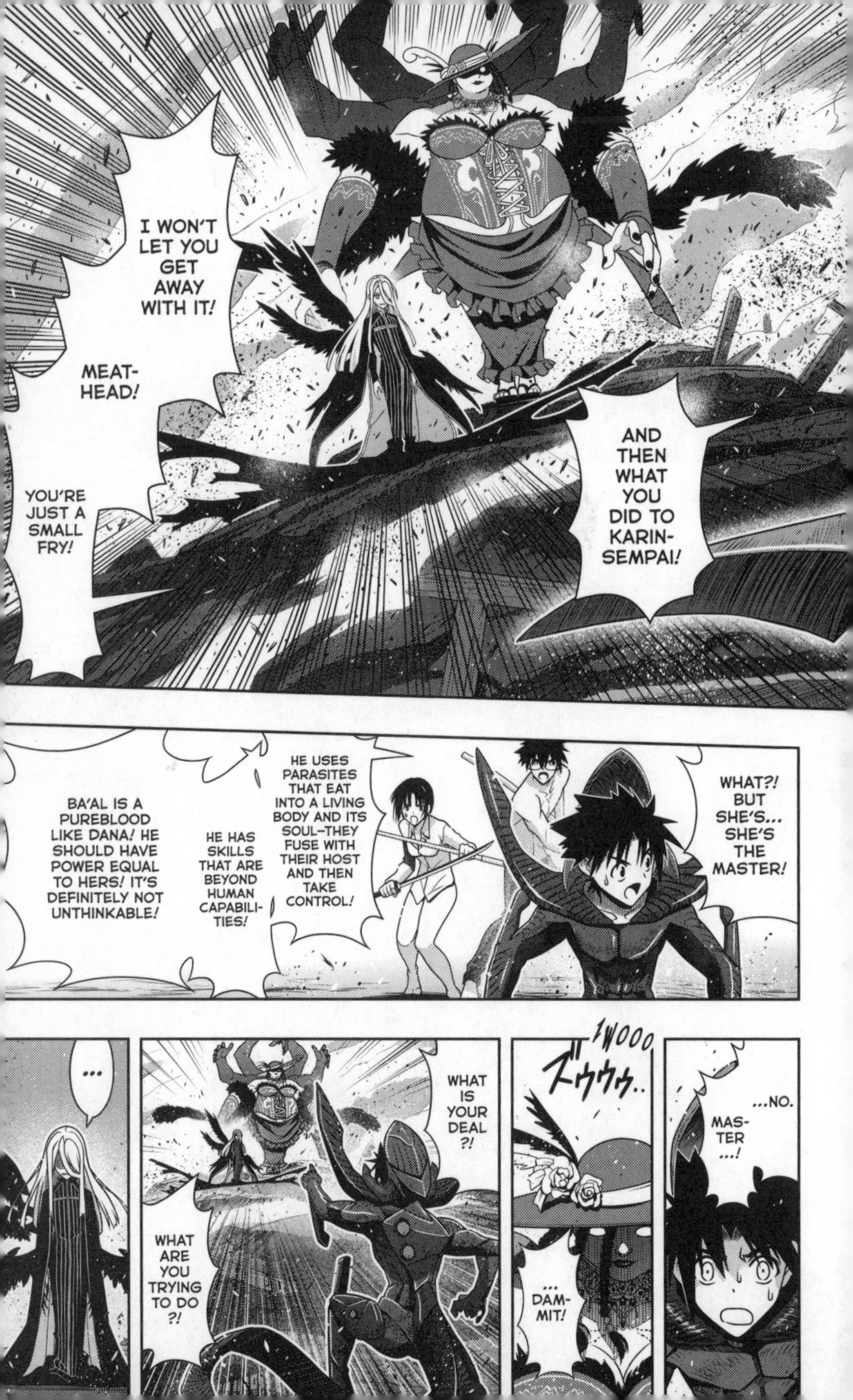
I WON'T LET YOU GET AWAY WITH IT!
MEAT-HEAD!
YOU'RE JUST A SMALL FRY!
AND THEN WHAT YOU DID TO KARIN-SEMPAI!
WHAT?! BUT SHE'S... SHE'S THE MASTER!
HE USES PARASITES THAT EAT INTO A LIVING BODY AND ITS SOUL—THEY FUSE WITH THEIR HOST AND THEN TAKE CONTROL!
HE HAS SKILLS THAT ARE BEYOND HUMAN CAPABILI-TIES!
BA'AL IS A PUREBLOOD LIKE DANA! HE SHOULD HAVE POWER EQUAL TO HERS! IT'S DEFINITELY NOT UNTHINKABLE!
...NO.
MAS-TER ...!
WOOO
ズウウウ..
... DAM-MIT!
WHAT IS YOUR DEAL ?!
WHAT ARE YOU TRYING TO DO ?!
...

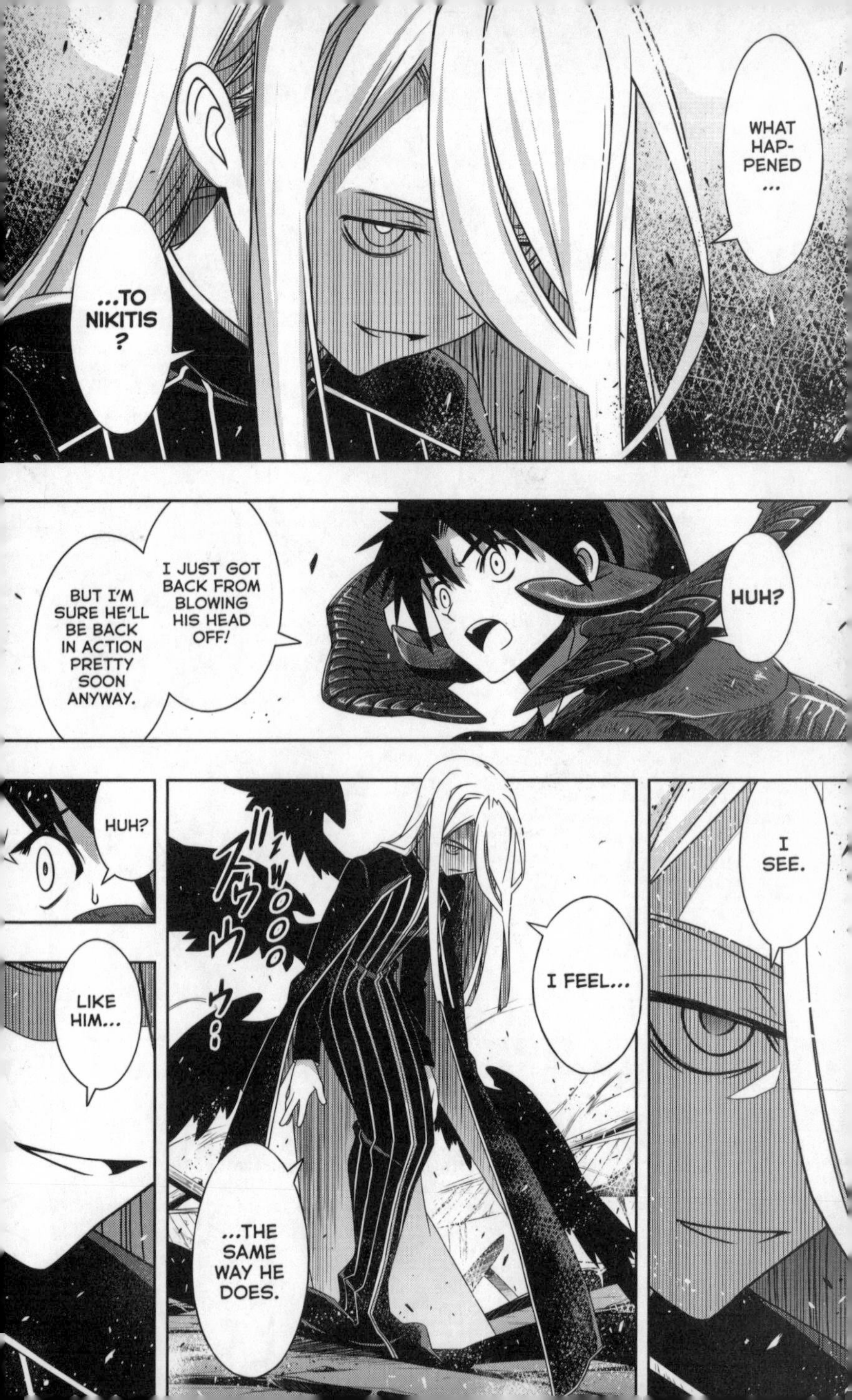
WHAT HAP-PENED...
...TO NIKITIS?
HUH?
I JUST GOT BACK FROM BLOWING HIS HEAD OFF!
BUT I'M SURE HE'LL BE BACK IN ACTION PRETTY SOON ANYWAY.
I SEE.
I FEEL...
WOOOO
...THE SAME WAY HE DOES.
HUH?
LIKE HIM...

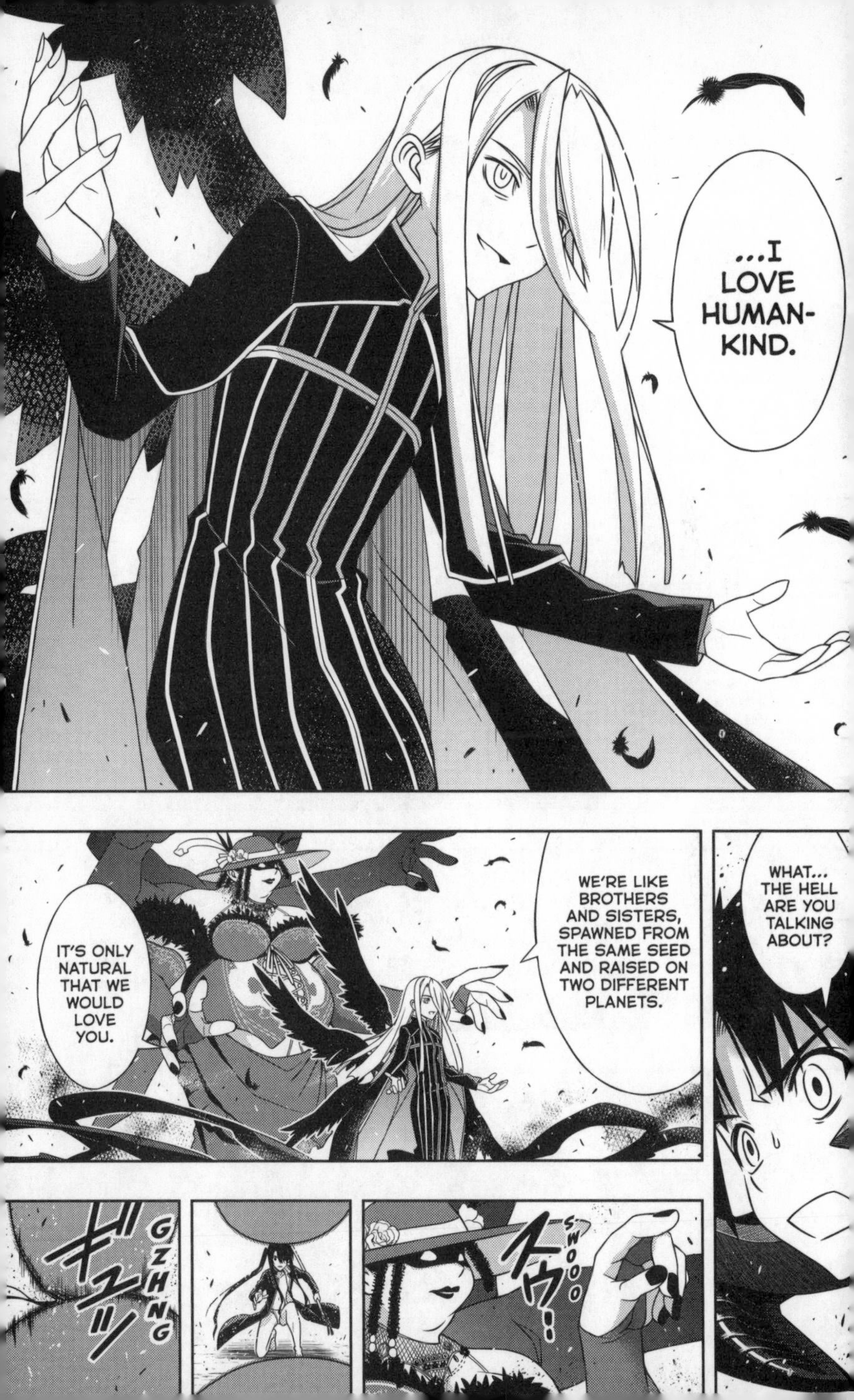

...I LOVE HUMAN-KIND.
WHAT... THE HELL ARE YOU TALKING ABOUT?
WE'RE LIKE BROTHERS AND SISTERS, SPAWNED FROM THE SAME SEED AND RAISED ON TWO DIFFERENT PLANETS.
IT'S ONLY NATURAL THAT WE WOULD LOVE YOU.
SWOOO
GZHNG

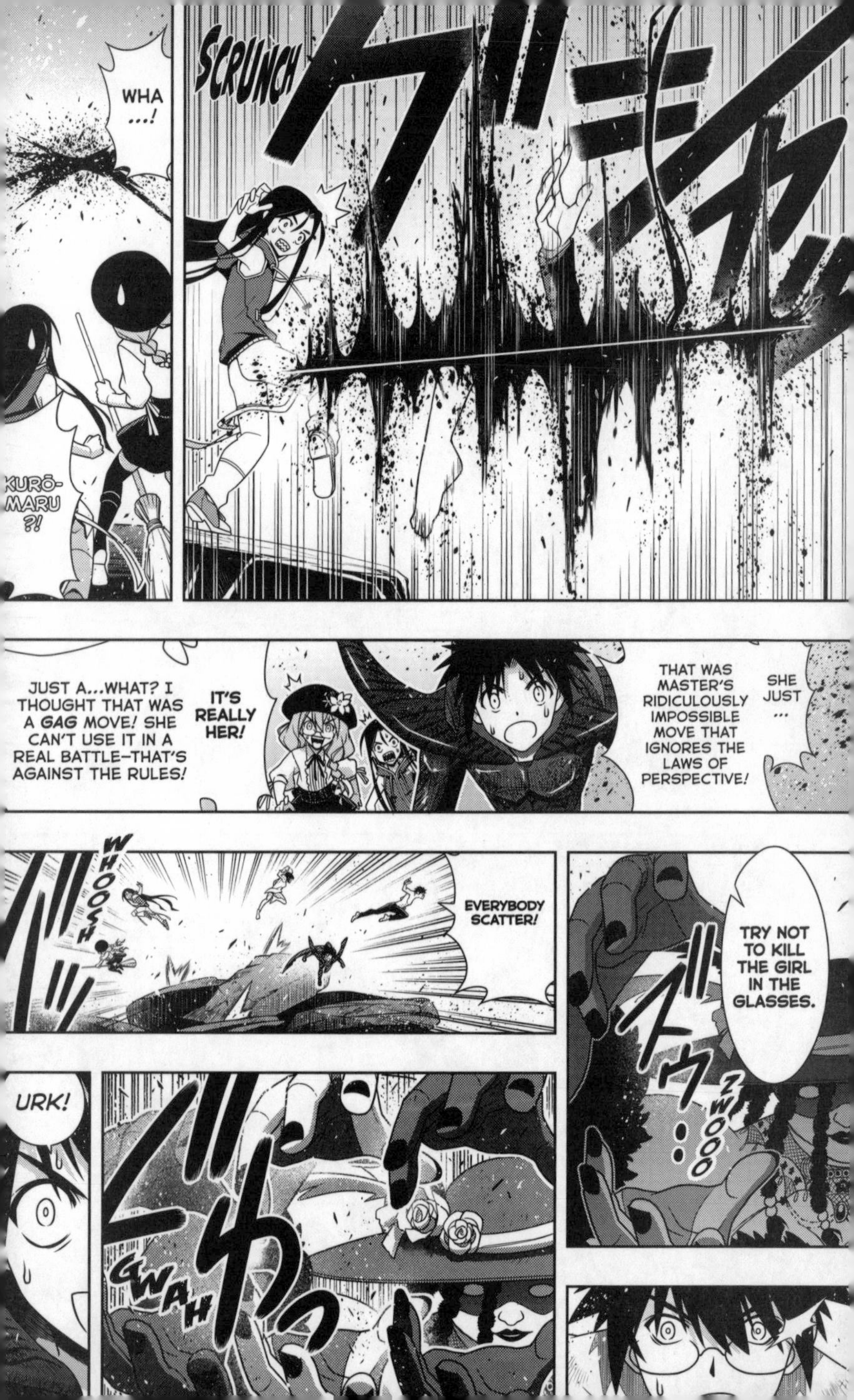
SCRUNCH
WHA ...!
KURŌ-MARU ?!
SHE JUST ...
THAT WAS MASTER'S RIDICULOUSLY IMPOSSIBLE MOVE THAT IGNORES THE LAWS OF PERSPECTIVE!
IT'S REALLY HER!
JUST A...WHAT? I THOUGHT THAT WAS A GAG MOVE! SHE CAN'T USE IT IN A REAL BATTLE—THAT'S AGAINST THE RULES!
TRY NOT TO KILL THE GIRL IN THE GLASSES.
ZWOOOO
EVERYBODY SCATTER!
WHOOOSH
GWAH
URK!

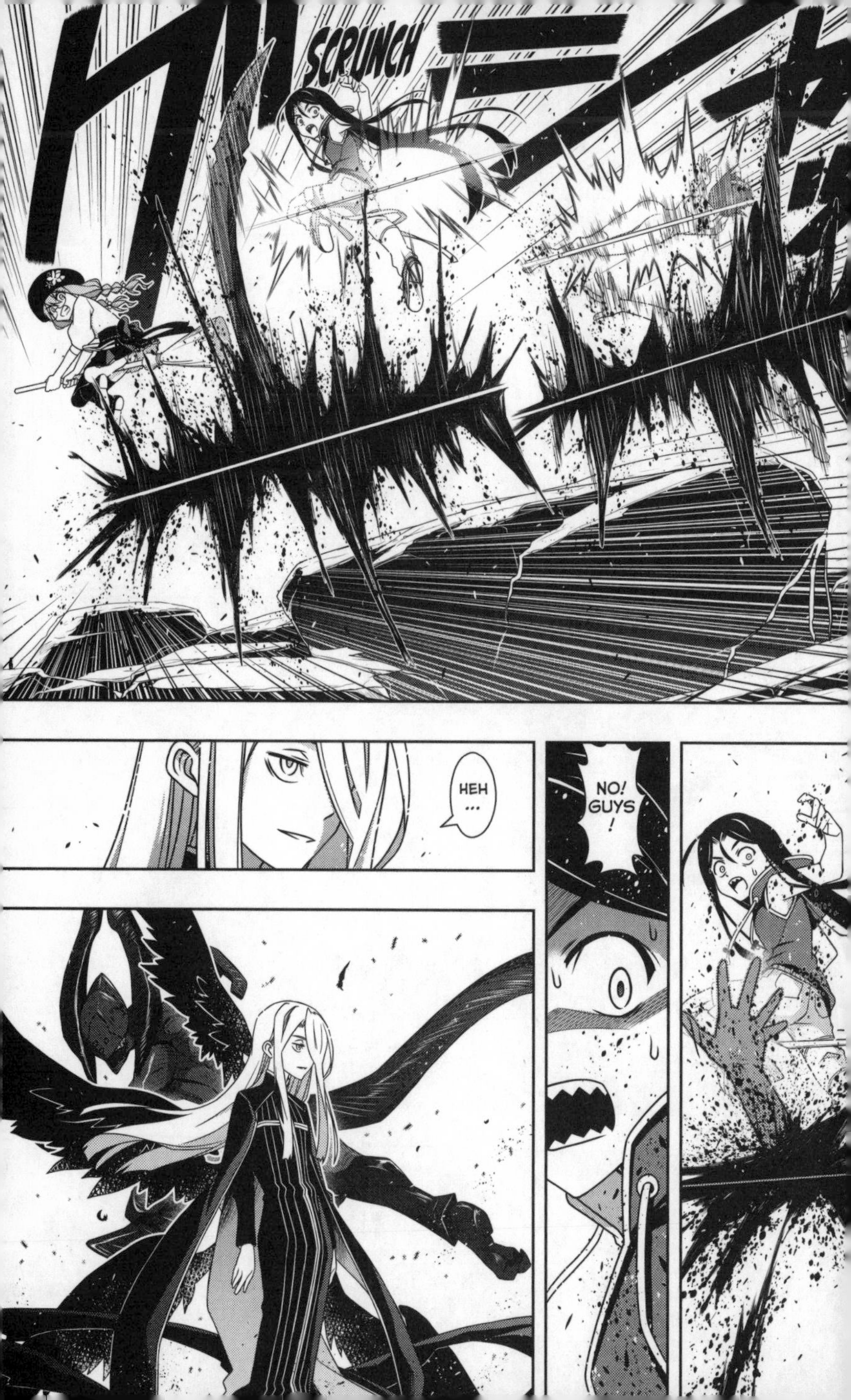
SCRUNCH
NO! GUYS!
HEH...

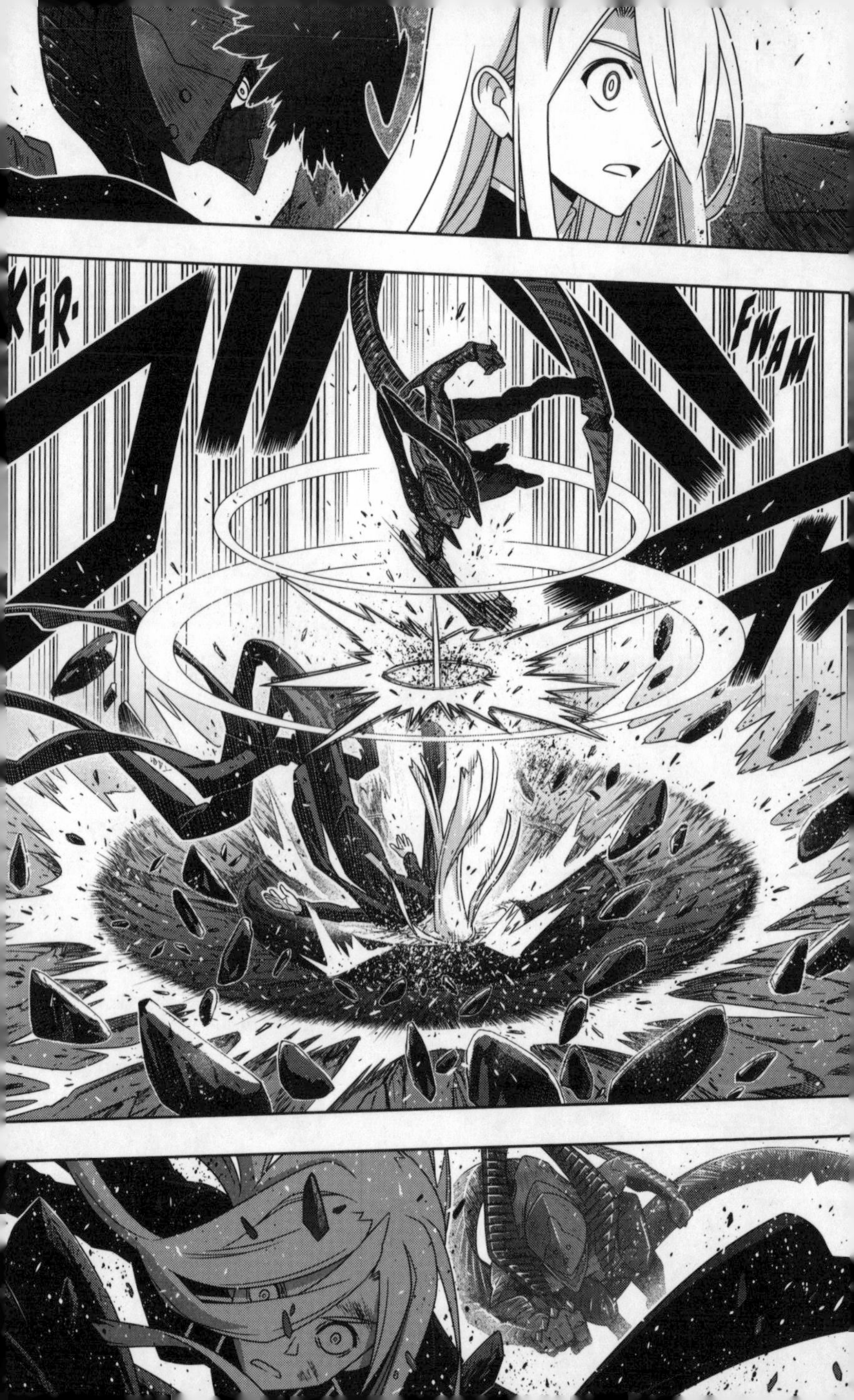

FWAM
KER-

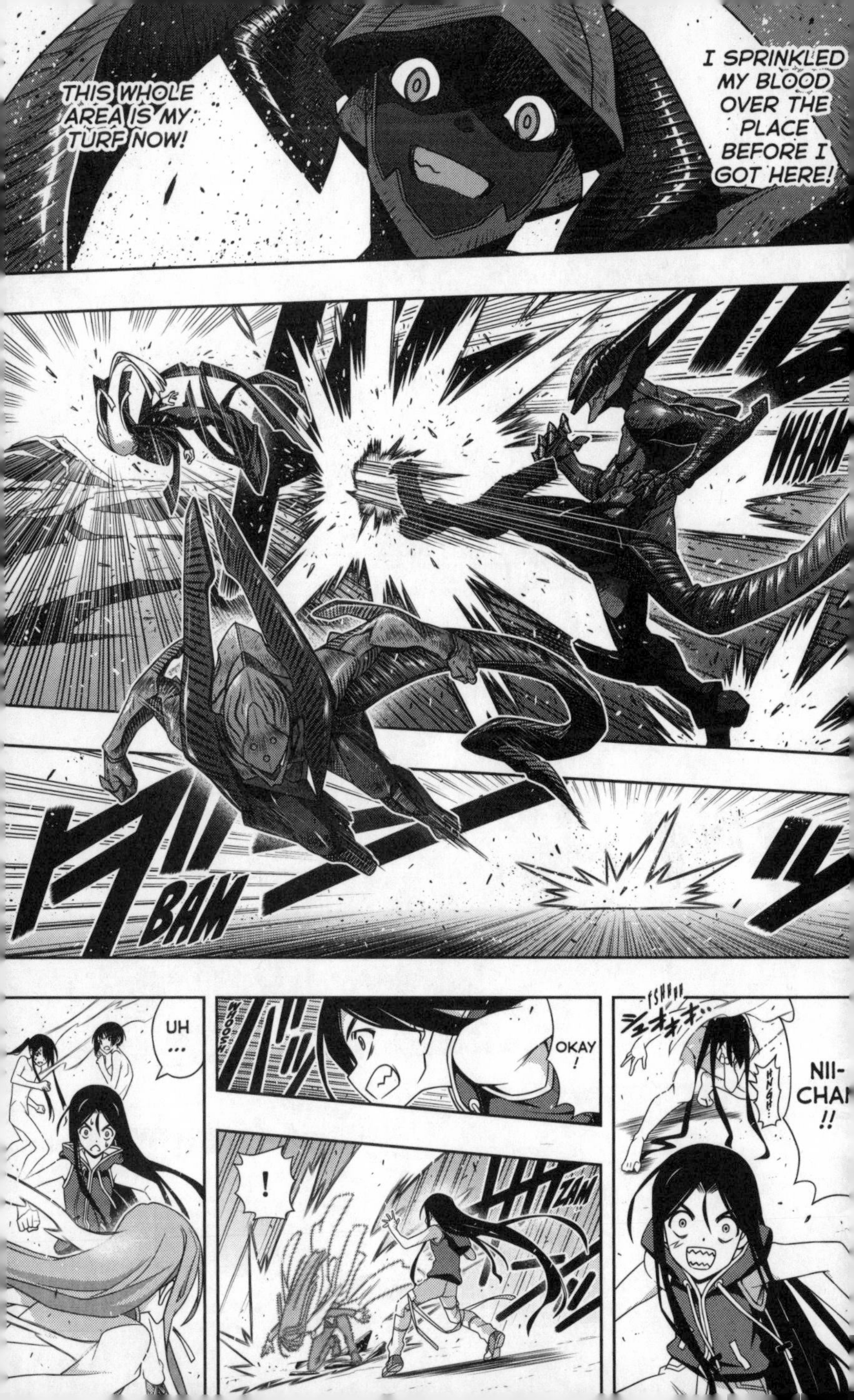
I SPRINKLED MY BLOOD OVER THE PLACE BEFORE I GOT HERE!
THIS WHOLE AREA IS MY TURF NOW!
WHAM
BAM
NII-CHAN!!
HNGH...
OKAY!
WHOOSH
!
ZAM
UH...

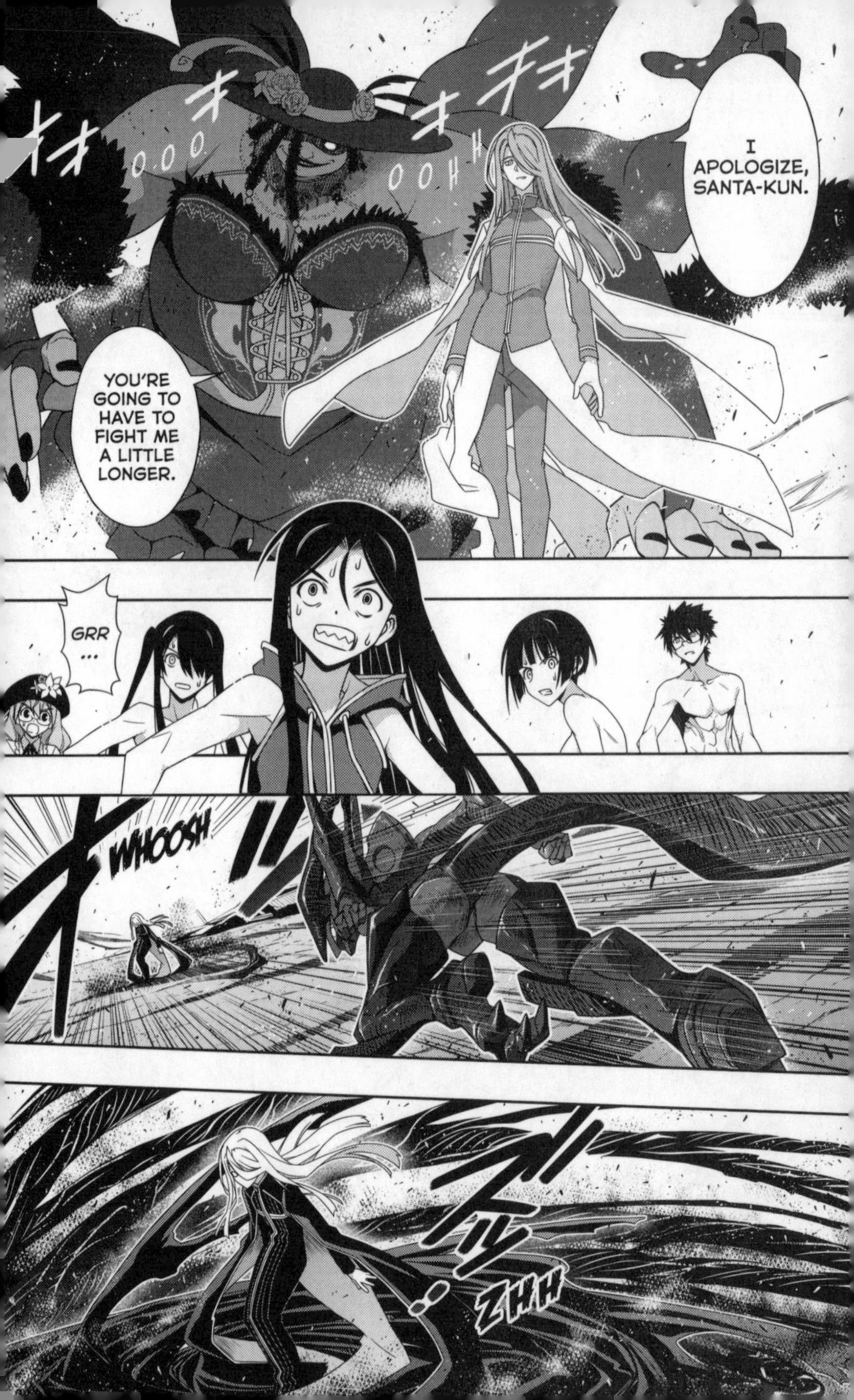
OOHH
I APOLOGIZE, SANTA-KUN.
OOO
YOU'RE GOING TO HAVE TO FIGHT ME A LITTLE LONGER.
GRR ...
WHOOSH
ZHH

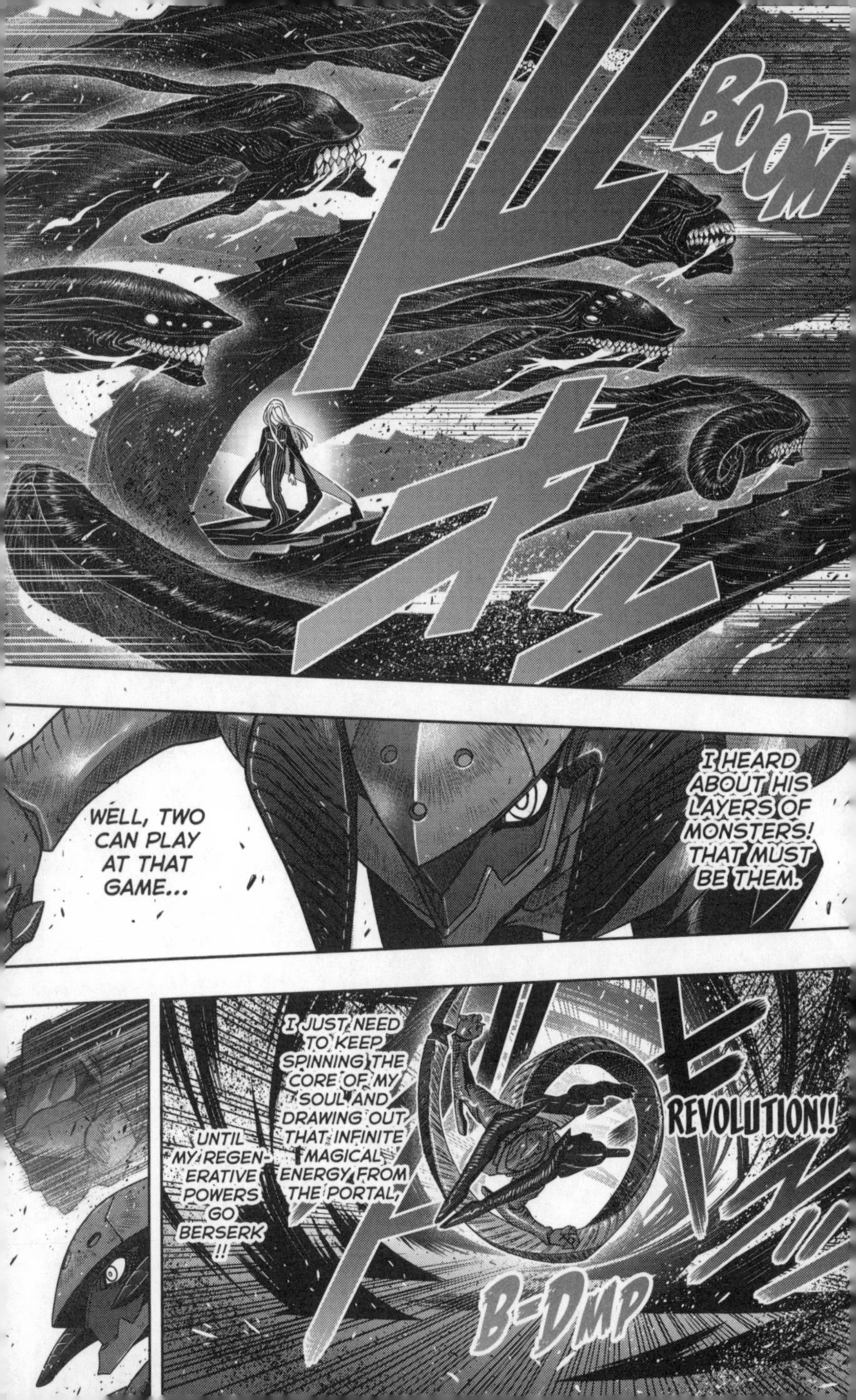
BOOM
I HEARD ABOUT HIS LAYERS OF MONSTERS! THAT MUST BE THEM.
WELL, TWO CAN PLAY AT THAT GAME...
I JUST NEED TO KEEP SPINNING THE CORE OF MY SOUL AND DRAWING OUT THAT INFINITE MAGICAL ENERGY FROM THE PORTAL,
UNTIL MY REGEN-ERATIVE POWERS GO BERSERK!!
REVOLUTION!!
B-DMP

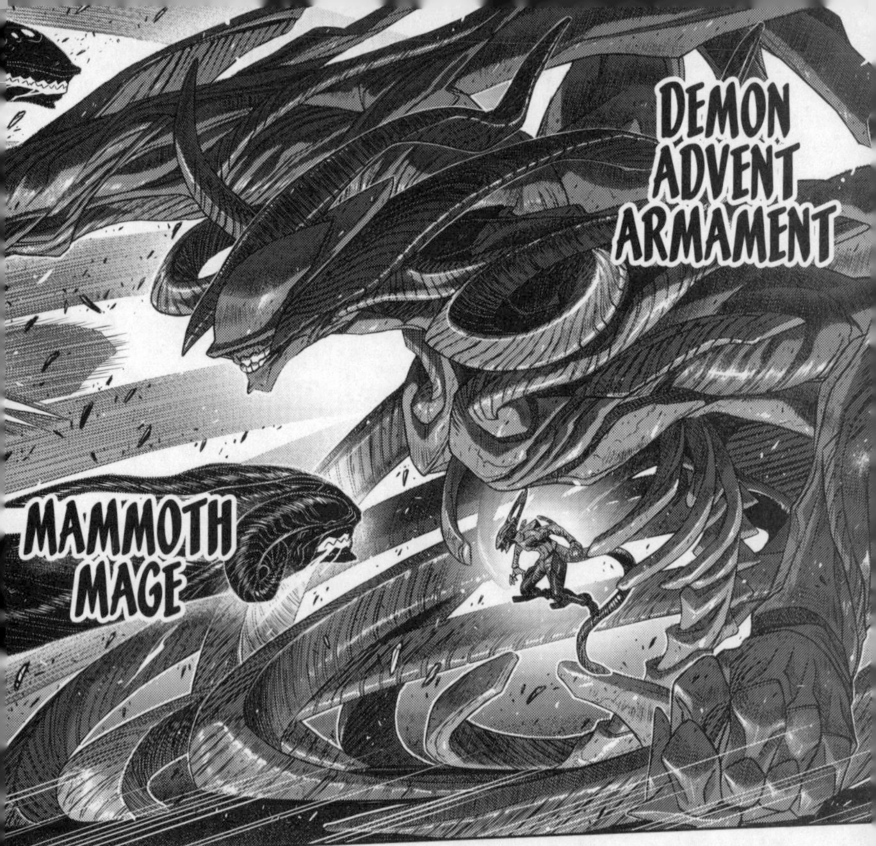
DEMON ADVENT ARMAMENT
MAMMOTH MAGE

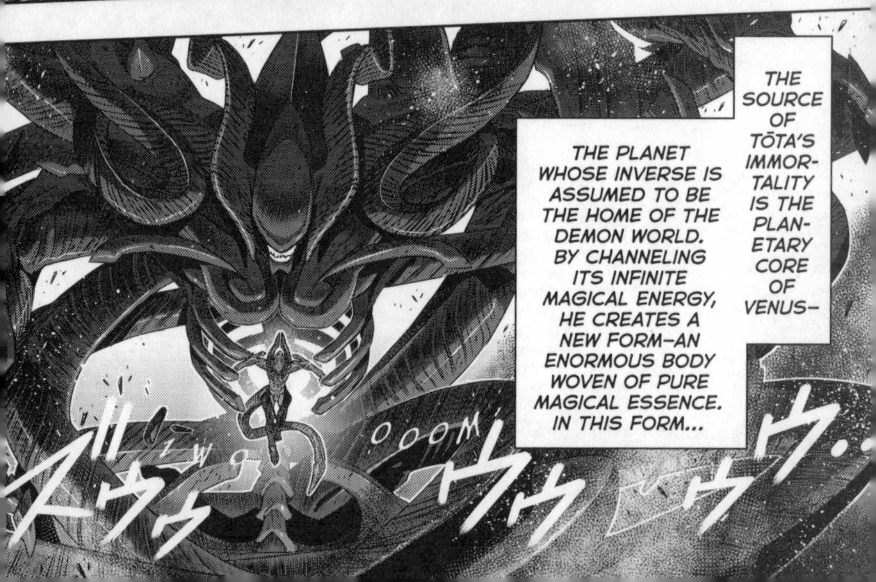
THE SOURCE OF TŌTA'S IMMORTALITY IS THE PLANETARY CORE OF VENUS–
THE PLANET WHOSE INVERSE IS ASSUMED TO BE THE HOME OF THE DEMON WORLD. BY CHANNELING ITS INFINITE MAGICAL ENERGY, HE CREATES A NEW FORM–AN ENORMOUS BODY WOVEN OF PURE MAGICAL ESSENCE. IN THIS FORM...

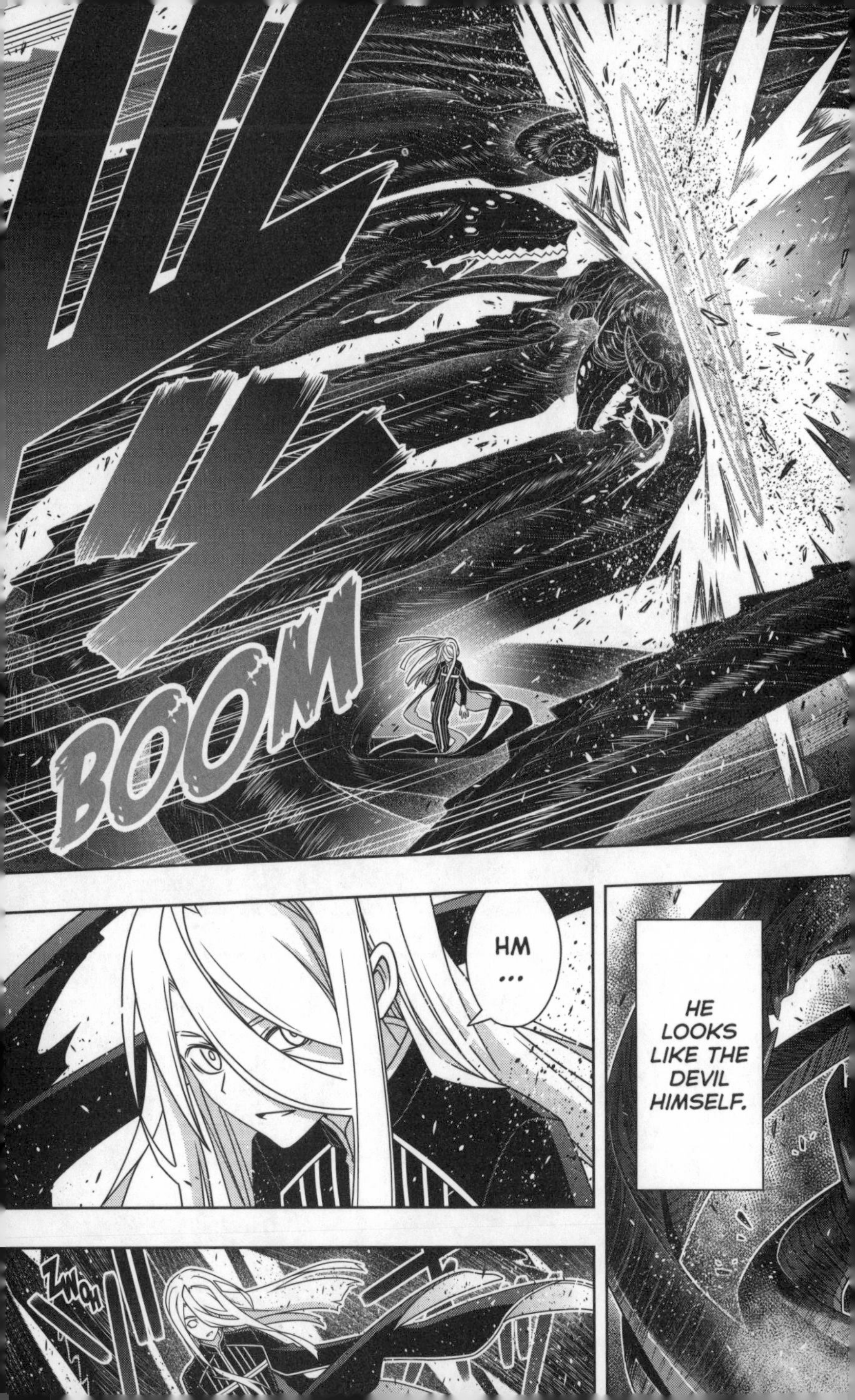
BOOM
HE LOOKS LIKE THE DEVIL HIMSELF.
HM ...
ZWOH

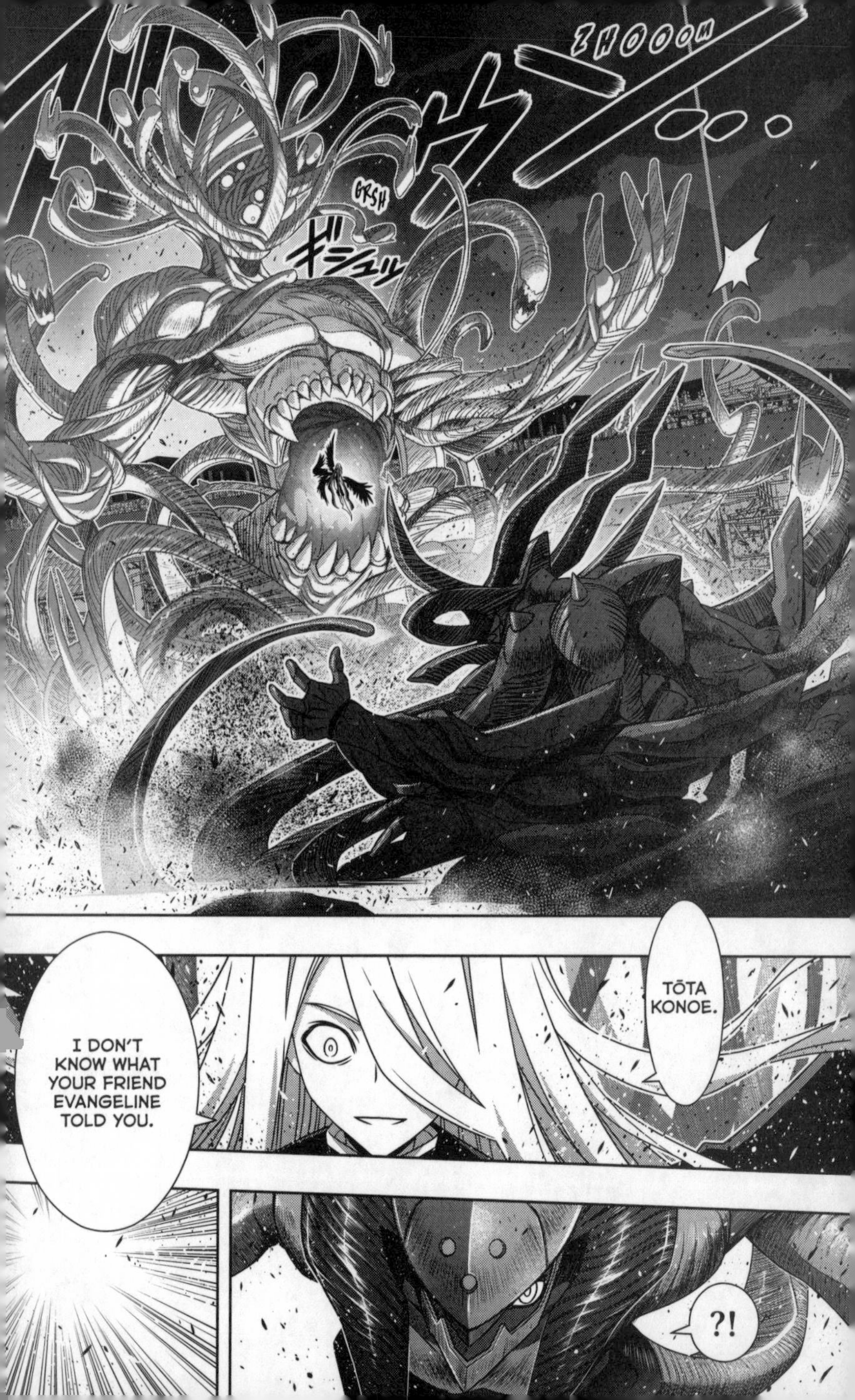
ZHOOOM
GRSH
TŌTA KONOE.
I DON'T KNOW WHAT YOUR FRIEND EVANGELINE TOLD YOU.
?!

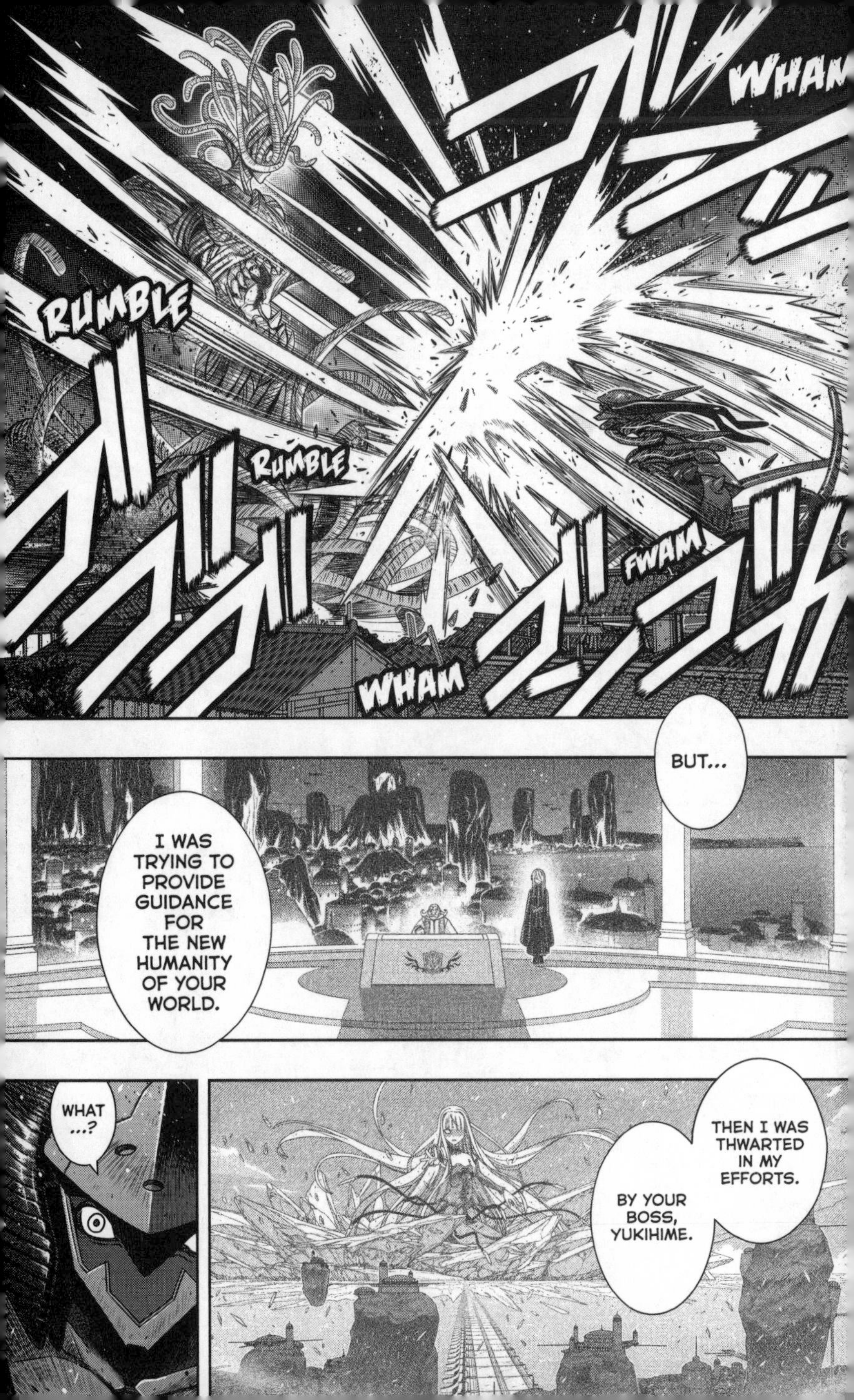
WHAM
RUMBLE
RUMBLE
FWAM
WHAM
BUT...
I WAS TRYING TO PROVIDE GUIDANCE FOR THE NEW HUMANITY OF YOUR WORLD.
THEN I WAS THWARTED IN MY EFFORTS.
BY YOUR BOSS, YUKIHIME.
WHAT ...?

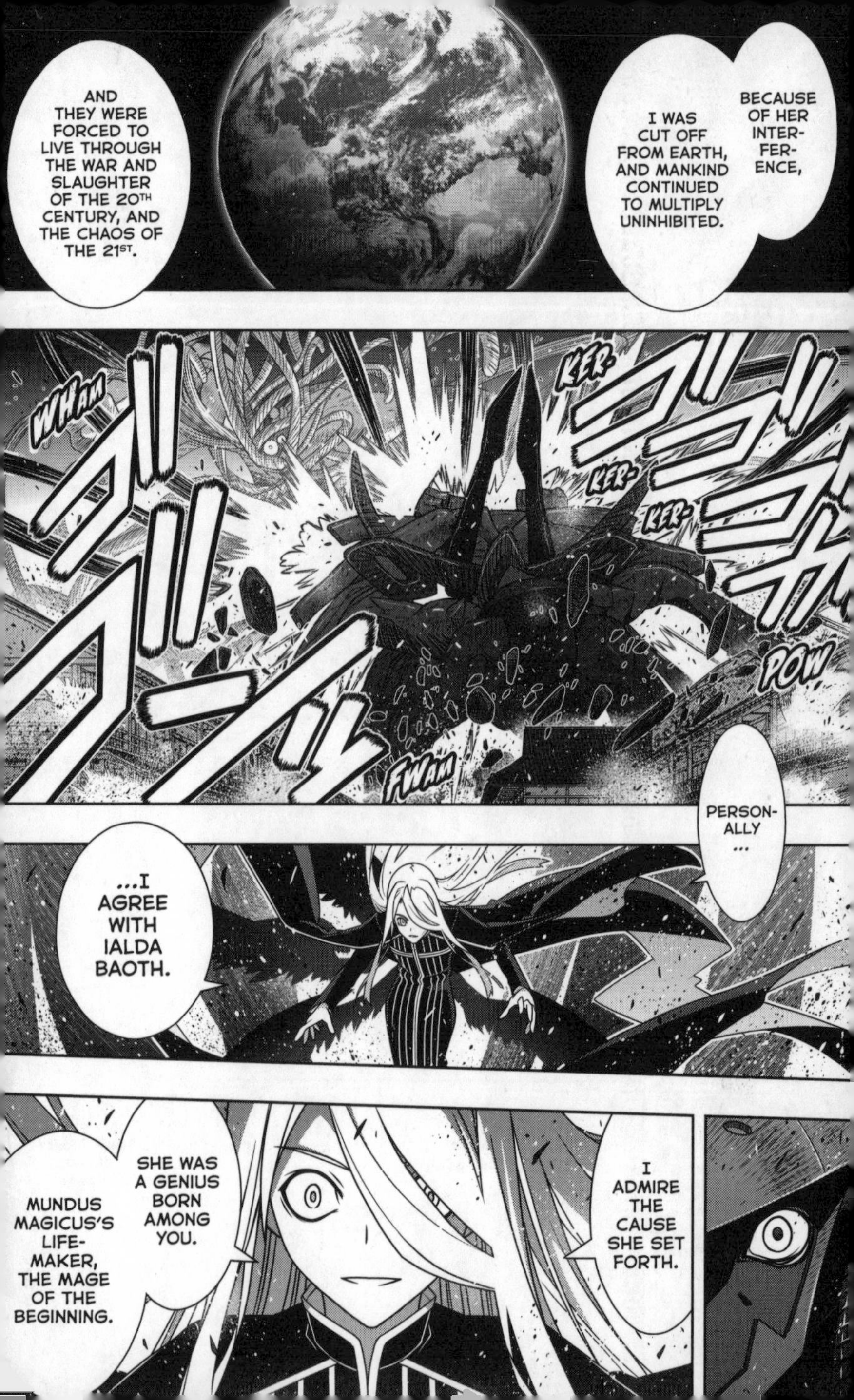
BECAUSE OF HER INTER-FER-ENCE,
I WAS CUT OFF FROM EARTH, AND MANKIND CONTINUED TO MULTIPLY UNINHIBITED.
AND THEY WERE FORCED TO LIVE THROUGH THE WAR AND SLAUGHTER OF THE 20TH CENTURY, AND THE CHAOS OF THE 21ST.
KER-
KER-
KER-
POW
WHAM
FWAM
PERSON-ALLY ...
...I AGREE WITH IALDA BAOTH.
I ADMIRE THE CAUSE SHE SET FORTH.
SHE WAS A GENIUS BORN AMONG YOU.
MUNDUS MAGICUS'S LIFE-MAKER, THE MAGE OF THE BEGINNING.

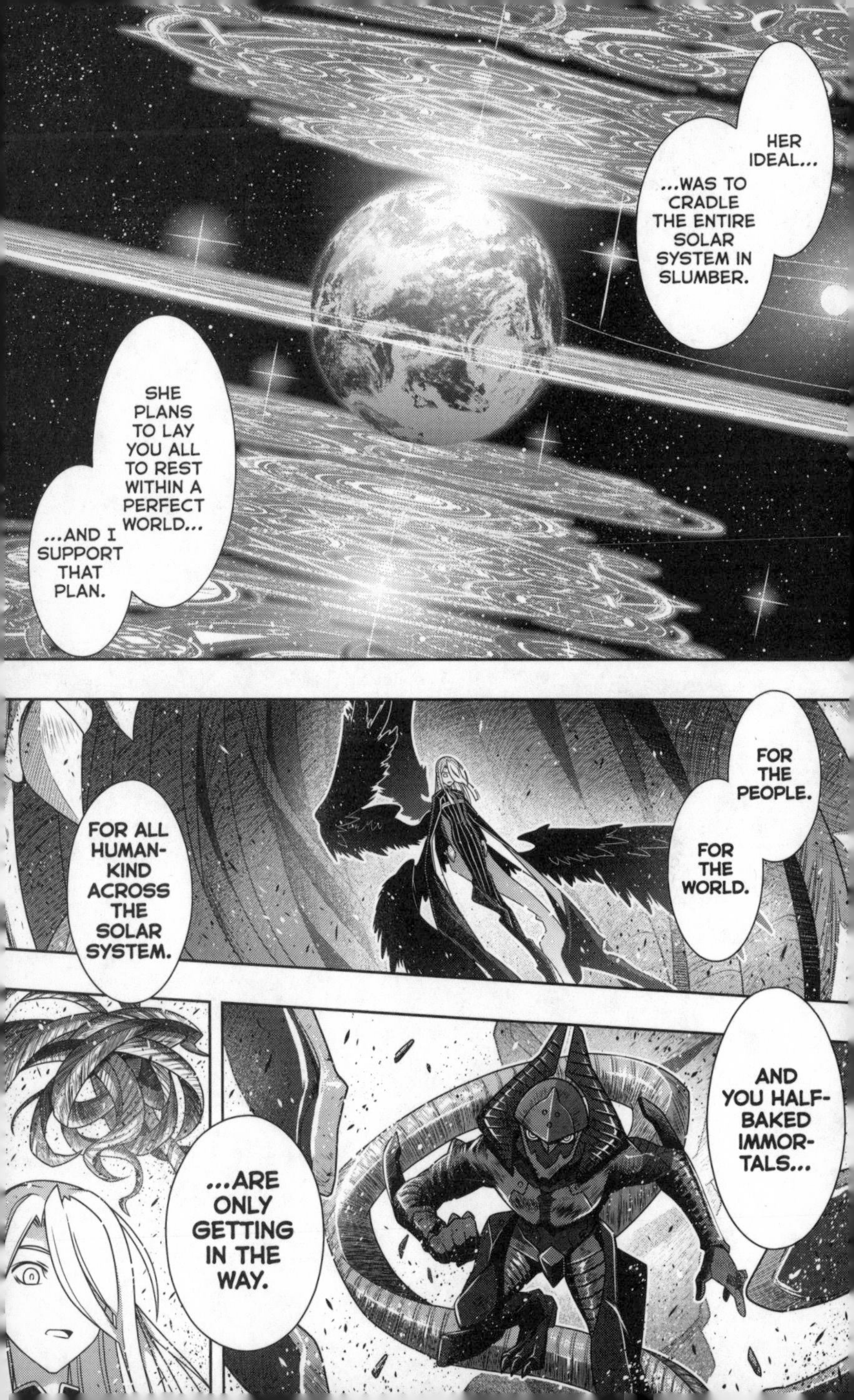
HER IDEAL...
...WAS TO CRADLE THE ENTIRE SOLAR SYSTEM IN SLUMBER.
SHE PLANS TO LAY YOU ALL TO REST WITHIN A PERFECT WORLD...
...AND I SUPPORT THAT PLAN.
FOR THE PEOPLE.
FOR THE WORLD.
FOR ALL HUMAN-KIND ACROSS THE SOLAR SYSTEM.
AND YOU HALF-BAKED IMMOR-TALS...
...ARE ONLY GETTING IN THE WAY.

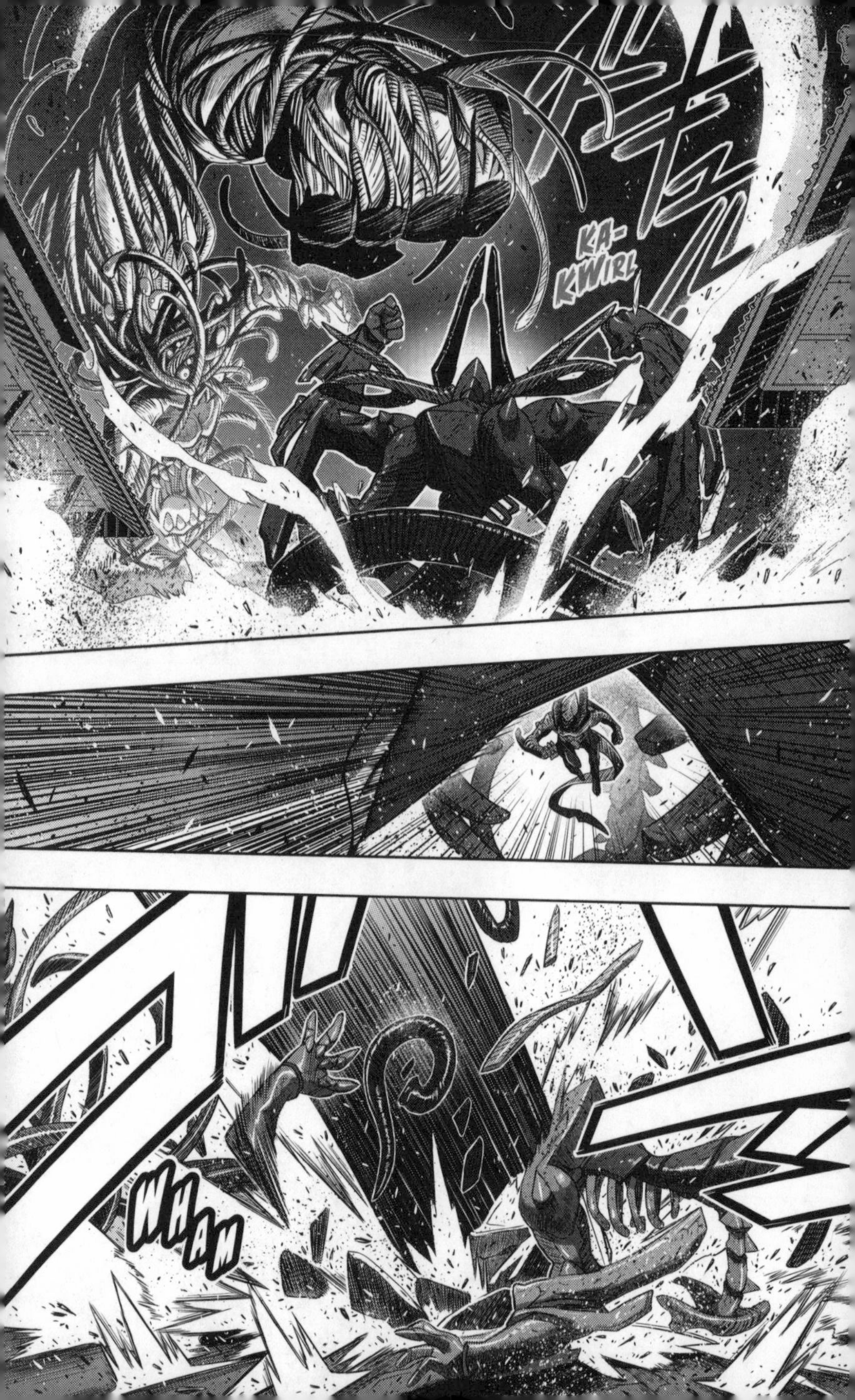
KA-KWIRL
WHAM

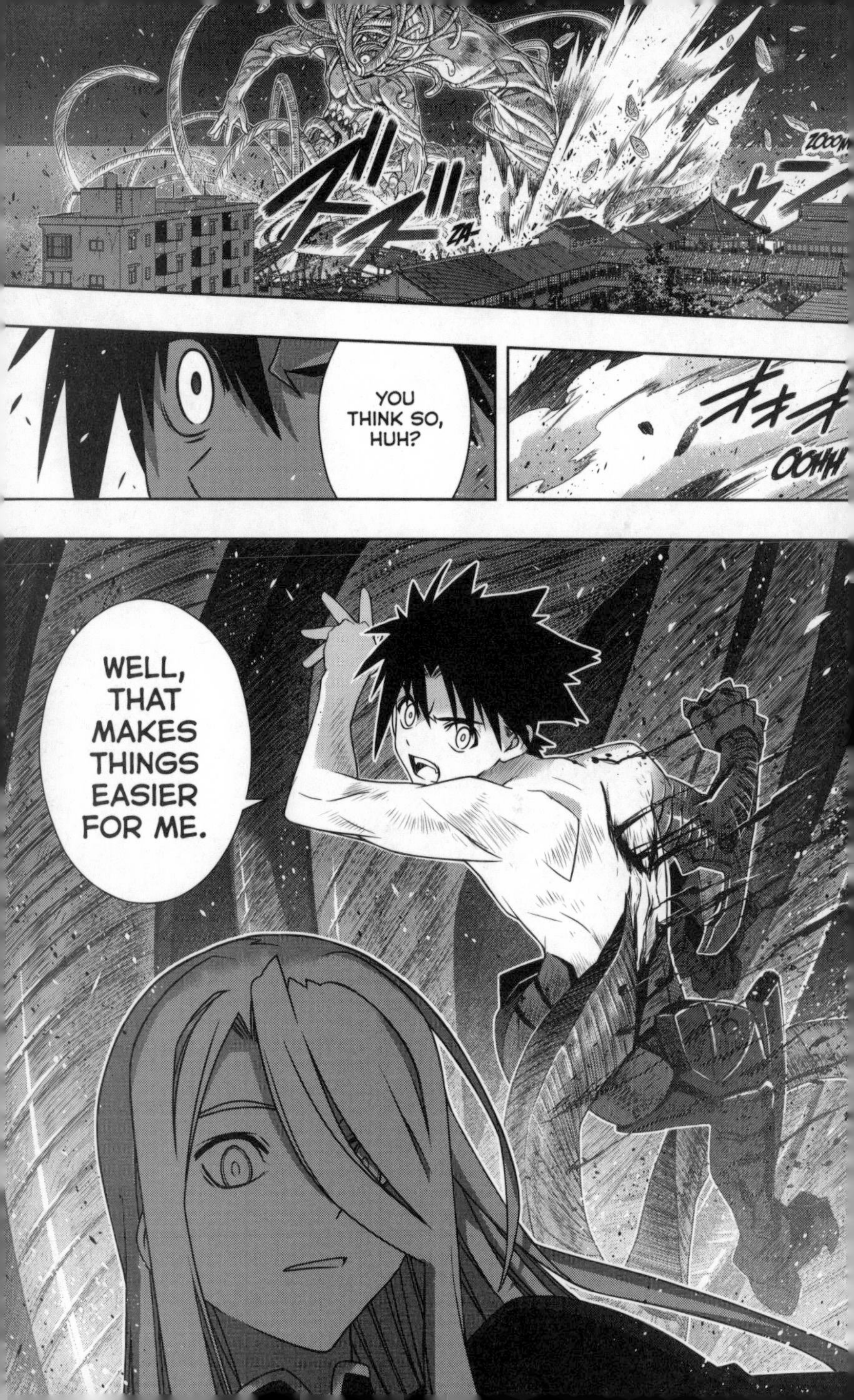
ZOOOM
ZA
OOHH
YOU THINK SO, HUH?
WELL, THAT MAKES THINGS EASIER FOR ME.

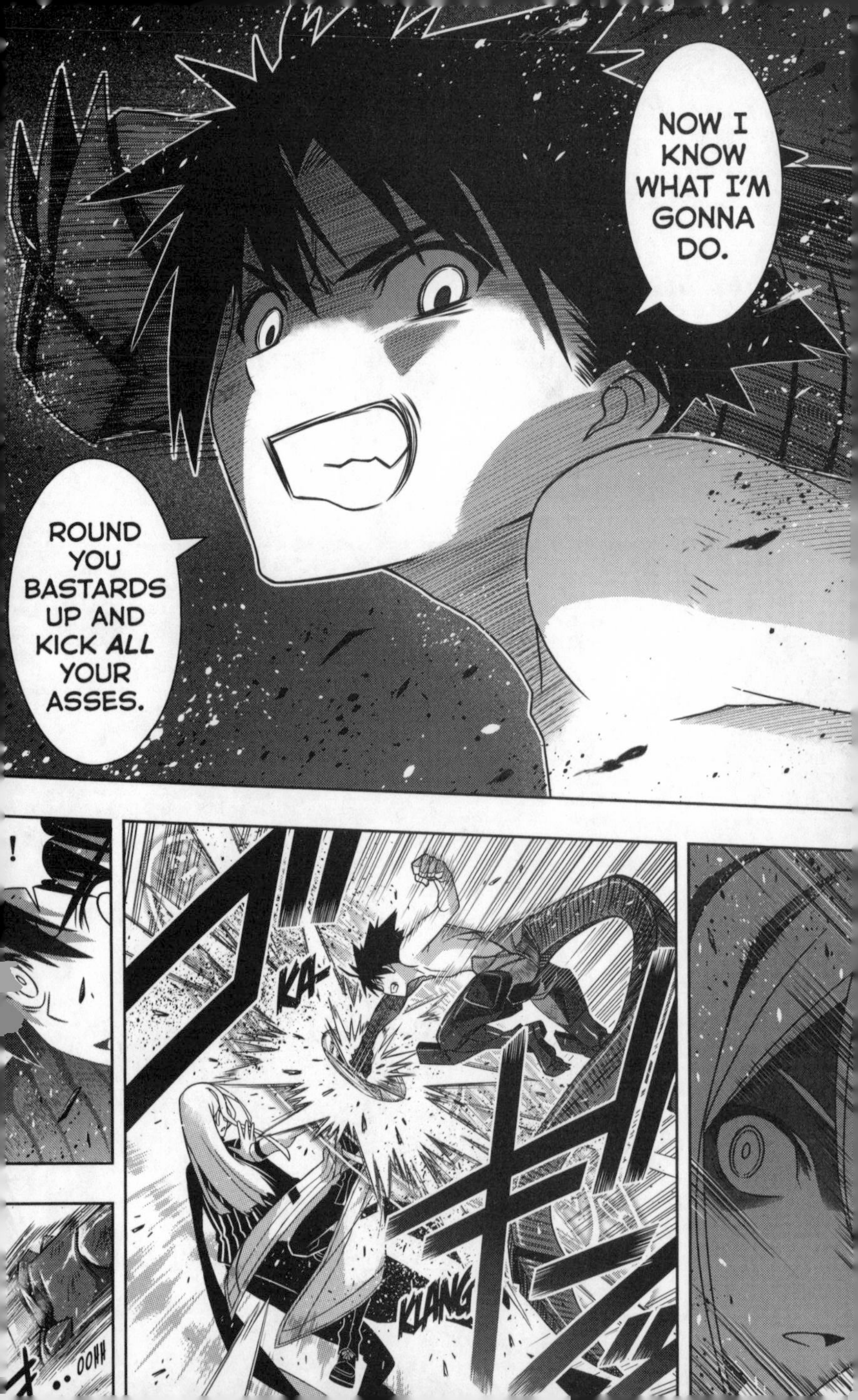
NOW I KNOW WHAT I'M GONNA DO.
ROUND YOU BASTARDS UP AND KICK *ALL* YOUR ASSES.
KA-
KLANG
!
..OOHH

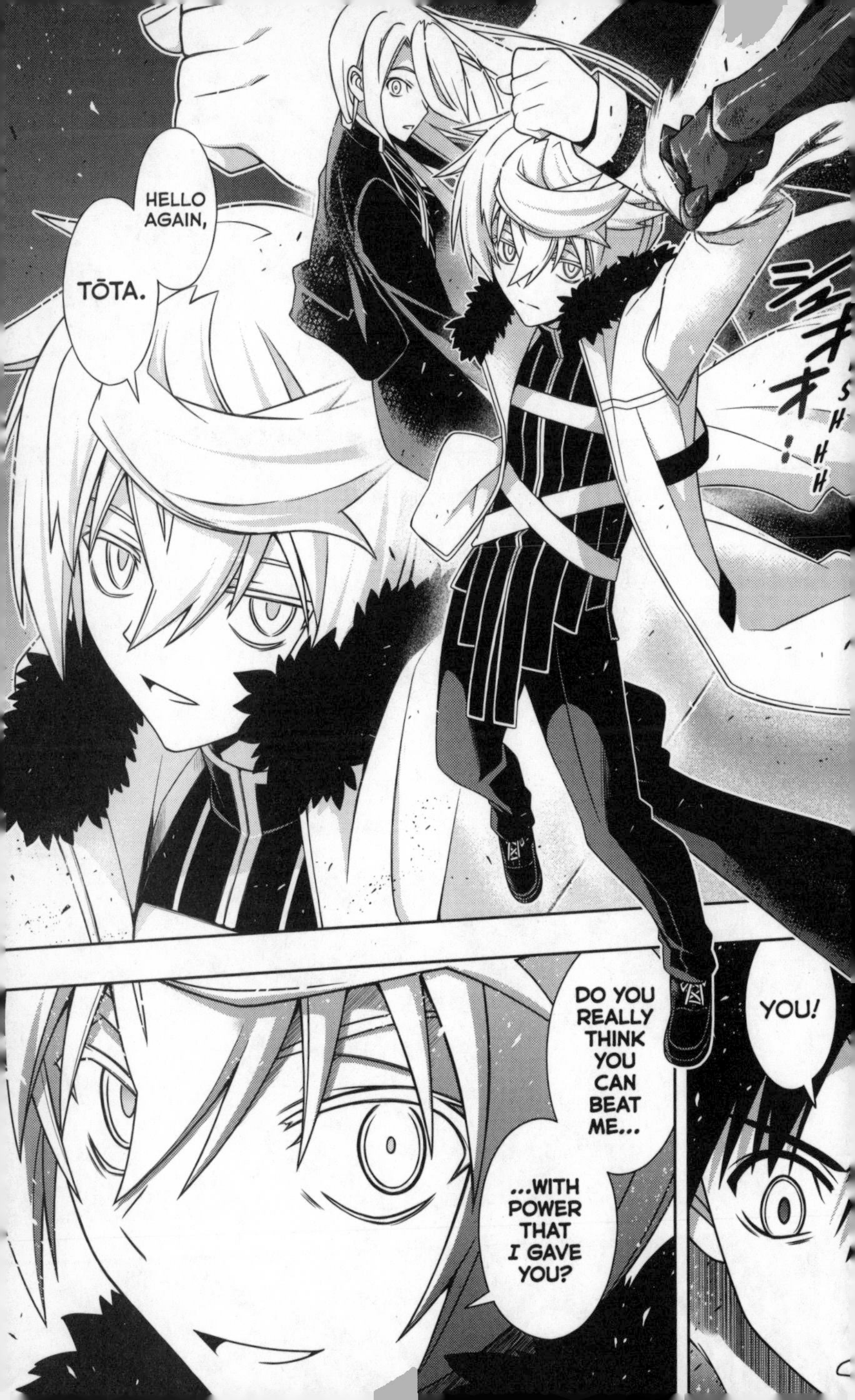
SHHHH
HELLO AGAIN,
TŌTA.
YOU!
DO YOU REALLY THINK YOU CAN BEAT ME...
...WITH POWER THAT I GAVE YOU?

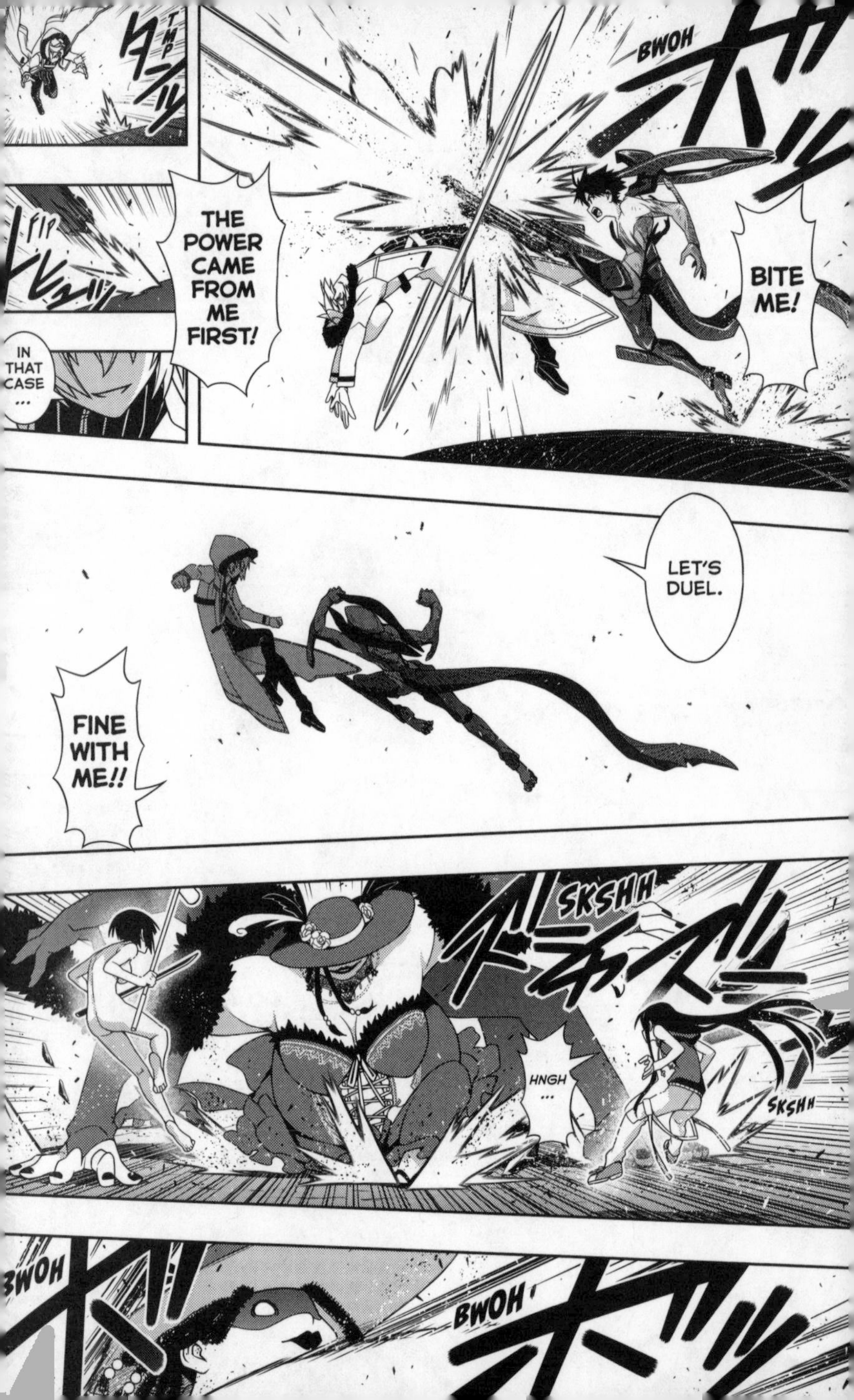
BWOH
BITE ME!
THE POWER CAME FROM ME FIRST!
TMP
FLIP
IN THAT CASE...
LET'S DUEL.
FINE WITH ME!!
SKSHH
SKSHH
HNGH...
BWOH
BWOH

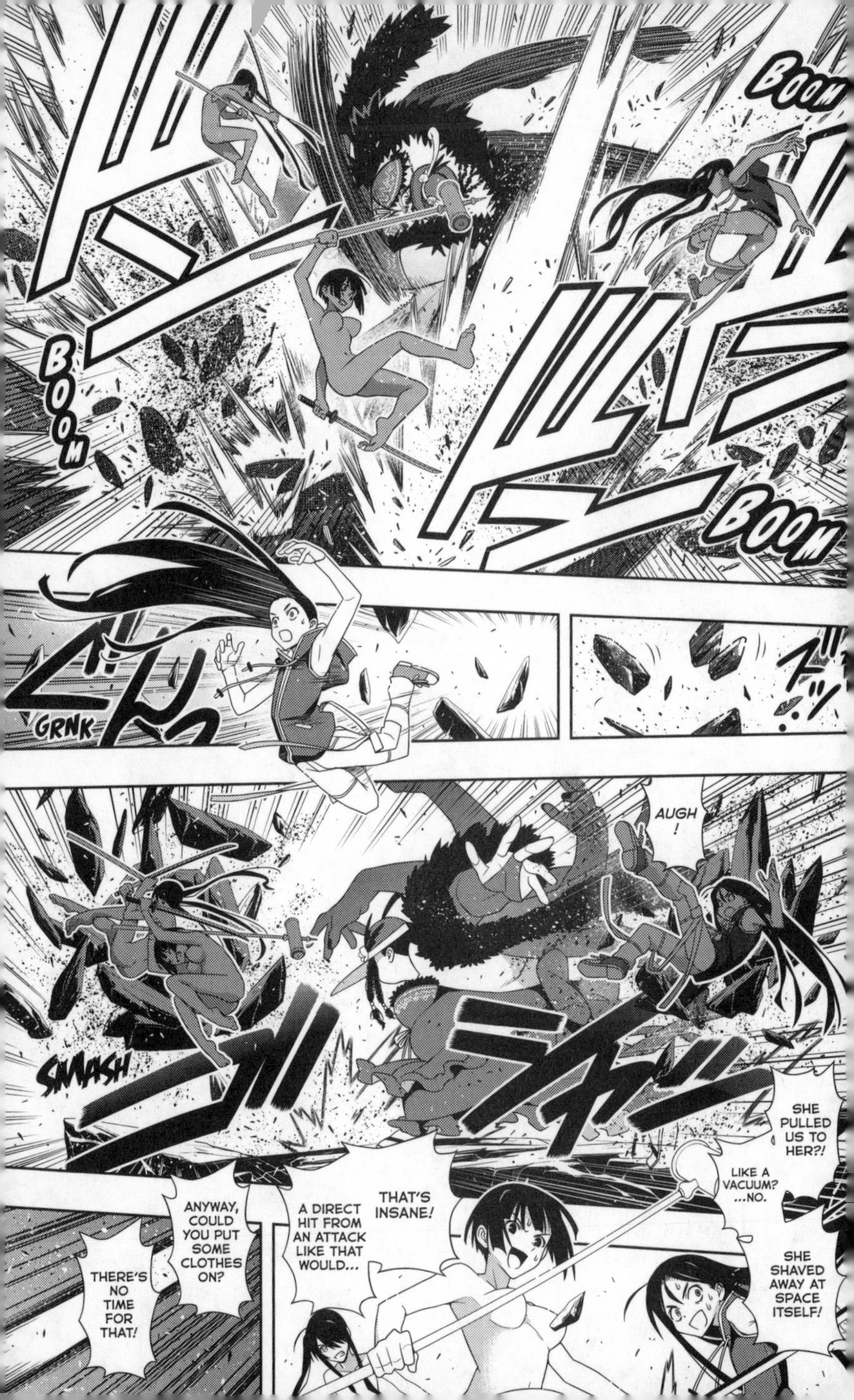
BOOM
BOOM
GRNK
AUGH!
SMASH
SHE PULLED US TO HER?!
LIKE A VACUUM? ...NO.
SHE SHAVED AWAY AT SPACE ITSELF!
THAT'S INSANE!
A DIRECT HIT FROM AN ATTACK LIKE THAT WOULD...
ANYWAY, COULD YOU PUT SOME CLOTHES ON?
THERE'S NO TIME FOR THAT!

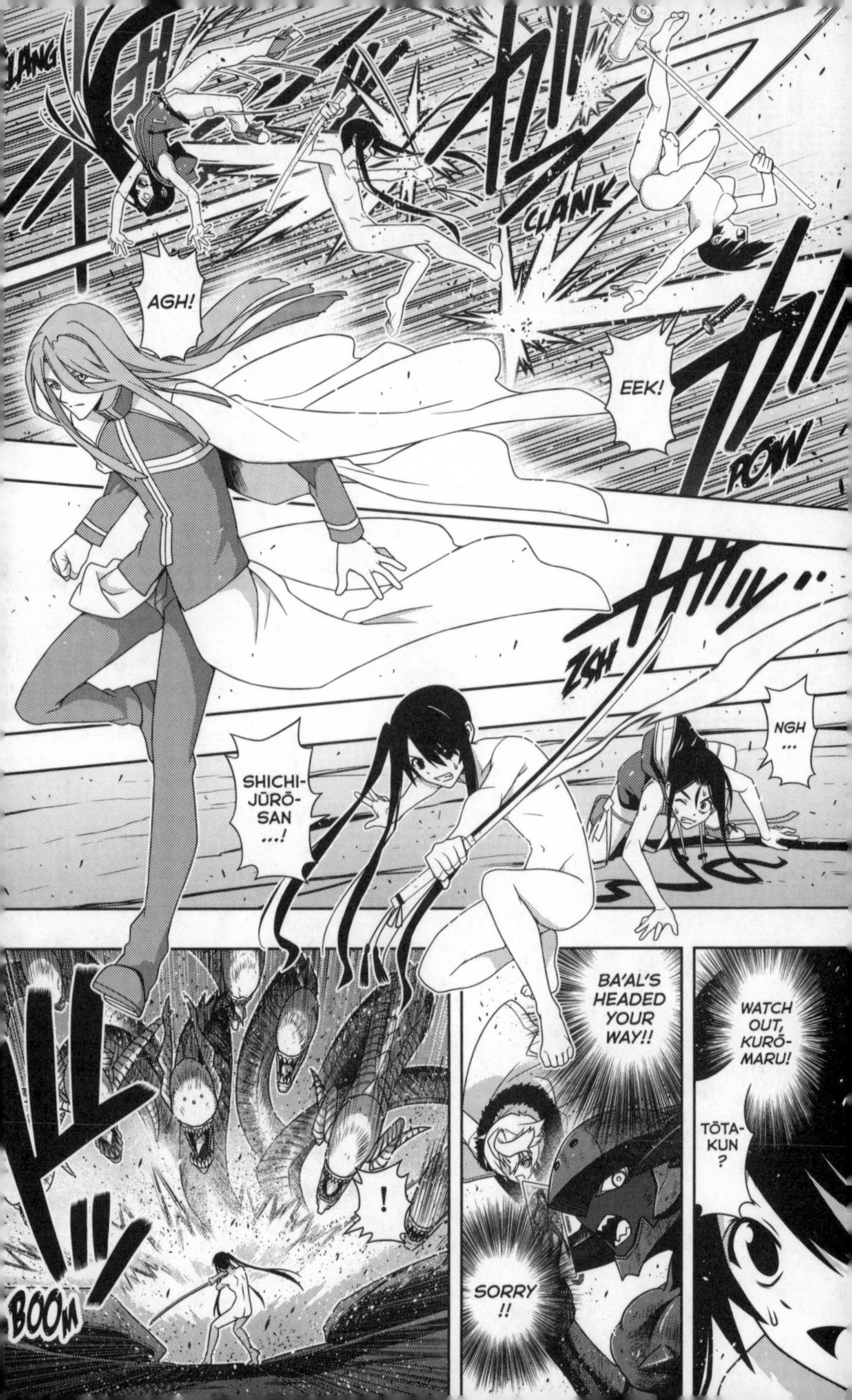
CLANK
CLANG
EEK!
AGH!
POW
ZSH
NGH...
SHICHI-JŪRŌ-SAN...!
WATCH OUT, KURŌ-MARU!
TŌTA-KUN?
BA'AL'S HEADED YOUR WAY!!
SORRY!!
!
BOOM

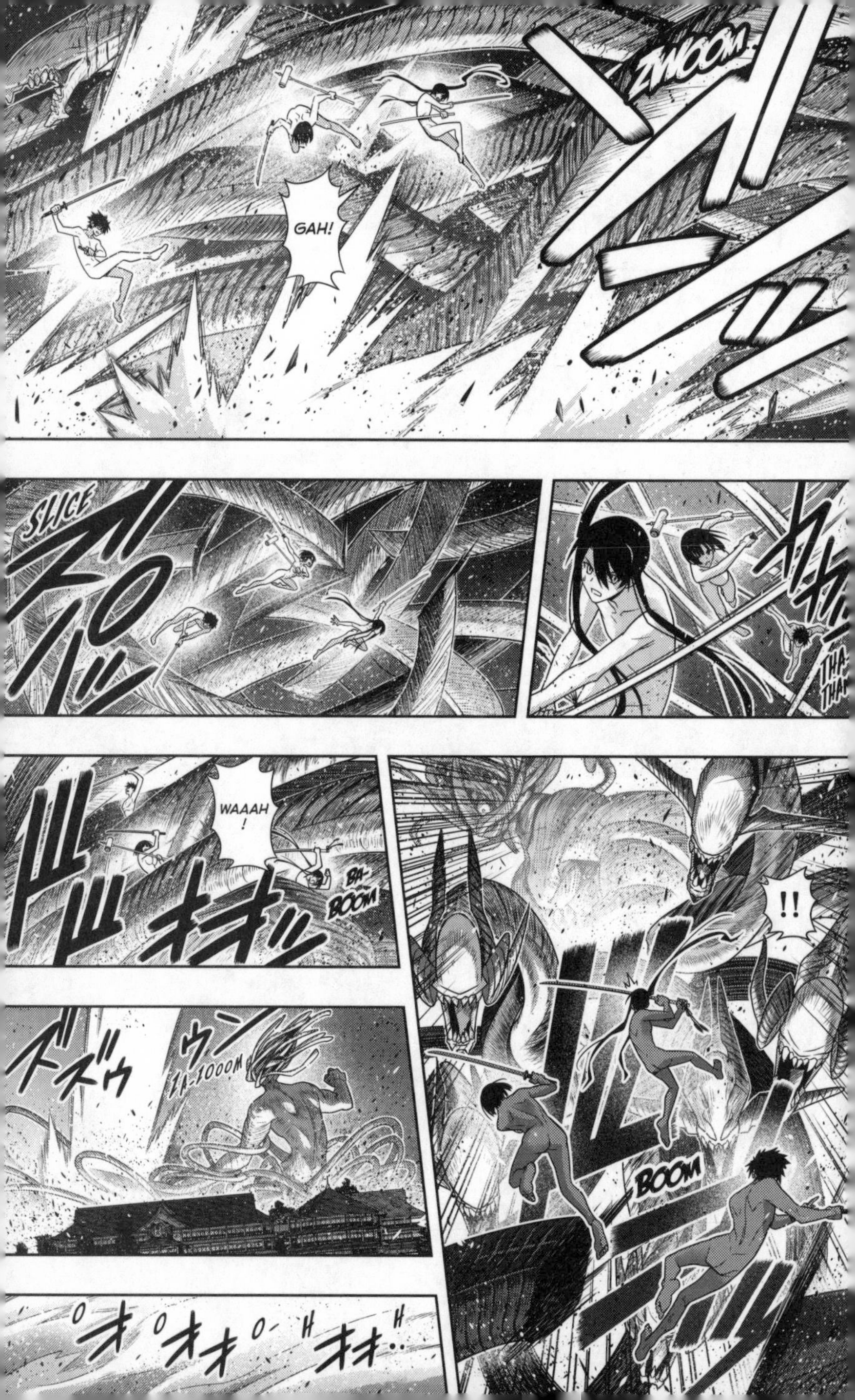
ZWOOM
GAH!
THA-
THA
SLICE
!!
BOOM
WAAAH!
BA-BOOM
ZA-TOOOM

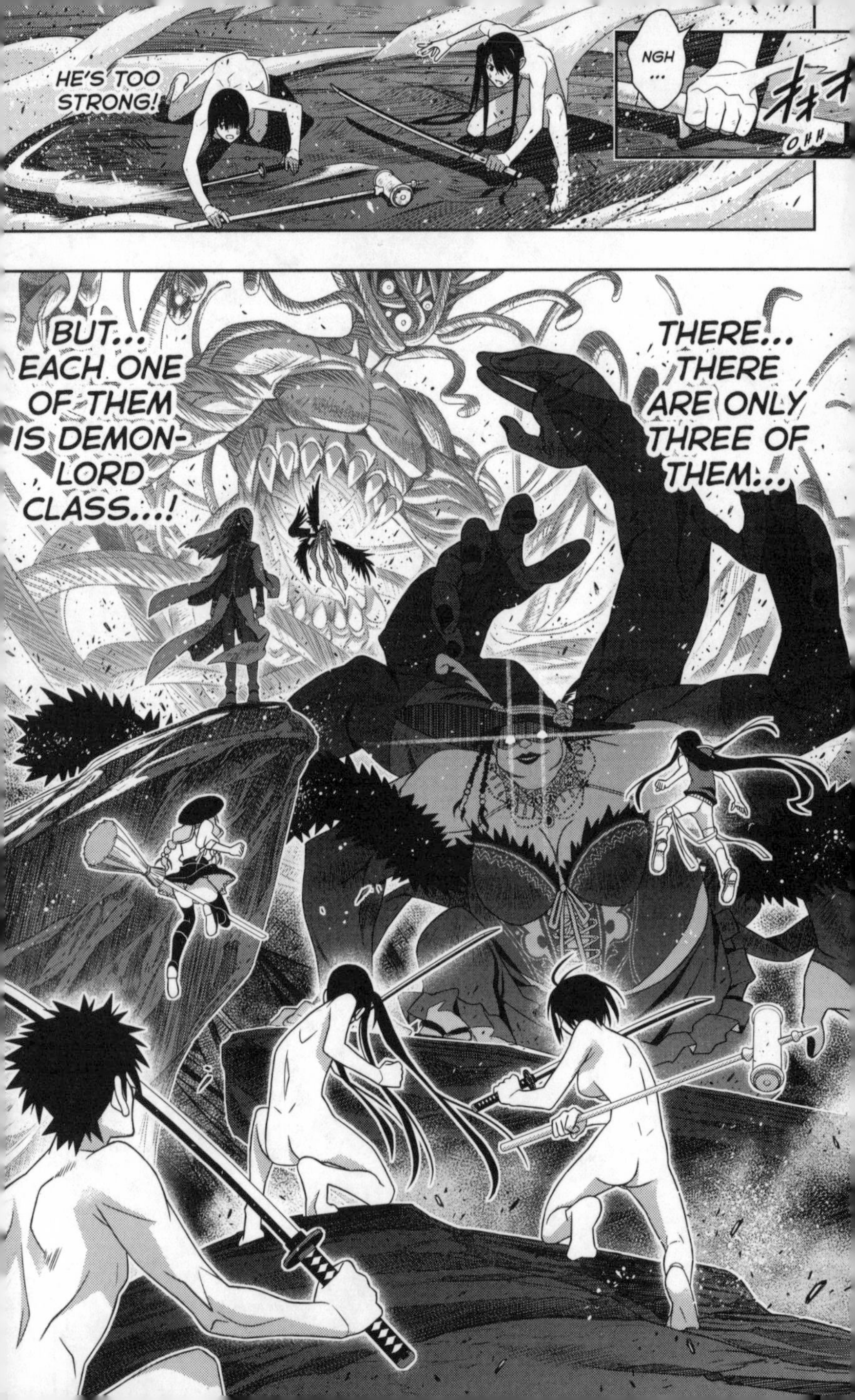
NGH ...
OHH
HE'S TOO STRONG!
THERE... THERE ARE ONLY THREE OF THEM...
BUT... EACH ONE OF THEM IS DEMON-LORD CLASS...!

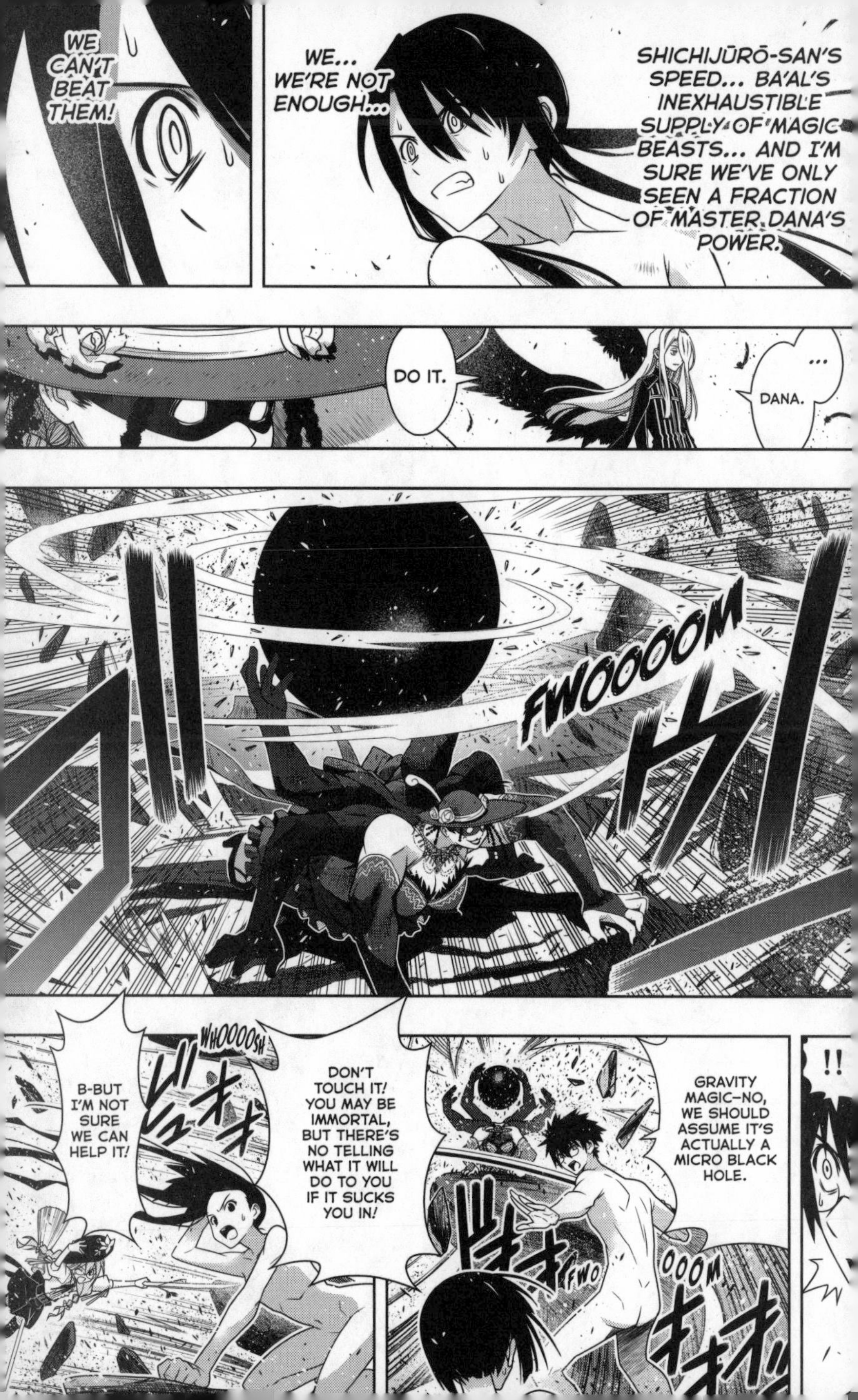
SHICHIJŪRŌ-SAN'S SPEED... BA'AL'S INEXHAUSTIBLE SUPPLY OF MAGIC BEASTS... AND I'M SURE WE'VE ONLY SEEN A FRACTION OF MASTER DANA'S POWER.
WE... WE'RE NOT ENOUGH...
WE CAN'T BEAT THEM!
... DANA.
DO IT.
FWOOOOM
!!
GRAVITY MAGIC–NO, WE SHOULD ASSUME IT'S ACTUALLY A MICRO BLACK HOLE.
DON'T TOUCH IT! YOU MAY BE IMMORTAL, BUT THERE'S NO TELLING WHAT IT WILL DO TO YOU IF IT SUCKS YOU IN!
FWO OOOM
WHOOOOSH
B-BUT I'M NOT SURE WE CAN HELP IT!

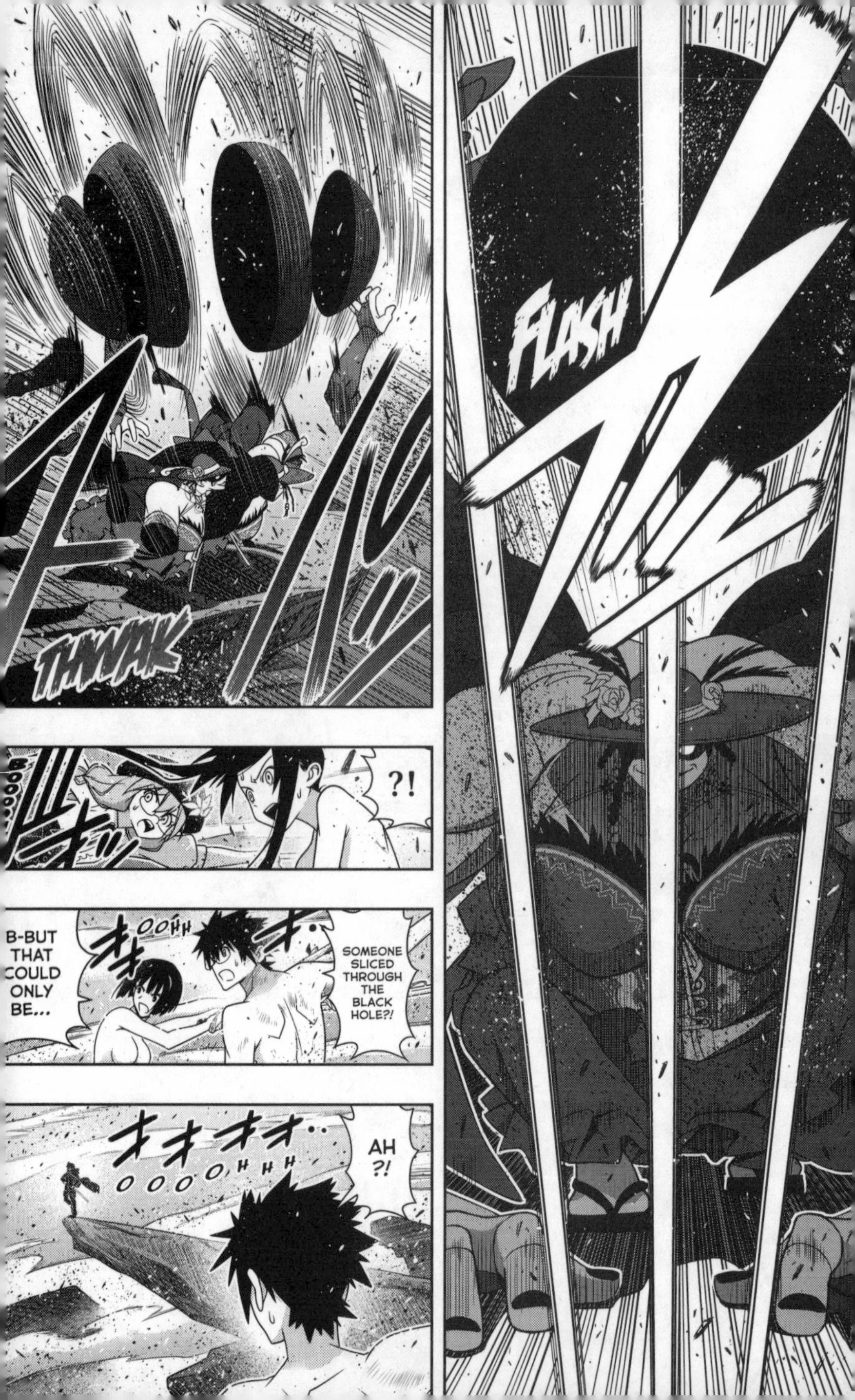
FLASH
THWAK
?!
BOOOO
SOMEONE SLICED THROUGH THE BLACK HOLE?!
OOOHH
B-BUT THAT COULD ONLY BE...
AH ?!
オオオオ
OOOOOHHH

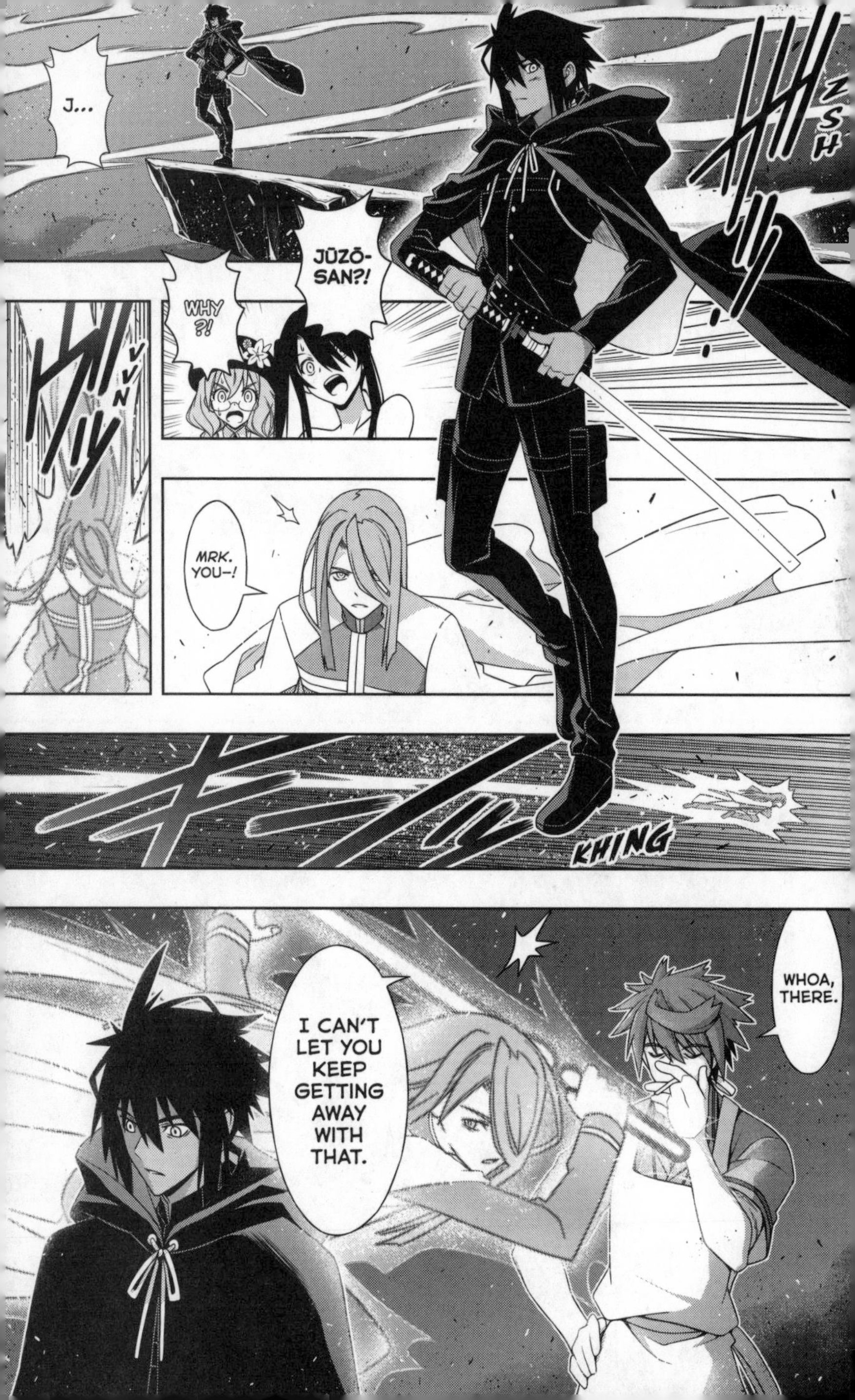
ZSH
J...
JŪZŌ-SAN?!
WHY?!
VVN
MRK. YOU—!
KHING
WHOA, THERE.
I CAN'T LET YOU KEEP GETTING AWAY WITH THAT.

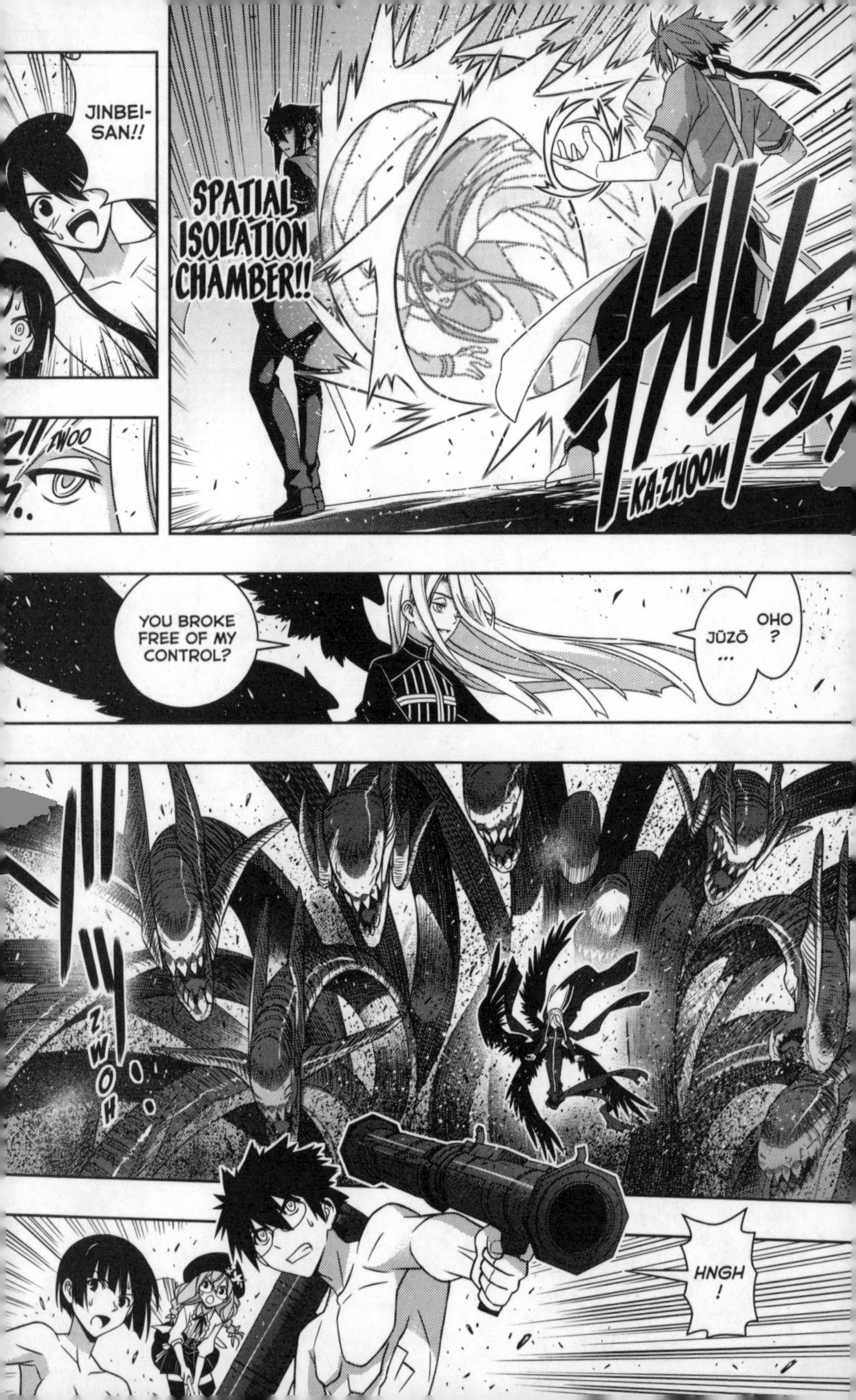
SPATIAL ISOLATION CHAMBER!!
KA-ZHOOM
JINBEI-SAN!!
ZWOO
OHO? JŪZŌ...
YOU BROKE FREE OF MY CONTROL?
ZWOOH
HNGH!

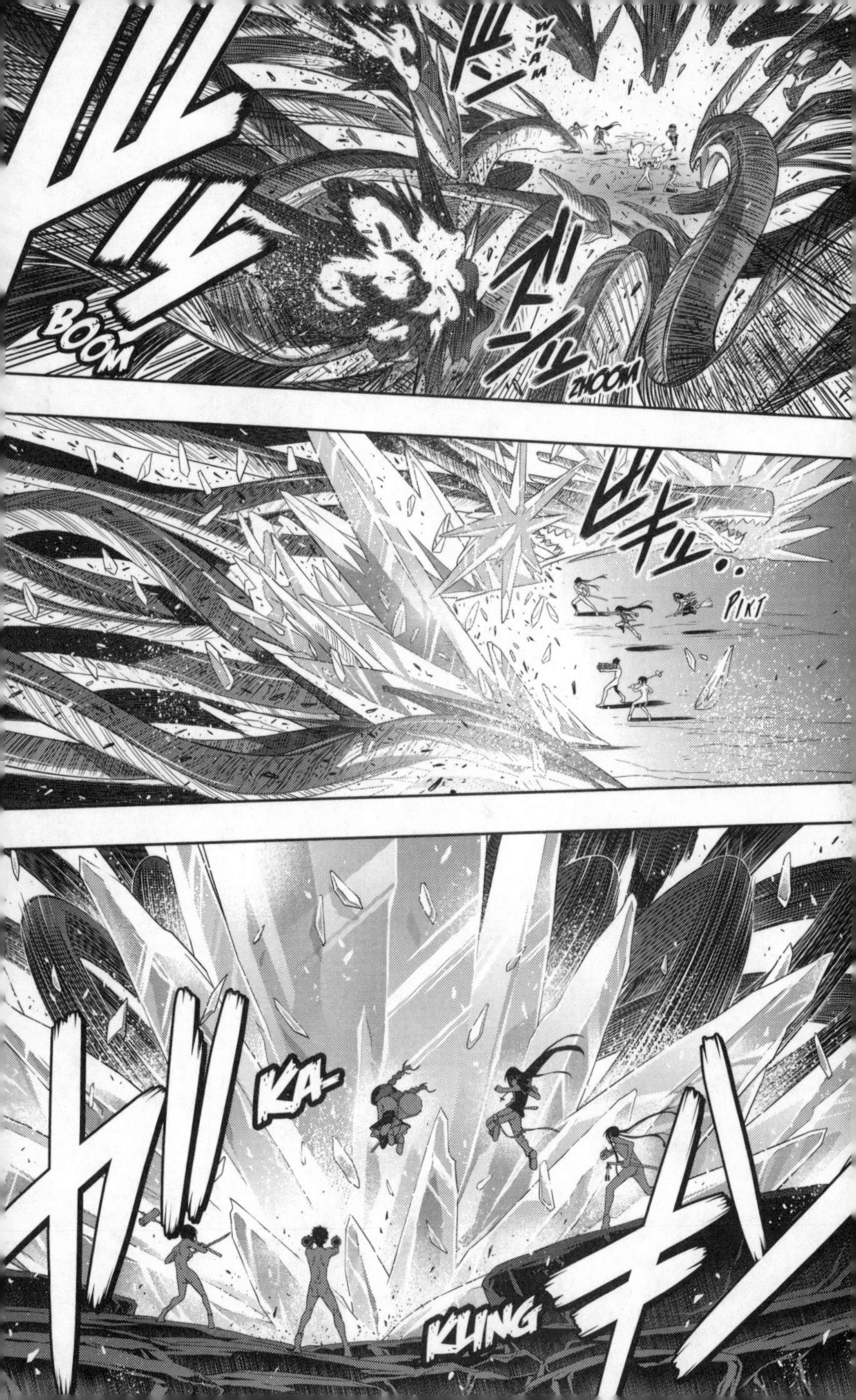
WHAM
ZHOOM
BOOM
PIKT
KA-
KLING

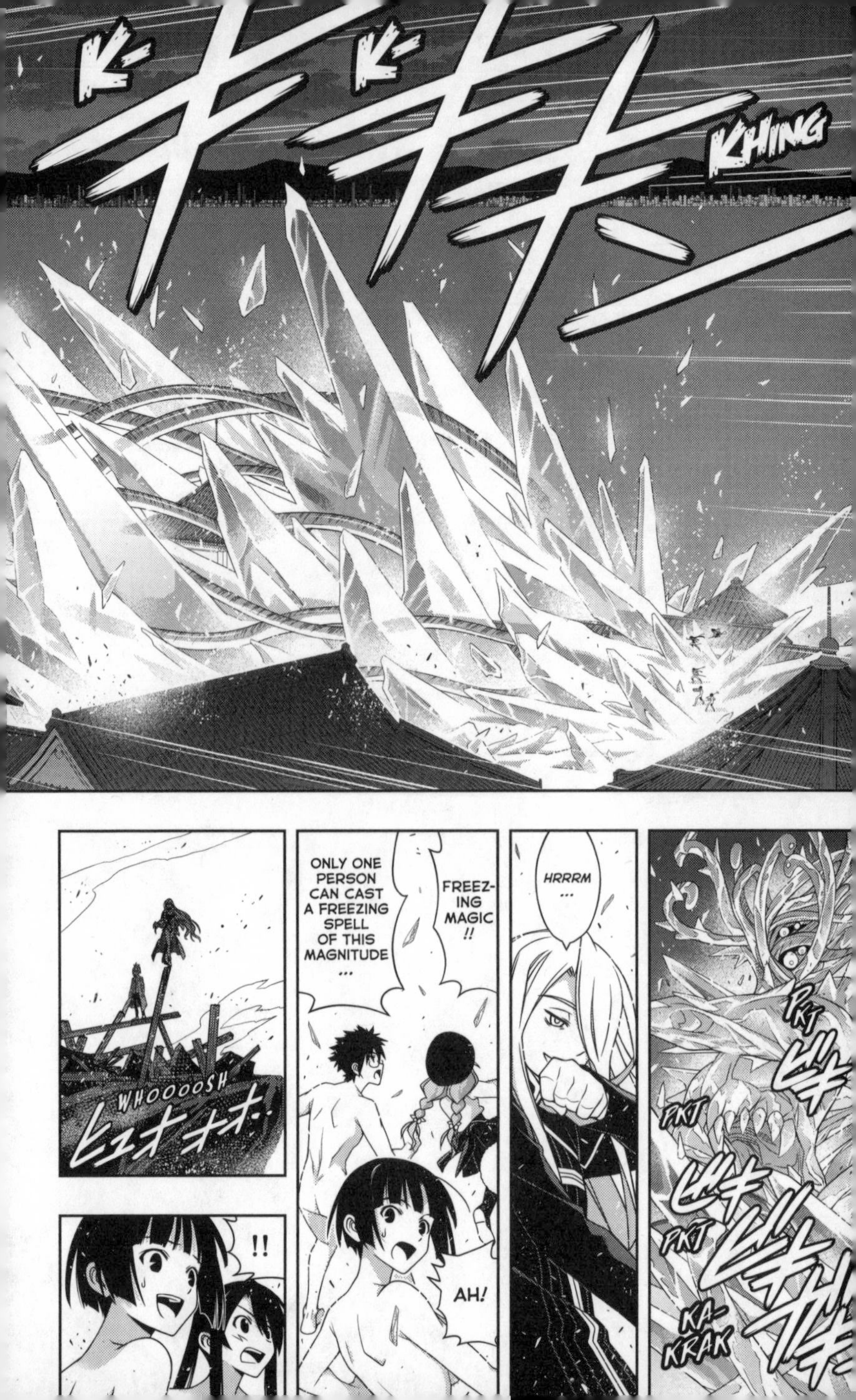
KHING
PKT
PKT
PKT
KA-KRAK
HRRRM ...
FREEZ-ING MAGIC !!
ONLY ONE PERSON CAN CAST A FREEZING SPELL OF THIS MAGNITUDE ...
AH!
WHOOOOSH
!!

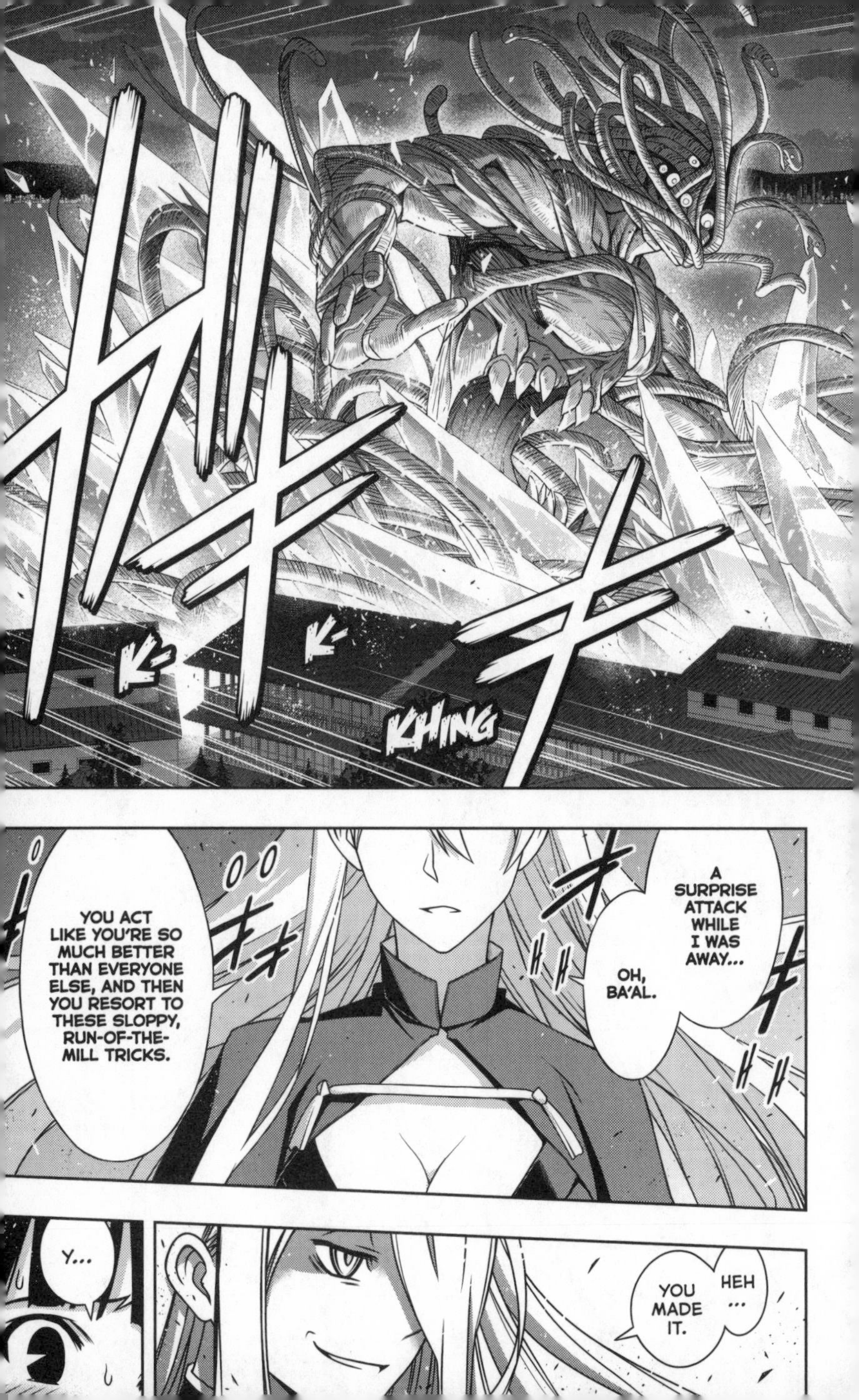
KHING
A SURPRISE ATTACK WHILE I WAS AWAY...
OH, BA'AL.
YOU ACT LIKE YOU'RE SO MUCH BETTER THAN EVERYONE ELSE, AND THEN YOU RESORT TO THESE SLOPPY, RUN-OF-THE-MILL TRICKS.
HEH...
YOU MADE IT.
Y...

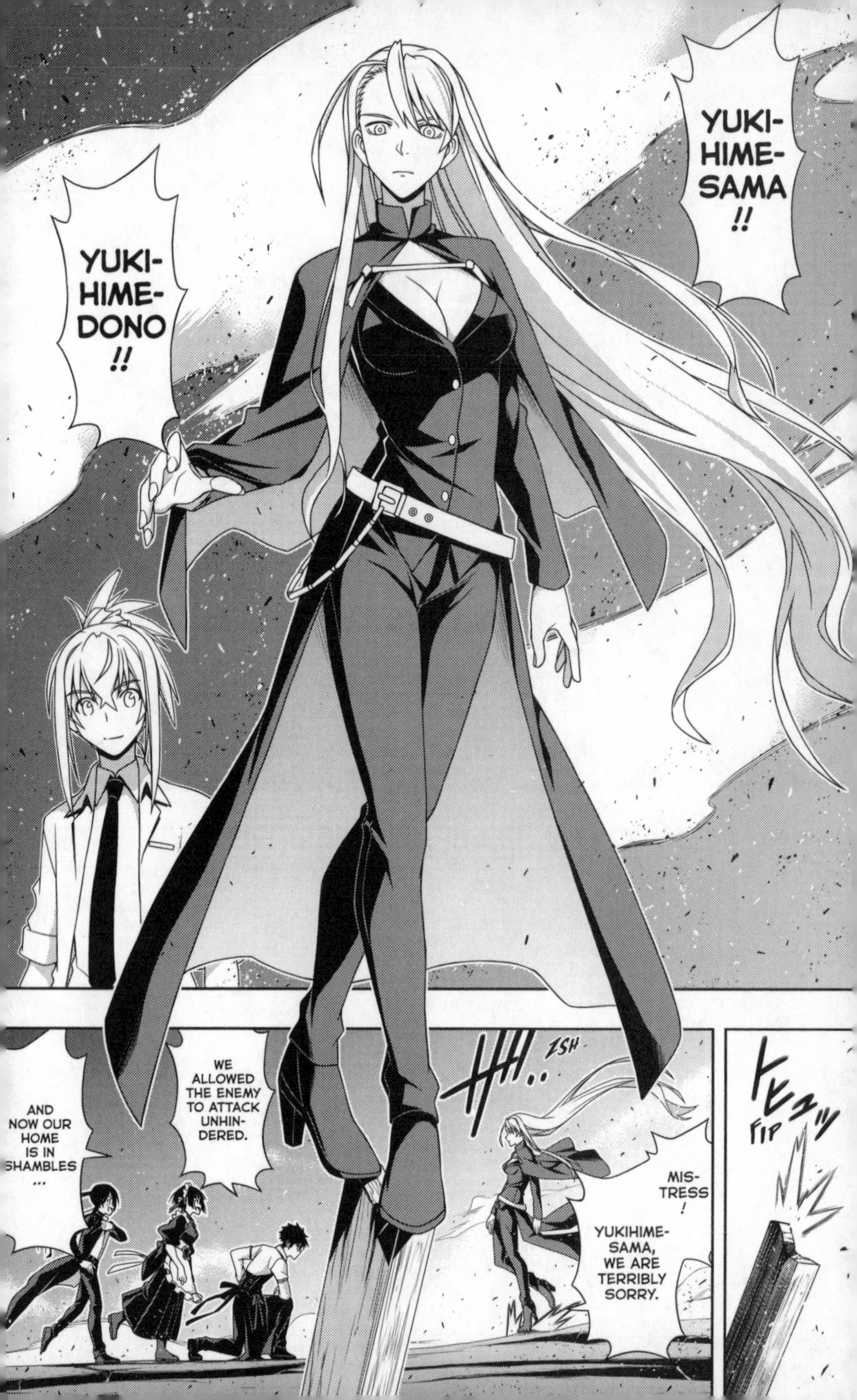
YUKI-HIME-SAMA!!
YUKI-HIME-DONO!!
FIP
ZSH
MIS-TRESS!
YUKIHIME-SAMA, WE ARE TERRIBLY SORRY.
WE ALLOWED THE ENEMY TO ATTACK UNHIN-DERED.
AND NOW OUR HOME IS IN SHAMBLES...

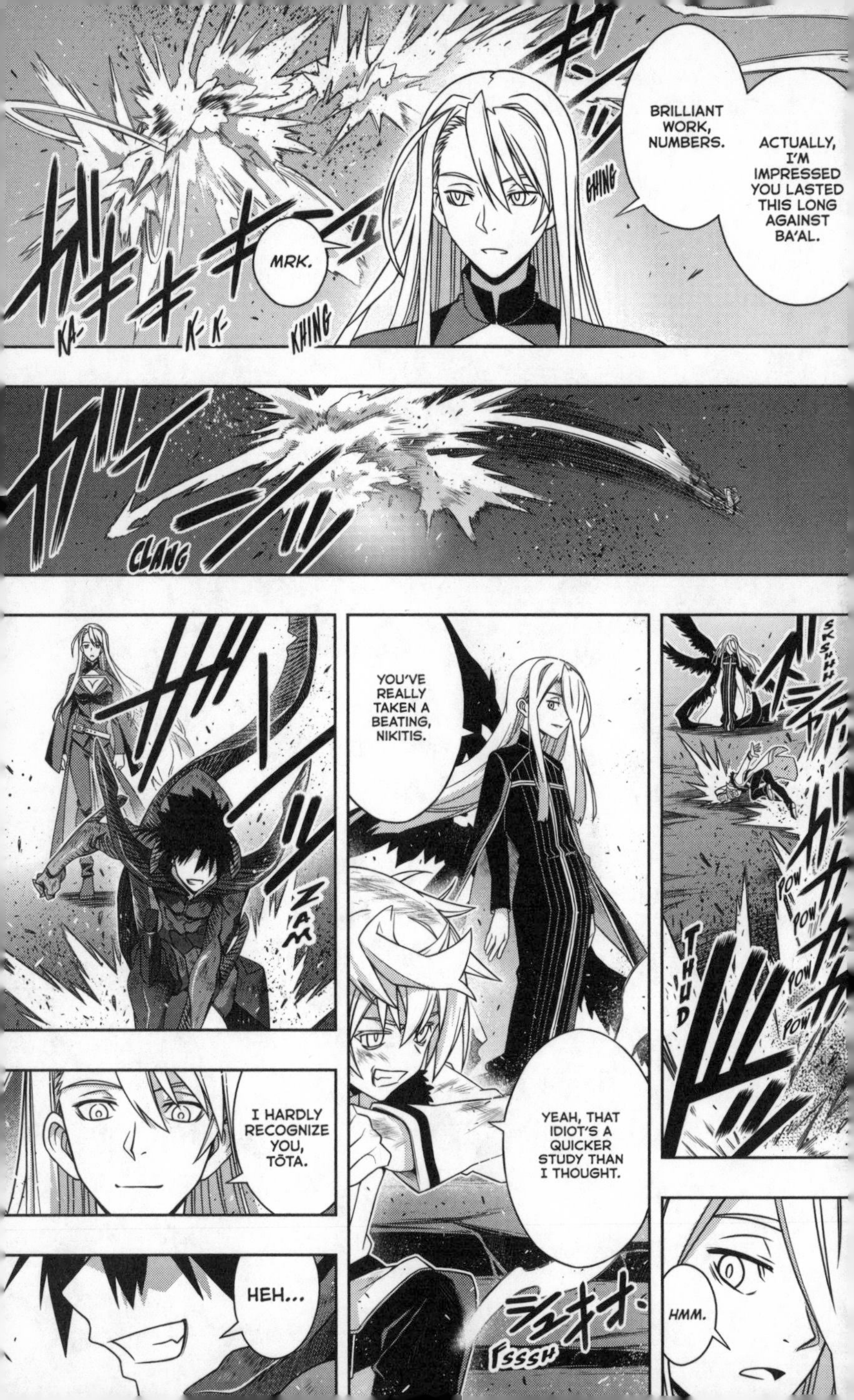
BRILLIANT WORK, NUMBERS.
ACTUALLY, I'M IMPRESSED YOU LASTED THIS LONG AGAINST BA'AL.
GHING
MRK.
KA-K-K-KHING
CLANG
SKSHHH
POW POW POW POW POW
THUD
HMM.
YOU'VE REALLY TAKEN A BEATING, NIKITIS.
YEAH, THAT IDIOT'S A QUICKER STUDY THAN I THOUGHT.
FSSSH
ZAM
I HARDLY RECOGNIZE YOU, TŌTA.
HEH...

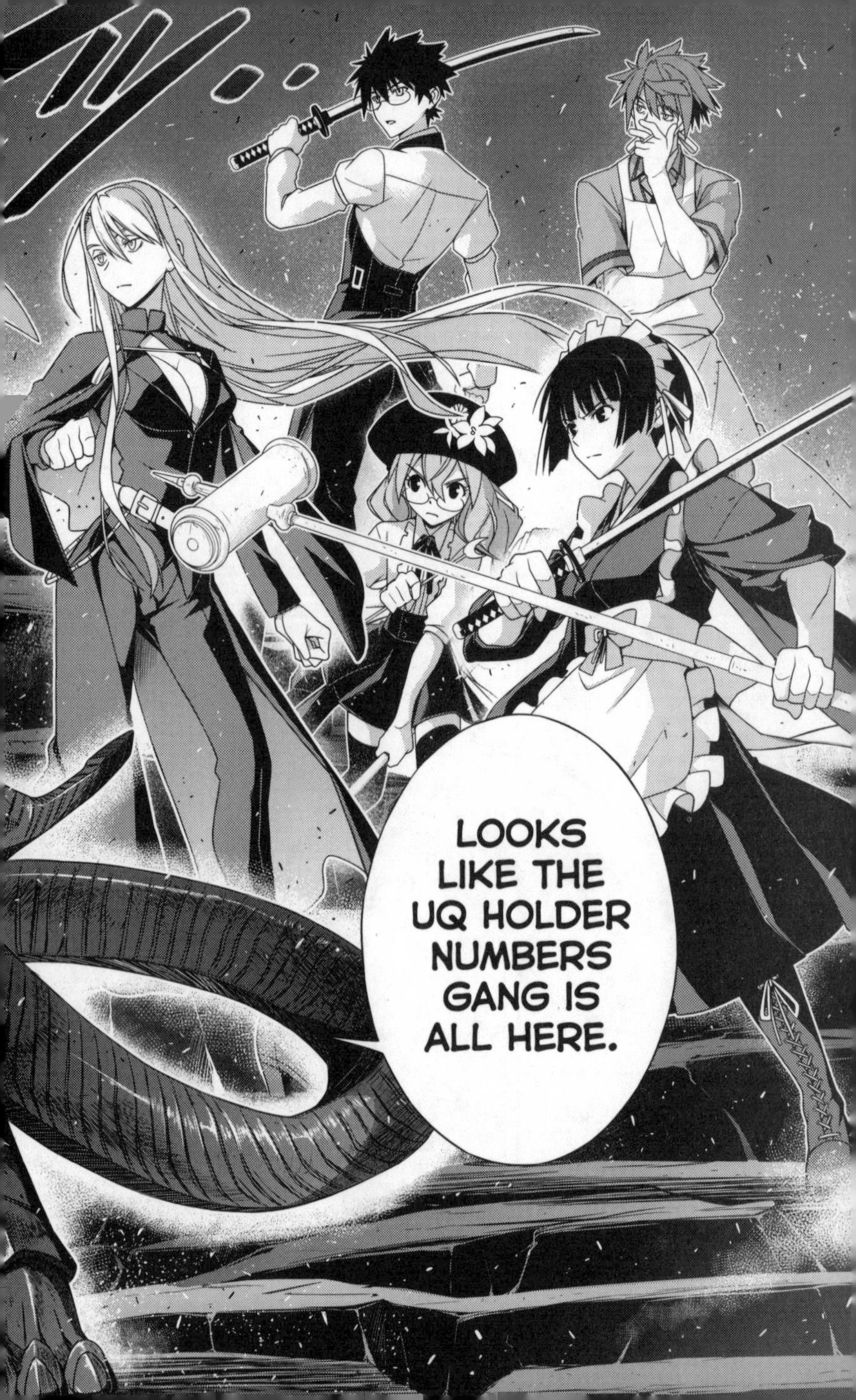
LOOKS LIKE THE UQ HOLDER NUMBERS GANG IS ALL HERE.

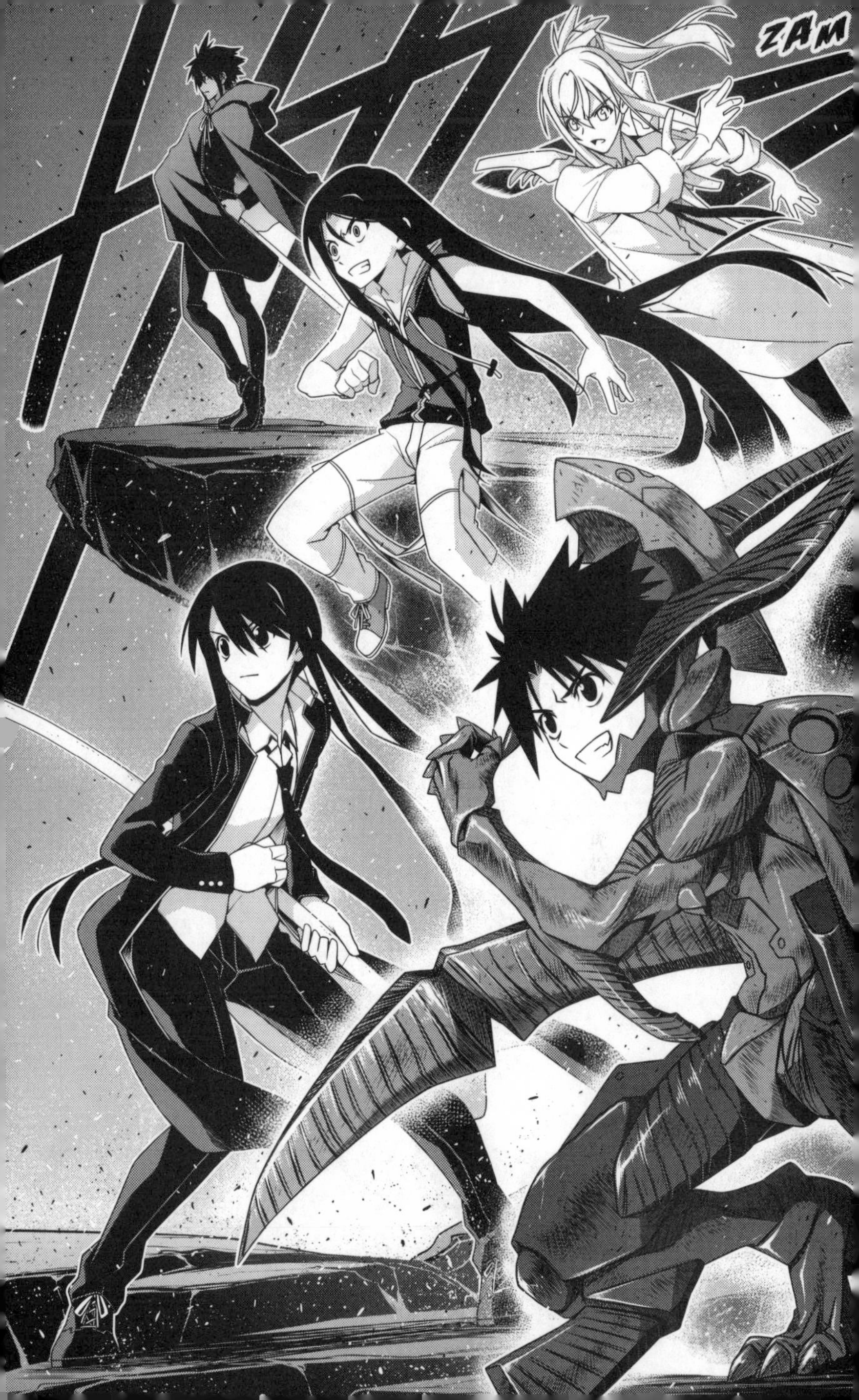
ZAM

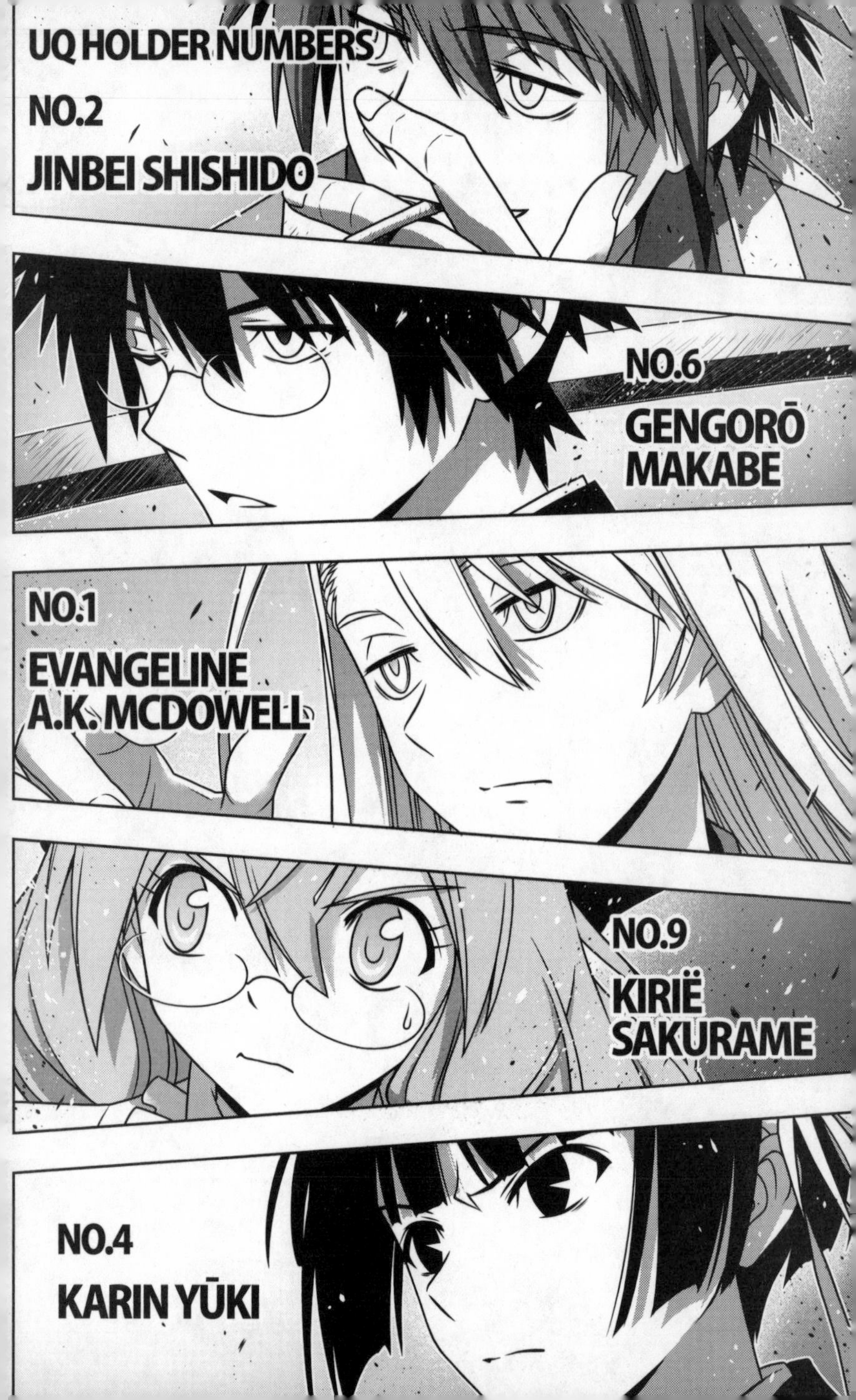
UQ HOLDER NUMBERS
NO.2
JINBEI SHISHIDO
NO.6
GENGORŌ MAKABE
NO.1
EVANGELINE A.K. MCDOWELL
NO.9
KIRIË SAKURAME
NO.4
KARIN YŪKI

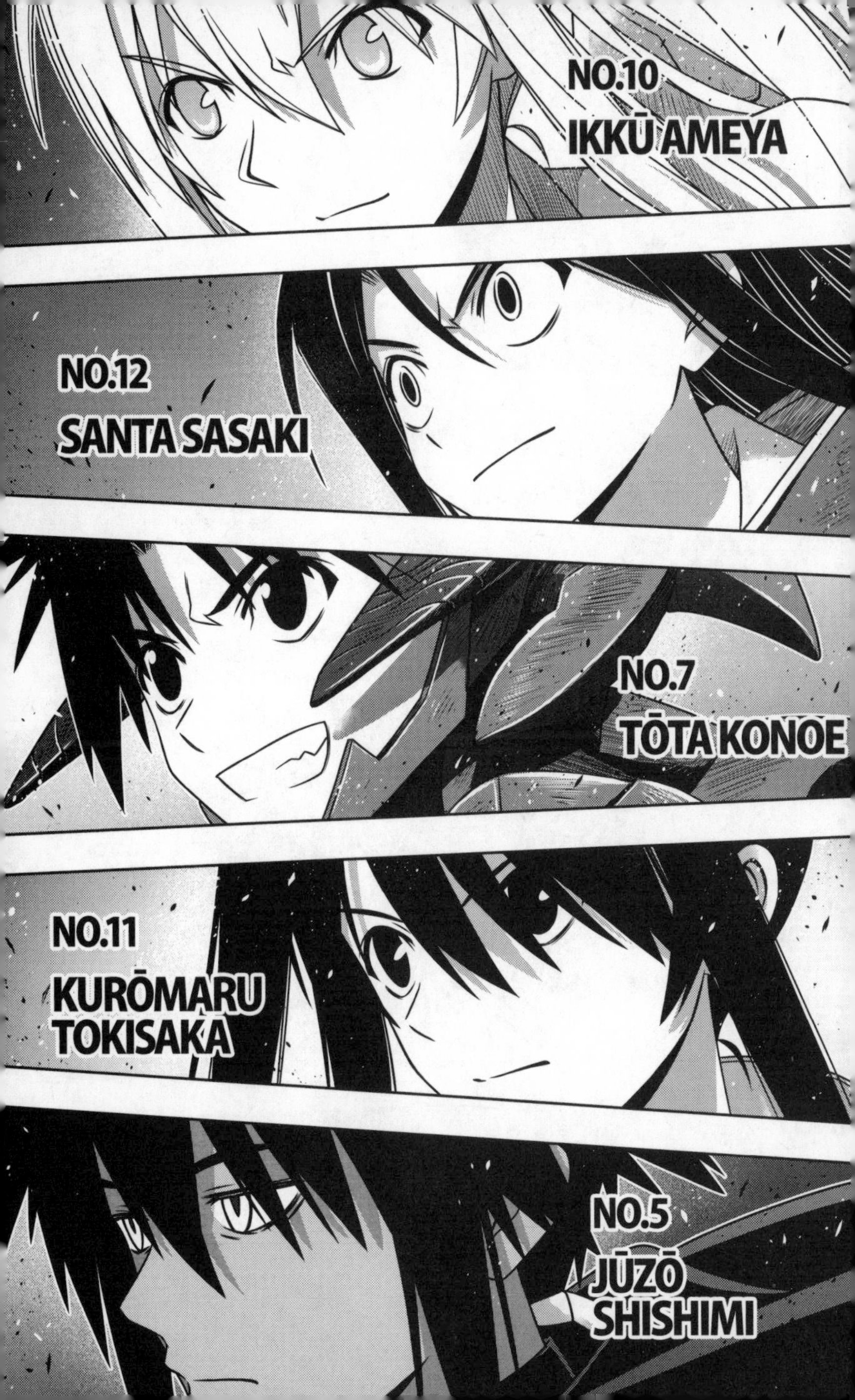
NO.10
IKKŪ AMEYA
NO.12
SANTA SASAKI
NO.7
TŌTA KONOE
NO.11
KURŌMARU
TOKISAKA
NO.5
JŪZŌ
SHISHIMI

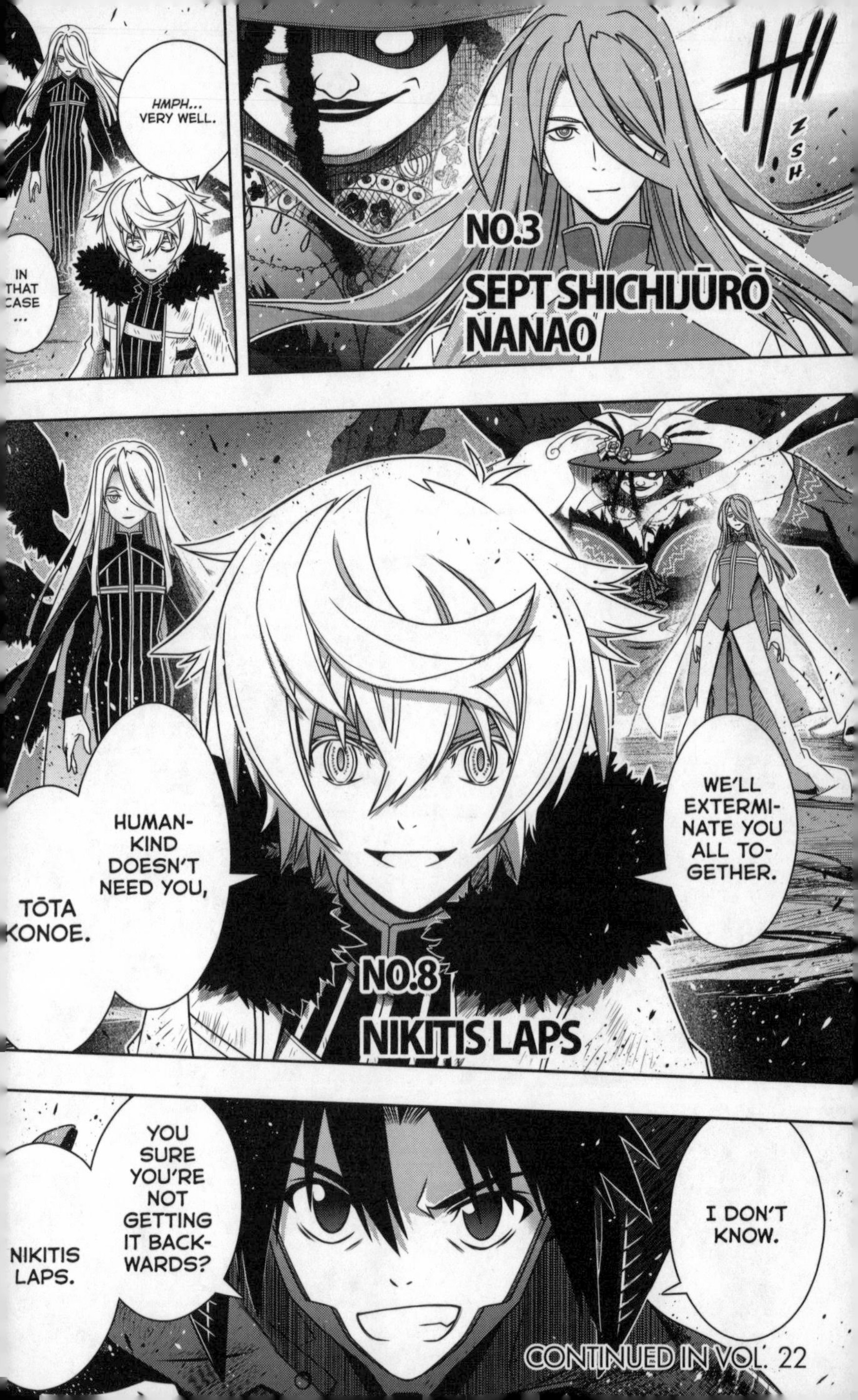
ZSH
NO.3
SEPT SHICHIJŪRŌ NANAO
HMPH... VERY WELL.
IN THAT CASE ...
HUMAN-KIND DOESN'T NEED YOU,
TŌTA KONOE.
WE'LL EXTERMI-NATE YOU ALL TO-GETHER.
NO.8
NIKITIS LAPS
YOU SURE YOU'RE NOT GETTING IT BACK-WARDS?
NIKITIS LAPS.
I DON'T KNOW.
CONTINUED IN VOL. 22

UQ HOLDER!

STAFF

Ken Akamatsu

Takashi Takemoto

Kenichi Nakamura

Keiichi Yamashita

Yuri Sasaki

Madoka Akanuma

Thanks to Ran Ayanaga

THE WORLD OF CLAMP!

Cardcaptor Sakura
Collector's Edition

Cardcaptor Sakura:
Clear Card

Magic Knight Rayearth
25th Anniversary Box Set

Chobits

TSUBASA Omnibus

TSUBASA WoRLD CHRoNiCLE

xxxHOLiC Omnibus

xxxHOLiC Rei

CLOVER Collector's Edition

Kodansha Comics welcomes you to explore the expansive world of CLAMP, the all-female artist collective that has produced some of the most acclaimed manga of the century. Our growing catalog includes icons like *Cardcaptor Sakura* and *Magic Knight Rayearth*, each crafted with CLAMP's one-of-a-kind style and characters!

The art-deco cyberpunk classic from the creators of *xxxHOLiC* and *Cardcaptor Sakura*!

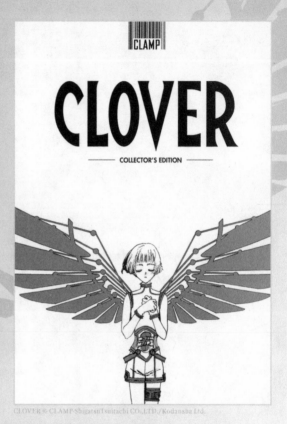

CLOVER © CLAMP-Shigatsu Tsuitachi CO.,LTD./Kodansha Ltd.

Su was born into a bleak future, where the government keeps tight control over children with magical powers—codenamed "Clovers." With Su being the only "four-leaf" Clover in the world, she has been kept isolated nearly her whole life. Can ex-military agent Kazuhiko deliver her to the happiness she seeks? Experience the complete series in this hardcover edition, which also includes over twenty pages of ravishing color art!

KC KODANSHA COMICS

MAGIC KNIGHT RAYEARTH
25TH ANNIVERSARY EDITION
CLAMP

A BELOVED CLASSIC MAKES ITS STUNNING RETURN IN THIS GORGEOUS, LIMITED EDITION BOX SET!

This tale of three Tokyo teenagers who cross through a magical portal and become the champions of another world is a modern manga classic. The box set includes three volumes of manga covering the entire first series of *Magic Knight Rayearth*, plus the series's super-rare full-color art book companion, all printed at a larger size than ever before on premium paper, featuring a newly-revised translation and lettering, and exquisite foil-stamped covers.

A strictly limited edition, this will be gone in a flash!

The boys are back, in 400-page hardcovers that are as pretty and badass as they are!

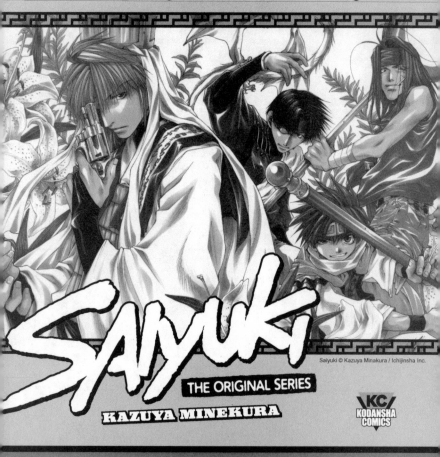

Saiyuki © Kazuya Minakura / Ichijinsha Inc.

SAIYUKI
THE ORIGINAL SERIES
KAZUYA MINEKURA

KC / KODANSHA COMICS

"AN EDGY COMIC LOOK AT AN ANCIENT CHINESE TALE." —YALSA

Genjo Sanzo is a Buddhist priest in the city of Togenkyo, which is being ravaged by yokai spirits that have fallen out of balance with the natural order. His superiors send him on a journey far to the west to discover why this is happening and how to stop it. His companions are three yokai with human souls. But this is no day trip — the four will encounter many discoveries and horrors on the way.

FEATURES NEW TRANSLATION, COLOR PAGES, AND BEAUTIFUL WRAPAROUND COVER ART!

Young characters and steampunk setting, like *Howl's Moving Castle* and *Battle Angel Alita*

Beyond the Clouds © 2018 Nicke / Ki-oon

A boy with a talent for machines and a mysterious girl whose wings he's fixed will take you beyond the clouds! In the tradition of the high-flying, resonant adventure stories of Studio Ghibli comes a gorgeous tale about the longing of young hearts for adventure and friendship!

A Kodansha Comics Trade Paperback Original
UQ HOLDER! 21 copyright © 2019 Ken Akamatsu
English translation copyright © 2020 Ken Akamatsu

Published in the United States by Kodansha Comics, an imprint of Kodansha USA Publishing, LLC, New York.

Publication rights for this English edition arranged through Kodansha Ltd., Tokyo.

First published in Japan in 2019 by Kodansha Ltd., Tokyo.

ISBN 978-1-64651-076-4

Printed in the United States of America.

www.kodanshacomics.com

9 8 7 6 5 4 3 2 1
Translation: Alethea Nibley & Athena Nibley
Lettering: James Dashiell
Editing: Jennifer Sherman
Kodansha Comics edition cover design by Phil Balsman

Publisher: Kiichiro Sugawara

Director of publishing services: Ben Applegate
Associate director of operations: Stephen Pakula
Publishing services managing editor: Noelle Webster
Assistant production manager: Emi Lotto, Angela Zurlo